UNDER SIEGE...

As Lincoln, Burnside, and the Army of the Potomac pushed the abolitionist crusade into the southland, Robert E. Lee and Thomas Jonathan Jackson prepared to dispute the Union hordes poised at Richmond.

"I am operating to baffle the advance of the enemy and retain him among the mountains until I can get him separated so that I can strike him," Lee said. "His force will thus be diminished and disheartened. His sick and stragglers must be going back. His advance cavalry is along the line of the Rappahannock River..."

But Burnside's real stratagem reached them soon enough, and by November 18–19 lead units of Longstreet's First Corps accompanied by Lee himself began marching into Fredericksburg from the west.

Jackson already knew that a juncture was in the offing, and by November 25 he was heading down the Valley Pike toward Strasburg; that was hours after Lee had told the president he thought "from the tone of the Northern papers, it is intended that General Burnside shall advance from Fredericksburg to Richmond...." Lee also told Davis: "I have waited to the last moment to draw Jackson's corps to me, as I have seen that his presence on their flank has defeated their purpose of advancing upon Gordonsville and Charlottesville." An additional message to Jackson implored him to hurry toward Fredericksburg by the best possible route.

—from *Lee and Jackson*

LEE
AND
JACKSON

Confederate Chieftains

PAUL D. CASDORPH

A LAUREL TRADE PAPERBACK
Published by
Dell Publishing
a division of
Bantam Doubleday Dell Publishing Group, Inc.
1540 Broadway
New York, New York 10036

The trademark Laurel® is registered in the U.S. Patent and Trademark
Office.

The trademark Dell® is registered in the U.S. Patent and Trademark Office.

ISBN: 0-440-50521-6

Reprinted by arrangement with Paragon House

Printed in the United States of America

Published simultaneously in Canada

June 1993

10 9 8 7 6 5 4 3 2 1

RRH

TO THE MEMORY OF MY GREAT FRIEND

Frank H. Smyrl

Contents

Preface

Ask Americans at random to name several Confederate generals from the Civil War and chances are the response will include Robert E. Lee and Stonewall Jackson. While almost everyone recognizes Lee, not many could identify Stonewall as Thomas Jonathan Jackson. Although Lee and Jackson have become household names for millions, few beyond Civil War specialists realize that together they were the nation's foremost soldiers from the summer of 1862 when Lee assumed command of the Army of Northern Virginia until Jackson's untimely death in May 1863. In a year's time—first Jackson alone in the Shenandoah Valley, and then Jackson and Lee together during the Seven Days, at Second Manassas, Antietam, Fredericksburg, and finally Chancellorsville—their combined genius and fighting prowess not only brought Abraham Lincoln's war machine to a standstill but also created a military legacy that survives undiminished to the present.

The lives of Lee and Jackson have been recorded by master biographers, including Douglas Southall Freeman, Robert E. Lee, Jr., Fitzhugh Lee, John Esten Cooke, Thomas L. Connelly, Burke Davis, A. L. Long, J. William Jones, Robert L. Dabney, Thomas Jackson Arnold, Frank E. Vandiver, Clifford Dowdey, Mary Anna Jackson, Margaret Sanborn, and Thomas Alexander White. The breadth of biographical insight and detail set down by these and other writers affords the modern reader an intimate glance at both men; their volumes have unquestionably molded the present work. Where this book differs from past studies is in its emphasis upon the "interconnectiveness" of the lives and careers of Lee and Jackson, which led to the great Confederate triumphs of 1861–1863. The close connection between Lee and Jackson started long before their glory days upon the fields of northern Virginia in the opening months of Civil War, and it was an association, however sporadic, that enabled each man to test the other's mettle. Their first presumed meeting took place in 1843 when Jackson was a West Point cadet and Lee a young engineering officer in the regular army. Their mutual admiration developed during the Mexican War and ripened through the 1850s, flourishing until Jackson's death at Chancellorsville twenty years later.

A more unlikely pair to form one of history's great fighting bonds would be difficult to imagine. Robert Edward Lee represented one of the country's most prestigious families; his father, Light-Horse Harry Lee, had been George Washington's devoted cavalryman during the Revolution, and Robert E. Lee himself had married a direct descendant of Washington's adopted son. Other Lee ancestors included signers of the Declaration of Independence, as well as statesmen of every stripe, and through his mother he was related to the aristocratic Carters of Virginia. Beyond his social standing, Lee was possessed of a flawless composure and self-control that made him a natural leader.

Jackson, on the other hand, at least during much of his early life, was a chronic complainer who worried his family and excited more than a little comment among his contemporaries. Yet his frontier forebears had instilled in him a long tradition of Calvinistic plainness and devotion to hard work that stood the young Tom Jackson in good stead; his family owned sizable tracts in western Virginia, operated a well-known gristmill on the West Fork River, and produced five United States congressmen. One uncle even married a sister of Dolly Madison. Although orphaned at an early age, Jackson was a young man whose family contacts enabled him to rise quickly. By age seventeen, he had become a Lewis County constable because of family influence throughout the region. An acceptable West Point career after an uncertain beginning followed by a brilliant performance in the Mexican War pointed his entry into the Virginia Military Institute (VMI) as professor of natural philosophy and artillery tactics.

At the opening shots of Civil War, Lee and Jackson were extraordinarily cosmopolitan for their time and place. Both had a West Point education, which was among the best available on this side of the Atlantic. Both had traveled widely: Lee had been west to Chicago and St. Louis as well as south to the Georgia coast and Florida in addition to his army service in Texas and Mexico. Jackson had been in Mexico followed by a brief tour pursuing Seminole Indians across the Florida swamps; he had also been to Canada, England, and several continental countries during the 1850s. By 1861 Lee had served as superintendent of West

Point, and Jackson, although disliked by his students, had spent a decade teaching at VMI. Working in the elevated atmosphere of Lexington, with Washington College—later Washington and Lee University—nearby, exposed the young professor to a sophisticated milieu indeed. Jackson had married twice, and both his fathers-in-law had been college presidents. Further, the travels of Jackson and Lee before and during the Civil War produced a formidable body of letters to family and associates, which coupled with their voluminous orders and other military correspondence, 1861–1865, show both to have been literate, cultured men.

Despite their disparate backgrounds, Lee and Jackson were in sporadic contact for the fifteen years before 1861. As an untried officer in the opening battles at First Manassas and in the Shenandoah Valley, Jackson steeled himself for his great contributions to Lee's later successes. After Lee took command of the army in June 1862, and Jackson marched across the Blue Ridge to join him for the Seven Days around Richmond, he quickly became the one lieutenant trusted to carry out the commander's wishes without hesitation. But it developed into a two-way street. Jackson could also be counted upon to restrain Lee's inherent inclination to be always on the attack. Once Jackson's steady hand was gone, Lee suffered the debacle of Gettysburg within weeks of his death, and though Lee was brilliant in his delaying maneuvers against Grant throughout the campaigns of 1864, he never again found an obliging subordinate to implement his plans while detached from the main army. After Chancellorsville, when Jackson tramped off through the wilderness undergrowth with Lee's Second Corps, as he had done at Second Manassas, the Antietam, and to a lesser extent at Fredericksburg, the Army of Northern Virginia was on the defensive until the final collapse of April 1865. Lee had placed his abiding confidence in Jackson's willingness to act alone, and when death took his "right arm," the prospects for Confederate victory also vanished.

The staggering abundance of printed material about every conceivable facet of the Civil War confronts the modern scholar with the need for selectivity. Although I have made considerable effort to draw upon memoirs and other writings by those who actually knew and fought with Lee and Jackson, contemporary scholarship has not been ignored. Readers should expect that most if not all of the older accounts present both campaigners in a favorable light. While it is not my intent to demean anyone, the reader should realize that other Confederate generals, such as James Longstreet, come off second best in the pages that follow; fighting in the Deep South and the West has largely been neglected because Virginia was the scene of the military operations of Lee and

Jackson, at least until the last months of war, when Lee was placed in command of all southern armies.

I am uncertain what first set me to work on the Confederate chieftains—for I attended Stonewall Jackson High School in Charleston, West Virginia, with its portrait of Stonewall himself hanging inside the front entrance, and I afterward devoured several classic biographies of both soldiers while an undergraduate at Victoria College, which is located in a Texas town where Lee once stayed briefly. The host of college students who have patiently sat through my Civil War lectures over the past twenty-five years unwittingly contributed to this book with their often lively discussions. Others who helped include Kim Suiter, Shonette Koontz, Sue Forrest, and Lois McCarthy who secured more library loan materials than any patron has a right to expect. As always, Elizabeth Scobell and Ron Wiley were more than helpful when I prowled their library stacks looking for special favors.

Carol Vandevender and Chris Kreiser were unfailingly knowledgeable when I called or visited the West Virginia Department of Archives and History, and Kathleen Bledsoe of the Marshall University Library helped in several important ways as did P J Dempsey and Chris O'Connell, my editors at Paragon House. In addition to my wife, Patricia Barker Casdorph, who helped constantly, several colleagues and scholars lent a willing hand at critical junctures: Edwin D. Hoffman of West Virginia State College always had time to listen and comment upon the latest battle to fall under my pen; Stephen W. Brown of the West Virginia Institute of Technology gave me important clues about Jackson's family and early career; Otis K. Rice, also of the West Virginia Institute of Technology, made this a much better book following his careful examination of an early draft; Sanford E. Lehmberg of the University of Minnesota pointed me in the right direction when I needed help with the English Civil War; and Robert W. McAhren of Washington and Lee University graciously checked a last minute detail that made my work much easier.

Paul D. Casdorph
Charleston, West Virginia

LEE

AND

JACKSON

1

Beginnings

They were heirs of Virginia and the Old South born seventeen years apart: Robert E. Lee in 1807; Thomas Jonathan Jackson in 1824. While both were Virginians born and bred, each descended from a different world. Yet their common love for the Old Dominion, the jewel of the South, enabled them to work in total harmony during the glory days of southern nationhood, 1861–1863. Lee, born into one of America's premier families, was a son of pure English stock, Episcopalian, as well as cavalier in spirit and outlook. "Stonewall" Jackson—after the fight at Manassas in July 1861 he was always Stonewall—was Appalachian born to Scotch-Irish forebears with a long tradition of Calvinist simplicity. Although Lee wavered when the time came to join the southern cause because of long personal and familial affiliations with the Union, Jackson embraced the Confederate banner without hesitation. Since the 1790s his family had been loyal Democrats with lasting ties to the men who forged the southern breakaway on the eve of Civil War; Jackson's ancestors were unique among their frontier neighbors, who became Republicans and created the pro-Union State of West Virginia twenty-five months after Jackson left the Virginia Military Institute in the summer of 1861 for Richmond, Manassas, and immortality.

Their worldviews were handed down by the first Lee and Jackson forebears to cross the Atlantic. Richard Lee, who died in 1664, established his illustrious family in America following 1642, when he arrived in Virginia. Six generations removed from Robert E. Lee, Richard Lee was descended from ancient Shropshire stock. The family could trace its origins from Reyner de Lega, or de Le, a Norman knight who followed William the Conqueror across the channel. "The Emigrant" Lee enjoyed strong bonds with the Stuart monarchy as well as with William Berkeley, the Stuarts' handpicked overseer who governed Virginia from 1642 until 1677; this affiliation with the English ruling class placed the Lee clan above the average colonist. After reaching Virginia by way of London, where his coat of arms was registered with the royal herald, he took up a one thousand–acre grant in present Gloucester County. A decade later, he had established another large plantation in nearby Northumberland County along the shores of Chesapeake Bay.

While amassing a fortune and instilling in his family a high moral and civic purpose, Richard Lee nearly lost everything because of a stubborn loyalty to Berkeley and the Stuarts. When the Puritan Roundheads under Oliver Cromwell won the English Civil War after 1648 to create the Commonwealth, Lee remained firmly entrenched with the monarchy. He even traveled to England on Berkeley's behalf after Charles I lost his head on the chopping block at Whitehall because he would not bow to parliament and the Puritans. Lee not only surrendered Berkeley's commission as colonial governor but also had enough influence to intervene with the exiled Charles II; besides obtaining a questionable patent for his friend from the exiled monarch, he invited Charles himself to make his home among friends in Virginia. Lee was able to trim his sails by swearing allegiance to the Commonwealth after Cromwell's men subdued several rebellious Virginians. Richard Lee and his growing clan actually prospered under Cromwell, who allowed several of his sons to be educated at English universities.[1]

Although the Emigrant Lee died in 1664, four years after the Restoration of Charles II, one of his surviving eight children, Richard II (1647–1715), an appellation to distinguish him from the first Richard, maintained the family obsession with gaining wealth and prestige. This great-great-grandfather of Robert E. Lee used his influence to help the Fairfax family obtain its royal charter for 5,282,000 acres along the Potomac. Under the tutelage of Thomas Fairfax, Sixth Baron (1692–1782), the grant encompassed seven counties in present West Virginia and eighteen in Virginia; it also made up the northern neck of Virginia—said to resemble a goose's neck when plotted on a map—which extended from the Potomac to the Rappahannock; and from Chesapeake Bay to the famed Fairfax Stone at the far southwestern corner of Maryland. The grant from Charles II to the Lords Fairfax dominated much of Virginia and indeed American legal history until its final disposition in the celebrated 1816 case of *Martin v. Hunter's Lessee*. The sixth Lord Fairfax, a bachelor who lived to the age of ninety nursing a hatred for women and an equal love for hunting dogs, worked with the Lees to erect a feudal domain along the Potomac. A "white post" installed by Fairfax near Winchester to direct perspective land buyers to his seat at Greenway was used as a marching beacon for Jackson's "foot cavalry" when they crossed the Blue Ridge to join Lee at Fredericksburg in the winter of 1862.[2]

Richard II's offspring marked a branching of the clan into the Stratford Hall and Leesylvania Lees. One son, Thomas, who built the great showplace at Stratford Hall in Westmoreland County, sired a remarkable brood that included Richard Henry (1732–1794), Francis Lightfoot (1734–1797), William (1739–1795), and the bachelor Arthur Lee (1740–1794). This group alone produced two signers of the Declaration of Independence, diplomats, writers, and congressmen—some of the most illustrious figures of the colonial and revolutionary eras.

Small wonder that Robert E. Lee enthusiastically pursued his family tree while a young officer on garrison duty. But his family, the Leesylvania Lees in Prince William County, branched from Henry Lee I (1691–1741), another son of the second Richard. Henry Lee I, according to Douglas Southall Freeman, incomparable biographer of Robert E. Lee, "lived at Lee Hall on the Potomac, adjoining the older Lee Mansion of Mount Pleasant. While probably not as wealthy as his father or grandfather, Henry Lee became a planter of ample means." He married Mary Bland, "daughter of Colonel Richard Bland, representative of a family of high station." His grandson, Light-Horse Harry Lee (Henry III, 1756–1818), of Revolutionary War fame, notes in his *Memoirs* that Leesylvania was "situated on a point of land jutting into the Potomac, three miles above Dumfries, then the county town of Prince William." This place, which boasted "a lively theatre," had been founded by Scottish merchants for the export of tobacco. An earlier master of Lee Hall was Henry II (1729–1787), who took over in 1747 on the eve of the French and Indian War; this Lee ancestor gained enduring notoriety by winning the hand of Miss Lucy Grymes, a great Virginia beauty, also courted by a youthful, love-stricken swain named George Washington. The celebrated wedding took place at Green Spring on the James River, Saturday, December 1, 1753, under the guidance of the Reverend William Preston of James City, a well-known Episcopal clergyman along the tidewater. Henry Lee II, notes his son, "was apparently a great favorite in the community, and represented the county, either as a burgess or a delegate, for more than twenty years."[3]

Light-Horse Harry might have added that his Lee forebears never strayed from their High Church Anglicanism while building their fortunes. For the Lees and their tidewater kin, an elevated social position implied an adherence to the Church of England. And that social milieu was strengthened by the influx of English Cavaliers who flooded colonial Virginia after Oliver Cromwell took over following the Civil War. After all, when the University of Virginia plays football to this day, it is the "Cavaliers" who take the field.

In contrast to the Cavaliers, who settled the Chesapeake country, another migration from the British Isles fanned over the Shenandoah Valley and the western reaches of Virginia a generation later. The lowland Scots who began arriving in the first decades of the eighteenth century by way of Northern Ireland—thus their designation as Scotch-Irish—mostly bypassed the tidewater. This hardy race, destined to bear the brunt of the Indian wars, used Philadelphia as their port of entry and then traveled westward along the Philadelphia Wagon Road into the Great Valley of Virginia and beyond. One John Jackson (c. 1715–1801), first American ancestor of Stonewall Jackson and a contemporary of Robert E. Lee's grandfather, Henry II, joined the Scotch-Irish exodus across the Atlantic during 1748.

Essentially the same information about John Jackson appears in Robert Lewis Dabney's chronicle of Thomas Jonathan Jackson published in 1866 (although others brought out earlier biographies) and in Mary Anna Jackson's *Memoir* of her husband printed some years later. Subsequent Jackson biographers, including Roy Bird Cook, Frank E. Vandiver, G. F. R. Henderson, and others, have relied heavily upon these first accounts. Unlike Robert E. Lee, who survived the Civil War by five years and who penned a family history in his edited treatment of his father's Revolutionary War *Memoirs*, Jackson's untimely death precluded a personal history. While Mrs. Jackson surely had access to family documents, Dabney, who worked with Jackson throughout the Confederate years, undoubtedly heard Stonewall's own reminiscences about his family origins.[4]

The value of Dabney's account, although it was not the first, lies in the author's proximity to Jackson during his climb to fame. Once the Stonewall sobriquet became a household word, those around Jackson and no doubt the warrior himself began to think about a postwar biography. Dabney had his *Life and Campaigns of Lieut-Gen. Thomas J. Jackson* in print within three years of Jackson's death; and he was well fitted to compose his early account. Thomas Jackson Arnold, Stonewall's nephew and himself a Jackson biographer, says Mrs. Jackson encouraged Dabney to bring out the work. The Presbyterian clergyman, a graduate of Hampden-Sydney, the University of Virginia, and the Union Theological Seminary, first joined the Confederate service as an army chaplain. By 1862, however, he had become Jackson's chief of staff and remained in that post until he was replaced by younger officers; further, Dabney lived until 1898, producing an endless stream of prosouthern tracts as well as religious and philosophical works. He gave up teaching at Union Theological Seminary during 1883 to become professor of mental and moral philosophy at the newly created University of Texas. From Victoria, Texas, where he spent his last days in total blindness at the home of a son, Dabney pursued a lengthy, detailed correspondence with Jed Hotchkiss—Jackson's chief topographer during the Civil War—about every conceivable facet of the Virginia fighting.[5]

John Jackson was born in northern Ireland, near Coleraine, about 1715. His ancestors had surely joined the Scottish migration to Ulster in the northeastern corner of Ireland during the seventeenth century, when "the Scotch-Irish came into existence to settle the Irish problem, a perennial nettle to royal politicians." English attempts to subdue the Irish over five centuries had been compounded by Irish refusal to embrace the Reformation and its precepts, so dear to Englishmen. The same Stuart kings who worked with the Lees in seventeenth-century Virginia, escheated the Ulster lands of two Roman Catholic lords, the Earls of Tyrone and Tyrconnel, to create something called the Ulster Plantation. Then, throughout the 1600s, Lowland Scots by the thousands crossed the Irish Sea to push aside the native Irish as they carved out successful homesteads and built a Presbyterian church at every crossroads. And therein lay their problem; the Scotch-Irish became too successful in their religious and economic takeover of Ulster. From the 1690s onward, absentee landlords in England gradually increased their quit rents; and parliament began to enact a string of laws designed to stem the importation of Ulster agricultural products into the mother country.

When additional legislation placed political and social restrictions upon the Calvinist Ulstermen because they were outside the Anglican establishment, the seedbed of their migration to America had been prepared. An estimated quarter of a million crossed the Atlantic between 1717 and the Revolutionary War, bringing with them a unique, stouthearted view of life; as one writer put it: "Believing that freedom to bear arms and to still whiskey were part of every man's birthright, they migrated to America in the 1700s, fetching their muskets and their thirst with them, to settle an area vaster than New England, a roadless wilderness of crags and coves." Although they went to many parts of the colonies, they spread over the Shenandoah Valley and the southern Appalachians like the plague, not only grabbing land but also pushing

Indians aside, just as they had attacked the Catholic Irish a century earlier; three generations later, these sons of Ulster formed the core of Stonewall Jackson's legions from 1861 to 1863.[6]

John Jackson, who reached Maryland in 1748 following a brief stay in London, like his kinsmen joined the migration after his rents had been raised. Dabney says he "became a respectable and prosperous trades-man" before his trans-Atlantic voyage at age thirty-three. He settled first in Calvert County, Maryland, but soon moved to Cecil County near Elkton in the extreme northeastern corner of the colony. On the voyage, he met his future wife, Elizabeth Cummins, whom he married shortly after reaching the new world; "she had the stature of a man, six feet in height, and as remarkable for strength of intellect as for beauty and physical vigor," remarks Stonewall's wife. "Elizabeth Cummins was well-educated, her father having been in sufficiently easy circumstances to own and rent out a public-house in London called the 'Bold Dragon,' from which he derived a good income, and he was supposed to own landed estates in Ireland." Her father's death and mother's remarriage prompted Elizabeth Cummins to move to America. Thomas J. Jackson was four years old when his great-grandmother Elizabeth died in 1828 at the advanced age of 105 years.[7]

The Jackson-Cummins marriage took place in July 1755, and within two years the young couple had joined the westering of the Scotch-Irish into backcountry Virginia. John Jackson located first near Moorefield in present Hardy County, West Virginia; the homestead six miles south of the county seat was almost certainly in what is now Lost River State Park. Jackson stayed there on the South Branch of the Potomac during the French and Indian War but left in 1768 when he relocated 150 miles westward near Buckhannon in Randolph County, Virginia. He was "a spare, diminutive man, of quiet but determined character, sound judg-ment, and excellent morals." Besides rearing a family of eight children and fighting Indians along the frontier, John Jackson and his wife amassed sizable land holdings along the Buckhannon and West Fork Rivers. Like Robert E. Lee's forebears east of the mountains, Jackson and his sons lost no time in acquiring all the land and wealth at their disposal.[8]

Although Stonewall Jackson himself had an unfortunate childhood because of his father's premature death, the Jackson family was clearly among the frontier elite. None other than Light-Horse Harry Lee ap-pointed John Jackson an Indian scout in western Virginia during his term as governor, and Elizabeth Cummins Jackson held patents to three thousand acres of land in her own right that encompassed the present city of Buckhannon. In addition to his service in the Indian wars and the Revolution, John Jackson served as Randolph County justice, and as late as 1789, at age seventy-four, he served as captain of a frontier company.

Three of John Jackson's sons reached even higher plateaus, including stints in Congress. Roy Bird Cook, a local historian and pharmacist who searched deeply into Jackson's background, reports that John Jackson's second son, Edward (1759–1828), also held numerous offices. This grandfather of Thomas Jonathan Jackson, whose life overlapped his famous grandson by four years, was successively appointed Randolph County surveyor, colonel of militia, commissioner of revenue, and high sheriff; he must have followed his older brother, George, to Clarksburg, because he was a magistrate in Harrison County after 1792. By 1801 Edward Jackson was situated near Weston, Lewis County, on the West Fork River, which joins the Tygart a few miles north of Clarksburg. He even represented Lewis County in the Virginia Assembly, 1822–1823; according to Cook, "he acquired some knowledge of medicine, was an expert millwright, and a farmer of more than usual ability." Dabney calls him a "respectable physician."

George Jackson (1757–1831), eldest son of John and Elizabeth Cummins Jackson, was elected to three congressional terms starting in 1794. As a young man of nineteen, he had marched with George Rogers Clark on the expedition against Cahokia and Vincennes during the Revolution. After reaching the rank of colonel, a sure political career beckoned with the return of peace and independence for the new nation; he was admitted to the bar at Clarksburg in 1784, elected to the Virginia Assembly two years later, and sat in the state conclave that ratified the United States Constitution.[9]

While a member of the Fourth Congress (1795–1797), George Jackson struck an enduring friendship with a one-term representative from Tennessee named Andrew Jackson, who came to Washington late in the 1796 session upon his state's admission to the Union. Although the two talked about their ancestors at length, they were unable to establish a positive connection between the two family branches other than they both had originated in the same Ulster parish. The two Jackson congressmen continued a long correspondence that reached Andrew Jackson's presidency. George Jackson was defeated for reelection in 1796 but managed to regain a seat in the Sixth and Seventh congresses, 1799–1803.[10]

In the election of 1802, George Jackson was replaced by his son, John George Jackson (1777–1825). This great uncle of Thomas Jonathan Jackson had a broken congressional career that reached into the 1820s, and became a leading spokesman for the new frontier. Stonewall's father in fact prepared for the bar by reading law in the Clarksburg office of John G. Jackson, and it is understandable how Thomas Jonathan Jackson was excellently connected to receive a congressional appointment to West Point in 1842 from Samuel L. Hays, a later Democratic congressman from Jackson's old district and a member of the Jackson clan. John G. Jackson first married Mary Payne of Philadelphia, a sister of Dolly Madison, a further asset for young Thomas Jonathan Jackson when he left Jackson's Mill and Lewis County for the larger world. Uncle John was nearly killed in a notorious duel with Joseph Pearson of North Carolina, which resulted from his steadfast support of his brother-in-law's stand on the Yazoo land controversy. Madison's successor, James Monroe, later named him to the first federal judgeship for the western district of Virginia. John G. Jackson, permanently lamed in his fight with Pearson, was sitting on the federal bench at the time of his death in 1825—one year after the birth of his famous nephew. His brother, Edward Brake Jackson (1793–1826), an army surgeon during the War of 1812 and like his father a respected Clarksburg physician, served in the Sixteenth and Seventeenth congresses, 1819–1823.[11]

Stonewall Jackson's uncles not only gave him an entrée to the larger world but also established ties with the Lee family long before the Civil War. When the Virginia convention of 1788 met to ratify the Federal Constitution, tidewater Lees and frontier Jacksons were present. Both George and John G. Jackson sat in the state assembly with Richard Bland Lee, younger brother of Light-Horse Harry, and George Jackson shared a legislative term with Arthur Lee. Light-Horse Harry and George Jackson served together in the Sixth Congress (1799–1801) during the former's only term in the House of Representatives.

But as the Jacksons were launching political careers as Jeffersonian Democrats, Henry Lee's role in public affairs ended when he left the executive mansion to enter congress. Lee made the mistake of his life by actively supporting Burr for the presidency when the Sixth Congress convened to decide the disputed election of 1800 between Thomas Jefferson and Aaron Burr. Yet he was a gentleman, writes his biographer Noel Gerson, "and when the House waited on Jefferson to extend its congratulations, he accompanied the other congressmen. It was evident from the frigid greetings exchanged that Harry was banished to a political wilderness. Both men bowed coldly, and neither extended a hand. 'I offer you my felicitations, sir,' Harry said. 'I thank you, sir,' Jefferson replied." That ended the conversation and, for practical purposes, Light-Horse Harry's political career. As a Federalist and confidant of George Washington, Lee had long been anathema to Jefferson and his political associates. And now Jefferson and his cronies had taken over in both Washington and Virginia.[12]

Harry Lee had used a spectacular military career to establish himself in politics. Following graduation from Princeton at age seventeen, he zoomed to meteoric heights during the Revolution. Three years out of college, he had joined Washington's continental army and by 1778 he had been promoted major; afterward, Washington put him in charge of an irregular cavalry troop. Lee rapidly became a great cavalryman—one of America's foremost soldiers with his brilliant maneuvers and surprise capture of Paulus Hook, New Jersey, from a British garrison. Even greater exploits awaited him after 1780 as cavalry officer under General Nathaniel P. Greene in the southern theater of operations. His enduring sobriquet, "Light-Horse Harry," resulted from dashing raids with the light cavalry at Guilford Court House, Camden, and Eutaw Springs. Lee served Greene with such distinction and valor throughout the Carolinas fighting that his family took the dying old soldier into their Georgia home in 1818.

The Revolution had no sooner ended than Harry Lee sat in the Virginia Convention to ratify the Constitution; always the loyal follower of Washington and the Federalists, he endorsed ratification without hesitation. When the first president died in 1799, Lee immortalized himself and Washington with a funeral oration delivered before a large crowd in Philadelphia's German Lutheran Church that included President John Adams. Associates said he wept openly upon hearing that his friend and mentor was dead. Initially fearful lest Jefferson's followers, who dominated the House of Representatives, might deny Washington due respect, Lee prepared his ringing tribute to the nation's founder: "First in war, first in peace, and first in the hearts of his countrymen, he was second to none in the humble and endearing scenes of private life; uniformly dignified and commanding, his example was edifying to all around him as were the effects of that example lasting. . . ."

In March 1782, Harry Lee had married a young cousin, Matilde Lee, at Stratford Hall; with his marriage into the Stratford Hall Lees, descendants of his great-uncle Thomas Lee, Light-Horse Harry became master of that great Westmoreland house. Not content with the planter's life, he embarked anew upon the public stage; there followed seats in the state assembly and Confederation congress as well as three one-year terms in the executive mansion at Richmond. But his world came crashing down when Matilde died in August 1790 while Lee sat in the same Virginia legislature as George Jackson. Undoubtedly, Jackson offered his condolences to his grieving colleague from the tidewater.

Lee was devastated by his wife's premature death during childbirth; with both Matilde and her newborn child dead, he was unconcerned about his wife's foresightedness in providing for her children's future. Light-Horse Harry had a serious defect of character that marred an otherwise idyllic life: a mania for financial speculation that had caused his wife deep concern. Five children, only two of whom survived, were born during the eight-year marriage, including Harry Lee IV, always known as Black-Horse Harry to distinguish father and son. Matilde had recognized her husband's weakness by seeing that her children were given Stratford as well as other properties by an inviolate deed of trust. Wild investment in several get-rich schemes had prompted her resolve. Continued speculation following Lee's tenure as governor resulted not only in financial ruin but also in a jail term.[13]

Three years after Matilde's death, Harry Lee married Ann Hill Carter, a girl of twenty who was descended from one of Virginia's foremost clans; the union took place in June 1793 at Shirley, her father's plantation along the James not far from Richmond, and proved as enduring as Lee's first marriage. Although Lee moved his bride to Stratford, the marriage was plagued from the start by ongoing obligations that he could never meet. Amid signs of approaching disaster, Robert E. Lee was born at Stratford on January 19, 1807, thirteen years and several children after the union of Henry Lee III and Ann Carter; finally, in 1809, when the boy was barely two years old, Major General Light-Horse Harry was jailed for failure to pay his debts. The birth took place in the same room where his cousins, Richard Henry and Francis Lightfoot Lee, had been born, both signers of the Declaration of Independence, a sure omen of future greatness. Upon the father's release, within a twelvemonth the family moved to a modest home in Alexandria. Thus, from an early age, Robert E. Lee was thrown into close contact with nearby Mount Vernon and the Washington legacy. Ownership of Stratford Hall had passed to Black-Horse Harry, and though he encouraged his father's new family to remain, the second Mrs. Lee never liked the place. Fortunately she had her own funds, a trust from her father that allowed the young family to live in meager comfort.

Light-Horse Harry was not disgraced by his prison sentence—after all, he was still a Lee and even became a justice of the peace following his release. But in June 1812, after going to Baltimore with Alexander C. Hanson, a Federalist newspaper editor, to propagandize against the War of 1812, he was nearly killed by an irate mob with Jeffersonian sympathies. He had picked the worst of places, because the city was not only Republican in sentiment but also favored a renewed conflict with England. Lee and several companions, including Revolutionary War general James Lingen, were attacked by a rowdy mob in the city jail, where authorities had put them in protective custody. In the ensuing melee that resulted from Hanson's editorializing against Republican policies, Lee was beaten, cut upon, and nearly killed. Douglas Southall Freeman's account reports that "one fiend nearly cut his nose off while another poured hot candle wax into his half-conscious eyes."

Sick and unable to withstand the damp winters in Alexandria, Lee left his wife and children for a self-imposed exile in the Caribbean. When he realized death was near, he started for home in a greatly weakened condition. However, death came in March 1818 at the Cumberland Island, Georgia, home of Mrs. Nathaniel P. Greene, wife of his old comrade in arms. Disfigured and maimed from the Baltimore affray, Harry Lee told young officers from a nearby naval base who kept a death vigil at his side that he had not known a moment without pain since the beating. [14]

Lee had commenced working on his *Memoir* of the Revolution while imprisoned, although the work was not completed until his return to Alexandria in 1812. It did not become the hoped-for financial success, but it graced military bookshelves on both sides of the Atlantic and fixed the author as an authority on war. Even today, *Memoirs of the War in the Southern Department of the United States* is widely accepted as a major work on the Revolution. Some years later, while he served as president of Washington College, Robert E. Lee brought out a revised edition with a touching memorial to the father he scarcely knew.

Much of what is known about the early life of Robert E. Lee comes from a series of letters between Charles Carter Lee, his elder brother, and Light-Horse Harry published as part of the revised *Memoirs*. Young Robert remained with his mother until 1825 when he left home for West Point; from an early age, the notion spread that he kept a watchful eye over Ann Carter Lee in Light-Horse Harry's absence. Except for his sisters, Anne Kinlock and Cathrine Mildred, Lee was the only child at home after his brother Smith left for the navy in 1820. Charles Carter Lee, nine years older than Robert, was a student at Harvard during his father's sojourn abroad. A February 1817 letter from Nassau to Charles asking for news about the younger children has helped the legend that mother and son formed a close bond at Alexandria: "You know how I love my children; how dear Smith is to me. Give me a description of his person, mind, temper, and habits. Tell me of Anne; has she grown tall? and how is my last in looks and understanding? Robert was always good, and will be confirmed in his happy turn of mind by his ever-watchful and affectionate mother. Does he strengthen his native tendency?"[15]

As an impressionable lad of seven, Robert and his mother witnessed the hubbub and excitement generated by the British capture of Alexandria and Washington during the War of 1812; it took place at the same time Light-Horse Harry, still opposed to the conflict, worked unofficially to negotiate an amicable settlement between the warring nations. Little is recorded about Ann Carter and her children throughout August 1814, when Major General Ross and his veterans from the Napoleonic wars marched through the Chesapeake. But surely the burning of government buildings across the Potomac and President Madison's flight from the capital while "the gardner and doorkeeper saved the Stuart portrait of Washington" had a strong impact upon a boy of Lee's perception. It was his first experience, however transitory, with things military.[16]

Robert became his mother's constant companion and helpmate in the years after 1814; he did marketing, cared for the horses, and shielded her from the outside world. A favorite incident with all Lee biographers has been the youngster's attention to his mother's well-being during frequent after-school drives in the family carriage. In keeping with Harry Lee's assessment of his youngest son, cousin Edmund Jennings Lee has noted:

> At the hour when other school-boys went to play, he hurried home to order his mother's drive, and there would be seen carrying her cushions with the gentleness of an experienced nurse. . . . When she complained of colds or "draughts," he would pull from his pocket a great jack-knife and newspapers, and would make her laugh with his efforts to improvise curtains, and shut out the intrusive wind, which whistled through the crevices of the old family coach. . . . When he left her to go to West Point, his mother was heard to say: "How can I live without Robert? He is both son and daughter to me."[17]

Moreover, the father kept a strong influence from exile. Light-Horse Harry's letter of February 1817 admonished his sons to be clean in person and appearance: "[I]t is indispensable to sanctity of body. Trained by your best of mothers to value it, you will never lose sight of it. To be plain and neat in dress, conforms to good sense and is emblematic of a right mind. Many lads who avoid the practice mentioned, fall into another habit which hurts only themselves and stupefies the senses— immoderate sleeping. . . ."[18]

Harry Lee's admonitions from afar undoubtedly had their intended effect because a manly bearing and simplicity of dress became Robert E. Lee's hallmark throughout the convulsions of 1861–1865. "During the war," notes J. William Jones, an early biographer, "he usually wore a suit of gray, without ornament, and with no insignia of rank save three stars on his collar, which every Confederate colonel was entitled to wear. But he always kept a handsomer (though equally simple) uniform which he wore on occasions of ceremony. . . ." And there is the oft-quoted account of the final surrender at Appomattox by General William Pendleton, his chief artillery officer: Pendleton, an Episcopal clergyman, found him on that fateful morning in "his neatest style" and chided Lee about his dress: "If I am to be General Grant's prisoner today, I intend to make my best appearance," was the reply. [19]

Caricatures about Lee's stature at the height of his powers can only lead to speculation about his appearance as a boy. When he returned to Alexandria in 1827 during a break in his West Point studies, a younger female relative commented upon his "manly beauty and attractiveness." He was then nineteen years old; these assets never left him in a lifetime devoted to public service. "General Lee, on horseback or off," writes Kyd Douglas, aide-de-camp to Stonewall Jackson, "was the handsomest man I ever saw." After that, Douglas continues: "It was said of Wade Hampton that he looked as knightly when mounted as if he had stepped out from an old canvas, horse and all. John C. Breckinridge was a model of manly beauty, John B. Gordon, a picture for the sculptor, and Joe Johnson looked every inch a soldier." Many top commanders in the Confederate service were models of masculine deportment, although Lee outclassed them all—a legacy of good breeding and upbringing. [20]

Meanwhile, Light-Horse Harry kept a watchful eye on the intellectual development of his sons. In November 1817, shortly before his hegira to Cumberland Island, he told Charles: "While I indulge myself every hour I am able in reading, it is more with a view of your, Smith's and Robert's good than any satisfaction to myself." He then launched into a description of Sir Isaac Newton's *Principia*. And Harry Lee was not a man to pull his political or intellectual punches: He thought the English physicist-astronomer had erred in his notions about gravity, but that St. Pierre, a French philosopher, had set the record straight. This was only one of many letters to suggest intellectual and scholarly pursuits for the boys' consideration. A family affinity for academic excellence was not lost on the impressionable Robert, who sat in Alexandria with his mother studying mathematics and natural philosophy—today it's called physics—in preparation for West Point. This influence propelled Robert E. Lee to a second-place finish in the class of 1829. [21]

Perhaps a greater force in molding the Confederate captain was the omnipresence of George Washington in Alexandria and the surrounding countryside. The legendary house at Mount Vernon was a stone's throw down the Potomac; as a boy, Lee must have strolled past the Masonic Hall where Washington had gone through the secret rituals. Although hard put to make ends meet in her husband's absence, Ann Carter Lee made regular jaunts to Shirley, ancestral home of the Carters, where young Robert gazed at the Peale portrait of the nation's founder. Carlyle House also stood in Alexandria during Lee's boyhood, the site where Washington and General Sir Edward Braddock had plotted their assault on the frontier during the French and Indian War.

Harry Lee often chided his sons to copy the letters of Washington and Nathaniel P. Greene as character-building exercises, and George Washington Parke Custis, who called himself "the child of Mount Vernon," lived nearby, regaling neighborhood children, Lee among them, with endless tales of the sainted Washington. The lad even attended Christ Church in Alexandria, where Washington had kept a pew. "To be thrown into constant association with Washington," concludes Burton Hendrick, "must have exercised a powerful influence on the growing boy. The chief devotion of Washington's latter days was the constitution and the Federal Union; and Lee's great love of the Union marked even at the time of his great decision, probably here had its inspiration."[22]

No member of the Lee family was present when Light-Horse Harry Lee died in 1818 at age sixty-two; the miserable state of roads and transportation between Alexandria and the Sea Islands of Georgia precluded a five hundred–mile journey for Ann Lee and her children. Yet the death of a beloved father—one who wrote genuine letters of concern and encouragement—affected eleven-year-old Robert. "I send you, for the work you are engaged upon, as the best history that can be furnished of the close of our father's life, his letters to me of that sad period. How much of them it is necessary to publish, I leave to you," brother Charles had written to Robert E. Lee in July 1866 when he was working on their father's *Memoirs*. Lee visited his father's grave while inspecting Carolina and Georgia coastal defenses during the Civil War; those who watched said his eyes were moist as he gazed down upon Harry's resting place. The remains were removed in 1913 to the Lee chapel on the grounds of Washington and Lee University, where famous father and renowned son were united at last.[23]

Jackson, too, worried about the resting place of his own family in later life. His mother had died in 1831—five years after his father, besides an older brother, Warren, in 1841, and a sister, Elizabeth, in 1826. Six-year-old Elizabeth had succumbed to an unknown fever three weeks before his father; the same malady apparently killed both daughter and father. During the 1850s while teaching natural philosophy at the Virginia Military Institute in Lexington, Stonewall Jackson wrote repeatedly to his sister, Laura Arnold, about their deceased family. In May 1856, when he was thirty-two, he did not know where some of the graves were located: "I wish to put stones to Warren's grave, and also to mother's if I knew certainly the spot."

Jackson's mother and brother had been buried at Ansted, in present Fayette County, West Virginia, where the family, including Thomas Jonathan himself, had resided briefly after 1826, while his father and sister rested near the ancestral home in Clarksburg. And the father he scarcely knew occupied his attention for many years; when Laura requested a miniature of Jonathan Jackson, he replied from Lexington in 1853 that he would not send it for fear it would be lost in the mail but indicated he would do so later "when a more favorable opportunity should present itself." Although he persuaded a cousin, "Aunt Katy Williams," to visit his father's grave in 1855, Jackson remained disturbed about a headstone: "I wish you would drop a letter to Mr. Criss or to cousin Elizabeth and ascertain whether he could see to putting up the stones at the graves of father and sister. And if you can get it attended to, I will advance the money at any time for the purpose," he told Laura three years later.[24]

Jonathan Jackson died in Clarksburg (now West Virginia), March 23, 1827, when Stonewall Jackson was a mere toddler. Although descended from hardy stock that produced Indian fighters and congressmen, he died at age thirty-seven before he had an opportunity to amass fame or fortune. Family connections and legal standing would have guaranteed political office and community position had he lived a normal life span. John Gittings and other writers who obviously enjoyed Jackson family confidences hint that he already had a flourishing legal practice. Born September 25, 1790, in present Upshur County, West Virginia, Jonathan Jackson was the third son of Edward Jackson and his first wife, Mary Haddon.[25]

Following study at Randolph Academy in Clarksburg, and the Old Male Academy in Parkersburg along the Ohio River, he had studied law in the office of his cousin, Congressman John George Jackson. Although western Virginia remained a rough frontier region throughout the antebellum era, it was also known for its numerous academies; these privately funded precursors of the modern high school afforded thousands of Appalachian youths like Jonathan Jackson with a solid education in mathematics and the classics. In quick succession, he was admitted to the Harrison County (Clarksburg) bar in 1810, Randolph County in 1813, and Lewis County (Weston) in 1817. Along the way, he courted and married Stonewall Jackson's mother, Julia (Judith) Beckwith Neale of Parkersburg on September 28, 1817.

The Northwestern Turnpike—first suggested by George Washington in 1784—which connected the Ohio River at Parkersburg with Winchester and eastern Virginia via Clarksburg—provided easy access for the Jackson clan with their Parkersburg relatives. Julia Neale and Jonathan Jackson had been childhood chums and classmates; while he struggled to establish himself as a frontier lawyer, a family of two daughters and two sons arrived between 1819 and 1826—Elizabeth in 1819, Warren in 1821, Thomas in 1824, and Laura Ann in 1826. His third child was christened simply Thomas at birth; the middle name Jonathan was added after the father's death.[26]

The fathers of Robert E. Lee and Stonewall Jackson had little in common except that both left their families to be reared by others in poor financial condition. Jonathan Jackson, who had been born while Light-Horse Harry Lee was governor of Virginia, died penniless; because he had a penchant for contracting long-term obligations, Roy Bird Cook reports that "every vestige of his property was swept away." Death resulted from a fever—probably typhoid—and his insistence upon nursing his eldest daughter during her own fatal illness. Elizabeth died March 5, 1826, and the father, who never recovered, passed away the following March 26.[27]

Thomas Jonathan Jackson, who was born in a "little story and a half brick house which stood opposite the courthouse in Clarksburg," was not as fortunate as the young Lee; Robert E. Lee was still a Lee, and his mother could always rely upon her own Carter money as well as numerous relatives in times of distress. Julia Jackson, on the other hand, was "almost destitute" after her husband's premature death, which forced her to remain in Clarksburg among her Jackson in-laws. Yet she managed to survive with the help of Jacksons, Neales, and a donation from the Masonic lodge. Jonathan Jackson had been "an officer in the order of Freemasons (who had presented him with a gold medal in token of their respect)." Then, continues Anna Jackson: "They now gave her a small house of only one room, and from this humble abode, with her fatherless children, she spent the greater part of the few years of her widowhood. Here she taught a little school and added to her support by sewing."

Widowhood and money cares must not have pressed too heavily upon

Julia Jackson. A brother, Minor Neale, was her frequent social companion as she and the children vacationed at a Wood County retreat, known as "The Ridge." In 1827, a short time after her husband's death, a Parkersburg friend noted: "She looked as cheerful and animated as usual, her easy graceful manners and pleasant conversation always making her a welcome guest." Three years later, Julia Neale Jackson married Captain Blake B. Woodson, a recently established lawyer in Clarksburg.[28]

About the time Robert E. Lee was reading mathematics in Alexandria and getting ready for West Point, six-year-old Thomas Jonathan Jackson was first beset by a host of upheavals that plagued his childhood. It started in 1831, when his stepfather was appointed clerk for the new county of Fayette, 125 miles south of Clarksburg. The small family moved immediately to Ansted, a stop on the stage line from Lewisburg to Charleston and the Great Kanawha Valley. Although family records call Blake Woodson "a gentle stepfather," the Jackson children were separated by the move: Ten-year-old Warren was sent to Uncle Alfred Neale in Parkersburg, while Thomas and Laura traveled to Ansted, located on a plateau overlooking the spectacular New River Gorge.

When Julia Woodson, already in delicate health, began a complicated pregnancy, the two children were hurried off to their step-grandmother, Elizabeth Brake Jackson, at Jackson's Mill in Lewis County. This widow of Edward Jackson, who lived at the ancestral home on the West Fork River near Weston until her death in 1835, quickly made "pets" of Thomas and Laura. Family biographers make a point of the boy's hesitancy to leave his mother and stepfather: When a Jackson uncle arrived for the children from Jackson's Mill, writes T. J. Arnold, "Thomas, now six years of age slipped off to the near-by woods, where he concealed himself, only returning to the house at nightfall. The uncle after a day or two of much coaxing, and the offer of numerous bribes, finally with the mother's aid, induced the children to make the visit, a journey of several days."[29]

His mother gave birth to a son, William Wirt Woodson, in October 1831; he was the half brother of Stonewall Jackson frequently mentioned in the latter's correspondence. Wirt Woodson, who lived with various Neale relatives, removed to California in the 1840s, and later lived at New Harmony, Indiana, until his death in 1875. After the birth, Julia Woodson's health deteriorated so rapidly that Thomas and Laura were summoned from their grandmother Jackson's home. The Jackson's Mill-to-Ansted trip, which included Warren, was made in the company of "Uncle Robinson," a trusted slave of the Jacksons who brought the children to a death-room reunion with their mother; his wife describes

Stonewall Jackson at the time as a "rosy-cheeked, blue-eyed boy, with wavy brown hair, to whom she clung with all of a mother's devotion." His nephew, Arnold, whose mother Laura was present, says they arrived in time to receive "the dying blessing and prayers" of their mother. Julia Woodson, age thirty-three, died on December 3, 1831; not until 1855, when he was teaching at the Virginia Military Institute, did Jackson again visit Ansted in search of his mother's grave.[30]

Jackson and his sister lived at Jackson's Mill until death claimed their adoring grandmother in 1835. Then he stayed briefly with an uncle in Clarksburg, while Laura joined Warren at the Neale home in Parkersburg; a family misunderstanding precipitated another move, this time to the Jackson's Mill home of another uncle, Cummins E. Jackson. Except for brief intervals, the boy remained with this bachelor uncle until he left Lewis County for West Point.

Cummins Jackson, according to Gittings, "was a man of ample means, very kind to his young relative, and let him have pretty much his own way. He kept race horses and was fond of the sport generally. . . . The writer has been told by men who knew him that he was a fine specimen of physical manhood. They said he was a giant in stature and built in proportion." Besides horse racing at his own track, Cummins Jackson had extensive business interests around Weston and the West Fork Valley, which included operation of the family gristmill. The Jacksons had owned and operated mills of different kinds in the region from at least 1806 and probably earlier; the building housing the mill, last used for milling in the 1890s, is still standing on the state 4-H grounds at Jackson's Mill. Young Jackson and his uncle lived in the homestead built during 1801 by grandfather Edward; although the house was destroyed by fire in the early 1900s, a granite block marks "the site of the boyhood home of General T. J. (Stonewall) Jackson, a soldier of great military genius and renown, a man of resolute, pure Christian character."[31]

After fame engulfed Jackson, all kinds of tales about an exemplary childhood at Jackson's Mill came to the attention of biographers. And there can be little doubt that he was influenced by his congressional uncles as well as a family tradition to excel. Dabney says he sought "to prove himself worthy of his forebearers" from an early age: "It gives us a key to many of the singularities of his character; to his hunger for self-improvement; to his punctilious observance from a boy of the essentials of a gentlemanly bearing."

Johnson Newlon Camden, a boyhood chum at Jackson's Mill, confirms that Jackson the boy became Jackson the man. The stuff that produced the toughness of mind and spirit to fight at Robert E. Lee's side through the battles of 1861–1863 was formed early. Another contemporary, William E. Arnold, a distant relative, notes that Jackson the boy "learned slowly, but what he got in his head he never forgot. He was not quick to decide, but when he made up his mind to do a thing, he did it on short notice and in quick time." Four years younger than Jackson, Camden became a United States senator from West Virginia and John D. Rockefeller's right-hand man to exploit the state's oil and gas resources; he entered West Point in 1846, the year of Jackson's graduation.[32]

Cummins Jackson, who joined the California Gold Rush and died during 1849 near Redding, California, encouraged the boy to develop his intellectual prowess. Amid the fun times and horse racing, Thomas was educated in schools at Jackson's Mill, Weston, and Clarksburg. But his studies did not prevent him from joining his older brother, Warren—a country schoolmaster in neighboring Upshur County—on a journey to visit their sister, Laura, in Parkersburg. With Uncle Cummins' approval, the young Thomas undertook the eighty-mile trek westward. Alfred Neale was then living on an 150-acre island upriver from Parkersburg, where the brothers learned that money could be made from chopping wood for steamboats plying the Ohio and her tributaries. Wanderlust also seized the boys, and just as Abraham Lincoln a decade earlier rafted downriver from Illinois in search of fortune and adventure, Thomas and Warren Jackson headed down the Ohio from their Uncle Alfred Neale's home. Although Lincoln made it to New Orleans, the Jackson boys barely reached the Mississippi. Thomas J. Arnold, who relied upon his mother's account, reports that "the two brothers traveled as far south as the southwestern corner of Kentucky, where they remained through the winter and spring. As to their life there little is known, as they were ever afterward reluctant to talk much of their experience. They did not acquire their fortune, however." Upon the return by steamboat, Thomas resumed his life with Cummins Jackson and Warren went back to his schoolroom, but Warren never recovered from a bout of malaria or related disorder contracted during the trip. He died in November 1841 at age twenty.[33]

Shortly after the Kentucky adventure, young Thomas secured a brief appointment as a surveyor's assistant for construction of the Staunton and Parkersburg Turnpike; the famous route, which was not completed until 1847, connected the Shenandoah Valley with the Ohio River during the antebellum period. As it passed through Weston and Lewis County, Minter Bailey, a family friend who operated a hotel in Weston, was appointed commissioner of contracts for the road's construction through the county. Bailey saw to it that thirteen-year-old Tom Jackson was put to work with one of the surveying gangs through the summer of 1837. "Problems of engineering and the compass and the level seemed to appeal to him very much," writes Roy Bird Cook. "He was described as being one of the best fellows on the job, always doing just what he was told and doing it well." It was also his first experience with a large-scale, organized endeavor.

Although it is difficult to understand that a lad of his age would be handed a responsible job, he was named constable for the Freeman's Creek District of Lewis County a few years later. Alexander Scott Withers, a political ally of the Jackson family, had been appointed justice of the peace in August 1841 by Virginia governor Thomas Gilmer, and under state law he was empowered to designate constables to carry out court functions. Since young Thomas Jackson had shown his mettle to the folks around Jackson's Mill, Withers knew the lad could discharge his duties as bill collector and process server. Anna Jackson relates an earlier incident in which Jackson took offense at an "overgrown rustic" who insulted one of the girls at school. He became fired at the cowardly conduct, and told the boy to apologize at once, or a thrashing would follow. The big fellow, supposing that he was an overmatch for Jackson, refused, whereupon he was handed a thorough pounding. This was the kind of story that sailed through a frontier community like Jackson's Mill; and the jaunt to the Mississippi with Warren made him a local hero.

The warrant, dated June 8, 1841, that named him constable was countersigned by Uncle Cummins, who encouraged the endeavor. Many Jackson biographers point to an episode in which he was attempting to seize a man's horse to satisfy a court-assessed debt. But the offender, who knew of a tradition that an animal could not be taken with the owner astride, would not dismount. The ingenious officer grabbed the reins and started for the partially opened door of a Weston livery barn. Sensing that the low structure would not accommodate horse and rider, the fellow jumped to the ground, leaving Jackson in sole possession. Mrs. Jackson says that her husband did not like the job and looked for any opportunity to escape. A six-by-eight–inch ledger kept by Jackson in which his legal transactions were recorded is now located in the Alderman Library at the University of Virginia, and indicates that he stayed at the job until June 1842, when he left for West Point. Thomas Jonathan Jackson was five months past his nineteenth birthday when his career as Lewis County constable ended.[34]

Robert E. Lee, who entered West Point at age seventeen, graduated in 1829, when Jackson was a toddler traveling from Jackson's Mill to Ansted with his mother and stepfather. Ann Carter Lee encouraged her son to seek the appointment as part of a scheme to launch her children on professional careers before her death. With her estate diminished by debts and family obligations—Lee received but $3,000 of the once-proud Carter money when she died in 1829—she could do little to help him toward financial independence. His elder brother Carter had already graduated from Harvard and established himself in a Washington law practice, and Smith was serving with the fleet. His sisters, Anne and Mildred, still at home, were supported by his mother, who was already in failing health when he left Alexandria for the Hudson.

In 1820, however, another scandal sent shock waves through the family and affected Robert E. Lee to the day of his death. His half brother Henry Lee IV, born in 1787, made the fatal mistake of violating the gentleman's code that permeated tidewater society. A plantation gentleman did not do certain things, and when Light-Horse Harry's eldest son forgot his upbringing, he became forever known as Black-Horse Harry. Twenty years older than Robert E. Lee, he was already recognized for his literary and leadership skills. Following graduation from William and Mary in 1808, Henry Lee got himself elected to the Virginia Assembly from Westmoreland County before the outbreak of war with England. Then, at the start of hostilities that Light-Horse Harry opposed and got himself beaten senseless over in the bargain, the master of Stratford was appointed major in the newly formed American army; active service followed in the Great Lakes fighting with Generals James Wilkinson and Ralph Izard.[35]

Henry A. Wise, later governor of Virginia and a Civil War general, describes Henry IV as "rather ugly in face but one of the most attractive men in conversation we ever listened to." In March 1817, he married Anne McCarty, daughter of a wealthy Westmoreland planter, Daniel McCarty. After the marriage, young Robert always found a welcome hearth at his half brother's home during visits from Alexandria, and the Stratford Lees seemed an idyllic household to the outside world until disaster struck; "the change began with a tragic accident," writes Clifford Dowdey. "His two-year-old daughter Margaret, playing in the great hall, darted through the front door and, unable to check herself, fell to her death down the high flight of stone steps. Anne McCarty Lee became inconsolable and her grief, on the border of dearrangement, could be assuaged only by morphine. In a short time the mistress of Stratford Hall became a drug addict."

Unable or unwilling to content himself, Major Henry Lee turned to the arms of his wife's teenage sister, Elizabeth. An heiress in her own right, she made her home at Stratford Hall when her brother-in-law not only became her legal guardian but also her lover. He became Black-Horse Harry when Elizabeth gave birth to a stillborn child and word leaked out that he had used her money to restore Stratford Hall to its former grandeur. A bad situation became worse when the girl cut off her hair and went into public mourning. [36]

By the time Robert E. Lee reached his thirteenth birthday, he had seen his father jailed for debt as well as beaten, watched his ailing mother struggle to keep up appearances, and witnessed his half brother's disgrace. Not only that, but Harry Lee was forced to liquidate Stratford Hall when his wife left with her McCarty money. It was the house where the future Confederate leader had been born and the place that linked him to the plantation South that he defended from invasion during the Civil War. Most importantly, having the Black-Horse Harry episode come on the heels of other family misfortunes stiffened his resolve to lead a life of moral rectitude. Lee became what Thomas L. Connelly has termed "The Marble Man," a man whose life had no closets—he simply had nothing to hide from that moment forward. And when his time of trial came in 1861, Lee commanded the unflinching loyalty of his troops as much for his personal conduct as for his military prowess.

Although Harry Lee and his wife were later reconciled, their life was never pleasant following earlier difficulties. In the 1820s, he became adviser and speech writer for Andrew Jackson and even moved into the Hermitage at Nashville to be near his patron. Upon entering the White House, Jackson named him consul to Algiers as reward for his services; Jackson was a man who knew about the need for personal support amid domestic upheaval. The Senate, however, rejected confirmation by a solid negative vote. Since he had traveled to Africa with Mrs. Lee, he never returned to the United States. Black-Horse Harry and Mrs. Lee made their home in Paris until his death on January 30, 1837, at age fifty. But the exile produced a notable literary output that included a history of the American Revolution, a treatise on the writings of Thomas Jefferson—intended as a vindication of his father's ill treatment by the third president—and a biography of Napoleon, who had become his lifelong idol. [37]

Although Robert E. Lee was subjected to more than his share of adversity in childhood, his mother did not neglect a proper schooling for the maturing boy. In a family like the Lees, and indeed the Carters, exposure to books and lively conversation dominated his early life. While very young, Lee was sent to school at Eastern View in Fauquier County on the estate of Robert Randolph, husband of Elizabeth Carter, his mother's sister. The Carter clan maintained two schools for their numerous offspring—one for girls at Shirley, and Eastern View for the boys. Apparently little is known about Lee's stay at Eastern View other than that the boy was "a little headstrong" beyond his mother's grasp; he became rebellious enough for Aunt Elizabeth to recommend the rod and prayer as a remedy.[38]

Lee's first academic teacher was W. B. Leary, a cultured Irishman who kept a private academy in Alexandria. Leary's instruction was laced with those writings of antiquity that gentlemen were expected to know throughout the early nineteenth century. Lee must have learned his lessons well because his familiarity with the classics impressed his military colleagues for years afterward. When Leary, who lived to advanced age, called upon his famous student at Lexington after the Civil War, Lee dispatched a word of appreciation from his Washington College study: "Your visit has recalled to me years long since passed, when I was under your daily tuition and instruction. . . . I have felt all my life for the affectionate fidelity which characterized your teaching and conduct. . . ."[39]

When his West Point appointment arrived in March 1824, Lee immediately entered a school near his mother's Alexandria home conducted by James Hallowell to acquire the necessary mathematics for success at the academy; he quickly developed the same esteem from his new instructor that he had enjoyed with Leary. Hallowell, described as "well over six feet in height, of massive frame, clothed in Quaker simplicity, dignity, and kindness," obviously did his work well. "His specialty was finishing up," Hallowell wrote in later life about Lee: "He imparted a neatness and, as he proceeded, to everything he undertook. One of the branches of mathematics he studied was Conic Sections, in which some of the diagrams are very detailed. He drew the diagrams off a slate; and although he well knew that the one he was drawing would have to be removed to make room for another, he drew each one with as much accuracy and finish, lettering and all, as if it were to be engraved and printed." It was the same attention to detail that carried him to a second-place finish in the West Point class of 1829 and to command of the Army of Northern Virginia.

Hallowell, who outlived his student by seven years, remained a staunch Unionist because of his Quaker background. Although a warm friend to Lee until his death, he supposedly "rejoiced" when the Confederate chieftain was beaten at Gettysburg. After the Civil War, Hallowell was named superintendent of Indians for Nebraska by President Grant.[40]

Though Lee and Jackson entered West Point at different times, each man was able to finish with distinction. When Lee graduated with the class of 1829, he immediately confronted the stagnation of the old army; Jackson, however, entered the army a brevet second lieutenant of artillery on the eve of war with Mexico, which increased his prospects for rapid promotion. Other than a sense of duty and a devotion to family tradition, the tidewater gentleman and the frontier youth had little in common except a consuming desire for success and recognition. Although their families had been intertwined by remote connections in generations past, the casual observer in 1846, when Thomas Jonathan Jackson finished seventeenth in his class of sixty members and Robert E. Lee was a struggling captain of engineers, would have noticed little to suggest their future greatness as military commanders. Yet their upbringing and training prepared the two warriors to stymie the whole might of the federal government from the summer of 1862 through May 1863, when Jackson gave his life at Chancellorsville; though Lee carried on with other subordinates until the inevitable collapse at Appomattox, the two were able to sustain the Confederate cause through its initial fiery trial.

2

Cadets

After years of academic preparation, Robert E. Lee sought admission to the United States Military Academy during the spring of 1824—a decision unquestionably designed to relieve his mother's financial burden and to insure a career that would lead to his own independence. And, says his nephew Fitzhugh Lee, the move "probably resulted from a son's desire to follow in his father's footsteps especially when the father had been so distinguished in the profession of arms." The Lee family interceded in his efforts to secure a cadetship by sending him to the Washington office of Andrew Jackson in the company of his aunt, Mrs. Nellie Lewis. Known as the "Belle of Mount Vernon and George Washington's favorite grandchild," Nellie Lewis had been a longtime friend of Jackson.

Old Hickory, about to fight the 1824 presidential canvas in which he eventually lost to John Quincy Adams, was United States senator from Tennessee and chairman of the military affairs committee; Jackson was sufficiently impressed with his old comrade Harry Lee's youngest that he wholeheartedly endorsed his application to Secretary of War John C. Calhoun. The appointment, dated April 1, 1824, was duly signed by President James Monroe before the famous "corrupt bargain" between John Quincy Adams and Henry Clay to deprive Jackson of the presidency sullied national politics. Others, including his mother and Congressman C. F. Mercer of Virginia, helped his cause, and his brother Henry Lee IV, although now known as Black-Horse Harry and soon to launch his own career under the tutelage of Jackson, made a special plea to Calhoun:

> I know of no principle of *rational* selection that should exempt him from the hazards of fair competition on the ground of personal advantages and

mental qualifications, (for which he is well prepared) but the just and admitted one of referring to the services of the Father in estimating the claims of the Son. . . . On this principle I beg to rest the claims of Robert. To a person of your enlarged sentiments, and accurate knowledge of our national history it will be unnecessary to enumerate the exertions of my father in the cause of this country, or to trace the grand and beautiful process of mortality, by which orphans of public benefactors, become the children of the State. . . .[1]

With endorsements from some of the most prominent personages in American life, Robert Edward Lee, age nineteen years and four months, entered the academy on July 11, 1825; seventeen years later, on July 1, 1842, Thomas Jonathan Jackson entered West Point at nineteen years and five months. Though a mere toddler in 1825, Jackson, like Lee, was destined to compile a brilliant record on the Hudson. The academy more than any other institution molded both into world-renowned fighting men; their paths as soldiers first intersected on the grounds at West Point during the summer of 1843, when Lee was a captain of engineers and Jackson had finished his first year of study.

Official academy records list Lee's "parent or guardian" as Colonel Henry Lee of Washington, D.C. Family connections and a solid academic background surely helped Lee at West Point, but an extraordinary discipline also fitted him for the soldier's regimen: "[V]ery few young men enter that institution so well prepared for military life as was Lee, for he had been accustomed to responsibility and had thoroughly mastered the art of self-control many years before he stepped within its walls." Then, continues a 1911 biography, "he was neither a prig nor a 'grind,' but he regarded his cadetship as part of the life's work which he had voluntarily chosen, and he had no inclination to let pleasure interfere with it."[2]

Lee's steadfastness enabled him to graduate second in a class of forty-six; he did so without a single demerit under the rating system conceived by Sylvanus Thayer. A graduate of Dartmouth College, Thayer had gone to West Point in 1804, where he raced to a commission after a single year of study; following a stint teaching mathematics at the academy, he fought with distinction in the War of 1812. Thayer became a devotee of Napoleon and the French military tradition, which led him to a tour in Paris, where he not only studied European tactics but also purchased books to form the basic West Point library during the early nineteenth century. Earlier slipshod methods led him to devise a ranking scheme that eliminated "subjective feelings, while it took into account nearly everything a cadet did for four years, both in and out of the classroom. . . . It was the most complete, and impersonable system imaginable. Every cadet was graded on every activity, in the classroom and on the drill field in a positive manner, and in every other way negatively. In his subjects, the cadet received marks ranging from 3.0 for perfect to 0.0 for complete failure; the more points he had, the higher he stood. But no matter how brilliant he was, his class rank could be low if his behavior was poor, because Thayer set up a system of demerits for each infraction of the regulations, and the demerits lowered a cadet's standing."[3]

Even a cursory review of Lee's "Academic Records" indicates that he mastered Thayer's scheme from the beginning. At the end of his fourth term (years of study at West Point are numbered in reverse), he stood third in a class of eighty-seven; third term, second in a class of sixty; second term, second in a class of fifty-four; and first term (his last), second in a class of forty-six. As academy demands caused his classmen to diminish by nearly one-half between 1825 and 1829, Lee was obliged to watch Charles Mason, a classmate from New York, beat him for top honors in every academic and military exercise. And though Lee left no comment about his fellow student, Mason resigned from the army soon after his graduation. "He practiced law for a number of years in New York, Wisconsin, and the District of Columbia, became a judge, edited a newspaper for awhile, and finally served as an official of various railway corporations." Mason apparently did not reenter the army at the outbreak of Civil War in 1861.[4]

Although Lee was not known to take a youthful liberty or visit nearby "fleshpots" during his near-perfect time at West Point, many of his contemporaries were not so fortunate. Future commanders such as Samuel P. Heintzelman, (class of 1826), Albert Sidney Johnston (1826), Leonidas K. Polk (1827), William N. Pendleton (1830), and Theophilus H. Holmes (1829), all had their difficulties. His close friend Joseph Eggleston Johnston, a fellow Virginian, only graduated thirteenth in Lee's class of forty-six. His future commander in chief, Jefferson Davis, amassed so many demerits that he finished twenty-third out of thirty-three men in the class ahead of Lee and Johnston. An exuberant Davis, something of a gay blade at the Point, fell over the Hudson cliffs during one escapade, which required an extended hospital stay. Edgar Allan Poe, who entered West Point in the class following Lee's graduation, had such a poor record that he left after one year to escape a court martial; nevertheless, he managed to publish a volume of poetry during his abbreviated studies.[5]

West Point without doubt was the foremost engineering and scientific school in the country during Lee's cadet days; many thought it superior to Harvard as an institution of higher learning. Under Thayer's watchful eye, a distinguished faculty had been assembled, including David B. Douglass as professor of mathematics and engineering before Dennis Hart Mahan assumed the post three years after Lee's graduation. Douglass, a Yale graduate and veteran of the War of 1812, had followed the Frenchman Claudius Crozet, who left West Point in 1823 to become chief engineer of Virginia and founder of the Virginia Military Institute. Like Crozet, Douglass relied upon Colonel Guy de Vernon's textbook on the "science of war and fortifications," which in turn drew upon the writings of Baron Antonie Henri de Jomini. Thus, Lee, like other American soldiers of his generation, had been heavily embued with Jomini's interpretation of Napoleonic strategy during his formative years at West Point.[6]

Jomini, a Swiss banker, had made his way to Paris at the outbreak of the Napoleonic wars and subsequently served on the staffs of Marshal Ney, Napoleon himself, and later the Czar Alexander. An intense student of campaign maneuvers and a prolific writer, he churned out a string of masterpieces, including his chief work, entitled, *Précis de l'Art de le Guerre*. Known as the *Art of War* following its English translation by another West Point officer, Captain J. M. O'Conner, the work quickly became a staple for the men who would make up the officer corps for both armies in the American Civil War, including Lee and Jackson. Interestingly, Ulysses S. Grant later admitted that he had not read Jomini before the war. Although the master's influence upon Lee is open to speculation, one Jomini scholar opines: "Among the earliest words that Jomini wrote when he began the *Art of War* were those which enumerated the prerequisites of a good general. First in position on the list of importance was the quality of 'high moral courage, capable of great resolution.' Next in importance was the virtue of 'physical courage which takes no account of danger.' " Moral and physical courage if nothing else characterized Lee's career in the Mexican War and in the Civil War.[7]

Lee's other instructors included Jared Mansfield, who taught natural philosophy—or physics—during his third class year of 1827–1828; Mansfield, who argued with academy administrators, was replaced during Lee's final year by Edward H. Courtenay, and, ironically, it was the latter's death twenty-five years later that occasioned the first positive contact between Lee and Jackson. It came about during 1853, when Major Thomas J. Jackson, then professor of natural philosophy at the Virginia Military Institute, secured a letter of recommendation from Lee in his unsuccessful bid to replace Courtenay at the University of Virginia, where he had been a member of the faculty for several years following a distinguished career at West Point and the University of Pennsylvania.

The persistent notion that Lee's class studied William Rawle's *A View of the Constitution of the United States,* with its eloquent defense of a state's right to secede from the Union is open to question. Samuel Heintzelman, class of 1822, left several diary entries suggesting Rawle had been used by his class; although the book was in use at the academy, Douglas Southall Freeman contends: "As for Lee there is no first-hand evidence that he was instructed in Rawle, or that he ever read the book." And, Charles Dudley Rhodes, who studied Lee's cadet days with care, cites Professor Albert E. Church that the 1825 class did not use Rawle but relied upon another text by James Kent, a Federalist interpreter of the constitution. There is conflicting evidence that Lee even studied constitutional law as a cadet.[8]

Lee sat through the usual curriculum designed to mold a competent soldier—French, drawing, ethics and history, mathematics, artillery tactics, chemistry, and the rest. A natural proficiency in mathematics earned him the position of "acting assistant professor" early in his career, although the post was generally reserved for first classmen who excelled in the subject; he was also named a cadet officer because of his high standing in the corps. Life was hard and nothing short of Spartan in the no-frills simplicity of West Point during the early nineteenth century, yet Lee left in 1829 with an abiding love for the place.[9]

According to custom throughout the antebellum era, Lee was granted his only furlough during the summer of 1828 between his second and first terms. With only one year left on the Hudson, he traveled to his mother's home and the familiar surroundings of Alexandria. Also waiting for him was a childhood sweetheart named Mary Randolph Custis. After his three-year absence, Lee renewed his close friendship with twenty-year-old Mary, a granddaughter of Martha Washington. Following a summer of frequent visits to Arlington, her father's great mansion on the Potomac overlooking Georgetown and the capital city, an understanding developed between the two lovers. Mary Custis was the only child of George Washington Parke Custis, a playwright of some reputation who always referred to himself as the "child of Mount Vernon"; "a unique character," writes Burton Hendrick, "Custis spent his time in leisurely and not too thrifty cultivation of his acres, in making Fourth of July speeches devoted largely to eulogies of the great American Washington, to writing garrulous reminiscences of early days at Mount Vernon and composing plays for the 'poor rogues of actors,' as he called them, on such obvious themes as *Pocahontas,* The *Pawnee Chief,* and *Baltimore Defended.*" He was not only George Washington's adopted son but was also descended from the Calvert-Baltimore family of Maryland, all of which gave his daughter unparalleled social status.

The necessity for a respectable engagement period and the need for young Robert to finish his studies and establish himself delayed the wedding until the autumn of 1831. Although Parke Custis had reservations about his future son-in-law, largely due to the well-known Lee insolvency, young love triumphed. The marriage lasted until Lee's death forty years later, without the slightest hint that it was anything other than a true love match. Mrs. Lee was a notoriously poor housekeeper, yet the man she referred to as "Mr. Lee" remained her devoted companion. When Lee left Virginia in the autumn of 1828, he had reinstated the tight bond between his family and George Washington established by Light-Horse Harry more than four decades earlier. And nothing better illustrates the Lee-Washington connection than a visit to the Washington and Lee museum in Lexington and a gaze at the first president's christening dress deposited there by Mrs. Lee when her husband served as president of Washington College.[10]

Lee's standing in the class of 1829 earned him a commission as second lieutenant in the corps of engineers; that army branch was considered the most prestigious, and only top West Point graduates were admitted to its ranks. Interestingly, Lee's eldest son, George Washington Custis Lee, whom the family always called "Custis," was likewise commissioned into the corps after he graduated first in the class of 1854; but Tom Jackson, class of 1846, because of his seventeenth place finish among fifty-nine men, ended up in the artillery. Lee understandably made straight for the fellowship of Alexandria, where he found his mother desperately ill at Ravenswood, a relative's home nearby. "Manliness, true and noble, was stamped upon the form and the face of the second lieutenant of engineers who hastened to the waiting mother at the close of his four years' course. She was granted only time to smile upon him with a mother's pride in her best-loved child." Twenty-two-year-old Robert quickly became her faithful sickroom attendant during her last painful days. Ann Carter Lee, the woman who said she could not live without Robert, died on July 10, 1829, six days after her son's West Point graduation. She was fifty-six years old.[11]

Lee's first military orders, dated August 11, 1829, commanded him to report to the officer in charge at Cockspur Island in the Savannah River. After a mournful summer settling his mother's estate and seeing his sisters situated, he bade Mary Custis good-bye and headed south on his first sea voyage with Nat, a trusted family servant. Lee had known the man since childhood and meant to care for him after his mother's death, but, writes J. William Jones, "the springtime saw the faithful old servant laid in the grave by the hands of his kind young master." Although deprived of this link with his family and Alexandria, Lee found other outlets in close-by Savannah. Through Jack Mackay, a Savannah native and his West Point classmate, he was introduced to fashionable society in the grand old city. And, Eliza Mackay, sister of his fellow officer, soon became his companion at balls and teas during his stay on the Georgia coast that lasted until April 1831. A flirtation of sorts developed between the handsome young engineer and Eliza, later Mrs. John Stiles, even though he married Mary Randolph Custis two years after he left Cockspur. Lee and his family kept a close bond with the Mackays, and when Eliza died in December 1867, she left him, he wrote, "with one less earthly tie to bind me."[12]

Lee's twenty-four-month tour on the Georgia coast was devoted to raising the elevation of Cockspur Island, a low-lying mud flat at the mouth of the Savannah River; it was mean work with difficult technical obstacles that made the gaiety of Savannah and the Mackays a pleasing relief indeed. Although an earlier fortification, Fort George, was on the island, the construction of Fort Pulaski was a more formidable undertaking; named for the Polish patriot Count Casimir Pulaski, who died at Savannah while fighting during the Revolution, the replacement fort was not completed until 1847. The project had scarcely advanced beyond initial efforts to raise the tidal island above the surrounding water level when Lee was reassigned to different engineering duties at Fortress Monroe. A furlough during the summer of 1830 enabled him to renew his courtship at Arlington House and to escape the often frustrating toil, when, as he told a confidant, he was "constantly damp." Lee's stay on the island relaxed somewhat after his return from Virginia to find Joseph King Fenno Mansfield, nephew of Jared Mansfield, his old instructor at West Point, as commanding officer. Mansfield, an 1822 graduate of West Point who would die leading an attack against Lee's positions at Antietam, was four years older than Lee; the two officers developed a lighthearted camaraderie during the fall and winter of 1830 that lasted until Mansfield's untimely death.[13]

In 1831 Lee was assigned a new billet at Fortress Monroe on the Virginia Peninsula; he did not realize that he would be asked to develop a plan for its destruction thirty-one years later. Although regulars had been garrisoned since 1823 at Old Point Comfort where the James River meets Chesapeake Bay, a military installation of sorts had been there since shortly after the founding of Jamestown. Captain Andrew Talcott, engineer in charge at Fortress Monroe, immediately directed Lee to oversee preparatory work for the erection of Fort Calhoun, located on a shoal called the Rip Raps a few hundred yards from the mainland. Again he was summoned to build up a low-lying and partially submerged island with rock and ballast, so his job was similar to what it had been in Georgia: "The construction of a heavy fort on an insecure foundation."[14]

When Lee arrived for his military duty in Virginia, he was twenty-four, while Talcott, a recent widower, was ten years older. Talcott, a Connecticut-born West Pointer, class of 1818, had already amassed a world of engineering experience at army outposts from the Missouri and Yellowstone Rivers in the West to several forts along the East Coast. As the two worked together, they formed a partnership that lasted well into the future. During what has been termed "the happiest period of his life," Lee joined his brother officers in the "pleasures and fascinations of Virginia social life." And, continues Fitzhugh Lee, "as soon as he unbuckled his sword belt there was but a step to take to get into the gay world. . . . He went much in the society of ladies—always most congenial to him. His conversation was bright, his wit refined and pleasant. Cement, mortar, lime, curves, tangents, and straight professional lines disappeared then." Talcott remarried in April 1832, and Lee's own wedding occurred but two months after his arrival at Fortress Monroe. For Lee it was a time for hard work and enjoyable interludes; later he would write to his friend Jack Mackay that the "ladies of Old Point are formed of the very poetry of nature, and would make your lips water and your fingers tingle."[15]

Lee's marriage took place on Thursday evening, June 30, 1831, "in the right-hand drawing-room of that fine old mansion" at Arlington. The hefty wedding party, which included his brother, naval lieutenant Smith Lee, accompanied by Miss Catherine Mason, was treated to a gala entertainment that lasted through the following Tuesday; some partying even spilled over to the nearby estate of General John Mason. General Long relates that the Reverend William Meade, later Episcopal bishop of Virginia and Lee's mentor during the Civil War, who officiated, reached Arlington "thoroughly drenched" after being stranded in an unexpected storm. A suit belonging to Parke Custis was hurriedly summoned, but "unluckily for the fit of these garments, Mr. Custis was short and stout, the clergyman tall and thin. . . . However, the ample folds of the surplice covered all defects of raiment, and the guests generally were un-aware of the awkward predicament of the dignified divine." Though the newlyweds were by all accounts supremely happy, they presented a study in contrasts that even their contemporaries had difficulty under-standing. A portrait for the occasion "shows Lieutenant Lee in his dark-blue uniform, gold epaulettes on his broad shoulders, and his youthful face adorned with the fashionable side whiskers of the day." But, writes another Lee biographer, "Mary Randolph Custis was not typical of Southern-raised girls in her attitude to gentlemen; instead of looking to their comfort, she expected them to look after hers. Nor was she any beauty. She was frail, bony of figure, and her patrician face was thin, sharp-featured and imperious. She had brown hair and eyes, like Lee's mother, but, careless of her appearance, her hair was the despair of the maids who helped her dress. . . ."[16]

After the customary furlough of one month for marrying officers, Lee returned to Fortress Monroe with his bride. She brought with her an inheritance that included not only Arlington House with its broad acres but also White House plantation on the Pamunkey River where George Washington had married her grandmother, Martha Custis. General Long is correct that the match was "a brilliant one for Lieutenant Lee." Yet Lee did not resign his commission for the life of a plantation gentleman, and Mary Custis Lee was ever complimentary of her husband as well as his constant companion. In later life, she avowed "the advantage of the wedding was largely on her side, since her husband's management of her estate was so skilful [*sic*] and judicious as to make it more valuable and remunerative than she could possibly have done."

At Fortress Monroe, where the army maintained its training school for artillery officers, the young couple joined the swirl of activity that en-gulfed the place; when Mrs. Lee remained at Arlington for an extended visit during the spring of 1832, the lonely husband was moved to write his "Dear Molly," a pet endearment: "I am greatly delighted at the near approach of your return to one, who is constantly thinking of you. I will be ready to receive you next Saturday, but will try & be not much disappointed should you not come till Wednesday. . . ." Their first child, George Washington Custis Lee, was born at Fortress Monroe in September 1832, and three years later in the summer of 1835, a second child, Mary, arrived while Lee served under the chief of engineers in Washington. This child, Lee's eldest daughter, who attracted the amo-rous attentions of a young cavalryman named Jeb Stuart, was born at Arlington; the birth apparently aggravated the mother's already frail constitution, although she bore another five children. Family members hinted that a prolonged pelvic infection caused her to cut off her hair in a fit of depression.[17]

While stationed at Fortress Monroe, Lee and his wife had occasion to observe the ugliness of slavery at close quarters when soldiers from the garrison were dispatched to help quell the infamous Nat Turner insurrection. Turner, a slave preacher near New Jerusalem, now Courtland, in Southampton County, led a rebellion that resulted in the deaths of fifty-five whites and chilled slaveholders across the South. The uprising in August 1831 lasted but forty-eight hours; it could have but one outcome once organized military force was brought to bear against it. Three companies "with a field piece and 100 stands of spare arms with ammunition" marched from Fortress Monroe commanded by Lieutenant Colonel William Jenkins Worth, Lee's old commandant at West Point. Although Lee did not accompany the troops, he wrote to Mrs. Parke Custis afterward that "the plot was widely extended, and the negroes [sic] anticipating the time of rising by one week, mistaking the third Sunday for the last in the month, defeated the whole scheme and prevented much mischief. It is ascertained that they used their religious assemblies, which ought to have been devoted to better purposes, for forming and maturing their plans, and that their preachers were the leading men."

Militia companies and marines from a United States warship at Norfolk converged on isolated Southampton County to assist the regulars under Worth; one detachment shot a number of black prisoners near New Jerusalem "and had their heads stuck on poles." Accounts vary about the number of blacks who marched with Nat Turner, but a total forty-six were brought to trial, seventeen of whom were convicted of murder. The incident induced widespread fear across the South and led to a rigid enforcement of the famed "slave codes" to control its black population. Northern abolitionists rose to Turner's defense, and the incident became one of the opening dramas in the heated controversy over slavery that culminated in the Civil War thirty years later. Lee told his mother-in-law just six weeks after his marriage in 1831: "The whole number of blacks taken and killed did not amount to the number of whites murdered by them."[18]

The horrors of slave insurrection were soon forgotten as Lee and Talcott resumed their work at Hampton Roads until October 1834, when Lee departed for a new post as assistant to Brigadier General Charles Gratiot, the army's chief engineer in Washington. A nasty squabble between the artillery and engineers over which should complete construction at Fortress Monroe reached even the secretary of war and darkened Lee's last days at Old Point; when the artillery won out, Talcott was sent to another project in New York harbor, while Lee made his way to Washington a few months later. Life brightened again when he joined his wife and two-year-old Custis at Arlington; Mrs. Lee, especially, was pleased to be back in the familiar social milieu along the Potomac, although a complicated pregnancy with her second child would soon present difficulty. At Arlington Lieutenant Lee could live the gentleman's life within easy reach of his office. During his rides from the Custis mansion into the city, as one writer puts it, "his handsome figure drew attention as the gallant horseman who passed daily along Pennsylvania Avenue."[19]

Although Lee was bored by the routine of office work and longed for more active duty, he also found time to enjoy himself. The conviviality of Mrs. Ulrich's boarding table attracted his notice on those days when a return home was not feasible because of weather or official obligations. Daily gatherings at her table, often called "The Mess," included not only Joseph E. Johnston and other young officers but also men who had already made their mark, men who offered Lee an entrée into the world of public affairs: "Mahlon Dickerson, Secretary of the Navy; William C. Rives, who had been minister to France, and who at the time was senator from Virginia; Hugh Swinton Legare of South Carolina, an eminent lawyer, then a member of Congress, but at an earlier period minister to The Hague; and Joel R. Poinsett, Secretary of War."

Another regular at "The Mess" was John Macomb, a West Point cadet in Lee's days at the academy and close friend of his brother, Smith Lee. Macomb said later that Lee was "the most beloved and admired by men and women" of all his acquaintances over an active lifetime. During the spring and summer of 1835, the two found time to amuse themselves: "As Lieutenant Lee was about to start for Arlington on one occasion on his spirited Virginia horse, seeing Macomb approach, he hailed him, saying, 'Come, get up with me.' To the surprise of Lee, Macomb approached, put his foot in the stirrup, and mounted behind him. Thereupon they rode down Pennsylvania Avenue, and just as they were in front of the President's House they met the Hon. Levi Woodbury, Secretary of War to whom they both bowed with great dignity: A more astonished gentleman has not been seen before or since." The comforts of Arlington and the good times at Mrs. Ulrich's notwithstanding, Lee not only found himself without promotion but also little more than "a dignified clerk" burdened with a monotonous work load.[20]

Lee's friend from Fortress Monroe, Andrew Talcott, came to his rescue in July 1835, when he secured his services as "assistant astrono-mer" to survey the Michigan-Ohio boundary. Talcott had already con-ducted one survey but had been summoned to run another as part of the fight over something called the "Toledo Strip." An interminable legal dispute had developed after the Northwest Ordinance of 1787 estab-lished the southern limit of Michigan Territory at "the southernmost point of Lake Michigan due east to Lake Erie"; thereafter, Congress admitted Ohio to statehood in 1803 without a clearly delineated north-ern border. When Michigan attained the requisite sixty thousand inhabi-tants for admission to the Union, Ohio authorities discovered that Toledo, at the western tip of Lake Erie would be in the new state. A number of surveys, including one known as the Talcott Line—first established in 1834 and resurveyed with Lee's help in 1835—were con-ducted over several years. The Talcott Line, which placed Toledo in Michigan, was rejected when the present boundary was established some years later.[21]

Lee's trip into the Old Northwest involved demanding work with a number of astronomical and surveying instruments that Talcott had obtained for their use; Talcott in fact established a scientific reputation by designing some of the telescopes himself. The journey also entailed physical hardship after the pleasures of Washington City. "We are en-camped on the verge of the Lake, in a wilderness of Land, with nothing around us but dwarf Wild Poplar & Pine," Lee wrote to his wife on September 2 from "South Bend of Lake Michigan." "The water of the Lake is beautifully clear, almost too cold to tempt bathing. There are no inhabitants near us & even the Indians that live in the country back of us, are in Chicago, on the West Shore of the Lake waiting to receive their annual annuities." An earlier letter from Detroit scolded Mrs. Lee for urging his early homecoming: "But why do you urge my *immediate* return, & tempt one in the *strongest* manner, to endeavor to get excused from the performance of a duty, imposed on me by my Profession, for the pure gratification of my private feelings. Do you not think that those feelings are enough of themselves to contend with, without aggravation; and that I rather require to be strengthened & encouraged to the *full* performance of what I am called on to execute, rather than excited to a dereliction, which even our affection could not palliate, or our judgment excuse." Although he was sympathetic to his wife's slow recovery from the birth of their second child, he was clearly committed to an uncom-promising devotion to duty that epitomized his entire military and university career.[22]

Upon his return to Washington in October 1835, Robert E. Lee remained at his desk in the War Department until July 1837, when he received his first independent command. Mrs. Lee, still incapacitated from the birth of Mary, had traveled to Ravensworth, but her husband had her transported to Arlington, where he took personal charge of her convalescence. His endeavors must have been successful, because another child arrived twenty months later, in 1837, while Lee struggled with his office duties. William Henry Fitzhugh Lee, always called Rooney by the family, was born May 31 at Arlington. Little did the young father know that his two eldest sons would serve him throughout the Civil War and that both would achieve distinction on their own merits after Appomattox: Custis as president of Washington and Lee University following Lee's death in 1870 and Rooney as a three-term member of Congress. During 1836–1837, however, Robert E. Lee, faced with a growing family and a sick wife, received his first promotion: He was made first lieutenant of engineers on September 21, 1836, seven years after leaving West Point.[23]

Meanwhile, fifteen hundred miles to the west, a new, different assignment beckoned Lee after the city of St. Louis convinced official Washington that its access to steamboat navigation on the Mississippi needed remedy. Although St. Louis had but six thousand inhabitants in 1833, its population increased to thirty thousand within a decade because of expanded river traffic that carried an avalanche of people headed for new homes in the West as well as trade and commerce of every description. But city fathers became alarmed that several sandbars opposite the waterfront were dangerously close to making it an inland city. "The apprehension was so great that persons refused to invest in real estate at St. Louis," writes one scholar. "And while the city was saved, Kaskaskia, the first capitol of Illinois, went to a watery grave. Napoleon, Arkansas is no longer remembered." While other river towns had similar difficulties, at St. Louis the two major bars known as Bloody Island—named for the duels fought on its shores—and Duncan's Island were formed by "gyrations" of the great river a few miles below its junction with the Missouri.

After St. Louis was declared an official port of entry in 1831 and Congress approved a meager appropriation, the Army Corps of Engineers was appointed to alter the main channel as it passed the city. General Gratiot first sent Captain Henry M. Shreve to develop a suitable plan for the river, but Lee was shortly dispatched from Washington in August 1837 to undertake construction of a series of dams and dikes. It was not only his first independent command but also the first opportunity to demonstrate his engineering abilities. He was no sooner on the site than his keen analytical powers enabled him to develop a detailed plan for attacking the river. "The works planned consisted of: first, a dam at the head of Bloody Island to cost $63,574; second, a dike running down the west side of Bloody Island, $80,680; and third, the protection of the head of Bloody Island, $14,300." At some point Lee had apparently read widely including a study of the Dutch dike system before starting his work; and, as early as July 1838, he "had pushed Duncan's Island a considerable distance downstream." Lee's efforts gained him recognition throughout the country as he shifted the main course of the river to accommodate the St. Louis waterfront. "The plan devised for this purpose by Captain Lee promises to be eminently successful," editorialized the *Missouri Republican* in September 1838. "Since the commencement of the work it has been prosecuted with great activity, and with unexpected dispatch, when the character of the locality, the scarcity of laborers and other difficulties are considered."[24]

As Lee signaled to his workmen in the river from an office on the second story of a levee warehouse, he also kept an eye on Mrs. Lee and the children at Arlington. About this time, he became concerned that Master Rooney was increasingly "hard to manage." His instructions to his wife on how best to discipline the boy also say much about the father: "I have endeavored in my intercourse with him to require nothing but what is in my opinion necessary or proper, and to explain to him temperately its propriety," the thirty-year-old father wrote on October 17. "I have also tried to show him that I was firm in my demands, and constant in their enforcement, and that he must comply with them; and, I let him see that I look to their execution in order to relieve him, as much as possible, from the temptation to break them. Since my efforts have been so unsuccessful, I fear I must have altogether failed in accomplishing my purpose, but I hope to profit from my experience."

In a letter to his cousin, Cassius F. Lee, dated August 20, 1838, Lee requested a handwritten copy of the Lee family tree that "I once saw in the hands of Cousin Edmund [Lee], for the only time in my life." And he implored C. F. Lee's assistance in securing the Lee coat of arms, which "I think is due a man of my large family to his posterity, and which I have thought, perhaps foolishly, enough, might as well be right as wrong." Isolated from his wife and children, Lee developed a serious interest in his lineage for the first time as he worked "at mastering the Mississippi."[25]

Family matters again intruded during the summer of 1839, when Mrs. Lee became confined with her fourth child. Lee journeyed to Arlington but returned to St. Louis before the child's birth on June 18; his second daughter, Anne Carter Lee, was born with a defective or impaired eye, which caused the family great concern. "You do not know how much I have missed you and the children, my dear Mary," a lonely Lee wrote from Louisville on his return west. "To be alone in a crowd is very solitary. In the woods I feel sympathy with the trees and birds, in whose company I take delight, but experience no pleasure in a strange crowd. . . ."[26]

General Long's account has Lee first traveling to St. Louis by way of Pittsburgh and then down the Ohio by steamboat; but the letter to Mrs. Lee says that he traveled by stagecoach in the summer of 1839 from Staunton to Guyandotte (present Huntington, West Virginia) on the Ohio. His journey westward along the James River and Kanawha Turnpike—completed by Virginia in 1830 to connect Richmond and the Ohio Valley—took him through Ansted, where Thomas Jackson had spent his young childhood. Lee, however, could hardly have had contact with the future Stonewall at this early date as his stage rolled through the small Fayette County community; fifteen years of age, the young Tom Jackson had lived with his bachelor uncle, Cummins Jackson, at the ancestral home in Lewis County since his mother's death in 1831. It would be fascinating to speculate if the Confederate warriors ever discussed Lee's brief visit to Jackson's childhood home during their countless war discussions.[27]

Upon his return to St. Louis in June, Robert E. Lee spent another two years working with his "dams and dikes" before he was transferred to another engineering project at Fort Hamilton, New York. His efforts not only earned him a captaincy during 1838 but also an offer to join the West Point faculty as "assistant professor," although he rejected teaching at the academy as the accolades rolled in for his work on the Mississippi. When Captain Lee left in 1841, the project was far from complete, yet he had laid the foundation for St. Louis's future greatness as a trading center and "gateway to the West." With his assistant, Lieutenant Montgomery C. Meigs—later quartermaster general of the federal army during the Civil War, Lee "went in person with the hands every morning about sunrise, and worked day by day in the hot, boiling sun—the heat being greatly increased by the reflection of the river." Afterward, continues John F. Darby, a St. Louis mayor during the 1830s and 1840s: "By his rich gift of genius and scientific knowledge Lee brought the Father of Waters under control."[28]

Lee reported to his duty station at Fort Hamilton, which guards New York Harbor at the western tip of Long Island, in the summer of 1842 and remained there until August 1846, when he joined the army in San Antonio at the outbreak of war with Mexico. Because of his closeness to

West Point, he visited the academy in an official capacity on at least three occasions while stationed in New York. Thomas Jackson entered West Point in July 1842 as a plebe in the class of 1846, which means their lives crossed, although evidence is speculative at best that personal contact between them resulted during Lee's visits. Lee was assigned to engineering new fortifications at the New York facility and was also able to have his family with him for the first time since leaving the War Department for St. Louis.

When Jackson arrived two weeks early to make his preparations for entering West Point, he may have briefly encountered Lee, who sat as examiner for the class of 1842. Lee visited West Point a second time in the summer of 1843—as Jackson completed his fourth term—with two other officers to locate a new cadet barracks. Lee again sat on the board of examiners for the class of 1844 at the conclusion of Cadet Jackson's second full year of study. Given the preoccupation of students everywhere with examinations, it is inconceivable that a shy, yet precocious Tom Jackson would have missed the handsome captain of engineers who called at the circumscribed world of West Point. Whether Lee would have singled out Jackson as a lower classman is more doubtful, unless he discussed the cadet roster with school officials. In view of Lee's great love for the place, it is entirely possible that he first became aware of Jackson at this time; whatever happened in 1842–1844, it is certain that Lee and Jackson were in the same place at the same time.[29]

Although Tom Jackson had an interest in formal education long before 1842, his entry into West Point was accidental except for a young man's desire to succeed. When Alexander Scott Withers, a writer of note, told the boy that Virginia gentlemen had servants for menial tasks and "worked their heads instead of their hands," Jackson supposedly replied: "Well, when one has money to go to William and Mary College, then he knows how to work his head." *The Chronicles of Border Warfare,* authored by Withers in 1831, remains a classic in frontier literature, and the writer, who doubled as local schoolmaster, had an unquestioned influence upon the young Jackson. The boy's association with men like Withers as well as his political uncles and J. M. Bennett, a Lewis County politico who attained statewide office as Virginia state auditor, indicate further that Jackson was a young man with contacts. His confession of ignorance to Congressman Samuel L. Hays notwithstanding, he attended local schools and briefly taught school himself while serving as Lewis County constable; nevertheless, he did not attend any of the numerous private academies that dotted the landscape in transmontane Virginia.[30]

When a West Point appointment became vacant for the fourteenth congressional district in the spring of 1842, Jackson joined two other youths—Gibson J. Butcher and Joseph A. J. Lightburn—in sitting for a competitive examination; arranged by Hays and conducted at the Bailey House in Weston, a few miles from Jackson's Mill, the exercise determined the qualifications of each candidate. It was also a means of relieving the pressure on Hays, a longtime political ally of the Jackson family. "The result of the test was that Gibson J. Butcher received the recommendation and subsequently a provisional appointment to the academy. He went to West Point in the closing days of May 1842, only to find the code of military discipline and the requirements for the course of study not to his liking." When news reached Lewis County that the cadetship was still vacant, the Jackson clan, including George Jackson, who had conducted the original examination, launched a campaign to secure the post for young Thomas.[31]

Leaving nothing to chance, Jackson made his way to Washington with a bundle of hurriedly gathered recommendations, including one from Withers, which he delivered to Hays in person. Roy Bird Cook, a careful student of Jackson's early life, traces the route:

Accompanied by one [of the Jackson family slaves], likewise mounted, to bring the horse back, he set out for Clarksburg to catch the stage. The stage line at the time was operated by the Kuyendalls and, as the Pioneer Stage Line allowed one to travel 210 miles for $10. Arriving at Clarksburg and finding the stage gone, Jackson overtook it near present Grafton, and the servant returned with the horse. Jackson's route to Washington from this point is obscure, but it may be said that he did not "walk 300 miles," "arrive covered with mud," or "sell his horse," etc. Instead it seems that he left the stage at Green Valley Depot, sixteen miles east of Cumberland [Maryland], and from there took his first ride on a train, the Baltimore and Ohio, which to a boy from the interior was no doubt interesting and exciting. . . .[32]

After he reached Washington on June 17, events developed quickly for the would-be cadet. Although his biographer Cook questions the fast-paced scenario, Jackson's widow asserts that Hays took him to the office of John C. Spencer, secretary of war in John Tyler's cabinet, for a personal interview; Hays, an illegitimate son of Congressman George Jackson (1757–1831) and therefore a relative, insisted that he stay in his own home and loaned him money to travel northward once the appointment was secured. Jackson, however, apparently took time to climb the capitol dome, and, says Anna Jackson, "took a view of the magnificient panorama before him, and immediately proceeded on his journey." On June 18, one day later, he penned a brief note to Spencer: "I have the honor to acknowledge the receipt of your communication of the 18th June 1842, informing me that the President has conferred upon me a conditional appointment as Cadet in the service of the United States and to inform you of my acceptance of same." That document now in the National Archives carried an endorsement by his guardian, "E. Jackson," authorizing him "to sign articles by which he will bind himself to serve the United States eight years unless sooner discharged." Unless the appointment was back dated, it is difficult to explain his uncle's codicil of the same day, although Jackson did enter a document of guardianship—signed by Cummins E. Jackson and Alexander Scott Withers—in the Lewis County courthouse before he left home.[33]

Armed with a letter of recommendation from Hays to the superintendent, Jackson proceeded at once to West Point; and, comments Anna Jackson, Spencer admonished him, "You have a good name. Go to West Point, and the first man who insults you knock him down, and have charged to my account." Interviews with a congressman and a cabinet officer must have been heady stuff for the "mountain youth" from western Virginia as he traveled toward the Hudson with an appointment in his vest pocket. Jackson may have toured New York City briefly—a place Robert E. Lee visited daily during his tenure at Fort Hamilton.

"The 'West Point Hotel Register' shows that a T. J. Jackson registered around noon Sunday, 19 June 1842; he stayed in room 48 located in the 'Attick,' " reads an official summary of his West Point experience. "The next day Cadet Candidate Thomas J. Jackson reported to the Adjutant's Office and signed his name in the Descriptive List of New Cadets for the year 1842. The Cadet Candidates were examined for admission on 23, 24, and 25 June. At 3:00 P.M. Saturday 25 June, the Academic Board announced the names of the Cadet Candidates found qualified for admission as Cadets to the United States Military Academy. Thomas J. Jackson's name was last on the list."[34]

Jackson's poor beginning, instead of working as a deterrent, served to spur him onward. "With his whole soul Jackson was bent upon passing," a classmate said later about the entrance examination.

> When he went to the blackboard the perspiration was streaming from his
> face, and during the whole examination his anxiety was painful to witness.
> While trying to work out his example in fractions, the cuffs of his coat,
> first the right and then the left, were brought into requisition to wipe off

the perspiration. Finally one of the faculty told Jackson he had passed and could take his seat. As he gratefully did so, "every member of the examining board turned away his head to hide the smile which could not be suppressed."

That bulldog determination not only drove Jackson to a respectable West Point career but also led him to his great achievements at Lee's side twenty years later, but the anxiety of youth soon gave way to the maturity of manhood. "Quick as lightning to take in the situation confronting him, he knew exactly when, where and how to strike, and when he did strike he was as irresistible as a tornado—he swept all before him. Never excited, he was as cool under fire as he would have been if attending to his devotions in his church," his fellow cadet, Henry Heth, who commanded one of his divisions at Chancellorsville, observed later.[35]

Without question, West Point had a maturing influence upon Jackson; it molded the raw Virginia youth into the disciplined soldier. When he entered, writes an always complimentary Dabney, "his demeanor was somewhat constrained, but by reason of its native dignity always pleasing; nor had he gained his full stature, but he was muscular of frame, and had a fresh, ruddy appearance." His early biographers are agreed that other cadets learned quickly not to jest or roughhouse with the former constable; his only difficulty took place during his second term, when another cadet attempted to switch an uncleaned musket for Jackson's clean one—an episode that resulted in the other man's reprimand. Still, he was known for eccentricities of habit that plagued him for life; he would sit bolt upright, suck on lemons for days at a time, or stand with an arm reaching skyward. When done in polite society, these mannerisms invariably attracted attention and comment. "The recollection is still preserved of many of his peculiarities—his simplicity and absence of mind, awkwardness of gait, and evident indifference to every species of amusement," John Esten Cooke, who knew him personally, wrote in 1866.[36]

Despite his drawbacks, Jackson was a dutiful student and, with the help of William H. C. Whiting (class of 1845 and one of his future commanders), he rose quickly in the class standings following a slow start. During his fourth term (1842–1843), he stood fifty-first in a class of eighty-three; in general conduct, he was eighty-eighth in a corps of 223 cadets. The third class year of 1843–1844 found him thirtieth in a class of seventy-eight; significantly, his position in mathematics had risen from forty-fifth to eighteenth. Under the regulations of 1839,

Jackson was granted a furlough in the summer of 1844, after Uncle Cummins sent a request to the academy superintendent indicating that he would be welcome at home. Thus, he visited Jackson's Mill in lieu of the customary summer encampment. When he left for western Virginia, Dabney reports, he had grown "by a leap, to a height of six feet" and "his bearing, though still deficient in ease, was punctiliously courteous and dignified. He was scrupulously neat in all his appointments, and, in his handsome cadet uniform, made a most soldierly appearance." This newly acquired demeanor not only impressed family and friends along the West Fork River but also "Miss Caroline Norris," who accompanied him to several social functions. As Jackson, Miss Norris, and several friends rode to church services, "his horse slipped on a stone, fell, and precipitated the future general into the river." And, continues, Roy Bird Cook, "he gallantly remounted, though thoroughly wet, and continued on his way—with a stoicism that marked many of his acts and no doubt with a feeling that he was simply keeping faith with the doctrines of the Broad Run Baptist church." Sharply clad in his blue uniform, Jackson also visited Sister Laura Arnold and her family at Beverly on his return to West Point.[37]

Although Jackson reminisced later that he "worked very hard for what I got," at West Point, his second term of 1844–1845 was a tour de force. "During my furlough, I was made an officer, consequently my duties are lighter than usual," he informed Laura on September 8; his official academy profile indicates: "Militarily, Cadet Jackson served as Sergeant of Company 'D,' during his Second Class year." Jackson was plainly becoming a soldier, and his fellow cadets as well as faculty recognized his improved performance. He did not receive a single demerit during the 1844–1845 school year, so that in general conduct he stood first in a corps of 204 cadets. Academically, he completed the year twentieth in a class of sixty-two. Though he rose to eleventh place in philosophy (his best performance), he finished fifty-ninth in drawing, his worst subject and one that helped preclude his entry into the engineering corps.

As the school year drew to a close, Jackson told Laura that General Winfield Scott was scheduled to conduct the final examinations, but when Captain Robert E. Lee served the same function in the summer of 1844, his letters home said nothing about the visit. Moreover, the commander of Company D, with a single year before graduation, had become concerned about the future. At least he was interested enough about down-home politics to ask Laura on May 17: "Who is elected from Lewis (County) to the Legislature, and who is Senator from the District." And he wanted the name and terms of subscription to the

Democratic newspaper in Clarksburg. Whether Jackson was entertaining a political career for himself as he later confessed or had an eye for those local politicians who might further his career, his politics was plainly obvious; he would live and die a Democrat![38]

Jackson's first term (1845–1846) brought an improvement in his individual and class standings: twelfth in engineering, fifth in ethics, eleventh in artillery, twenty-first in infantry tactics, and seventeenth in mineralogy and geology; at his graduation in July 1846, he stood seventeenth in a class of sixty. His entering class of eighty-three had fallen by twenty-three men, which was not unusual at West Point or at public colleges and universities across the country. By comparison, Lee's class of 1829 had fallen by twenty-one men at the time of his graduation. Jackson accrued seven demerits during his first term, which lowered his overall conduct position to twenty-first among 213 cadets.[39]

Jackson's classmates included future generals on both sides of the Civil War: Union, George B. McClellan, who graduated second, fifteen slots ahead of Jackson, John G. Foster, Jesse Reno, George Stoneman, and Darius N. Couch; and Confederate, George E. Pickett, who finished dead last, Dabney H. Maury, D. R. Jones, W. D. Smith, and Cadmus Wilcox. Before his own commission as brevet second lieutenant with orders to active duty in Mexico, Jackson again told Laura that his future was uncertain: "I have before me two courses, either of which I may choose," he wrote in the summer of 1845. "The first would be to follow the profession of arms; the second that of a civil pursuit, such as law. If I should adopt the first I could live independently and surrounded by friends I have already made, and have no fear of want. My pay would be fixed; the principal thing I would have to pay attention to would be futurity." Like graduating seniors in every age, he was worried about leaving the safe haven of school, but Jackson soon recognized that war would alter his plans. "Rumor appears to indicate a rupture between our government and the Mexican. If such should be the case the probability is that I will be ordered to join the army of occupation immediately, and, if so, will hardly see home until after my return, and the next letter that you will receive from me may be dated Texas or Mexico," he told Laura on April 23, 1846. Jackson was correct in his assessment of the international situation. Within six weeks of his graduation, he had been posted to Winfield Scott's force at Vera Cruz, although, contrary to his predictions, he did have time to call upon Laura and Uncle Cummins before heading south.[40]

War with Mexico likewise halted Robert E. Lee's stint in New York Harbor, where he upgraded the defenses at the same time Jackson was struggling with his West Point studies. Before the conflict interceded, Lee spent five happy, productive years in total charge of construction, and he built upon the engineering reputation he had already established in St. Louis; he became known throughout the army as a man who got results. Actually, he had command of four installations, with Fort Hamilton as the most important; in addition, Fort Lafayette was located a little way offshore, and there were two gun emplacements on Staten Island across the Verrazano Straits from Fort Hamilton. Lee's duties were purely technical: "First, there were seawalls and leaky casements to repair, gun positions to be strengthened and modernized. . . . Beyond this rehabilitation, he was to make such changes and advance such suggestions—especially on the number, caliber, and position of the guns—as he believed would make the chain of forts impregnable against warships." Fitzhugh Lee adds: "He perfected the defenses of the splendid harbor of that great city [New York]."[41]

As he toiled with cement and stone, Lee matured into the loving father and family man. Perhaps a lack of intimacy with his own father caused him to devote more attention to his growing family. When his daughter, Eleanor Agnes, was born at Arlington during 1842, Lee playfully told his friend Henry S. Kayser at St. Louis that he had "another black-eyed daughter." Although Agnes died unmarried at age thirty-one, Robert E. Lee, Jr., born in October 1843, not only served under his father during the Civil War but also, along with Rooney, became Lee's only child to leave an heir. His last child, another daughter, Mildred Childe, named after Lee's sister, was born during late 1845 or early 1846—the date of birth was seemingly never entered in the family archives. Lee did not see this child for several months after her birth, as Mrs. Lee did not return to Fort Hamilton after her confinement. Mildred died unmarried at New Orleans in March 1905, and, like Agnes, is buried with her mother and father in the family crypt at Lexington.[42]

Lee visited Manhattan every day and absorbed the city's rich cultural offerings: "I drove Mr. & Mrs. Wm. Barry to the Italian opera the other night & heard Pico & Borghese," he told his kinswoman "Markie" Williams in December 1844, while Mrs. Lee was at Arlington with the children. Mostly, however, Lee remained the caring father, particularly in his dealings with Custis and eight-year-old Rooney. "I received last night, my dear son, your letter of the 25th inst, and was much gratified to perceive the evident improvement in your writing and spelling and to learn that you are getting on well in your studies," he told Custis in November 1845. "You must endeavor to learn, in order to compensate me for the pain I suffer in being separated from you, and let nothing discourage or deter you from endeavoring to acquire virtue and knowledge."[43]

When Lee returned from one of his New York visits, he found that an adventuresome Rooney had severed the tips of "the fore and middle fingers of the left hand" with a straw cutter in the family barn. Then, after telling thirteen-year-old Custis details of the mishap, Lee cautioned: "I hope, my dear son, this may be a warning to you to meddle or interfere with nothing with which you have no concern, and particularly refrain from going where you have been prohibited, or not have permission of your parents and teachers." But Rooney was a high-spirited lad who continually upset the family. A year earlier, in April 1844, Lee permitted the boy to accompany him into the city, although the lad complained of pains about the legs before leaving home. Lee chose to ignore the complaint, convinced that his son was imagining the discomfort, but became alarmed when the condition worsened while the two called at city shops. "At home, Lee carried his son into the house and began a series of old-fashioned remedies. As with plantation people, it did not occur to Lee to call a doctor at once. After he discovered that scalding hot baths brought relief, the captain daily administered to the little boy just as he had to his mother and did for his wife." Whatever his tribulations in life, Robert E. Lee put his family and others first.[44]

The work at Fort Hamilton may have been boring as he toured the outer forts in a small tug known as *Flash,* but Lee made several influential friends as he broadened his reputation. In June 1844 he favorably impressed Winfield Scott when the two sat on the same examining board at West Point. Although Cadet Tom Jackson told his sister that Scott returned the following year, Lee was not a member of the 1845 board. Lee's newly established relations with the commanding general led to his quick recognition under Scott's tutelage at the outbreak of war. General Henry J. Hunt, who served at Fort Hamilton after his 1839 graduation from West Point, confirms the prevalent impression of Lee on the eve of war with Mexico: "He was a fine-looking man as one would wish to see, of perfect figure and strikingly handsome. Quiet and dignified in manner, of cheerful disposition, always pleasant and considerate, he seemed to me the perfect type of a gentleman."[45]

Throughout Lee's stay in New York, he served as vestryman of the Episcopal parish at Fort Hamilton. But when the tractarian movement reached his congregation from England, resulting in a high church position—advocated by the Reverend E. B. Pusey—versus a low church approach, both sides attempted to draw Lee into the controversy. He may have cultivated an aloof bearing when dealing with others, but Lee was not above a bit of fun with his subordinates. Henry Hunt, who arrayed the fearsome artillery barrage against Lee at Malvern Hill in the summer of 1862, penned the following vignette about the religious debate for inclusion in General Long's biography:

> One evening he came into the quarters of one of us youngsters, where a number of officers and one or two of the neighbors were assembled. . . . Captain Lee was quiet, but, to those who understood him, evidently amused at the efforts to draw him out. On some direct attempt to do so he turned to me and in his impressive, grave manner said, "I am glad to see that you keep aloof from the dispute that is disrupting our little parish. That is right, and we must not get mixed up in it; we must support each other in that. But I must give you some advice about it, in order that we may understand each other: Beware of *Pussyism*! *Pussyism* is always bad, and may lead to unchristian [*sic*] feeling. Therefore beware of *Pussyism!*"

The famous joke aside, Lee remained an active member of his parish until he left New York for Mexico.[46]

3

From the Rio Grande to Vera Cruz

Lee at Fort Hamilton and Jackson at West Point kept an eye on developments in Texas and along the Rio Grande during 1844–1846 as the United States and Mexico drifted toward war. In the event of open hostilities, like soldiers on both sides of the border, each man hoped to enter the fray at the earliest opportunity. War with Mexico carried dreams of personal glory, of quick recognition, and, above all, the possibility of rapid promotion in a moribund army. Although Lee remained circumspect in his letters about Mexico, the twenty-two-year-old Jackson, fresh out of West Point, made no secret of his longing: "Notwithstanding my present situation," he wrote to Laura following the capture of Jalapa. "I have some hope of getting forward by and by, when more troops get in from the United States. . . . I throw myself into the hands of an all wise God, and that it may yet be for the better . . . and after having accomplished His purpose, whatever it may be, He in His wisdom may gratify my desire." Jackson's thirst for recognition did not go unnoticed, he emerged from the conflict a brevet major of artillery. Within two years after leaving the academy, he had advanced from brevet second lieutenant to major; promotion of that order in the peacetime army would have been unthinkable.[1]

Lee had been commissioned for seventeen years and still entered the Mexican War as a captain of engineers. Just as the fates smiled on Jackson, Lee, too, climbed rapidly in prestige and rank. Unlike the ambitious youngster from Western Virginia, he did not openly court recognition. "I hope my friends will give themselves no annoyance on my account, or any concern about the distribution of favors," he told his father-in-law, Parke Custis, from Mexico City following the Mexican collapse. "I know how these things are awarded at Washington, and how the President will be besieged by the clamorous claimants. I do not wish to be numbered among them. Such as can be conscientiously bestowed, I shall gratefully receive, and have no doubt that those will exceed my deserts." But Lee did earn his "deserts" because of his spectacular work on Scott's staff as the army marched on the Mexican capital from Vera Cruz: "In a brief six month's campaign he had demonstrated in a wonderful manner his qualities as a soldier," writes Fitzhugh Lee, who later followed his uncle across the battlefields of Virginia. "Brevet major, brevet lieutenant colonel, and brevet colonel followed each other in rapid succession." And with a prophetic burst, the future cavalry commander continues: "An examination of his record in Mexico will show that the flanks of the hostile army were his favorite points of reconnaissance. If they could be successfully turned victory would save human life; a reference to his campaigns when he afterward became an army commander, will show that flanks of his enemy were still objects of his greatest attention."[2]

Like every officer of note in the Civil War, whether Confederate or Union, Lee and Jackson gained notoriety in Mexico because the United States faced a civilized military force for the first time in thirty-one years. Following Andrew Jackson's victory over the British at New Orleans in 1815, the country had fought nothing more strenuous than occasional Indian campaigns; but now the officer corps was called upon to fight a sovereign nation. In the years following independence from the Spanish crown in 1822, Mexico had taken her place among the family of nations. Although the troops under Generalíssimo Santa Anna, composed mostly of poorly fed, illiterate Indians, proved no match against the United States when war finally arrived, many observers thought otherwise at the outbreak of hostilities. In the summer of 1846, the Mexican army had four times the number of men under arms as its American counterpart.

A London *Times* correspondent in Mexico was positive that Mexican soldiers were superior to those from the United States. Another British newspaper thought American troops were "contemptible and fit for nothing but to fight Indians." The British minister at Mexico City announced grandly that an American victory south of the Rio Grande was impossible because of superior European training given the Mexican army. A deep dislike for the "gringo" prompted Mexican leaders to rush into war during 1845–1846 with a mistaken notion of their own resources.

North of the Rio Grande in the Protestant United States, Manifest

Destiny surged through the country, a feeling that heaven itself meant for the Anglo-Saxon race to inhabit the North American continent from sea to sea. Simply put, the dark-skinned peoples who professed allegiance to Roman Catholicism below the border stood in the way of divine progress. Midwestern and New England abolitionists might decry war with Mexico as part of a "plot" to annex additional slave territory, and congressmen like Abraham Lincoln and David Wilmot sought to block American intervention, but the country as a whole unhesitatingly shouted for war.[3]

Endless tales of atrocities along the Texas-Mexican frontier reaching back to the first contact between Anglo-Saxons and Spaniards in the New World also stirred passions. Just two hundred years earlier, Englishmen had been obliged to place the Jamestown Plantation along the inland shores of Chesapeake Bay to escape Spanish raiding parties; in New Orleans and in the Southwest, people remembered that Anson Jones, last president of the Lone Star Republic, although an obscure physician, had zoomed to political prominence because of his Masonic activities among those early Texans in Stephen F. Austin's colony; Jones had secured the first Masonic charter in Texas from the host lodge at New Orleans. People throughout Texas and their Yankee kinsfolk longed for union with the United States because Mexican law nettled the Anglo-Saxon conscience; among other things, they had to be married before a priest according to the hated rites of Roman Catholicism. A horrible resentment toward all things Spanish and popish had precipitated the Texas Revolution of 1836 against Mexican authority. Though Sam Houston and his "Texicans" won the day and succeeded in joining the United States after nine years as an independent country, the old animosities lingered because Mexico never recognized the legitimacy of Texas, let alone its annexation by a foreign power. When several Texans were slain along the Rio Grande during the so-called Federalist Wars of 1839–1842, they were denied burial in a Mexican churchyard because they were "heretics" or non-Catholics. These ingrained hatreds culminated in war to complete the North American revulsion against the ethos of Roman Catholicism and to ensure the goals of Manifest Destiny.[4]

Although the Texans, with their memories of the Alamo and Goliad, had a healthy respect for Hispanic prowess, most Americans never doubted that the "inferior Mexican" could be easily beaten. Yet the United States was ill suited for war with anyone in 1846, particularly with a formidable country like Mexico. The army that sent Lee and Jackson into battle had less than seven thousand men under arms during the autumn of 1845: "Along a three thousand mile northern border in menacing contretemps with Great Britain, manning seaboard fortifications, holding posts in Florida, on a great arc from the Falls of St. Anthony at the north for fifteen hundred miles through the Indian country to New Orleans, and in newly annexed Texas where more than half the army was stationed, there were only fourteen regiments—two of dragoons, four of artillery, and eight of infantry."[5]

Planners estimated an army of twenty-five thousand men beyond the existing force was needed to subdue the enemy; as the army expanded, Lee and Jackson were able to advance rapidly because they were in the right place at the right time. In the beginning, Washington requisitioned those areas nearest the border—in the South and Southwest—to supply the twenty-five thousand with a quota of forty thousand additional men levied upon the remaining states. The literature is replete with colorful incidents as recruiting sergeants raised the all-volunteer force among the recalcitrant. Lieutenant Tom Jackson obligingly drilled a volunteer company at Weston when he visited Uncle Cummins on his way from West Point to join the army in Mexico; hundreds of similar groups were raised when men heard the cry for war. Thousands of recruits appeared for muster from all parts of the country, but the army never came near its anticipated strength. Commanders were frequently short of men throughout the conflict, and troops had to be detached from Zachary Taylor's army in northern Mexico for the landings at Vera Cruz. The shift of men from Taylor to Winfield Scott, who had an invasion force numbering only eighty-five hundred, included Lee and Jackson.[6]

After joining Scott's army for the march on Mexico City, recognition was not long in coming to each man; before the Treaty of Guadalupe-Hidalgo in 1848, Lee and Jackson found ample opportunity to distinguish themselves on the battlefield. As Scott's chief of engineers, Lee was constantly in the limelight as the army marched inland; following entry into the Mexican capital, the commanding general singled him out for special praise: "Capt. Lee, so constantly distinguished, also bore important orders from me, until he fainted from a wound and the loss of two nights sleep at the batteries."[7] Tom Jackson managed to land an assignment with John B. Magruder's artillery because that officer was an impetuous fighter. As Magruder prodded his men into more than one fight, Jackson found his own place in the army. In his reports to headquarters, Magruder said Jackson's conduct was exemplary: "If devotion, industry, talent and galantry are the highest qualities, of a soldier, then he is entitled to the distinction which their possession confers."[8] Moreover, none other than Winfield Scott himself recognized Jackson. In a dispatch from the Mexican National Palace on September 18, 1847, "Lieutenant Jackson" was mentioned twice with "merited praise"; apparently, the commanding general did not know about Jackson's promotions to captain and brevet major.[9]

Although Lee is mentioned on nearly each page of Scott's account of the war, Jackson, too, had received his due in high places—recognition indeed for an officer barely fifteen months out of West Point. Lee and Jackson thus emerged from the Mexican conflict with established reputations as fighting men. Each had experienced the grim reality of an adversary who meant to kill him, and each had learned how to handle himself and his command under fire. Lee had been in uniform since 1829, yet he had never fired a shot nor seen a shot fired in anger. Other than his days as a constable in frontier Virginia and the customary give-and-take of hardy young men, Jackson likewise had not encountered men with hostile intent. Mexico, however, was different! Here Jackson and Lee fired guns and directed troops; they met the enemy on the enemy's own terms. Their ingenuity and physical courage in battle marked them as officers on the rise.

The published record simply does not indicate whether Lee and Jackson came into personal contact during the war. Yet they were constantly near enough to make it entirely plausible that they met on the field of battle. As a member of Scott's staff until the conflict ended, Lee enjoyed a high profile throughout the ranks. The biographer can only speculate, but Lee must have heeded the young cannoneer in Magruder's battery as the army raced toward Chapultepec and victory; and Jackson—albeit several years younger—could scarcely have missed Lee's spectacular career in Mexico.

The first time their paths crossed during this period was at Fort Hamilton, before the journey southward. Although a formal declaration of war had come on May 13, 1846, and hostilities had been underway for some weeks, Lee remained at his post in New York until August 19, when he received instructions to join General John E. Wool at San Antonio. As he awaited his own summons to join the fighting, Lee wrote his cousin, Markie Williams, a month earlier about the steady parade of men through New York: "There is nothing here but preparation for battle: Sharpening of Swords, the grinding of bayonets and equipping for the field, occupy all thoughts and hands." All the while, Lee watched patiently as thousands of men trooped through Fort Hamilton en route to the Mexican fighting; one of those passing through was Tom Jackson, who arrived the very day Lee received his marching orders to San Antonio.[10]

While it is fascinating to speculate that Lee noticed the young lieutenant among all the men and officers departing for Mexico, it is more likely that neither man was aware of the other amid the intense activity. Jackson was surely a wide-eyed second lieutenant as he searched for his billet in the artillery company of Captain Francis Taylor, a man he had never seen. Captain Lee, busy with plans to visit Mary and the children at Arlington as he headed for the Southwest, had little time for the parade of men through his old post. Jackson was one of many; yet Lee and Jackson—two soldiers who spearheaded the Confederate cause fifteen years later on the fields of northern Virginia—were at Fort Hamilton on the same day in August 1846. Their paths would cross many times before that fateful day in May 1863 when Jackson lay dead in Dr. Chandler's house at Guiney Station.

Jackson reached Fort Hamilton seven weeks after his June 30 graduation from the academy; actually, he was ordered to Governor's Island, also in New York Harbor, but was unable to locate Taylor, who had proceeded to Hamilton with his company. Jackson had earlier traveled to Washington with several classmates for a farewell fete in Brown's hotel; among his fellow travelers was Cadmus Wilcox, who afterward penned a first-rate history of the Mexican War. Wilcox, who served as aide to General John A. Quitman in Mexico, served as groomsman for the wedding of Ulysses S. Grant and also fought with Lee and Jackson at First and Second Bull Run, the Peninsula, Fredericksburg, and Chancellorsville. Following the Washington interlude, Jackson had used a furlough to visit Jackson's Mill as well as Laura and her new family at Beverly, located on the Tygart River—thirty miles east of Jackson's Mill—in present Randolph County, West Virginia. The Tygart River Valley around Beverly was an area that Robert E. Lee would know well during his ill-fated campaign in western Virginia during the autumn of 1861.[11]

When Jackson arrived, Laura's household included eight-month-old Thomas Jackson Arnold, who became his uncle's future biographer. Arnold, who used the copious letters between his mother and Jackson as centerpieces for his 1916 work, *The Early Life and Letters of General Thomas J. Jackson*, later married Eugenia, daughter of General D. H. Hill. Two years younger than her brother, Laura had married Jonathan Arnold in September 1844, about the time Cadet Jackson commenced his junior studies at West Point. Although Laura bore four children between November 1845 and December 1853, only the eldest and her brother's namesake had arrived at the time of Jackson's visit. The familial bond between Jackson and his sister is reflected in their published letters—although none describe the 1846 stay.[12]

Jackson stayed with Laura about two weeks because he arrived in Jackson's Mill on July 20 to visit his uncle, Cummins Jackson. A widely cited letter to Arnold after the Civil War from a cousin, Sylvanus White, gives an entertaining glimpse into the sojourn; White, who joined Cummins on the latter's journey to California during the gold rush, was a member of the militia at nearby Weston when Jackson reached his uncle's home. What transpired must have been his first attempt at command: "While he was here our county militia was called out, with a view of getting up a company of volunteers for the Mexican War. Our Colonel (McKinly) asked him to take command of a company in the day's muster. He (Thomas) said, 'No, I probably would not understand your orders!' But the Colonel insisted. When we got on the parade ground, the Colonel did not give the proper command, and Tom's company was headed up-town, so he went on, afterwards explaining that he was obeying orders."[13]

Jackson's visit ended abruptly two days into his stay, when he received orders assigning him to Company K, First Artillery. Since Cummins Jackson died three years later in the California gold fields, Thomas Jackson never saw his uncle again. After taking leave of his loved ones, Jackson finally caught up with Captain Francis Taylor and Company K at Fort Hamilton; as Lee prepared to leave for Arlington on his journey to Texas, Jackson traveled first to Pittsburgh and then to New Orleans.

Company K had been detailed to General Zachary Taylor's Army of Occupation at Point Isabel, Texas, at the mouth of the Rio Grande. Jackson told Laura in a letter posted from the Texas port on September 25 that he had landed the previous day after a thirty-six-day journey from Fort Hamilton. Although written while still aboard his transport, the letter contains a surprisingly detailed account of his travels. When Jackson left New York with Captain Taylor, Company K had thirty men and forty horses for the four-hundred mile first lap to Pittsburgh. Next, the group moved down the Ohio to Parkersburg, where Jackson had spent happy boyhood days with his Neale relatives, then past the island in western Kentucky, where Jackson and his now-deceased brother Warren had attempted to earn a living by selling cordwood to passing steamboats. Following a short layover at New Orleans, he apparently had an uneventful passage to the Rio Grande. "My health is better than it has been for some time," he told Laura; "the good people of Beverly," he added, "occupy a high place in my esteem, especially your husband, whose kindness as well as yours has been indelibly written on my heart and memory."[14]

As Jackson trudged overland to Pittsburgh, Lee left Fort Hamilton for the Southwest. Their paths would not cross again until December 1846, when Lee arrived at Saltillo in northern Mexico with Wool's column; Jackson reached the same place after Company K had been assigned to Worth's division of Taylor's command. In the four-month interval, Lee traveled first to Arlington, where he apparently saw his baby daughter, Mildred Childe, for the first time. Although the exact birth date was never recorded, she clearly arrived during December 1845 or January 1846. Lee, who was preoccupied at Fort Hamilton, had not been at Arlington for the birth. In a March 1846 letter to fourteen-year-old Custis and nine-year-old Rooney, Lee admonished the boys: "I hope to come on soon (from Fort Hamilton) to see that little baby you have got to show me. You must give her a kiss for me and one to all the children, and to your mother and your grandmother."[15]

Sensing the dangers of impending battle, Lee provided for his now-completed family by making a will during a brief stay at home. According to Freeman, it was filed September 1st in the Fairfax County courthouse. "This document was never changed, even after the War between the States. It left all his property to Mrs. Lee for life and provided that after her death it should be distributed equally among his children unless Annie, who remained in delicate health, should need more than the others."

Six-year-old Anne Carter—the family called her Annie from birth—died at White Sulphur Springs, North Carolina, in 1862, during the height of the Civil War. When a group of "ladies" unveiled a monument for her in 1866 and invited Lee to attend the ceremony, he sent a warm note of appreciation: "I do not know how to express to you my thanks for your great kindness to her while living, and for your affectionate remembrance of her since death." Lee said further that he intended to visit his daughter's resting place near Warrenton, "but it must be done with more privacy than I can hope for on the occasion you propose." That privacy did not come until after the war, when a dying Lee visited the grave with his daughter Agnes while he served as president of Washington College.[16]

The brief family reunion of August–September 1846 ended when Lee boarded a steamer for New Orleans and the war zone. Though he reached Texas before Jackson, both men were constantly on the move once they left Fort Hamilton. Two weeks after Lee filed his will at Fairfax, he stepped ashore at Port Lavaca on the Texas coast. The seacoast hamlet, founded in 1840 as a shipping outlet for the Texas longhorn, was a place Lee would know again. Fifteen years later, in April 1861, he sailed from nearby Indianola—a few miles down Matagorda Bay—when he left the Second Cavalry to cast his fortune with the Confederacy.

Lee and Jackson surely passed through New Orleans within days of each other; they must have wandered the city's ancient thoroughfares with thousands of others awaiting sailing berths for Mexico. But Lee, who had been assigned to Wool's force in Texas, took a different route than Jackson; going first to Port Lavaca and then overland through Victoria—a small town on the Guadalupe River named for an early president of the Mexican republic—he reported to Wool on September 21 at San Antonio de Bexar. Three days later, Jackson's transport reached the mouth of the Rio Grande at Point Isabel, 180 miles down the coast from Matagorda.[17]

By the time each man landed in Texas, momentous events had engulfed the border with Mexico. Warships had been ordered into the Gulf of Mexico by President John Tyler some months earlier to guard against Mexican intrusion while talks were underway for the annexation of Texas. Tyler also commanded General Zachary Taylor to form an "Army of Observation" to stand at the ready along the Texas-Louisiana border; during the summer of 1845, Taylor's force was strengthened and renamed the "Army of Occupation." When Texas was formally admitted to the Union by joint congressional resolution and Mexico broke diplomatic relations with the United States, Taylor was ordered across the border on June 15. Although Lee and Jackson were still at Fort Hamilton and West Point, another young officer, Lieutenant James Longstreet, a man both would know in another war, marched south with the Army of Occupation.[18]

Taylor did not leave Louisiana until July 26, but five days later he was encamped along the south bank of the Nueces at Corpus Christi. He had now crossed into territory that the enemy considered its own with thirty-five hundred effectives, about one-half the total fighting force of the United States. The government in Mexico City, which had never recognized Texan independence, steadfastly insisted the limits of Texas and hence any international boundary lay at the Nueces and not the Rio Grande. The incoming Polk administration sought in vain to reach an understanding with Mexican authorities while the army remained at Corpus Christi. Finally, Secretary of War William L. Marcy instructed Taylor on January 13 "to move his force to the Rio Grande." Months of wrangling by Polk's special envoy, John Slidell of Louisiana, with the

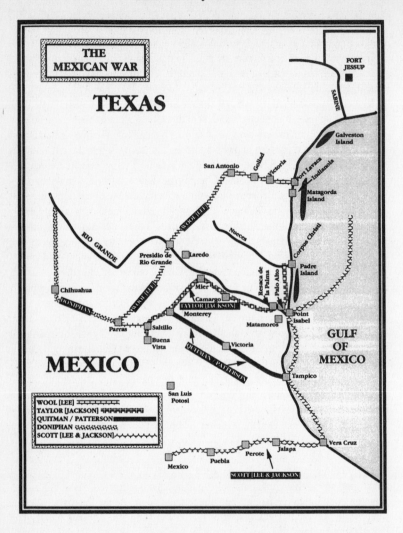

changing guard south of the border had ended in failure. When Taylor resumed his trek southward, a shooting war had become inevitable.[19]

Events shifted rapidly from the negotiating table to the battlefront. After Taylor started his command from Corpus Christi following intense preparations, he got to the Rio Grande on March 28; although part of his army had gone by sea, the bulk marched overland through the hot, dry brush country of south Texas. Upon striking the road along the north bank of the river, Taylor divided his troops; part were dispatched eastward to the coast at Point Isabel, while the remainder established a fortified emplacement—dubbed Fort Texas—opposite Matamoros. Meanwhile, Mexican contingents under General Mariano Arista occupied the town south of the river and prepared to resist further intrusion into Mexican territory. Arista promptly erected Fort Paredes—named for the current Mexican president, Mariano Paredes—and sent word to Taylor contesting his presence beyond the Nueces; from the Mexican viewpoint, "hostilities had already commenced," he added.[20]

As the two armies lay in wait, Arista sent a force of sixteen hundred across the Rio Grande to probe the Americans. Led by General Anastasio Torrejón, the force "isolated Captain William Thornton and about sixty American dragoons that afternoon [April 24] and after an intense skirmish forced Thornton to surrender." The affair was one of numerous encounters between troops and bushwhackers that dominated the region for weeks; the engagement forced a harassed Zachary Taylor to dispatch a rider toward Washington with news of the opening shots. James K. Polk, who swept into office by supporting the annexation of Texas in the 1844 presidential canvass with Henry Clay, was a man who believed in direct action as well as Manifest Destiny. In short, he meant to have war. Even before word from the Rio Grande, Polk had told his cabinet that the country could wait no longer; when Taylor's message reached the White House on the evening of Saturday, May 9, the president was spurred to action. Within two days, he stood before Congress to urge a declaration of war. The war message, writes his major biographer, "drew a touching picture of an aggrieved and long-suffering nation, whose patient efforts to preserve peace had been thwarted by Mexican belligerence and unreasonableness." Abolitionists in both houses, who viewed war with Mexico as a ruse to gain additional slave territory, attempted to check the national will, but Polk got what he wanted, and on Wednesday, May 13, he signed the war edict into law.[21]

Arista did not wait for the niceties of congressional mandates; he crossed the Rio Grande in force on May 7 to block the road connecting Point Isabel and Fort Texas. Taylor's army had not been enlarged to any great extent when he set out from Point Isabel to confront the enemy. At a water hole known locally as Palo Alto, midway down the pike to Matamoros, twenty-three hundred Americans with two hundred supply wagons met six thousand enemy troops spoiling for an easy victory. But Yankee fighting prowess was never in question; when the three-hour confrontation ended, Mexican troops had been forced from the field by Taylor's superior artillery. When Taylor himself came upon the scene during the May 8 melee, he was a sight to inspire confidence. "There he was," writes Holman Hamilton, "in a blue-checkered gingham coat, blue trousers without any braid, a linen waistcoat and a broad-brimmed straw hat. Neither his horse nor his saddle had any military ornament. Simplicity! This well-born son of Virginia gentlefolk personified simplicity. And every time his privates saw him, plain, and unpretending, mounted on Old Whitey they felt that impelling urge to obey his orders and to march or ride wherever he might lead."[22] For a brief time at least, Lee and Jackson were attached to Taylor's Army of Occupation, and whether influenced by Taylor's example or not, it is worth noting that neither man exhibited outward military display during the glory days of the Confederacy.

Taylor won another lopsided victory the following day, May 9, when he advanced to Resaca de la Parma, a dry creek bed along the road to Matamoros. Although still outnumbered, he delivered Arista's army a crushing blow. The twin victories made Taylor an instant hero, and they fixed him as a potential presidential candidate, because Palo Alto and de la Parma forced Arista to abandon his positions along the Rio Grande. Moreover, Taylor's force was augmented during May and June until it reached nearly fifteen thousand men; and Polk, anxious to avoid further bloodshed, even flirted with Santa Anna, who had taken the helm at Mexico City after the collapse of the Paredes government. This ill-conceived move to secure peace without further military operations had the opposite effect of lengthening the war. Santa Anna, like his predecessors, could never agree to American demands upon Mexican territory. As Tom Jackson traveled south to join the swelling army, Taylor occupied Matamoros on May 18, following Polk's decision to press the conflict.

A new phase in the war opened on July 6, 1846, when Taylor marched out of Matamoros to begin his descent on Monterrey via Camargo and Mier—the latter place the scene of a brutal massacre of eighteen Texans during an 1842 raid below the river. Although Texas troops with the army shivered at reminders of the so-called Black Bean episode at Mier, when every tenth prisoner had been shot by the Mexicans, Taylor made quick progress toward Monterrey. By September 25, the city had capitulated after a heroic flanking movement by General William J. Worth, Taylor's second in command. Located on the Santa Catarina, a tributary of the Rio Grande, Monterrey—capital of Nuevo León—remains to this day the chief city of northern Mexico. Its loss was a powerful blow to enemy pride and it prompted a counteroffensive by Santa Anna. But while the Mexicans gathered their forces, Taylor consented to an eight-week armistice before he entered the city; now more than one hundred miles into the heart of Mexico, he agreed to stay in place with the now-enlarged Army of Occupation.[23]

Robert E. Lee and Thomas Jackson began their Mexican service during the unpopular truce that was disavowed shortly by President Polk. Lee set out for the Rio Grande on September 28 as captain of engineers in Wool's contingent when that officer was summoned to move against Chihuahua, like Monterrey, another strategic point in northern Mexico. When the 2,000-man force left San Antonio four days after his arrival from Port Lavaca, Lee was second to Captain William D. Fraser, a New Yorker, who served as Wool's chief of engineers. The sixty-two-year-old Wool, born at Newburgh, New York, up the Hudson from West Point, had not attended the academy but made his way through the ranks; after receiving a captaincy during the War of 1812, he had not been elevated to general rank until 1826. Although he had not seen a shot fired in anger since the Battle of Plattsburg in 1814, he was a stern disciplinarian who was not well liked by his troops. During Lee's duty at Fortress Monroe, Wool, who was inspector general of the army after 1826, had toured the Virginia facility.[24]

Wool led his command southward through the barren reaches of south Texas without mishap. Lee had little to occupy his time except observe a military column on the move through hostile country, a new experience after years in the engineering service. "After an eleven-day march," writes Robert S. Henry, "the little column reached the riverbank opposite the town of Presidio de Rio Grande. The river was nearly 300 yards wide and more than four feet deep, with a rapid current, but . . . General Wool had made timely preparation. Captain William D. Fraser, his engineering officer, had brought along the pontoons and framed timbers for a so-called 'flying bridge,' prepared at San Antonio, and on October 12, three days after reaching the river, the army with all its wheeled and animal transport marched across dry-shod." It was also Lee's first service along the Rio Grande—he would return in the 1850s—when he helped Fraser transport the army into Mexican territory.[25]

Once beyond the river, Wool's force encountered a Mexican subaltern and his outriders who told the Americans about Taylor's armistice following the occupation of Monterrey. But Wool pushed aside suggestions that his presence violated the pact; he quickly issued orders for the column to march on Monclova, 150 miles beyond the Rio Grande yet north of Monterrey and Taylor's army. Lee penned a letter to Arlington, dated October 11, in which he told Mrs. Lee that his companions "had met no resistance yet. The Mexicans guarding the passage retired upon our approach." And reminiscent of his letter to "Cousin Markie" from Fort Hamilton, he added, "there has been a great whetting of knives, grinding of swords, and sharpening of bayonets ever since we reached the river."[26]

Although Wool's expedition was a peripheral operation at best, events at Mexico City a few days before Lee reached the Rio Grande produced a dramatic turn in the war when Antonio López de Santa Anna—already president on eight separate occasions since 1833—again assumed power. "Every day that passes without fighting at the north is a century of disgrace for Mexico," he crowed while admonishing his countrymen to resist the advancing gringos. By October 8—the same day Wool reached Mexican territory—he pushed his own troops to San Luis Potosí, roughly 150 miles south of Taylor at Monterrey. And when Wool learned of Santa Anna's movements, he abandoned the Chihuahua project and began to maneuver in the direction of Taylor. After a brief halt at Monclova because of the armistice, he reached Parras on November 28.[27]

Meanwhile, Zachary Taylor, also wary of the Mexican threat, dispatched Worth's division to Saltillo, a few miles below Monterrey; Wool remained at Parras until December 17, when a hurried note from Taylor summoned him to join the main army. Due to the engineering and road-building skills of Fraser and Lee, Wool was able to join Worth four days later following an uneventful march. Although heavy fighting lay on the horizon, Captain George W. Hughes, chronicler of the expedition, wrote that the column had "met nothing but kindness and hospitality" on the five-hundred mile trek from San Antonio. Lee, however, had his first encounter with a large military force when Wool's arrival at Saltillo swelled Taylor's army to more than six thousand effectives.[28]

For the second time since leaving Fort Hamilton, Lee and Jackson found themselves in the same vicinity. Jackson reached Saltillo as commissary officer for Company K, of Worth's division, although no record exists that they met in Taylor's enlarged army. Still, it is possible that Lieutenant Jackson would have noted Lee's December 24 promotion to chief engineer under Wool when Captain Fraser was ordered to Taylor's staff at Monterrey. Jackson surely heard about Lee's famed scout a few weeks afterward to locate Santa Anna's army when word of that ill-fated scenario raced through the encampment.

Jackson had been garrisoned at Saltillo for several weeks before Lee arrived with Wool's column. Yet more than a little confusion exists concerning his activities with the First Artillery between September 24 when he arrived at Point Isabel and his posting to Saltillo on December 2. Was he fledgling artillerist or company commissary officer? Most likely he was both; during the trip from Fort Hamilton, Captain Taylor had placed him in charge of guns as well as provisions for men and horses.

Although letters to Laura trace Jackson's movements along the path from Point Isabel to Matamoros, Camargo, Mier, Monterrey, and finally Saltillo, they do not indicate when he was at each place or how long he stayed. His journey along the road followed by Taylor and Worth is also confirmed by his nephew Arnold. But another Jackson biographer, Lenoir Chambers, writes in detail about the march; he indicates that Jackson reached Camargo by steamer on October 3 at the limit of navigation on the Rio Grande. Like numerous units, Company K had been trapped in the babel of men and supplies pouring into northern Mexico. "How shall I be able to get this [letter] to New Orleans I cannot say," Jackson told his sister in his September missive from Point Isabel. "I could say much more, but I am writing in a strong gale of wind, and where all is confusion. I am in hopes of starting up the Rio Grande tomorrow and of reaching General Taylor as soon as possible." The young hot spur was anxious for the front, although his letters also point to considerable sight-seeing along the slow march. "His detachment reached Monterrey November 24 and joined the remainder of Company K," Chambers continues. "The newcomers had arrived just in time to join Zachary Taylor's southward movement toward Saltillo on November 29. They arrived December 2 and remained until January."[29]

A disappointed Jackson was marooned aboard his transport in the breakwater at Point Isabel during the capture of Monterrey. Yet he found time to sightsee through the city during a five-day sojourn on the march to Saltillo. "Whilst I was in Monterrey, my quarters were in the outskirts of the city, having a large back lot attached, which contained a beautiful orange orchard. . . . Monterrey is the most beautiful city I have seen in this distracted country," he informed Laura.

Ere that, Jackson termed northern Mexico beyond the cities "a barren waste"; at Saltillo, capital of Coahuila and two thousand feet higher than Monterrey, he was told that a single grandee had an estate larger than the state of New York. And perhaps imbued with his later religious zeal,

Jackson noted the city's ecclesiastical life: Saltillo's Roman Catholic church was "the most highly ornamented in the interior of any ediface which has come under my observation." In contrast to the austere churches of frontier Virginia, he said the "music is of the highest character. The priests are robed in the most gorgeous apparel. . . ."[30]

Jackson's letters indicate that he served with a "light battery" during the journey to Saltillo, yet G. F. R. Henderson, his British biographer, had him attached to a heavy unit; "his first duty was to transport heavy guns and mortars to the forts which protected Point Isabel." Since Taylor was already fighting at Monterrey when Jackson arrived at the Texas port, it is difficult to fathom why the place needed fortification; also, Mexican forces had no navy to attack anyone. Because operations had shifted from the border, he understandably told his sister that he hoped to be in "at least one battle." Dabney H. Maury, Jackson's West Point classmate, found him manhandling his guns along the muddy roads to Saltillo. Other Jackson biographers have been equally confused about this phase of his career. Dabney is painfully silent about Jackson in northern Mexico, and Vandiver, his foremost modern biographer, cites Henderson to have him "installing guns in the Point Isabel defenses, which soon became more an exercise than anything else."[31]

Although Jackson struggled with Captain Taylor and his Company K companions to move the guns, he clearly had other duties. He wrote to Brigadier General George Gibson, the army's chief subsistence officer since 1818, complaining that he had received no pay for acting as company commissary from August 13 through November 27, 1846. The December 26 letter posted from Saltillo said he had acted on Captain Taylor's orders.[32]

Lee spent Christmas 1846 writing to Mary and the children. A December 24 letter to his eldest sons, Custis and Rooney, flowed with warm affection for his growing brood: "I hope good Santa Claus will fill my Rob's stocking; that Mildred's and Anna's may break down with good things. . . ." And a Christmas-day letter to Mrs. Lee also swelled with thoughts of home: "It is the first time we have been entirely separated at this holy time of year since our marriage [and] I hope it does not interfere with your happiness. . . . I trust you are well and happy, and that this is the last time I shall be absent from you during my life." Apparently "Spec," the family pet, had been moping after Lee because he told his wife "to take him to walk with you and tell the children to cheer him up." Robert E. Lee, Jr., said the dog was beside himself upon his father's return from Mexico.[33]

Lee's yule letter to Arlington noted that "false rumors" about a Mexican attack had spread through the army. During the next weeks, everyone from Zachary Taylor to privates in the ranks cast a wary eye toward San Luis Potosí, where Santa Anna gathered his forces. Wool had heard enough by early January, and he directed Lee, now his chief engineer, to locate the enemy. All Lee biographers, starting with J. William Jones, "a local Baptist preacher and Lee family confidant," have recounted his one-man scout from Saltillo with great relish. Jones wrote with authority after he befriended Mrs. Lee at Lexington following Lee's death. "In 1874 Jones's *Personal Reminiscences, Anecdotes and Letters of General Lee* was published and it became the source book for all future Lee biographers." He not only had access to Lee's personal correspondence but he also consulted with the family while compiling this and other Civil War writings. [34]

Actually, Lee had volunteered to search for Santa Anna; and though Wool ordered a cavalry troop to accompany his chief engineer and his young guide, a Mexican lad, Lee missed the picket line. He resolved to ride into the night alone, after his youthful companion was warned to expect "the contents of a pocket-pistol should he play false." Five miles into the darkness, Lee stumbled across wagon tracks but no sign that heavy artillery had passed; a puzzled Lee likewise found no enemy outposts. Leaving his frightened guide behind, he rode onward to investigate several hillside fires and what he thought to be white army tents.

"By this time," General Long's account reads, "he was near enough to be able to make better use of the moonlight, and discovered that his tents were simply a large *flock of sheep,* and that his army was a train of wagons and the drovers of a large herd of cattle, mules, etc. Riding into their camp, he quickly learned that Santa Anna had not yet crossed the mountains, and that there were no Mexican forces in the locality." Within hours of his return from his nighttime ride, which approached forty miles, Lee set out a second time with a cavalry escort to pinpoint Santa Anna's actual whereabouts. [35]

About the time Lee returned to Wool's encampment at Saltillo, President Polk made his decision to press the war. Zachary Taylor and the Army of Occupation, it was reasoned, could never crush the enemy from the position in northern Mexico, and a direct assault on Mexico City from Monterey was deemed impossible. Following a period of indecisiveness and soul-searching about elevating a Whig general to prominence, it was decided to open a second front—to send an army under Winfield Scott for an amphibious landing at Vera Cruz. Once ashore, Scott was expected to march inland for a descent upon the central valley of Mexico and the capital itself. His path would parallel the route followed by Hernando Cortes three hundred years earlier when the Spanish had first captured the Halls of Montezuma. And to the eternal disgust of Zachary Taylor, a portion of his army was handed over to the new conquerors.[36]

Both Lee and Jackson were ordered to Scott's army at Vera Cruz in the military shake-up of January 1847. When Taylor beat the Mexicans at Buena Vista—the decisive battle in the north—on February 22–23, both men were wending their way southward. Jackson told Laura that he left Saltillo in January, and records in the National Archives pinpoint the departure of Company K as January 7.[37]

Jackson had been in Mexico since September 24 and besides his descriptions of Monterey and Saltillo, he surely observed other facets of Hispanic life. "From the moment the Americans crossed the Rio Grande, they were besieged by Mexican vendors with wares to sell, mostly fresh fruit and vegetables, bread, milk, and more spirited beverages that were locally produced from the cactus and grain. Mexican women who flocked around the Yankee camps supplied the soldiers with food, articles of clothing, and assorted souvenirs. The meager fare supplied by army quartermasters caused many to seek the highly-spiced and often unclean Mexican foods. . . ." Under these conditions, continues Robert Johannsen, "it is not surprising that disease took a heavy toll, accounting for seven times the number of battle deaths. Epidemics swept the army camps, including measles and the dreaded vomito, or yellow fever, but by far the greatest cost was exacted by those illnesses traceable to unsanitary conditions, strange and unclean food, polluted water and an often hostile climate."[38]

Lieutenant A. P. Hill, like Jackson a recent West Point graduate, informed his father: "The ladies of Mexico *are* beautiful, oh, how beautiful. However, very few of them ever read Wayland's 'Moral Science.' " Unlike hundreds of men who came down with gonorrhea or syphilis, Jackson avoided the debilitating effects of camp life; nevertheless, he did not escape the captivating lure of Mexico. His idle hours were devoted to the study of Spanish, and he recalled his stay below the border with fondness until his death; the alien, if romantic, culture and the swirl of military preparation made a deep impression upon the twenty-two-year-old officer from western Virginia. Throughout the Civil War, he constantly referred to the second Mrs. Jackson as his "*esposita*," a pet name adopted from his Mexican service.

Company K did not disembark at Vera Cruz until March 9, which means Jackson was on the march for nearly two months. About the time

Lee sailed from Lobos Island aboard Winfield Scott's flagship, the USS *Massachusetts,* Jackson received a more or less automatic promotion to second lieutenant to replace his brevet rank. He had done little since leaving West Point the previous June except help Captain Taylor on the journey from Fort Hamilton; he had not seen a hostile enemy. The commission, dated March 3, 1847, became his first military recognition. Although unrelated to his new rank, Jackson and Company K were placed under General David Twiggs when Worth's division was reorganized during operations at Vera Cruz. Jackson had joined his new comrades at Point Isabel and then followed the army southward to Tampico and Lobos, where Scott assembled his thirteen thousand–man force for the assault on the Mexican capital.[39]

As Jackson waited on the beach at Point Isabel for suitable transport, he encountered his future brother-in-law, Captain D. H. Hill, also looking for a berth to Vera Cruz. Hill's recollection of the meeting, published five years after his own death, has become a staple for subsequent Jackson biographers: "I strolled over to the tent of Captain George Taylor of the artillery, and as we were conversing, a young officer was seen approaching, 'Do you know Lieutenant Jackson?' asked Captain Taylor. 'He will make his mark in this war. I taught him at West Point; he came there badly prepared, but was rising all the time, and had the course been four years longer, he would have graduated at the head of his class. He never gave up on anything, and never passed over anything without understanding it.' " After Taylor departed, Hill and Jackson walked alone along the gulf shore; and Jackson, heretofore "reserved and reticent," opened up to his newfound companion. "I really envy you men who have been in action; we who have just arrived look upon you as veterans. I should like to be in one battle. . . ."[40]

Jackson, Lee, and the entire army did not have long to wait for their first taste of war. By March 4, two hundred ships laden with men and supplies had arrived off the island of Antón Lizardo within sight of Vera Cruz—the City of the True Cross; as officers and men gazed outward at the fortress of San Juan de Ulloa, a great sense of jubilation swept the armada. "On the decks of the various ships the regimental bands played such favorites as *Love Not, Some Love to Roam, Alice Gray,* and *Oft in the Stilly Night.* Ammunition and three days' rations were issued, swift boats sped from ship to ship with orders for the landing, which was planned for the next day." And while Jackson remained on board his ship at Vera Cruz, General Scott and his staff reconnoitered the landing site already spotted by Commodore David Conner. Like other junior officers anxious to prove their mettle, he was forced to take a backseat as the men around Scott surged forward; Robert E. Lee, Pierre G. T. Beauregard, Joseph E. Johnston, and George Meade, all destined for Civil War glories, were the officers who accompanied the commanding general. Little wonder that Jackson told his sister: "It is such that only those who have independent commands are as a general rule spoken of [in the newspapers] . . . if any officer wishes to distinguish himself he must remain long in service until he obtains rank; then he receives praise not only for his efforts, but for the officers and men under him."[41]

Lee's star was rising fast when he accompanied Scott and his generals to sound the Mexican coast. The March 7 reconnaissance aboard a captured vessel of shallow draft, the *Petrita*, not only gave Lee his first taste of enemy gunfire, it nearly ended in disaster. After Matthew Calbraith Perry, brother of Oliver Hazard Perry, of Lake Erie fame, assumed command of the naval flotilla upon the retirement of Commodore Conner, it was decided that a seaward attack upon San Juan de Ulloa with the ships at hand was out of the question. Scott and his men were forced to search for a suitable site to begin a land assault. But when the *Petrita* closed on the Mexican stronghold, shots rang out. "One shot went over her, one short," writes Alfred Hoyt Bill: "The next was fairly in the middle of the bracket, but by good luck burst high above the little vessel, or the expedition might have been brought to a sudden stop then and there by the loss of its commander and every one of its senior officers."

Still, Conner's original landing place was deemed best as Scott ordered the troops ashore about three miles down the coast from Vera Cruz; the exact spot was well beyond the castle guns and opposite the offshore island of Antón Lizardo. By March 9, the transports had arrived with the main force—Jackson among them—and the landing was made on a "surf-beaten beach surrounded by high sandhills." As swarms of spectators aboard foreign warships watched, sixty-five surfboats ferried the men inland with Worth's division in the lead followed by the troopers under Twiggs. More than ten thousand men had landed by ten o'clock on the same night without a single casualty. All the while Lee observed the operation from his berth aboard the *Massachusetts*.[42]

Lee had accompanied the army from Point Isabel-Brazos via Tampico and Lobos to the beach at Vera Cruz. But unlike Jackson who remained with his guns, Lee traveled with the general staff as Scott's chief engineer. Lee himself has left an account of the journey in a February 27 letter to Arlington posted from the "Ship Massachusetts Off Lobos"; he says, "General Worth's and General Twiggs' divisions have arrived," indicating that Jackson, still under Worth's command, was nearby when the armada passed through Lobos. Again there is not a hint that either man was aware of the other's presence.[43]

Although Freeman attempts to show that Winfield Scott did not specifically ask for Lee's transfer, other writers who knew him personally say otherwise. General Long maintains that Lee was ordered to leave his engineering post with Taylor "by the particular request of General Scott," and Fitzhugh Lee is equally firm: "The American commander [Scott] promptly availed himself of the talents of the engineer and summoned Lee to his side, and in the memorable campaign which followed, Lee was his military advisor and possessed his entire confidence."[44]

When Lee did become Scott's confidant and member of the "little cabinet," he also found himself entangled in the politics of command during the army shake-up of January–February 1847. Zachary Taylor had unquestionably fallen from favor with President Polk and his advisers; Winfield Scott had become the chief instrument of Washington military planning. "Old Rough and Ready" even wrote to Scott regarding the raid on his force in northern Mexico: So many men had been removed that he "was left with less than a thousand regulars and a volunteer force partly of new levies to hold a defensive line, while a large army of more than twenty thousand men is in my front." As he faced Santa Anna at Buena Vista, Taylor also complained that he had "lost the confidence of the government. . . . But however much I may feel personally mortified and outraged . . . I will carry out in good faith . . . the views of the government though I may be sacrificed in the effort."[45]

Eighteen months later, Taylor capitalized on the sacrificial lamb argument during the 1848 presidential canvass—that Polk and the Democrats had thrown him to the dogs to advance others. Taylor's major biographer says flat out: "His command was depleted in compliance with the instructions of Winfield Scott." And Lee was not the only officer to join the Vera Cruz exodus. Men assigned to the new army besides Generals Worth and Twiggs included Ulysses S. Grant, Gordon Meade, Charles F. Smith "and a host of equally promising officers," including Lieutenant Thomas Jackson. "Not a single general officer of importance who had been under fire remained with Zachary Taylor." A man of Lee's contacts throughout the army surely knew about the high-level bickering. Yet he lost no time in finding new friends and in throwing himself into the tasks at hand; and though direct evidence is lacking, he no doubt did what he could to ingratiate himself with the new Caesar. He certainly did nothing to dissuade Scott from adding him to the general staff. When the two met at Brazos in January 1847, writes Lee confidant William P.

Snow, three years before Lee's death: "Captain Lee was one of the first selected to be on his personal staff and council, and the high opinion Scott entertained of him is well known."[46]

In his lengthy letter of February 27 addressed to his elder sons, Lee not only admonished them "to grow in goodness and knowledge," but also gave a detailed account of his movements from Saltillo. Upon getting orders to leave Taylor and Wool, he had ridden 250 miles to the coast on his mare Creole. The horse "was the admiration of every one at Brazos and they could hardly believe she had carried me so far, and looked so good." Jim Connally, a servant whom Lee called "Jem" in his letters to Arlington, thought "there was nothing like her in the country." Although the transports had berths for the officers' horses, Lee became fearful lest Creole and another mount would be injured at sea. When he boarded the *Massachusetts* at Brazos, Connally stayed behind with instructions "to come on with the horses."

A "grand parade" took place upon Scott's arrival at Tampico, which Lee described for his sons: "The troops were all drawn up on the bank of the river, and fired a salute as he passed them. He landed at the market, where lines of sentinels were placed to keep back the crowd. In front of the landing the artillery was drawn up, which received him in the center of the column and escorted him through the streets to his lodgings. They had provided a handsome gray horse, richly caparisoned, for him to ride, but he preferred to walk with his staff around him, and a dragoon *led the horse behind us.* . . ." In the two or three weeks between his arrival at Brazos and the parade through Tampico on February 19, Lee had obviously carved a niche in Scott's command scheme. And one can only speculate that Jackson was present with his artillery battery when Scott, Lee, and the staff passed in review.

Lee left Tampico February 19, and after a stopover at Lobos Island until March 3, reached Anton Lizardo three days later. Once ashore he played a key part in the reduction of San Juan de Ulloa and subsequent occupation of Vera Cruz itself. After the city's surrender on March 29, Lee remained near the coast until mid-April, when Scott started the march inland. His letters to Mary and the children as well as his frequent mention in official dispatches afford insight into his role in the ensuing campaign. Cadmus Wilcox, who first saw Lee at Vera Cruz, noted a fighting man at his peak: "I was much impressed with his fine appearance, either on horse or foot. Then he was in full manly vigor, and the handsomest man in the army."[47]

4

To the Halls of Montezuma

The endeavors of Lee and Jackson during the race for Mexico City make it all but impossible that either man could have escaped the other's attention from the instant Scott started his inland march. Although possible meetings during Lee's visit to West Point and during the first hectic preparations for war at Fort Hamilton remain speculative, they had more than ample opportunity for close association during the siege of Vera Cruz. Dabney insists that Jackson "bore his part" in the city's bombardment but that he did nothing to merit "special distinction." Yet he clearly participated in Scott's buildup to secure the army after the initial beachhead along a seven-mile perimeter that engulfed the city's inland defenses while carefully avoiding its guns. "There followed days of maddening delays," writes Alfred Hoyt Bill: "Northers slowed the debarkation, hurling high waves up the beach to work havoc among the wagonloads of shells, the tentage, the mess-bags and the barrels of bread that were stacked at the foot of the sandhills. Transports were driven ashore with crews and soldiers clinging to the shrouds. By the end of the siege the wrecks of thirty brigs and schooners lay amid the surf. In the wreck of one vessel between one and two hundred horses were drowned."[1]

In spite of countless headaches, Winfield Scott had no sooner landed than he told Robert E. Lee, Pierre G. T. Beauregard, and Lee's buddy, Joe Johnston to stymie the enemy's feeble artillery. "Natty Lieutenant Beauregard" not only tore his new uniform to pieces in the undergrowth as he worked to place the American guns but Lee also took a hand in directing Scott's fieldpieces toward the Vera Cruz ramparts. Captain Taylor's battery, like others in the invading force, were needed when units under Twiggs were placed along the coast north of the city. James

Dabney McCabe's account of the ensuing bombardment, published within a year of Jackson's death, has him "assigned the command of one of the batteries erected for the destruction of the devoted city. Exposed to great hardships, he exhibited the most unvarying cheerfulness, and, the object of heavy fire, he worked his guns with such skill and courage as to attract the attention of the commanding general and receive his highest commendation." Jackson himself appeared to confirm his West Point classmate's report when he wrote to Laura from his "camp near Vera Cruz" one day after the capitulation: "While I was at the advance batteries a cannon ball [sic] came in about five steps of me." If Jackson was trying to reassure his sister, his future in-law, D. H. Hill, was more direct: "After a night of toil at Vera Cruz [Jackson and an unnamed companion] sought shelter under a sand-bank to snatch a few hours sleep, when an enormous shell from the Castle of San Juan de Ulloa came crushing through their shelter and nearly ended their earthly career."[2]

Jackson unquestionably pounded the Vera Cruz defenses with his guns, and it is more than probable that Robert E. Lee noted the young artillerist with Twiggs' division near Vergara, a small hamlet north of the city; as Lee and his fellow engineers rode through the encircling gun replacements to improve Scott's forward positions, he could hardly have missed him. Jackson's letter of March 30 hints that he was engaged in "the bombarding and cannonading" throughout the fight; and he was promoted first lieutenant—a rank that allowed him to join the intrepid "Prince" John Magruder a few weeks later—because of his "gallant and meritorious conduct at the siege of Vera Cruz." Although several officers received promotions in rank, but three brevets were issued, including Henry Hopkins Sibley—afterward Confederate commander during the occupation of New Mexico, 1861–1862. When contrasted to the profusion of honors parceled out following the fighting at Cerro Gordo, Contreras, Churubusco, and Chapultepec, Jackson's recognition was remarkable.[3]

Early shelling by army pieces, and by warships hugging the coast, made it obvious that the walls could not be breached without guns from the fleet. Moreover, the most forward emplacements were under steady fire from the city as well as San Juan de Ulloa. Lee himself had a narrow escape on the night of March 19 while returning from a scouting operation; "his coat was burned by the pistol flash of an excited lad who fired before he could establish identity." In order to break the stalemate, and fearful that upward of two thousand men would be sacrificed if he stormed the parapets, Scott called upon Commodore Perry for help. It was a blow to army pride, but Scott did not have the resources to proceed; Perry and his tars were proud to assist, but they made it plain that his men would fire navy guns even on land.

Amid the interservice rivalry, Scott detailed Lee to oversee positioning of the guns. "Three long 32-pounders and three 8-inch shell guns were hoisted out of the warships and ferried to the beach, where pairs of huge timber wheels awaited them. They weighed more than three tons apiece, and it was more than three miles to the well-concealed platform that Lee had built for them within eight hundred yards of the city wall." Hundreds of sailors assisted by army volunteers struggled to get the guns in place—and by the 24th they were ready to open fire. Foreign consular officials, who watched the growing armament with alarm, rushed to Scott's headquarters early in the morning of March 25 to seek a truce so that women, children, and foreign nationals might leave. But the commanding general said, "No!" That courtesy of war had been offered earlier and then summarily dismissed by the Mexican defenders.[4]

Raphael Semmes, a young fleet officer who watched the fearful hammering, wrote that it was the heaviest gunfire ever mounted in a siege. The future commander of the Confederate raider ship C.S.S. *Alabama,* by all accounts a man who knew his military history, was a careful observer at Vera Cruz; his 1851 classic, *Service Ashore and Afloat during the Mexican War,* even added to the Lee mystique when he penned a closely reasoned account of Scott's chief engineer: "The services of Captain Lee were invaluable to the chief. Endowed with a mind which had no equal in his corps, . . . he examined, counseled, and advised, with a judgment, tact, and discretion worthy of all praise. His talent for topography was peculiar, and he seemed to receive impressions intuitively, which it cost other men much labor to acquire." Semmes, who watched Lee throughout the march to Mexico City, wrote his assessment twelve years before the Civil War hurled Lee to international prominence.[5]

At Vera Cruz, meanwhile, Lee had more guns to place the following day, March 25, when an additional four 24-pounders and two 8-pound mortars arrived from the fleet. The Mexican defenders returned his fire, but their artillery—part of it cast at the West Point Foundry in New York—could not long withstand the superior American armament. Finally, writes A. H. Bill, "the morning of the 26th saw another flag of truce from the lofty arched gateway of Fort Santiago, which formed the southern end of the fortifications. It came from the Mexican commander this time." The siege of Vera Cruz had ended.[6]

While the surrender negotiations proceeded, Lee sent a letter to his brother, also at Vera Cruz, although he said nothing about his near wounding. Smith Lee, on duty with the fleet guns, was asked if he could obtain wine and other articles from a "French bark" offshore. "Can you through any of your comrades, get me a box of claret, one of brandy, and four colored shirts. The latter are seventy-five cents each (I have two of them) and the brandy thirty-seven and a half cents per bottle." It is not clear if Lee wanted the spirits for his own use or for entertaining fellow officers; he also asked Smith to purchase a telescope to replace one he had lost. Lee had attempted to visit his naval brother when he came ashore with "the naval battery" but failed. "I was too thankful that you were saved through that hot fire. I felt awful at the thought of your being shot down before me."[7]

Although some writers downplay Lee's role in the surrender talks, Dabney H. Maury, who was present, says that he was one of the negotiators. "General Scott selected Captains Joseph E. Johnston and Robert E. Lee to represent us, and nobly they did also. This selection gave great satisfaction throughout the army. In rich uniforms, superbly mounted they were the most soldierly, as they were the ablest, men in the army. We young Virginians were proud that day to see them, and to know our two victorious armies were led by two great Virginia generals. . . ." Maury's bravado resulted from news of Zachary Taylor's victory at Buena Vista which overtook Scott's army during the siege of Vera Cruz, although the Virginia-born Taylor had long since removed his residence to Kentucky.[8]

The articles of capitulation signed on March 28 and sanctioned by Scott were generous to the vanquished. When General Juan Morales realized that no help was coming from the interior, he had no choice but to surrender before the American pounding. His troops were accorded the honors of war; they were paroled on word not to fight again—a provision quickly forgotten; their personal property and the free exercise of religion respected. First Lieutenant Thomas Jackson, however, had reservations: "I approve of all except allowing the enemy to retire," he told Laura. "That I cannot approve of inasmuch as we had them secure, and could have taken them prisoners of war unconditionally." Lee's published letters are silent about his feelings.

American troops—Lee and Jackson amongst them—occupied Vera Cruz the following day, March 29, 1847, but Scott, fearful lest the *vomito* might ravage his precariously small force, gave the order to advance inland from the coastal lowlands. While he waited for reinforcements and prepared for the march, Scott reorganized his army on April 6 into two divisions; the first was commanded by Worth with brigades under Colonels John Garland and N. S. Clark, and the second fell to

Twiggs with Brigadier General Persifor Smith and Colonel Bennet Riley as brigade leaders. By April 8, Scott's entire complement was on the move down the National Highway toward Jalapa and the highlands of central Mexico. Twiggs's division which included Jackson's artillery battery led the way. Brigadier General Robert Patterson—the same Patterson who faced Jackson at Harpers Ferry in the spring of 1861— followed the next day with a division of volunteers.[9]

The national roadway ran northwestward from Vera Cruz toward Jalapa, the first town of size on the route to Mexico City; within three days, across "nothing but sand—sand as far as the eye could see," lead units under Twiggs reached the Río del Plan, a small river that flows through a canyon from the Sierra Madre into the Atlantic. Here, sixty miles from the coast, the Yankee column met a determined force under Generalíssimo Santa Anna, who had placed his cannon on two hills overlooking the line of march. "Just north of the point where the road returned to the rim of the canyon above the river rose a conical hill, sometimes called El Telegrafo because it was surmounted with the remains of one of the old line of visual telegraph towers used to communicate between Vera Cruz and Mexico, but more commonly known as Cerro Gordo—which is to say 'Big Hill.' Half a mile to the northeast of Cerro Gordo was another hill, Atalaya, nearly as high and as steep." Mexican batteries had been placed atop the seven hundred-foot peak of Cerro Gordo as well as Atalaya; and Santa Anna put more emplacements at the Ranchero Cerro Gordo, a short distance beyond the peaks. Scott's meager eighty-five hundred-man army could not continue until the guns were silenced.[10]

After a day or so of helpless stalemate, Scott called upon Lee to find a route to attack the entrenched enemy. As he gazed upward from the National Highway at El Telegrafo and Atalaya, Scott realized intuitively that the Mexican line which extended from Atalaya on his right to the Río del Plan offered formidable resistance. His only hope of success by a costly frontal attack lay in finding a path through the jumbled undergrowth and gullies around the enemy's left flank—around Atalaya. Accompanied by Beauregard, Lee set out on a series of reconnaissances during April 15–17 that resulted in the hoped-for route. Lee's engineering-scouting exploits again captured wide notice through the ranks; Scott accounted they "were conducted with vigor . . . and at the end of the third day a passable way for the light batteries was accomplished without alarming the enemy, giving the possibility of turning the extreme left of his line of defense and capturing his whole army. . . ." Although the "whole" enemy was not routed, the Mexicans were sent scurrying down the road toward Mexico City. It was a great day for American arms because of Lee's exertions; Santa Anna later proclaimed that he did not think a goat could climb those hills. "Hence the surprise was greater," Scott added.[11]

Scott's plan called for Twiggs, with Patterson, Shields, and Harney in support, to assault the Mexican left while Pillow's division probed at the enemy front. After he oversaw construction of the trailways around Atalaya, Lee personally directed the artillery under Twiggs—Captain Taylor and Jackson included—into position on the 17th. For a brief interval, Jackson found himself under his direct command—the first Lee-Jackson association.

Lieutenant Ulysses S. Grant, who accompanied one of the units under Lee's temporary command, recounted the rough march against Cerro Gordo and Atalaya thirty-eight years later: "Under the supervision of the engineers, roadways had been opened over the chasms to the right where the walls were so steep that men could barely climb them. Animals could not. These had been opened under the cover of night, without attracting the notice of the enemy. The engineers, who had directed the opening, led the way and the troops followed. Artillery was let down the steep slopes by hand, the men engaged attaching a strong rope to the rear axle. . . ." Grant's close memory of the fighting reflected the lasting imprint that Mexico had upon the young officers who marched with Winfield Scott and Zachary Taylor; it was their first encounter with the wider world, and not only Grant but also men like Lee and Jackson must have spent countless hours in barracks-room talk about the war. In April 1865, when Lee and Grant met in the McLean House at Appomattox, to end another, much crueler war, the discussions opened with a reminiscence of their Mexican service. As for Cerro Gordo, "the attack was as ordered, and perhaps there was not a battle of the Mexican War, or of any other, where orders issued before an engagement were nearer being a correct report of what afterward took place," Grant added.[12]

Lee's scouts played a key role in the victory, and when the army barreled into Jalapa one day later, he described his part in the affair for Mrs. Lee: "I reconnoitered the ground in the direction of the ravines on their left, and passed around the enemy's rear," an April 25 letter said.

On the 16th a party was set to work in cutting out the road, on the 17th I led General Twiggs division in the rear of a hill in front of Cerro Gordo, and in the afternoon, when it was necessary to drive them from the hill where we intended to construct a battery at night, the first intimation of our presence or intentions were known. . . . Soon after sunrise our batteries opened, and I started with a battery to turn their left and to get on the Jalapa road. Notwithstanding their efforts to prevent us on this, we were perfectly successful, and the working party, following in our footsteps, cut out the road for the artillery.[13]

Either out of modesty or because he did not want to frighten his wife, Lee failed to mention that he was nearly killed at Cerro Gordo. As General Long tells the story, Lee strayed from his guides in the Mexican darkness and found himself near enemy outriders. "He was forced to take refuge beneath a fallen tree, near which was a spring to which Mexicans frequently came for water. While he lay hidden in this perilous covert hostile soldiers frequently passed over the tree, and even sat down on it and entered into conversation, without discovering the somewhat nervous individual beneath it. He was obliged to remain there until the coming of light enabled him to return from the dangerous locality." The yarn, Long relates, came from John Fitzwalter, who acted as Lee's guide throughout the Cerro Gordo operation.[14]

Jackson also left a narrative of his duty at Cerro Gordo with the batteries under Twiggs. When he reached the battle site, he told Laura from Jalapa, "we learned that General Santa Anna held the pass in force. Consequently we waited for reinforcements, which finally arrived, and on the 17th inst. we attacked the Mexicans, but did not succeed in routing them until the 18th, when we took some thousands of prisoners and completely routed the remainder." When the enemy commenced his headlong retreat down the National Highway, Jackson's guns were not far behind. "We followed close on the retreating column until night and came near enough to give them a few shots from the battery, but they succeeded in effecting their escape for want of our dragoons." Always ready to let Laura know about his progress, Jackson added that "Captain Taylor in his report to General Twiggs has spoken of me in very flattering terms." It was more than idle boasting for family consumption— Jackson was making a name for himself as Scott plunged toward the prize at Mexico City. "Through the great exertions of Lt. Jackson," Taylor noted, "the caissons were brought up early in the night."[15]

While Jackson wrestled his "caissons" under Taylor, he watched with awe as "Prince" John Magruder shot to prominence by storming the enemy with his light pieces. In a calculated move that hurled him to the forefront of the subsequent fighting and enabled him to leave the country a brevet major, Jackson launched an instant campaign to join the "flying battery" of his fellow Virginian. Magruder's reputation for heavy fighting and a penchant for being at the center of every action heightened

Jackson's determination. According to John Esten Cooke's biography published in 1866, Jackson told several contemporaries: "I wanted to see active service, to be near the enemy and in the fight; and when I heard that John Magruder had his battery, I bent all of my energies to be with him, for I knew if any fighting was to be done Magruder would be 'on hand.' " A close camaraderie developed between the two, which caused Magruder to speak favorably about his young subordinate in official dispatches.

During a later period of boredom following the capture of Mexico City, Magruder called upon Jackson to deliver his famous challenge to General Franklin Pierce; some memoirs suggest Pierce's face was "slapped" by Magruder during a card game, although it is not certain that Jackson was present. In the presidential campaign of 1852, when Pierce's personal honor was under attack, Magruder, then living in California, ended the affair with a public letter "which showed the very best feeling." Jackson—then professor of natural philosophy in the Virginia Military Institute—kept his counsel.[16]

Jackson was obliged to wait several weeks before he joined Magruder at Puebla. A very disappointed young lieutenant explained the delay in a May 25 letter to his sister: "I have the mortification of being left to garrison the town of Jalapa. Captain Taylor used his influence to keep me with him, in which event I should have gone forward. But Colonel Childs, who was made Military Governor of this place got General Scott to issue an order requiring me to join my company which was under the command of the Governor." Actually he missed little if any of the fighting when the army waited at Puebla until early August before making a final descent upon the enemy capital; Jackson apparently moved forward during mid-June with General George Cadwalader, who passed through Jalapa with three regiments to reinforce Scott. "I am in fine quarters and making rapid progress in the Spanish language, and an idea of making some lady acquaintances shortly," he informed Laura. He also asked to hear from his brother Wirt.[17]

When Lee moved forward with Worth's division, the retreating enemy had left an open roadway; by the time Cadwalader followed from Jalapa on June 18, marauders had not only destroyed bridges and blocked the National Highway they also posed a threat to supply columns. Cadwalader's five hundred-man force ran into trouble with guerrillas a few miles west of town; "the garrison of Perote had to turn out to extricate him from a serious situation at the pass of La Hoya." Moreover, A. H. Bill's detailed treatment continues, "the Perote troops, bored and disgusted by the continual scrimmages in which they generally had several killed and wounded and frequently came off second best, had reached a state of mind in which they noted with satisfaction that Captain Walker of the Texans seldom brought in any prisoners. In the La Hoya combat they burned the near-by town of Las Vegas, which they knew to be a veritable nest of guerrillas." Cadwalader, new to the bushwhacking game, aroused a storm among the Americans when he ordered the offending troops punished.

A month or so afterward, Jackson told Laura about his own part in the affair: "As I was coming from Jalapa I was detached with a few men in the vicinity of La Hoya and succeeded in killing four and taking three prisoners together with a beautiful sabre and some other equipment." One wishes the letter from Mexico City contained more detail, but the fight was probably his first experience with killing enemy soldiers at close quarters, his artillery encounters notwithstanding. Although Jackson said nothing about Cadwalader's conduct, he asked for his brother Wirt's address as well as that of another relative. "I wish to write them both," he acknowledged.[18]

At Perote, Cadwalader found an order from General Gideon J. Pillow, also bringing up reinforcements amid constant guerrilla attacks, to await his arrival before proceeding toward Scott at Puebla. A combined column, Pillow reasoned, would enjoy better odds. So Jackson must have tarried a few days on his way to Magruder's command, looking over the city and castle that Lee had seen in April. "The castle or fort of Perote is one of the best finished that I have ever seen—very strong, with high, thick walls, bastioned front, and deep, wide ditch," Lee had written his wife. "It is defective in construction and is very spacious, covers twenty-five acres, and also there is within its walls nearly three thousand troops, and it is not yet full. Within the fort is a beautiful chapel, in one corner of which is the tomb of Guadalupe Victoria." When one of the brigade chaplains conducted a hastily arranged Episcopal service, Lee took time from his map-making chores to attend. "I endeavored to give thanks to our heavenly Father for all of his mercies to me, for his preservation of me through all the dangers I have passed. . . ."[19]

Meanwhile, the combined Calwalader-Pillow column had no sooner reached Puebla on July 8 than Magruder appointed Jackson his commissary officer. Magruder's was one of four light batteries created by Scott while the army regrouped until August 7 before moving forward; and though Jackson's new post was contingent upon his promotion for his service at Vera Cruz, his commission as first lieutenant was not dated until August 20, 1847. But his letter of October 6 to General George

Gibson in Washington makes it clear that Magruder used his previous experience with Captain Taylor before the promotion became final. Upon requesting appointment as "assistant commissary," he asked for it "to date from the 16th, of July that being the time at which I was assigned to duty in the commissary and quartermasters Department with light company I First Arty by written orders from Captain Magruder its commanding officer." Though Magruder seconded his petition, the request was shelved until the following April.[20]

When Magruder's command was dissolved following the capture of Mexico City, Jackson was reposted to Captain Taylor's battery; nevertheless, he did not spend all of his time at Puebla supplying I Company with "various amounts of pork, beef, bacon, salt, candles, etc." With keen interest in the world around him, he watched every move in the preparation for battle as the light batteries awaited Scott's command to advance. Because of his own doing in searching out Magruder, Jackson now found himself in the right place at the right time. The flying battery concept became the military organization of the moment because of its speedy maneuverability—just what was needed for the final thrust at the Mexican capital. Dabney, who talked with him daily during the Virginia campaigns, wrote that Jackson "foresaw this arm of warfare was henceforth destined to be used in every battle, and to be always thrust forward to the post of danger and honor." It is easy to see why Jackson, yearning for recognition, wanted to leave Taylor and the heavy guns. "The old artillery, cumbersome in moving and slow in working," Dabney observes, "was usually posted at some permanent point, and must needs remain there for the day. If the tide of battle flowed toward it, it might render important service; if away from it, it was condemned to inactivity, and a partial disaster could compel its surrender. . . ." That changed with the new service.[21]

Jackson continued his close observation of the Mexican countryside as he waited and readied himself for the onslaught. "The next place of importance [after Perote] on the national road is Puebla, which is, from its manufacturing character, the Lowell of Mexico, but to an American the place is extremely interesting; but sixty odd miles further west is situated the ancient city of the Aztecs which contains people of most every clime," he told his brother-in-law, Jonathan Arnold.[22]

Although Scott was obliged to send several thousand volunteers home at the expiration of their enlistments, the May 15–August 10 "hiatus" at Puebla was not a complete stalemate. Like Jackson, Lee was deeply embroiled with preparation for the coming campaign as Scott awaited reinforcements. The wartime diary of General Ethan Hitchcock, Scott's

Inspector General, hints that Lee sat at the commanding general's elbow throughout the wait. Interestingly, Hitchcock's own impressions parallel those of Lee: "A semicircle of mountains is on the north and west—Orizaba, Popocatpetzl, etc.,—all constantly covered with snow. Puebla contains some seventy or eighty thousand people. Buildings all of stone, the finest and largest being religious edifices."[23]

Douglas Southall Freeman cites a collection of maps in the Virginia Military Institute archive to demonstrate that Lee and Major William Turnbull, Scott's chief topographical engineer, spent their time in the preparation of charts outlining possible routes to the capital. It is reasonable that Lee was too preoccupied with his plats to notice Jackson and the flying batteries, although the fast-moving artillery played a key role in Scott's planning. "The limited range of the musket and the close order formations that it necessitated made it possible for artillery to be used extensively on the offensive," writes two recent scholars about the Mexican campaign. "Artillery could advance close to a defending infantry line before entering effective musket range." Magruder and Jackson did exactly that at the subsequent battle of Contreras.[24]

Winfield Scott may have been "aloof and pompous during the long hiatus at Puebla," and he may have failed to inspire an indifferent home front that thought the war was finished once he left Vera Cruz, but he made a lasting impression upon Lee with his attention to detail and its boldness of execution. "Our Genl. [Scott] is our great reliance," Lee wrote from Mexico. "He is a great man on great occasions. Never turned from his object. Confident in his powers and resources, his judgement is as sound as his heart is bold and daring." Lee's high admiration for Scott, who died in 1866—four years before his engineering subordinate— continued to the end of his life. "I have put in the bag Genl. Scott's autobiography which I thought you might like to read," Lee informed his wife from the trenches around Petersburg. "The Genl. of course stands out very prominently & does not hide his light under a bushel, but he appears the bold sagacious truthful man as he is." And Lee was not the only officer influenced by Scott's tactics on the road from Vera Cruz to Chapultepec—Grant, McClellan, Joe Johnston, Beauregard, and a host of Civil War commanders, North and South, extolled their old chieftain in later years. Although Jackson's letters from Mexico disagreed with aspects of the campaign, he told Laura in 1847 that the siege of Vera Cruz "must in my opinion excel any military operation known in the history of our country."[25]

The interlude at Puebla ended abruptly on August 6, when General Franklin Pierce arrived with a three thousand–man contingent from the

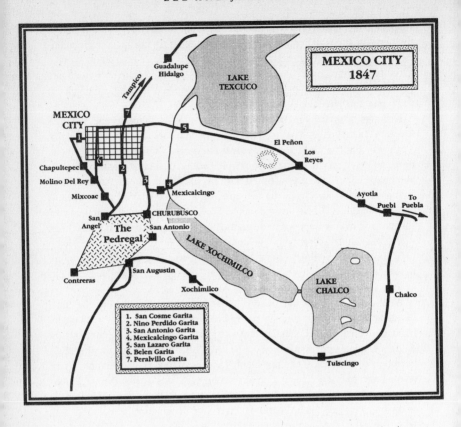

MEXICO CITY
1847

LAKE
TEXCUCO

Guadalupe
Hidalgo

Tampico

MEXICO
CITY

El Peñon

Los
Reyes

Chapultepec

Molino Del Rey

Mixcoac

Mexicalcingo

Ayotla

Puebl   To
         Puebla

San
Angel

CHURUBUSCO

San Antonio

The
Pedregal

LAKE XOCHIMILCO

LAKE
CHALCO

Chalco

Contreras

San Augustin

Xochimilco

1. San Cosme Garita
2. Nino Perdido Garita
3. San Antonio Garita
4. Mexicalcingo Garita
5. San Lazaro Garita
6. Belen Garita
7. Peralvillo Garita

Tuiscingo

coast and Scott issued his marching orders for the next morning. Harney's cavalry was first followed by Jackson's old commander, Brigadier General David E. Twiggs; "pointing down the street leading out of the garita toward the City of Mexico, Twiggs gave the command 'Forward,' " Cadmus Wilcox recounts. "His division with drums beating and banners flying, left the plaza, and in a little time had passed the city limits. It was a thrilling spectacle, of serious and intense interest, being regarded as the beginning of an enterprise that admitted of no failure, either victory or a soldier's grave; in success, safety, in failure, annihilation." Though a small garrison under Colonel Thomas Childs was left to guard the rear, the Duke of Wellington supposedly exclaimed, "Scott is lost," upon hearing that he had descended into the Valley of Montezuma with his entire force.

Quitman left on the 8th, followed two days later by the divisions of Worth and Pillow—the latter included Magruder's light battery. Lee remained close to headquarters as the army renewed its march down the National Highway; because Scott kept an engineer company with his lead columns, he was summoned to more scouting duty within days of leaving Puebla. Like his previous reconnaissances, they earned wide recognition. Although Jackson far back in the ranks with Pillow's units did not enjoy Lee's high visibility at Scott's side, his long-sought-after distinction came twelve days later at Contreras; both men were to have their share of fighting before Santa Anna's capitulation.

Scott's fourteen thousand-man force was a pitifully small band to attack the heart of a civilized nation, but it never questioned that Anglo-Saxon resoluteness which had carried it inland from Vera Cruz. Opposition to the American spearhead collapsed with startling quickness when Scott breached the walls of Mexico City six weeks after leaving Puebla, but on the morning of August 7 eighty miles of enemy-infested roads and causeways lay between the units under Twiggs and victory. Along the northern shore of Lake Chalco at Ayotla, Scott ordered a halt to reconnoiter possible routes into the capital. His first obstacle was El Peñon, "an immense hill of volcanic lava, seven miles from the Garita de Lazaro. Over three hundred feet high, well fortified, and with thirty guns in position, it commanded all the approaches to the causeway directly at its base; there was a battery six or eight hundred yards in front of it on the road and one similiarly situated a like distance beyond on the side next to the city." With his most direct route blocked, Scott was obliged to find another once he descended from the mountains; even a cursory glance at a map of central Mexico reveals a great depression in the center of the country, which encompasses a series of lakes—Zumpango, San Cristóbal, Texcuco, Xochimilco, Chalco—each surrounded by impassable swamps and morasses. Moreover, the valley which is rimmed by mountains "is over 7,500 feet above sea level, elliptical in outline, the longest diameter being eighteen, the shortest twelve and a half Spanish leagues; with a slight declivity toward Lake Texcuco northeast of the capital."

The only entrances into the city lay along causeways—some constructed by the Aztecs—each straddled by a garita or fortified custom-house stationed by sentries in more peaceful times. When the army reached the road junction at Ayotla, Lee was ordered forward to seek the best route; accompanied by Captain James L. Mason and Lieutenant I. I. Stevens, he probed the defenses at El Peñon. "At the same time, Beauregard rode along the north and west shore of Lakes Chalco and Xochimilco, and ascertained that the road on the east and south shore of the former was practicable, thus corroborating the news received before leaving Puebla." Additional scouting by Lee convinced Scott that an assault against El Peñon would prove too costly but that the army could proceed toward the Halls of Montezuma from the south through the village of San Augustín.[26]

With Lee by his side, Scott established his headquarters at San Augustín on August 17, a mere ten miles from the capital. Although Santa Anna shifted his main force to encounter the maneuver, Twiggs was left at Ayotla to threaten what remained of his force at El Peñon and Mexicalcingo. While Lee was plunged into the fray immediately, Jackson, still under Pillow's command, did not reach San Augustín until the 18th with Magruder's company. In the ensuing fight at Contreras—called Padierna by Mexican chroniclers—they were not only in close association but Lee again had Jackson under his command when he directed the light battery into position.

The shorter path from San Augustín lay through San Antonio and Churubusco; directly west lay the infamous Pedregal, extending from Churubusco to the village of Padierna. General Henry Jackson Hunt, who was present, described it as "a vast surface of volcanic rocks and scoria broken into every possible form, presenting sharp ridges and deep fissures, exceedingly difficult even in daytime for the passage of infantry, and utterly impassable for artillery, cavalry, or single horsemen. . . . By taking advantage of the small open places a difficult, crooked, and hardly passable road—not much better than a mule-track—had been opened from San Augustín to the plateau, in front of which it joins the road from the city of Mexico." The great road south from the capital branched at Churubusco because of the Pedregal with the main thoroughfare leading to San Augustín and the other to Contreras and "the elevated plateau" described by Hunt. The future Union officer likewise pointed out that Lee found a way through the lava when General Gabriel Valencia ensconced his troops on the plateau at Contreras to guard Santa Anna's flank. Scott could not march from San Augustín until the force at Contreras was eliminated—until Lee replicated his exploits at Cerro Gordo. General Long's *Memoir,* which reproduces Hunt's 1871 assessment—with lithograph depicting troopers struggling through the lava—of Lee's renewed scouting during August 18–20, has led subsequent biographers to paint the episode as a major boost to his later career.[27]

Lee's task was to locate a final approach around the San Antonio causeway defended by Santa Anna himself. Other roads leading south passed through San Angel beyond the lava from the American camp clustered about San Augustín. With Beauregard as his companion, Lee quickly spotted the hoped-for route. "To the hacienda of San Pobre, a mile and a quarter from San Augustin toward the west, they had found a good road; and then proceeding about an equal distance by a mule-path to the top of a sharp ridge, they had seen the path continue to Padierna and the turnpike, and they believed it possible to make a road by that line." Padierna was a small ranch four miles directly west of Scott's headquarters on the western rim of the Pedregal. Less than a mile southward lay the sleepy village of Contreras, where Valencia held the southern-most flank of Santa Anna's army.

Once Lee's intelligence reached headquarters, the entire army was set in motion. "The next morning, August 18, while Quitman unwillingly remained at San Augustín to guard the base, and Worth, with his engineers and troops, continued to reconnoiter and threaten on the San Antonio road, Scott ordered a force of engineers to build a road in the other direction. Pillow's division was to furnish the working-parties, and Twiggs to clear away whatever Mexican detachments might undertake to hinder the operations; and the implied instructions were to gain and hold the San Angel turnpike so that San Antonio could be turned." When the lead columns reached Valencia with his entrenched guns, Pillow immediately directed the mounted rifles to advance with the batteries of Magruder and Franklin D. Callender in support. There is no question that Lee and Jackson were in close contact during the fighting of August 19; Captain George Brinton McClellan, an officer both would know well in future battles, even helped Lee direct Magruder's guns during the action. Jackson, who took charge of one section upon the death of Lieutenant Preston Johnstone, nephew of Lee's friend Joe Johnston, found his niche when Magruder's battery was "emplaced behind a slight rise in the rocks within less than 1,000 yards of Valencia's heavier and more numerous guns. Beyond this point there was no advance but the batteries stayed from two in the afternoon until ten at night."[28]

Besides Lee and Jackson, a veritable who's who of future Confederates distinguished themselves at Contreras and in the next day's fight at Churubusco—George B. Crittenden, Arnold Elzey, P. G. T. Beauregard, Richard S. Ewell, Daniel H. Hill, James Longstreet, Earl Van Dorn, George W. Smith, Simon B. Buckner, George Pickett, and Samuel B. Maxey, all received brevet promotions. Jackson's steady pounding of Valencia's position that August afternoon won him a promotion to brevet captain as well as the commendation of his superiors. Pillow spoke of Jackson's "gallant services" in his battle summary and, continues Jackson's friend, James Dabney McCabe:

> Captain Magruder in his report (which singularly enough was addressed to Captain J. Hooker), speaks as follows: "I reported to General Twiggs, and was ordered, by him to advance toward the enemy's battery. . . . About 2 o'clock P.M., the battery was placed in front of the enemy's entrenchments at a distance of about nine hundred yards. . . . My fire was opened . . . and continued with great rapidity for about an hour. . . . In a few moments Lieutenant Jackson, commanding the second section of the battery, who had opened a fire upon the enemy's works from a position on the right, hearing our own fire still further in front, advanced in handsome style . . . kept up the fire with great briskness and effect . . . Lieutenant Jackson's conduct was equally conspicuous throughout the whole day, and I cannot too highly commend him to [the] major general's favorable consideration."

Although Jackson's letters to Laura say nothing about the Contreras episode, he did mention Pillow's commendation; he also stated that he earned $104 per month while assigned to Magruder.[29]

Lee was poised for greater honors when darkness fell over both armies staring at each other across an impassable ravine in spite of the day-long cannonade by Magruder and Callender. During the early evening, Lieutenant Z. B. Tower, an officer assigned to Colonel Persifor Smith, found a path around the abyss; when a coterie of officers met in the village chapel at nearby San Geronimo to discuss Smith's hurriedly revised plan of action, Lee characteristically volunteered to recross the Pedregal to inform Scott. "In a cold, heavy rain which, throughout the night poured upon Mexican and American alike," he hiked to headquarters at San Augustín: "The gallant and indefatigable Captain Lee, of the Engineers, who has been constantly with the operating forces, (eleven o'clock P.M.,) just in from Shields, Smith, Cadwalader, etc., to report, . . . and to ask that a powerful diversion be made against the center of the entrenched camp toward morning." Thus Winfield Scott informed Secretary of War William L. Marcy on the night of August 19 from "Headquarters of the Army, San Augustín, Nine Miles From Mexico."

Scott continued: "Brigadier General Twiggs cut off . . . from part of his division beyond the impracticable ground, and Captain Lee are gone, under my orders, to collect the forces remaining on this side with which to make that diversion at about five o'clock in the morning." Although Scott did not mention Jackson by name in his Report No. 31, he added: "All our corps, including Magruder's and Callender's light batteries, not only maintained the exposed positions early gained, but all attempted charges upon them."

Thereupon, in the dead of night, Lee recrossed the lava beds for a third time to assist Twiggs and his staff collect the remaining troopers in the Pedregal—near a rise called the Hill of Zacatepec—for the early morning thrust. The actual attack that followed Persifor Smith's quick march around Valencia's rear via the San Angel road while Twiggs and Shields charged his front, was a stunning victory—a victory executed in large measure by Captain Robert E. Lee, which sent the hapless Mexicans running toward Mexico City. Smith looked at his timepiece when the fight commenced and noted that Valencia's position was firmly secured within seventeen minutes of the opening shots. Little wonder that Scott penned another tribute to his captain of engineers in his official report: Lee's actions was "the greatest feat of physical and moral courage performed by any individual" during the Contreras-Churubusco campaign.[30]

A relentless momentum now seized the army! Soldiers throughout the ranks knew that Santa Anna could never keep them from the capital. He had after all lost upward of seven hundred men in the seventeen-minute fracas at Contreras, while American losses were but sixty dead and wounded. Valencia was branded a traitor as Santa Anna rallied his forces to stem the Yankee drive and withdrew from San Angel with his panic-stricken force to the Churubusco River, which flows into Lake Xochimilco near Mexicalcino; the stream was little more than "a drainage ditch running between high embankments planted with maguey." Close by, however, was a massive church and convent where the roads around the Pedregal converged from San Angel and San Antonio. "At the Churubusco bridgehead and convent and at San Antonio, where the erection of defenses had begun some time before, laborers could be seen working—particularly at San Antonio—like bees; and with all possible haste guns, as well as troops, were brought over from Peñon. Here, said the President, he 'desired to have the battle fought.' "[31]

Santa Anna's good intentions notwithstanding, Scott had another victory under his belt by midafternoon, August 20, when the Mexicans broke from Churubusco in a frenzied mob; Lee was again active in the fight, although Jackson and the light battery were held in reserve when Pillow's command was posted toward San Antonio. At the village of Coyoacán, less than a mile from the Churubusco road junction, Scott ordered Lee to reconnoiter the avenues into Mexico City at the same time Pillow was sent in the opposite direction. But Lee, who traveled with the mounted rifles and Stephen W. Kearny's company, soon encountered enemy units fleeing northward from San Antonio—driven by Worth's division—and returned to headquarters. Scott immediately placed the brigade of Franklin Pierce under Lee's command and told him, according to Cadmus Wilcox, "to move by the road leading north from Coyoacán, across the Churubusco River by a bridge on that road, then turn to the right and seize the causeway in the rear tête-du-pont." Afterward, General James Shields, ordered forward to relieve Lee, soon found himself heavily engaged all along the line of contact; but Lee, who returned to Scott's command post, was instantly put in charge of Henry H. Sibley's company of dragoons, and with William W. Loring's mounted rifles rushed forward to reinforce Shields. "Meanwhile the attack was persistently pressed at all points along the whole front, and now very seriously in danger of having their retreat cut off by increasing forces in their rear, the Mexican lines gave way and fell back, pursued by the victorious Americans." Lee's arrival had tipped the balance.[32]

Henry A. White's 1910 biography cites a letter, which also appears in Freeman, reputedly penned by Lee himself, detailing his part in the battle. After he crossed the river, the letter says, Lee came across Santa Anna's massed infantry on the bridge leading north from Churubusco on the road to Mexico City; he had crossed by the enemy's right flank with Shields and Pierce to get behind the Mexicans:

Apprehending a fire from batteries to defend the rear, I drew out towards the city of Mexico until I reached the large hamlet on the Mexican road about three fourths of a mile in the rear of Churubusco [Los Portales]. Throwing the left of his brigade upon this building which offered protection against the masses of cavalry stretching towards the gates of Mexico, and his right upon the building in the field in rear of which we had approached, General Shields formed his line obliquely to that of the enemy, who not to be outflanked, had drawn out from his entrenchments and extended his line to nearly opposite our left. General Pierce's brigade coming up just after General Shields' brigade had commenced the attack, took position to his right, enveloping the building in the field. Our troops being now hotly engaged and somewhat pressed, I urged forward the Howitzer battery under Lt. [Jesse L.] Reno, who very promptly brought the pieces to bear upon the head of their column with good effect. . . .

Lee left the attacking force and again returned to Scott's headquarters at Coyoacán, but by that time the rout was nearly complete: "I hastened back to the General-in-Chief, who directed Major [Edwin V.] Sumner to take the Rifle regiment and a squadron to the support of that wing. About the time this force reached the open country in the rear of Churubusco, the enemy began to give away. . . ." The letter, if written by Lee, is as near as he ever came to tooting his own horn.[33]

Although Shields and Pierce chased the Mexicans "right up to the gates of the city," mean fighting engulfed the Americans at the church of San Pablo. Santa Anna rallied his troops to hold the church at all costs and "one of the defending batteries was composed largely of American Deserters, who could expect no mercy. Repeated American attacks were beaten back with heavy losses." Units under Twiggs met a determined resistance at the San Pablo convent, where the desperate garrison held out for several hours. While Santa Anna got the worst of it, including 4,200 dead and wounded, "American losses for the day were 131 killed, 865 wounded, and 40 missing. One of Scott's first orders was to execute members of the Batallón de San Patricio who were among the Mexican captives."[34]

Four months earlier, Lee had been breveted major "for gallantry at Cerro Gordo," and now he was elevated to brevet lieutenant colonel for his services at Contreras and Churubusco. Jackson, too, was breveted at Contreras and, though he was forced to the rear in the second fight, he watched closely as the battles of August 19–20 unfolded. "But the lieutenant was able to once again observe the advantages of a flank attack, as at Padierna (called Contreras in the official reports), over a frontal assault so brutally demonstrated at Churubusco."[35] Jackson's great victory over Joe Hooker at Chancellorsville was nearly a replay of Smith's flanking march around Valencia at Contreras; a strategy endorsed by General Robert E. Lee as the two Confederate soldiers sat on discarded Yankee biscuit boxes in the early morning hours of May 2, 1863.

Negotiations commenced a few days after Churubusco, resulting in the Truce of Tacubaya that extended from August 27 until September 6 when Scott determined to renew the battle. Arranged ostensibly to allow President Polk's envoy, Nicholas P. Trist, time to open peace talks, the truce was used by Santa Anna to resupply his army. During the lull, Lee remained close to Scott's headquarters around Tacubaya and worked with Beauregard to scout approaches to Mexico City from the south. He also worked quietly to heal a distressing rift between the commanding general and several junior officers; and he managed to console his old comrade Joe Johnston upon the death of his nephew. Johnston, who lived until 1891, later penned his own account of the incident that tells much about Lee the man: "I saw strong evidence of the sympathy of his nature the morning after the first engagement of our troops in the Valley of Mexico (Contreras). I had lost a cherished young relative in that action, known to General Lee only as my relative. Meeting me, he suddenly saw in my face the effect of that loss, burst into tears, and expressed deep sympathy as tenderly in words as his lovely wife would have done."[36]

A recent graduate of the military academy as well as promising young officer, Preston Johnstone's death had been felt throughout the ranks. Although the record is unclear, Lee must have known that Lieutenant Tom Jackson had taken the place of his friend's nephew with Magruder's battery; but Jackson, like Lee, was too busy with the coming fight to think about letters to Laura as he sat out the truce near Mixcoac with Pillow's division. Also, the military and physical isolation of Scott's army made mail dispatches a near impossibility when Jackson would likely have mentioned the matter.[37]

Although Lee and several other engineers advised Scott to attack the capital from the south—along the Piedad and Niño Piedad causeways, he decided otherwise when the truce terminated abruptly on September 6. The army would advance from the west via Molino del Rey, the fortress of Chapultepec, and thence along the causeways of San Cosme and San Belen. "Across the highway leading into the city from the southwest the Mexicans concentrated their troops for defense," writes Henry A. White. "In front they presented a fortified line five hundred yards in length. At the front of this line was Molinas-del-Rey, the Mills of the King, and at the right stood a fort, within which was a large building termed the Casa Mata. Along the front of this entire line extended a deep ditch. On a height, in the rear of the line towered the fortified castle of Chapultepec. Hovering on the right wing were the Mexican cavalry." It was Santa Anna's last opportunity to check the onslaught. Beyond Chapultepec lay the capital gates.[38]

When Scott ordered Worth to make a frontal assault on the ancient foundry because of a mistaken notion that church bells were being reduced to cannon, there was little for Lee to do but watch the unfolding battle. Jackson, however, entered the fray with the light battery when the enemy cavalry charged Worth's left; he had arrived on the field from Mixcoac in time for the final repulse. At Molino del Rey, Dabney says, "Jackson had no other part than to protect the flank of the force engaged from the insults of the Mexican cavalry, which he accomplished with a few well-directed shots." The September 8 battle resulted in another American victory, but at a terrible cost. Worth suffered 117 killed as well as 700 wounded and missing; although enemy casualties exceeded 2,000, with more than 650 prisoners taken, Scott could ill afford such losses. Jackson again watched the fruitlessness of a direct assault upon an entrenched foe; little wonder that General Hitchcock's diary was not kind to Scott: "We were like Pyrrhus after the fight with Fabricius—a few more such victories and this army would be destroyed."[39]

A few hundred yards east of Molino del Rey through a stand of ancient cypress stood the symbolic fortress of Chapultepec; an "isolated mound of rock, one hundred and fifty feet high, surmounted by a large building constituted the castle; a solid wall enclosed the building and grounds. Breastworks added strength to the hill, and heavy batteries commanded the approaches. Along the steep western slope was a series of mines." Since 1833, it had served as the national military academy—the Mexican West Point—although in more peaceful times it had been a retreat for Aztec caciques and Spanish viceroys. Two miles beyond lay the gates to Mexico City.[40]

Although Lee continued to counsel a southern approach, Scott resummoned his staff following the capture of Molino del Rey. Lieutenant P.G.T. Beauregard, who had scouted with Lee for days argued forcibly

that on account of the marshy nature of the ground and the numerous inundations the southern attack would have to be confined almost entirely to the causeways, which had been cut in many places and strongly fortified in others, and on which the advancing columns would be exposed to heavy enfilading fire without being able to receive adequate support from their own artillery. He held that, whichever side of the city might be attacked afterward, Chapultepec ought to be taken as a pivot from which a movement could be made against any part of the city's perimeter.

Following Beauregard's talk, Scott renewed his command: The army would continue its advance through Chapultepec.[41]

Preliminary to the assault by Pillow's division—which included

Jackson's pieces—and Worth, Lee was directed to oversee placement of siege guns. Thereupon, reminiscent of his assignment at Vera Cruz, he worked with Benjamin Huger throughout the night to erect four batteries; Huger, who served under Lee without distinction in the Seven Days battles, was Scott's chief ordnance officer. The next morning, at Lee's command, a fourteen-hour bombardment pounded the Chapultepec defenders, including the entire corps of young cadets eager to fight the hated invaders. All during September 12, "the great guns and mortars sent their 8-inch and 12-inch shells screaming over the five-hundred-year-old cypress grove that had been the delight of Montezuma and Cortes to burst against the castle walls. By nightfall some shot holes had been observed in these, but the bombardment had not forced evacuation of the place, as Scott had hoped that it would, and the return fire from its batteries was too close for comfort."[42]

Unable to dislodge the garrison by gunnery alone, Scott ordered a direct assault for September 13. "Quitman's division was to attack from the south in a diversionary move, Pillow from the southwest, and Worth from the extreme west. At 5:30 A.M., a cannonade was begun; at 8:00, the attack was made in force. In spite of a number of appalling mistakes, not the least of which was the failure to have scaling ladders in the proper place at the proper time, the Americans were able to take the castle after a bitter struggle. By 9:30 in the morning the Mexicans had surrendered the last major obstacle in the path of Scott's aggressive little army."[43]

Although Joe Johnston led Pillow's men up the steep western incline, Lee had been placed in overall charge; once more he had Jackson under his direct authority since Magruder and the light battery were still attached to Pillow. American losses were substantial during the assault; when Lieutenant James Longstreet fell wounded, another future Confederate, Lieutenant George Pickett—who would lead a more famous charge sixteen years later at Gettysburg—took a battle standard from his grasp and carried it to the castle heights. But Scott's great victory came in large measure because several well-aimed shots from Jackson's guns discouraged Mexican cavalry reserves from joining the battle at a critical juncture.

Scott singled out both men for recognition at Chapultepec—Lee was breveted colonel and First Lieutenant Jackson, brevet captain, was elevated to brevet major. In his official report to the secretary of war, "Old Fuss and Feathers" noted that Lee received a minor wound while leading Pillow's division through the cypress grove that was also crisscrossed with bothersome irrigation trenches: "Captain Lee, so constantly distinguished, also bore important orders from me (September 13), until he fainted from a wound and loss of two nights sleep at the batteries." Although he toppled from the saddle while riding over the battlefield with Scott, Lee had recovered sufficiently to don his full dress uniform the next morning and to enter the capital with the general staff. The commanding general included Jackson's exploits in his report to Secretary Marcy: "To the north [of Chapultepec], and at the base of the mound, inaccessible on that side, the 11th infantry under Lieutenant-Colonel Herbert, the 14th, under Colonel Trousdale, and Captain Magruder's field battery, 1st Artillery, one section under Lieutenant Jackson, all of Pillow's division, had, at the same time, some spirited affairs against superior numbers, driving the enemy from a battery in the road, and capturing a gun. In these, the officers and corps named merited praise." Jackson even received a second commendation for his brief service under Worth during a later phase of the fighting.[44]

Scott's praise aside, most subsequent chroniclers have drawn upon Dabney for Jackson at Chapultepec. At the opening shots, Pillow told Magruder to divide his company—Jackson was sent forward with William B. Trousdale's two companies of infantry toward "the northwest angle" while Magruder himself remained near Pillow. Although Magruder soon rejoined his subordinate, Jackson, who had been pushed forward by Trousdale, "found himself unexpectedly in the presence of a strong battery of the enemy, also at short range, that, in a few moments, the larger portion of his horses was killed, and his men either struck down, or driven from their guns by a storm of grapeshot; while about seventy of the infantry were holding a precarious tenure of the ground in the rear."

General Worth, meanwhile, arrived on the scene and perceiving Jackson's predicament, ordered him to retire.

He replied, that it was more dangerous to withdraw his pieces than to hold his position; and that if they would send him fifty veterans, he would rather attempt the capture of the battery which had so crippled his. Magruder then dashed forward, losing his horse by a fatal shot as he approached him, and found that he had lifted a single gun across a deep ditch by hand to a position where it could be served with effect; and this he was rapidly loading and firing, with the sole assistance of a sergeant; while the remainder of his men were either killed, wounded, or crouching in the ditch. Another piece was brought over, and in a few moments, the enemy was driven from his battery by the rapid fire of Jackson and Magruder.

Not only Dabney but other early Jackson biographers—his wife, his nephew Thomas J. Arnold, James D. McCabe, Markenfield Addey, John Esten Cooke—have quoted extensively from the battle reports of Pillow, Worth, and Magruder, which mention Jackson in glowing terms, stating that his guns helped blast the enemy cavalry off the causeways beyond Chapultepec. His earlier battles were mere preludes to the siege of September 13; here, in the closing minutes of the war, Jackson found his long sought-after, even planned-for recognition as he rushed into Mexico City—fieldpieces at the ready—with the victorious columns of Pillow, Worth, and Quitman. Twenty-three-year-old Thomas Jonathan Jackson was suddenly the toast of the army.[45]

Lee and Jackson stayed in Mexico until the following summer, and though both were part of the occupation force, neither seems to have taken a hand in policing the countryside. Jackson told Laura in February "that you may expect to hear from me by every mail until I am ordered from this city which, may or may not be at all, as I am in General Smith's brigade and he is governor of the city"; Jackson had been back in Taylor's company since the previous December. And his former commander, Jeb Magruder has left a vignette about Lee's duty at Mexico City: When an assembly of Americans proposed to toast "the captain of engineers who found a way for the army within the city," Prince John was dispatched to find the absent Lee; he was found "in a remote corner of the National Palace" poring over several maps. "Magruder accosted his friend and reproached him for his absence. The earnest worker looked up from his labors with a calm, mild gaze which we all remember, and, pointing to his instruments, shook his head.

'But,' said Magruder in his impetuous way, 'this is mere drudgery. Make somebody else do it and come with me.'

'No,' was the reply—'no, I am doing my duty.' "

As both men went about their not-too-strenuous tasks, the months of squabbling between the new government that assumed power upon the resignation of Santa Anna as president culminated in the Treaty of Guadalupe-Hidalgo. Named for a village north of Mexico City, the pact required Mexico "to relinquish all her claims to Texas above the Rio Grande and to cede New Mexico and California to the United States. In return, the United States would pay $15 million and assume the outstanding claims, which totaled $3.25 million, of its citizens against the Mexican government." Lee and Jackson followed the protracted arguments with keen insight before President Polk proclaimed the treaty in effect on July 4, 1848. "The treaty has arrived from Washington with its amendments," Jackson informed Laura on April 20. "Many think that it will receive the ratification of this government but some think it will not. For my own part I hope it will."[46]

Lee, however, told his wife some weeks earlier: "I still have hopes that the treaty will be ratified, though I think some of our leading men, and probably by this time some action of Congress, may so confuse the Mexican mind in reference to her future course as to encourage the recusant to absent themselves so as to defeat it." On February 8, he had told her that the terms were not harsh on Mexico, "considering how the fortune of war has been against her." Although abolitionists in and out of Congress thought otherwise, Lee was convinced the American cause had been just, notwithstanding Senate failure to incorporate the Wilmot Proviso into the treaty designed to eliminate slavery in territories annexed by the United States. "It is certain we are the conquerors in a regular war, and by the law of nations are entitled to dictate the terms of peace. We fought well and we fought fairly," he added. When the Mexican senate voted to accept the pact, he told his brother Smith Lee: "We all feel quite exhilarated at the prospect of getting home. . . . As soon as it is certain that we march out, and I make the necessary arrangements, . . . I shall endeavor to be off."[47]

While Lee, Jackson, and thousands more awaited shipment home, several disruptive trials sent waves through the army. A conflict of ambitions between Winfield Scott, General William J. Worth, a career officer hungry for recognition, and Gideon Pillow, a former law partner of James K. Polk who had been appointed brigadier general by the president, generated the trouble. Charges and countercharges filed in separate actions embittered partisans of the three officers. And though Lee worked to pacify the warring factions, his place on Scott's inner circle drew him into the maelstrom; "the dissensions have clouded a bright campaign," he told his brother. "It is a contest in which neither party has anything to gain and the army much to lose, and ought to have been avoided." Mostly, the difficulty cost Scott the 1848 presidential nomination, and Jackson, who had no part in the affair, mentioned Pillow's troubles in a letter home—that he thought the trouble would be terminated in the United States and not Mexico. But the new brevet major of artillery was wrong; though Lee testified in Scott's behalf—and made a lifelong ally in doing so, the unfortunate incident ended when all parties agreed to drop charges.[48]

Jackson appears to have experienced his first religious encounter while waiting to go home; according to his wife, who surely knew that religious sincerity permeated the remainder of his life, "Captain Francis Taylor, an earnest Christian . . . was the first man to speak to Jackson on the question of personal religion." Although his mother belonged to a Methodist congregation and he flirted with Roman Catholicism in Mexico, he decided to embrace "a simpler form of faith and worship." Lee also toured the religious shrines around Mexico City, but like Jackson he was never in danger of becoming a Roman Catholic. Following a visit to Our Lady of the Remedios, he sent Mrs. Lee a description of the Holy Image, which stood on a "large silver maguey-plant, with a rich crown on her head and an immense petticoat on." Near her statue he noted "representations in wax of the parts of the human body that she had cured of the diseases which they had been afflicted. And I may say there were all parts. I saw many heads severed from the trunks. Whether they represented those she had restored I could not learn." A skeptical Lee had his doubts! "It would be a difficult feat," he proffered.[49]

Jackson's habit of visiting the homes of prominent families apparently brought him into contact with at least one young woman; the record is not clear, but it is easy to speculate about the charms of a señorita of high breeding upon a frontier lad who had undergone the rigors of West Point and the ordeal of battle. His letters to Laura hinted that an interlude had taken place: "Do not allow my words about marrying in Mexico disturb you. I have sometimes thought of staying here, and again of going home. I have no tie in this country equal to you." The romance must have gone sour, because his letters after February 1848 were full of longings for the United States. When not otherwise occupied, Jackson spent his time studying Spanish—something he remembered for the rest of his life— and reading. Among his other pursuits, including the works of Shakespeare, he told Laura that he was reading "Lord Chesterfield's Letters to his son translated into Spanish; so that whilst I am obtaining his thoughts, I am also acquiring a knowledge of the Spanish tongue."

At the same time, Lee told his cousin Markie Williams that he was too busy for letter writing or anything else. General Long, Fitzhugh Lee, the Reverend Jones, and other writers vouch for his constant industry at Scott's headquarters; nevertheless, he found time to join the prestigious Aztec Society, a combination social-fraternal group with General Franklin Pierce as presiding officer. The organization, designed to while away the evening hours, remained in tact until after the turn of the century; it had a distinguished roster, including Ulysses S. Grant, George B. McClellan, Bernard Bee, and William J. Hardee. Jackson unexplainedly was never a member, although he surely held comparable rank.[50]

The Mexican venture ended for Jackson in late June with a posting to Fort Hamilton in New York Harbor. Lee left a month earlier, on May 27, for a joyous reunion with family and friends at Arlington; within weeks, he was assigned to an engineering project at Fort Carroll outside Baltimore. Both Lee and Jackson were left with lifelong memories and a mutual respect developed over twelve months of joint service since the landings at Vera Cruz. They had toiled together with Scott's army to forge a great national triumph. Throughout the 1850s, when the country inched its way toward Civil War, they pursued different paths—Lee in the army, Jackson in civilian life.

5

The Schoolmen, 1848–1859

Within months after the return from Mexico, Lee and Jackson became schoolmen—Lee as superintendent of West Point and Jackson as professor of natural and experimental philosophy and military tactics at the Virginia Military Institute (VMI) in Lexington. It was the common pursuit of academe that next brought them into personal contact during the autumn of 1853, five years after Chapultepec. Lee arrived at the academy September 1, 1852, after a stint at Arlington overseeing disposition of his father-in-law's will followed by a four-year tour of duty rebuilding the defenses of Baltimore Harbor. Brevet major Jackson, however, was already professoring at Virginia's military establishment when Lee took over at West Point; his appointment from March 27, 1851, followed a frustrating year in the Florida swamps during the last gasps of the Seminole Wars. Jackson's disastrous stay at Fort Meade— forty miles from Tampa Bay on the Peace River—contributed to his decision to leave the army.

Jackson's company, still commanded by Captain Francis Taylor, arrived at Fort Columbus on Governor's Island in New York Harbor August 16, 1848; he had passed through New Orleans, July 17–20, and unlike Lee, who traveled up the Mississippi and Ohio Rivers to reach home, Jackson arrived in New York by sea. Within days, he was posted to nearby Fort Hamilton. He had been there in July 1846 on his way to Mexico, but now Jackson had time to enjoy the pleasures of a great city, even if garrison life brought renewed aggravation as commissary officer. His letters to Laura reveal a great deal about his time at Lee's old post, although he was unwilling to depart immediately for Beverly: "If I should leave, some other officer might be attached during my absence who would rank me in case of his remaining so long as I remain with the company," he told his sister. His trust in Captain Taylor notwithstanding, "my absence might reduce the number of officers so much as to render another officer necessary."[1]

Jackson spent much of his time away from Fort Hamilton sitting on court martial panels throughout the east. In September 1848, he was dispatched to Carlisle Barracks for a "general court martial about a hundred miles east of Pittsburgh." Jackson visited the Pennsylvania post on two additional occasions, 1849–1850, for the same purpose, and though his letters to Beverly describe the countryside, they leave no hint of actual court proceedings. In May 1850, he passed through Fort Ticonderoga and Crown Point on his way to Plattsburg Barracks, near the Canadian border, "to try some prisoners"; lack of time, however, kept him from visiting Montreal and Quebec "before returning south." Those places would have to await his honeymoon trip to Niagara Falls and Canada three years later. His travels also took him to Fort Ontario and West Point during August 1850. At the Point, Jackson found that his old barracks had been demolished, but, he told Laura, "among the existing and unaltered objects are the garden of Kosciuszko, his monument, Fort Putnam, in which Andre was confined, and from which [Benedict] Arnold escaped after his unsuccessful attempt to sell his command. Here too is the Plain, the military works, and, above, all the grand and lofty mountains." It is uncertain whether Jackson took notice of Custis Lee, Robert E. Lee's eldest son, then a plebe in the class of 1854.[2]

Jackson decided to leave Company K long enough to spend Christmas 1848 with Laura and her family at Beverly. According to his nephew Arnold, he traveled westward to visit relatives around Clarksburg and Weston, although his sister was too ill to accompany him on the prearranged journey. On the return to Fort Hamilton, Jackson stopped in Richmond for a visit with John S. Carlile, member of the state senate for the district around Beverly; the practice of singling out prominent men was already a part of his modus operandi; there can be little doubt that Jackson had an eye on higher attainments, and politicians like Carlile could help boost him up the army ladder. Carlile later sat in the Virginia Constitutional Convention of 1850–1851 with Jackson's kinsman William L. Jackson. Further, Jackson kept in touch with Carlile, who became a leader in the movement to create the new state of West Virginia, although in the final stages of statehood he worked to scuttle the scheme. That would have pleased Jackson, who fretted about the loyalty of western Virginia to the Confederate cause in the first months of Civil War; before 1863 and admission of West Virginia as the thirty-fifth state, Carlile represented reorganized Virginia—or the state's loyalist government—in the United States Senate.[3]

Upon the return from western Virginia and his court martial duty, Jackson was beset with health problems and spiritual uncertainty. "I caught the rheumatism in your salubrious mountain air, which is harassing me no little," he wrote Laura on February 13; nearly every letter during his stay at Fort Hamilton and his assignment in Florida mention some physical complaint—especially that he was plagued with poor vision. Other letters written about the same time make no mention of health problems, which lead to the possibility that Jackson was either hypochondriacal or that he had found an attention-getting device to use with a beloved family member—as bachelors who spend much time alone often suffer from imaginary illnesses. Army surgeons, after all, did nothing to curtail his activities, and it is difficult to believe that a man who traveled extensively over nineteenth-century byways had a serious complaint. A decade later, writes Erasmus D. Keyes, "General Lee designated Stonewall Jackson as his right arm and the loss of the officer [at Chancellorsville] could no more be replaced than the great southern chief himself." A sickly officer could not have carried the burden of command as Lee's pillar throughout the Virginia campaigns; nor could a weakling single-handedly heave his fieldpiece across the ditch at Chapultepec. About the poor eyesight that interfered with his studies at Fort Hamilton and later at VMI, Dabney ascribes it to reading by "artificial light." Though Jackson never read at night "except for a short portion of scripture" and watched his health constantly, General Keyes, who knew Jackson at West Point, pronounced him "manly."[4]

The conversations about a "personal religion," which had commenced in Mexico, undoubtedly continued on the voyage to New York. "The chaplain of the garrison," notes Jackson's wife, "is said to have been a Rev. Mr. Parks, to whom Major Jackson became much attached, and at whose hands it has been reported that he received the sacrament of Baptism." His entry into the Episcopal church at Fort Hamilton—the same chapel Lee served as vestryman—took place on April 29, 1849; a family tradition that his mother had him baptized in infancy by a Presbyterian clergyman, the Rev. Asa Brooks, was brushed aside, although D. H. Hill insists that Jackson was received into the church across the street from the post—sometimes called the "Church of Generals"—but that he was never confirmed. "All must pay the debt," he told Laura, "and my sincere desire and thrice daily prayer is, that when your exit comes that your previous preparation will have been made. How glorious it will be in that august and heaven-ordained place to meet with mother, brother, sister, and father around the shining throne of Omnipotence. . . ." And when he wrote to his benefactor, former congressman Hays, in 1850, Jackson proposed to call upon the "blessing of Providence" to help him become "a hard student, and to make myself not only acquainted with Military art and science; but with politics, and of course, I must be well versed in history."[5]

Jackson was immersed with Rollin's *History of the Ancient World* when orders arrived from Washington assigning him to Fort Meade in Florida. Upon his arrival, he was made second in command to Captain William H. French, also a brevet major from the Mexican conflict; Jackson also found his old nemesis—he was made "commissary officer and acting quartermaster." Other officers present were Absalom Baird, second lieutenant, West Pointer, and adjutant, as well as Dr. Jonathan Letterman, post surgeon. As usual, he fired off a letter to Laura describing his new assignment: "Florida, so far as I have seen it, is a vast plain, with occasional slight elevations. It is covered with beautiful forests of pine—the yellow pine growing on the elevations, and the pitch pine on the lowlands. The country is filled with lakes and swamps. . . ." Jackson spent the next year in the pine and palmetto-studded interior arguing with his commanding officer and chasing renegade Indians.[6]

Named for Lieutenant George G. Meade, Lee's adversary at Gettysburg, who had established the place, Fort Meade was a new installation when Jackson arrived in October 1850. Situated on "bluffs overlooking Peace River which afforded them an unobstructed outlook for miles in every direction (the country on both sides of the river being bare of timber)," it was one of several outposts across the peninsula. The earlier Seminole Wars, which resulted in the removal of Indians to Arkansas and Oklahoma, had terminated in the late 1830s; in 1842, General William J. Worth "had made an agreement with the few remaining Seminole allies in Florida that they could stay in their everglade retreats if they did not bother their white neighbors. For seven years the Indians kept their promise and, unmolested by whites, grew in numbers to between four and five hundred." But occasional raids prompted construction of Fort Meade in raw frontier country forty miles east of Tampa Bay, where isolated farmers and ranchers eked out a living on widely separated homesteads. Its new commandant, William F. French, and his second in command had little to do but make the place livable and pursue an occasional raider. "To make this country accessible," writes a local historian, "to open communication with the outside world, for the purpose of hauling their ammunition, guns and supplies, the troops built a road as straight as the bird flies from Tampa to Fort Meade and beyond to other forts on both sides of the river."7

Fort Meade was French's first command, and he was anxious to please his superiors as well as fearful settlers in the surrounding country-side. Sporadic Indian outbursts—nearly always in response to white provocation—led French to send Baird and Jackson on scouting expeditions amongst the sparse settlements. "Baird took a detail across the Peace River and scouted eastward for several days, returning without seeing any signs of Indian activity. Several weeks later Captain French, alarmed about the possibility of Indian depredations against settlements around Lake Tohopekaliga, about forty miles northeast of Fort Meade, sent Jackson there to scout." Jackson, who made two scouts—February 1 and 25—did not locate the elusive lake until his second outing; he also visited the "fashionable homes" of sugar planters who, like their small-farmer neighbors, were happy to have military patrols in their midst. Clearly disappointed, Jackson wrote his sister on March 1: "I have just returned from an eight days' scout, in which I saw about twenty deer in the afternoon. I could find no Indians. I travelled more than one hundred miles without seeing a house. I like scouting very much, as it gives me a relish for everything; but it would be more desirable if I could have an occasional encounter with Indian parties. . . ."8

Jackson's running feud with French worsened when news of "lavish entertaining" during his scouts reached Fort Meade; he told Laura that he had been on several sugar plantations that "resembled large farms covered with luxuriant corn." But the downward spiral between lieutenant and captain—though both were brevet majors—started months earlier, when French overrode several of Jackson's decisions as commissary. Furthermore, French carped about Jackson's scouting performances and insisted that his subordinate was leading a conspiracy against him; Jackson, too, fired off counteraccusations to General David E. Twiggs at New Orleans—the same Twiggs who had been his commander in Mexico. A nasty situation got out of hand on April 12, when Jackson grilled two sergeants about French's relationship with "Julia," a house servant to the commander and his wife. His insistence that moral improprieties had taken place resulted in French's order for Lieutenant Baird to place Jackson under arrest for "conduct unbecoming an officer and a gentleman."

Although French was compared "to one of those lethargic French Colonels, who are so stout, and who look so red in the face, that one would suppose someone tied a cord tightly around their necks," he maintained that nothing untoward had taken place. Dr. Letterman assumed the role of peacemaker, but an obstinate Jackson held his ground. "An officer," writes D. H. Hill, "went to Jackson to get him to withdraw the charges, lest the wife [of Captain French] should learn of her husband's unfaithfulness. Jackson shed tears, and said that the thought of inflicting pain upon her was agony to him, but his conscience compelled him to prosecute the case." The same singleness of purpose in the face of moral circumstance would enable him to drive his Confederate troopers to victory after victory on the battlegrounds of Virginia. The voluminous French-Jackson correspondence went all the way to the secretary of war; the affair ended when General Roger Jones, adjutant general of the army, scrawled across the front: "The General-in-Chief [Winfield Scott] sees no sufficient reason why the appeal should be entertained. . . . The decision of Brevet Major General Twiggs is confirmed."9

Washington therefore sided with Twiggs, who ordered Jackson set free and rejected French's bid for a court of inquiry; French's reproof did not totally exonerate Jackson in the affair, which Twiggs and other army brass considered "silly." Jackson's decision to leave the service, which came at the height of the controversy, was also influenced by other events. As early as April 2, he told Laura that he had been approached about joining the faculty at the Virginia Military Institute; unbeknownst to Jackson, his friend from West Point and the Mexican War, D. H. Hill—professor of mathematics in Washington College at Lexington—had suggested him for a vacant professorship to Colonel Francis H. Smith, superintendent at the Virginia school. Acting on Hill's recommendation, Smith attended a hurriedly summoned meeting of the VMI Board of Vistors, March 27, 1851, in Richmond, and advanced Jackson's name. After his advocate, John S. Carlile, who was also present, heartily endorsed his candidacy, Jackson got the appointment. "Good news," he wrote his sister on April 22: "I have been elected Professor of Natural and Experimental Philosophy in the Virginia Military Institute, and you may expect to see me home in the latter part of June." But the "good news" was tempered by his lingering complaints: "I am recovering," a postscript said, "from a recent attack of sickness and owing to the weakness of my eyes I do not like to write myself."10

Although Jackson was fitted for the appointment, his election was undoubtedly influenced by Virginia politics. Since colonial times, the transmontane sections of Virginia, including Jackson's home county of Lewis, had been aggrieved with the power monopoly of the tidewater and piedmont sections of the state. The Constitution of 1830 had discriminated further against the western counties by allotting greater representation in the general assembly and state senate to the east; the slave-owning regions made certain that yeomen farmers beyond the Blue Ridge were denied the franchise and thus any meaningful influence in governing the state. By midcentury, however, whites in the western counties outnumbered their eastern cousins 271,000 to 269,000; when a new constitutional convention—the so-called reform convention—assembled in October 1850, the old differences were rectified somewhat by giving all white males the franchise. Jackson must have followed the convention debates from his Florida outpost: "I see that Mr. Carlile has been making two speeches in the convention. . . . I hope before long to see him in congress. I am much pleased at seeing Cousin Wm. L. Jackson also in the convention. Indeed I have some hopes that our ancient reputation may yet be revived."[11]

The Board of Visitors met in Richmond, where Carlile and other of its members likewise held seats in the constitutional convention; the intricacies of Virginia politics led to Jackson's success. Politicos and board members from the eastern counties agreed to the nomination in return for support from Carlile, William L. Jackson, and their allies in rewriting the state constitution. Jackson, after all, won the professorship over a formidable list of candidates: George B. McClellan, Jesse L. Reno, William S. Rosecrans, and George W. Smith, all of whom attained general rank in the Union or Confederate armies. "It was thought desirable," writes Anna Jackson, "to elect a professor from Western Virginia to secure the patronage from that quarter, most of the cadets coming from the East." Whatever the reason, twenty-seven-year-old brevet major Thomas J. Jackson left Fort Meade on May 21, 1851, for the Shenandoah Valley, Rockbridge County, and the Virginia Military Institute.[12]

Jackson was able to leave because he had been granted a leave of absence by the secretary of war due to poor health and impaired eyesight; upon his release from arrest, he was free to travel, although he did not resign his commission until February 29, 1852, seven months after he commenced his teaching duties. Dabney says he arrived in Lexington during July 1851 and took up residence in one of the cadet barracks. Colonel Francis H. Smith issued initial teaching assignments on August 13 for the 1851–1852 term, and he met his first classes on September 1.[13]

Problems arose for Jackson from the beginning in the intellectual milieu of Lexington, one of the country's most sophisticated, which included not only VMI but also Washington College—now Washington and Lee University. Margaret Junkin Preston, his future sister-in-law, labeled him "eccentric in our little professional society, because he did not walk in the conventional grooves of other men"; and by all accounts he was "no talker." Eccentricities in speech and personal demeanor soon caused difficulties with the cadets under his charge; numerous complaints about Jackson as a harsh taskmaster, and perhaps uncertainty over his teaching future, prevented his early resignation from the army. "As professor of Natural and Experimental Philosophy Jackson was not a success," wrote a subsequent superintendent at VMI: "He had not the qualifications for so important a chair. . . . He was *no* teacher, and he lacked the tact required in getting along with his classes. . . . He was a brave man, and a good man, but he was no teacher." Even Dabney comments that "he had no particular gift for teaching; yet teaching was at Lexington his profession."[14]

Although he joined the Franklin Society, a local debating group, and worked at improving himself, he was unable to rein the inherent melancholy that made him seem odd to others. D. H. Hill, who observed him closely during this period, notes that "his health was bad, but he imagined that he had many more ailments than he really did have." He insisted on wearing a wet shirt next to the body on the advice of "hydropathic physicians," and according to Hill, existed on a diet of stale corn bread and buttermilk. The young professor became famous for his drowsiness in church, for never putting "a morsel in his mouth after supper," and for retiring promptly at nine o'clock no matter the occasion.[15]

"Dyspeptic and something of a hypochondriac," to use Hill's words, Jackson nevertheless found time to pursue the ladies in Lexington. Apparently the trysts in Mexico had been long forgotten when he caught the eye of Eleanor Junkin; although Jackson did not solicit any available young lady, he now pursued the daughter of Dr. George Junkin, Presbyterian divine and president of Washington College. Ever ambitious, he wooed "Elie"[16] and probably her family connections as well; following her death and his own remarriage, he found time to correspond with Dr. Junkin during the trials of Civil War. "Eleanor's family," writes her sister, "while honoring Major Jackson for his dignified and substantial character, were perhaps just a little surprised that such a grave and ungraceful man should capture her heart." Jackson fell head over heels in love with Elie Junkin, although, notes the ever-present Hill, "they were engaged soon after [their first encounter] but a rupture took place, and the engagement was broken off." The lovers' quarrel, which lasted "two or three months," may have been caused by a visit by Mary Anna Morrison to her sister Eugenia—wife of D. H. Hill in Lexington; Anna

Morrison, daughter of the Reverend Robert H. Morrison, president of Davidson College in North Carolina, in time became the second Mrs. Thomas J. Jackson. Yet love triumphed, and the marriage between Eleanor Junkin and Professor Jackson took place in a quiet ceremony on August 4, 1853, in the Junkin home. The Reverend Dr. Junkin officiated.[17]

After his marriage, Jackson left the VMI barracks and moved into the Junkin home on the Washington College campus; in a strange twist, Robert E. Lee moved into the same house twelve years later when he became president of the college following the Confederate surrender.[18] Elie's pious nature and the influence of her family led Jackson to join the Presbyterian congregation at Lexington a few months before the wedding. D. H. Hill was convinced "Elie's faith wore new attractions in his eyes," while Anna Jackson said he found the Presbyterian congregation "the largest and most influential, embracing many of the most influential families, although the professors of the Institute were mostly Episcopalians." Jackson also fell under the influence of Dr. William S. White, Presbyterian minister at Lexington, who became his spiritual mentor.[19]

Following the ceremony, Jackson and his bride left on an extended honeymoon trip that took them to a number of northern cities and Canada; his subsequent letters and Mrs. Preston's diaries indicate the party toured Baltimore, Philadelphia, West Point, and Niagara Falls. The Jacksons were accompanied by the bride's sister, Margaret, a fact that apparently passed unnoticed in nineteenth-century Virginia. After the obligatory boat ride into the mists at Niagara, the entourage made its way up the St. Lawrence to Montreal and Quebec; Jackson obviously enjoyed himself, and not even the Sabbath interfered with visits to French and Indian War battlegrounds from a century earlier. "It was a matter of surprise, in Montreal," Margaret Junkin observed, "to find Major Jackson going out on Sunday afternoon to witness the drill of a Highland regiment. When the matter was reverted to by some of our party, he defended himself stoutly for having done so, [saying] that if anything is right and good in itself, and circumstances were such that he could not avail of it anytime but Sunday, it was not wrong for him to do so. . . ."[20]

When the party reached West Point during August 1853, Robert E. Lee had been superintendent of the academy for twelve months. And Jackson mentioned the visit in the inevitable letter to Laura upon his return to Lexington—not even marriage could impede that bond: "We proceeded to West Point where I was delighted with my early associations." Neither Jackson nor Margaret Preston say a word about meeting

Lee. Lee's logbook as superintendent is likewise silent about a Jackson visit; though direct evidence is lacking that the two men met during Jackson's honeymoon jaunt through West Point, it is inconceivable that Jackson, always attentive to leading men would have passed an opportunity to call upon his old comrade in arms. Furthermore, as Jackson traveled northward, Professor Edward E. Courtenay, who held the chair in mathematics at the University of Virginia, lay dangerously ill and Professor Jackson had an eye for his position. Lee later supported his formal petition to replace Courtenay, and Dabney leaves a tantalizing hint that the two discussed the upcoming vacancy at Charlottesville: "When Jackson mentioned his project to his friend [Lee], he said to him: 'Have you not departed from what you told me upon coming to this military school, was the purpose of your life.' [He referred to the declaration that war was his proper vocation.] Jackson, who never seemed to forget his most casual remarks, or to overlook an obligation to maintain consistency with what he had once said, replied, 'I avow that my views have changed.' " Since he returned to Lexington for the start of the fall term, Jackson must have discussed the job at Virginia with Lee before Courtenay's death in December; the inference is clear that while Mrs. Jackson and her sister took in the sights, Lee and Jackson discussed his possible move to Charlottesville.[21]

Lee had arrived at West Point in September 1852, when he replaced Captain Henry Brewerton following a four-year stint as chief engineer for the construction of Fort Carroll in the harbor at Baltimore. Earlier, he had been away from Arlington since 1846, and he was permitted to spend but six weeks with family and friends before the Baltimore assignment. Lee rejoined his loved ones June 29, 1848, following a boat trip up the Mississippi and Ohio Rivers from New Orleans to Wheeling in western Virginia, where "he took the cars" to Baltimore and Washington. "There was visiting us at this time Mrs. Lippitt, a friend of my mother's, with her little boy, Armistead, about my age and size, also with long curls," writes Robert E. Lee, Jr., not quite five years of age when his father returned from Mexico. "After a moment's greeting to those surrounding him, my father pushed through the crowd, exclaiming: 'Where is my little boy.' He then took up in his arms—not me, his own child in his best frock with clean face and well arranged curls—but my little playmate, Armistead. . . ."[22]

Lee had a lot of catching up to get done. "It is not surprising that I am hardly recognizable to some of the younger eyes around me and perfectly unknown to the youngest," he wrote to Smith Lee a week after reaching home. "But some of the older ones gaze with astonishment and wonder at me, and seem at a loss to reconcile what they see and what was pictured in their imagination." His children ranged from Custis at age sixteen—soon to enter the West Point class of 1854—to baby Mildred born in January 1846; the happy father took his children on family outings to Baltimore and Middleburg, even though a trip to the Baltimore home of his sister Ann, wife of Judge William L. Marshall, may have been for other reasons: "I remember being down on the wharves," writes Robert, Jr., "where my father had taken me to see the landing of a mustang pony which he had gotten for me in Mexico, and which had been shipped from Vera Cruz to Baltimore in a sailing vessel."

Although he was "perfectly surrounded by Mary and her precious children, who seem to devote themselves to staring at the furrows in my face and the white hairs in my head," Lee was still an army officer. Brigadier General Joseph G. Totten, chief engineer in Washington, had him posted to his office in July, which proved a blessing because he could remain at home with Mary and the family as well as his aging father-in-law. His duties in Totten's office even took him to the Florida coast with a group of engineers "to recommend locations for new fortifications." And Lee made his Florida tour while Jackson was stationed at Fort Hamilton. Near the end of his stay at Arlington, he received official confirmation of the brevet ranks earned in the Mexican fighting. The general orders, dated August 24, 1848, made him Colonel Robert E. Lee, his highest rank in the old army.[23]

Colonel Lee's departure for Fort Carroll and Baltimore did not break up his family reunion: Mrs. Lee and the children went with him to a large "house on Madison Street, three doors above Biddle." But the press of work and nearness of his family kept him from writing many letters during 1848–1852; the Reverend Jones in fact offers none for this period and relies solely upon Robert E. Lee, Jr., to describe his services at Sollers Point. A letter to his beloved Markie at Georgetown indicates that he was a busy man: "My days are pretty much spent at Fort Carroll (Sollers Point); My thoughts are engrossed with driving piles & laying stone; and my imagination is exercised in the construction of cranes, Diving bells, Steam Pile drivers &c. Poor subjects for correspondence with young ladies." Away from his work, Lee was able to enjoy the pleasures of a growing family. "In Baltimore," writes Robert, Jr., "I went to my first school, that of a Mr. Rollins on Mulberry Street, and I remember how interested my father was in my studies, my failures, and my little triumphs. Indeed, he was always. . . ." In spite of his unquestioned devotion to duty and family, Lee added a curious note to his young cousin in the District of Columbia: "If it was not for my heart

Markie, I might as well be a pile of stone myself, laid quietly at the bottom of the river."[24]

There can be little doubt that Lee's association with Totten led to the Baltimore assignment. Totten, already acknowledged as the army's leading expert on fortification construction, had designed Fort Carroll— named from Charles Carroll of Carrollton, last surviving signer of the Declaration of Independence—and he sent Lee, whom he had known in Mexico, to oversee its completion. It was located on a submerged shoal in the Patapsco River between Sollers and Hawkins Points, not far from the present interstate tunnel under Baltimore Harbor. "One of its six faces looks right down the main channel along which big ships must come, and the fire from the guns from that face of Fort Carroll would rake them from stem to stern." The project had been started by others during 1847, but actual construction did not commence until Lee's arrival in September 1848; situated near Fort McHenry, where Francis Scott Key had penned "The Star Spangled Banner," it was originally intended to have 225 guns arranged in three levels. Under Lee's direction, it was built in water twelve to fifteen feet deep. "Its walls are on piles which are driven as far as they would go. On top of these was placed a wooden grillage, and upon the grillage the massive stones of the foundation were laid with the use of a diving bell. The space thus enclosed was filled with material excavated from the channel nearby. The walls were faced with granite and filled with concrete," writes a later officer at the fort. Although Lee's 1851 letter to Markie Williams contained an accurate rendering of his construction methods, Fort Carroll was never completed according to its original design. Following several years of neglect, during which Congress refused appropriations to complete the project, it became something of an eyesore; "a fifteen-inch smooth-bore gun was hurriedly mounted there at the outbreak of the Spanish American War."[25]

Amid a busy social swirl in Baltimore, Lee for the first time was drawn into national and, indeed international, events. In March 1849, he was one of 230 "prominent Americans" who sponsored a grand soiree in the city hall at Washington to honor the inaugurations of Zachary Taylor and Millard Fillmore. Taylor had just won the 1848 presidential canvass, but Lee was unable to join "the outstanding event" because of army business in Florida, "far from the amenities of capital society." The nonpartisan group assembled in honor of the new president included "the tall, angular, good natured Abraham Lincoln," who was there with his political friends. The historian can only speculate about a meeting had Lee been on hand instead of surveying coastal defenses. He may have missed the premier festivity of Taylor's brief presidency, but back in Baltimore Lee and his wife were in constant demand at social gatherings; "when he and my mother went out," says a son, "my father was always in full uniform, always ready, and always waiting for my mother, who was generally late . . . and I would go to sleep with this beautiful picture in my mind, the golden epaulets and all—chiefly the epaulets."[26]

Lee's encounter with international intrigue occurred in 1849, when a group of Cuban revolutionaries suggested he take command of their army of liberation; the New York-based junta led by Narciso López, according to Jefferson Davis, "offered him every temptation that ambition could desire, and pecuniary emoluments far beyond any which he could hope otherwise to acquire. He thought the matter over, and, I remember, came to Washington, to consult me as to what he should do." He must have been sufficiently attracted to the offer of leading an insurrectionist band to end Spanish rule over that troubled island to seek advice from his friend. Davis, then United States senator from Mississippi and shortly secretary of war when Franklin Pierce and the Democrats moved into the White House, had been offered $200,000 himself to lead the Cuban cause, but, like Lee, had spurned the scheme. Lee, Davis reflected, "felt it would be wrong to accept service in the army of a foreign power while he held his commission."[27]

When Lee became superintendent at West Point, he spent all but five of his thirty-month tenure under Davis's supervision, thereby strengthening the bond between soldier and future president that survived the Civil War. But he was ordered from Fort Carroll by Charles M. Conrad, Fillmore's secretary of war, a Louisiana Whig and later member of the Confederate Congress. And, Lee, a lifelong Democrat, entered upon his new duties with misgivings: "Although fully appreciating the honour of the station," he wrote to General Totten, "and extremely reluctant to oppose my wishes to the orders of the Department, yet if I be allowed any opinion in the matter, I would respectively ask that some other successor than myself be appointed to the present Superintendent." Lee, fearful that he did not possess "the skill and experience" to direct the academy, proved a respected administrator who enjoyed harmonious relations with Davis and President Pierce after March 1853.[28]

Upon his arrival, he found an educational schedule in which the cadets spent "71 percent of their total classroom time in the study of mathematics, natural and experimental philosophy, chemistry, topographical drawing, engineering, mineralogy and geology, while devoting 29 percent to French, drawing of the human figure, moral and political science, rhetoric, and tactics." The capstone of the entire program was "Denis

Hart Mahan's military and civil engineering and the science (sometimes called the art) of war, which first classmen took daily"; every cadet for two generations remembered the unbending Mahan, author of several books and father of naval historian Alfred Thayer Mahan. The order of merit by which every cadet was ranked depended upon Mahan's assessment because of the heavy weight placed upon mathematics and engineering in the determination of class standing. In spite of the rigid curriculum inherited by Lee, it was thought inadequate for the preparation of informed fighting men. With the approval of Jefferson Davis, a short-lived fifth year of study in languages and the humanities was added to the entrenched four-year program; although it was implemented at the end of Lee's tenure, the expanded curriculum was soon dropped as impractical.[29]

Lee was able to keep his family with him at West Point, where Custis was already a second classman; the family—without two of his daughters who stayed with their grandmother Custis at Arlington—moved into the superintendent's house, which was "built of stone, large and roomy, with gardens, stables and pasture lots." Two horses, "Grace Darling" and "Santa Anna," which accompanied the family to New York, were used for afternoon rides with the young Robert at his side. Lee was the gracious host, often inviting cadets into his home for Saturday afternoon levies; pious Oliver O. Howard, who conducted regular Bible study groups at the academy, frequently called at the Lee home, and Lee, ever solicitous of his subordinates, later visited the future Yankee general at the post hospital during some youthful illness. James Ewell Brown Stuart, who became Lee's cavalryman eight years afterward, was another caller at the superintendent's residence, where he admired Mrs. Lee and especially her daughter Mary, age seventeen, "both as regards beauty and sprightliness."[30]

In his letters to Markie Williams, Lee complained that "the constant duty of 12 hours a day & the continual interruption of visitors, does not afford much prospective pleasure." Yet he found time to enjoy a solar eclipse during May 1854: "The curious & scientific are assembling in the observatory above me. . . . The Cadets & boys are scattered over the plain with pieces of smoked glass, each his own astronomer, begriming his face & hands. The glorious Sunlight is sensibly diminishing, & a blueish twilight covering the mountains. How unerring is the course & periods of the Heavenly bodies & how sure are the calculations of science." And he told his young cousin: "I would that our course were as true and our calculations as sure."[31]

Amid the near-constant entertaining and preoccupation with running the academy, Lee had a formal portrait made by R. S. Weir, professor of drawing and painting. "This portrait," writes his son, "shows my father in the dress uniform of a colonel of engineers. . . . To me, the expression of strength peculiar to his face is wanting, especially in the lines of the mouth. . . . My father could never bear to have his picture taken, and there are no likenesses of him that really give his sweet expression." A short time earlier, the Lee family experienced its first bereavement in the spring of 1853, with the death of Mrs. George Washington Parke Custis. That Lee had become an intimate of the Custis family was plain when he wrote to his wife at Arlington about his mother-in-law: "She was to me all that a mother could be, and I yielded to none in admiration for her character, love for her virtues, and veneration of her memory."[32]

One of Lee's last functions as superintendent was presiding over commencement exercises for the class of 1854, which saw a proud father recognize Custis as a number one on a roster of forty-six graduates; others in the class that produced twenty-three Union and fourteen Confederate officers included O. O. Howard, Stephen D. Lee, Archibald Gracie, Jeb Stuart, John Pegram, James Deshler, and John B. Villepigue. Although graduation day was the good time when honors were handed out and accomplishments recognized, Lee had his troubles with errant cadets. In an oft-repeated sequence, Robert, Jr., tells what happened during one afternoon ride with his father: "While rounding a turn in the mountain road with a deep woody ravine on one side, we suddenly came upon three cadets beyond limits. They immediately leaped over a low wall on the side of the road and disappeared from our view. We rode for a minute in silence; then my father said; 'Did you see those young men? But no; if you did, don't say so. I wish boys would do what is right, it would be so much easier on all parties.' " In two celebrated instances involving Archibald Gracie, who took a fatal wound during the siege of Petersburg after becoming a Confederate brigadier general, and James A. M. "Curly" Whistler, the American artist, Lee was forced to take drastic action. A playful Gracie was allowed to graduate with his class after his father, an Alabama businessman, interceded between Lee and the boy; but in Whistler's case not even the mother he painted for immortality could persuade Lee and Jefferson Davis to retain an indolent student who would not conform to academy standards. Lee, the gentleman in all things, induced both to speak about him with the utmost respect for the rest of their lives.[33]

In January 1854, a year and three months before he left West Point for the Texas frontier, Lee had his first positively recorded contact with Professor Tom Jackson; but five months after Jackson and Elie visited the academy during their honeymoon, Lee penned a formal letter of support for Jackson's application to join the University of Virginia faculty. Although Professor Edward Henry Courtenay did not die until December 21, 1853, the available evidence suggests that Jackson was thinking about the mathematics vacancy beforehand. He wrote to his kinsman Judge John J. Allen in Richmond about the position on December 28, only seven days after Courtenay's death; Lee posted his letter on January 26, indicating that Jackson either decided quickly to pursue the career change or that the two had already discussed his possibilities, as Dabney suggests. Otherwise, Jackson would have been hard put to approach Lee at such an early time.

The newly married Jackson undertook a formidable task when he sought to replace Courtenay. If not the leading university in the 1850s, the University of Virginia was certainly one of the nation's top schools and its professors, men such as Courtenay, enjoyed positions of distinction. They were also well paid. Born in Maryland in 1803, Courtenay had been at Charlottesville more than a decade in 1853; he had graduated in the West Point class of 1821 and, besides serving in the engineer corps, he had taught at the academy and the University of Pennsylvania prior to 1843. "His native efficiency had been invigorated by an officer's training, for at the age of sixteen he had graduated at the head of his class . . . ; and he had advanced to a full professorship in that great school by the time that he was twenty-six." Significantly, he had introduced the West Point system of instruction into the University of Virginia, where he had established himself as a mathematical scholar; he published at least two volumes on mechanics and calculus that became widely used texts. It was a set of credentials that Jackson at VMI could not match.[34]

Undaunted, Jackson sent his December letter to Judge Allen: "I am an applicant . . . at the University of Virginia. I shall have strong letters of recommendation from professors of mathematics at the Institute and Washington College; and taken in connexion [*sic*] with other recommendations from other scientific men I consider will be sufficient to satisfy the Board of Visitors of my qualifications." Allen, married to Mary Elizabeth Payne Jackson, daughter of Congressman John G. Jackson, a cousin of Jackson's father, was asked "to favor my election." Tom Jackson, who pulled the stops in his bid for Courtenay's place, attached a postscript indicating similar requests were being dispatched to nine others—all prominent Virginia politicians, including John Y. Mason, future Governor Henry A. Wise, Joseph C. Cabell, and Robert A. Thompson. It was not clear what role Allen, a judge on the Virginia

Court of Appeals was intended to play, but the others, including Thompson, a former congressman from western Virginia, were implored to help him.[35]

Four days later, Jackson sent a neatly penned—much neater than his letter to Allen—application on lined paper:

> To the Board of Visitors of the University of Va.
>   Gentlemen,
>   The object of this communication is to present my name as a candidate for the vacant mathematical chair in the University of Va. I graduated at West Point in 1846, and served as an officer in the U. S. Army until 1851, when I was elected Professor of Natural and Experimental Philosophy in the Va. Military Institute; and in the discharge of the duties of this office I have continued until the present time.
>   My recommendations are herewith enclosed.
>   I am, Gentleman
>   Very respectfully[36]

Lee's letter, written three weeks later, recounted Jackson's service in Mexico and mentioned his early life and education:

> U. S. Military Acad'y
>   West Point 26 Jan'y 1854
>   Understanding that Major Thomas J. Jackson, late of the U. S. Army, is a Candidate for the vacant chair of Mathematics in the University of Virginia, I take pleasure in bearing testimony to his Character and Merit. Entering the Mil. Acad'y in the year 1842, his career at the Institution evinced his determination of purpose & the Strength of his Intellect. Not having previous advantages, he steadily rose to the first sections of his Class in the various branches of their courses, & maintained an honorable position, until he graduated in the year 1846—His Conduct while at the Acad'y was in every way exemplary. Promoted on graduating into the 1st Art'y his Services in the Army were equally distinguished, & he was breveted for gallant & meritorious Conduct in the battles of Contreras, Churubusco & Chapultepec in the year 1847.
>   R E Lee Bt. Col
>   Supt Mil Acad'y
> The Hon'ble Board of Visitors
> University of Virginia[37]

Lee's references to Jackson's early life and preparation as well as his career at West Point suggest considerable prior, if not intimate, knowledge of his background other than his service in Mexico. The letter to

Charlottesville, although straightforward and matter-of-fact, reinforces the notion that Jackson had conversations with Lee during his honeymoon just five months earlier.

Two extant letters, both dated January 2, 1854, from D. H. Hill and John Lyle Campbell, professors of mathematics and chemistry, respectively, in Washington College, likewise support Jackson's petition. Said Hill: ". . . I have known him for about ten years and am well acquainted with his scientific attainments. I believe him eminently qualified to discharge the duties of the Chair to which he aspires and think that his appointment would reflect credit upon the University." Campbell, who had been Robinson Professor of Physical Science since 1851, echoed Hill's recommendation in a short note scrawled across the bottom. "I feel free to express a full concurrence in the opinion given above."[38]

Jackson's petition was marred from the beginning, which may or may not have affected the outcome. Lee's letter, while complimentary, was not particularly enthusiastic in support of his onetime subordinate; Hill and Campbell misdated their joint recommendation by one year; and Jackson himself wrote that he had left the army in 1851, when his resignation was not effective until February 29, 1852; surely, his reputation as a poor performer in the classroom reached the university as well as his lack of publications. Moreover, the widely respected Denis Hart Mahan refused to support him. "What are Jackson's prospects at the University," he asked VMI superintendent Colonel Francis H. Smith on March 8: "Say to him that I have since given a testimonial to another . . . a rule I have adopted—to say for any graduate of the Academy whatever his position and services give him a claim to. . . ." In the same letter, Mahan endorsed William Nelson Pendleton, later Lee's chief artillery officer and an 1830 graduate at West Point, for a teaching job at Washington College, although he balked in Jackson's case. Mahan's support would have carried considerable weight, especially among military men throughout Virginia.[39]

The man chosen to replace Courtenay was not Jackson but Albert Taylor Bledsoe, professor of mathematics at the University of Mississippi; he was not only a West Point man, class of 1830, and fellow student of Jefferson Davis and Robert E. Lee, with teaching experience at several schools, he was also a widely known writer on religious topics. "As between Jackson and himself at that time, the choice offered little room for hesitation," comments a historian of the university. Jackson wanted the job, writes Dabney, because "he regarded it as every man's duty to seek the highest cultivation of his powers, and the widest sphere of activity within his reach; and therefore he desired to be transferred to the

State University." When Bledsoe's appointment became public, Dabney continues, Jackson, "acquiesced with perfect cheerfulness." He may also have been relieved at not having to move into a new academic environment. "I am not certain about my election," he told Laura, "but be the result as it may be, my friends have acted nobly in my cause." Presumably, his friends included Brevet Colonel Robert E. Lee.[40]

After Lee's letter in January 1854, he had no contact with Jackson until November 1859, when the John Brown insurrection brought them together at Charles Town in northern Virginia. After the effort to help his young friend, Lee had another fifteen months at West Point before his departure for Texas upon formation of new cavalry regiments for frontier defense. While Jackson returned to his classroom at Lexington and experienced a great personal tragedy when his beloved Elie died unexpectedly in October 1854, Lee completed his duties on the Hudson. Besides his implementation of the new five-year curriculum, Lee oversaw a number of improvements at the academy, including construction of a new wharf and a riding school for cadet exercises. Although General Long pronounced his superintendency "highly efficient and successful," others have condemned it as "unhappy because he was too kindhearted and hated to discipline the boys." Cadet behavior unquestionably bothered Lee to the end. "I have just accomplished . . . the most unpleasant office I am called upon to perform," he wrote to Markie Williams after the 1854 commencement: "The discharge of those cadets found deficient at the examination. There were fortunately only nine of them, but all very nice youths, . . . who have neglected their duties, contrary to all advice & effort to the contrary, must now suffer the penalty, which they acutely feel, but which they could not be made to realize, I have just closed their connection with the Acad'y."[41]

Besides his other duties, Lee found time to improve his military prowess through the famed Napoleon Club, formed by George B. McClellan in 1848, for the systematic study of Bonaparte's European forays. Although Little Mac left his post as professor of military engineering in 1851, the group continued to hold "meetings several times each week in the rooms of the Academic building, on the walls of which large-scale maps were painted, showing the various theaters of war, and illustrating the strategical movements of each campaign." Denis Hart Mahan—the same Mahan who refused to endorse Jackson—presided and assigned each man a special topic for presentation; McClellan himself worked up a 120-page paper on the 1812 Russian invasion. Lee is known to have attended the intense study sessions, though no record exists that he made a formal lecture. Yet, "a close comparison will show many points in common with Napoleonic methods of war which may justify the conclusion that he had studied them well," concludes one student of his war record.[42]

Lee left the academy on March 31, 1855, when he handed keys to the superintendent's office to Captain Jonathan G. Brainard. At the time, he had spent but eight of his thirty-two years a commissioned officer in actual command of troops. Additional months in charge of cavalrymen followed during 1856–1857 and 1860–1861, when he chased renegade Indians across the remote prairies of Texas, but Lee had to wait another seven long years, until June 1862, at Fair Oaks near Richmond, when he took the Confederate reins from Joseph E. Johnston, before the opportunity arrived to use his command skills.

6

Old Brown

While Lee completed his tour at West Point, Tom and Elie Jackson continued their married life in the home of the Reverend Junkin; Lexington, with its close-knit academic community and the church connections of the Junkins, presented an opportunity for many learned and pleasant associations. "The nearest neighbors of the Junkins on College Hill," writes his sister-in-law, "were Major [D. H.] Hill and his wife, and Professor and Mrs. Dabney, and these interesting people became close friends." There were others, such as the daughters of former Governor James McDowell and young ladies from Lexington's Ann-Smith Academy, who joined the lively circle. As Elie, now pregnant, and Professor Jackson enjoyed their social swirl, his sometimes peculiar actions started to attract attention. His devotion to Dr. White's Presbyterian congregation got him dubbed "The Blue Light Elder," and, according to John Esten Cooke, "Jackson was the fartherest [sic] removed from any thing graceful." Even his "stiff and unbending" gait but mostly his hard attention to military detail caused the lads at VMI to call him "Old Tom Jackson" and "Tom Fool Jackson" behind his back. Many in the Lexington community agreed with them.[1]

Because of her upbringing, Jackson's young and vivacious wife had a pronounced impact upon him during their short life together. "Eleanor Junkin had more to do with the extraordinary piety which was afterward conspicuous in 'Stonewall Jackson' than has ever been told," writes her sister Elizabeth. And Margaret Junkin Preston continues the same theme: "The finely poised character of his wife had very much to do with the maturing of Jackson's character at the most formative period of his life. . . . The molding influence which she had over him, in intensifying and giving bent to his character, was a fitting crown for her short and beautiful life." D. H. Hill thought Elie and the Junkins pressured Jackson toward his intense Presbyterianism. Yet he could never embrace the denomination's strictures on predestination and infant baptism. "He had a good knowledge of the Bible and simply could not fit these Presbyterian doctrines into his understanding of the gospels," writes a recent Jackson scholar.[2]

The first break in Jackson's near-idyllic existence at Lexington came in February 1854 with the death of Mrs. Julia Junkin. Just as Lee lamented the death of Mrs. Custis, Jackson, along with the entire family, was saddened at the death of Elie's mother. "We have recently been called to mourn the death of my mother-in-law," he wrote to Laura ten days afterward. "She asked us to kiss her and told her children to live near Jesus and to be kind to one another. Her death was no leap in the dark. She died in the bright hope of an unending immortality of happiness. . . ."[3]

When the 1853–1854 school year ended, Jackson took his bride of twelve months across the mountains to the Arnolds at Beverly. A May 2nd letter to Laura hinted that Elie was having health problems and that she was well along with her pregnancy. Even so, Jackson, anxious to see his sister and to show off Elie, proceeded with his plans. Elie and Laura had exchanged locks of hair and snippets of ribbon after the custom of the day, but most trying was his sister's loss of a newborn child. Jackson had written to cheer her, and he was understandably ready to see Laura at the end of term. And Elie herself wrote a short note on July 1: "The Major is so busy with his duties at the Institute that he commissioned me to finish this letter for him; He wishes me to say that he hopes you will not exert yourself by making any preparations to receive us; he does not want you to weary yourself or injure your health on our account." The weather was hot, Elie said, and they hoped to find it "cooler among the mountains."

Thomas J. Arnold recounts the visit of his aunt and uncle in his 1916 biography of Jackson; although it was a joyous time, with sister and wife united at last, serious problems developed for Elie during the jerky stage ride to Randolph County. The miserable state of nineteenth-century roads complicated Elie's already advanced pregnancy; she never fully recovered from the incessant pounding of the journey before her death in October. When Laura wrote to say she could not come to his side, Jackson told his sister: "I would like to see you and appreciate your sisterly affection, yet I would not like for you to attempt coming over such a road, with all its harassments; so do not attempt it. . . . My dear Elie thought to pass over the state route from here to Beverley [*sic*] as a hard undertaking for her. . . . She has now gone on a glorious visit through a gloomy portal. . . . I look forward with delight to the day when I shall join her."[4]

There can be no question that Jackson was shaken by the death of his wife and baby. "About fourteen months after his first marriage," writes his second wife, "in giving birth to a child that never breathed, the mother died also, so that all he saw dearest to him was laid in the grave." And his foreboding was compounded by an eighteen-inch snow that blanketed Lexington two days after the tragedy. Although D. H. Hill tells about Jackson's daily visits to the snow-covered graves, an abiding faith saw him through what must have been a torturous school year. Still, friends and colleagues worried about his health and mental stability. "He had loved her—perhaps too much," Frank Vandiver opines. "The baby had been stillborn and never had a chance. But dear Elie had had so many years before her. It was Elie who was needed."[5]

"My dear sister," he wrote to Margaret Junkin Preston in February, "from my heart I thank God that though He had left me to mourn in human desolation He has taken dear Elie to Himself. I am well assured that He left her with us to the latest moment consistent with His glory, hers, yours, and my happiness." Already we can see the pious resignation and inner strength of the Scotch-Irish race, which not only fortified Jackson in his hour of grief but also sustained him on the battlefield during 1861–1863.[6]

Lee also developed a firm religious faith as he made a commitment to the Episcopal Church during his time at West Point; although he had been schooled from boyhood in the rites of the church, he did not receive confirmation until July 1856, while vacationing at Arlington. In company with his daughters, Mary and Annie, Lee knelt before the Right Reverend John Johns, Episcopal bishop of Virginia, in the chancel of Alexandria's Christ Church to receive the sacrament of confirmation. And, notes Freeman, "his vows were not taken lightly." Lee had considered himself an Episcopalian from childhood, and as early as his service at Fortress Monroe he had served as vestryman.[7]

"I never knew him late for Sunday service at the Post Chapel," writes his son about the West Point years. "There he sat very straight—well up in the middle aisle—as I remember, always became very sleepy, and sometimes took a little nap during the sermon." Robert Jr.'s dismay at his father's "drowsiness" aside, Lee worked with fellow parishioners in San Antonio to construct a new meetinghouse while stationed there in 1860–1861; his faithful church attendance continued until his death.

While leading the Army of Northern Virginia, notes J. W. Jones, "he always set the example himself, and never failed to attend preaching when his duties did not absolutely preclude his doing so." He frequently attended services at Jackson's headquarters; "and it was a scene which a masterhand might have delighted to paint—these two great warriors, surrounded by hundreds of their officers and men, bowed in humble worship before the God and Savior in which they trusted." The simple devotions of Lee and Jackson during the trying days of Confederate combat earned them a near-idolatrous respect throughout the ranks; it was a basic ingredient of their success as men and soldiers. [8]

When Lee left West Point in March 1855, four and one-half years elapsed before his next meeting with Jackson at Harpers Ferry. Twenty months of that time until October 1857 was spent with the Second Cavalry in Texas. Upon the urging of Jefferson Davis, still serving as secretary of war under Franklin Pierce, Congress authorized formation of two new cavalry regiments for frontier defense. The vast expanse of Indian-inhabited lands added to the country following the Mexican War prodded the politicos into action; the brutal massacre of an army detachment in present Wyoming was the clinching catalyst, and after congressional passage of the new law on March 3, 1855, Davis personally selected the officers for each regiment. The First Cavalry led by Edwin V. Sumner was assigned to Fort Leavenworth in Kansas, while the Second commanded by Albert Sidney Johnston was posted to Texas and contained one of the most illustrious duty rosters in American history. [9]

Jefferson Davis, a military man himself, assembled a galaxy of mostly southern officers destined for Civil War fame to lead the Second Cavalry. Albert Sidney Johnston, Kentucky born, West Pointer, and onetime private in the Texas war for independence, was hand chosen for the job because of his experiences with frontier warfare. Robert E. Lee, no longer eligible for the superintendancy at West Point when he accepted a transfer from the engineer corps to the line, was made his second in command. Johnston's junior officers were slated for equal distinction:

William J. Hardee and George H. Thomas were majors; included among the captains were Earl Van Dorn, E. Kirby Smith, Nathan G. Evans, Innis N. Palmer, George Stoneman, and Richard W. Johnson; and among the lieutenants were John B. Hood, Charles W. Field, William P. Chambliss, Charles W. Phifer, and Kenner Garrard. . . . The deeds of Johnston and Lee in the Confederate cause need no recounting. Hardee, Van Dorn, Smith, Evans, Field, Hood, Chambliss, and Phifer were well known southern generals in the great internecine conflict, while Thomas, Palmer, Stoneman, Johnson, and Garrard rose to a similiar station in the Northern army.[10]

At Arlington, where he had returned from the academy, Lee received orders on April 12 to join his new command. Following a stopover in Louisville, he finally reached Jefferson Barracks at St. Louis, where the Second Cavalry was recruited and trained. Although General Long says Lee "brought to bear with great effect his fine power of organization and discipline," formation of the regiment was not without its problems. "I have been busy all the week superintending and drilling recruits. Not a stitch of clothing has yet arrived for them, though I made the necessary requisition for it to be sent here more than two months ago in Louisville," he told Mrs. Lee on July 1.

> Yesterday at muster, I found one of the late arrivals in a dirty, tattered shirt and pants, with a white hat and shoes. . . . I asked him why he did not put on clean clothes. He said he had none. I asked him if he could not wash and mend those. He said he had nothing else to put on. I then told him immediately after muster to go down to the river, wash his clothes, and sit on the bank and watch the passing steamboats till they dried, and mend them. This morning at inspection he looked as proud as possible, stood in the position of a soldier with his little fingers on the seams of his pants, his beaver cocked back, and his toes sticking through his shoes, but his skin and solitary two garments clean. He grinned very happily at my compliments. . . .[11]

For all his effort, Lee did not accompany the regiment on its overland march through Missouri, Arkansas, and the Indian Territory to Fort Mason in Texas. When Johnston and the command departed Jefferson Barracks on October 27, Lee and Major George H. Thomas had been detached for court-martial duty. Among other army locations, Lee found himself at Forts Riley and Leavenworth in Kansas as well as Carlisle Barracks, Pennsylvania, and West Point throughout late 1855 and early 1856.[12]

At Fort Mason, northwest of San Antonio, Albert Sidney Johnston placed Lee in command of two squadrons at Camp Cooper another 170 miles north toward the Red River. During his brief stopover at Fort Mason, Lee encountered perhaps the first and only criticism of his official conduct after Mrs. Eliza Johnston, wife of his commanding officer, wrote in her diary for March 31: "Col. Lee was requested to stay and testify to Lieut Woods character as a gentleman. He humed and ha'd and at last said he was a mere boy when he knew him and had not observed him particularly and finally left for Clear Fork,[13] a mean act in my opinion when he knows the man's reputation as well as he does. I suppose the man feared to become unpopular." Mrs. Johnston's disdain grew from an incident during the regiment's march from Jefferson Barracks in which Lieutenant Robert C. Wood, Jr., son of Assistant Surgeon General Robert C. Wood, was accused of stealing by fellow officers. Although she wrote before his climb to fame, Lee probably did not have sufficient information to assist Wood in a court of inquiry; no doubt unaware of her hostility, Lee wrote to his wife after a visit to the Johnstons at Fort Mason that "Mrs. Johnston is a pretty and sweet woman, intelligent and well adopted to her position and life."[14]

Upon his arrival at Camp Cooper—named for Adjutant General Samuel Cooper and located on the Clear Fork of the Brazos—Lee had his initial encounter with Katumse, the local tribal chief, and with the troops under his command. "Katumse was every inch an Indian leader, about fifty years old, six feet in height, with a dark red-bronze complexion. His striking physique, however, was offset by his ludicrous attire. He wore corduroy leggings and buckskin moccasins, an old, greasy, checkered-cotton coat, and 'a six-penny straw hat.' " His wives, another observer noted, were "hardly more than immature girls, one about eighteen and the other sixteen years old." They were also shoddily dressed, while the Indian village under Katumse, writes a frontier historian, "was typically Comanche. Wolflike dogs, lean and snarling, snapped at the visitor's heels; the air was filled with a bedlam of noise." It was a poverty-stricken collection of one hundred or so lodges. In spite of his protestations of friendship, Lee told the wily chief at their first meeting that he would "meet him as an enemy the first moment he failed to keep his word."[15]

Lee's four company captains were Earl Van Dorn, George Stoneman, Charles H. Whiting, and Theodore O'Hara. The first three were West Point graduates with service records in the Mexican and Seminole wars; O'Hara, although not a West Pointer, "was a ripe scholar, a modest gentleman, a Mexican War veteran, and author of 'Bivouac of the Dead,' and other poems." Then, continues Carl Coke Rister, "each man was furnished a brass-mounted Campbell saddle with wooden stirrups; a spring, movable stock, or Perry carbine; a Colt navy revolver and dragoon saber, carried by saber belt and carbine sling; a gutta-percha cartridge box; and a cape or talma, with loose sleeves extending to the knees. He wore pale blue trousers, a close-fitting blue jacket trimmed with yellow braid, a silken sash, a black hat with looped 'eagle on the right side' with trailing ostrich plumes on the left." Presumably Lee's clothing requisition had arrived for the Camp Cooper cavalrymen.[16]

Fitzhugh Lee, who knew the Comanche firsthand, describes Lee's task: "The Indians of western Texas in those days roved over the prairies in small bodies, and would descend suddenly upon the frontier settlements scalping and killing settlers and driving off their horses and cattle. They were fine specimens of irregular cavalry, were splendid riders, and when compelled to fight, used the open or individual method of warfare, after the manner of the Cossacks." In response, Lee was told to march out from his post and corral the "marauders." He left on May 27, 1856, with troops from his own command as well as units from Forts Mason and Chadbourne, on an 1,100-mile trek across western Texas; it was a hot, miserable business as he scouted the headwaters of the Brazos, Colorado, and Wichita Rivers as far west as the Llano Estacado. But when it was done, Lee's troopers had little to show for their efforts— several abandoned campsites were spotted but no hostile braves. "They brought back a lone Indian woman, and when Lee learned that her father and mother lived on the Brazos reservation, he immediately sent her to them without delay."[17]

Upon the return to Camp Cooper, Lee wrote to Arlington about the abortive chase: "I hope your father continues well and enjoyed his usual celebration of the Fourth of July; mine was spent after a march of thirty miles on one of the branches of the Brazos, under a blanket, elevated on four sticks driven in the ground, as a sunshade. The sun was firey hot, the atmosphere like a blast from a hot-air furnace, the water was salt. . . ." His father-in-law, Parke Custis, had long made the national birthday at Mount Vernon into an annual event with "a patriotic speech of welcome to the many who visited him on such occasions."[18]

Before he left Camp Cooper, Lee learned that his sister Mrs. Mildred Childe had died in Europe. "Though parted from her," he told Mrs. Lee, "with little expectation but of a transient reunion in this life, this terrible and sudden separation has not been the less distressing because it was distant and unlooked for." His grief aside, Lee made it his practice to associate with his junior officers whenever possible; insight into his devotion to a responsible life has been noted by John Bell Hood, who rode with Lee on several afternoon jaunts from the post. "He said to me with all the earnestness of a parent: 'Never marry unless you do so into a family which will enable you to feel proud of both sides of the House.' " The twenty-five-year-old lieutenant had first known Lee while a cadet at West Point and, Hood's "affection and veneration grew to the end of his days."[19]

Lee departed his outpost in early September 1856 with George H. Thomas to sit on a court martial at Fort Ringgold in the Rio Grande Valley. Established in present Starr County, Texas, and named for Major David Ringgold, who died in the nearby Battle of Palo Alto, the post survived as an army installation until the Second World War. Lee got there on September 28 "after twenty-seven consecutive days of travel," he informed his wife. "The distance was greater than I had anticipated, being seven hundred and thirty miles. I was detained one day on the road by high water—had to swim my mules and get the wagon over by hand. My mare took me very comfortably, but all my wardrobe, from socks up to plume, was emersed [*sic*] in the muddy water. . . ." He also noted the realities of south Texas: "I am writing with much inconvenience from a stiff finger, caused by a puncture from a Spanish bayonet, while pitching tent on the road, which struck the joint. Every branch and leaf in this country nearly are armed with a point, and some seem to poison the flesh." Lee remained at Ringgold until October 30, when the tribunal adjourned several miles down the river to Fort Brown.[20]

While he remained in extreme south Texas, Lee took time to visit Matamoros—a place he had bypassed during his march into Mexico with Wool's column. He found the town "out at the elbow [with] nothing apparently going on of interest." Brownsville was a regular port of call for steamships, which afforded Lee a more direct link with Mrs. Lee and the family. After reading copies of the Alexandria *Gazette*, he penned a Christmas letter to Arlington that revealed his thoughts on slavery and the heated debates tearing at the country.

> In this enlightened age there are few, I believe, but will acknowledge as an institution slavery is a moral and political evil in any country. . . . I think it, however, a greater evil to the white than to the black race, and while my feelings are strongly interested in behalf of the latter, my sympathies are stronger for the former. The blacks are immeasurably better off here than in Africa, morally, socially, and physically. . . . How long their subjection may be necessary is known by a wise and merciful providence. Their emancipation will sooner result from a mild and melting influence than the storms and contests of fiery controversy.

Lee observed his fiftieth birthday a few weeks later at Fort Brown, unaware that he was about to lead a great army to decide the fate of American slavery.[21]

Professor Tom Jackson, meanwhile, spent Christmas 1856 with Mary Anna Morrison at Davidson, North Carolina—the same Miss Morrison, sister-in-law of his friend Professor D. H. Hill, he had encountered three years before when Elie Junkin had broken off their engagement. Although he had waited a respectable two years before approaching other women, Jackson by all accounts experienced some unhappy moments while coping with Elie's memory. It was difficult for a vigorous young man of thirty to forget the loss of a wife and child; friends and acquaintances even fretted that he might not survive the loss. He stayed on in the home of Dr. Junkin, which lessened the blow, and to forget he threw himself into a regimen of work and travel.

Eight months after his wife's death, Jackson set out for an extended visit with relatives in western Virginia at the close of the 1854–1855 school year. "I recall his visit at this time," writes his nephew. "He was more serious in manner than I had ever known him. I was too young to fully realize that this was the result of his late bereavement." When he left Laura and the Arnolds at Beverly, Jackson went to Clarksburg, where he visited the graves of his father and infant sister, Elizabeth; next he traveled to Jackson's Mill to see his aunts, uncles, and cousins along the West Fork River. Uncle Cummins Jackson had already gone to his death in the California gold fields. [22]

Jackson took the stage across the Staunton and Parkersburg Turnpike —along present U. S. route 50—to the Ohio River home of his uncle Alfred Neale above Parkersburg. Wirt Woodson, his half brother, who had been reared in the Neale home after his mother's death, was also there for the family reunion. Ever solicitous of his brother's well-being, Jackson wrote later: "I do not want him to go into a free state if it can be avoided for he would probably become an abolitionist; and then in the event of trouble between North and South he would stand on one side, and we on the opposite." His brother, like a majority of western Virginians, was already embracing the antislavery cause, and Jackson was also concerned about his delicate constitution. "In his early childhood," notes T. J. Arnold, "he got possession of some buckeyes or horse-chestnuts, considered quite poisonous, and which there was a great quantity growing on the island where his uncle resided. The child ate of these before the family were aware of what he was doing. He was badly poisoned and his life was despaired of, and although he recovered, the effects therefrom were apparent for many years."

At the same time Jackson left Neale Island for VMI, his brother headed west to carve out a life for himself in southern Indiana—a free state—where he eventually became a successful businessman. Besides his fears over Wirt's stand on slavery, Jackson, who remained a lifelong Democrat, had his own misgivings about the worsening North-South divisions—the same debates that troubled Lee at Fort Brown. When he called on relatives at Mineral Wells, a few miles southwest of Parkersburg, records Roy Bird Cook, he said in the event of trouble "it may be the duty of some of us to stand for some of the things we may not implicitly approve. It is inevitably so in a conflict of that kind." His words were for friends and family alone, writes William P. Snow, because "he was not known at any time to mix in the political questions of the day, though he must have watched, with keen anxiety, the violent agitation which resulted in the disruption of the Union."[24]

From Parkersburg, Jackson boarded a steamboat down the Ohio to Point Pleasant and thence up the Great Kanawha to Charleston, soon to become the capital city for the new state of West Virginia. A few miles east, along the James River and Kanawha Turnpike, he visited Hawks Nest, now a popular state park, but once called Marshall's Pillar from an 1812 description penned by John Marshall, the future chief justice. Within a few miles of the rocky crag that falls as a sheer cliff into the depths of New River Gorge was his mother's resting place at Ansted. When he finally reached Lexington by stage, Jackson wrote to his aunt, Mrs. Alfred Neale, describing his frustrated attempts to locate the twenty-one-year-old grave. "I stopped to see the Hawk's [sic] Nest, and the gentleman with whom I put up was at my mother's burial, and accompanied me to the cemetery for the purpose of pointing out her grave to me; but I am not certain that he found it. There was no stone to mark the spot. Another gentleman, who had the kindness to go with us, stated that a wooden head or foot board with her name on it had been put up, but it was no longer there. A depression in the earth only marks her resting place. . . ." It was a sad time for a man already sorrowing over the loss of his wife and infant child.[25]

In order to occupy himself and to foster their religious training, Jackson started a Sunday School for blacks upon his return to Lexington; there can be no question that he took the obligation seriously. He taught from eighty to one hundred pupils every Sunday afternoon from the autumn of 1855 until 1861, when he left to join the Confederate army. "His method was to make the sessions extremely short, continuing from three P.M. to a quarter to four P.M. At a quarter to three the bell was rung and precisely at three o'clock he began. The exercises were first, singing and prayer, then a brief, pointed, and perspicuous exposition of an assigned passage of the Scriptures addressed by him to the whole school." As late as Chancellorsville, just days before his death, Jackson begged travelers from Lexington for news about the progress of his students.[26]

Then, as Robert E. Lee chased renegade Comanches across the prairies of west Texas, Jackson left his charges in the hands of others for a three-month furlough in Europe. John Esten Cooke argued in 1866 that the trip through England, France, and Switzerland "had no influence upon his life and character"; Jackson's sister-in-law, Margaret Junkin Preston, thought the journey "full of enjoyment and profit," although she discounted any military sway upon the future Confederate. "And strange to say, he did not turn aside to visit battle-fields or to witness any military movements, but found more pleasure in the famed galleries of art and in the grand remains of ancient architecture than perhaps in anything else."[27]

Jackson's detailed itinerary can be found in his letters to Laura from Naples and Lexington. After landing at Liverpool aboard the steamship *Asia*, he traveled through northern England and Scotland to Glasgow, Stirling, and Edinburgh. "I returned to England, visiting York, the residence of Oliver Cromwell, the University of Cambridge and London. From London I took a steamer to the continent, landing at Antwerp, and passing on to Brussels, Waterloo, Naples, Rome, Genoa, Marseilles, Lyons, Paris, Calais, London, New York, home. . . ." A trip of this magnitude altered the ever-observant Jackson in subtle ways; and contrary to the statements of Mrs. Preston, his extant letters from and about Europe refer not only to Waterloo but also to Napoleon and Cromwell. "During his journey," observes Dabney, who lived near him in Lexington, "he carefully examined the field of Waterloo, and traced out upon it the positions of the contending armies. When he returned home he said that although Napoleon was the greatest of commanders, he had committed an error in selecting the Chateau of Hougomont as the vital point of attack upon the British line." Jackson, Dabney continues, agreed with other military men that the crucial thrust should have been elsewhere on the field. Bonaparte and Waterloo held a powerful sway over the nineteenth-century mind, and while Lee had absorbed the campaign through reading and Napoleon Club meetings at West Point, the future Stonewall walked the same ground as the great tactician.[28]

As he trekked across the continent, Major Jackson was beset with thoughts of matrimony. "After returning from Europe with restored health and spirits he began to realize that life could be made bright and happy to him again, and in revolving this problem in his mind his first impulse was to open communication with his old friend Miss Anna Morrison and see if she could be induced to become a participant in attaining his desired happiness." Continues the second Mrs. Jackson:

"To my great surprise, the first letters I ever received from him came to me expressing such blissful memories over reminiscences of the summer we had been together in Lexington that my sister Eugenia[29] laughed and predicted an early visit from the major." She goes on to describe Jackson's sojourn at her father's North Carolina home during his Christmas vacation in December 1856; Jackson passed his first hurdle when the Reverend Morrison, onetime president of Davidson College, pronounced him a "Christian gentleman."[30]

Apparently his overtures were not immediately accepted, despite his jaunt to North Carolina and a flurry of letters throughout the New Year. Jackson did not tell the ever-protective Laura about the impending marriage until May 1857, a short two months before the wedding. After buttering up his sister, he playfully said: "I will tell you that Miss Mary Morrison, a friend of mine, in the western part of North Carolina and in the southern part of the state, is engaged to be married to an acquaintance of yours living in this village, and she requested me to urge you to attend her wedding in July next."

Laura missed the wedding, and must have expressed misgivings, because Jackson hurried to Beverly as soon as the school year ended. Although his nephew remembered "the truly beautiful presents that he brought from Italy the preceding autumn for my sister and myself," he says nothing about the nature of the visit other than it was short. Jackson must have left western Virginia without delay; he arrived at the home of D. H. Hill, who had resigned his place at Washington College to join the Davidson faculty, on July 15. The following day he was married "in a quiet little home wedding, and the ceremony was performed by a favorite old ministerial friend of the family, the Rev. Dr. Drury Lacy."[31]

Two months after Jackson's marriage, Robert E. Lee who had returned to his post at Camp Cooper in April from the Rio Grande Valley, was summoned to regimental headquarters at San Antonio. Albert Sidney Johnston had been ordered to lead an expedition against the Mormons in Utah and to relinquish command of the Second Cavalry to Lee effective July 28, 1857. Although Jones reproduces several letters to Arlington from Camp Cooper, none apparently survives for his time in the Alamo City. During this first, brief tenure as an independent commander, relates General Long, "he examined everything thoroughly and conscientiously until master of every detail, ever too conscientious to act under imperfect knowledge on any subject submitted to him." But Lee had scarcely unpacked his bags as regimental commander than word reached him that his father-in-law, George Washington Parke Custis, had died in his seventy-sixth year. He left San Antonio on October 24 with a quickly secured leave of absence, and three weeks later on November 11 he reached his wife's side.[32]

Lee's homecoming after twenty months in Texas was beset with difficulty, not the least being Mrs. Lee's deteriorating health. Although she had complained to relatives in recent weeks, her letters to Texas had not burdened her husband with her sickness. "Arthritis had assailed her right hand and arm at that time and probably was slowly spreading," reads Freeman's account. "Often she was kept awake at night by the pain. Lee now found her scarcely able to move about the house, and, though she was only forty-nine, aging very rapidly. Overnight, and without warning, he had to face the fact that his wife had become an invalid." Besides Mrs. Lee's illness and the lingering gloom of Custis's death that pervaded the plantation, Lee's children were not there for his usual bright welcome. Of his seven offspring, only Mildred, age eleven, remained at home to cheer her father. The older boys, Custis and Rooney, were in the army, and the two middle girls, Annie and Agnes, as well as fourteen-year-old Robert, Jr., were at boarding school. Twenty-year-old Mary, his eldest daughter, technically at home, was so occupied with her own comings and goings that she offered her father little solace.[33]

Lee's chief dilemma, however, was how best to settle the tangled estate left by his father-in-law.

I give and bequeath my dearly beloved daughter, Mary Custis Lee, my Arlington House estate, containing seven hundred acres, more or less, and my mill on Four Mile Run, in the county of Alexandria, and the lands of mine adjacent to the said mill in the counties of Alexandria and Fairfax, in the State of Virginia, the use and benefit of all just mentioned during the term of her natural life. My daughter, Mary Custis Lee, has the privilege by this will of dividing my family plate among my grandchildren, but the Mount Vernon plate, together with every article I possess relating to Washington, is to remain with my daughter at Arlington House during said daughter's life, and at her death to go to my eldest grandson, George Washington Custis Lee, and to descend from him entire and unchanged to my last posterity.

Beyond that, Rooney was given White House, and Robert, Jr., Romancoke, both on the Pamunkey; Lee's four daughters were left bequests of $10,000 each. During the last years under Mr. Custis, Arlington and the other plantations had fallen into disrepair with heavy debts; the enslaved blacks had grown accustomed to a relatively easy existence under their former master and were reluctant to undertake the field work necessary to make the land pay. And Lee soon learned that plantation operations were impossible without slave labor, although he conscientiously carried out his father-in-law's wishes to free the Arlington laborers by 1863, five years after his death. He set out with a soldier's precision to bring order out of chaos. "He was always fond of farming," notes Robert, Jr., "and took great interest in the improvements he immediately began at Arlington relating to cultivation of the farm, to the buildings, roads, fences, fields, and stock, so that in a very short time the appearance of everything on the estate was improved."[34]

Lee's letters to Markie Williams relate that a steady parade of visitors did not dispel his gloom; and he was yet an officer in the United States Army, although his leaves of absence from the Second Cavalry were extended until 1860 to provide time for settling his wife's estate. Headquarters assigned him court-martial duty in such diverse places as Newport Barracks, Kentucky, West Point, Washington, and Fort Columbus, New York. Lee's spirits were bolstered somewhat in April 1859, when he journeyed to his mother's old home at Shirley for the wedding of twenty-two-year-old Rooney, the first of his children to marry. His new daughter-in-law was Charlotte Wickham, a distant cousin through the Carter clan. Both Lee and his wife became extremely fond of "the delicate patrician bride," who went off to White House plantation with their second son.[35]

Six months afterward, while working at his Arlington desk, Lee received word from the war office beyond the Potomac that some unknown revolutionary had seized the federal arsenal at Harpers Ferry, Virginia. A directive from Secretary of War John B. Floyd ordered him to take a contingent of marines commanded by Lieutenant Israel Green and hasten to the beleaguered town sixty miles to the northwest; within weeks, Major Tom Jackson also arrived at Harpers Ferry with a squad of VMI cadets, which brought the comrades in arms together for the first time since 1854, when Jackson had visited West Point with his beloved Elie.

When Lee reached the town during the early hours of October 17, he not only found the place astir but he soon learned that his adversary was John Brown. "Old Brown," as his admirers liked to call him, had returned east from the Kansas wars with the single-minded determination to destroy slavery in the American South. And he was willing to take up arms against a government that kept men in chains while others merely debated. As Lee tracked Comanche warriors along the Brazos and Jackson toured the continent and pursued the hand of Miss Anna Morrison, John Brown had set out on a one-man crusade that many believe started the Civil War, which was to propel Lee and Jackson to fame. Brown, a product of the "burnt over district" of western Pennsylvania and northeastern Ohio, where the abolitionist impulse was strongest, went beyond the moral suasion of other antislavery fighters. In doing so, he convulsed the national conscience; northern abolitionists who wanted to end the "peculiar institution" saw him as a martyr for human freedom, while apologists for slavery condemned him as a bleary-eyed madman bent upon destruction of the southland.

Although John Brown harbored an outrage against slavery from childhood, his first defiant acts surfaced during 1851 at Springfield, Massachusetts, where he managed a branch office of Perkins & Brown, his commercial partnership with Simon Perkins for the purchase and sale of wool; here, in response to the Fugitive Slave Law—part of the Compromise of 1850—he formed the League of Gileadites to help runaway blacks escape capture and prosecution. But his greatest enterprise took place in 1855–1858, when he fought with free-soil partisans to bring Kansas into the Union without slavery; Brown reached the territory in October 1855, and six months later he moved in swift retribution when a group of "border ruffians" from Missouri ravaged Lawrence, Kansas, a pronorthern town. "Three nights later, on March 24–25, 1856, he led seven compatriots, including several of his sons, in a counter raid near a spot named Dutch Henry Crossing at Pottawatomie Creek. News of the Pottawatomie Massacre which ended in the deaths of five prosouthern homesteaders at Brown's hands electrified the country." Brown achieved instant notoriety with his violent stab at slavery and those who supported it.[36]

More fighting followed before he left Kansas in the last months of 1857 and sequestered himself in the Rochester, New York, home of the black journalist and abolitionist Frederick Douglass. As he hid from federal marshals who hounded him with arrest warrants, Brown hatched plans for an armed thrust into the slave-holding South. According to Douglass, Brown mulled over plans "from the first thing in the morning until the last thing at night"; although he told Douglass, Harriet Tubman, and other black activists about his scheme "to build a string of fortifications in the mountains of western Virginia" to protect the runaway slaves he expected to sally forth once he raised the banner of insurrection, Douglass counseled against the plan. But Brown would not be denied and after he conferred with his backers, known as the Secret Six—Franklin B. Sanborn, Theodore Parker, Samuel Gridley Howe, Thomas Wentworth Higginson, Gerrit Smith, and George Luther Stearns—he prepared to march. He even held a convention at Chatham, Ontario, to draft a

"Provisional Constitution" for use after the hoped-for slave uprising: "We the Citizens of the United States, and the Oppressed people who by a recent decision of the Supreme Court[37] are declared to have no rights which the white man is bound to respect, together with all other People degraded by the laws thereof, do, for the time being, Ordain and Establish the following Provisional Constitution and Ordinances, the better to protect our persons, property, lives and liberties. . . ." That document, found among his belongings after his capture at Harpers Ferry, convinced Virginia Governor Henry A. Wise and the slaveholders that the possibility of slave insurrection was real; its capture, furthermore, became a prime factor in the insistence by Virginia authorities that Brown be charged with treason.[38]

After he rented a Maryland farm across the Potomac from Harpers Ferry and took an alias—Isaac Smith—Brown moved forward on Sunday evening, October 16, with a pitifully small band of fourteen men. Hostages, including Colonel Lewis Washington, a kinsman of the first president, were taken early in the raid, although the operation went badly from the start. By dawn on October 17, Brown had captured the brick engine house at the federal armory but little else. And as Brown's makeshift army floundered in indecision, Lee called at Floyd's office in the company of Lieutenant Jeb Stuart, who was on leave from the First Cavalry in Kansas. Stuart, who was trying to sell a new device to headquarters that would attach a cavalryman's saber to his belt, was quickly signed on as Lee's second in command. "Since no soldiers were available in the capital, a force of ninety marines was borrowed from the navy and supplied," writes a Stuart biographer, "with a proper number of ball-cartridges, ammunition, rations and two howitzers and shrapnel and placed aboard the 3:30 B & O train."[39]

When he arrived in Harpers Ferry during the night, Lee realized immediately that his artillery pieces were useless because of Brown's hostages. With a frontal assault out of the question, Lee sent Stuart under a white flag at 6 A.M. to the engine house door to demand a surrender. John Brown opened the barricade long enough to be recognized by Stuart from his cavalry service in Kansas, and when the Old Man said "No!" to Lee's ultimatum, the marines under Lieutenant Green charged with sledgehammers and battering ram. Captain Dangerfield, clerk of the armory and one of the hostages, tells what happened after Green and the marines gained entrance:

When he saw Brown he sprang about twelve feet at him, giving him an upper thrust with his sword, striking Brown about midway the body, and raising him completely off the ground. Brown fell forward with his head between his knees, while Green struck him several times over the head. . . . I was not two feet from Brown at the time. . . . It seems that Green's sword, in making the thrust struck Brown's belt and did not penetrate the body. The sword was bent double. The reason that Brown was not killed when struck on the head was that Green was holding his sword in the middle, striking with the hilt, and making only scalp wounds.

By 7 A.M., October 18, Brown was not only in Lee's custody, but his plan to end slavery in America had lasted less than forty-eight hours.[40]

Lee did not tarry in northern Virginia but returned to Arlington as the Virginians prepared to try the old abolitionist. Although he did not write Mrs. Lee from Harpers Ferry, Lee later penned a succinct account of his role in Brown's capture. "Received orders from the Secretary of War in person, to repair in the evening train to Harpers Ferry," his Memorandum Book reads for October 17: "Reached Harpers Ferry at 11 P.M., . . . Posted marines in the United States armory. Waited until daylight as a number of citizens were held as hostages, whose lives were threatened. Tuesday about sunrise, with twelve marines under Lieutenant Green, broke in the door of the engine house, secured the insurgents, and relieved the prisoners unhurt." Lee did not enjoy a national reputation in 1859 and when he was attacked for not using stronger measures, Jeb Stuart wrote to several Richmond papers praising his coolness in a difficult situation. The missives were never published, but they defended his chief for not charging without forewarning: "He chose to demand a surrender [contrary to the wishes of Governor Henry A. Wise] before attacking, because he wanted every chance to save the prisoners unhurt, and to attack with bayonets for the same reason. . . ."[41]

Brown's highly publicized trial, which lasted seven days, October 25 through October 31 "was technically fair as the Governor of Virginia boasted and the defendant admitted. Against the advice of counsel, the unchastened abolitionist scorned advice to seek refuge in a plea of insanity." Once Wise and the Virginians decided to make Brown an example, the trial could have only one outcome: He was found guilty and sentenced to death on the gallows. When his execution was set for December 2, 1859, a frenzied indignation swept the abolitionist North; Old Brown was one of their own and the slave-owning South was about to hang him. Thomas Wentworth Higginson, one of the Secret Six, even planned a commando-style raid to thwart their plans.[42]

Military units were assembled from across the state to guard against intruders at the actual execution. Lee arrived at Charles Town on November 30 with four companies of regulars from Fort Monroe three days after Major Tom Jackson brought a contingent of VMI cadets into town. Although Lee and Jackson wrote several letters from Charles Town, none leave a hint that they visited each other; nevertheless, it is incomprehensible that the two did not exchange pleasantries after years of separation. Both must have seen countless acquaintances among the scores of political dignitaries and military men on hand for the event. One wonders if either man took notice of a young private with one of the militia companies from Richmond who was also destined to leave a mark on the American saga. His name was John Wilkes Booth, assassin of Abraham Lincoln.[43]

Lee said without comment that he had been "introduced to Mrs. Brown" in a letter to his wife one day before the execution. Other than saying, "Tomorrow will probably be the last of Captain Brown," he remained silent about his role at Charles Town. Despite the seriousness of the affair, a certain levity must have pervaded as both Lee and Jackson took time to comment upon "the kindness of the people." And numerous scholars from J. William Jones in 1906 to Burke Davis in the 1950s are probably correct that Lee, Jackson, Jeb Stuart, and others "returned home with little thought of the influence upon their own lives and the destinies of his country which those events at Harpers Ferry exerted."[44]

Unlike Lee, Jackson penned a first-rate account of Brown's last moments. He had not wanted to leave his recently purchased home in Lexington for the northward trek; though he complained to Laura about a sore throat during the trip, he assured his wife that in spite of sharing sleeping quarters with four others he "was in good health and spirits throughout his military excursion."

"He behaved with unflinching firmness," Jackson wrote to Laura on December 2 immediately after the hanging:

> Brown rode on the head of his coffin from his prison to the place of execution. . . . He had his arms tied behind him and ascended the scaffold with apparent cheerfulness. After reaching the top of the platform, he shook hands with several who were standing around him. The sheriff placed the rope around his neck, then threw a white cap over his head and asked him if he wished a signal when all was ready. He replied that it made no difference, provided he was not kept waiting too long. . . . With the fall his arms, below the elbows, flew out horizontally, his hands clinched; and his arms gradually fell, but by spasmodic motions. There was very

little motion of his person for several moments, and soon the wind blew his lifeless body to and fro.

Jackson, who stood with his cadets in front of the gallows, told Anna that he prayed for Old Brown's soul.[45]

After the grim business at Charles Town, Lee bade his family farewell for the Texas frontier, while Jackson returned to his classroom at Lexington. Following John Brown's execution, Jackson and Lee did not meet again until the summer of 1861, when both soldiers arrived at Richmond with new promotions first in the forces of Virginia and afterward in the Confederate service. But Robert E. Lee, army veteran of thirty-four years counting his student days at West Point, must have pondered his future as he headed westward. Still a colonel with grandchildren and little prospect for promotion, he surely did not relish more Indian fighting at the same time worsening sectional tensions threatened to disrupt the Union. As the politicians debated the future of slavery, Lee rejoined his command at San Antonio during February, following a journey by land and sea through New Orleans and Indianola on the Texas coast.[46]

Within weeks of his arrival, Lee was ordered to Fort Ringgold to join the "Cortina Wars." Juan Nepomuceno Cortina, who died in 1894 at age seventy, was a mischief maker and brigand who led Texas Rangers and the regular army on a chase through the Lower Rio Grande for nearly three decades. Texas historian David Vigness describes Cortina, whose mother was heiress to extensive Spanish land grants in the Brownsville area, as "uneducated and illiterate, but a natural leader of men, a freebooter who became the champion and idol of the humble Mexicans as well as the high born living on both sides of the Rio Grande." In September, before Lee's arrival at the border, Cortina and his raiders had killed several Texans, including the town jailer while shooting up Brownsville. When frightened townspeople called for federal intervention, General David E. Twiggs, now commanding the Eighth Military department, dispatched Major Samuel P. Heintzelman to contain the Mexican usurper. Although Heintzelman's "stern, rather unkempt appearance with full beard and long, thin hair and lack of initiative" kept him from becoming a top commander during the Civil War, he made short work of Cortina. In something called the battle of Rio Grande City two days before Christmas 1859, he routed a force of 350 Mexicans, killing sixty bandits.

Yet Cortina was again raiding Anglo settlements and steamboats along the river by February 1860, which brought Lee to the Rio Grande; he was told to stop the Mexican outlaw once and for all. John Salmon "Rip" Ford, Texas newspaperman, politician, Texas Ranger, and Civil War officer, who had tangled with Cortina himself, has penned a telling description of Lee during the Cortina affair:

> His appearance was dignified without hauteur, grand without pride, and keeping with the noble simplicity characterizing a true republican. He evinced imperturbable self-possession, and a complete control of his passions. To approach him was to feel yourself in the presence of a man of superior intellect, possessing the capacity to accomplish great ends and the gift of controlling and leading men. It later inspired confidence when we saw Robert E. Lee announced as the commander of the Army of Northern Virginia. Once in his life the writer's estimate of a man was realized to the full extent.

From Ringgold, Lee moved down river to Brownsville, where he had seen court martial duty four years before, and sent "pointed notes" informing Mexican officials they had two choices—restrain Cortina from his cross-border raids or prepare for war with the United States. Although Ford, who commanded Texas Ranger forces in the area, said Heintzelman had already crushed the outlaw, he notes in his *Reminiscences* that the "Cortina War was at an end" following Lee's forceful letters to the Mexicans and a determined show of force around Fort Brown.[47]

Lee stayed on the Rio Grande for several weeks following what proved a temporary check of Cortina. The Mexican persisted in his dream of driving Anglo-Americans beyond the Nueces at Corpus Christi—the very strip of Texas that precipitated the Mexican War when President James K. Polk ordered Zachary Taylor to march into northern Mexico; as late as 1875, when he was taken into custody by General Edward C. Ord, Cortina was still wreaking havoc along the border. But the Cortina chase was pushed aside as Lee, still at Ringgold Barracks, turned his thoughts homeward in an April letter to the newly married Rooney. After acknowledging a March 10 missive from "My Dearest Fitzhugh" announcing the birth of his first grandchild, he continued: "You must kiss his dear mother [Charlotte] for me, and offer her my warmest thanks for this promising scion of my scattered house, who will, I hope, resuscitate its name and fame. Tell her I have thought much of her, and long to see you both, and your little treasure who must, I think greatly resemble his papa."

Rooney, who took nasty wounds in the Antietam campaign and at

Brandy Station, was trying to make a success of his farming operations at White House plantation following his marriage. Upon his graduation from Harvard in 1857, where he had been a classmate of Theodore Lyman, the future soldier-congressman served a brief hitch in the army as part of Albert Sidney Johnston's 1858 Mormon expedition. At the outbreak of Civil War, when both father and son donned Confederate uniforms, his mother, Mrs. Robert E. Lee, forced to flee Arlington, took up residence at White House; when she was required to abandon Rooney's home before McClellan's invaders during the Peninsula campaign, a note was tacked to the front door:

> Northern soldiers who profess to reverence Washington, forbear to desecrate the home of his first married life, the property of his wife, now owned by her descendants.
>
> *A Granddaughter of Mrs. Washington*[48]

In April 1860, however, Lee had his mind on more tranquil pursuits for White House: "And now the school-house must be commenced, or it will not be completed in time. I hope both mother and child are well and increasing daily in strength. . . . Your momma must have rejoiced at another *baby* in the house, and have all her former feelings brought back afresh. I never could see the infantine beauties that she did, but I will be able to appreciate him by the time I shall see him."[49]

Lee was back at his regimental duties in San Antonio from Ringgold by the last weeks of May; the new grandson must have remained in his thoughts: "In a letter to Charlotte," a June 2 missive to Rooney began, "I expressed gratification I felt at the compliment paid me. . . . I wish I could offer him a more worthy name and a better example. He must elevate the first, and make better use of the latter to avoid the errors I have committed. I also expressed the thought that under the circumstances you might name him after his great-grandfather. . . . [But] I should love him all the more, and nothing could make me love you two more than I do."

Besides these maudlin outpourings, Lee designed a fort for the Conchos River during the summer of 1860 that was never built, and he helped "the good people of San Antonio" construct a new Episcopal church. Yet his mind was never far from events in Virginia; in late August—as the 1860 presidential campaign reached fever pitch—Lee again wrote his son with more fatherly advice on how best to manage White House—advice that reflected his own concept of an ordered life: "I am glad to hear that your mechanics are all paid off, and that you have managed your funds so well as to have enough for your purposes. As you have commenced [Lee had a fondness for the word commenced], I hope you will continue, *never to exceed your means*. It will save you much anxiety and mortification, and enable you to maintain your independence of character and feeling. It is easier to make our wishes conform to our means than to make our means conform to our wishes. . . ."[50]

Lee was forced to deal with Texas governor Sam Houston, who wanted the federal government to create a protectorate south of the Rio Grande to guard against additional cross-border raids. Never a man to abandon a project once undertaken, Houston had advocated a filibustering expedition to secure the new state after Washington said no to his scheme. One of Houston's agents, A. M. Lea, who sought Lee's assistance, soon informed his chief: "As he [Lee] is a *Preux chevalier, sans peur, sans reproche,* he is careful to do nothing that would cast a slur upon his name. He would not touch any thing that he would consider vulgar filibustering"; but a determined Houston persisted with his plans.

Lee wrote to Lea on March 1 in no uncertain terms that "should military force be required to quiet our Mexican frontier, I have no doubt that arrangements will be made to maintain the rights and peace of Texas, and I hope in conformity to the Constitution and laws of the country. It will give me great pleasure to do all in my power to support both." Lee added that he had been an admirer of Houston since his student days at West Point, when the future Texas statesman had been president of the Board of Visitors during 1826. He said nothing, however, about a youthful Sam Houston's visits to Mount Vernon to woo Mary Custis before she became Mrs. Robert E. Lee.[51]

Lee also gave himself to experiments with camels as army pack animals and renewed his expeditions against renegade Indians. A debate had raged through army circles about the practicality of camels since their introduction into Texas by Jefferson Davis some years earlier, so Lee acted upon instructions from John B. Floyd, Buchanan's secretary of war, and ordered Lieutenant William H. Echols on an extended expedition into the Texas hinterland to determine their worth. Echols, leader of a previous march with the animals, left San Antonio in June with a company of "well-equipped men, heavily burdened camels trudging along in six detachments, and a train of mules, heading west to undergo the most severe trials for both man and beast yet undertaken." After rough going through the parched Big Bend country, Echols and his party returned in triumph to Lee's headquarters. Although Lee had not expected the men to encounter such harsh conditions—water had to be rationed to troopers and mules—he was enormously pleased when

Echols completed his tour without mishap. Despite their initial successes in Texas and later California, the beasts were slaughtered or left to roam across the Southwest when officials determined them impractical for military use. At least one was used as a pack animal by Confederate forces in Missouri during the Civil War.[52]

Additional Indian troubles soon goaded Lee into action. In response to Houston's cries that "51 persons had been killed as many more taken prisoner, 1,800 horses taken, and much property stolen," he stepped up surveillance from San Antonio and other posts under his command. In one episode, his nephew and future biographer, Second Lieutenant Fitzhugh Lee, intercepted a raiding party with several stolen horses; though other troopers overpowered the band, a lone brave led young Lee, says an official report, on a "chase over hills and ravines covered with dense cedar for six or seven miles." After overtaking the man, he "threw his foe by a 'back heel' fall and killed him." Increased pressure brought a temporary respite from raiding parties, but the Comanche was far from beaten during the summer of 1860. The Second Cavalry was unable to subdue the last renegade Comanche until 1876, six years after Lee's death.[53]

As Lee posted his patrols and watched the 1860 presidential canvass, news reached San Antonio of an event that echoed throughout the "Old Army": General Thomas Sidney Jesup, quartermaster general for the past forty-two years, died on June 10; active in not only army but also national affairs since the War of 1812, the Virginia-born Jesup had been a soldier since 1808. In April 1828, he had acted as second to Henry Clay in the Kentuckian's famous, albeit bloodless, duel with John Randolph of Roanoke. And because promotions were notoriously slow in the antebellum service, Jesup's death opened a new opportunity. Lee had long known the disappointment of slow recognition and the dream of reaching general rank certainly had its appeal. Even Joseph Eggleston Johnston, the man picked to become quartermaster general, although breveted lieutenant colonel in 1847 following the Battle of Chapultepec, waited until 1860 to attain a general's star.[54]

As a result of Jesup being next in rank to Winfield Scott, "the question as to the proper man to fill his vacancy was of great importance since owing to his advanced age, the appointee might be called upon at any moment to the chief command of the army." Like Jesup, Scott had been a fixture beyond living memory; "a year older than the federal constitution," Scott, who had distinguished himself in the War of 1812 and had generaled the Mexican War, had been general in chief since 1841. The old war-horse, also a Virginian and "the only non-West Pointer of southern origin to remain loyal to the Union," had carried the Whig banner against Democrat Franklin Pierce in the 1852 presidential canvass. He was seventy-four years old in the summer of 1860, and though he directed the opening rushes of the Civil War, Scott gave up active command in November 1861.[55]

Robert E. Lee could not have been unmindful of the prestige accompanying an appointment to replace Jesup. But Secretary of War Floyd, onetime governor of Virginia and a man soon to have his own troubles with the Confederate army, did not favor Lee for the post. To extricate himself from a difficult situation, President Buchanan asked Scott to name Jesup's successor, but the old warrior suggested four men instead: Joseph E. Johnston, Albert Sidney Johnston, Charles F. Smith, and Lee. All had long and notable army careers, and all but Smith sided with the Confederacy within the year; each reached general rank soon enough even if under altered circumstances. Joe Johnston, who argued with Jefferson Davis over rank when the Civil War opened, like Lee, became one of five army commanders for the Confederacy. That was after a nasty wound at Fair Oaks, when McClellan and the Yankee army got within sight of Richmond but no further during the Peninsula campaign. Charles Ferguson Smith, a Philadelphia native who graduated at West Point in 1825, had stormed the ramparts at Loma Federación during the capture of Monterey with the famed "red-legged infantry"; before promotion to major general in 1862, he had distinguished himself with Grant's army at Fort Donelson when "he personally led an assault against the Confederate outworks and secured the defenses, the immediate cause of the surrender of the garrison. . . . He was placed in command of the expedition up the Tennessee River, but an injury from an accident developed into an illness that caused his death at Savannah, Tennessee, a month later."

Lee's onetime superior in the Second Cavalry, whose statue stands today on The University of Texas campus with other giants of the Lone Star, once served as secretary of war for the infant Republic of Texas. The Kentucky-born Johnston had joined the exodus of southerners to Texas during the 1830s, and, writes Alfred Hoyt Bill: "Albert Sidney Johnston, thirty-three years old and sorrowing over the death of a beloved wife, resigned a lieutenancy in the United States Army and enlisted as a private in that of Texas. Very soon he rose to command of it—after taking a dangerous wound in the thigh in a duel with the Texan whom he superseded and who considered himself slighted by Johnston's appointment." He was already a brevet brigadier general after rejoining the American service following the admission of Texas into the Union and when the Civil War opened, he was considered the "number one soldier on the continent." Tragically, he failed to receive the simplest medical attention at Shiloh in April 1862, where he bled to death from a leg wound.[56]

Lee was dropped from consideration as the field narrowed to a consideration of the two Johnstons. Although Jefferson Davis, then senator from Mississippi, argued to the bitter end for confirmation of the Kentucky-born Johnston, the post went to another son of Virginia, Joseph E. Johnston. Always the essence of propriety and gentlemanly conduct, Lee had done nothing to advance his cause. Two days after Johnston received senate confirmation as quartermaster general, he wrote a characteristic letter of congratulation to his old comrade: "I am delighted at accosting you by your present title, and feel my heart exalt within me at your high position. I hope the old state may always be able to furnish worthy successors to the first chief of the new department. . . ."[57]

Lee lost no time in writing to Johnston—the letter was posted from San Antonio two days after the appointment—as he watched the unfolding national drama from the hot, dry prairies of central Texas. He was already pondering what Virginia's role would be should that "black Republican from Illinois" named Abraham Lincoln win the presidency in November. In his August 22 letter to Rooney—the same letter that cautioned his son to live within his means—Lee exclaimed: "Things look very alarming . . . And as a[n] American citizen I prize the Union very highly and know of no personal sacrifice I would not make to preserve it, save that of honor." Thirty-five years and more of agitation over the continuation or elimination of slavery in America came to a head during the 1860 campaign as southern extremists talked about leaving the Union if the result went against them—if the Republicans carried the day. The same wires that carried word of Johnston's promotion brought daily reports of the presidential canvass to his headquarters at San Antonio; within the year, Lee and Jackson would be drawn into the North-South maelstrom.[58]

7

Rendezvous at Richmond

Robert E. Lee remained with his Texas command as the sectional controversy intensified while thirty-six-year-old Thomas J. Jackson went
about his duties at the Virginia Military Institute. Although no evidence
suggests the two had direct contact through the summer of 1860, Jackson, like Lee, maintained a military presence while still a professor,
wrote to family members with regularity, and kept a close watch on
political developments. Seven months before Lee told Rooney he was
alarmed at the raging debates over slavery, Jackson did the same for his
aunt, Mrs. Alfred Neale, still living at Parkersburg. In a January 21 letter
from Lexington, Jackson posed a rhetorical question: "What do you
think about the state of the country," and proceeded with his own
answer. "Viewing things at Washington from human appearances, I
think we have great reason for alarm, but my trust is in God; and I
cannot think that He will permit the madness in men to interfere so
materially with the Christian labors of this country at home and
abroad." Jackson's world assessment with its characteristic religiosity
within six weeks of John Brown's execution at Charles Town came after
he told his aunt that he was "thankful to be living in his own house." He
also invited Mrs. Neale to visit Lexington, and, indeed, throughout the
war period Jackson was concerned about his relations in western Virginia
as well as political events in that part of the Old Dominion. Parkersburg
and Wood County were in Unionist territory, and within a short time his
aunt would be living in the new state of West Virginia, although separate
statehood for Virginia beyond the Alleghenies did not come in Jackson's
lifetime.

Mrs. Jackson, who lived to shake hands with President Woodrow
Wilson—she had a widowhood of fifty-two years—left a vivid descrip-

tion of her husband during their last summer together in Lexington. He remained a devoted professor until the outbreak of Civil War, and except for the Harpers Ferry episode he did not accompany the VMI cadets again until April 1861, when he took them to Richmond to be mustered into active service. "Several trips were made by the corps to the capital and to Norfolk, to grace state occasions," Anna relates, "but at such times he always requested that he might be permitted to have his holiday at home, while he lent his sword, epaulets, and sashes to his brother-officers who were more fond of display."[1]

While he loaned out his sword, Jackson found time to correspond with Laura and her young daughter, Grace, at Beverly; it was an area like Parkersburg, soon to be incorporated into West Virginia. His letters to Mrs. Arnold were unfailingly signed, "Your affectionate brother, Thomas," and those to Grace, "Your affectionate uncle, Thomas." Jackson left Lexington with his wife during July to visit a "hydropathic establishment" in Massachusetts with the hope that it would cure a nagging indisposition plaguing Anna. Much of his correspondence with Laura dealt with a plan for Jackson to purchase furniture for his sister when he passed through New York. But an April 16 letter concerned her eyes and offered some practical advice: "I wish you would try the simple remedy of washing them with cold water, lifting the water to the face in both hands, and washing the face until a little water gets into the eyes and they commence smarting. Do this just before going to bed, and again immediately after getting up. . . ." Following his exercise in telling relatives what is best, he and Anna sent their love.[2]

Jackson's letters to Grace during 1860–1861, which always opened with "My Dear Niece," were concerned with her welfare. They not only dealt with her education but also revealed marvelous insights into his own schooling. A letter of February 25, 1860, in fact, is a summation of his own philosophy of education: "And first of all, I want you to learn to spell well; give particular attention to spelling; for I don't care how much you know about other things, if you don't spell well you will be laughed at by educated people." A May 7 letter admonished his niece: "Remember that there are a great many ways of spelling a word wrong, but there is only one way of spelling it right."[3]

Jackson's mind was soon diverted from the pleasures of home and letter writing when a new Parrott gun and one hundred rounds of ammunition arrived at Lexington. The Virginia Military Institute had already been incorporated into the state's military apparatus subject to orders of the governor; and when a committee on public safety traveled northward to witness a demonstration by the gun's inventor, Colonel

Francis H. Smith was told to secure one of the pieces for examination by his professor of ordnance and artillery tactics. Smith, who was Jackson's academic and military superior, lost no time in complying with their wishes, though ordnance officers in the United States army considered Parrott's invention a toy. Virginia born in 1812, Francis Henny Smith had graduated in the West Point class of 1833, and following a short stint in the regular army, he became professor of mathematics in Hampden Sydney College. But, unlike Jackson, Lee, and most regular officers, he did not see action in the Mexican conflict. When VMI opened its doors during November 1839 with twenty-eight cadets, Smith and John T. L. Preston were its only professors—Smith became superintendent two years later, a post he held for the next fifty years. Further, Smith, who had a short, undistinguished Civil War career when the Institute closed for a few months, had been instrumental in bringing Jackson to Lexington in 1851, and he had no qualms about the major's ability to handle the new gun.[4]

As he made plans to take Anna northward for the summer, Jackson quickly prepared the tests. "Major Jackson," writes VMI historian Jennings C. Wise, "caused a number of tent flies to be set up as targets, on the ridge across the river, north of the Institute, and, manning the new piece was a detail of his artillery class, who gave it a thorough trial." Any number of Virginia military men, including his brother-in-law, D. H. Hill, and William Nelson Pendleton, rector of Lexington's Grace Episcopal Church and soon Lee's artillery chief, were on hand to watch the Parrott belch its deadly fire. Like other veterans of Scott's march on Mexico City, Jackson had been accustomed to smooth-bore howitzers, and the rifled marvel at his command dumbfounded him with its firepower.

Old smooth-bore pieces with a maximum range of eighteen hundred to two thousand paces were notoriously untrustworthy: An axiom from Prince Hohenlohe, Prussian prime minister, and his country's artillery chief in the Seven Weeks War, was well known to American fighting men: "When firing at 1,000 paces the first is for the devil, the second is for God, and only the third is for the King." Roughly one-third of all shot could be expected to strike a target six feet high and fifty yards wide.

Jackson not only demonstrated the gun's superior accuracy and range, but his report written before the departure for New England convinced Virginia authorities to purchase twelve Parrotts with ammunition. They were first used, June 10, 1861, at Big Bethel on the Virginia peninsula, when Benjamin F. Butler attempted to reinforce the garrison at Fort Monroe; Daniel Harvey Hill, who watched Jackson on the firing range at Lexington, used the guns to rout Butler's Federals. Although Big Bethel was a minor skirmish—the Confederates lost but eleven men out of fourteen hundred engaged, the rifled Parrotts changed the thinking of commanders, North and South; and while the Confederates were forced to rely on the small but efficient Tredegar Iron Works in Richmond, the South's only foundry capable of producing cannon, and weapons stolen from the Yankees, the federals could depend upon an unlimited supply. Before the Civil War ended, the United States Foundry at Cold Spring, New York, had supplied the northern army with twelve hundred Parrotts and nearly three million projectiles.[5]

Although the first three-inch Parrotts were replaced with the more effective twenty-pounder, or 3.67-inch gun, all of them were fearful things on the battlefield. Robert Parker Parrott, New Hampshire born and 1828 graduate of West Point, developed the piece after a long ordnance and metalworking experience. "For almost forty years he kept himself well-informed in these fields and, in addition, prosecuted a course of research and experimentation of his own." After learning that the German firm of Krupp had produced a workable rifled cannon in 1849, Parrott lost no time manufacturing the guns that found their way to Jackson at VMI. He worked on the piece for ten years before securing an 1861 patent that employed a wrought-iron ring around the breech to handle additional forces generated by the rifled piece. An exploding projectile with an expanding brass ring that forced it into the gun's rifling made his invention complete. Parrotts were easily recognizable on Civil War battlefields because of their distinctive "outside hoop" with an effective range exceeding two miles. It is easy to understand Virginia military authorities' approval of Jackson's results.[6]

Jackson's report, which circulated widely through army ranks, must have been composed quickly. By July 21, three weeks after the gun's arrival, he was writing to Laura from a "hydropathetic establishment" in New England. "I think my general health is better than it has been for a year or two at this season of the year; but exercise brings on increased trouble and pain," he informed his sister before leaving Lexington. A week or so later, he was in Northampton, Massachusetts, at "Round Hill Water Cure" under the care of "a skillful water cure physician" who brought him out of a "bilious fever." Jackson also told Laura that she could find him on a map because he was on the "west side of the Connecticut River."

The Jacksons remained at Round Hill, located "on an elevation overlooking the river," through August, when he returned to Lexington alone to commence the fall term. It must have been a happy summer, although Anna writes in her *Memoir* that her husband "heard and saw enough to awaken his fears that it might portend civil war; but he had no sympathy with those who differed from him." The arguments over slavery and the 1860 presidential canvass did not keep Jackson and his wife from enjoying the surrounding countryside. Northampton, Anna wrote later, "was once the home of Jonathan Edwards, and a large elm-tree which was planted by him was still standing as a memorial to the great theologian. In the old burying ground, a time-worn, moss-covered tombstone bears the name of the saintly David Brainard . . . altogether forming a landscape Jenny Lind thought one of the most beautiful she had seen in America." It is not clear that Jackson heard the famous Swedish singer as she toured the East Coast during 1850–1852, but he was quite at home prowling through century-old cemeteries and reflecting upon divines from an earlier time.[7]

Both Jacksons sought relief at Round Hill. "Our physician says that Anna will have to remain here until about the 1st of October if she wishes to be cured. He says that he can thoroughly cure her. He says that he could cure me of all my symptoms of disease in from four to six months. . . ." Though he could not stay the full course of treatment, another letter to Laura, on September 3, from Lexington, said his health was "much improved" and that he had purchased furniture for her in New York during his journey homeward. "Major Jackson's health improved wonderfully," Anna writes, but he was concerned about her as he prepared to face the fall term alone. And his "regular letters" to Anna before her return recounted a servant's tending of her garden, although Jackson would not "touch" the plot himself: "You have Lima beans, snap beans, carrots, cabbage, turnips, onions, parsnips, beets, potatoes, and some inferior muskmellons. Now do you think you have enough vegetables?"[8]

While Jackson spent his bucolic summer at Northampton and Lexington, and Lee tended his army duties in San Antonio, the first rumblings of Civil War broke across the land. It was not military, but political, events that drove the two soldiers together on the battlefields of Virginia during 1861. Unceasing arguments over slavery and festering sectional differences reached a climax during the 1860 presidential campaign, which opened officially on April 23, when the Democrats convened their national convention at Charleston, South Carolina. Although other factors entered into the shearing election, fresh memories of the "black horror" aroused by John Brown dominated the southern mind and its politicians. The episode at Harpers Ferry scared southern politicos, who had made the strengthening and preservation of slavery an article of faith since the first days of the republic.

The new Republican party, committed to the containment of slavery to those states where it already existed, had been formed during 1854 at an unlikely spot called Ripon, Wisconsin. As southern apologists realized that the great wave of antislavery fervor—fanned from countless evangelical pulpits and political hustings—sweeping the North and Midwest could ensure a "black republican" victory in November, talk of leaving the Union raced through the South. John Brown not only meant business about slave insurrection and a black takeover of the plantation South, but large blocs in the north encouraged his crusade. Lee and Jackson had played significant roles in the Brown saga, yet both observed events with alarm. As comparatively low-ranking officers concerned with careers and families, they could do nothing but watch and write letters to friends and loved ones. Every southerner knew that nothing less than slavery and their plantation-based economy were threatened by Republican success at the polls in November 1860. The closeness in time to John Brown's southern thrust fueled the fires of dread and anticipation.[9]

Brown's impact was captured eighty years later by Stephen Vincent Benet in his epic poem "John Brown's Body":

> Some Yankee named Old John Brown
> Has raised the debil back in Virginny
>
> And freed de niggers all over town,
> He's friends with de ha'nts and steel won't touch him.
>
> But the patrollers is sure to cotch him.
>
> How come he want to kick up such a dizziness!
> Nigger business ain't white folk's business.

Then follows the classic lines:

> John Brown's body lies a-mouldering in the grave
> He will not come again with foolish pikes
> And a pack of desperate boys to follow the sun. . . .

Benet had no doubts. John Brown and what he represented brought an end to the Old South:

> . . . I hear the unloosed thing,
> The anger of ripe wheat—the ripened earth
> Suddenly quaking like a beaten drum
> From Kansas to Vermont, I hear the stamp
> Of the ghost feet. I hear the ascending sea.
> Glory, Glory, Hallelujah
> Glory, Glory, Hallelujah.

And later:

> Bury the South with this man,
> Bury the bygone South
> Bury the minstrel with the honey mouth,
> Bury the broadsword virtues of the clan,
> Bury the unmachined, the planter's pride. . . .
>
> And all the chivalry that went to seed
> before its ripening. . . .[10]

John Brown went to the gallows on December 2, 1859, and three months later, on February 24, the Alabama legislature ordered its governor to withdraw the state from the Federal Union should the Republicans triumph in November. Abhorrent as slave rebellion might be to the white southern mind, an equal concern was slavery in the territories; southern attempts to introduce it into lands added to the country after 1848 had aroused a northern fire storm. Because the free-soil North and its political engine, the Republican party, steadfastly opposed any extension of slavery into the territories, not only the Alabamians but all the plantation South felt threatened. Alabama's price for staying in the Union, therefore, found ready acceptance among her sister states because it read like a litany of southern grievances. Prodded by William Lowndes Yancey, the legislature resolved that the "state would not submit to a 'foul sectional party' and provided for the calling of a convention in the event of the election of a 'Black Republican' president." Yancey, an Alabama newspaperman and former U. S. senator, was a party maverick who never wavered in his defense of southern interests. His resolutions demanded "the territories be common property and as such open for immigration by the citizens of every state with all property recognized by the Constitution." If that was not enough to rile the abolitionist North, the document "supported the principles enunciated by Chief Justice Taney in his decision in the Dred Scott case." That decision had thrown salt in the North-South wound by declaring blacks inferior to whites and thus unqualified for citizenship.[11]

The Democratic party was the chief agent for the southern viewpoint and when it assembled at Charleston a great unanswered question pervaded the deliberations: What would Democrats who lived and voted in the antislavery North do about the slavery issue—especially slavery in the territories? Yancey led the attack, demanding acceptance of the Alabama Platform, but the northern backers of Stephen A. Douglas shouted, "No!" Douglas, still wedded to his popular sovereignty doctrines, wanted a "nonintervenist" stance. Let people in the territories accept or reject slavery, the Douglasites said, because the federal government could never legislate on slavery before statehood. When the assembly opted for the "Douglas Platform," the convention and the Democratic party broke into pieces. The one vehicle that might have preserved the South and her institutions had disintegrated on the issue of popular sovereignty in the territories.

Unable to agree at Charleston, the Democrats reconvened on June 18 in Baltimore, where the fight flared anew. When the recalled delegates voted to seat several Douglas backers in a credentials fight, the southern hotheads—now called fire-eaters—withdrew from the convention and later from the Union itself. Douglas men, who still held the ground in Baltimore, proceeded to nominate their man for the presidency on a popular sovereignty, noninterventionist platform. Herschel V. Johnson, onetime governor of Georgia, "who deplored the division in the party," was named his running mate. Meanwhile, southern Democratic leaders chose John C. Breckinridge as their standard bearer. The Kentucky politician was Buchanan's vice president, who entered the United States Senate in 1861; although named by proslavery Democrats, he declared during the campaign that he "was an American citizen, a Kentuckian, who never did an act nor cherished a thought that was not full of devotion to the Constitution and the Union." Disruption of the Democratic party was complete when Joseph Lane of Oregon was picked as Breckinridge's running mate. A North Carolina native, onetime member of the Indiana legislature, and soldier in the Mexican War, Lane, although currently a northerner, was a secessionist during the convulsions of 1860–1861; James K. Polk had appointed him governor of the Oregon Territory and when Oregon attained statehood he entered first the House of Representatives and later the U. S. Senate. Although an effective speaker, "and an independent thinker on public questions," his support of slavery and secession destroyed his political career.[12]

As the Democrats were wrecking their party, a new force appeared on the already-muddied political scene. The old American or Know-Nothing movement revamped its scattered following into the Constitutional Union Party and held a nominating convention in Baltimore on May 9; hoping to gather what was left of the Whig vote and some Democratic support, the new organization confronted the slavery issue by ignoring it. "The Constitution of the country, the Union of the states, and the enforcement of the laws" was its only platform. John Bell, born on a farm near Nashville in 1797, who had been a leading member of the Tennessee bar since his graduation from Cumberland College, and a U. S. senator, was picked for president. As an oldtime supporter of Andrew Jackson, Bell was a strong Union man who opposed secession "both as a constitutional right and as a remedy for existing ills."

The Baltimore convention tapped Edward Everett of Massachusetts, Unitarian minister, teacher, statesman, and one of the country's foremost orators, to run with Bell. He had been a five-term congressman, but was best known for his brilliant and always patriotic oratory that continued straight through the war. Everett is remembered for his speech on the battlefield at Gettysburg before Lincoln gave his immortal Gettysburg Address. "I should be glad," he penned to Lincoln afterward, "if I could flatter myself that I came as near the central idea of the occasion in two hours as you did in two minutes." But in 1860 Everett had little enthusiasm for the Constitutional Union nod, and though he delivered speech after speech for the Union and the ticket, he was not surprised when it went down in defeat. In many ways Bell and Everett remained outside the major tug-of-war, although both made a determined effort in the border states.

Lincoln, however, had plenty of support in that broad expanse of the country from New England through the Midwest, where abolitionist, and hence Union, sentiment was strongest. It was the same area that had nourished and molded John Brown before his ordeal at Harpers Ferry. The Republican national convention opened in the old Wigwam at Chicago on May 16, one week after the Bell-Everett gathering, amid great consternation by the slave interests. In a stormy convention dominated by free-soil giants Edward Bates, who became Lincoln's wartime attorney general, Salmon P. Chase, and William H. Seward, famed for his "Higher Law" speech during the debates of 1850, Lincoln won the nomination on the third ballot. The "rail-splitter" had experienced years of political frustration following his single term in Congress during the Mexican conflict—an enterprise he opposed—but zoomed to national prominence after his 1858 debates with Stephen A. Douglas. Though

Lincoln lost his bid to enter the U. S. Senate from Illinois in 1858, he had fixed himself as a leading spokesman for the new party, and, most importantly, for the free-soil North. Abraham Lincoln was clearly the man of the hour, precisely because he spoke for the most populous section of the country—that part of America opposed to business as usual on the slavery question.

Although Lincoln reiterated that the Republicans had no intention of bothering slavery where it already existed, the party was adamant about slavery in the territories. "Resolved, that the normal condition of the territory of the United States is that of freedom," the platform announced, "and we deny the authority of Congress, or of a territorial legislature or of any individual, to give legal existence to slavery in any of the territories of the United States." Nor did Lincoln and the Republicans limit their appeal to antislavery sentiments: "Very conspicious were the planks in reference to economic policy and to immigration," writes historian Henry H. Simms. "River and harbor improvements, a protective tariff, free homesteads and transcontinental railroads were endorsed. Changes in naturalization laws were opposed. . . ."[13]

The Republicans rounded out their ticket with Hannibal Hamlin, U. S. senator from Maine, for the vice presidency. He had been governor of the Pine Tree State, and during a long career in the House of Representatives he had been conspicuous in the abolitionist crusade. Hamlin "had decided anti-slavery leanings," writes one biographer, "but, like many of his contemporaries, regarded slavery as an institution beyond the legislative authority of the national government." In 1860 his long reputation as a free soiler from New England made him a logical running mate for Lincoln.

Months before the November elections, strong talk swept the South about secession and war if Lincoln and Hamlin carried the day. And nowhere was the exuberance stronger than among the youthful cadets at the Virginia Military Institute. The Lexington school had been incorporated into the state's military establishment, and the young soldiers had guarded John Brown amid a wave of sectional excitement. War and military preparedness, after all, were the school's chief business, and during the autumn, writes Jennings Wise: "The newspapers were scanned with avidity in the Barracks, and the accounts of military preparations fired the cadets with an enthusiasm for war which youth, careless of consequences but longing for opportunities to win glory, alone can feel."[14]

Although Jackson sought to restrain the more boisterous among his charges, he was soon caught in the growing war fever. The New York

Herald, which he read daily during the election and secession crisis, was his chief source of information from the North; Virginia papers reaching Lexington were plastered with a southern view of the impending crisis. According to his wife, Jackson voted for Breckinridge, and as a military man he understandably had a yen for action should war result from the election. In an incident related afterward by General Henry T. Douglas, who was at VMI during 1860, Jackson's assistant, Edward Cunningham, asked if

> "he would like to see war, after the two schoolmen had been poring over the *Herald* in their section room." Cunningham, who served with Jackson at Harpers Ferry, remarked that he "stopped reading his paper, and for five minutes hung down his head before replying." He then looked up, and, in a low and deliberate tone, said: 'Mr. Cunningham, as a Christian, I wouldn't like to see war,' and then raising his voice until it rang like a bugle-call with eye flashing and every fiber of his body tingling, added, 'but as a soldier, sir, I would like to see war!'[15]

Jackson did not vote with a majority of his fellow Virginians in the tangled November elections. By the narrow margin of 358 votes, the Old Dominion chose Bell and the Constitutional Unionists over Breckinridge and the proslavery Democrats. Bell's triumph in Virginia was largely the work of Waitman T. Willey, a strong Union man from the mountainous west and shortly a United States senator from the new state of West Virginia! Bell's thirty-nine electoral votes came from the border states of Virginia, Kentucky, and Tennessee, where disunion fears were strongest. In Virginia, the final presidential tally stood: Bell, 74,681; Breckinridge, 74,323; Douglas, 16,290; Lincoln, 1,929. Though Lincoln ran poorly in Virginia and throughout the South—he did not receive a single vote in seven southern states, the combined Bell-Douglas-Lincoln vote in the state demonstrated a huge majority for the Union. Little wonder that Jackson was concerned for the northwestern section of Virginia, where that sentiment was strongest.

Nationally, Lincoln and the Republicans triumphed, although he did not receive a majority of the popular vote. In the electoral college, it was Lincoln, 180; Breckinridge, 72; Douglas, 12; Bell, 39. Abraham Lincoln had pulled in 1,866,452 popular votes, but his three challengers got a combined tally of 2,815,617. Breckinridge's electoral vote came from the cotton South, where he carried a band of states stretching from North Carolina to Texas; he had carried only the plantation states, with 849,781 votes out of a total 4,682,069 cast. Lincoln had won only the North, but a specter hung over the South in spite of all the brave talk about leaving the Union. Breckinridge had gotten a bare majority in those states soon to cast their lot with the southern Confederacy, but a majority vote was cast against him in all of the slave-holding states combined. Lee and Jackson soon found themselves leading an army against the very giant that had voted against the slave interests—a giant that ultimately overwhelmed them.[16]

The election results were no sooner fixed than the country became unstuck. It started in South Carolina, where the state legislature sent out a call for a "secession convention" less than a week after the election. When it assembled on December 20, the old resentments against the North were rehashed, including a Republican victory that denied equality to all parts of the country in the territories; even Lincoln's House Divided Speech during his 1858 debates with Douglas was added to the list. As honorable gentlemen, the conventioneers crowed, they could not remain in the Union with that "Black Republican" in the White House. They had voted themselves into the Union back in 1788 and now, they promised the world, South Carolina would vote itself out.

Although each southern state had varying numbers of Unionist sympathizers, all opposition was quickly squelched. And the South gave in to South Carolina like a deck of falling cards. Mississippi was next, voting herself out on January 8, 1861, following a quick debate on "whether the state could be better served in the Union or out of it." With the Republicans in command, they opted to leave. The remainder of the South followed in quick succession: Florida, January 10; Alabama, January 11; Georgia, January 19; Louisiana, January 26. In Texas, where proslavery elements had been flying the Lone Star since the election, an Ordinance of Secession was rammed through on February 1. Then six of the seceded states gathered on February 4 at Montgomery, Alabama, to form the Confederate States of America, even though the upper South remained in the Union. Yet the entire country kept an eye on Virginia, jewel of the southland, and asked but one question: What will The Old Dominion do?[17]

While Jackson read the *Herald*, Robert E. Lee kept a close feel on events from the Texas frontier. He apparently cast no vote in 1860, but like Jackson his sentiments lay with the southern Democrats. Freeman cites a letter from Texas during July from Marse Robert to his longtime friend Major Earl Van Dorn: Stephen A. Douglas, he thought, should withdraw from the campaign "and join himself and his party to aid the election of Breckinridge"; Lee wanted Lincoln beaten, but he thought "politicians are too selfish to be martyrs." A Mississippian as well as veteran of Mexico and the Indian wars, Van Dorn became a brigadier general in the Confederate service before he was shot dead during 1863 by a local physician. The doctor said Van Dorn, "a small, elegant figure," had violated the sanctity of his home.[18]

As the country broke apart in December 1860, Lee again stood on the periphery of a dramatic turn in the American drama; back in 1831, he had watched troopers leave Fortress Monroe to join the chase after Nat Turner; he had been at Scott's side during the march to Mexico City; and now cavalrymen from his command helped in the capture of Cynthia Ann Parker. The famed encounter between Parker and Lawrence Sullivan Ross—a future governor of Texas—took place near present Crowell, Texas, in something called the Battle of Pease River. After Ross had marched with a company of Texas Rangers and fourteen men from the Second Cavalry following reports of Comanche raids throughout the Pease–Red River country, a white woman indistinguishable from her companions except for her "blue eyes and fair complexion," was captured with a band of raiders. The thirty-four-year-old Parker had been taken captive during 1836 as a nine-year-old child; because she had married into a Comanche tribe and became the mother of several children, she returned to her relatives with great reluctance. More than any other white adopted by Indians, Cynthia Ann Parker stole the national imagination with her return; afterward, she became a heroic figure in American folklore and her son Quanah Parker lived to be a hunting companion of President Theodore Roosevelt.

Lee must have followed Parker's return with fascination from his headquarters at San Antonio until December 13, when he received orders to relinquish his command and rejoin the Second Cavalry at Fort Mason; located near the junction of the San Saba and Llano Rivers, Fort Mason had been a previous duty station for Lee and also for some of the most illustrious names in the army—Albert Sidney Johnston, George H. Thomas, David E. Twiggs, Earl Van Dorn, Joseph Eggleston Johnston. The secessionist movement gained momentum as Lee traveled northward to his new post; he received news of South Carolina's secession while riding to Fort Mason, which he reached two days before Christmas 1860. He remained at the outpost until word arrived from Winfield Scott to come east upon the outbreak of war.[19]

Meanwhile, Virginia joined the gallop toward secession. As early as November 7, ninety-four members of the general assembly had petitioned governor Letcher to summon a special legislative session to consider the consequences of Lincoln's election. "Honest John" Letcher, a Douglas Democrat who opposed secession, finally conceded to the southern extremists, and when the legislature met on January 7 a call was formally drafted for a secession convention; the Virginians not only dispatched commissioners to President Buchanan urging restraint in the worsening crisis but they also issued a call for a peace conclave to assemble February 4 in Washington. Sometimes called the Old Gentleman's Convention because of a preponderance of elder statesmen in its deliberations, the gathering was unable to resolve North-South differences. With John Tyler presiding, several constitutional amendments were proposed, including a provision to extend the Missouri Compromise line to the Pacific, before the convention collapsed in failure. [20]

Even before creation of the Confederacy at Montgomery, with Jefferson Davis and Alexander H. Stephens as president and vice president, the seceding states had embarked upon a systematic confiscation of federal property across the South; even Fort Mason was surrendered to the Knights of the Golden Circle, a Texas secessionist group, within a month of Lee's departure for the East. But it was the contention surrounding Fort Sumter in the harbor at Charleston, South Carolina, that gripped the country. It also immobilized the Buchanan administration, because proslavery members of the cabinet blocked the president's efforts to preserve Sumter and South Carolina for the Union. After the resignation of Secretary of War John B. Floyd, who once told confidants he would "rather have my hand chopped off" than send reinforcements to Major Robert Anderson holding the installation, Buchanan managed to dispatch an unarmed merchantman—the famed *Star of the West*—with men and supplies, but the vessel never reached its destination. The president's efforts were a classic case of too little too late as he sat helplessly watching one southern state after another march toward secession. Lincoln, however, did not hesitate after he entered the White House in March; his quick action to relieve Major Anderson led to the dramatic events of April 12, when Pierre Gustave Toutant Beauregard opened fire from his Confederate batteries around Charleston. Civil War had started!

Lincoln sent out his famous call on April 25 for seventy-five thousand men—Virginia, still in the Union, was given a quota—to put down the rebellion. Governor Letcher not only refused the presidential request, but the impact of Sumter and its aftermath jarred the normally serene Virginians. "There was a great parade of military mobocracy in the street," Robert Y. Conrad, a member of the Virginia Secession Convention observed:

A park of artillery was taken and placed in the public square, just before the Capitol, and one hundred guns fired in honor of the disgrace of our national flag, the governor was serenaded by a procession of Palmetto banners, and then the doors of the Capitol were forced, and the flag of the Confederate Southern States hoisted on the top of the Capitol, just over the Hall where we sat. The rejoicings, with procession, fire works, and music were kept up until midnight. . . . The worst of this matter is that men of standing and influence, including some members of the convention, openly countenance all these proceedings and avow their purpose to establish a provisional revolutionary government.

The intensity of the moment was not lost as the convention voted 88 to 55 to take Virginia out of the Union within three days.[21]

Buchanan, powerless to stem the flow of events, relied upon General Winfield Scott to salvage what he could of the national honor. By January 1861, Scott had moved "the headquarters of the army back to Washington, where at his advanced age he actively oversaw the recruiting and training of the defenders of the capital." Scott's reorganizational plans included orders issued on February 19 directing Robert E. Lee to abandon his post at Fort Mason and report to Washington at his first convenience. Although he complied immediately, Lee was subjected to enormous pressures from fellow southerners in the army and by Texas authorities to cast his lot with the new Confederate States of America. During a brief stopover in San Antonio, a Texas committee on public safety—Samuel A. Maverick, Thomas Devine, and Phil N. Luckett—told Lee that Texas was out of the Union and should he refuse to join the Confederacy transportation would be denied for his personal belongings. The Texans had been appointed to oversee seizure of federal property and munitions in the state after Sam Houston, who was unable to accept Confederate authority, resigned the governorship. But Virginia had not joined the parade to Montgomery, and Lee, son of Light-Horse Harry, the man who helped George Washington establish an independent Union seventy-two years before, kept his counsel as he headed for the warmth of Arlington.[22]

At the same time Lee wound up his affairs in Texas, Jackson was also watching the worsening crisis; although Anna insists that her husband was a states-rights man but never "a secessionist," Jackson felt Virginia should defend her interests. Before the secession convention opened in Richmond, he told his nephew, Thomas Jackson Arnold: "For myself I have never as yet been induced to believe that Virginia will even leave the Union." He felt secession was unnecessary because "northern people" loved the Union more than they disliked slavery. But Jackson also spoke out in the same letter of January 26: "I desire to see the state use every influence she possesses to procure an honorable adjustment of our troubles, but after having done so free states, instead of permitting us to enjoy the right guaranteed to us by the Constitution of our country, should endeavor to subjugate us, and thus excite our slaves to servile insurrection in which our families will be murdered without quarter or mercy, it becomes us to wage such a war as will bring hostilities to a speedy close."[23]

Jackson, like other white southerners, realized slavery was the root of the national discontent. And Anna herself was forced to admit he fought for the southern Confederacy "and her Constitutional rights" which included retention of slavery. Furthermore, she added, Jackson, although "a friend of the negro [sic]," thought the "peculiar institution" was sanctioned by Holy writ: "He therefore accepted slavery, as it existed in the Southern States, not as a thing desirable in itself, but allowed by Providence for ends which it was not his business to determine."

Jackson was also a bachelor through the spring, while Anna returned to North Carolina for a younger sister's wedding. Besides attending sessions of the Virginia Presbytery, which met in Lexington during April, he was forced to cope with growing rowdiness among the cadets. Old Jack's letters to his Beverly relatives had already mentioned that Lexington and Rockbridge County were hotbeds of Unionist sentiment, but serious confrontations arose when surrounding mountain folk took a dim view of prosecession activities at VMI.[24]

A nasty incident developed after cadets insisted on raising the "Stars and Bars" of the new Confederacy in Lexington at the same time townsmen were saluting Old Glory. Although the Richmond convention had not removed Virginia from the Union, some "unknown cadets" managed to bore holes in the pole supporting the national emblem; what was worse, several onlookers were injured as the flag crashed to the ground. When a number of cadets went into the city for their regular Saturday visit, a band of armed mountain boys lay in wait. After a few VMI men were "roughed up" in the ensuing melee, the remaining corps formed up to rush their antagonists.

School officials had long dissuaded their youthful charges from open secessionist displays, and to quell their red hot enthusiasm, Major Jackson entered the barracks room at the insistence of Commandant Smith. "His erect figure, flashing eye, energetic expression—short, quick, and to the point, disclosed to the commonest mind a leader of men," notes a school historian. Jackson the soldier also spoke: "Military men make short speeches, and as for myself, I am no hand at public speaking anyhow. The time for war has not yet come, but it will come, and soon; when it does come, my advice is to draw the sword and throw away the scabbard."[25]

"Tom Fool" Jackson and his cadets would unsheathe their swords sooner than any could have imagined. From the moment Virginia secessionists rammed through the Ordinance of Secession, VMI was plunged into a growing war fever. On April 17, the same day as the convention vote for secession, Letcher appointed a three-man council of war: John J. Allen, member of the State Court Appeals and Jackson's kinsman, Commodore Matthew Maury, onetime superintendent of the naval observatory in Washington, and VMI superintendent Francis H. Smith. And Smith added to the anxiety by his quick departure for Richmond to advise Letcher about the sure-to-come onslaught. Three days later, a summons to action arrived in Lexington: "Send courier to Major Preston immediately to send Corps of Cadets to Richmond. Let sufficient cadets remain to aid as guard, and get volunteers from Lexington to act as guard. Bring down all ordnance stores with full supply of ammunition. . . ." Instantly, more than two hundred cadets were alive with preparations for the 150-mile journey; further instructions put Jackson in charge of the eastward trek by way of Staunton across the Blue Ridge, through Gordonsville to Richmond.[26]

At half past noon, sharp, Professor Jackson roared, "Forr-ward march," and the VMI corps along with four 6-pounder artillery pieces, and impressed farm wagons to carry their knapsacks, started the first of Jackson's Civil War marches. A mile or two beyond Lexington, the cadets were loaded into waiting stagecoaches, which took them thirty miles northward to Staunton, where they spent the first night, April 21; the lads were billeted in city hotels to await rail transportation the next morning, and the fair lasses of Staunton's prestigious schools with their "matronly guardians" turned out to console them before their departure. And depart they did for the rail junction at Gordonsville and the remaining sixty-five miles into Richmond aboard the Virginia Central.

Jackson and his charges were needed at Camp Lee, located on the state fair grounds, to act as drillmasters for the swarms of raw recruits and volunteers flocking to the capital. For a worried Anna, Old Jack took time out to write his first wartime reassurance to his beloved esposa: "April 22, 1861. My little darling, the command left Staunton on a special train at about quarter past ten this morning. We are stopping for a short time on the eastern slope of the Blue Ridge. . . . The war spirit here, as well as at other points of the line, is intense. The cars had hardly stopped before a request was made that I leave a cadet to drill a company."[27]

Actually, the letter was composed while the cadets and train crewmen worked to right their derailed engine near Waynesboro. The delay was temporary, however, and "by late afternoon" the cadets were in Richmond, where Jackson formed them for a march to the capitol grounds on their way to Camp Lee. As townspeople and politicians looked on and hurrahed the lads from Lexington, "Honest John" Letcher made a speech of appreciation.[28]

Robert E. Lee arrived in Richmond on the same day as Jackson to confer with Letcher and the war council. Surely the two soldiers, if they did not actually meet on that April afternoon, were aware of each other's presence. From that day, the destiny of the Confederate experiment in separate government was linked to the fighting caliber of Lee and Jackson. For the next twenty-five months—until Jackson lay mortally wounded on the field at Chancellorsville—they were fated to become the South's most famous soldiers.

Lee had arrived at Arlington on March 1 from his Texas command in a personal dilemma. Too proud to draw his sword against the Old Dominion, he stayed at home pondering and waiting while the Richmond convention debated her fate. Always the devout churchman, Lee led his family in daily devotionals from the *Book of Common Prayer* and looked after the plantation as the secession fury raged to a climax. He reached home three days before Lincoln's inauguration, and as every visitor to Washington knows, his house at Arlington lay within eyesight of the federal capitol and its preparations to recoup an errant South. Winfield Scott, who personally directed troops at the inauguration to insure Lincoln's safety, was one of many who implored Colonel Lee to remain firm for the old flag. In spite of great persuasions, writes J. W. Jones: "Lee turned his back upon wealth, rank, and all that a mighty nation could offer him, severed the strong ties which bound him to the 'old service' and his brother officers, and offered his stainless sword to his mother state."[29]

Lee's moment of truth came one day after the prosecession vote at Richmond. Upon the invitation of Francis Preston Blair, a Kentucky lawyer who was a Democrat and Lincoln's confidant, Lee rode to his Washington home on April 18 for the famous encounter offering him command of the federal army. No greater honor could be paid any man than the offer to command the armies of each people at the outbreak of Civil War. Confusion exists about the true sequence of events, although the world knows Lee spurned the overture; Jones says flat-out that Lincoln offered him the post through Blair as emissary. Douglas Southall Freeman, who studied Lee in unsurpassed detail, quotes a memorandum of the Lee-Blair meeting left by Montgomery Blair, son of Francis P., and himself a politician of note: "General Lee said to my father, when he was sounded by him, at the request of President Lincoln, about taking command of our army against the rebellion, 'Mr. Blair I look upon secession as anarchy. If I owned four millions of slaves in the South I would sacrifice them all to the Union but how can I draw my sword upon Virginia, my native state?' " Although the younger Blair was not present at the tête-à-tête—which took place in the family home at 1651 Pennsylvania Avenue, not far from the White House—he continues: "Lee could not determine then; said he would consult with General Scott, and went on the same day to Richmond, probably to arbitrate; and we see the result." Blair is in slight error, because Lee did not leave Arlington until the 22nd—four days after the interview. Still, Montgomery Blair graciously acknowledged: "It is hard for a noble mind to tear itself from home, kindred, friends, and native soil, and go into the opposite ranks to crush them."[30]

Carl Sandburg, moreover, concludes in his massive biography of Lincoln: "Scott and Old Man Blair made it plain that Lee was the choice for high command of the Union armies, Blair having authority from Lincoln to 'ascertain Lee's intentions and feelings,' and the consent of Secretary Cameron to offer high command." Sandburg suggests the interview was merely exploratory but Scott obviously considered Lincoln's offer valid. "Lee, you have made the greatest mistake of your life," his old commander told him upon hearing about the refusal.[31]

Lee left his own account in an oft-quoted letter written during 1868 to Maryland senator Reverdy Johnson. A great friend of the South who generaled a drive to rescue President Andrew Johnson in the impeachment trial of 1867, he was told by Lee:

> I never intimated to anyone that I desired the command of the United States Army; nor did I ever have a conversation with but one gentleman, Mr. Francis Preston Blair, on the subject, which was at his invitation, and, as I understood, at the instance of President Lincoln. After listening to his remarks, I declined the offer he made me, to take command of the army that was to be brought into the field; stating as candidly and as courteously as I could that, though opposed to secession and deprecating war, I could take no part in an invasion of the Southern States. I went directly from the interview with Mr. Blair to the office of General Scott; told him of the proposition that had been made to me, and my decision. Upon reflection after returning to my home, I concluded that I ought no longer to retain the commission I held in the United States Army, and on the second morning thereafter I forwarded my resignation to General Scott.

Lee was as good as his word and sent letters of resignation to Scott and Lincoln's secretary of war, Simon Cameron, which are reproduced in toto in the collection of letters by his son. Lee surely spent all of April 20 at his writing desk; besides letters to Scott and Cameron, he wrote missives to friends and relatives, all dated April 20, justifying his course. Since the letters were written three days after Virginia's secession, he clearly had some notion that high military rank awaited him in Richmond. "Now we are in a state of war which will yield to nothing," he penned to his sister, Mrs. Anne Marshall of Baltimore: "The whole South is in a state of revolution, into which Virginia, after a long struggle has been drawn; and though I recognize no necessity for this state of things, and would have foreborne and pleaded to the end for redress of grievances, real or supposed, yet in my own person I had to meet the question whether I should take part against my native State. . . ."[32]

And to his brother, Smith, still on active naval duty: "After the most anxious inquiry as to the correct course for me to pursue, I concluded to resign, and sent my resignation this morning. . . . War seems to have commenced, and I am liable at any time to be ordered on duty which I could not conscientiously perform. To save me from such a position, and to prevent the necessity of resigning under orders, I had to act at once, and before I could see you again on the subject, as I had wished. . . . Save in defense of my native State, I have no ambition ever again to draw my sword."

Although a formal referendum on the secession ordinance did not follow until May 23, Lee was caught in the swirl of military preparations from the moment he reached Richmond. He conferred with Letcher immediately, and the following day, April 23, as Jackson watched over his cadets at Camp Lee, he was invited to address the still-in-session convention. Clearly the man of the hour, Lee was escorted to the podium by a venerable Virginian named Marmaduke Johnson; after a formal introduction by John T. Janney, an ardent Unionist from Loudoun County, not far from Arlington, who nonetheless presided as convention chairman, Lee made an extraordinarily brief reply. He not only thanked the gathering for "the honor conferred upon me" but also added a justification for his actions: "Trusting to Almighty God. . . . I will devote myself to the defense and service of my native State, in whose behalf alone I have ever drawn my sword."[33]

Lee's address followed a ceremony in which he had been placed in command of all Virginia forces. When he arrived on April 22, Letcher informed him about a law enacted immediately after the vote on secession creating the rank of major general to serve at the governor's pleasure; and Honest John Letcher had appointed him to the post with unanimous approval of the Committee on Public Safety. The late colonel of infantry in the United States Army lost no time in accepting the honor. [34]

That very night, April 23, Jackson wrote to Anna back in Lexington, also the home of Letcher, about Lee's elevation to command: "Colonel Robert E. Lee of the army is here, and has been made major general. This I regard as of more value to us than to have General Scott as commander; as it is understood that General Lee is to be our commander-in-chief, and I regard him as a better officer than General Scott." Jackson told his wife that God had intervened in the appointment. [35]

8

Getting Ready

Jackson remained at Camp Lee four or five days before Letcher announced his appointment as colonel in the state forces of Virginia and ordered him to Harpers Ferry. His Richmond letters to Anna reveal a diligent drillmaster absorbed in whipping thousands of raw recruits into fighting men as well as a commander obsessed with the need for secrecy. This latter trait, his fanatical, closed-mouth approach to command, not only dogged relations with his wife but also with superior and subordinate officers to the very end. "I am unable to give you the information I would like respecting things here. The State troops are constantly arriving," he wrote from the Fair Grounds on the 24th. And a day later: "The scene here, my darling pet, looks quite animated. The troops are constantly arriving. Yesterday about seven hundred came from South Carolina. . . ."[1]

More than twenty thousand men swarmed Camp Lee in the first weeks after secession to be drilled by Jackson's cadets. It was Old Jack's youthful charges who made the soldiers that stood firm at Falling Waters and First Manassas as the long civil conflict opened, and within months practically every VMI man had been commissioned into the Confederate officer corps. Unassigned recruits and volunteer companies, many with grandiose names and outlandish ambitions, were trained and organized into fighting units. A memoir by James A. Bosang, who fought with the Stonewall Brigade, describes the adventures of a group called the Pulaski Guards. Like most volunteer companies, it was composed initially of mere lads; although organized in 1859, Bosang relates the disappointment at not being mustered for the John Brown hanging. "The boys were coming nearly all night and we town boys were up and looking after them the best we could," he wrote about the order to assemble one day after Virginia secession. "Oh, what a day it was! The tears, the farewells, the parting with loved ones, the heartaches of those who were left behind. My younger brother Henry and myself had joined at the organization of the company. A younger brother, only 16 years of age, insisted on going with us and finally with the consent of our dear mother, Henry and I agreed he should go, thinking it would probably be better for us to go together." Bosang's experience was not unique; Virginia and the South needed men, and few questions were asked as whole families and entire communities answered the muster.[2]

The Pulaski Guards commenced their northward march first to Dublin and thence by train to Camp Lee. At Christiansburg in neighboring Montgomery County, the company was joined by the Montgomery Fencibles, the Blacksburg Highlanders, as well as groups from Wythe and Smyth Counties. Several who were already versed with the *Manual of Arms* were detailed to assist other recruits, but it was Jackson's cadets from Lexington who carried the ball at Camp Lee. The secession convention voted a $20 per month bonus to each VMI drillmaster for his services. In July 1861, the Institute's board of supervisors announced that "one third the field officers in the provisional army were graduates or ex-cadets while the number of captains and lieutenants were in proportion to the field officers." Old Jack's great popularity among the Valley men who formed the later Stonewall Brigade unquestionably sprang from his tenure at the Virginia Military Institute.[3]

Jackson told his wife in the letter of April 24 that "Major General Lee is commander-in-chief of all the land and naval forces of the State." He also told Anna that her brother, William W. Morrison, late major in the Federal service, had passed through Richmond on his way home. Morrison, who helped Jackson obtain a North Carolina marriage license ten years earlier, had resigned his position in Washington—he told Jackson about "great uneasiness" in the capital—to cast his sword with the South. Jackson's good words about "William (my brother), Major W. W. Morrison" was followed by an admonition to Anna on the eve of his departure for Harpers Ferry. "I received your precious letter, in which you speak of coming here in the event of my remaining. I would like very much to see my sweet little face, but my darling had better remain at her own home, as my continuance here is very uncertain."[4]

It was just as well that she stayed in Lexington, because Jackson received his marching orders two days later. With fighting on the horizon, he found his duties at Camp Lee distasteful, which prompted his Richmond friends to intercede with the convention. Letcher sent an April 27 dispatch to Lee that ordered Jackson to Harpers Ferry "to organize into regiments the volunteer forces which have been called into the service of the State, and which may be assembled in the neighborhood." Lee's subsequent directive told him to transfer machinery and rifle-making equipment at the Harpers Ferry armory to Richmond and to complete "as quickly as possible any guns and rifles partially constructed, should it be safe and practical." Beyond a doubt, Lee had seconded the decision to put Jackson in the Shenandoah Valley; since he left Richmond on the 26th, it is reasonable to say the two had talked before his departure.[5]

One delegate reportedly asked during the convention debates about Jackson's appointment: "Who is this Major Jackson, that we are asked to commit to him so responsible a post?" And in an oft-quoted reply, Samuel McDowell Moore, convention representative from Lexington and neighbor of the Junkins, gave the answer: "He is one, who if you order him to hold a post, will never leave it alive to be occupied by the enemy." Moore, a onetime Whig congressman and state legislator, like others around Lexington, had observed their man closely during his teaching years.[6]

Harpers Ferry, with its strategic location at the head of the Shenandoah Valley and critical rail junctions, was crucial to southern war plans from the beginning. Located at the confluence of the Shenandoah and Potomac rivers, Harpers Ferry was the gateway to the great valley of Virginia; here, between the Blue Ridge and Alleghenies, lay the breadbasket of the Old Dominion, and any Yankee army threatening the Shenandoah would have to overtake the town. When war came, Lee and Letcher knew Jackson was the man to organize its defense. When Old Jack's appointment became public, his fellow professor at VMI, John T. L. Preston, now a colonel himself at Richmond, dashed off a letter to his wife, a sister of Jackson's first wife, at Lexington: "Jackson with the rank of colonel goes to supersede General Harper at Harpers Ferry. It is most flattering to him. Say to his wife that it is the command of all others which he would most prefer. He is a noble fellow and I rejoice in his success." It was the same Preston, professor of foreign languages and English, who welcomed Jackson to the Institute back in 1851.[7]

Although Virginia had been out of the Union but eleven days when Jackson arrived on April 28, he was not the first to command at Harpers Ferry. One day after Virginia's Ordinance of Secession, Letcher, on his own initiative, had placed Major General Kenton Harper in command of state forces in the town and told him to hold fast. A militia appointee and captain during the Mexican conflict, Harper had little notion of the realities of war, although he later commanded the Fifth Virginia Infantry at First Manassas. When Jackson arrived, he found that Harper had done little more than bide his time with five thousand militiamen under his command; he had not organized the local units. With the entire post in shambles, Jackson inherited enough to occupy his restless energies.[8]

Even before Virginia yoked itself with the Confederacy, military men and politicians wondered if the old state could be defended. Yet Letcher did not waver in his defensive actions—besides Harper at Harpers Ferry, Philip St. George Cocke, Daniel Ruggles, W. B. Taliaferro, and Andrew Talcott were hurried to command in various places. St. George Cocke, a former student at the University of Virginia, 1832 graduate of the military academy and a writer on agricultural policy, was sent to the area facing Washington. A wealthy plantation owner in Virginia and Mississippi, he had been at West Point with Lee. Although he was commissioned a brigadier general in the Confederate army, Cocke was a "naturally impetuous fellow," who took his own life in December 1861. He was fifty-two years of age.[9]

Daniel Ruggles, on the other hand, who lived to the ripe old age of eighty-seven, was marched off to supervise preparations in the Fredericksburg area. Unlike Cocke, he had fought in the Indian wars and Mexico after leaving West Point in 1833; Ruggles was a northerner by birth who married a Virginia lass and cast his lot with the South. The Massachusetts native fought at First Manassas and Shiloh, before ending his Confederate career in the West under Braxton Bragg, Earl Van Dorn, and Joe Johnston. William Booth Taliaferro entered the Confederate service by way of William and Mary, Harvard, and the Virginia legislature; Letcher sent him to secure the naval yard at Norfolk and to oversee fortifications along the lower Chesapeake. Although not a West Point man, Taliaferro, a veteran of Mexico, fought brilliantly under Jackson in the Valley and later with Beauregard in Georgia and Florida. He reentered the Virginia legislature after Appomattox and he served as the state's Masonic grand master during the 1870s; "six feet tall and full-bearded," says the *Dictionary of American Biography*, "Taliaferro was by tradition and character a Virginia gentleman and a leader, temperamentally akin to Washington and Lee."[10]

Letcher's other appointee, Andrew Talcott, Lee's old army buddy, was asked to build fortifications along the York River between Gloucester Point and Yorktown because of his engineering skills. A Connecticut native, West Pointer, class of 1818, he had wide experience with the engineering corps before he resigned in 1836 to pursue a private career. Already sixty-five years old when the Civil War started, Talcott did not see active duty but returned to Mexico, where he built a railroad from

Vera Cruz to Mexico City. A long list of honors befell Talcott before his death in 1883 because of the so-called Talcott Method. Besides his surveying and railroad ventures, he had an interest in practical astronomy; while running the Ohio-Michigan boundary in the 1830s, "he devised a method of determining terrestrial latitudes through the observation of stars near the zenith, adapting the zenith telescope to the purpose."[11]

Meanwhile, Jackson left Richmond on April 26 for Harpers Ferry by the Orange and Alexandria Railroad. Although it is but 175 miles by modern highway, he was two days on the road. Military exigencies required him to change trains at Manassas Junction instead of going on to Washington and then direct to Harpers Ferry via the Baltimore and Ohio. At Manassas, a place he would get to know soon enough, Jackson boarded a westbound train on the Manassas Gap Railroad through White Plains, Salem, and Rectortown; then it was across the Blue Ridge at Manassas Gap to Front Royal and Strasburg; in the latter place, the railroad turned south along the North Branch of the Shenandoah River to Mount Jackson. From Strasburg to Winchester, a twenty-two-mile stretch, Jackson and his two cadet companions were obliged to use the stage. No tracks yet connected the two valley towns. He stopped briefly in the Frederick County seat at Winchester to dash off a few lines to Anna: "Little one you must not expect to hear from me very often, as I expect to have more work than I ever had in the same length of time before; but don't be concerned about your husband, for our kind Heavenly Father will give every needed aid." He told his wife that he was taking the train from Winchester to Harpers Ferry "at halfpast two o'clock" for the remaining thirty-two miles along a branch of the Baltimore and Ohio. The next day, Jackson telegraphed a recommendation to Letcher suggesting a hurry-up project to complete construction of a railroad link from Strasburg.[12]

While Jackson made preparation for war at Harpers Ferry until May 23, when Joe Johnston arrived to relieve him, Robert E. Lee was caught up in not only planning for war but also with negotiations between Virginia and the newly formed Confederacy. General Long, who became his aide on the eve of First Manassas, has left a telling description of Lee during those first days at Richmond. After commenting on his "ease and grace of bearing" as well as his "courteous and mild but decided manner," Long proceeds: "Though at that time he had attained the age of fifty-four years, his erect and muscular frame, firm step, and animated expression of his eye made him appear much younger. He exhibited no external signs of rank, his dress being a plain suit of grey." A quiet, unaffected Lee proceeded to mold the Army of Northern Virginia into a deadly fighting machine in the weeks following the appointment. And he did it with a dignity that inspired what amounted to awe in friend and foe alike. Little wonder that John Bell Hood's Texans later crowed that they "would charge hell with a bucket of water" if Lee gave the word.[13]

The Memoirs of Robert E. Lee: His Military and Personal History, published by Long in 1886, is a trove of basic information about Lee and the war. Along with *The Recollections and Letters* by Robert E. Lee, Jr., Long's work has been a mainstay for all subsequent writers about the South's most illustrious soldier. Every scholar of consequence since 1886 has drawn heavily upon his interpretations. Born in Campbell County, Virginia, in 1825, and an 1850 graduate of West Point, Long wrote his lengthy memoir under extreme circumstances. Following Appomattox, he became chief engineer for a Virginia canal company, but by 1870 he was totally blind because of exposure to the elements during his Civil War campaigning. Long used a special slate fitted with mechanical guides to write the seven hundred-page work at his Charlottesville, Virginia, home. He joined Lee's personal staff in June 1861 and remained through the Gettysburg campaign; for the remainder of war, he served as an artillery officer in Jackson's old corps.[14]

Lee's organizing efforts at Richmond, where first Letcher and then Jefferson Davis refused his pleas for active command, were nothing short of Herculean. Davis himself wrote that Lee "possessed my unqualified confidence, both as a soldier and a patriot, and the command he had exercised over the Army of Virginia, before her secession to the Confederacy, gave him that special knowledge which at the time was most needful." By the end of May 1861, Lee had overseen the organization of more than thirty thousand men into fighting units.[15]

Lee's task was all the more remarkable because of a scarcity in arms and ammunition throughout the South. Yet his knack of recognizing able subordinates allowed him to succeed. Colonel Josiah Gorgas, who became his chief of ordnance during the Richmond period, according to Long, "found in all the arsenals within the Confederacy only 15,000 rifles and 120,000 muskets at Richmond and Hall's rifles and carbines at Baton Rouge. There was no powder, except small quantities at Baton Rouge and at Mount Vernon, Alabama, holdovers from the Mexican War." Nor could he find artillery pieces or equipment for cavalry units. In the first weeks of war, Gorgas molded the Confederate ordnance arm by capitalizing on importations from Europe as well as building new powder mills and foundries at home.

Like Lee, the West Point soldier and veteran of the Mexican conflict gathered a remarkable team to do his work. Gorgas had been born into a German family in Dauphin County, Pennsylvania, but had married a daughter of governor and U. S. senator John Gayle of Alabama while he was stationed at the Mount Vernon Arsenal near Montgomery in the 1850s. Upon joining the Confederacy, Gorgas rose to brigadier general before the final collapse; after the war, he served as president and later, because of ill health, librarian of the University of Alabama. In spite of crippling deficiencies, his organizing genius permitted Lee to assemble sixty regiments of infantry and cavalry besides numerous artillery units, a total of sixty thousand men, before First Manassas.[16]

As early as April 23, Lee conferred with Alexander H. Stephens, vice president of the Confederacy, regarding military cooperation between Virginia and the Montgomery government. The two came to fundamental agreement in quick order; although Virginia's hookup with the Confederacy was never discussed, Lee agreed the state should act in concert with other southern states after Virginia had adopted an ordinance of secession. And then "Little Aleck" trailed off into an area that had never occurred to Lee: Volunteer officers under Lee's command in Virginia state units held their commissions from the convention—in other words, any military understanding might necessitate Lee as major general and his subordinate officers taking orders from Confederate officers of lesser rank.

Lee, however, told Stephens he had not resigned from the old army to advance his own career; nevertheless, lesser officers became upset when Confederate authorities systematically reduced them in rank a few weeks later. The Confederate vice president wrote in his monumental *A Constitutional View of the Late War Between the States* that Lee had told him: "He did not wish anything connected with himself, or his official rank or personal *position*, to interfere in the slightest degree with the immediate consummation of an alliance." Lee was unquestionably favorable in his report to Letcher and the war council about his tête-à-tête with Stephens. The following day, April 24, Virginia took its first step toward joining the Confederacy by signing a formal military treaty.

Alexander H. Stephens, whose heart was never in the cause, made a strange negotiator for the new government. While he apparently believed secession meant war, he also argued that southern nationhood would lead to a mutually agreed-upon settlement. Stephens had grown to manhood in central Georgia, the son of a poor dirt farmer and sometimes schoolmaster. His entire existence was spent reconciling a frail, sickly body with a superior intellect and unbounded political ambition. Vernon Parrington, the American intellectual historian, wrote it was a miracle how that physique never weighing a hundred pounds held together for seventy-one years. Neither war, imprisonment, nor poor health dampened his fighting heart; Stephens was serving in the Georgia governor's mansion when he died in 1883.[17]

In spite of a sickly, even melancholy, disposition, Stephens was a gamecock when the occasion demanded; he was nearly killed in a notable fight with Francis Cone, a three hundred–pound jurist. Stephens remained a lifelong bachelor, although he maintained a lasting friendship with a half brother, Linton, whom he educated at Harvard and the University of Virginia; he was also a confidant of Robert M. Toombs, his fellow Georgian. "Pessimistic and embittered, he did incalculable harm to the Confederate cause by obstructionist tactics and violent opposition to the Davis policies," writes Confederate historian Clement Eaton. At Savannah, one month before his conference with Lee, Stephens proclaimed the new government's position on slavery and blacks. After saying the founding fathers of 1787 had contemplated a theoretical equality of man, he got down to business: "Our government is founded upon exactly the opposite idea; its foundations are laid, its corner-stone rests upon the great truth that the negro [*sic*] is not equal to the white man; that slavery—subordination to the superior race—is a natural and normal condition."[18]

Lee may have wished for a more humane approach to the slavery issue, but Virginia had yoked itself with men who thought otherwise. Although his letters from Richmond say nothing about Stephens and Confederate politics, Lee's dread of approaching war as well as concern for the safety of Mrs. Lee and the younger children permeated his thoughts. "I am very anxious about you," he said on April 26: "You have to move and make arrangements to go to some point of safety, which you must select. The Mount Vernon plate and pictures ought to be secured. Keep quiet while you remain and in your preparation. War is inevitable, and there is no telling when it will burst around you. Virginia, yesterday, I understand joined the Confederate States. What policy they may adopt I cannot conjecture."[19]

Four days later, as General Irvin McDowell assembled a Union force for the invasion of northern Virginia, Lee was yet concerned that military operations along the Potomac would engulf his wife and children. "I think therefore that you had better prepare all things for removal, that is the plate, pictures, etc., and be prepared at any moment. Where to go is the difficulty. When the war commences no place will be exempt, in my opinion, and indeed all the avenues into the State will be scenes of military operations." Lee lapsed into a brief political discourse; he told

Mrs. Lee that Virginia would not propose or accept a truce. The soldier in him admonished his wife not to be deceived by rumors of sectional compromise.

Although Lee was barely one hundred miles from his wife, he was in no position to help. At the same time, he was organizing his army brigades and sending communiqués to field officers, he wrote constantly first to Arlington and then Ravensworth, where his wife resettled, offering advice and soothing. When he heard she was moving to a relative's home ten miles or so down the road toward Fairfax Court House, Lee was concerned for her happiness while living in another's home: "I grieve at the necessity that drove you from your home," he wrote on May 8. "I can appreciate your feelings on the occasion and pray that you may receive comfort and strength in the difficulties that surround you. When I reflect upon the calamity impending over the country, my own sorrows sink into insignificance. . . . Be content and resigned to God's will."

Yet he found time to enjoy some of life's pleasures amid his Richmond duties and family cares. Like Jackson, who attended a Presbyterian gathering in Lexington while Anna was away, Lee went to a state Episcopal convention in Richmond and listened to an address by his old friend Bishop William Meade of Virginia. A well-known speaker and religious writer, Meade became presiding bishop of the General Council of the Protestant Episcopal Church for the Confederate States during October 1861. "I witnessed the opening of the convention yesterday, and heard the good Bishop's sermon, being the 50th anniversary of his ministry," he told his wife on May 16: "It was a most impressive scene, and more than once I felt the tears coming down my cheek. . . ."

The family was gone from Arlington by the end of May; Lee's eldest son, George Washington "Custis" Lee, had moved into Richmond's Spotwood Hotel with his father while the younger daughters joined relatives in Fauquier County. Eighteen-year-old Rob (Robert E. Lee, Jr.), his youngest son, left the university at Charlottesville and at Lee's urging accompanied his mother into exile from Arlington. Mrs. Lee went to the Fairfax County home, Ravensworth, of her aunt, Mrs. A. M. Fitzhugh. Fearful that Mary and "Cousin Anna" might not hit it off, Lee wrote repeatedly to encourage his wife. A May 25 letter: "I sympathise [sic] deeply in your feelings at having to leave your dear home. I have experienced them myself, and they are constantly revived. I fear we are not being grateful enough for the happiness there within our reach, and our heavenly Father has found it necessary to deprive us of what He has given us. I acknowledge my ingratitude, my transgressions, and my unworthiness, and submit with resignation to what He thinks proper to inflict upon me." With that insightful assessment of his own serenity and resignation to divine will, Lee concluded: "We must trust all then to Him, and I do not think it prudent or right for you to return there, while the United States troops occupy that country. I have gone over all this ground before, and have written to Cousin Anna on the subject. . . ." Mrs. Lee never returned to her home again, with its spectacular view of the Potomac and the federal city.[20]

Meanwhile, earth-shattering political and military events had prompted Lee's transfer to the Confederate service on May 25, the very day he wrote to his wife at Ravensworth. Virginia had joined the Confederacy May 7, and the Montgomery authorities immediately started their trek eastward. Their eagerness was entirely understandable. "The statesman of the Confederacy," writes Clement Eaton, "worked under irritating and uncomfortable conditions in the hot, provincial capital at Montgomery. This capital in the black belt was teeming with office seekers, and was cursed with miserable hotel facilities; moreover, mosquitoes were eternally biting the statesmen and their ladies."[21]

Virginia, after all, was the jewel of the South; Richmond with its forty thousand inhabitants, many the most cultured of any people on this side of the Atlantic, was an urbane, desirable place to live. The Old Dominion had more people than any southern state, as well as a plentiful supply of raw materials; both were needed for the coming war! Although Jefferson Davis did not favor the move, he was easily overridden by an overzealous congress. And the Montgomery assembly rammed through a resolution on May 21, "That this Congress will adjourn on Tuesday next, to meet again on the 20th day of July at Richmond, Virginia."[22]

Although levees reaching Virginia from the lower South had already been placed under Lee's command before Davis and the cabinet arrived, Lee and his staff were also handed a perplexing military dilemma: From the moment Davis switched his official residence to the Old Dominion until the final surrender at Appomattox, the capture of Richmond became the great obsession of Lincoln and his generals. Over the next four years, the Virginia countryside from the James to the Potomac was destined for one long bloodbath. All other campaigns in the war inevitably became secondary to the Yankee strategy of crushing Lee's Army of Northern Virginia as it guarded the Richmond approaches.

The federal battle cry, "On to Richmond," caused military men to become divided on the best avenue south. One faction favored the route followed later by George B. McClellan—land by sea at Fortress Monroe, which remained under the Stars and Stripes, and advance up the historic peninsula between the York and James Rivers to the Confederate capital. An equally inviting route was the more direct path—march straight down the Orange and Alexandria tracks and then turn southward through Fredericksburg. In the end that was the route followed by Ulysses S. Grant during the Wilderness campaign of 1864–1865.

Since federal military options in Virginia were obvious, Lee moved quickly to develop a counter strategy. He created a defensive barrier extending from the mountains of western Virginia to the dismal swamp country around Norfolk on the Atlantic coast; it stretched in a great slanting arc from the Shenandoah Valley, where Jackson held the keep at Harpers Ferry, along the Orange and Alexandria and Manassas Gap railroads, down the lower reaches of the Potomac to Yorktown and beyond. Moreover, Letcher's earlier appointments, many of them resentful at loosing their grandiose military titles, were hardly the men to hold the federals at bay. By the time Davis arrived at his Virginia residence in late May, Lee had started making organizational changes that continued for several weeks. His new officers commanded roughly sixty-five thousand men along the western Virginia–Chesapeake line when his plans were finally in place.[23]

As Lee gazed northward, his extreme right was held by a descendant of French Huguenot parents named Benjamin Huger. A West Pointer and veteran of Mexico, Huger was put in charge of the small detachment at Norfolk on May 23; his subsequent actions when McClellan marched up the Peninsula in 1862 became a disappointment to the Confederate high command. After convincing himself that his Norfolk position was untenable, Huger "dismantled his fortifications, removed the stores, set fire to the naval yard, blew up the *Merrimac,* and withdrew." He got into trouble with Joe Johnston and Longstreet a couple of months later, because of inaction during the Seven Days fighting; although he was finally promoted to major general, he was shunted to the Trans-Mississippi, where he sat out the remainder of the war.[24]

A few miles away, at Yorktown on the Virginia Peninsula, "Prince John" Magruder, another West Point man and Jackson's chief in Mexico, was stationed with a small detachment. But, unlike Huger, he was not a man to run from the first test of steel. Known far and wide in both armies for his flamboyant lifestyle, "Prince John" directed a successful defense of the lower peninsula until the federal invasion of May 1862; Magruder won the celebrated fight at Big Bethel on June 10—the first land battle of consequence—when Benjamin F. "Beast" Butler marched out from his base at Fortress Monroe and ran into the Parrott guns from VMI eight miles up the road from Hampton. Yet, like Huger, Magruder did not live up to his early promise; in spite of temporary fame for his showmanship and quick marching from Richmond to deceive a gullible McClellan during the Peninsula campaign, he lost Lee's confidence because of his slowness at Savage Station and Malvern Hill in the Seven Days operations. Magruder, who sat out the conflict on the remote Texas coast, spent the rest of his life protesting his imagined shabby treatment by the Confederate high command.[25]

The bulk of Lee's commanders on station when Jefferson Davis got to Richmond had been seconded by Confederate authorities following Virginia's link with the Confederacy. A case in point was Theophilus Hunter Holmes, West Point classmate of Jefferson Davis, who officered eight thousand men at Aquia Creek between Alexandria and Fredericksburg. The Confederate president personally appointed him brigadier, major, and even lieutenant general before the war ended. Holmes, son of a North Carolina governor, like other early appointees, did not measure up as the war progressed. After proving himself a "capable officer" at Bull Run, he ran afoul of his superiors at Malvern Hill, where "he allowed the day to pass and the battle to be decided in his hearing without doing anything more than forming his men in line." Even so, Davis put him in charge of the Trans-Mississippi, but the work proved too strenuous and he assumed a subordinate role under E. Kirby Smith; a nasty dispute between Holmes and General Sterling Price in Missouri caused Davis to send him home as commander of North Carolina reserves.[26]

Pierre Gustave Toutant Beauregard, "Old Borey," the man who fired the first cannon at Fort Sumter, had command of twenty thousand troops in the Manassas Junction–Bull Run sector. The elegant Louisianian, twice wounded in Mexico, had recently been fired as superintendent at West Point for advising a southern cadet to resign from the academy if his state left the union. Beauregard, who had been commissioned a Confederate brigadier general immediately upon his resignation from the federal army, faced Irwin McDowell's force within sight of Washington. Although replaced as overall commander by Joe Johnston before the Manassas fight in July, Beauregard was in charge after June 1 when he arrived from South Carolina.[27]

The extreme Confederate left was held by Robert S. Garnett with a force of five thousand along the present West Virginia–Virginia border. Garnett, whose father had been a longtime Virginia congressman, was another West Point man with a distinguished record in the Mexican War; after service as aide-de-camp to Zachary Taylor, he stayed in the army until 1858, when he gave up his commission, got married, and left for an extended European tour. Returning home upon Virginia's secession, he was appointed adjutant general of state forces and worked closely with Lee to organize the state's military might. By early June, Garnett had been commissioned brigadier general and sent to command in northwestern Virginia. But confronted with a hostile population and an overwhelming Union force under McClellan, he was doomed to failure; he was killed instantly in July 1861 while directing the withdrawal of his force during the action at Carrick's Ford.[28]

At Harpers Ferry, Colonel Tom Jackson remained in command until May 23, 1861, when he was replaced by Lee's old comrade Joseph E. Johnston. This contingent grew until it reached nearly fifteen thousand men on the eve of First Manassas. Johnston had bypassed Virginia service and traveled to Montgomery following his resignation as quartermaster general in the old army. After receiving a brigadier's cap from Jefferson Davis, he was sent directly to Harpers Ferry, where he superseded Jackson. But Old Jack had done yeoman service by molding hundreds of raw recruits into soldiers following his April 27 appointment, although he was summarily replaced by Confederate orders. In a few short weeks, he had organized what became known as the "Stonewall Brigade," destined to become one of the most renowned units in the entire war. Jackson, who maintained constant communication with Lee during his Harpers Ferry sojourn, did not hold another independent command until Lee sent him back to the Valley following the Manassas campaign.[29]

While Lee directed his far-flung command with daily dispatches from an inconspicuous office in Mechanics' Hall near the Confederate statehouse, Jackson at Harpers Ferry steeled his troops for the inevitable thrust from a federal force under General Robert Patterson clustered about Chambersburg, Pennsylvania. And Jackson was quickly added to Lee's dispatch list; it was the beginning of their military correspondence, which continued until the tragedy at Chancellorsville two years later. No fewer than fifteen communiqués—some of them lengthy—appear in the *Official Records* for the interval Old Jack stayed in command at the Ferry. Lee and Letcher had not sent Jackson on an idle expedition into the lower Shenandoah. A directive from Richmond, dated May 1 and signed by "R. E. Lee, Major General, Commanding," authorized him to call out the militia in seven surrounding counties in addition to companies around Harpers Ferry.

Lee's May 1 order written three or four days after Jackson reached his command told him further: "You are desired to urge the transfer of all the machinery, materials, etc., from Harpers Ferry as fast as possible, and have it prepared in Winchester for removal to Strasburg, whence it will be ordered to a place of safety. The machinery ordered to this place must be forwarded with dispatch, as has already been directed. . . . All the machinery of the rifle factory, and everything of value therein, will be removed as rapidly as your means will permit." Lee admonished him to keep a tight watch on the federals in Pennsylvania: "You will keep yourself as well informed as possible of any movements against you. Should it become necessary to the defense of your position, you will destroy the bridge across the Potomac."[30]

Old Jack was secrecy personified as he proceeded with dogged determination. He moved quickly to establish spit and polish among his troops who had grown lax under easygoing militia officers; while earlier commanders had been all pomp and circumstance, Jackson and his cadet aides went about their duties clad in "the plain blue uniforms of the Military Institute." His British biographer, George F. R. Henderson, writes "there was not a particle of gold lace about him. He rode his horse as quiet as himself. His seat in the saddle was ungraceful. His well-worn cadet cap was always tilted over his eyes; he was sparing in speech; his voice was very quiet, and he seldom smiled." Jackson held no military parades, and "even with his officers he had little intercourse." He confided his orders to no one, and not a "single item of information, useful, or otherwise, escaped his lips," Henderson added.[31]

Jackson did not neglect the spiritual well-being of his command. A pattern of religious concern, which he established at Harpers Ferry, continued until his death; deeply spiritual himself, Jackson encouraged visiting clergymen and evangelists to sermonize among the men. And the Virginia lads under his command reciprocated his feelings. The Reverend C. F. Fry, a member of the Baptist Colportage Board, who visited his Valley command, wrote later: "I . . . could have sold more than $100 worth of books a month if my assortment had been larger—especially if I could have had a good supply of Testaments. A captain said to me, 'I am a sinner, and wish you to select some books to suit my case.' I did so; and at night he called his men into line and asked me to pray for them." Nineteenth-century devotion to the distribution of religious tracts—tractarianism—as well as Bible reading raced throughout the southern armies during 1861–1865.[32]

When it came to the deadly sins and demon rum in particular, Jackson showed no mercy; he no sooner appeared at Harpers Ferry than he moved to squelch vice wherever he found it. John N. Opie, who was present, tells what happened in his first-rate memoir: "Finding there was great quantities of liquor in the town, he ordered it to be poured out. The barrels were brought forth, the heads knocked in and the contents poured in the gutter; but the men dipped it up in buckets, and there was a sound of revelry at night. Finally, he ordered the whiskey poured into the Potomac River. . . ." Jackson's attempts at moral suasion among the troops unquestionably had the support of Lee and Davis since neither moved to dampen his efforts.[33]

Still, Jackson and Lee disagreed over strategy at Harpers Ferry. Although a good portion of their correspondence through May 1861 reveals a division about fortifying parts of Maryland, no long-term animosity disturbed their mutual confidence. Jackson took one look at the town, with its mountain precipices where the Potomac cuts through the Blue Ridge on its way to Chesapeake Bay, and decided the high ground beyond the river needed guns and men to guard against intruding Yankees. The Old Line State after all—though it technically remained in the Union—had long entrenched loyalties to the South, and more than a few Confederate sympathizers; visits from several state legislators who encouraged Jackson to enter the state emboldened him to act without Lee's approval. "I have occupied the Virginia and Maryland Heights," he telegraphed on May 6, "and I am fortifying the former with blockhouses of sufficient strength to resist any attempt to carry them by storm. Whenever the emergency calls for it, I shall construct similar works on Maryland Heights." Jackson had placed troops on Maryland soil but apparently no entrenchments.[34]

Three days later, Jackson informed Lee that the Maryland overlooks had been seized by five hundred men from Kentucky and Augusta County. And the same day Lee warned him: "[I]t is considered advisable not to intrude upon the soil of Maryland, unless compelled by the necessities of war." Jefferson Davis and the cabinet hoped the state might yet cast its lot with the Confederacy, and Jackson was ordered to do nothing that might sway public opinion northward. Lee uncharacteristically repeated his command to quit the state in two dispatches dated May 10: "I fear you have been premature in occupying the Heights of Maryland with so strong a force near you. The true policy is to act on the defensive, and not invite an attack. If not too late, you might withdraw until the proper time."[35]

Jackson, who signed his dispatches, "T. J. Jackson, Colonel, Virginia Volunteers, Commanding," further informed Lee on May 11 that, besides his placements at Harpers Ferry, he had stationed troops at Berlin, Point of Rocks, Shepherdstown, and Martinsburg to guard the Potomac crossings. Uncertain, Lee telegraphed the following day: "I presume the points occupied by you at Point of Rocks, Berlin, and Shepherdstown are on our side." Since their correspondence in the *Official Records* falls silent about Maryland, the issue was presumably ended.[36]

Another headache for Jackson was Richmond's insistence that the Baltimore and Ohio Railroad (B & O) continue operation. Completed in 1853, the all-important link with northwest Virginia and the Ohio Valley ran sixty miles from Baltimore to Harpers Ferry and thence 319 miles to Wheeling on the Ohio River. With the exception of one or two overland turnpikes—which played a major role in Lee's efforts to hold the region for the Confederacy—the B & O was the sole economic and cultural tie between the rebellious northwest and old Virginia. At Harpers Ferry, a branch line ran southwest to Winchester in the Shenandoah Valley; at Grafton, in present West Virginia, another line, the Northwestern Virginia, leased by the B & O in 1857, ran to Parkersburg, also on the Ohio—eighty-one miles downstream from Wheeling. Roughly fifty miles of the main line passed through Jackson's command, and he was told to watch helplessly as supply-laden trains rolled east and west. "I was very much astonished," Opie noted, "that the military authorities permitted thousands of cars loaded with livestock, breadstuff and bacon to pass from the fertile fields of the West to our Northern enemies."[37]

Yet Jackson was not above harassing the trains which carried among other western produce a steady supply of coal for the federal navy; he struck with a vengeance on May 23 when he ordered Kenton Harper, now a colonel in command of the Fifth Virginia at Martinsburg, twenty miles from Harpers Ferry, to close the line. By taking advantage of double tracks along the main line, Jackson and Harper acted on the very day Virginia ratified its ordinance of secession. "Then at noon sharp," observes Festus P. Summers in his 1939 classic *The Baltimore and Ohio in the Civil War*, "Harper closed the road and the scoop was complete. In this single hour the Virginians had bottled fifty-six locomotives and more than three hundred cars. Within the limits of their operations also were the railroad shops at Martinsburg with costly equipment. All were now in the hands of the Confederacy."[38]

Although southern mastery of the B & O was far from complete, Jackson obtained "Little Sorrel," his faithful horse for the rest of the war, during an early foray against the line. Old Jack's sense of right living kept him from appropriating federal property for his personal use, but when he saw "a small sorrel horse" aboard a captured train, he mused that Anna might like the mount. The horse soon fell under the control of Colonel John A. Harman, his chief commissary and quartermaster officer—the same Harman, another Shenandoah man from Staunton,

who supplied his troops during the Valley campaigns and later constructed pontoon bridges across a rain-swollen Potomac for Lee's army
following the disaster at Gettysburg. Jackson secured the animal, but not
before he gave Harman sufficient cash to cover its fair market price; he
liked the horse so much, he forgot about Anna's needs.³⁹

Busy as he was, Jackson found time to send off several letters to his
wife, even if they contain no mention of Little Sorrel. After confirming
his deep love, he told Anna that he was "in tolerable health, probably
better than usual, if I had enough sleep." Jackson again complained
about his inability to rest in a May 8 letter: "I am strengthening my
position, and if attacked shall, with the blessing of Providence, repel the
enemy"; he said nothing about his tiff with Lee over fortification of
Maryland Heights. At Jackson's urging, his wife closed the house in
Lexington—which became a hospital and today a museum—and placed
the servants "in good homes among the remaining residents." She subsequently accompanied a younger brother, who had been dispatched as her
escort to her parents' home in Cottage Hill; except for brief interludes at
her husband's side, she stayed there throughout the war.⁴⁰

Senator James M. Mason, an influential Confederate politician, wrote
to Lee on May 15 following a two-day sojourn at Harpers Ferry: "I
spent the evening and night at Colonel Jackson's headquarters, and even
my limited observation there confirmed the general tone of all around
him, and that all were in good hands under his command." Mason, who
resigned his Senate seat when Virginia left the Union, joined the Maryland fray on Jackson's side; "Maryland is not *suo jure*," he informed Lee:
"She remains one of the United States, a power now foreign to Virginia
and in open and avowed hostility to us. Occupying her territory, therefore, is occupying territory of the enemy." Although Mason was about
to gain notoriety himself when he was seized with John Slidell aboard the
British ship *Trent* while sailing for Europe as Confederate envoy to
England, Lee told him in reply: "Colonel Jackson was directed to give
their occupation (Maryland Heights) the appearance of its being done by
the people of that State, and not to take possession himself till necessary;
but the time has been left to his discretion which I am sure will be wisely
exercised. There is no doubt under the circumstances, of our right to
occupy these heights."⁴¹

Jackson, however, was replaced by Johnston on May 23; though Old
Jack had the confidence of men like Lee and Mason, Jefferson Davis and
his Confederate advisers preferred another for command at Harpers
Ferry. Anna wrote in her *Memoirs* that Johnston was chosen because of
his "higher rank, age, and greater experience." Johnston, who arrived

unannounced to take charge, had known about his command for nearly two weeks. "Having been appointed a brigadier general in the Army of the Confederate States," telegraphed adjutant general Samuel Cooper, and an old friend of Davis, "you have been assigned by the War Department to the command of the troops near Harpers Ferry." Oblivious that his position had been undercut, Jackson even dispatched a lengthy status report to Lee about his command two days before Johnston's appearance. It contains no clue that he was about to be replaced. Lee, who surely knew the particulars of Johnston's elevation, had not bothered to tell Jackson about the power transfer. And the historian can only speculate why.[42]

When Johnston got to Harpers Ferry accompanied by E. Kirby Smith, W. H. C. Whiting, Edward E. McLean, and Thomas L. Preston, he tersely informed a disbelieving Jackson: "In obedience to the orders of the Secretary of War, the undersigned assumes command of the troops at and in the vicinity of this place." Although Johnston had his staff in place—McLean to be quartermaster in place of Harman and Whiting chief engineer—he met a stone wall of resistance before that term found its way into the Confederate lexicon. "Until I receive further instruction from Governor Letcher or General Lee, I do not feel at liberty to transfer my command to another, and must therefore decline publishing the order. . . ." And he signed the reply with his formal title: "T. J. Jackson, . . . Commanding at Harpers Ferry."[43]

Jackson was caught in the events surrounding Virginia's official admission to the Confederacy and the shift of government from Montgomery to Richmond. The new regime was far too busy after the move eastward to worry about the untested colonel at Harpers Ferry. While Old Jack did his best to hold firm, he received his overdue order from Lee on May 25, whereupon he quickly relinquished command. Fearful that Anna would be upset with newspaper accounts of the Johnston takeover, he fired off a quick note to his wife on May 27: "I will now have time to write longer letters to my darling pet," he said in an effort to soften the blow. And he admonished his wife not to "concern yourself with the change."[44]

Although the question remains—Did Lee fail to inform Jackson about Johnston's appointment to spare his feelings or did he simply overlook the matter?—Lee had more than enough to occupy his attention while Jackson commanded at the Ferry. After his visit to the state Episcopal meeting, Lee undertook a hurried trip southward to correct an organizational snafu; before leaving, he wrote to his wife: "I am called down to Norfolk and leave this afternoon. . . . I write to advise you of my absence, in case you should not receive my answers to any letters that may arrive. I have not heard from you since I last wrote. . . ." Lee concluded his May 16 letter with news that his brother Smith, now serving with the Confederate navy, was escorting a Mrs. Stannard around Richmond. "The charming women, you know, always find him out," he mused. Lee had reason to worry about things at home; like Jackson, who encouraged Anna to find refuge with her father in North Carolina, he urged his wife to move from Ravensworth to the home of Edward Turner in Fauquier County. Her abrupt departure from Mrs. Fitzhugh was prompted by the gathering federal army around Centreville and Fairfax Court House on the eve of Bull Run.[45]

The May 16 trip to Norfolk was brought about by Brigadier General Walter Gwynn, whose gesturing had made a mess of his command. Gwynn, who had not seen army service since 1832, had bombarded Richmond with confused dispatches and demands for men and matériels during the initial war preparations. He not only argued with Flag Officer French Forrest at the Norfolk Navy Yard over who was in charge but also with Lee over additional men for his command; after Lee's visit, Gwynn again asked Richmond's approval to call upon the governor of North Carolina for help if "Federal troops in large numbers begin arriving at Fort Monroe." Although Lee gave his blessing to the North Carolina plea, he had had enough of Gwynn's carping. The next day, May 23, Adjutant General R. S. Garnett, who had not yet left on his ill-fated rendezvous in western Virginia, issued Special Order, No. 109. At Lee's behest, Gwynn was told to hand over his troops to Benjamin Huger.[46]

Lee had no sooner returned to Richmond than all Virginia troops were transferred from state to Confederate service. Since Congress recognized no officers above brigadier general, he found himself reduced in rank by one notch. Although he was later reinstated major general by Confederate authorities, his demotion occurred two days after Virginia's official affiliation with the new government. Nevertheless, he supported Davis and Letcher, who worked as one in the days following Virginia's secession ordinance in April, but the state's popular referendum on leaving the Union did not take place until May 23.

Statewide, the official tally—at least the one endorsed by Richmond—overwhelmingly favored secession: 127,950, for; 20,373, against. These numbers, however, did not include the vote of thirty-one counties beyond the Shenandoah Valley. A careful study by historian Otis K. Rice insists the secession vote in transmontane Virginia "cannot be determined" because northwestern Virginia, including Jackson's home county of Lewis, clearly did not favor secession, nor Virginia's link with the Confederacy. The secession referendum became the signal for western Virginia to break away from the mother state and thus confirm the worst fears of Lee and Jackson.

Long-standing differences between the Virginias reached a breaking point in the secession convention of January–April 1861, with ominous consequences for the future; even the convention vote to leave the Union was far from unanimous: eighty-eight, for; fifty-four, against. "Of the 47 delegates from what is now West Virginia in the Secession Convention, 32 voted against secession, 11 for it, and 4 did not vote. Two of those who did not vote later signed the ordinance, as did also two of those who had voted in the negative. The number of those favoring secession was therefore 15." After considerable trepidation and downright personal bravery in war-charged Richmond, the western delegates headed across the mountains to make certain their part of Virginia remained firmly in the Union. One day after the convention vote, a gathering in Wheeling—at the western terminus of the B & O and far from Confederate Richmond—met to lay plans for the region. Following lengthy debate over immediate statehood versus reorganization of Virginia along Unionist lines, the meeting adjourned to await results of the referendum. The northern panhandle town had long been a hotbed of Unionist sentiment, which caused Jackson to write Lee on May 6 from Harpers Ferry: "The news from the northwest shows great disaffection, especially in Ohio County."

Once Virginia was officially out of the Union, the pronorthern men at Wheeling moved with dispatch. Another convention on June 11–25 not only rejected immediate statehood but opted for a reorganized state government. "With flags flying and the delegates and onlookers singing the *Star Spangled Banner,* the convention condemned the Virginia Ordinance of Secession as treason." A loyalist attorney from western Virginia named Francis H. Pierpont was chosen governor of reorganized Virginia. Before adjournment, the convention added the words "Liberty and Union" to the official seal of the commonwealth. When Lincoln immediately recognized the new government, Virginia fought the Civil War with two governors until 1865, although West Virginia became a separate state two years earlier: Letcher in Richmond and Pierpont in Wheeling and Alexandria. The westerners also elected two U. S. senators, Waitman T. Willey and John S. Carlile, to assume the vacated seats of R.M.T. Hunter and James Mason. Jackson's friend and supporter at Harpers Ferry found himself replaced in Washington by another of his former allies from western Virginia.[47]

Before that, the actions at Wheeling were legitimatized by Yankee firepower, when George B. McClellan crossed the Ohio River into Virginia on May 26 and commenced his trek eastward along the B & O. McClellan's proclamation "To the Union Men of Virginia" before the invasion from Ohio greatly emboldened the westerners to oppose the Confederates in Richmond: "Now, that we are in your midst, I call upon you to fly to arms and support the general government. Sever the connection that binds you to traitors; proclaim to the world that a faith and loyalty so long boasted by the Old Dominion, are still preserved in Western Virginia, and that you remain true to the stars and stripes." And he appealed to the soldiers under his command: "When under your protection, the loyal men of Western Virginia have been able to organize and arm, they can protect themselves, and you can return to your homes with the proud satisfaction of having saved a gallant people from destruction. . . ."[48]

Once across the river, McClellan sped toward the Shenandoah Valley with little or no Confederate opposition. By May 30, Colonel Benjamin F. Kelley, a New Hampshire native, merchant, and railroad agent in western Virginia, had reached Grafton without the loss of a single Union trooper; Jackson had warned Lee three weeks earlier from Harpers Ferry that the important rail junction where the B & O split into lines reaching Wheeling and Parkersburg should be occupied by Confederate forces. But, McClellan noted in his official reports, "the Secessionists had abandoned the town upon Kelley's approach." Confederates in the Monongahela region, commanded by Colonel George A. Porterfield, withdrew southward toward the Staunton Turnpike and passage to safety through the mountains. At Philippi, where a covered bridge—built in 1852 and still in use during the 1980s—crossed the Tygart River, Kelley and Colonel Ebenezer Dumont sprang the trap. "Shortly after dawn on June 3," writes Otis K. Rice, "when their six-pounders heralded their approach at one end of town, the Confederates fled by the other. Neither side lost a single life, but Kelley was severely wounded in what has been called 'the first important inland engagement of the Civil War.' Discredited by the 'Philippi Races' as the action was humorously dubbed, Porterfield retreated to Beverly. On June 8 he was replaced by Brigadier General Robert S. Garnett."[49]

While Lee sat in Richmond, watching Union strength mushroom in front of Washington in anticipation of Bull Run, and Jackson chafed under Johnston at Harpers Ferry, great chunks of western Virginia fell under solid Union control; as the area worked its way toward separate statehood, it remained a constant irritant to Lee and Jackson. Secessionist Virginia, after all, was unable to retain control over her own territory, although former governor and now brigadier general Henry A. Wise dreamed of marching on Wheeling from the Great Kanawha Valley to thwart the new-state makers. When Jackson assumed his Valley command after the Bull Run fight, he experienced repeated difficulties in the region—at Romney and elsewhere. Lee, too, suffered when he took command at Huttonsville following the untimely death of his onetime adjutant Robert S. Garnett. Because Lee and the Confederate high command were forced to concentrate on the western mountainous regions of Virginia herself, they found themselves having to fight a multifront war. Like Germany in two future world wars, Lee and the Army of Northern Virginia were unable to achieve ultimate victory in part because they could never overcome a two-edged military threat.

9

Stonewall

Military reverses in western Virginia were soon overshadowed by Irvin McDowell's gathering army along the Potomac. From the moment Jefferson Davis moved his headquarters to Richmond, Abraham Lincoln meant to strike down the Orange and Alexandria Railroad toward the Confederate capital. "On to Richmond," became the rallying call throughout the North, and McDowell was the man appointed for the initial thrust. "Squarely and powerfully built with a frank and agreeable manner," the forty-three-year-old McDowell had served with Lee in northern Mexico as General John E. Wool's aide-de-camp. And, like Lee at Richmond, he had performed miracles by whipping disorganized northern units into a potent fighting machine in the weeks following his May 28, 1861, appointment to command the Army of Northeastern Virginia. By July 16 when he crossed the river into Virginia, he had a thirty thousand man army organized into five divisions with numerous cannon. His subordinate commanders were likewise seasoned soldiers: generals Daniel Tyler and Theodore Runyon, and colonels David Hunter, Samuel P. Heintzelman, and Dixon S. Miles. [1]

As McDowell marshaled his army around Washington, aging General Robert Patterson amassed another eighteen thousand men at Chambersburg, Pennsylvania, to threaten Harpers Ferry and the Shenandoah. Although Winfield Scott—still nominal commander of the northern army—held the sixty-nine-year-old holdover from the War of 1812 and Mexico in considerable esteem, Patterson himself had reservations about active field command. Still, he intended, in his own words, "to move through Hagerstown, Maryland, where the railroad from Harrisburg ended, cross the Potomac at Williamsport, and attack Harpers Ferry." Patterson's planned attack against Joe Johnston and Tom Jackson had been conceived by Scott as a coordinated attack with McDowell's move into northern Virginia. But Patterson's timidity in mid-July, when he marched south, failed to halt Johnston's march across the Blue Ridge on the eve of battle.[2]

Meanwhile, Lee and Jackson played major roles in the Confederate strategy to counter Scott's two-pronged threat. Feverish preparations on both sides of the Potomac propelled North and South toward the first grand engagement of the war. And the hard years of military discipline hurled both Lee and Jackson into the national conscience during the resulting battle of Bull Run, or First Manassas; six hectic weeks had passed since the warriors parted company at Camp Lee—Jackson for the defense of Harpers Ferry and Lee to fret away his time as military adviser first to Governor Letcher and then Jefferson Davis. Nor would they meet face-to-face until June 1862—nearly a year later—and their famous conference in Mr. Dabbs' house outside Richmond on the eve of the Seven Days campaign. Jackson not only marched over the Blue Ridge with Johnston's command at the first word of McDowell's advance, but he soon found himself at a crucial juncture on the Manassas battlefield, where, opposite the Stone Bridge across Bull Run creek, his performance on July 21 put him in the American lexicon as "Stonewall." Although Lee did not accompany Davis and his entourage to Bull Run to view the battle, it was his fertile mind that sent McDowell and his Yankee columns reeling back upon the Washington defenses.

Twelve days before the official transfer of Virginia troops to Confederate command, Lee had traveled to Manassas Junction and Fairfax Court House. His trip was part of the general preparations for war; when he inspected the southern positions under General Milledge L. Bonham strung out along the Warrenton Pike beyond Centreville, he was seemingly satisfied that all had been done that could be done. "While at Manassas," he wrote a nervous Joe Johnston at Harpers Ferry,

I made the following arrangements of light troops: A corps of observation, of cavalry and infantry has been established under Colonel [Richard S.] Ewell, in advance of Fairfax Court House, the right extending toward Occoquan, the left to the Leesburg Road. Col. Eppa Hunton, commanding at Leesburg, has been ordered to have an advance post at Dranesville, and to extend his scouts down the Alexandria and Leesburg roads, to communicate with Colonel Ewell. He is to inform you of any movement of the U. S. troops in the direction of Leesburg, tending to threaten your rear, through Captain [Turner] Ashby at Point of Rocks. In the event of such a movement, I would suggest a joint attack by you and General

Bonham, commanding at Manassas, for the purpose of cutting them off. . . .

Although Beauregard and others who actually directed the campaign would make minor adjustments to Lee's plans, the basic scheme to thwart McDowell's march toward Richmond had been fixed: Joe Johnston would head for a linkup with the main Confederate force around Manassas Junction at the first sign of trouble.[3]

Lee presented his plan to Jefferson Davis and the Confederate brass at Richmond; yet any thoughtful soldier might have reached the same conclusions. Colonel Philip St. George Cocke, first ordered to northern Virginia by Governor Letcher, had foreseen the plan now propounded by Lee. "It is obvious sir, with a strong *corps d' armee* at Manassas, and at least a division at Winchester, these two bodies being connected by a continuous railway through Manassas Gap, there should be kept at all times upon the road ample means of transportation," he informed Lee on May 15 from Culpeper. "The two columns—one at Manassas and one at Winchester," he added, "could readily cooperate and concentrate upon one point or the other, either to make head against the enemy's columns, advancing down the Valley, should he force Harpers Ferry, or, in case we repulse him at Harpers Ferry, the Winchester supporting column could throw itself on this side of the mountains, cooperate with the column at Manassas and all that can come up in the rear of this line, to hurl back the invader, should he attempt to march beyond the Potomac upon Virginia's soil."[4]

The opening moves did not take place in the Manassas sector, where Beauregard had assumed command on June 2, but in the Shenandoah Valley against Joe Johnston. And Colonel Tom Jackson played a conspicuous part in the ensuing actions. Patterson left his bivouac near Chambersburg on June 12, and three days later he had occupied Hagerstown, Maryland, within three or four miles of the Williamsport crossing; just as Lee and Davis meant to bring the armies of Johnston and Beauregard together at the critical moment, Union strategists applied their whole energy to keeping them apart. Winfield Scott personally telegraphed an anxious McDowell: "If Johnston's force joins Beauregard he should have Patterson on his heels." With that assurance, writes William Swinton, "which provided that Johnston's force in the Shenandoah Valley should be neutralized, General Patterson was, on the 2nd of July, again ordered across the Potomac from Maryland. He made the passage of the river at Williamsport, and took possession of Martinsburg. The specific duty assigned to Patterson was, in view of the impending battle in front of Washington, to defeat Johnston or prevent his making a junction with Beauregard at Manassas." It was Patterson's second intrusion into Virginia within two weeks, but this time the old campaigner did not fall back; although he continued to pressure the Confederates with his eighteen thousand-man force, he failed to keep Johnston in the valley, and he was forced to resign his commission a few weeks afterward.[5]

Once Johnston assumed the reins at Harpers Ferry, Jackson's official correspondence with Lee in Richmond ceased; still, no less than thirteen of his letters before the fight at Manassas to Anna and to his political friend from northwestern Virginia, J. M. Bennett, appear in the compilations by his wife and nephew. And they afford an insight into his personal and military frustrations during the opening drama of Civil War. When Anna chided him for not keeping her posted about his movements: "I suppose you meant military news, for I have written you a great deal about your *esposo* and how much he loves you. What do you want with military news? Don't you know that it is unmilitary and unlike an officer to write news respecting one's post? You wouldn't wish your husband to do an unofficer-like thing, would you? I have a nice green yard, and if you were here, how much we could enjoy it together! But do not attempt to come, as before you get here [Harpers Ferry] I might be ordered elsewhere." He added: "The troops here have been divided into brigades, and the Virginia forces under General Johnston constitute the First Brigade, of which I am in command."[6]

Jackson was clearly disenchanted with his subordinate position as well as Johnston's subsequent decision to abandon Harpers Ferry. His men were "dispirited," he told Anna, when ordered to retire: "I hope the general will do something soon. Since we left Harpers Ferry an active movement towards repelling the enemy is, of course, expected. I trust that through the blessing of God we shall soon be given an opportunity of driving the invaders from this region." His hope of victory aside, Jackson explored the possibility of transfer before he marched from the Potomac; when Bennett wired from Richmond suggesting that he be promoted to brigadier general and sent to command in northwestern Virginia, he was quick to respond. "Your very kind letter . . . has been received and meets my grateful approbation. The sooner it is done the better. Have me ordered at once. That country is now bleeding at every pore. I feel a deep interest in it and have never appealed to its people in vain, and trust it may not be so now. . . ." Unsatisfied with that attempt to leave Johnston, Jackson dispatched an identical letter "by private hands" the same day.[7]

Harpers Ferry had been Tom Jackson's first command, and he desperately wanted to hold it for personal and strategic reasons, although Johnston took one look at the surrounding terrain and said no. "Maps and intelligent persons of the neighborhood, told me that the principal route into 'The Valley' from Pennsylvania crossed the Potomac, and the railroad at Martinsburg, at least twenty miles west of the garrison, and of course beyond its control," Johnston later penned. And he was correct—if Patterson traveled down the Valley Pike he would completely bypass the place. "Harpers Ferry is untenable against the army of any force not strong enough to hold the neighboring heights north of the Potomac and east of the Shenandoah, as well as the place itself," Johnston continues. "Artillery on the heights above mentioned to the north and east could sweep every part of this place. As the rivers are fordable at various points it is easy to turn or invest the place, or assail it from the west." Although Jackson sought to fortify the Maryland Heights before Lee reversed him, Captain William Poague, who was present, thought Johnston demonstrated "fine military judgment in giving up Harpers Ferry." After a barrage of letters between Harpers Ferry and Richmond, Johnston's command left on June 15 for Winchester.[8]

With the arrival of fresh troops during mid-June, Johnston reorganized his force into four brigades under Bernard Bee, Tom Jackson, Arnold Elzey, and Francis S. Bartow. A fifth brigade under E. Kirby Smith was added later; besides Johnston, who was wounded at Fair Oaks, not one of his commanders escaped the war unscathed: Bee and Bartow were killed at First Manassas, and Smith was severely wounded; Jackson died at Chancellorsville, and Elzey received nasty wounds at Cold Harbor.

Jackson's First Brigade, composed of four regiments broken into forty-nine companies, was made up entirely of men from the Shenandoah. Shortly immortalized as the "Stonewall Brigade," his outfit consisted of the Second, Fourth, Fifth, and Twenty-Seventh Virginia regiments, each with its own moniker. "The Second was called The Innocent Second because it refrained from pillaging," writes a brigade historian. "The Harmless Fourth received that name for its good behavior in camp, and the Fighting Fifth for the opposite reason. The large element of Irishmen was partly responsible for the sobriquet, The Fighting Twenty-Seventh, though in time it justified its name by an extraordinary casualty rate in battle." Also attached to Jackson was the Rockbridge Artillery, led by William Nelson Pendleton, the Episcopal clergyman, and later, the Thirty-Third Virginia, which became known as "The Lousy Thirty-Third." Johnston's other brigades had units from Georgia, Mississippi, Alabama, Tennessee, Maryland, and Kentucky.[9]

Upon Johnston's withdrawal to Winchester, Jackson was posted to Camp Stephens, near Martinsburg, to guard against any enemy intrusion; cavalry patrols under Patterson and Stuart had sparred for weeks along the Potomac until July 1, when infantry units crossed the river at Williamsport. Jeb Stuart, a man about to make his own mark in this war, instantly alerted Jackson that Patterson was on the march. Never a man to equivocate before shot and steel, Jackson rushed down the Valley Pike to meet the oncoming Yankees on the morrow; and near Falling Waters, where the Potomac makes a giant westward bend to almost touch the Shenandoah roadway, the First Brigade fought its initial engagement.[10]

One day after the fight, Jackson wrote in his official report:

Having received instructions from you [Johnston] not to fall back unless the enemy were in force. . . . I immediately ordered forward Colonel [Kenton] Harper and Captain Pendleton's battery. . . . After advancing a short distance I left three pieces of the battery. On reaching the vicinity of Falling Waters I found Federal troops indicated by Colonel Stuart. . . . From a house and barn we took possession of an apparently deadly fire was poured on the advancing foe until our position was being turned, when, in obedience to my instructions, Colonel Harper gradually fell back. Soon the enemy opened with his artillery, which Captain Pendleton, after occupying a good position in the rear and waiting until the advance sufficiently crowded the road in front, replied with a solid shot, which entirely cleared the road in front.[11]

Although subsequent writers have embellished the clash, his own report remains the best account. The battle—Joe Johnston dubbed it the "affair at Falling Waters"—not only earned Jackson a commendation from the general commanding and a brigadier's star, it also made him known throughout the army and by the general public. "Jackson had met the enemy with the skill and nerve of the trained soldier," writes John Esten Cooke. "And his men told afterward with admiration how, while writing a dispatch in the midst of the action, a cannon ball which tore the tree above his head to splinters had not made him move a muscle or discontinue his occupation. . . . Such incidents are not trifles in war." Beyond that, Cooke's oft-repeated assertion that Pendleton had called out, "Aim low, men! and may the Lord have mercy on their souls," when his six-pounder opened fire may not have been correct. William

Thomas Poague, who served the gun, says flat-out that it never happened, and Pendleton himself relates only that when the enemy came within range: "I instantly had the gun directed, with careful instructions on how it should be aimed. In another moment the messenger of death was on its way. Not a man or a horse remained standing in the road. . . . Our next shot was aimed with equal care at one of their cannon in a field on the left of the road. The effect was scarcely less." In a postscript, he declared: "The instructions for aiming the gun on this occasion were: 'Steady now; aim at the horses' knees.' " Jackson says nothing in his battle account about the incident.[12]

Whatever the particulars, Jackson had carried the day with 'a whiff of grapeshot' and a victory-starved Confederacy was quick to show its appreciation. He had lost but two men killed and less than ten wounded during the fleeting encounter in which Harper had only 380 men engaged besides Pendleton's complement of gunners. And, writes John W. Thomason, "James Ewell Brown Stuart, riding alone in the woods on the edge of the fight, came unexpectedly upon a company of Pennsylvania volunteers, ordered them to surrender before they could decide what to do about it, and brought them in prisoners." Jackson singled out Stuart for praise, but it was Joe Johnston's dispatch to Richmond that conveyed the hoped-for news: "I therefore respectfully recommend that Colonel Jackson be promoted without delay to the grade of brigadier general and Lieutenant Colonel Stuart to that of Colonel."[13]

Although Anna was told that his troops had "behaved beautifully," Poague hints that the First Brigade had been bloodied: "A curious mental exaltation seized us; an inward questioning as to whether it was all a dream. But then came a boom from our gun! And another! Presently a limping man supported by a comrade comes: Blood dripping from his sleeve! Yes, the war is on!"[14]

Victorious gunfire also brought military recognition. Within hours of Falling Waters, Robert E. Lee wrote to Jackson from his Richmond office: "My dear general, I have the pleasure of sending you a commission of brigadier-general in the Provisional Army, and to feel that you merit it. May your advancement increase your usefulness to the State." Lee's commendation did not reach him until later, but an ecstatic General Jackson forgot his pledge not to burden Anna with his military exploits; he dashed off a lengthy letter from his camp near Darkesville that practically recounted all particulars in his official report. "On the 3rd I did nothing more than join General Johnston," he told her in a later missive from Winchester. "My promotion was beyond what I had anticipated, as I only expected it to be in the volunteer forces of the State. One of my greatest desires for advancement is the gratification it will give my darling. . . . I have all that I ought to desire in the line of promotion. I should be very ungrateful if I were not contented, and exceedingly thankful to our kind Heavenly Father." He said nothing about the entreaties to Bennett to win promotion and an independent command. [15]

Significantly, Jackson had strengthened his position two weeks earlier, when Johnston moved his headquarters to Winchester and directed him to disrupt the B & O as the army withdrew southward. And he later informed Anna: "It was your husband who did so much mischief at Martinsburg [on June 20]. To destroy so many fine locomotives, and railroad property was a sad work, but I had my orders, and my duty was to obey. If the cost of the property could only have expended in disseminating the gospel of the Prince of Peace. . . ." Jackson may have been as religious as ever, but destroy he did! More than forty engines and pieces of rolling stock were burned or rolled into Opequan Creek. Several engines were sent down the tracks to Harpers Ferry and Winchester as the roadbed and bridges were destroyed before Patterson's advance. [16]

After Falling Waters, Jackson and the First Brigade fell back to Darkesville, a few miles below Martinsburg, to await the onslaught, but Patterson contented himself with an occupation of the latter place. Reinforcements were rushed to the crossroads hamlet six or seven miles south of Patterson and, writes Joe Johnston: "We bivouacked there in order of battle as the Federal army was supposed to be advancing to attack us. We waited in the position four days, expecting to be attacked because we did not doubt that General Patterson had invaded Virginia for that purpose." But an ever-timid Patterson overestimated the size of Johnston's force and refused to press the offensive, although he later moved down the Valley Pike as far as Bunker Hill. James Dabney McCabe opines that "the lesson taught him at Falling Waters was not without its effect." Once convinced that Patterson had no intention of attack, Johnston withdrew to Winchester while the former remained at Martinsburg. A two-week hiatus ensued, as Yankee and Confederate stared at each other until July 18, when word came that Jackson and the rest of Johnston's army were needed on the field at Manassas. [17]

Meanwhile, McDowell's advance units had occupied the area around Alexandria as Confederate vedettes under Bonham and Ewell kept a close watch. Vice President Hamlin visited the front at Falls Church because "he was intent upon seeing how a rebel picket looked at short range." Then, two weeks after Falling Waters and more than a little prodding from President Lincoln, the blue-coated legions were set in motion at 2 P.M., July 16, when Ambrose Burnside led his regiment across the Long Bridge out of Washington. McDowell's order of march had been set the previous evening at a general staff meeting: Three great columns would proceed along the Orange and Alexandria Railroad, the Little River Turnpike, and the Vienna Post Road. One column veered off to march down the road built by Sir Edward Braddock during the French and Indian War. McDowell's converging columns were intended to envelop Bonham's outposts at Fairfax Court House, but those units fell back toward the safety of Bull Run Creek before the massed federals.

Except for occasional firefights with retreating skirmishers and fallen abatis, McDowell's columns went forward without mishap other than picayunish delays of the march; primarily, his men were unprepared for extended tramping across the Virginia countryside. "We did not follow altogether the country roads, but tried to shorten the distance by short-cuts across the country, through wheat and corn-fields," writes Edwin S. Barrett. "Women scowled at us from the doors and windows of their houses, children fled in terror, but the slaves could not conceal their delight, and were always ready to do us service. We had captured some rebel scouts on the march, but they were sullen and silent, and not interesting to look at. . . ." In the opening campaign of the great crusade, northern soldiers, conditioned by decades of abolitionist rhetoric, made no secret of their intention to help southern blacks toward freedom; the oncoming Yankees knew where the main conflict lay—slaves had to be released from bondage. When General Daniel Tyler's division encountered several blacks along the route to Centreville, he told them "to go where they pleased!" "These were the first slaves manumitted under martial law, my procedure antedating General [Benjamin] Butler's action at Old Point Comfort," he noted proudly. When summoned before Winfield Scott, Tyler insisted that his "captured slaves had been turned over to the quartermaster and told to take care of themselves." Scott, he added, "appeared satisfied."[18]

At Richmond, however, Robert E. Lee was distressed and perhaps ill as McDowell's troopers lay concentrated about Fairfax Court House by nightfall on July 17. Forced to the sidelines as the two armies maneuvered for advantage, his discomfort stemmed in part from Mrs. Lee's forced abandonment of her home during the federal advance; Arlington House overlooks the Capital City, and McDowell himself soon took the plantation as his headquarters. "I am temporarily in camp on the grounds, preferring this to sleeping in the house, under the circumstances which the painful state of the country place me," he assured Mrs. Lee on May 30. "It has been and will be my earnest endeavor to have all things so ordered that on your return you will find things as little disturbed as possible. In this I have the hearty concurrence of the courteous, kind-hearted gentleman in the immediate command of the troops quartered here, and who lives in the lower part of the house to insure its being respected." She had written to admonish Union officers about the house and its furnishings. McDowell, conscious of the social standing of Mrs. Lee as George Washington's granddaughter, promised that she could return "whenever she desired." But neither of the Lees ever lived at Arlington again; the historic mansion and grounds were sold for delinquent taxes later in the war by Virginia's Unionist government.[19]

Permanent loss of Lee's home lay in the future as McDowell made ready for his drive to Richmond. Yet Lee was not a contented man! "I am very anxious to get into the field, but am detained by matters beyond my control," he wrote to Mrs. Lee four days before Burnside tramped across the Long Bridge below Arlington. "I have been labouring to prepare and get into the field the Virginia troops, and to strengthen those from other States, the threatened commands of Johnston, Beauregard, Huger, Garnett, etc. Where I go I do not know, as that will depend upon President Davis. As usual in getting through a thing, I have broken down a little and had to take to my bed last evening, but am in my office this morning [July 12] and hope will soon be right again."

When James Chesnut of South Carolina, a former U. S. senator and member of the Confederate Congress, arrived from Manassas July 16 with an appeal from Beauregard to change from a defensive to an offensive posture, Jefferson Davis retained his high confidence in Lee's judgment. Although the Confederate president was incapacitated by an attack of nervous prostration himself, he joined Lee and Adjutant General Samuel Cooper to hear Beauregard's somewhat fanciful scheme. "General Johnston should with the bulk of his forces, say twenty thousand, unite with [Beauregard], leaving from three to five thousand men to guard the passes of the Blue Ridge and to hold Patterson in check. Then, with the combined forces of General Johnston and [Beauregard], move rapidly forward on Fairfax Court-House, establish yourself with larger masses, and thus exterminate them or drive them into the Potomac." After disposing of McDowell, the combined army would then turn its attention to Patterson. According to Chesnut, the plan was thought "brilliant and comprehensive," but "objections were urged by the President and General Lee." Lee's earlier plans would remain in place because "they thought the enemy was too close" for Beauregard's strategy to succeed. "Mr. Chesnut left at day light, disheartened," his wife wrote on July 14. "Beauregard sent him to get permission for Johnston and himself to join & rush the enemy over the Potomac," but Mary

Chesnut added later: "At Manassas the President proved right & Beauregard wrong!"[20]

Lee, too, had reason to be downcast when the battle commenced. When a wire arrived that fateful Sunday morning saying Beauregard and Johnston had engaged the enemy, Davis immediately headed north on a commandeered train. "With total disregard of the desperate urge of Lee to be at the scene where he laid the foundation of defenses, the President ignored the soldier. As acting aide-de-camp, he took along his nephew, Joseph R. Davis, a lawyer," notes historian Clifford Dowdey. And the question persists about whether Jefferson Davis purposely ignored his military confidant or whether it was a mere *faux pas*; further, he could have well chosen to rely upon his training and judgment in an hour of crisis. Outwardly undaunted, Lee's letter to his wife after the First Manassas could not mask his disappointment: "That was indeed a glorious victory and heightened the pressure upon our front amazingly. Do not grieve for the brave dead. . . . I hope God will again smile on us and strengthen our hearts and arms. I wished to partake in the former struggle, and am mortified at my absence, but the President thought it more important that I be here. I could not have done as well as has been done, but I could have helped, and taken part in the struggle for my home and neighborhood."[21]

As Lee sat helplessly and Jackson anticipated a quick march from Winchester upon McDowell's advance, Beauregard and the Confederate defenders at Manassas made their troop dispositions behind Bull Run, a tributary of the larger Occoquan, which flows into the Potomac three or four miles downstream from Mount Vernon. "The country in the valley of Bull Run and its tributaries was for the most part woodland. The current of Bull Run was not rapid, but the banks were abrupt, often rocky and precipitous, so that it could not readily be crossed except at bridges and fords. The higher ground afforded quiet slopes and plateaus, but everywhere so many trees had been allowed to grow that the farms were like glades of more or less expanse in the midst of the forest." Level terrain and the scarcity of reference points meant Beauregard and McDowell were forced to rely upon maps and charts to develop their battle plans. West of Centreville—a distance of three miles, Bull Run was spanned at the soon-to-be famous Stone Bridge along the Warrenton Pike and by the Orange and Alexandria Railroad bridge three and a half miles to the southeast. In between, lay several fords easily accessible to both armies.[22]

The Bull Run crossings were critical, and by July 17–18 Beauregard had his defensive line in place: From right to left, the fords and the brigade at each, designated by the commander, were Union Mills, Richard Ewell with Jubal Early in reserve; McLean's, D. R. Jones; Blackburn's, James Longstreet; Ball's and Lewis's, Philip St. G. Cocke; at the Stone Bridge on the extreme left, N. G. Evans's demibrigade. "The Confederate line was nearly eight miles in length," and, comments T. Harry Williams, "even before he received one soldier from Johnston, Beauregard had concentrated his forces on the right." His strength was not at the Stone Bridge and Warrenton Pike but along the southern fords.[23]

Beauregard sprang to action during July 16, when a ciphered message reached Fairfax Court House from his contact in Washington, Mrs. Rose O'Neale Greenhow. The courier was "young Betty Duval who had concealed the small note in the coils of her long black hair and proceeded down the Potomac on the Maryland side, crossed near Dumfries, and reached General Bonham's headquarters." The message was short but powerful: "McDowell has certainly been ordered to advance on the sixteenth." Although "Old Borey" would soon know that McDowell was on the march when Bonham was obliged to abandon his forward lookout, he immediately dispatched the news from Mrs. Greenhow to Richmond. The official record is silent about Lee's role in the subsequent war preparations, but Jefferson Davis lost no time with his order to Johnston at Winchester: "General Beauregard is attacked. To strike the enemy a decisive blow, a junction of all your effective force will be needed. If practicable, make the movement, sending your sick and baggage to Culpeper Court House, either by railroad or by Warrenton." And Davis told him: "Exercise your discretion" on the march.[24]

The directive reached Johnston at 1 A.M., July 18, and by noon the Valley command had started its fifty-seven-mile trek to Manassas. Tom Jackson and the First Brigade, who took the van, had reached the Blue Ridge crest at Ashby Gap by 8 P.M., when his Shenandoah boys bivouacked for the night. "Bright and early the next morning we resumed the march, and the head of our column arrived at Piedmont on the Manassas Gap Railroad, about six o'clock in the morning. After getting our breakfast, the brigade commenced going aboard the cars, and the same day all that could be carried arrived at Manassas about four o'clock in the afternoon without much suffering to my men or myself," he told Anna. The overstrained railroad from Piedmont Station—present Delaplane—not only broke down from the constant transport, it also experienced time-consuming delays and at least one wreck; operating engineers even insisted on a night's rest amid the going and coming. Though Jackson's men reached the vicinity of Bull Run in record time, the last Confederate units under E. Kirby Smith did not arrive until July 21, when the battle had already started.[25]

At the very hour Jackson's men were wading the waist-deep Shenandoah on the afternoon of July 18, generals Tyler and Longstreet fought the opening duel at Blackburn's Ford, a mile or so from Centreville. McDowell had every intention of pounding the Confederate right and summoned Tyler forward to reconnoiter the southern fords; when four regiments under Colonel I. B. Richardson ran into Longstreet's units, an artillery and infantry fight broke out. Blackburn's Ford, where Confederate infantrymen had been chastised the night before because they left the line to chase rabbits, became a baptism for many on both sides at Bull Run. "About nine o'clock while standing on the breastworks, the loudest cannon I ever heard was fired from the Yankee line," James Franklin, a private in the Eleventh Virginia, later commented.

> The shot struck the ground very near a piece of the Washington artillery. . . . The second struck just to our left, and just in front of General Bonham's South Carolina Brigade, and very near Kemper's Virginia Battery of Artillery. The third shot was shell and exploded. In a short time we heard the bugle order of forward from the Yankee line, and then it advanced. The enemy marched right down to the edge of the water, and his two lines did the best they could, but it lasted only a few minutes; when the enemy retreated, then all was as still as midnight.

The "sharp repulse" handed Tyler and Richardson convinced McDowell to abandon his attack at Blackburn and Union Mills Fords and to send his scouts in search of a path around Beauregard's left. He had already decided to attack beyond the Stone Bridge.[26]

When Jackson and the First Brigade arrived the following afternoon, they were posted in a reserve position behind the commands of Bonham and Longstreet; nearby were the brigades of Bee and Bartow. Johnston's entire force, although some were still traveling over the Manassas Gap Railroad, remained "right down to the water's edge" behind Mitchell's, Blackburn's, and McLean's Fords throughout July 20. "Not a sound or shot disturbed the quiet of that long Saturday, and we slept peacefully in the pines that night," writes D. B. Conrad. It was the lull before the storm! Jackson and his fellow brigade captains were kept near the fords as part of Beauregard's persistent dream that he could yet lunge across Bull Run and attack McDowell's main army around Centreville.[27]

> Jackson appeared perfectly calm when the guns began to roar. He was a man who never spoke unless spoken to; never seemed to sleep; had his

headquarters under a tree; the only tent used was that of the adjutant. He walked about alone, the projecting visor of his blue cap concealing his features; a bad-fitting, single-breasted blue coat, and high boots covering the largest feet ever seen, completed his picture. . . . He ate the queerest food, and he sucked lemons constantly; but where he got them during the war, no one could find out—but he always had one. In fact no one knew or understood him. No man ever saw him smile—but one woman, his wife.

Neurotic though he was, according to Conrad, Jackson became the supreme soldier once the battle opened on July 21. At Bull Run, notes John Esten Cooke, Jackson saved the day with only 2,611 muskets. "Without them the Federal column would have flanked and routed Beauregard. Bee, forced back, shattered and overwhelmed, galloped up to Jackson and groaned out, 'General, they are beating us back.' Jackson's face did not move. 'Sir,' he said, 'we will give them the bayonet.' Without those 2,611 muskets that morning, goodby Beauregard!" And D. H. Hill, who knew him as well as anyone, thought the excitement of war caused him to forget his hypochondria—that it made him into a new man.[28]

While the First Brigade lay idle throughout Saturday, July 20, Irvin McDowell was busy with his own plans for battle. Federal scouts had located a route up Cub Run, a short distance from Centreville, that would enable his lead divisions to cross the Sudley Ford without difficulty; Daniel Tyler, an experienced railroad man, moreover, recognized the telltale sounds of overtaxed engines beyond the Confederate defenses and alerted McDowell that Johnston's army had given Patterson the slip. Undeterred, the federal commander perfected his offensive strategy for the early hours of July 21: Richardson's brigade of Dixon's Fourth Division would strike south toward Longstreet at Blackburn's Ford while most of the division was held in reserve around Centreville; Tyler's First Division was ordered straight down the Warrenton Pike toward the Stone Bridge, where Nathan G. "Shanks" Evans—his nickname "was a matter of his thinnest members receiving the loudest acclaim"—waited with his demibrigade. Tyler's attack, as well as Richardson's, was intended as a feint or sideshow to the main thrust under David Hunter (Second Division) and Heintzelman (Third Division), who headed for Sudley Ford to outflank Beauregard's left.[29]

The first Yankee brigades reached the Sudley crossing about 9:30 A.M., and immediately turned south toward Evans and Philip St. George Cocke, who held the Confederate left. Tyler reached the Stone Bridge around 6:00 o'clock, "when he opened an artillery fire on the enemy on

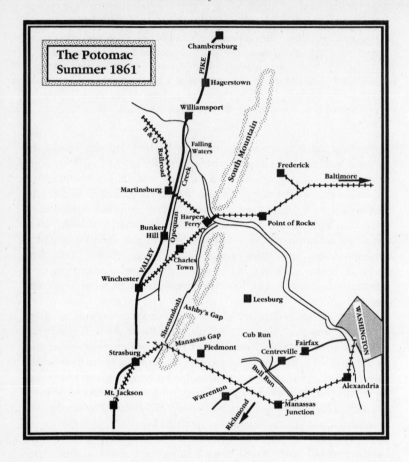

The Potomac
Summer 1861

Chambersburg

PIKE

Hagerstown

Williamsport

B & O Railroad

Falling
Waters

South Mountain

Frederick

Baltimore

Martinsburg

Creek

Opequan

Harpers
Ferry

Point of Rocks

Bunker
Hill

VALLEY

Charles
Town

Winchester

Shenandoah

Ashby's Gap

Leesburg

WASHINGTON

Strasburg

Manassas Gap

Piedmont

Cub Run

Fairfax

Centreville

Bull Run

Mt. Jackson

Warrenton

Richmond

Manassas
Junction

Alexandria

the opposite side of Bull Run." But the wily Evans, a West Pointer, class of 1848, and veteran of the Indian wars, kept his meager infantry well hidden, although his field pieces roared back at Tyler's cannon; not to be outdone, he divided his small band into two units—one opposite Tyler at the Warrenton Pike and the other facing the oncoming columns of Hunter and Heintzelman. As Evans prepared to meet the onslaught, Beauregard climbed an observation tower to catch a glimpse through his spyglass of glistening bayonets crossing Sudley Ford. The beleaguered Evans faced the whole federal fury with "two regiments of infantry, and a squadron of cavalry, and two guns" before Johnston's Valley command rushed to his side.[30]

The brigades of Bartow and Bee rushed to reinforce Evans; they formed a new line, albeit a thin one, a few hundred yards beyond the pike with a streamlet called Young's Branch at their backs. Bee had been afraid to advance lest his colleagues Bartow and Jackson be in positions of greater advantage, and Jackson did not immediately join the movement to assist Evans. "About four in the morning I received notice from General Longstreet that he needed a re-enforcement of two regiments, which were accordingly ordered." Then, continues Jackson's battle report, which is probably the best source for his movements throughout July 21: "Subsequently I received an order from General Beauregard to move to the support of General Cocke, and finally to take such position as would enable me to re-enforce either." Instead of heading toward Bonham and Cocke, whose troops were concentrated around Mitchell's and Ball's Fords on Beauregard's southern flank, Jackson marched to the sound of guns and battle—to the Confederate left—where Bernard Bee was under attack at the Stone Bridge.[31]

By 11:30 A.M., Jackson had posted his guns and John Imboden's battery of Bee's command, as well as his regiments along the south slope of Henry House Hill. "So soon as I had nearly reached the summit of the [Henry] hill, I placed two pieces of Captain Stannard's battery in position, firing at the enemy," Jackson wrote to his Richmond benefactor J. M. Bennett. "I also placed two regiments of infantry (Colonel Preston's and Colonel Echols') in the rear of the battery concealed from the enemy's view. One regiment (Colonel Harper's) was placed on the right of the battery, and principally in the woods. One regiment (Colonel Allen's) was placed on the left of the battery, and the remaining one (Colonel Cummings') on the left of this." And, he told Bennett, all regiments had instructions to charge with bayonets when the federals got within fifty yards. Jackson subsequently had his troops crouch behind the crest of the hill as his line—later intermingled with those of Evans,

Bartow, and Bee—extended about six hundred yards from the home of James Robinson, a free black, and that of Mrs. Judith Henry, aged widow of a former naval officer. Mrs. Henry, who spurned pleas to leave her house, later died in the intense shelling.[32]

Near the Robinson House beside the Warrenton roadway, however, the Confederate right began to waver as Bee's South Carolinians fell back before the federal hordes now commanded by Irvin McDowell himself. With Jackson's shells screaming over their heads from the Henry House Hill, the soldiers under Bee and Wade Hampton became disenchanted and scared. "Now it was time for the birth of a legend," writes William C. Davis. "As the Confederates on Hampton's right were retiring in disorder, men in Jackson's right-flank saw a rider approach. 'He was an officer all alone, and as he came closer, erect and full of fire, his jet-black and long hair, and his blue uniform of a general officer made him the cynosure of all.' " It was Bernard Bee, come to tell Jackson that his brigade was crumbling, and it was here that Old Jack told him, "Sir, we will give them the bayonet!"[33]

As Bee left to rally his men, Jackson, according to Kyd Douglas, turned to a subordinate: "Tell the colonels of this brigade that the enemy are advancing; when their heads are seen above the hill, let the whole line rise, move forward with a shout and trust to the bayonet. I'm tired of this long range work!" And Jackson himself relates what happened next: "At 3:30 P.M. the advance of the enemy having reached a position, I gave the command for the charge of more than brave Fourth and Twenty-seventh, and, under commanders worthy of such regiments, they, in order in which they were posted, obliquely to the left of our batteries, and through the blessing of God, who gave us the victory, pierced the enemy's center, and by cooperating with the victorious Fifth and other forces soon placed the field in our possession." Jackson's battle report listed several trophies—the colors of the First Michigan Regiment and an artillery flag. The First Brigade also had its losses: Eleven officers, fourteen noncoms, and eighty-six privates killed; twenty-two officers, twenty-seven noncoms, and 319 privates wounded; one officer and four privates reported missing.[34]

The undying words that he was "standing like a stone wall" were apparently shouted by Bee as Jackson checked the federal drive. A persistent confusion surrounds what he actually said and, indeed, what he meant to imply, but most writers have relied upon an article in the Charleston (S.C.) *Mercury* announcing Bee's death at Bull Run:

The name of this officer deserves a place in the highest niche of fame. . . . Overwhelmed by superior numbers and compelled to yield before it, Gen.

Bee rode up and down the lines, . . . to stand up and repel the tide which threatened them with destruction. At last his own brigade dwindled to a mere handful, with every field officer killed or disabled. He rode up to Gen. Jackson and said: "General, they are beating us back." The reply was: "Sir, we'll give them the bayonet." Gen. Bee immediately rallied the remnant of his brigade, and his last words were: "There is Jackson standing like a stone wall. Let us determine to die here and we will conquer!"[35]

Since the *Mercury* article, which appeared four days after the battle, refers to the "bayonet story" confirmed by Jackson himself, it is reasonable that the unknown correspondent had the facts about a stone wall correct as well. The debate hinges on whether Bee was speaking about Jackson the man or his entire brigade; as he lay dying at Dr. Chandler's house two years later, Old Jack told his aide-de-camp Kyd Douglas that the honor belonged to his men. But according to General W. H. C. Whiting and others who visited the dying Bee, he complained "that his and Bartow's brigades were hard pressed and that Jackson refused to move to their relief and in a passionate expression of anger he denounced him for standing, like a stone wall and allowing them to be sacrificed." Others on the field at Manassas insist that Bee referred only to Preston's battery of Jackson's brigade. Bee unfortunately died the next day and therefore could never tell the world what he said, or what he meant.[36]

R. M. Johnston, a meticulous student of the battle, is unquestionably right that "someone said something" during the fight, because the nickname was circulating widely within days. Biographies of Jackson that came out in 1863 ("A Virginian") and 1866 (John Esten Cooke) had Stonewall prominently displayed on their title pages; none have been published since without it. Jackson and his wife, moreover, recognized immediately that the fresh acclaim had its advantages. "I commanded the centre more particularly, though one of my regiments extended to the right for some distance. . . . Whilst credit is due to other parts of our gallant army, God made my brigade more instrumental than any other in repulsing the main attack," he wrote home after the battle. And, he admonished: "This is for your information only—say nothing about it. Let others speak praise, not myself." But Jackson was not so modest in his letter of July 28 to Bennett: "You will find when my report shall be published, that the 1st brigade was to our army what the Imperial Guard was to the First Napoleon—that, through the blessing of God, it met the thus far victorious army and turned the fortunes of the day."

There can be no questions that Jackson stood the test, although he said nothing about the timely arrival of E. Kirby Smith—called by some, the

Blücher of Manassas—and others to bolster Beauregard's entire position. Nor did he escape unharmed, a fact he relayed to his Richmond benefactor; to Anna, however, he poured out the details: "Although under a heavy fire for several continuous hours, I received only one wound, the breaking of the longest finger of my left hand; but the doctor says the finger can be saved. It was broken about midway between the hand and the knuckle, the ball passing on the side next to the fore finger." Jackson said his horse was also wounded but like himself had escaped serious injury; his coat received "an ugly wound near the hip," which his servant repaired "so that it doesn't show very much." Realizing that his wife, who remained his champion until the end of her long life, would read newspaper accounts of the battle, he may have been reassuring her that he was not hurt. "Though he was so reticent of his own part in the battle, it was well known that his brigade saved the day, the credit of which was justly given to its commander," Anna Jackson wrote later. Because of Bee, she added, "he was christened in the baptism of fire, with the name that he was henceforth to bear, not only in the Southern army, but in history, of STONEWALL JACKSON, while the troops that followed him that day counted it glory enough to bear on their colors the proud title of the 'Stonewall Brigade.' " Mrs. Jackson is perfectly correct. Whatever happened on the Henry House Hill that July afternoon, her husband has been Stonewall Jackson ever since.[37]

Once Jackson "gained possession of the field," Beauregard ordered the entire Confederate line to move forward at four o'clock. Although he held superior rank, Joe Johnston stayed in the rear upon his arrival from Winchester and left the actual fighting to Old Borey, but he took an active part by directing newly arriving troops under Jubal Early and Theophilus H. Holmes besides those of E. Kirby Smith to the line. Jackson held the crucial ground and, with bayonets and captured guns— at one time, says one biographer, he had twenty-six pieces in action—he charged the federals until McDowell's whole center collapsed; and the once-proud Yankee army broke for the safety of Bull Run. The fearsome cannon fire that sent federals scurrying for cover was heard by Private John H. Worsham of the Twenty-first Virginia Infantry as he trekked westward from Staunton and Buffalo Gap toward the fighting in transmontane Virginia, more than one hundred miles from the battleground. "The firing was as distinct that day as I heard afterwards that was five to six miles off."[38]

What began as a retreat soon degenerated into a pell-mell debacle, as blue-coated soldiers, tired and thirsty under a grueling July sun, ran for safety. And they lost no time in getting there! By the next morning,

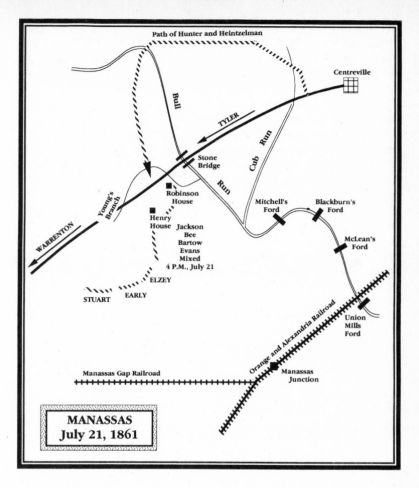

writes Bruce Catton, "human fragments of the routed army drifted up and down the streets of Washington, clotting the sidewalks and alleys, eddying sluggishly about the bars, as soiled and depressed to see as the fragments of the broken republic itself. President Lincoln, like everyone else including Confederate sympathizers in the capital, saw McDowell's dispirited army roaming the streets, realized the need to revamp Federal strategy." Still, Lincoln faulted neither McDowell nor Patterson for the debacle, although two days later he issued a detailed "Memoranda of Military Policy Suggested by the Bull Run Defeat," and summoned General George B. McClellan from western Virginia to reorganize the army "Around Washington and Arlington."[39]

Serious northern weaknesses were evident in the battle returns: McDowell had lost 2,645 killed, wounded, and missing out of 28,500 men engaged; the same figures for Beauregard and Johnston were 1,981 casualities out of 32,232 effectives. The northern army had not only been outnumbered it had also suffered greater losses; the defeat might have been even worse had the Confederates charged toward Washington following the rout. But Jefferson Davis, who had arrived while the guns roared, said no! upon conferring with his commanders. The great Napoleon, after all, had cautioned against an organized army attempting to chase down a broken and retreating mob; besides, the Confederate brass said, the heavily defended Potomac lowlands, more than two miles across, lay between them and the capital. Tom Jackson, flushed with victory and the sound of guns, openly protested that the army should pursue the vanquished, but he was forced to bide his time before higher authority. A subordinate commander, although covered with laurels, could hardly overrule the provisional president. The First Brigade had already won lasting fame on the field at Manassas, and the South had won its first great triumph. It was time to rest and to fight elsewhere.

At this point, Winston Churchill asserted nearly a century later, "few outside the Confederacy had even heard of Lee or Jackson," which was unquestionably correct because the enduring reputations of each lay beyond the horizon. As Jackson remained encamped with the army near Centreville and Lee toiled at his desk in Richmond, the prospect of future acclaim seemed remote indeed. Although circumstances would change in the months ahead, Lee was headed for near oblivion when Jefferson Davis unexpectedly ordered him into western Virginia one week after Bull Run to bolster Confederate fortunes among the Old Dominion's transmontane counties. With Richmond aglow in the aftermath of victory, Lee quietly "took time to congratulate Beauregard and his old comrade Joe Johnston on their work at Manassas despite his own

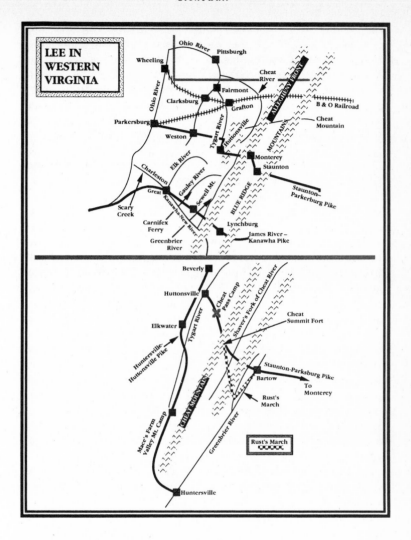

disappointments." "I cannot express the joy I feel at the brilliant victory of the 21st. . . . You and your troops have the gratitude of the whole country," he told Beauregard. And to Johnston, who had just rejected the command Lee was undertaking, Lee wrote: "I almost wept for joy at the glorious victory. . . . The feeling of my heart could hardly be expressed on the brilliant share you had in its achievement." Mrs. Lee remained at White House plantation with Rooney's wife, Charlotte, as her husband set upon a campaign that could only reinforce his feelings of frustration.[40]

Virginia beyond the Shenandoah Valley was federal territory after McClellan's stab along the B & O Railroad right up to the Allegheny crest; ironically, McClellan, who had pushed his lead units beyond the Tygart River at Huttonsville, was traveling east to assume higher command in the Potomac sector at the same moment Lee headed west to undo his advances. But the difficulties confronting Lee were greater than an entrenched and determined foe. The entire region was infested with Yankee sympathizers intent upon destroying the Confederacy and creating a new state loyal to the Union. Lee and other southern commanders in western Virginia were obliged to campaign among a hostile populace who constantly helped the very forces they were trying to defeat. "The Kanawha Valley is wholly traitorous," former governor Henry A. Wise telegraphed from the west at the same time Lee conducted his Cheat Mountain campaign. "It was gone from Charleston down to Point Pleasant before I got here. Boone and Cabell [counties] are nearly as bad, and the state of things in Braxton, Nicholas, and Greenbrier is awful. . . . You cannot persuade these people that Virginia can or ever will reconquer the northwest." Try as they might, not only Lee but also John B. Floyd and Wise could not overcome federal might in the region following McClellan's defeat of General Robert S. Garnett at Carrick's Ford. Within eighteen months of Lee's return to Richmond in failure, the new state of West Virginia had been created from the Old Dominion's fifty westernmost counties.[41]

Meanwhile, Lee trekked out of Staunton on July 29 with his aide, Captain Walter H. Taylor, who later penned an account of the campaign, and arrived at Huntersville on August 4; Colonel John A. Washington, nephew of the first president and owner of Mount Vernon, also served him as aide-de-camp before his tragic death at Elkwater a few weeks later. At Huntersville, described by one trooper "as a most wretched and filthy town, where there were many sick soldiers in a public meeting-house, in public and private buildings, and in tents," Lee encountered Brigadier General William W. Loring. The forty-four-year-old Loring, a lifelong bachelor who lost an arm at Chapultepec, had been ordered by Lee himself to command "the Army of the Northwest" barely a week earlier; when Lee arrived without specific authority from Jefferson Davis other than to oversee military contingencies, Loring was neither pleased nor cooperative. Lee suddenly found himself among hard men who did not take kindly to the genteel aristocrat; he necessarily assumed the role of diplomat in order to calm a delicate situation—his inability to chastise rebellious subordinates became a problem that plagued Lee for the remainder of the war. Not until August 31, when he was promoted to full general, did Loring demonstrate an inclination to work in the common effort; Lee's indecisiveness at Huntersville increased his frustrations, and it also shifted the momentum to his adversaries.[42]

"I travelled from Staunton on horseback," he wrote to Mrs. Lee on August 4. "A part of the road as far as Buffalo Gap, I passed over in the Summer of 1840, on my return to St. Louis, after bringing you home. If anyone had told me then that the next time I travelled that road would have been on my present errand, I should have supposed him insane." He had hoped to visit Rob, Jr., still a student at the university, but failed to locate his youngest son when passing through Charlottesville; he relayed the news that Rooney, whom Lee always called Fitzhugh, then serving with one of Loring's cavalry units, was in good health. Many of the men, he noted, were not as fortunate: "The soldiers everywhere are sick. The measles are prevalent throughout the whole army, and you know that disease leaves unpleasant results, attacks on the lungs, typhoid, etc., especially in camp where accommodations for the sick are poor." After giving his wife a surprisingly accurate description of his troop dispositions, Lee observed: "We must always be on the alert. My uneasiness on these points brought me out here. It is so difficult to get our people, unaccustomed to the necessities of war, to comprehend and promptly execute the measures required for the occasion."[43]

Lee had to deal with Loring's mulishness as well as foul weather; it had rained every day since July 24, he told Mrs. Lee on September 1. Mountainous roads were muddy to the point of uselessness and every stream was overflowing; it was cold enough for ice to form on the night of August 24. Loring, furthermore, refused to march from Huntersville until his slow-moving wagon trains arrived from the Shenandoah Valley. "After remaining several days at Huntersville without gaining any positive information from Loring in regard to his probable advance, he proceeded to join Colonel William Gilham at Valley Mountain," notes General Long. Here, near present Mace, West Virginia, Lee fell back upon his experiences in Mexico and thoroughly reconnoitered the countryside with the help of Taylor, John Washington, and his own son, who had moved his cavalry unit forward to Valley Mountain; one of these scouting expeditions down the Tygart Valley resulted in the September 13 death of Colonel Washington.[44]

When Loring decided to join him a few days later, Lee had about eleven thousand men at his disposal positioned on both sides of Cheat Mountain. At present Bartow, where the Staunton and Parkersburg Pike crossed the Greenbrier River, General Henry R. Jackson, whom Lee had met on his journey to Huntersville, and a onetime congressman from Arkansas, Colonel Albert Rust, had two brigades. Four additional brigades commanded by General D. S. Donelson, and Colonels Jesse S. Burks, William Gilham, and S. R. Anderson, were on the Tygart River or west side of the mountain. "I find that our old friend J. J. Reynolds, of West Point memory, is in command of the troops immediately in front of us," he informed Mrs. Lee. "He is a brigadier general. You may recall him as the Assistant Professor of Philosophy, and lived in the cottage beyond the west gate, with his little pale-faced wife." Rooney Lee had gone into the federal camp under a white flag a few days earlier and had recognized him. Reynolds, who had command in northwestern Virginia after the departure of McClellan, had approximately nine thousand troops encamped at Huttonsville, Elkwater, Cheat Mountain Pass, and Cheat Mountain Summit.[45]

As Lee studied the terrain with its steep precipices from his camp at Valley Mountain, he became convinced that Reynolds had to be attacked at the "fort" on Cheat Mountain Summit; otherwise, he could not unite his own forces located on both sides of the mountain. Then, writes Captain Taylor,

> one of the citizen volunteers, a professional surveyor, having been informed that General Lee was particularly anxious to obtain accurate information of the nature and extent of the enemy on the center-top of Cheat Mountain, undertook the task of reaching such a point on the mountain as would enable him to take a deliberate and careful survey of the fortified position. . . . The only route other than the turnpike by which this point could be reached was by pursuing a course along and up the ragged sides of the mountain, through undergrowth and trees, over rocks and chasms, and with nothing save the compass or the stars to indicate the direction of the summit. The *quasi* engineer made the assent successfully, and obtained a complete view of the enemy's works.

A second reconnaissance followed, in which the Arkansan Rust personally climbed the mountain "to obtain a full, unobstructed view of the entire line of works occupied by the enemy." When Rust reported that a pathway had been found, Taylor continues, "General Lee decided to give battle." It was Mexico all over again—like Lee's route through the Pedregal fifteen years earlier, this one could accommodate neither cavalry nor artillery. It would be only men on foot, struggling along lofty mountainsides and through soggy laurel thickets. But Lee depended upon others to climb the mountain for him and did not make the assent himself; here, perhaps, is where the campaign went astray.[46]

Although Lee initiated a well-conceived attack on the morning of September 12, it was doomed to failure because of inept officers and foul weather. The scheme involved three converging columns; Rust was to leave his bivouac on the Greenbrier River and make his way to the summit; H. R. Jackson was to march from the same point via the Staunton-Parkersburg Pike to assist Rust; and S. R. Anderson was ordered to invest Elkwater on the Tygart from the Valley Mountain Camp along the Huntersville-Huttonsville road. Donelson and Burks were told to rush down both sides of the Tygart in support of Anderson; Gilham was kept in reserve at Valley Mountain. Everything depended upon Rust, who was supposed to fire a single cannon to start the remaining columns once the summit "fort" had been secured.

Rust's march up Cheat Mountain in September 1861 started a fiasco that caused the entire operation in western Virginia to collapse. "With what was supposed to be three days' rations we started out on that memorable march," writes A. C. Jones, one of Rust's officers. "At least thirty miles of the way we had to travel in single file through a trackless wilderness, a good part of it climbing mountains sometimes sloping at an angle of forty-five degrees and frequently compelled to hew our way through thickets of mountain laurel. I do not remember how many streams we crossed, but at one point we were compelled to wade for a mile and a half down the bed of Cheat River, the water nearly waist-high and cold as ice." Upon reaching the summit, Rust and his "miserable human beings" attacked the wrong place and were beaten back by the entrenched federals. Many of his tired, hungry troops threw rifles into the sodden laurel and started back down the mountain without reaching their objective. Meanwhile, Lee, tired of waiting for Rust's cannon shot, launched an uneventful attack down the Tygart Valley and was "stopped cold" at Elkwater. Rust's failure upset the Confederate timetable, as Reynolds quickly seized the opportunity to checkmate Lee's advance.[47]

The Cheat Mountain debacle unquestionably tarnished Lee's reputation at the same time Jackson was basking in the aftermath of Manassas. When Jefferson Davis ordered Lee to undertake an evaluation and strengthening of coastal defenses in the south, the Confederate president was obliged to reassure several governors that he could do the job. And though Lee renewed the attack on September 13, he was again repulsed "when a rifled, 10-pounder Parrott gun from Loomis's battery was run forward and opened fire on the gray-clad ranks, supporting the riflemen who were blazing away without doing much damage." Moreover, Lee was clearly disappointed with his own performance during the campaign. "I cannot tell you my regret & mortification at the untoward events that caused the failure of the plan," he wrote home. "I had taken every precaution to ensure success and counted on it. But the Ruler of the Universe ruled otherwise & sent a storm to disconcert a well-laid plan, & to destroy my hopes."[48]

Although Lee did not file a formal report, he wrote to Governor John Letcher—"for your eye only"—at Richmond in a similiar vein. "We waited for the attack on Cheat Mountain, which was to be the signal till 10 A.M.; the men were cleaning their unserviceable arms. But the signal did not come. All chance for a surprise was gone. . . ." After describing the fighting, Lee concluded: "It was a grievous disappointment to me, I assure you. But for the rain storm it would have succeeded. . . . Please do not speak of it; we must try again." And Rooney's brush with disaster must have shaken him: "Our greatest loss was the death of my dear friend Colonel Washington. He and my son were reconnoitering the front of the enemy. They came unawares upon a concealed party who fired upon them within twenty yards, and the Colonel fell pierced by three balls. My son's horse received three shots, but he escaped on the Colonel's horse." Lee added that he had taken seventy prisoners in the encounter, and again complained about the constant rain and poor roads. But Reynolds had endured the same conditions and managed to turn back his advance. Upon his return to Richmond, writes his nephew, "there were no shouts from the populace . . . the chaplet of victory was missing from his brow, the scalps of Rosecrans and Reynolds missing from his belt. The public looked at the cold facts, and were interested in actual results." Lee never responded to the outcry but quietly resumed his post as military adviser to the provisional president.[49]

Before he left the mountains, Lee had another distasteful task that led to a stalemated engagement with General William S. Rosecrans along the James River and Kanawha Turnpike. After a tiresome and difficult journey over impossible roads, Lee reached Meadow Bluff in Greenbrier County about one hundred miles south and west of Cheat Mountain; he rode into the camp of General John B. Floyd on September 21 and found that discontented commander encamped ten miles east of a second Confederate force, the Wise Legion, under General Henry A. Wise, at the crest of Sewell Mountain. Facing both was Rosecrans, who had moved eastward from Parkersburg on the Ohio River. Lee arrived with only Captain Taylor and a small cavalry escort, but once he studied the countryside Loring was ordered to join him with the brigades of Donelson and Gilham as well as Alexander's cavalry.[50]

Lee walked into a hornet's nest when he entered a festering quarrel between Floyd and Wise—both former governors of the Old Dominion that had thwarted Confederate prospects in the region for several months. Wise, who had been governor during the John Brown insurrection, had organized his "Legion" in western Virginia at the suggestion of Jefferson Davis; he quickly made his headquarters at Charleston, where he encountered a hostile populace as well as a ticklish military situation. Although a part of his force had defeated General Jacob D. Cox at Scary Creek on July 17, when the two crossed swords fifteen miles west of Charleston, Wise was forced to abandon the Kanawha Valley before superior numbers. Captain George S. Patton, whose grandson achieved greater honors during World War II, served under Wise in the battle, which saw minimal Confederate losses. Wise—a brother-in-law of Lee's future nemesis at Gettysburg, George G. Meade—destroyed bridges across Elk and Gauley Rivers as he retreated before Cox's advance up the Kanawha.[51]

John B. Floyd, who had been governor in 1852 as well as Buchanan's secretary of war during the secession crisis, arrived in northwestern Virginia as Wise's senior after raising a company of volunteers; from the first moment, he was determined to exert his authority. What amounted to a war within a war erupted when Wise absolutely refused to accept orders from Floyd—not even military necessity could overcome the memory of nearly forgotten political battles. Proud and strong willed, Wise had bombarded Lee at Valley Mountain with requests to be transferred from the region. The Wise-Floyd correspondence consumes dozens of pages in the *Official Records,* with Wise imploring Lee at one point: "I am willing, anxious, to do and suffer anything for the cause I serve, but I cannot, nor can I consent to command in dishonor. I have not been treated with respect by General Floyd, and co-operation with him will be difficult and disagreeable, if not impossible." Even though Wise refused to support him when Rosecrans attacked earlier, Floyd managed to defeat a federal force at Keslers Cross Lanes on August 26 and at Carnifex Ferry two weeks later.[52]

Although Floyd won two small battles and received a nasty arm wound at Carnifex Ferry, he soon joined Wise in a eastward retreat toward Richmond. When Lee arrived on September 21, he found the two encamped within ten miles of each other and arguing over the best defensive position against Rosecrans's advance. Lee rode to the crest of Sewell Mountain one day after reaching Floyd's camp at Meadow Bluff and quickly determined that Wise held the favorable ground; with the combined forces of Rosecrans and Cox numbering about fifteen thousand, Lee had no choice but to order Floyd westward for a union with Wise. "No little diplomacy was required, therefore, to produce harmony and hearty cooperation, where previously prevailed discord and contention," writes Captain Taylor. "It will be readily understood that the partisans of Floyd at first viewed in no pleasant frame of mind the apparent endorsement of Wise's judgment if not, by a forced construction, the approval of his disobedience and insubordination, implied in General Lee's order that Floyd should forsake his chosen position and return to that persistently held by Wise." Lee said nothing about his troubles when he wrote to Mrs. Lee on September 26 from his "Camp on Sewell's Mountain"; instead, he devoted himself to family matters and complaints about the weather: "It is raining heavily. The men are all exposed on the mountain, with the enemy opposite us. We are without tents, and for two nights I have lain buttoned up in my overcoat. To-day my tent came up and I am in it. Yet I fear I shall not sleep for thinking of the poor men. . . ."[53]

Rosecrans had occupied an adjacent crest of Sewell Mountain and with nothing but intervening crevices the two armies stared at each other until October 8; while he waited atop the peak for Rosecrans to attack, Lee first laid eyes on the immortal Traveller—destined to become his lifelong companion. That great horse belonged to Captain Joseph M. Broun, quartermaster of the Third Virginia Infantry; his brother, Major Thomas L. Broun writes: "He was raised by Mr. Johnson, near the Blue Sulphur Springs, in Greenbrier County Virginia (now West Virginia); was of the Gray Eagle stock, and as a colt, took the premium under the name 'Jeff Davis' at Lewisburg fairs for each of the years 1859 and 1860. He was four years old in the spring of 1861." Lee seemingly did not purchase the animal until February 1862, when he again encountered his owner in South Carolina: Captain Broun had traveled south with units of the Wise Legion after that command was broken up and sent to other theaters. "My brother wrote to me of General Lee's desire to have the horse, and asked me what he should do. I replied at once: 'If he will not accept it, then sell it to him at what it cost me.' He then sold the horse to General Lee for $200 in currency, the sum of $25 having been added by General Lee to the price I paid for the horse in September, 1861, to make up the depreciation in our currency from September, 1861 to February, 1862." General Long, however, cites a letter that Lee dictated to his daughter Agnes after the war which presents a different view: "I purchased him in the mountains of West Virginia in the autumn of 1861, and he has been my patient follower ever since—to Georgia, the Carolinas, and back to Virginia."[54]

Although Lee had nothing but praise for Traveller, the animal was high spirited; at Second Manassas, he bolted while Lee was dismounted, dragging him across a stump and breaking both hands. That episode induced Jeb Stuart to purchase "Lucy Long," a more gentle mare, as a present to Lee. Yet Lee's affection for Traveller remained to the end, though he had several mounts during the course of the war. "Of all his companions in toil," he told Agnes, " 'Richmond,' 'Brown Roan,' 'Ajax,' and the quiet 'Lucy Long,' he is the only one that retained his vigor to the last." A few months following Lee's death in 1870, General Long comments, "Traveller had become almost milky-white having grown hoary with age and honors. He died very soon after the decrease of his master, his death arising from lockjaw caused by his treading on a nail which penetrated his foot and could not be withdrawn."[55]

In September–October 1861 atop Sewell Mountain, both Lee and Rosecrans waited several days for the other to attack; neither man wanted to abandon his defensive works. Rosecrans, however, withdrew first, which may have been something of a Confederate victory, although Lee suffered no delusions about his second setback in western Virginia. The roads were too primitive and the terrain too mountainous for serious campaigning; as he left for Richmond within days of the federal retreat to resume his post as adviser to Jefferson Davis, Lee was not unmindful of the mounting criticism. "I am sorry," he wrote ahead to Mrs. Lee, "that the movement of armies cannot keep pace with the expectations of newspaper editors. I know they regulate matters on paper. I wish they could do so in the field." And then, he added, "no one wishes them more success than I do and would be happy to give them full swing." As a failed leader, Lee incurred the wrath of southern newspapers at the very moment Jackson remained the toast of the hour after his performance at Manassas. In October 1861, Jackson unquestionably enjoyed greater esteem among his countrymen.[56]

10

Intuitive Collaboration

After Lee arrived in Richmond from his abortive campaign in western Virginia, and Jackson remained encamped with the Manassas army at Centreville, the two men had not seen each other since April 1861, when the Confederate forces had mustered at Camp Lee. But Lee had not forgotten the intrepid artillerist he had known in Mexico, nor the physics professor who marched the VMI cadets to John Brown's hanging in December 1859; like others, he was surely aware of Jackson's recent reputation as Stonewall. Although his duties at the president's side were soon interrupted by a four-month tour through the Carolinas, Georgia, and Florida to look after southern coastal defenses, Lee opened a momentous correspondence during April 1862 with Jackson, who had assumed command in the Shenandoah Valley, a correspondence that shaped one of America's most successful military operations. It also led to what one writer later termed "an intuitive collaboration" between the two soldiers that continued unabated until Jackson's death.

The offensive strategy formulated by Lee and implemented by Jackson against Nathaniel P. Banks and John C. Fremont in the Shenandoah established Jackson and his "foot cavalry" among the first rank of military men and also led to George B. McClellan's failure to capture Richmond by marching up the great peninsula formed by the York and James Rivers. When Lee took charge of the Army of Northern Virginia on June 1, 1862, after Joe Johnston's brush with death at Fair Oaks, he already knew that Jackson was the man to carry out his wishes from afar. And their lengthy dispatches in the *Official Records* reveal a subordinate officer who went to great lengths to keep his superiors informed about his every move. Jackson may have been secretive when dealing with his own subordinates to avoid gossip and loose talk while on the march, but when he dealt with Lee he was the most candid of officers.[1]

Jackson remained in northern Virginia until November 4, when he received orders to command in the Shenandoah Valley at Winchester. Lee did not leave Richmond for the southern coast until November 6, which means the Lee-Jackson collaboration did not start until his return and after Jackson had received his independent station; all the while, Jackson and the Stonewall Brigade watched as Joe Johnston sent his outriders to Munson's Hill within sight of Alexandria and Washington to erect the notorious "Quaker guns" fashioned from painted logs. When McClellan balked at an advance against Johnston's "wooden ordnance," one of his critics proclaimed, "we have been humbugged by the rebels." Nor was that the last of it: "On another occasion our people fired at a balloon with cannon shot, and down came the balloon," observes Private David Johnson. "A short while after this, the balloon was up again, when our boys concluded at least to give the man in the basket— Professor Lowe—a scare; so, rigging up the rear gears of a wagon with a stovepipe they ran the improvised artillery to the hilltop, in full view of the aeronaut, pretending to load. The professor descended quickly." Yet Jackson and his company commanders never relaxed their guard at Centreville. Despite the fun and frolic, daily firefights with the enemy demanded that Jackson enforce a rigid military discipline. When Johnston decided to abandon his position around Manassas and withdraw to the Peninsula, Private John Casler observed that "the rail fence all around the field we were camped in had disappeared, and we all had strict orders not to burn a rail. But they were gone, and, of course, nobody did it." At Jackson's order, Colonel A. C. Cummings sent his men into a nearby wood to split enough wood to replace the absent rails.[2]

Jackson spent some of his time around Centreville in a "Sibley tent," but mostly he found accommodations with local families anxious to have prominent officers in their homes. His tent, he told Anna, "is of a conical form, so constructed as to allow a fire to be used, having an opening at the top for the escape of smoke." During August, Jackson complained about the cold weather at night and that his "wounded finger suffered." When a nephew of Napoleon—fresh from a White House reception— passed through the Confederate lines on his way to Manassas, Jackson told his wife: "He spent the night (August 8–9) with General Johnston, took a view of the battle-field yesterday morning and then returned to Washington. I saw him only at a distance." Jackson called upon Jefferson Davis in the company of several officers when he visited Beauregard's headquarters. Never one to pass up a conversation with prominent men, he described the encounter for his wife: "His voice and manners are very mild. I saw no exhibition of that fire which I had supposed him to possess." When Davis discussed conditions in western Virginia, Jackson told him that he had "a very deep interest in it." The president, Jackson added, "spoke very hopefully of that section and highly of General Lee" as the latter struggled with Rosecrans atop Sewell Mountain.[3]

Mrs. Jackson, who left a detailed account, visited her husband at Centreville during September. Jackson had been promoted to major general in August—with Earl Van Dorn, G. W. Smith, and James Longstreet, which made the reunion particularly joyous after their five-month separation. The couple secured accommodations with a family named Utterbach, although Anna took her meals with "him and his staff at their mess-table under the trees" in the family yard. Jackson took his wife on a tour of the Manassas field, no doubt showing her where he had stood "like a stone wall," and when she called upon Joe Johnston for the first time she was impressed with his "soldierly appearance and polished manner." According to her memoir, everyone, including Jackson's head cook, a hired black named George, catered to her every wish.[4]

Anna Jackson no sooner left the Utterbach farm for her father's home in North Carolina than Major General Tom Jackson was caught up in the army reorganization of October 1861. In the aftermath of Davis's visit to the army, he apparently decided to revamp the entire command structure. "About the 1st of November a new military arrangement was made on the northern frontier of Virginia," writes Joe Johnston, "by which my command was extended to the Allegheny on one side and the Chesapeake on the other. . . . It was composed of the 'Valley district,' lying between the Allegheny and Blue Ridge, commanded by Major General Jackson; 'the District of the Potomac,' commanded by General Beauregard, and extending from the Blue Ridge to Quantico; and that of the Acquia [sic], lying between the Quantico and the Chesapeake, commanded by Major General Holmes."[5]

Although Jackson remained under the nominal direction of Johnston, he could not hide his pleasure at going home to western Virginia with his own command of roughly five thousand square miles in the Shenandoah Valley from the Potomac to Staunton. But when he departed Centreville on November 4 for the west, he did so without the Stonewall Brigade, which had been ordered to remain behind. In a near-tearful parting, he rose in his stirrups to address his faithful legion: "In the Army of the Shenandoah you were the First brigade; in the Army of the Potomac you were the First brigade; you are the First brigade in the affections of your general; and I hope in your future deeds and bearing that you will be handed down to posterity as the First brigade in this our second War of Independence. FAREWELL!" Private John Casler who was present, says: "For a moment there was a pause, and then arose cheer after cheer, so wild and thrilling that the heavens rang with them." Jackson watched the outpouring for a few moments, waved his hat, spurred Little Sorell, then rode westward. "We all had the blues," Casler continues, "for we did not want to part with him as our commander. Besides we all wanted to go with him, as nearly all of us came from the different counties in the Shenandoah Valley."[6]

Upon his arrival at Winchester, there can be little question that Jackson had greater ambitions than a mere defense of the Valley. Immediately, he set about organizing and drilling a small band of militia units already at hand, and he launched a campaign to gather troops for a stab into northwestern Virginia. First, his trusted kinsman by marriage Colonel J. T. L. Preston was dispatched to Richmond in an effort to have the Stonewall Brigade transferred to his Valley command. Preston also visited Generals Edward "Allegheny" Johnson at Staunton and William W. Loring, who had taken charge in the northwest upon Lee's departure from Sewell Mountain.

Jackson's efforts began to pay dividends on November 5, when his old company was ordered to Winchester. "Not even a cold rain on Friday, November 8, could dampen the spirits of the Stonewall Brigade as it left camp at Fairfax Court House and marched to Manassas to board trains for the west," writes a brigade historian. "Several jubilant men fortified themselves along the way with whiskey, and according to a member of the Thirty-third regiment, 'there was a jolly time quieting them.' " Now a major general, Jackson could hardly command the brigade himself, so Colonel Preston was made interim commander until the first weeks of December, when General Richard B. Garnett was named as Jackson's permanent replacement. The First Brigade not only had a new chief but most important of all they were back where they belonged—with Old Jack.[7]

Jackson also asked for William W. Loring's command at Huntersville—the same Loring who balked under Lee's orders during the Cheat Mountain fighting and who would presently cause trouble for Jackson himself. Although Robert E. Lee seemed to agree with Loring that his force should remain in northwestern Virginia "to guard the passes," Secretary of War Judah P. Benjamin on November 24 ordered Loring to join Jackson at Winchester. Loring, however, retained independent command over his "Army of the Northwest" and was merely instructed to cooperate with Jackson in what became known as the Romney expedition. The arrival of Loring in late December as well as William B. Taliaferro's brigade a few days earlier, according to the Reverend Dabney, "brought his command to about eleven thousand men, of whom three thousand were militia, while the remainder were volunteer forces of the Confederacy."[8]

While Jackson waited for his army to assemble, he perfected the personal staff that served him throughout the Valley campaign. In his selection of subordinate officers, comments his wife, Jackson never appointed a man "without knowing all about him. He would make inquiries. Was he intelligent? *Did he get up early?* This was a great point with him. If a man was wanting in any of these qualifications, he would reject him, however highly recommended. No feeling of personal friendship, was allowed to interfere with his duty." Major John A. Harman, whom he had used earlier, stayed on as quartermaster; Harman's great knowledge of the Valley, as owner-operator of a stage line along its thoroughfares, served Jackson well in spite of his great fondness for profanity. Wells J. Hawks, a carriage manufacturer in more tranquil times, remained as chief commissary—a chore Jackson knew well from his days in Mexico and Florida. And Jackson's ability to pick the right man for the right job brought him Jedediah "Jed" Hotchkiss as topographical engineer and chief mapmaker. The schoolmaster from New York who settled in the Valley after 1851 became famous for his maps of the country between Harpers Ferry and Lexington, "which showed all the points of offense and defense between those points."[9]

Jackson's perception of men included Captain Turner Ashby, who joined his coterie as cavalry chief; "with his sad, earnest gray eyes, jet-black hair and flowing beard, his lithe and graceful form mounted upon a superb steed, he was a typical knight of the Golden Horseshoe, and his daring and intrepid exploits soon shed a romance around his name," writes Jackson's wife. Ashby became a fighting man personified during the Valley campaign, although his notion that his was an independent command caused some anxious moments before Jackson extended his tight discipline to the cavalry. Following the death of a beloved brother, Captain Richard Ashby, early in the war, Turner Ashby became a changed man, a man with one great commission—to kill as many Yankees as humanly possible. "He evidently regarded his life as no longer his own, and contemplated habitually its sacrifice in the war," notes Dabney. "He was, in his own eyes, a man already dead to the world. His exposure of his person to danger became utterly reckless, and, wherever death flew thickest, thither he hastened, as though he courted its stroke." Ashby and his Black Horse Cavalry harassed Jackson's enemies throughout the Valley fighting until his death near Cross Keys.[10]

As his army assembled in the countryside around Winchester, Jackson laid out his plans for Secretary Benjamin: He would concentrate his entire force on Romney to drive the enemy—about six thousand men—from the South Branch Valley. He thought his thrust against the town might induce McClellan to come out of his fortifications around Alexandria, where Little Mac was opposed by Joe Johnston. But if McClellan did take the offensive, he told Benjamin, "I would at once be prepared to reenforce [*sic*] [Johnston] with my present volunteer force, increased by General Loring's. . . . After repulsing the enemy at Manassas, let the troops that marched on Romney return to the Valley, and move rapidly westward to the waters of the Monongahela and Little Kanawha. . . . I deem it of great importance that Northwestern Virginia be occupied by Confederate troops this winter." Jackson, although he did not say so, proposed to succeed where Robert E. Lee had failed because "the enemy are not expecting an attack there." After considerable debate between Davis and his advisers, who rejected a scheme by Beauregard to invade Maryland, the attack on Romney was approved during the last days of December.[11]

While he waited for Loring, Jackson took Turner's cavalry and the Stonewall Brigade northward to destroy Dam No. 5 on the Chesapeake and Ohio Canal near Martinsburg. The B & O railroad bridge at Harpers Ferry had been destroyed, as well as the tracks to Martinsburg, but the canal connected Washington and Cumberland, Maryland, which gave the federals easy access to coal and other supplies from the west. Running along the northern shore of the Potomac, the canal got its water from a series of sluice dams in the river, the most important being Dam Number 5, "built within a sharp curve, concave toward the south, north of the town of Martinsburg." Jackson transported twenty flatboats with him to the Potomac to mislead federal spies into thinking he was on his way to Maryland; but, writes John Casler, who joined the march, "we halted at the dam and began to destroy it. The enemy on the other side of the river, kept up such a continuous firing that we could not work, so we took the boats up the river opposite Little Georgetown, Md., unloaded them, and made preparations as if we were going to cross. The enemy at once drew all of their forces up there in order to intercept us, and left us free to tear open the dam, which we did." Only one infantryman was lost in the venture.[12]

Jackson returned to Winchester on Christmas Day 1861, to find both

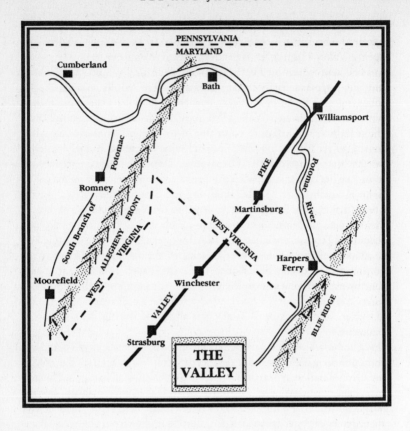

his wife and Loring waiting for him. After her arrival at Taylor's Hotel "in the latter part of cold, dreary December," Mrs. Jackson tells what happened when she could not locate her husband following a tiresome stage journey. As she passed a group of soldiers on the hotel staircase, she thought one of the men looked familiar. "I felt that I must be mistaken. However, my backward glance did reveal an officer muffled up in a military coat, and cap drawn down over his eyes following me in rapid pursuit, and by the time I got to the top step a pair of strong arms caught me in the rear; the captive's head was thrown back, and she was kissed again and again by her husband. . . ."

Six days later, Jackson marched out of Winchester with eighty-five hundred men and five artillery batteries toward Bath (present Berkeley Springs, West Virginia) and Romney, but not before he secured lodgings for his wife with the Reverend J. R. Graham, a local Presbyterian minister. Anna Jackson later penned a memorable passage describing that ideal time in her married life, which included a constant social swirl with Confederate bigwigs and townspeople. "The Winchester ladies," she says, "were among the most famous of Virginia housekeepers, and lived in a great deal of old-fashioned elegance and profusion. The old border town had not then changed hands with the conflicting armies, as it was destined to do many times during the war. Under the rose-colored light in which I viewed everything that winter, it seemed to me that no people could have been more cultivated, attractive and noble-hearted." Jackson returned to Winchester on January 24 to occupy himself with the federal buildup under General Nathaniel P. Banks before he was forced to abandon the place some weeks later: "Early in March," Anna Jackson continues, "he thought it was no longer safe for me to remain, and I was sent away on the same train which conveyed the sick to a place of safety."[13]

Offensive operations by Banks lay in the future as Jackson set out on January 1 for Romney, a mere forty miles to the west; spirits were high as the Confederates trooped out of Winchester in weather that many thought too mild for midwinter. By nightfall of the first day, a snow and ice storm dampened enthusiasm and nearly caused the march to collapse in disaster. On January 8, notes Private John Worsham of the 21st Virginia, "the road had become one sheet of ice from marching on it, and the men would march in the side ditches and in the woods where it was practicable. Guns were constantly being fired by men falling. In some instances the horses had to be taken from the cannon and wagons, which were then pulled by men with chains and ropes." Men and animals suffered in the raw climate, and Kyd Douglas relates that Jackson took a belt from what he supposed to be wine, but was really "fine old whiskey" to combat the cold. The bottle had been given to him by "a gentleman of Winchester." If Old Jack discovered his mistake, he said nothing, but "in a short while the General complained of being very warm, although it was still getting colder." He even unbuttoned his greatcoat and part of his uniform, which prompted Douglas to speculate that Jackson had become "incipiently tight."[14]

Complicating the operation was Jackson's circuitous route, which more than tripled his distance from Winchester to Romney. First, he marched to Bath, which he occupied on January 4 following a brief skirmish. Next, he headed for the Potomac in worsening weather; but when Ashby and Colonel Albert Rust—the Arkansan who failed Lee on Cheat Mountain—met a heavy fire opposite Hancock, Maryland, Jackson abandoned plans to capture the place. "As the U. S. troops had repeatedly shelled Shepherdstown, and had done so while there were no troops in the place and it was not used as a means of defense, I determined to intimate to the enemy that such outrages must not be repeated, and directed that a few rounds from McLaughlin's battery be fired at Hancock," Jackson included in his battle report. That done, he headed south toward Romney but had to halt at a crossroads named Unger's Store to rest men and horses because of cold weather. The "winter march" resumed on January 13, with Jackson entering Romney the next day. The town had been abandoned by Colonel Samuel H. Dunning, who decided that his two thousand bluecoats were no match for eighty-five hundred Confederates. Jackson, who almost alone considered Romney a place "of great strategic importance," closed his report with a stinging reproach of "reprobate Federal commanders" in northwestern Virginia. "In Hampshire County (Romney) they have not only burnt valuable mill property, but also many private houses. Their track from Romney to Hanging Rock, a distance of 15 miles, was one of desolation. The number of animals lying along the road-side, where shot by the enemy, exemplified the spirit of that part of the northern army."[15]

When Jackson returned to the Shenandoah with the Stonewall Brigade on January 24, Loring was left behind to guard against renewed incursions. Dissatisfied with spending the winter in poor quarters while "Jackson's pet lambs" basked in the luxury of Winchester, some of Loring's officers started a letter-writing campaign to discredit Jackson; their innuendo about his judgment and mental stability became downright rancorous. Loring and his friends, who enlisted the aid of several Confederate congressmen, succeeded on January 30, when Jackson received the following directive from Secretary of War Benjamin: "Our news indicates that a movement is being made to cut off General Loring's command. Order him to Winchester immediately." Although flabbergasted because he knew that Loring was in no danger, Jackson sent an order for him to withdraw and immediately forwarded his own resignation to Richmond: "With such interference in my command I cannot expect to be of much service in the field, and accordingly respectfully request to be ordered to report to the superintendent of the Virginia Military Institute in Lexington, as has been done in the case of other professors. Should this application not be granted, I respectfully request that the President will accept my resignation from the army."

Joe Johnston, still Jackson's superior, fought to have the resignation nullified. And as Jackson told confidants that the war office "needed to be taught a lesson," Governor Letcher likewise interceded to save Old Jack's military savvy for the Confederacy. Although Jackson stayed in the army and Loring was sent to another theater after his sudden promotion to major general, the episode kicked up a stir at Richmond and throughout the army. Both men had their champions in and out of the service. "By God, sir," Loring is supposed to have said, "this is the damnedest outrage ever perpetrated in the annals of history, keeping my men out here in the cold without food." Before it ended, Jackson not only preferred court martial charges but also told fellow officers that Loring should be "cashiered from the army." John Esten Cooke, who knew both men, wrote in 1866 that Loring's behavior "negatived [sic] at one blow the results of the expedition, and all the sufferings of the troops had been for nothing. Moorefield, Romney, and Bath were again defenceless [sic], and the counties of Hardy, Hampshire, and Morgan once more at the mercy of the enemy." All three counties were subsequently included in the new state of West Virginia.[16]

As Jackson sat in Winchester and watched Banks recapture the west, Robert E. Lee struggled to improve Confederate coastal defenses in the Carolinas, Georgia, and northern Florida. Although Lee and Jackson had no direct communication until Lee returned from the south, Jackson exchanged several notes with Alexander R. Boteler, a Confederate congressman who persuaded him to withdraw his resignation during the Loring affair. He intended to maintain a bold front throughout the Shenandoah Valley while he reorganized his command, Jackson told Boteler on March 3; nor had he forgotten Lee during his own difficulties with the Richmond bureaucrats. "I trust that General Lee will become Secretary of War. You ask me for a letter respecting the Valley. . . . I have only this to say, that if this Valley is lost, Virginia is lost." Jackson continued to think that western Virginia, including the Shenandoah region, was the key to Confederate success; his words about Lee no doubt reached the latter's ears, although no record exists that they did.[17]

Lee, meanwhile, had established his new headquarters at Coosawhatchie, South Carolina, located on the railroad between Charleston and Savannah; he could conveniently direct his attention to either southern bastion if threatened by Union gunboats. He had rushed to South Carolina on November 6, following a conference with Jefferson Davis. The presidential concerns stemmed from reports that a naval flotilla under Admiral Samuel DuPont and Thomas W. Sherman had sailed from Hampton Roads with twelve thousand men bound for the southern coast. Then, on November 7, as Lee traveled southward, DuPont's fleet steamed into Port Royal Harbor near Hilton Head to establish a federal foothold. Although the intruders showed no inclination to expand their beachhead other than to offer sanctuary for runaway slaves, governors in North and South Carolina, as well as Georgia, demanded protective measures. Lee's job was not only to reassure the governors, who viewed him with a jaundiced eye—Joseph Brown of Georgia was an exception— but also to arrange a defensive barrier that extended fully six hundred miles from Wynyah Bay in South Carolina to the St. John's River, which forms the Florida-Georgia border. Confounding his job was the great number of inlets and coves that punctuated the entire coastline, any one of which might serve as a Yankee springboard.[18]

From his quarters near Port Royal Harbor, which he shared with Major A. L. Long and Captain Walter H. Taylor, both of whom became his future biographers, as well as other aides, Lee rushed to the federal landing site with General R. S. Ripley, local militia commander. He learned soon enough that neither men nor guns were available to stem the encroachment. "The enemy having complete possession of the water and inland navigation, commands all the islands of the coast, and threatens both Savannah and Charleston," he informed Richmond on November 9. Although Lincoln added to Lee's worries by proclaiming a blockade of the southern coast, the Confederate steamer *Fingal* arrived at Charleston with "ten thousand Enfield rifles ordered from England by President Davis. Four rifled cannon likewise came aboard the runner." Lee got but half the cache, with the remainder assigned to Albert Sidney Johnston's command in Tennessee.[19]

Lee parceled out the guns as best he could to regulars in the vicinity, and hurried down the coast toward Savannah and Fernandia on Florida's Amelia Island. After inspecting his available resources, Lee wrote his daughter Mildred, then attending school in Winchester, that he "was on a forlorn expedition worse than West Virginia." From Savannah, he extended his inspection to Charleston Harbor, where he conferred with Governor F. W. Pickens and visited Fort Sumter. At the latter place, Lee was observed by Paul Hamilton Hayne, South Carolina poet-philosopher, who left a telling portrait: ". . . he was every inch the gentleman and soldier. Had some old English crypt or monumental stone in Westminister Abbey been smitten by a magician's wand and made to yield up its knightly tenant . . . with a chivalric soul beaming from every feature, some grand old crusader or 'red cross' warrior who, believing in a sacred creed . . . looked upon mere life as nothing in comparison, we thought that thus he would have appeared, unchanged in naught but costume and surroundings." Yet Lee had his detractors, which led Governor Pickens to inform Jefferson Davis that his critics "may do injury to the public service." And during a subsequent tour Lee was at the Mills House in Charleston with several aides when a great fire engulfed much of the city. "While standing atop the hotel with Major Long, he watched a scene of awful sublimity; more than one-third of the city appeared a sea of fire shooting up columns of flame to mingle with the stars. From King Street eastward to the river, extending back more than a mile, stores and dwellings, churches and public buildings, were enveloped in one common blaze, which marched steadily and rapidly across the city." Lee was forced to abandon the Mills House "with a baby in his arms" as he helped several guests to safety.[20]

Earlier, following his initial trip along the coast, Lee informed Adjutant General Samuel Cooper about his basic strategy: "The guns from the less important points have been removed, and are employed in strengthening those considered of greater consequence. The entrance to Cumberland Sound and Brunswick and the water approaches to Savannah and Charleston are the only points which it is proposed to defend." Although Captain Taylor and John Esten Cooke say that he accomplished "nothing of interest," Lee pressed forward with his plans. Savannah, Charleston, and one or two other places were indeed fortified with earth-invested batteries, and strategic spots along the Charleston and Savannah Railroad were strengthened with militia postings. In short, Lee realized the futility of guarding the whole coast and sea islands, and chose instead to concentrate upon a land-based defense. By the middle of June, when Jefferson Davis recalled him to Richmond, Lee had, according to Long, "established a strong interior line of defense from Wynyah Bay to the mouth of St. Mary's River. This line being bravely and skillfully defended, proved to be an impenetrable barrier to the combined efforts of the land and naval forces of the enemy constantly employed on the coast, until it was carried by Sherman in his unopposed march through Georgia and South Carolina."[21]

Added to Lee's worries was a concern for his wife's well-being as McDowell and others maneuvered across northern Virginia. On Christmas Day 1861, as Jackson returned to Winchester and a joyous reunion with Anna after the destruction of Dam Number 5, Lee wrote to his wife about Arlington House: "As to our old home, if not destroyed, it will be difficult to ever recognize. Even if the enemy had wished to preserve it, it would have been impossible. With the number of troops encamped around it, the change of officers, etc., the want of fuel, shelter, etc., and all the dire necessities of war, it is vain to think of its being in a habitable condition." Lee added that he wished he could purchase Stratford Hall "in the absence of a home." Two weeks later, on January 18, he recounted a visit to his father's grave at Dungeness, the Cumberland Island estate of General Nathaniel P. Greene. "The spot is marked by a plain marble slab, with his name, age, and date of his death." If the desecration of Arlington made him sad, Dungeness must have made a deep impression upon Lee as he used nearly a page to describe the plantation and burial site to Mrs. Lee.[22]

An impossible situation confronted Lee throughout his stay at Coos-awhatchie: There were insufficient resources to keep the enemy from landing on the coast almost at will. General Long may have been technically correct that Lee's "interior lines" held until the arrival of Sherman during 1865, but great stretches of the coast and offshore islands were another matter. In February 1862, while Lee was still in the south, a federal flotilla overpowered General Henry A. Wise on historic Roanoke Island in Pamlico Sound; notes James M. McPherson, "by April 1862 every Atlantic harbor of importance except Charleston and Wilmington (N.C.) was in Union hands or closed to blockade runners." Lee had done his best with the resources at hand, but as he "took the cars" for Richmond in the first week of March, he surely hoped for a more rewarding assignment than had been his lot in western Virginia and the Carolinas.[23]

Robert E. Lee was recalled to the president's side because the grand drama of the war was about to unfold. Confederate spies around Washington and along the Potomac had warned Joe Johnston for weeks about increased military activity—that General George B. McClellan was about to march. McClellan, the West Point acquaintance of Lee and Jackson and veteran of the Mexican War, had been appointed to lead the federal onslaught on November 1 by President Lincoln. Although he fought with Lincoln and the war cabinet over his place in the command structure after the retirement of Winfield Scott, McClellan had definite ideas on how best to capture Richmond, with its munitions factories, transportation hub, and government buildings.

But Little Mac waited too long to start his offensive! Abraham Lincoln, impatient for action, had issued his War Order Number 1 on January 31, 1862, directing him to advance no later than February 22, George Washington's birthday; McClellan did not march until March 17, nearly two weeks after Lee's return to Richmond, and then he did not take the direct land route favored by Lincoln and his cabinet but conceived an amphibious assault on the Confederate capital by way of the James River Peninsula. With great reluctance, Lincoln had agreed to his incessant badgering for the Peninsula plan only if sufficient troops were kept in front of Washington to guard his own seat of government.[24]

Lee was no sooner at his old desk than Davis assigned him the task of "superintending under the direction of the president, all military operations in defense of the southern Confederacy." The authorization was dated March 13, but, observes John Esten Cooke, "the Confederate forces in Virginia did not number in all one hundred thousand men; and it is now apparent (1871) that, without the able strategy of Johnston, Lee, and Jackson, General McClellan would have been in possession of Richmond before the summer." Lee's first priority was to strengthen Johnston's army of forty thousand, which faced General McDowell around Centreville and Manassas, as well as Jackson's force of nineteen thousand, which guarded the Valley against Banks; smaller forces were positioned about the state under Richard S. Ewell, Theophilus H. Holmes, and John B. Magruder. In the weeks ahead, Lee scoured every troop return to see if additional men could be transferred to the vital points; once Johnston was obliged to move most of his men to the Peninsula as a counter to McClellan, Lee's job became increasingly urgent. Johnston had to be augmented at the same time sufficient numbers were required to thwart an overland assault on Richmond by McDowell.

As Lee applied his every energy to finding new companies for Johnston and Jackson, he called upon William Meade, Virginia's Episcopal bishop, who lay dying at his Richmond home after a long and useful life. Lee had known the ecclesiastic since boyhood, and, reported observers, tears streamed down his cheeks as he bade his friend and mentor goodbye. Meade's last words, Cooke's account continues, were, "Heaven bless you! and give you wisdom for your important and arduous duties."[25]

Arduous days, indeed, lay on the horizon not only for Lee but also for Jackson following March 11, when Banks swept into Winchester as part of McClellan's advance. This forced Jackson's retreat up the Valley before superior numbers; before he left, however, Anna was sent from Dr. Graham's house "on the same train that carried the sick to a place of safety." Although he wanted to counterattack immediately, Jackson was forced to abandon the attempt when his wagon train was found to be in the wrong place to support an offensive. Jackson continued up the Valley Pike first to Strasburg and then Mount Jackson, at the southernmost terminus of the railroad. Here, he learned from Ashby that Banks had marched away from the Shenandoah toward McDowell's army, and that only Shield's division remained at Winchester. "With the Stonewall

Brigade in the van and convinced that he was attacking the rear flank of the retreating Federals, Jackson hit Shields, whom he had known in Mexico, on March 23 at Kernstown, a small village three or four miles south of Winchester. All proceeded as planned until Garnett's men were in danger of a cutoff." Then, continues a modern writer, "in spite of desperate rallying efforts by Jackson, who was opposed to the withdrawal, the men continued to fall back. After retreating southward for about four miles, they bivouacked at Newtown (present Stephens City), where their train was parked. Although the victorious Federals did not pursue very far, Shields had gained an honor that he enjoyed for the rest of his life—he had defeated Stonewall Jackson in a battle."[26]

Following Kernstown, Jackson fell back to Mount Jackson, where he informed Major J. A. Harman: "Our little army here is in good spirits." In spite of the repulse at Kernstown, Jackson had reason to rejoice because he had accomplished his objective of frightening Lincoln into withholding McDowell's thirty thousand from the peninsula. While Jackson reorganized and replenished his army, McClellan arrived at Fortress Monroe on April 2 to take personal command. Alarmed that the Confederate ironclad *Virginia* might interfere with naval operations on the James, he ordered a thrust upon the Confederate entrenchments around Yorktown. Although he enjoyed vastly superior numbers, McClellan put Yorktown under siege rather than attack the ingenious southern positions along the Warwick River. Dark moments befell Little Mac when he learned that McDowell would stay in front of Washington and that Blenker's division had been ordered to join Fremont in the South Branch Valley. McClellan remained convinced that Jackson was merely posturing in the Shenandoah as a tactic to divert men and supplies from his campaign on the peninsula. As he directed the Yorktown investment, which continued until May 4, a festering hatred of Lincoln and the war cabinet began to gnaw at the otherwise rational commander.[27]

Joe Johnston, newly arrived from Centreville, spent one day on the Yorktown ramparts peering at McClellan's siege guns and decided this was not the place to fight; he hurried to Richmond, where Jefferson Davis had little choice but to meet with him. Also invited to the April 15 strategy session were Lee and George Wythe Randolph, who had replaced Judah Benjamin as secretary of war and who sided with Lee against Johnston. At the meeting, Lee found himself in the uncomfortable position of disagreeing with his old friend and comrade: He felt McClellan should be opposed on the Lower James, while Johnston wanted to concentrate all available forces—drawn primarily from the Carolina coasts—for a grand battle near Richmond. The debate became heated, a Davis biographer records: "Lee became very emotional and with tears in his eyes declared that Richmond must not be given up." As the gathering adjourned, Davis sided with Lee, although, as we will see, Joe Johnston had no intention of abiding by the presidential directive; he sulked, and refused to visit the capital for new conferences. "Lee, wonderfully tactful and self-effacing, acted as peacemaker between the president, dissatisfied with Johnston's behavior, and the general in command of defense."[28]

Lee's conviction that Richmond had to be defended at all costs formed the basis of his quiet but determined alliance with Jackson; within a week of the showdown in Davis's office, Lee opened a correspondence with "Tom Fool" Jackson—Quartermaster General Harman even told his wife that he was "cracked-brained," which led to Jackson's great campaign in the Shenandoah designed to worry Lincoln into withholding Irvin McDowell from the Peninsula. Lee clearly comprehended that Jackson should keep the pressure on Banks and McDowell as the key to victory against McClellan. And when Lee walked away from the Richmond meeting, Jackson had been encamped at Rude's Hill between Mount Jackson and New Market since April 2; he remained in good spirits about the army and told his wife on April 11: "Although I was repulsed in the attempt to recover Winchester, the enemy's loss appears to have been greater than ours. In addition to this, the great object which required me to follow up the enemy as he fell back from Strasburg seems to have been accomplished very thoroughly. I am well satisfied with the result." Jackson was also pleased, he informed Anna, that the Confederate Congress tendered its thanks "to Major General Thomas J. Jackson, and the officers and men under his command, for . . . a successful engagement with a greatly superior force of the enemy near Kernstown, Frederick County, Virginia."[29]

One of Jackson's first acts after the battle was his removal of Richard B. Garnett from command of the Stonewall Brigade. Garnett, a cousin of General Robert S. Garnett, who fell at Carrick's Ford during the campaign in western Virginia, enjoyed the respect of his men, but Old Jack was convinced that his dalliance had cost the victory at Kernstown. General Charles S. Winder was put in Garnett's place, but, relates Kyd Douglas, he was "received in a sulky and resentful silence, and for nearly three weeks General Jackson was permitted to ride past his old command without hearing a shout." Jackson later brought charges against Garnett, but the proceedings lapsed when the Second Manassas diverted Jackson's attention. Garnett fell at Gettysburg the following year, while leading a new brigade in Pickett's charge.[30]

Prior to Jackson's retreat into Harrisonburg before a rejuvenated Banks, his men spent a good part of their time moving Engine 199 from Mount Jackson, up Rude's Hill, to Staunton. The Confederates had captured the locomotive at Harpers Ferry and brought it down the tracks to the stopping place at Mount Jackson. "Stonewall resolved to get the valuable engine to Staunton and the only way was up the Valley Pike," writes a Valley historian. "Squads of scavenger machinists were put to work. They hoisted the locomotive with jacks, stripped everything removable except the huge rear driver wheels, swung it around and lowered it onto the Pike. The strongest teams in the Valley were hitched to the engine by means of an ingenious rigging of front wheels and a chain with harnesses of forty horses. These stood more than one hundred feet ahead of the locomotive in ten rows of four animals abreast." After a great toil, the Valley Army got Old 199 to its destination, but during the entire operation, federal cannoneers were shelling Jackson's positions south of Mount Jackson.[31]

Unable to withstand the continued pressure, Jackson fell back toward Harrisonburg and around the southern tip of the Massanutten; by April 19, his army was concentrated along Elk Run, which flows from Swift Run Gap in the Blue Ridge to the South Fork of the Shenandoah at Conrad's Store, or present Elkton. Jackson's great strategic sense told him as he fell back that a union with Ewell's eight thousand men near Brandy Station would enhance his options. In one of the remarkable endeavors of the war, Jackson dispatched Henry Kyd Douglas, recently attached to his personal staff, on an urgent mission to locate Ewell. The young lieutenant left immediately, rounded the forbidding Massanutten at Port Republic, passed through Luray, and made his way across the Blue Ridge at Thornton's Gap to Standardsville in eastern Virginia. Every Jackson chronicler, including Douglas himself, has recounted the harrowing adventure as he traveled in pitch darkness over a totally unfamiliar roadway. "One hundred and five miles over mountainous country, no foot of which he had even known before, came this messenger to start the wheels of one of the world's great campaigns in motion. He had ridden continuously for twenty hours, using five horses," writes a Ewell biographer. Douglas literally collapsed on Ewell's cot as the general prescribed sleep and special food for the exhausted messenger.

The message to Dick Ewell, known throughout the army as Old Bald Head, was simple enough: Head for Swift Run Gap at the instant! Yet Jackson, now at Conrad's Store, was secretive as ever, and Ashby's outriders were bringing him conflicting reports about Banks. An order to Ewell halted his march while still east of the Blue Ridge at Stan-

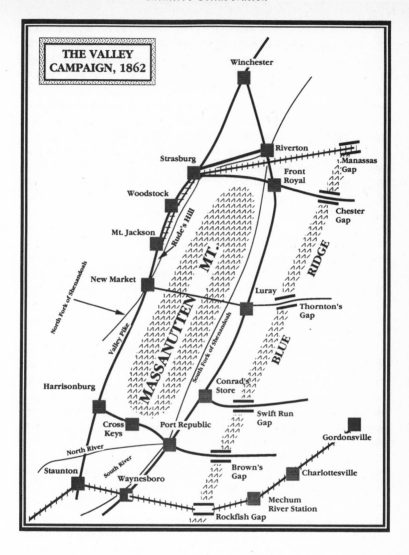

dardsville which caused him to snort that Jackson was "crazy as a March Hare." Ewell, who wanted to attack Shields before he could leave the Valley, took a ride himself across the Blue Ridge to confer with Jackson after receiving confused orders for several days—Lee and Jackson needed him in the Valley, while Joe Johnston repeatedly summoned him to the Peninsula. But Jackson remained adamant. Close up to Swift Run Gap, and stay there until further orders, he told his visitor, who became increasingly uneasy about his commander's sanity.[32]

With Banks at Harrisonburg, fourteen miles west of Swift Run Gap, Jackson pondered his next moves, and opened his close correspondence with Lee. No fewer than ten dispatches between them appear in the *Official Records* while Jackson lingered atop the Blue Ridge, and, strangely, he did not comment on his new association with Lee to his wife. Lee necessarily kept a wide-ranging communication with commanders throughout Virginia, and, although Joe Johnston had to remind him during mid-May that he was in command in the Valley, Lee directed his primary attention toward Jackson. His message was straightforward and to the point: Combine with Ewell to keep Banks beyond the Blue Ridge and away from McClellan. Here, their hearts beat as one, and when Jackson told Lee on April 28 that Banks showed no inclination to attack, their grand design was ready to unfold.

The following day, April 29, Jackson sent a detailed analysis of his options that simply ignored Johnston. He proposed to leave "General Ewell here [at Swift Run Gap] to threaten Banks' rear in the event of his advancing on Staunton, and move rapidly with my command on the force in front of General Edward Johnson, or else, co-operating with General Ewell, to attack the enemy's detached force between New Market and the Shenandoah, and, if successful in this, then to press forward and get in Banks' rear at New Market, and thus induce him to fall back; the third to pass down the Shenandoah to Sperryville, and thus threaten Winchester via Front Royal." Jackson's intelligence network had told him that General John C. Fremont was massing an army to threaten Staunton from the west, and that General Louis Blenker's force of seven thousand had recently joined him from McDowell's army. Thus, Fremont had an eight thousand–man force spread throughout the South Branch Valley with outposts at Moorefield, Franklin, and McDowell. "Of the three plans," Jackson confessed, "I give preference to the force west of Staunton." Two days later, Lee informed Jackson to use his own judgment about which plan was best, because he had nothing better to offer. When Ewell encamped at the old campgrounds of the

Stonewall Brigade at Swift Run Gap to keep Banks from advancing beyond Harrisonburg, Jackson, who had all the orders he needed, had already marched westward.[33]

Without a word to anyone save Lee, Jackson slipped past Fort Republic and through Brown's Gap of the Blue Ridge to lull Banks into thinking he had left the Valley for good; it was hard marching for his men who were quickly earning a new name—Jackson's Foot Cavalry. When one trooper complained of hunger, relates Private John W. Fravel, "our colonel told him to tighten his belt a notch or two." On they marched to Mechum River Station on the railroad to Staunton, where, Fravel adds, "our mess got some chickens and we had a feast." Joy overtook the town when the engines rolled into Staunton on May 5 with the Valley Army; Jackson had arrived from eastern Virginia, and he promptly sealed off the place to prevent travelers and farmers from tipping Banks that he was on the move. Near Mechum River Station, he told Anna, "I received a dispatch that part of the enemy's force arrived within one day's march of Brigadier General Edward Johnson's camp. Under the circumstances I felt it encumbent upon me to press forward, and I arrived here [Staunton] last evening [May 4] where I am stopping at the Virginia House. The troops are still coming in. The corps of cadets of the Virginia Military Institute is here." Jackson's soul swelled with pride when the lads from Lexington all decked out in smart uniforms joined his veterans. He linked up with Allegheny Johnson's force of three thousand rifles a few miles west of Staunton and continued his westward trek toward the Highland County town of McDowell.[34]

At the town on the upper reaches of the Bullpasture River, Jackson's army of twelve thousand encountered the federals under General Robert H. Milroy, reinforced by Robert C. Schenck. Schenck, a former Ohio congressman and onetime railroad president, was not only senior officer, but he also attacked the oncoming Confederates before Jackson had an opportunity to reconnoiter or deploy his troops. Although Fravel says that "we whipped them," as the federals, mostly Ohio and West Virginia regiments, charged Jackson's hastily drawn positions on a mountainside called Sitlington's Hill, it was not a thumping victory. Milroy and Schenck were forced to retire after what appeared to be an initial success, but they did so having inflicted "twice as many casualties on the southerners as they, themselves, suffered." Jackson, however, was ecstatic when the disheartened federals fled toward Franklin (now West Virginia), thirty miles down the South Branch Valley. "I congratulate you on your recent victory at McDowell," Old Jack proclaimed to

"The Army of the Valley and Southwest," and he urged his troopers to thank "Almighty God for thus having crowned your arms with success."[35]

At the same time Lee, Jackson, and Ewell were exchanging daily letters about the Valley, Lee was also dispatching words of encouragement throughout the army. "Exercising a constant supervision over the condition of affairs at each important point, thoroughly informed as to the resources and necessities of the several commanders of armies in the field, he was enabled to give them wise counsel, as well as of the dangers which respectively threatened them, assistance and support to such an extent as the limited resources of the Government would permit," Walter H. Taylor comments. "It was in great measure due to his advice and encouragement that General Magruder so stoutly and gallantly held his lines on the Peninsula against General McClellan until troops could be sent to his relief from General Johnston's army." Taylor is correct, as anyone reading the *Official Records* for this period will agree; just as Jackson was expending great efforts marching and countermarching against Fremont and Banks, Lee was preoccupied not only with military matters but also with personal concerns. On May 6, he had ridden down to White House, where Mrs. Lee had been "refugeeing" with Rooney's wife, Charlotte, since leaving Arlington and Ravensworth. That historic old place, near the confluence of the Mattaponi and Pamunkey rivers which form the York estuary, once owned by George Washington, had been willed to Rooney Lee by his grandfather, George Washington Parke Custis. When McClellan decided to shift his headquarters from Fortress Monroe to West Point on the Richmond and York River Railroad into the Confederate capital, the plantation was suddenly surrounded by federal troops. When Rooney visited the plantation during the Seven Days fighting, he "found that only the two chimneys remained." Margaret Sanborn, a Lee biographer, continues: "It was thought at the time that it had been burned in the fire of the night before. Later, Rooney learned that the Federals had carefully guarded it out of deference to its associations with George Washington, but that an incendiary had eluded the guards and set fire to it."[36]

Lee's letter writing to Old Jack and others, which unquestionably had the sanction of Davis, led to a near blowup with Joe Johnston. McClellan had shifted his headquarters to the York so that he could both advance along the railroad to Richmond and be nearer to a linkup with McDowell. And just as McClellan sent hourly telegrams to Washington clamoring for McDowell to join his offensive, Joe Johnston appealed for more troops to help defeat him. Lee's determination to keep McDowell close to Washington and away from Richmond by encouraging Jackson and Ewell, caused Johnston to explode. "When Lee came back to his office on May 8 [the same day that Jackson repulsed Milroy and Schenck], a scorching letter from Joe Johnston was on his desk," writes Clifford Dowdey, "complaining about his lack of recognition of authority." Johnston charged that "Lee had given orders to troops under his command. . . . 'My authority does not extend beyond the troops around me,' he raged. 'I therefore request to be relieved of a merely geographical command.'" Still, both men, friends since West Point and Mexico, held to their respective courses. Johnston continued to withdraw toward Richmond, abandoning Yorktown on May 3 and then another hastily deployed defense near the ancient capital at Williamsburg on May 5; by May 17, he had settled into a line of earthen works constructed the year before within three miles of Richmond; rumors swept the army that he intended to abandon the city for a better defensive position.

Neither Lee nor Davis knew about the withdrawal until John H. Reagan, Confederate postmaster general, rode out from the city to greet some fellow Texans serving in Hood's brigade and stumbled across the army within sight of the capital. In an effort to justify himself, Johnston wrote in his official report that "before taking command on the Peninsula I expressed to the President my opinion of the defects of the position then occupied by our troops there. After taking command I reported that the opinion previously expressed was fully confirmed." Although Johnston said the troops "displayed high courage, and on the march endured privation and hardship with admirable cheerfulness," Lee was aghast that McClellan's army of 105,000 men had been allowed to approach Richmond without a major battle.[37]

Lee was not commander in chief and therefore could do little but use his influence with Davis as he watched events unfold on the Peninsula; with Jackson, however, it was another matter, as neither man was prepared to lose Richmond without a fight. Lee told him on May 16 not to "lose sight of the fact that it may be necessary for you to come to the support of General Johnston, and hold yourself in readiness to do so if required"; nevertheless, the Valley remained uppermost in Lee's plans: "Whatever movement you make against Banks do it speedily, and if successful, drive him back toward the Potomac, and create the impression, as far as practical, that you desire threatening that line." No further letters appear in the *Official Records* until June 8, which placed Jackson, and, indeed Ewell, in an awkward position.

After McDowell, Jackson had pursued the retreating federals northward toward Franklin (present West Virginia), but his prey managed to impede the march "by setting the woods on fire." Jackson gave up his plan to crush Fremont's mountain army, ordered a return to McDowell, and then swung eastward toward Harrisonburg and the Valley Pike. At Lebanon White Sulphur Springs, at 5 A.M. on March 17, he sent an order to Ewell, still encamped at Elk Run and Swift Run Gap, to move his command to New Market on the double quick. Two additional dispatches, both dated May 17, crossed each other, and given the expected time lag for horse-borne couriers, presented difficulties for the Valley commander. "We want troops here [the Peninsula]; none, therefore, must be kept away, unless employing a greatly superior force of the enemy." And, Johnston told Old Bald Head, if Banks was fortifying himself at Strasburg "General Jackson can observe him and you come eastward. After reading this send it to General Jackson, for whom it is intended as well as yourself," he added. That very morning, Jackson told Johnston from Mount Solon that he was going after Banks: "If I do not hear from you soon I will continue my march until I get within striking distance of him."

A worried Ewell "brought forth his best horse, and, riding hard" set out to find Jackson, who was pushing his command toward Harrisonburg like the furies. At the meeting, writes Ewell's biographer, "Jackson found himself forever in Ewell's debt." His visitor not only decided to remain in the Valley of the Shenandoah but he also drafted the order issued by Jackson on May 18, 1862:

> Your letter of this date, which you state that you have received letters from Generals Lee, Johnston, and myself requiring somewhat different movements, and desiring my views respecting your position, has been received. In reply I would state that as you are in the Valley District you constitute a part of my command. . . . You will please move your command so as to encamp between New Market and Mount Jackson on next Wednesday night, unless you receive orders from a superior officer, and of a date subsequent to the 16th instant.[38]

Jackson and Ewell consciously elected to ignore Johnston, and Lee, who surely discussed details with President Davis, did not intervene. Still, Jackson had qualms about committing his army against Banks's formidable entrenchments at Strasburg: "I am of the opinion that an attempt should be made to defeat Banks, but under the instructions just received from General Johnston I do not feel at liberty to make an attack. Please answer by telegraph at once," he implored Lee on May 20. But no reply can be found in the official correspondence; writes Anna Jackson about the Jackson-Ewell tête-à-tête: "Both were sorely perplexed as to what was their duty under the circumstances . . . but Ewell proposed that if Jackson, as his ranking officer, would take responsibility, he would remain until the condition of affairs could be represented to General Johnston, which was decided upon." When Jackson filed his battle summary over one year later, he said nothing about the incident. Lee, however, had plenty to say when he wrote to Jackson on June 8 and 11, after he had assumed command of the Army of Northern Virginia and after Jackson had concluded the Valley campaign. On the 8th: "I congratulate you upon defeating and then avoiding your enemy"; and three days later: "Your recent successes have been the cause of the liveliest joy in this army as well as in the country. The admiration excited by your skill and boldness has been constantly mingled with solicitude for your situation." A gnawing question remains: Did Lee wait until after the fact before endorsing Jackson, or was he too busy with the Peninsula operations to respond to Jackson's letters? Interestingly, Joe Johnston, in his 1874 memoir, says merely that "instructions were given at once to advance and attack, unless [Jackson] found the enemy too strongly intrenched [*sic*]."³⁹

Jackson's success in the valley was far from certain when he joined Ewell's troops at New market on May 20 to begin his offensive. Ashby's cavalry had learned that Banks, although positioned at Strasburg, had a detached unit at Front Royal under Colonel John R. Kenly; put another way, the main federal army was astride the Valley Pike west of Massanutten Mountain, while Kenly guarded the eastern or Luray entrance to the Shenandoah at Front Royal. Jackson characteristically headed for the weakest point; he crossed the Massanutten from New Market to Luray and traveled the South Fork of the Shenandoah toward Kenly. "The troops were accustomed to severe marches, but this was a most trying one," writes Colonel John M. Patton. "All day long they pushed forward under a boiling sun—unusual for that season—and with a dense and stifling dust." Although "men frequently staggered from the ranks overcome by the heat," Jackson's "foot cavalry" reached Kenly's pickets by 9 P.M., May 22; they had marched 120 miles from Franklin in ten days. The next day, Jackson routed Kenly's outpost, took seven hundred prisoners, including twenty officers, an entire section of Parrott guns, and a trove in supplies from the federal quartermaster. "The enemy's flank was turned and the road to Winchester opened," reads his official battle report.⁴⁰

After first contact by Ewell's brigade, Jackson's triumph at Front Royal was aided by a remarkable woman and Confederate spy named

Belle Boyd. Jackson, Ewell, and their staffs were standing on a hillock overlooking the town when they saw "a tall, supple, graceful, figure of a girl" running toward them waving a bonnet frantically through the air. At Ewell's suggestion, Jackson dispatched Kyd Douglas to see what she wanted. Douglas, who recognized her as a childhood chum from Martinsburg, recounts her message for Old Jack: "Go back and tell him that the Yankee force is very small—one regiment of Maryland infantry, several pieces of artillery, and several companies of cavalry. Tell him I know, for I went through the camp and got it out of an officer. Tell him to charge right down and he can catch them all. I must hurry back. Good-by. My love to all the dear boys. . . ."[41]

"All the dear boys" prompted Banks to form his own foot cavalry as officers and men scrambled thirteen miles down the Valley Pike from Strasburg to his old entrenchments at Winchester. Actually, Jackson and Banks had become locked in a triangular race—Jackson and Ewell left Front Royal on May 24 by the Front Royal–Winchester route, while Banks and the main Yankee force sped up the Valley Pike from Strasburg. When Jackson reached Cedarville—six or seven miles from Front Royal, he became alarmed that Banks might escape behind him through the Blue Ridge. He decided to leave Ewell in place with Trimble's brigade as he took a side road through Reliance to Middletown on the Valley Pike. It was here at Middletown that Ashby's cavalry and Poague's artillery first encountered the retreating Banks; a veritable slaughter ensued as the federal troopers with their cumbersome wagon trains, trapped behind stone walls that lined both sides of the Pike, were gunned down without mercy. Nor could the Valley Army be restrained from ransacking and plundering another cache of quartermaster supplies; even Jackson himself could not resist the temptation to get his evening meal from an abandoned wagon. "Ashby's boys tempted by first choice of the spoils as they chased the enemy north from Middletown, went wild. Many roped two or three horses and rode off to their homes." The looting of the federal stores and Jackson's decision to allow his troopers a brief rest unfortunately gave Banks time to regroup.[42]

The next morning, May 25, found the two adversaries arrayed in parallel lines on the southern edge of Winchester. Dick Ewell, whatever his faults, was not a man to run from a fight, and he rushed up the Front Royal–Winchester road at the first sign of trouble. An early morning fog enveloped both armies as they jockeyed for position—some opposing units even bumped into each other in the mist—but Jackson was determined to occupy the high ground south of town and west of the Valley Pike. Banks, also west of the Pike, soon turned his long-range guns at the

Confederate lines, and an extraordinary sight of the war followed when Old Jack ordered Richard Taylor's Louisianians to charge the federal right. A son of President Zachary Taylor, and one of the last Confederate commanders to surrender in 1865, he led his men with parade-ground precision through a blistering fire straight at the bluecoated position. Other fighting followed, including an attack on Banks's left by Ewell and another artillery blast by Poague's battery, but Taylor's Louisiana boys had broken the Union line. Jackson had "shattered Banks's force to bits in a hotly contested battle," observes George Cary Eggleston, "and having cut off the Federal general's retreat to Harpers Ferry, sent him flying through Martinsburg to Williamsport on the upper Potomac."[43]

Winchester erupted into an extravaganza of unrestrained rejoicing when Jackson's gray-clad ranks swept through town in hot pursuit. An opportunity to crush the federal army vanished when hundreds of men stopped to loot another cache of Union supplies, but a worse disappointment took place when Old Jack could not find sufficient cavalry to chase down his disarrayed enemy. Ashby was in the wrong place, and General George H. Steuart, "Maryland Steuart," refused an order to charge without a direct command from Ewell, who was his immediate superior. Steuart, who survived the war by forty years, although he was captured in the Wilderness fighting, finally went into action along the Winchester-Charles Town road following a stern rebuff by Ewell. But he was too late. Banks had escaped. Jackson soon gave up the pursuit because his men had done all that mortal flesh could do, and, observes Dabney, "the general rode slowly back to town. Having procured quarters in the chief hotel, he refused all food, and throwing himself upon his breast, booted and spurred, was sleeping in a moment, with the healthy quietude of infancy." Once revived, however, Jackson dealt swiftly with those who stopped to ravish captured quartermaster wagons, although he did offer congratulations to the rest of his command. And, he dashed off a quick note to Anna: "Our entrance into Winchester was one of the most stirring scenes of my life. . . . Your friends desired to see you and me. Last night I called to see [Rev.] and Mrs. Graham who were very kind. . . . Time forbids a longer letter but it does not forbid my loving my *esposita*."[44]

After a brief pause to rest his "foot cavalry," Jackson pushed toward the Potomac; by May 26, he had reached Halltown, within sight of Harpers Ferry, but halted because of a force commanded by Rufus Saxton that had been quickly assembled after the Winchester rout; Jackson made several feints at the old citadel over the next several days, but he was unable to retake it. And his return to the Potomac proved to be temporary. Unbeknown to him, Lee's strategy to worry Lincoln began to pay dividends—dividends that nearly spelled disaster for the Valley Army. The Republican president at this point clearly seized the initiative from his own generals, and even a cursory perusal of his correspondence for late May–early June reveals that he had more than a mere defense of Washington in mind. He meant to drive Jackson from the Shenandoah.

Lincoln set his plan in motion before the Jackson-Banks confrontation at Winchester, when he telegraphed Fremont on May 24 at Franklin "to move against Jackson at Harrisonburg and operate against the enemy in such a way to relieve Banks." And, on the day of Winchester, May 25, at 4 in the afternoon, he informed McClellan, while Jackson was hunting his errant cavalry to harass Banks's retreat, that McDowell's orders to march for the peninsula had been "suspended." Another telegraph was dispatched an hour later to Irvin McDowell, commanding at Fredericksburg: "You are instructed laying aside for the present the movement on Richmond to put twenty thousand in motion at once for the Shenandoah moving on the line or in advance of the line of the Manassas Gap Railroad. Your object will be to capture the forces of Jackson and Ewell, either in cooperation with Gen. Fremont or in case want of supplies and transportation interferes with his movement, it is believed that the force with which you move will be sufficient to accomplish the object alone."[45]

Dispatches and telegrams flowed hourly as Lincoln directed Fremont from the South Branch Valley and McDowell from the Rappahannock to close on Strasburg and Front Royal in a pincer movement designed to trap Jackson before he could move up the valley to safety. At Halltown, according to Jackson's own words, "to avoid such a result orders were issued for all the troops, except Winder's brigade and the cavalry, to return to Winchester on the 30th. Directions were given to General Winder to recall the Second Regiment from Loudoun Heights [Harpers Ferry], and as soon as it should return to its brigade to move with its command, including the cavalry, and rejoin the main body of the army." Couriers had informed Old Jack during May 28–29 that Fremont and McDowell were converging on him, and before he could reach Winchester by train, McDowell's lead division under James Shields marched into Front Royal. By 5 o'clock on the afternoon of May 31, Shields had his main force in place, and Fremont, opposed by Ewell, was strung out along Cedar Creek, a mile or so northwest of Strasburg. In spite of the tightening noose, Jackson halted the army at Strasburg to await Winder and the Stonewall Brigade. "Toward evening," Jackson wrote about the events of May 31, "Winder arrived, part of his brigade (the Second

Virginia regiment) having in one day marched 36 miles. The command being united, the retreat was resumed toward Harrisonburg." Stonewall Jackson and the foot cavalry had escaped Lincoln's trap.[46]

Once through the McDowell-Fremont vise, the Valley Army "continued south from Strasburg and then fell out to bivouac." Then, continues, James I. Robertson, "most of the men simply dropped into the muddy road where they had been standing. In the condition of indifference that comes from fatigue, hunger, and dampness, troops fell asleep with unconcern for the dangers about them." Jackson now had fifteen thousand effectives, but the combined federal force was more than twice as large. The enemy had the advantage, with Shields pushing through the Luray Valley on June 2, and Fremont a day or so later marching up the Valley Pike to threaten the Confederate rear as Jackson's withdrawal continued over the next several days. With Union armies pressing south along both sides of the Massanutten, Jackson left the Valley Pike at Harrisonburg and commenced an eastward movement. By June 7, he had the army astride the South Fork of the Shenandoah at two small villages called Cross Keys and Port Republic.[47]

Since Fremont and Shields had been unable to join forces across the Massanutten after Jackson destroyed several key bridges in the Luray Valley, Fremont became his immediate pursuer; constant firefights between federal cavalry and Ashby's horsemen as the armies parried down the North Fork of the Shenandoah resulted in Turner Ashby's untimely death on June 6. Just north of Harrisonburg while Jackson was securing his headquarters at Port Republic, Ashby encountered the First New Jersey commanded by Sir Percy Wyndham, an English soldier of fortune. Wyndham had bragged throughout both armies that he was the man to capture Ashby, but he was captured himself in a brief cavalry clash. As he postured—one observer said Wyndham was mad enough to engage his captors in fisticuffs, Fremont hurried two infantry units including the famed Pennsylvania Bucktails, toward Ashby's position.

"Ashby, always mounted, ordered up the 58th Virginia, a small company. Here a hot and stubborn fight ensued with Ashby everywhere animating his men. Seeing his men suffering under this heavy fire and making no headway, he ordered the 58th to cease firing, and, putting himself at their head, directed a charge with the bayonet. His horse being killed, and instantly recovering his feet, he gave his last ringing order for the cold steel, as a ball pierced his heart." Jackson was interrogating the still-fuming Wyndham when word came that Ashby had fallen; after the body was carried into Port Republic, "General Jackson," writes Dabney, "came to the room where he lay, and demanded to see him.

They admitted him alone; he remained for a time in silent communion with the dead, and then left him, with a solemn and elevated countenance." Although Jackson often quarreled with the impetuous cavalryman, he later wrote that "the close relation which General Ashby bore with my command . . . will justify me in saying that, as a partisan officer, I never knew his superior."[48]

Most of Jackson's contemporaries concede that Ashby's rearguard fight gave him time to position the army at Port Republic. The village is situated at the southern extreme of Massanutten Mountain, where the South and North Rivers join to form the South Fork of the Shenandoah. A bridge spanned North River into town from Harrisonburg, but South River had to be forced to reach Brown's Gap in the Blue Ridge as well as the road to Luray. Jackson left the main army on the Harrisonburg side of the North River bridge while he established his headquarters in the Port Republic home of Dr. George Kemper. Ewell's troops were left on the road from Harrisonburg a few miles west of his headquarters, and the wagons were placed south of town on the road to Staunton.

When the battle opened on June 8, Jackson was nearly captured by a troop of federal cavalry that surprised the pickets around the Kemper house; although he managed to escape, members of his staff were taken. If that was not enough, after he mounted Little Sorrel and bolted across the North River bridge, he was almost killed by another party of federals. An enemy gun, according to Captain Poague, which startled everyone, was aimed at Old Jack:

> I had just come from army headquarters, and, although I had met a cavalryman who told me the enemy were advancing up the river, still I did not think it possible they could have gotten any guns into place in so short of time. It thereupon occurred to me that the gun at the bridge might be one of Carrington's who was on that side of the river whose men had a new uniform something like those we saw at the bridge. Upon suggesting this to the General, he reflected a moment, and then riding a few paces, he called in a tone loud enough to be heard by them, "Bring that gun up here," but getting no reply, he raised himself in his stirrups and in a most authoritative and seemingly angry tone shouted, "Bring that gun up here, I say." At this they began to move the tail of the gun so as to bring it to bear upon us, and when the General perceived what was happening, he quickly turned to the officer in charge of my gun, and said in his sharp, quick way, "Let 'em have it."

The blast from Poague's battery was enough to drive the enemy in retreat.[49]

Along the road from Harrisonburg, meanwhile, one of Fremont's detachments under Louis Blenker, who commanded several regiments of German recruits, encountered Trimble's brigade of Ewell's command. Isaac Trimble, Kentucky born and more than sixty years of age, like Ewell, was not a man to withdraw when the armies met at Cross Keys, a crossroads hamlet three miles west of Port Republic. Jackson had already decided to throw the Valley Army at Shields, who was advancing up the South Fork of the Shenandoah and to leave Cross Keys to Ewell and Trimble. Stationed among an elevated copse of oak trees near Mill Creek, a tributary of North River, Trimble met Blenker's initial charge, and his vigorous counterattack sent Fremont reeling toward Harrisonburg. Although Trimble lost 288 men, federal losses at Cross Keys were listed at 684; mostly, however, the fight disabused Fremont of any further inclination to attack, thereby enabling Jackson to concentrate against Shields.[50]

Jackson's instructions during the night of June 8–9 suggest that he intended to pound Shields and then turn on Fremont's army. Unforeseen obstacles, including a makeshift bridge made from wagons across the South River fords that failed, sending troopers into the water, and a stubborn defense by the enemy upset his plans for victory. After innumerable delays in crossing the river, the Confederates went into battle around Lewiston, the home of General Samuel Lewis, a descendent of one of the first Scotch-Irish families in the valley; the home was also a favorite stopping place for Jackson and his staff. Situated three miles from town on the Port Republic-Luray road, Lewiston and its outbuildings was an oasis in an otherwise heavily forested area. The federal left rested on a hillock behind the house, where Lewis operated a coaling for the manufacture of charcoal, and extended to the South Fork of the Shenandoah along a country lane that was lined by steep ravines. Atop the hill, a Yankee battery of seven guns had been positioned to dominate the entire field.

Reminiscent of Wellington's confession that Waterloo had been "a damned close run business," Jackson ordered Poague's battery supported by infantry to rush the gun emplacements at the coaling, but the attack wavered miserably. At the same time, "Charley" Winder and the Stonewall Brigade charged the enemy right, where the federals were entrenched in the ravines along the road to the Lewis gristmill on the river and were stalled with heavy losses. But Ewell, who left but two brigades beyond the North River to restrain Fremont, arrived in time to attack the federal center commanded by General Erastus B. Tyler. The fight did not favor Jackson until Richard Taylor moved up his Louisiana troops, who, reinforced by part of Ewell's command, overpowered Tyler's guns and drove in his entire left flank. As the enemy broke toward Luray, the captured pieces were turned upon the retreating army with Old Bald Head himself joining in the cannonade. The battle at Port Republic ended with Fremont threatening to rejoin the fray from across the Shenandoah but never quite getting his forces into action, and Jackson pursuing the vanquished federals almost to the road through Swift Run Gap at Conrad's Store.[51]

After Cross Keys and Port Republic, where Confederate losses exceeded one thousand men, Jackson gathered his command at Brown's Gap in the Blue Ridge, until Lee sent for his assistance around the capital. Although he had been forced to fight on the Sabbath, Jackson told Anna that "God has been our shield, and to His name be all the glory . . . How I do wish for peace, but only upon the condition of our national independence!" The valley campaign, while it did not bring the hoped-for nationhood, demonstrated Jackson's superb generalship and proved that he could handle an independent command. When it ended, Robert E. Lee realized that Old Jack could be trusted to carry out his wishes under difficult circumstances. Jackson, furthermore, had accomplished his objective: With Abraham Lincoln's help, he had ruined McClellan's peninsula campaign by keeping Banks, Fremont, and McDowell occupied in the valley. Yet the federals under Samuel S. Carroll and Erastus B. Tyler at Port Republic—Shields himself never got beyond Luray—showed unmistakenly that Yankee farm boys were also learning the art of war. "Riding over the field after the battle," records John Esten Cooke, "Jackson said [he] never saw so many dead in such a small space in all my life before."[52]

1)

An 1861 "photograph" of
Robert E. Lee taken from an
1850 print by Mathew B.
Brady. *(West Virginia State
Archives.)*

2)

Robert E. Lee, 1864. *(West
Virginia State Archives.)*

3)

Left: One of six photographs of Robert E. Lee taken April 16, 1865, by Mathew B. Brady. *Left to right:* Lee's son, G.W.C. "Custis" Lee, Lee, and Walter H. Taylor, Lee's Aide Colonel. *(Massachusetts Commandery Military Order of the Loyal Legion and the United States Army Military History Institute.)*

5)

Below: Nineteenth-century composite of Lee accompanied by Generals Jeb Stuart, Braxton Bragg, Sterling Price, and Kirby Smith. *(West Virginia State Archives.)*

4)

Lithograph of Robert E. Lee that was in wide circulation during the war. *(Massachusetts Commandery Military Order of the Loyal Legion and the United States Army Military History Institute.)*

6)

Lee at his Richmond home in 1865, photographed by Mathew B. Brady. *(National Archives.)*

7)

Lee on his horse, Traveller, at Lexington, Virginia. *(West Virginia State Archives.)*

8)

Last meeting of Lee and Jackson: an 1869 painting by E.B.D. Julio. *(West Virginia State Archives.)*

9)

Lee's early home, Stratford Hall, the south facade. *(Robert E. Lee Memorial Association.)*

10)

Mother's room, Stratford Hall, the room in which Lee was born. *(Robert E. Lee Memorial Association.)*

11)

James Longstreet, Lee's "Old War Horse." *(Massachusetts Commandery Military Order of the Loyal Legion and the United States Army Military History Institute.)*

12)

General Joseph Eggleston Johnston. *(Massachusetts Commandery Military Order of the Loyal Legion and the United States Army Military History Institute.)*

13)

"The Gallant" Major John Pelham, C.S.A. *(Massachusetts Commandery Military Order of the Loyal Legion and the United States Army Military History Institute.)*

14)

James Ewell Brown Stuart. *(United States Army Military History Institute.)*

15)

First Lieutenant Thomas J. Jackson during the Mexican War. *(Massachusetts Commandery Military Order of the Loyal Legion and the United States Army Military History Institute.)*

16)

An 1851 photograph of professor T. J. Jackson by Mathew B. Brady. *(National Archives.)*

17)

Famed 1862 photograph of Jackson with crooked coat button. *(National Archives.)*

18)

Left: Nineteenth-century litho-graph of Lieutenant General T. J. Jackson with signature. *(West Virginia State Archives.)*

19)

Below: Jackson homestead, 1907, with famous gristmill in the fore-ground. *(West Virginia State Archives.)*

20)

Contemporary view of Jackson's mill. *(West Virginia State Archives.)*

21)

Jackson and his staff. *(West Virginia State Archives.)*

22)   Last photograph of Jackson, two weeks before his death. *(National Archives.)*

11

Seven Days in June

While Robert E. Lee continued to seek his place in the Confederate sun as military adviser to Jefferson Davis, Jackson had already secured his reputation; First Manassas and the Valley had made him a household name in both North and South. Walter Taylor, Lee's loyal confidant, terms Jackson's performance "brilliant," and Longstreet says flat-out that he was the talk of the army and the country. Besides Lee's own praise and recognition for the Shenandoah campaign, Fitzhugh Lee labels it "splendid." After all, Lee's nephew records, "in three months he had marched six hundred miles, fought four pitched battles, seven minor engagements, daily skirmishes, defeated four armies, captured seven pieces of artillery, ten thousand stand of arms, four thousand prisoners, and a very great amount of stores."[1]

At the same time, Lee had his detractors as he remained chained to his Richmond desk from March 13 until June 1, when Davis appointed him to command following Joe Johnston's misfortune at Fair Oaks. Prior to his elevation, argues General Long, "the name of General Lee had scarcely appeared, and his position, while of great importance, kept him from public prominence." Although "from this time forward he became the central figure of the war," Lee had already established his great liaison with Jackson during the valley fighting; in spite of his quiet efforts to bolster Johnston's defenses in front of the capital, many line officers, men who felt the sting of Yankee steel, resented his favored place. James Longstreet, who would fail Lee at Gettysburg and who decried Virginia's domination of the Confederate effort, says that Lee's appointment did not "reconcile" the army: "General Lee's experience in active field work was limited to his West Virginia campaign against General Rosecrans, which was not successful. His services on our coastal defenses were known as able, and those who knew him in Mexico . . . , knew that as military engineer he was especially distinguished; but officers of the line were not apt to look to the staff in choosing leaders of soldiers, either in tactics or strategy. There were, therefore, some misgivings as to the power and skill for field service of the new commander." Yet Longstreet concedes that Lee was better than the "halting policy under Johnston."[2]

Although Lee surely knew about his unappreciative subordinates, he moved to do what Joe Johnston had not done—defeat McClellan and, indeed, drive him from the peninsula. Lee was no sooner in command than he took several actions designed to accomplish his mission: He summoned his generals together at the Dabbs home located on the Nine Mile Road just inside the Confederate lines; he moved quickly to reestablish discipline—which had grown lax under Johnston—and an esprit de corps, and he set his men to digging. At the Dabbs House, which he used as his headquarters throughout the Seven Days, the generals assembled on June 2 for "a frank discussion" of not only strategy but also their prospects for victory. All but Jackson—A. P. Hill, James Longstreet, D. H. Hill, John Magruder, Benjamin Huger— were present for a free exchange of ideas. "This novelty was not reassuring, as experience had told that secrecy in war was an essential element of success; that public discussion and secrecy were incompatible," Longstreet notes in his memoirs. When President Davis happened on the Dabbs House during his daily ride to the front and joined the meeting, he found it permeated with gloom: "The tone of the conversation was quite despondent, and one [general], especially, pointed out the inevitable consequence of the enemy's advance by throwing out *Boyaux*, and constructing successive parallels." Davis "expressed, in marked terms, his disappointment at hearing such views, and General Lee remarked that he had, before I came in, said very much the same thing." Still, Lee did not tip his hand, although Longstreet and Davis agree that his momentous decision to summon Jackson from the Shenandoah grew out of these discussions.[3]

Fitzhugh Lee, who probably observed his uncle as closely as anyone during the war, explains the beginnings of the great confidence and affection that Lee began to enjoy throughout the Army of Northern Virginia: "Almost every day now a soldierly-looking man, clad in neat but simple gray uniform, conspicuous by the absence of wreath, gold braid and stars usually found on the uniforms of general officers, sitting his horse like a dragon, might be seen riding along the lines." He seldom rode about with couriers or staff at his side as he looked after every detail of the army; it was a practice he had developed in Mexico, when he rode among the gun emplacements surrounding Vera Cruz.

Lee likewise incurred more than a little grumbling among the commands of A. P. Hill, Huger, Magruder, Longstreet, and D. H. Hill when he set them to digging trenches and erecting earthworks in front of McClellan's growing army. Although he ached to take the offensive, Lee also knew that McClellan was bringing up siege guns to bombard Richmond, a scant five miles beyond the Dabbs House. Lieutenant Robert H. Miller, a Louisianian who had fought his way up the peninsula with Johnston, told his father what he thought of Lee's tactics when he heard that Jackson was marching for the Chickahominy: "Jackson has used his army as a Hercules would his club hurling it irresistibly against the enemy at all points utterly routing and scattering two of their large armies flying from place to place with such rapidity that they not only did not follow him but are bewildered to know his whereabouts till he strikes again as he has done all this and in doing it I am fully convinced that he is the only General on either side in this War who shows any of that *Genius* which is necessary to the managing of armies to affect anything but dig ditches." But Lee had learned the value of good defensive position in Mexico, and he perfected the art in front of Richmond. Margaret Sanborn, his 1967 biographer, calls the "use of intrenchments for infantry Lee's greatest contribution to military art."[4]

Lee suffered no illusions that easy victory was near as sullen troopers carped about the incessant digging. "The war may last ten years," he had written to Mrs. Lee in April when nineteen-year-old Robert, Jr., wanted to leave the university at Charlottesville for the army. He thought Rob, Jr., and boys like him should remain in school because there were sufficient men to fill the ranks. All of that would change as Lincoln's war of attrition began to take its toll upon Confederate manpower, and Lee's youngest son was allowed to join Jackson's command in the valley. Throughout his life, Robert E. Lee was always concerned about his children; even as he led the army into battle, he did so without showing the least parental favoritism. "Suddenly I was rudely awakened by a comrade, and was told to get up and come out, that someone wished to see me," Robert, Jr., wrote about his arrival from the Shenandoah with Jackson. "Half awake I staggered out, and found myself face to face with General Lee and his staff. Their fresh uniforms, bright equipments and well-groomed horses contrasted so forcibly with the war-worn appearance of our command that I was completely dazed. It took me a moment to realize what it all meant, but when I saw my father's loving eyes and smile it became clear to me that he had ridden by to see if I was safe and how I was getting along."⁵

Two letters from the Dabbs House to Mrs. Lee as Lee prepared for battle reflect a further concern for his family. Mrs. Lee, forced to abandon the White House plantation after its destruction by McClellan's forces, had retreated to Richmond with her young daughters. Before she left the Pamunkey, according to an early biographer, Lee's wife fired off a "resolute" note to the intruding Yankees: "Sir: I have patiently and humbly submitted to the search of my house, by the men under your command, who are satisfied that there is nothing here which they want. All the plate and other valuables have long since been removed to Richmond, and are now beyond the reach of any Northern marauders who wish their possession. . . ."

Lee, although confronted by McClellan's army, said that he was "strongly tempted to visit [her] in the city." Besides telling Mrs. Lee to look after Custis, about whom he had been "uneasy," he hoped the mother's influence might restore his eldest son. And when he learned that his only grandson, the child of Rooney and Charlotte Wickham, had died in North Carolina, Lee poured out his feelings: "I cannot help grieving at his loss & know what a void it will occasion in the hearts of his parents. But when I reflect upon his great gain by his merciful transition from earth to Heaven, I think we ought to rejoice. God grant that we may all join him around the throne of our maker to unite in praise & adoration of the Most High forever . . ."⁶

Lee had been in charge of the army since June 1—one day after Joe Johnston's near-mortal wounds at Seven Pines–Fair Oaks. Although Johnston had finally resolved to challenge the advancing Yankees in front of Richmond, President Davis had grown increasingly disenchanted with his hesitant command tactics; "in face, figure and character, General Johnston was thoroughly the soldier," notes John Esten Cooke, who observed him during the campaign. "Above the medium height, with an erect figure; in a close-fitting uniform buttoned to the chin; with a ruddy face, decorated with close-cut side-whiskers, mustache and tuft on the chin; reserved in manner, brief of speech, without impulses of any description, it seemed General Johnston's appearance and bearing were military to stiffness and he was popularly compared to a 'gamecock,' ready for battle at any moment." Yet he looked for every opportunity to avoid a head-on confrontation as McClellan inched his way toward the Confederate capital. As the impasse between Davis and Johnson lengthened, Lee, writes a Johnston biographer, "also thought that Johnston should advise the President of his plans, and requested, 'Let me go see him, and defer this discussion until I return.' When Lee came back from an interview with the field commander, he had good news. Johnston planned to attack McClellan on the coming Thursday on the north side of the river." But he did not attack the main Yankee force beyond the Chickahominy. After learning that McDowell had been sent to chase Jackson in the valley and that the normally sluggish Chickahominy was swollen by heavy downpours over the night of May 29–June 1, he decided to confront the isolated federal units south of the river.[7]

The Chickahominy and its tributary, White Oak Creek, dominated much of the fighting around Richmond. The stream, which originates a few miles north of the city, meanders in a southeasterly direction until it strikes the James between Charles City and Williamsburg. Because of the low-lying tidewater country, the Chickahominy has poorly defined banks that, depending on local rainfall amounts, are lined with not only swampy morasses but also heavy, tangled vegetation. White Oak Swamp Creek, which enters the river from the south, presents a formidable barrier in the country east of Richmond. Four major thoroughfares crossed the area from Mechanicsville, four miles north of the capital, southwestward to White Oak swamp: the Mechanicsville Road, the Nine Mile Road, the Williamsburg Stage Pike, and the Charles City Road. Also crossing the region was the Richmond and York Railroad that roughly paralleled the Williamsburg Road. By May 24, Silas Casey's division of Keyes Corps had advanced to a copse of trees at the Seven Pines crossroads, where the Williamsburg and Nine Mile roads intersect. Less than a mile away was Fair Oaks depot on the railroad, and it was along this line that federal batteries were implanted within sight of Richmond.[8]

Once he decided to act, Johnston devised a straightforward plan of concentrating his divisions against Keyes and Heintzelman, who was threatening him along the Williamsburg Road. Longstreet's Heavy Division was ordered down the Nine Mile Road with fourteen thousand; D. H. Hill's ninety-five hundred passed down the Williamsburg Pike; Huger's five thousand down the Charles City Road. W. H. C. Whiting's division was directed to support Longstreet, while A. P. Hill was kept in reserve around Mechanicsville. John Magruder, under the command of Gustavus W. Smith—senior major general after Johnston—was posted to watch McClellan's right flank north of the Chickahominy.[9]

When the army marched on May 31, Longstreet did not follow his assigned path but proceeded to split his command between the Williamsburg and Charles City roads. Benjamin Huger, newly arrived from

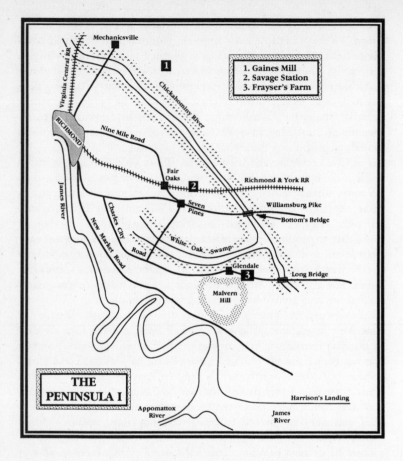

Mechanicsville

Virginia Central RR

Chickahominy River

1

1. Gaines Mill
2. Savage Station
3. Frayser's Farm

RICHMOND

Nine Mile Road

James River

Fair Oaks

2

Richmond & York RR

Seven Pines

Williamsburg Pike

Bottom's Bridge

Charles City Road

New Market Road

White Oak Swamp

Glendale

3

Long Bridge

Malvern Hill

THE
PENINSULA I

Harrison's Landing

Appomattox River

James River

Norfolk and unaware that Longstreet was "in an overall tactical command," was unable to move for several hours because of the mix-up. Although Johnston and McClellan soon lost control of their respective armies, D. H. Hill became tired of waiting for the jumbled columns to sort themselves out and finally went into action about 1:30 in the afternoon. Longstreet, his force depleted by the confused marching orders, entered the fray with only two of the seven brigades at his disposal. In the meantime, Old Edwin Sumner, who had marched his troops to the water's edge on the north side of the Chickahominy, commenced crossing the river at the first sound of battle. "It was only after 5:00 P.M. that the first of Sumner's men began arriving on the field, and just one of his divisions got into action before dark, but along with the reinforcements Heintzelman had sent forward from his corps it was enough to halt the Confederate drive," writes McClellan's biographer. [10]

The bloodbath at Seven Pines was a stalemate, although Johnston managed to drive Keyes and Heintzelman approximately one mile down the Williamsburg Pike. Casualties were high on both sides, with Johnston losing just over sixty-one hundred men to McClellan's five thousand. Longstreet's unexpected changes on the battlefield bungled the Confederate effort, and the blame was not long in coming. Gustavus W. Smith, who commanded the army during the fighting on June 1, writes in his 1891 memoir: "In spite of Longstreet's letter of June 7, and his official report, and the official report of General Johnston, and all that has been said by both of them in censure of Huger and Huger's division, the facts now established, show, beyond doubt, that General Longstreet should be held responsible, under General Johnston, for the failure of the Confederate army to destroy Keyes corps at Seven Pines, on the 31st of May, 1862." Still, Longstreet mounted a halfhearted attack on the morning of June 1, but it was quickly broken off; the damage had been done by nightfall on May 31, when both armies had decided to end the engagement, "the whole of the thirteen brigades had quietly filed by, and the rear guard moved off, not a Yankee in sight or a puff of smoke." [11]

According to General Long, Robert E. Lee, who "took no part" in the battle, arrived at Gustavus Smith's headquarters on the Nine Mile Road "on the morning of the 31st, just before 9 o'clock." Jefferson Davis was with him, and Long positively states that Johnston joined them. Johnston, however, who was "greatly disappointed" with Longstreet's performance, says that he placed himself "on the left, where I could learn soonest the approach of Federal reinforcements from beyond the Chickahominy." Others, including several Johnston biographers, indicate that he saw Lee and Davis riding into camp and mounted his horse to avoid a confrontation with the president. Davis charitably says that Johnston left for the front "soon after our arrival." All agree, however, that Joe Johnston was severely wounded on the evening of May 31, and "as soon as an ambulance could be obtained, he was removed from the field." As late evening approached, a musketball penetrated his right shoulder and within moments a shell fragment "struck him in the breast and knocked him from his horse unconscious." Although Gustavus Smith took immediate command, Lee replaced him the next day at the president's order.[12]

"General Robert E. Lee was now in immediate command, and thence-forward directed the movements in front of Richmond," Jefferson Davis later observed: "Laborious and exact in details, he was vigilant and comprehensive in grand strategy, a power, with which the public had not credited him, soon became manifest in all that makes an army a rapid, accurate, compact machine with responsive motion in all of its parts." And Davis was correct in his assessment; although he was already "collaborating" with Jackson to use the Valley Army to keep reinforcements from the Peninsula, Lee soon employed every resource at his command to foil McClellan's drive toward Richmond. He meant to protect the capital by shifting the main theater of operations as far away as possible. In short, he meant to crush McClellan, and in the days that followed he was in constant motion as he conferred with his generals and rode among the troops. Not even Mrs. Lee's arrival in the city could induce him to leave the front.[13]

Lee had obviously determined to take the initiative within a week or so of his appointment, but to do so he needed Jackson at his side. The notion of a Lee-Jackson merger had been in his mind for at least a month—even before he replaced Johnston—and now was the time to move from intuitive collaboration to active participation. Following his victory at Winchester, Jackson had formulated a scheme to cross the Potomac for an intrusion into northern territory; Old Jack had even dispatched his friend and sometime aide A. R. Boteler to ask for the necessary troops from Richmond. "Tell them that I now have fifteen thousand men. I should have forty thousand; and with them I would invade the North." Then, continues Dabney's account: "When this message was delivered to General Lee, the Commander-in-Chief replied: 'But first he must help me drive these people away from Richmond.'"[14]

Although Lee congratulated Jackson on the valley campaign in his communiqués of June 8 and 11, and started to hint at Jackson's march to Richmond, the impact of the valley on McClellan is open to question.

Traditional Confederate wisdom dictates that Jackson and the foot cavalry upset federal operations on the peninsula, yet a recent McClellan biographer suggests otherwise: "Despite all of Jackson's efforts at creating a diversion, two of McDowell's three original divisions—Franklin's and McCall's—had already joined McClellan. Moreover, during the course of the peninsula campaign up to the last week of June, the threat that McDowell's corps might march south had kept Jackson's entire command out of the ranks of Richmond's defenders. Mr. Lincoln often pointed out, every Confederate soldier otherwise occupied meant that many fewer Confederates facing the Army of the Potomac." And it should be noted: Although Jackson with Lee's blessing had bloodied Shields and Fremont in the valley, he had not destroyed them.[15]

Be that as it may, Lee set his plans into motion during the second week in June with an order to reinforce Jackson as a means of deceiving McClellan. "It was determined to do so at the expense of weakening this army," he informed Old Jack on June 11. "Brigadier-General [Alexander R.] Lawton with six regiments from Georgia is on his way to you, and Brigadier-General [W. H. C.] Whiting with eight veteran regiments leaves here today. The object is to enable you to crush the forces opposed to you. Leave your enfeebled troops to watch the country and guard the passes covered by your cavalry and artillery, and with your main body, including Ewell's division and Lawton's and Whiting's commands, move rapidly to Ashland by rail or otherwise." John Bell Hood who joined in the ruse to mislead McClellan, said later that his command, reinforced by Hampton's Legion, marched from Richmond via Lynchburg to Charlottesville, and then across the Blue Ridge to Staunton. "Upon our arrival, we received orders to retrace our steps, return to Charlottesville, and there take the train to Hanover Court Junction. On the 25th I conducted my command, which now formed part of Jackson's army, to Ashland." Throughout, Lee demanded that extreme care be exercised to conceal Jackson's movements; he even implored the new secretary of war, George W. Randolph, to intercede with the Richmond newspapers to say nothing about Jackson or the additional troops ordered back across the Blue Ridge.[16]

The evening before his letter to Jackson, Lee, anxious about McClellan's troop dispositions, called James Ewell Brown Stuart, his twenty-nine-year-old cavalry commander, to the Dabbs House and set in motion one of the heroic episodes of the war; then, on June 11, he sent a formal directive to the intrepid cavalryman: "You are desired to make a secret movement to the rear of the enemy now posted on the Chickahominy, with a view to gaining intelligence of his operations, communications, etc;

and of driving in his foraging parties, and securing such grain, cattle, etc., for ourselves as you can make arrangements to have driven in. Another object is to destroy his wagon trains, said to be daily passing from the Piping Tree Road to his camp on the Chickahominy. . . ." Stuart worked throughout June 11 to assemble twelve hundred sabers, including light guns—the famed horse artillery—under the command of Lieutenant James Breathed. Four abreast, Stuart and his horsemen rode north from Richmond—infantrymen said they were going to reinforce Jackson—past a way station on the Telegraph Road named Yellow Tavern, and then the column turned eastward away from the Shenandoah and headed toward the Yankee lines. [17]

Stuart's company commanders included Colonels Rooney Lee (9th Virginia Cavalry) and his cousin, Fitzhugh Lee (1st Virginia Cavalry), as well as Breathed and his guns; also accompanying the troop was a giant of a man, newly enlisted in the Confederate cause while on leave from the Prussian dragoons, named Heros Von Borcke. The big German fought throughout the war, eventually becoming Stuart's chief of staff, and he also penned a two-volume memoir that captures the élan and devotion of Lee's cavalrymen. The Chickahominy expedition, if it accomplished little else, shot Stuart to the first rank among Confederate warriors.

In June 1862, according to Von Borcke, "Stuart was a stoutly-built man, rather above middle height, of a most frank and willing expression, the lower part of his fine face covered with a heavy beard. His eye was quick and piercing, of a light-blue in repose, but changing to a darker tinge under high excitement. His whole person seemed instinct with vitality, his movements were alert, his observation keen and alert, and altogether to me he was the model of a dashing cavalry leader." Before his death at the hands of Phil Sheridan's cavalry in the fight at Yellow Tavern two years later, Stuart had indeed become the archetypical cavalryman. Another of his trusted lieutenants, "the boy artillerist from Alabama," who became a mighty contributor to the Stuart legend until his own death at Kelly's Ford in May 1863, did not ride with the cavalry that June morning. Pelham, who usually commanded the batteries that traveled with Stuart's troop, instead remained behind as James Breathed marshaled the horse artillery. Twenty-four years old, a West Point dropout, blue eyed and gallant, John Pelham became a charming beau to numerous Richmond belles, and he also fought with Stuart and Von Borcke on other fields. [18]

When Stuart swung eastward, crossed the Virginia Central railroad and approached Hanover Court House, he encountered federal cavalry for the first time. His own father-in-law, General Philip St. George Cooke, commander of Fitz-John Porter's cavalry, sparred with him over the next two days as the column sped across Totopotomoy Creek toward Old Church. Although Porter would later complain that Cooke had not pressed hard enough, Stuart fought a running battle with enemy horsemen until he crossed the Chickahominy near Sycamore Springs; his biographer, John W. Thomason, a fighting man in another war, has pieced together a first-rate account of the contending forces:

> When two cavalry units ride into each other there is a screaming confusion and a dusty tumult, wherein nothing is very clear, then or afterward; and where, after the fewest frantic minutes, one party or the other runs. The horses, already brought to the highest excitement, plunge and rear, trying to get free of the press, and their men hack and slash, each trooper just as likely to shear an ear from his own mount, or to rake a comrade's ribs, as to get home on the enemy. All things being equal, the men and horses will break first who are least hardened by discipline against their natural aversion to getting hurt. . . .[19]

Once Stuart crossed the Chickahominy, his famed "ride around McClellan" progressed without mishap; that leg of the trip, beyond the enemy's left flank, took him through Charles City Court House, past a slight rise called Malvern Hill, and up the New Market Road to Richmond. "When he strode into Lee's headquarters before sunrise on the 15th," relates Thomason, "Stuart's column had with it 165 prisoners and 260 animals, and had burned and destroyed notably, and suffered just one casualty. The regiments reported four enlisted men missing, straggled, or lost in the woods." And though couriers were dispatched to Lee while the troopers rode through the Virginia countryside, the affair produced questionable results other than its obvious propaganda value. It became a great morale boost for Confederate arms as Richmond lasses threw flowered bouquets before the horsemen. Still, intelligence about Fitz-John Porter's positions, which enabled Jackson to attack with precision a few days later, had been garnered on the first day out; Stuart could easily have returned to the Dabbs House with that news without his foray across McClellan's line of communications. The ride, concludes McClellan's biographer, "demonstrated the vulnerability of the York River base, particularly to cavalry raiders." McClellan himself boasted that Stuart "was a minor consideration," although he probably saved the federal army from certain destruction by shifting his base of operations to the James immediately afterward.[20]

As Lee pondered his options, Jackson made ready to leave the valley following the letter of June 11. From his bivouac "Near Weyer's Cave," a tourist attraction in more peaceful times, Jackson wrote to Anna on the 14th: "Our God has again thrown His shield over me in various apparent dangers to which I have been exposed. This evening we have religious services in the army for the purpose of rendering thanks to the Most High for the victories . . . and to offer earnest prayer that He will continue to give us success, until, through His divine blessing, our independence shall be established." At Jackson's invitation, the Reverend Dabney preached the message of thanksgiving. And he reminisced with his "esposita" about a visit the two of them had made from Lexington to the cave. He informed his friend Jonathan M. Bennett on the same day that while he trusted "no hostile foot will in the Providence of God ever be permitted to enter our honored capital, but should that calamity befall us, I will be very glad to have you with us in the field." Bennett, still Virginia state auditor, had apparently asked to join Jackson's army should Richmond fall to Mc-Clellan.[21]

If Bennett was worried about a potential collapse, others were not. According to some accounts, Richmond assumed an almost carnival atmosphere when thousands of soldiers flooded into the city. "A few weeks before the Seven Days campaign" observes one scholar, "a newspaper reported a large influx of prostitutes of both sexes into the capital, and remarked that they have been disporting extensively on the sidewalks, and in hacks and open carriages. . . . Indulging in smirks and smiles, winks and . . . remarks not of a choice kind in a loud voice."[22]

At the front, however, Lee started to act one day after Stuart's news that McClellan's right flank north of the Chickahominy was vulnerable. Since Fremont and Shields "were apparently retrograding," he informed Jackson on June 16: "The present seems to be favorable for a junction of your army and this. If you agree with me, the sooner you can make arrangements to do so the better." And, Lee admonished: "To be efficacious, the movement must be secret. Let me know the force you can bring, and be careful to guard from friends and foes your purpose and your intention of personally leaving the valley. The country is full of spies, and our plans are immediately carried to the enemy." Jackson wasted no time in obeying Lee's instruction, although his tight-lipped stratagems aroused a storm among his staff. The drive for secrecy as well as rapidity of movement caused him to fall silent for the next weeks; both Anna's memoir and the *Official Records* contain no Jackson letters until the Seven Days campaign had run its course. Before he left the Shenandoah, relates Dabney, "the Confederate cavalry [under Munford] drew a cordon of pickets across the country so tight that the befooled enemy never learned that General Jackson's whole army was not on his front, until he discovered it by the disasters of McClellan."[23]

After he put the army in motion on the 17th, Jackson left his Port Republic campsite for Staunton to confer with Whiting and Colonel Thomas T. Munford, who had taken command of the cavalry upon Ashby's death. Old Jack himself left on Wednesday, June 18, for Waynesboro and Rockfish Gap; he crossed the Blue Ridge to Mechum Station and "took the cars" for Charlottesville; by Friday, June 20, he had reached the rail junction at Gordonsville. True to Lee's orders, Jackson confided in no one about his destination until Gordonsville, when he swore Dabney to secrecy and told him that the army was headed for Richmond. While two hundred decrepit railroad cars shuttled his troops from Mechum Station, Jackson's penchant for secrecy even permeated the army. "One of Hood's men left the ranks on the march, and was climbing a fence to go to a cherry-tree in a field near at hand, when Jackson rode by and saw him," relates John Esten Cooke:

> "Where are you going?" asked the General.
> "I don't know," replied the soldier.
> "To what command do you belong?"
> "I don't know."
> "Well, what State are you from?"
> "I don't know."
> "What is the meaning of all this?" Jackson asked of another. "Well," was the reply, "Old Stonewall and General Hood issued orders yesterday, that we were not to know anything until after the next fight." Jackson laughed and rode on.[24]

Nothing, not even mulish subordinates like Whiting and the ever-swearing Major Harman, who resented being kept in the dark, could deter Jackson. "We could break any cavalry brigade on a long march," recalls John Casler, who trekked along with the Stonewall Brigade. "As the cars reached their destination they would return and meet us, and take another load; but we still had to march." Jackson and the foot cavalry remained in constant motion until he reached Gordonsville, when he ordered a halt to rest his foot-weary infantrymen. A "groundless rumor" that a federal column was approaching from the Rappahannock also prompted the one-day layover. Ewell's division was ordered to remain near the Stonewall Brigade, but Whiting and Lawton were rushed forward on the road to Ashland.[25]

At Gordonsville, Jackson asked Dabney to take a train ride with him; by late Saturday night, the two had reached Fredericks Hall. Here, fifty miles north of Richmond, Jackson paused at the home of Nathaniel Harris to observe the Sabbath; after he attended church services, again conducted by Dabney, and enjoyed the hospitality of the Harris family, he mounted Little Sorrel at 1 A.M., June 23, and rode toward Richmond. Lee, after all, in the letter of June 11, had urged him to "keep me advised of your movements and, if practicable, precede your troops, that we might confer and arrange for simultaneous attack." Without a word and accompanied by Major Harman, Mr. Harris, and a local guide, Major General Thomas J. Jackson set out for the Dabbs House and a face-to-face meeting the general commanding.[26]

Several hours after he left Fredericks Hall "by relay of horses," Old Jack reached his destination. Longstreet's account has him arriving first with the others being summoned to headquarters afterward. Others at the conference say that D. H. Hill was leaning against a gate post when Jackson rode up, and that, following an exchange of pleasantries, the two brothers-in-law entered Lee's "private office" to join Lee, A. P. Hill, and Longstreet. Although Lee asked if he wanted refreshments, Jackson apparently said little throughout the meeting; countless commentators have speculated that the fatigue which plagued his movements over the next several days had already started to cloud his judgment.

After the opening amenities, Lee got down to business. He had developed a straightforward scheme, which he spelled out in the famed "General Orders, No. 75." Issued the following day, June 24, it called upon the troops to cook three days' rations and prepare for action by the 26th. Jackson was expected to arrive at Ashland on June 25 and to make contact with Lawrence O. Branch's brigade of A. P. Hill's division; he was further commanded to march the next morning at 3 A.M., and "turn the enemy's works at Mechanicsville and Beaver Dam Creek." In Lee's own words, although assistant Adjutant General R. H. Chilton signed the actual order:

General Jackson will advance on the road leading to Pole Green Church, communicating his march to General Branch, who will immediately cross the Chickahominy and take the road leading to Mechanicsville. As soon as the movements of these columns are discovered, General A. P. Hill, with the rest of his division, will cross the Chickahominy near Meadow Bridge and move direct upon Mechanicsville. To aid his advance, the heavy batteries on the Chickahominy will at the proper time open upon the batteries at Mechanicsville. The enemy being driven from Mechanicsville and the passage across the bridge opened, General Longstreet, with his division and that of General D. H. Hill will cross the Chickahominy at or near that point, General D. H. Hill moving to the support of General Jackson and General Longstreet supporting General A. P. Hill. The four divisions, keeping in communications with each other and moving en echelon on separate roads, if practicable, the left division in advance, with skirmishers and sharp-shooters extending their front, will sweep down the Chickahominy and endeavor to drive the enemy from his position above New Bridge, General Jackson bearing well to his left, turning Beaver Dam Creek and taking the direction toward Cold Harbor. They will press forward toward the York River Railroad, closing upon the enemy's rear and forcing him down the Chickahominy.[27]

John Magruder and Benjamin Huger were told to hold their positions between Richmond and Fair Oaks Station. Lee had observed Joe Johnston's loose commands during the Seven Pines fight and he sought to spell out the maneuvers for each division. Strangely, his drive for precision did not include a reliable timetable for detailed executions on the battlefield. And he attempted an exceptionally difficult operation—the combination of two separated forces while the battle progressed. Everything depended upon Jackson. If he reached his assigned place at the appointed hour, Lee's plan had a chance; if he was deterred on the road, then trouble lay on the horizon. And Jackson, accustomed to fast marches through the well-manicured Shenandoah with the ever-present Valley Pike for direction, appeared confused from the beginning about the low-lying topography around Richmond. Longstreet's recollection of the Dabbs House conversations has Jackson certain that he could reach the Virginia Central Railroad at Ashland by June 25. When Lee withdrew briefly from the room, Longstreet turned to him and "expressed doubt of his meeting that hour, and suggested that it would be better to take a little more time, as the movements of our columns could be readily adjusted to his. He then appointed the morning of the 26th." Lee must have agreed upon his return. The attack was set for 3 A.M., June 26.[28]

Jackson did not await Lee's written order but left immediately to rejoin his marching columns. By nightfall on June 25, his force had reached "the village of Ashland, 12 miles north of Richmond." Here, Jackson secluded himself in fervent prayer during much of the night and when the march was resumed on the 26th, observes Percy Hamlin: "A native of the section, Lincoln Sydnor, who had been sent to guide Jackson found so many new roads cut and familiar landmarks gone, that he became confused and led the column some distance on the wrong road. It was necessary to countermarch, with greatest difficulty and loss of time, turning guns, limbers and caissons in the narrow woods road. Ewell was furious and threatened

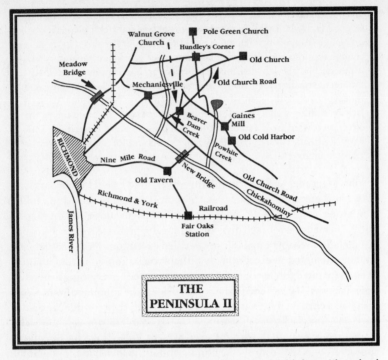

THE
PENINSULA II

to hang Sydnor at once, but Jackson intervened and told the guide to lead them back." Jackson was not only fighting personal fatigue from riding to and fro but now he had become lost and temporarily bogged down; he was also short of his destination.[29]

What was worse, McClellan had learned about his approach from a Confederate malingerer and decided to open the campaign. Little Mac pleaded hourly with Secretary of War Edwin Staunton to send additional forces as he prepared to act before Jackson could reinforce Lee north of the Chickahominy. On the 25th, he "determined to move his line in front of Seven Pines forward to a large clearing on the other side of a heavily timbered piece of ground, through the middle of which ran a small stream whose swampy borders had until that time formed the extreme picket line of the opposing forces in that direction." In what became known as the "affair at Oak Grove," continues Alexander Webb, "Heintzelman's corps, part of Sumner's and Palmer's brigade of Keyes's corps, advanced in good order through the timber, met and repulsed a strong force of the enemy and occupied the position throwing out pickets within four miles of Richmond." Thereupon, as Jackson pressed toward his rendezvous with Lee, McClellan halted the attack with the onset of darkness. A spirited counterattack by Huger and Magruder had blunted his thrust south of the Chickahominy.[30]

Undaunted by the engagement—also known as the Battle of King's School House—Lee proceeded with his plans for the 26th; his entire strategy nearly collapsed, however, when Jackson failed to reach his assigned attack point by 3 A.M. After Old Jack left Ashland and approached Totopotomoy Creek, a tributary of the Pamunkey, on the day in question, he wrote in his own battle summary: "The Federal picket crossed to the south side of the stream and partially destroyed the bridge, and by felling trees across the road farther on attempted to delay our advance. After the Texas skirmishers [Hood's brigade] had gallantly crossed over and Reilly shelled the woods for the purpose of driving the enemy from it, in order that we might safely effect a lodgement beyond the creek, Whiting rapidly repaired the bridge and the march was resumed." The Valley Army had only reached the crossroads at Hundley's Corner by nightfall of the 26th, two miles or so north of where it should be, yet close enough to hear the sounds of battle. Jackson's artilleryman, Captain Poague, says that "the continuous and tremendous roar of musketry exceeded anything I heard during the war."[31]

What Poague and his messmates heard from their Hundley's Corner bivouac was the last gasp of fighting around Mechanicsville and Beaver Dam Creek. Lee, and, indeed, the entire army, had listened in vain for the sound of Jackson's guns against the federal right until mid afternoon on June 26, when A. P. Hill crossed the Chickahominy to open the fight on his own initiative. After the enemy was driven from Mechanicsville with heavy Confederate losses, Lee ordered the commands of D. H. Hill and Longstreet into the bloody fray to do what Jackson had been expected to do—drive in McClellan's northernmost flank. Yet Fitz-John Porter managed a technical victory by withdrawing into his entrenchments behind Beaver Dam Creek at nightfall; although Lee, who rushed to the scene, lost fourteen hundred men on the 26th, he still held the advantage. With the exception of Huger and Magruder, who guarded the Richmond roads, his entire force including Jackson lay concentrated against the federal right. "And thus it happened," notes William Swinton, "that, while on the north side of the Chickahominy thirty thousand Union troops were being assailed by seventy thousand Confederates, twenty-five thousand Confederates on the south side held in check sixty thousand Union troops."[32]

Although a recent Jackson biographer maintains that a Confederate victory would have resulted had Jackson been there, Lee maintained an outward serenity in dealing with his tardy commander. General Long, who was on the field at Mechanicsville, writes that Lee was "disappointed" with Jackson's lateness. Lee told Jefferson Davis on the 26th that Jackson had been detained "by high water and mud"; his official report, written two months before Old Jack's death, says only: "In consequence of unavoidable delays the whole of General Jackson's command did not arrive at Ashland in time to enable him to reach the designated point on the 25th. His march on the 26th was consequently longer than had been anticipated, and his progress also being retarded by the enemy." Lee had already started to exhibit his rare qualities of great leadership, which included an innate ability to mask his displeasure at the poor performance of others, thereby preserving an atmosphere of future cooperation.[33]

When A. P. Hill ordered Maxcy Gregg and his South Carolinians to reopen the offensive on June 27, Jackson was still absent; described by one participant in the Gaines Mill fight as "a very modest, quiet gentleman, of about fifty," with grey hair, full whiskers, and a ruddy complexion, Gregg was "thick-set, of medium height, and jocular in manner." Known as a fighting man soon to fall dead at Fredericksburg, he drove the enemy from the country around Beaver Dam Creek and Ellison's Mill without Jackson's help. And Old Jack's late arrival for the second time in as many days did not win him many friends. During Porter's early morning retreat down the Chickahominy, observes Longstreet's chief of artillery, E. P. Alexander: "Had Jackson's corps made an early morning start, and pushed as Jackson was wont to push, both before and after the Seven Days, he would have struck Porter's corps on the flank as it marched toward Cold Harbor. But the advance was so slow that when at last, at about eight o'clock, it appeared in rear of Porter's position, having marched about three miles, the last Federal soldier had withdrawn, and Jackson's artillery fired by mistake into the head of Hill's advancing column. The trap was sprung, but the bird had flown." Although Jackson had difficulty reaching the field, he combined with Longstreet and A. P. Hill later in the day, and, contrary to Alexander's fuming, the Valley Army soon tipped the Confederate scales north of the Chickahominy.[34]

Lee rode to the fighting from his new headquarters at the Hogan farm on the Nine Mile Road at the same time Magruder remained positioned at the Garnett Farm, directly across the river in Lee's line of sight. Inexorably drawn to the scene once A. P. Hill set Gregg and his other brigades on the march, Lee "now witnessed in person the fighting of his troops, who charged under his eye, closing in a nearly hand-to-hand conflict with the enemy." Then, continues John Esten Cooke:

This was the first occasion in which a considerable portion of the men had seen him—certainly in battle—and that air of supreme calmness which always characterized him in action must have made a deep impression on them. He was clad simply, and wore scarcely any badges of rank. A felt hat drooped low over the broad forehead, and the eyes beneath were calm and unclouded. Add a voice of measured calmness, the air of immovable composure which marked the erect military figure, evidently at home in the saddle, and the reader will have a correct conception of General Lee's personal appearance in this the first of the great battles of his career.[35]

Lee ordered a three-pronged advance for the 27th: A. P. Hill took the center and moved down the Cold Harbor Road or the chief route from Mechanicsville toward Gaines Mill; Jackson, with D. H. Hill, formed the Confederate left and marched by "a road which intersected the Cold Harbor Road between Gaines Mill and Cold Harbor"; Longstreet, who brought up the extreme right, headed eastward along a road that paralleled the Chickahominy; and Stuart's cavalry screened the columns of Jackson and Hill.[36]

Jackson, however, moved with extreme difficulty throughout the day after he left Hundley's Corner. It was 11 o'clock before he reached the Walnut Grove Church at a crossroads along A. P. Hill's advance; after he talked briefly with his fellow commander, who rode off on some errand of command, Jackson and Lee, who still traveled with Powell Hill, held their first battlefield conversation. Burke Davis recites what happened as "curious Alabamians" who marched with Isaac Trimble's brigade watched the two warriors from afar. "Jackson reined short and dismounted. Lee's grandly attired staff stared at the strange figure of the army's most famous field officer as Stonewall took orders from the commander. Lee sat on a cedar stump at the roadside, himself looking so undistinguished that the Reverend Dabney had to be told who he was. Jackson listened with his disreputable cap in hand, and soon mounted to ride away."[37]

Lee's "final instruction" to Jackson included a summary of his plan of attack; Old Jack was told to prevent any retreat McClellan and Fitz-John Porter might attempt toward their base on the York. But Jackson and his staff, including Ewell and Whiting, had no grasp of the swampy, heavily wooded terrain between the Walnut Grove Churchyard and Cold Harbor not two miles distant. Two roads in fact led to his destination, and when he found two of Stuart's cavalrymen who resided in the area, he instructed them to lead the Valley Army toward his rendezvous with A. P. Hill and Longstreet. "They naturally pointed him to the direct and larger road, as the route to Cold Harbor." And, Dabney continues:

After marching a mile and a half, the booming of cannon in his front caught his ear, and he demanded sharply of the guide near him: "Where is that firing?" The reply was, that it was in the direction of Gaines Mill. "Does this road lead there?" he asked. The guide told him that it led by Gaines Mill to Cold Harbor. "But," exclaimed he, "I do not wish to go to Gaines Mill. I wish to go to Cold Harbor, leaving that place on the right." "Then," said the guide, "the left-hand road was the one you should have taken; and had you let me know what you desired, I could have directed you aright at first."

Once again his urge to secrecy had gotten Jackson into trouble; as the fight between A. P. Hill and Porter shook the countryside, he was lost in the undergrowth with no choice but turn his columns and artillery amid the narrow, nearly impassable roads. Then, as he hurried toward the battle, he told his fretting staff: "Let us trust that the providence of our God will so overrule [our delay], that no mischief will result."[38]

As Jackson struggled with his columns, A. P. Hill had moved forward about two o'clock without him. "My division was engaged a full two hours before assistance was received," Hill noted later. "We failed to carry the enemy lines, but we paved the way for the successful attacks afterward. . . . About four o'clock reinforcements came upon my right from General Longstreet and later Jackson's men on my left and center, and my division was relieved of the weight of the contest." Hill did not break the enemy lines because Fitz-John Porter had drawn behind Powhite and Boatswain Creeks, a position that not only gave him an escape southward across the Chickahominy but also proved a formidable defense along his rear. General Long reports that Porter occupied a "plateau bounded on the north-west side, by a bluff eighty or ninety feet in elevation, which curving to the north and east, gradually diminished into a gentle slope. The plateau was bounded on the north side by a stream [the Powhite] flowing along its base, whose banks gradually widened and until, when reaching the bluff, they had gained a width of five or six feet, thus forming a natural ditch." The enemy, strengthened by fieldpieces atop the plateau and from guns beyond the Chickahominy, was arrayed in three tiers along the bank.[39]

Although Longstreet entered the brawl after four o'clock, Jackson's men were needed to turn Porter's extreme right along the creek. "Ah, general, I am very glad to see you. I hoped to be with you before," was Lee's greeting when Jackson finally reached Old Cold Harbor around five o'clock. And, continues John Esten Cooke's account: "Jackson made a twitching movement of his head, and replied in a few words, rather jerked from his lips than deliberately uttered."

Lee had paused, and now listened attentively to the long roll of musketry from the woods, where Hill and Longstreet were engaged, then to the still more incessant and angry roar from the direction of Jackson's own troops, who had closed in upon the federal forces.

"That fire is very heavy," said Lee. "Do you think your men can stand it?"

Jackson listened for a moment, with his head bent toward one shoulder, as was customary with him, for he was deaf, he said, in one ear, "and could not hear out of the other," and replied briefly:

"They can stand almost any thing! They can stand that."

After he received a final word from Lee, both Cooke and Kyd Douglas agree that Jackson rode to the sound of battle with a lemon clenched between his lips—an incident that has been dutifully repeated by every Civil War chronicler since. The instant he mounted his horse, "someone handed him a lemon—a fruit of which he was specially fond." Thereupon, continues Douglas, "a small piece was bitten out of it and slowly and unsparingly he began to extract its flavor and its juice. From that moment until darkness ended the battle, that lemon scarcely left his lips except to be used as a baton to emphasize an order."[40]

Dr. Hunter McGuire, Jackson's medical officer who served him to the moment of his death, maintains that Old Jack's performance at Gaines Mill simply reflected Lee's orders at the Walnut Grove Church, that Jackson had been told "to form in line with D. H. Hill and wait until McClellan retreated toward the Pamunkey, and then to strike him a side blow and capture him." When he reached Gaines Mill and found Hill already engaged, "Jackson obeying Lee's instructions sent an aide to inform Hill of the orders of the commander-in-chief, and it was with some difficulty, that he was withdrawn from the fight." Once he recognized that the enemy was not retreating in the direction Lee had anticipated, McGuire adds, Jackson "put every man he had [about 25,000] into the battle."[41]

Although shouts of "Jackson, Jackson" greeted his arrival, most observers concede that Old Jack was hollow eyed from fatigue. "His appearance on this day was not imposing. He rode a gaunt sorrel horse, slow, and somewhat awkward in movement, and his seat in the saddle was in strong contrast to that of General Lee, who was very erect and graceful on horseback. Jackson leaned forward like a tyro in riding; was clad in a dingy gray uniform, without decorations, and wore his famous old sun-scorched cap drawn low upon the forehead." Complicating his conduct was the fact that his command had become disarrayed when forced to turn its direction of march on the Cold Harbor Road; D. H. Hill had already joined the battle to bolster Powell Hill's troops before he reached the field.

Jackson, however, when he did get there, lost no time in sending Whiting and the Stonewall Brigade against Porter. His difficulties with Whiting aside, Old Jack was unstinting in his praise of what followed:

> Advancing thence through a number of retreating and disorganized regiments General Whiting came within range of the enemy's fire, who, concealed in an open wood and protected by breastworks, poured a destructive fire for a quarter of a mile into his advancing line, under which many brave officers and men fell. Dashing on with unfaltering step in the face of those murderous discharges of canister and musketry General Hood and Colonel Law, at the heads of their respective brigades, rushed to the charge with a yell. Moving down a precipitous ravine, leaping ditch and stream, clamoring up a difficult ascent, and exposed to an incessant and deadly fire, these brave and determined men pressed forward, driving the enemy from his well-selected and fortified position.

In spite of Jackson's elegant words, Hood's brigade incurred one thousand casualties, although the Texans broke the federal line and captured "nearly a regiment of prisoners." While Jackson called Hood's men "soldiers indeed," another charge was needed to drive Porter from the field.[42]

As both armies counted their losses—Lee, eighty-seven hundred; McClellan, sixty-eight hundred—Jackson was nearly captured by lingering federals north of the river. In a move that presaged his death less than a year later, Jackson rode beyond his lines near the Chickahominy crossing and encountered several federal pickets in the darkness. Luckily, the episode had a happy outcome when he boldly commanded the men to lay down their arms; at least one trooper was heard boasting that he had been "captured by Stonewall hisself" as he marched to the Confederate rear; if Jackson escaped injury in this, the first pivotal battle of the Richmond fighting, others of his official family were not so fortunate: Chatham Roberdeau Wheat, who led "the rough and unruly Louisiana Tigers," was among the dead at Gaines Mill; the Stonewall Brigade under Charles S. Winder lost Colonels Samuel V. Fulkerson and J. W. Allen. The entire Confederate army suffered terribly in the same fight that Lee called the "Battle of Chickahominy." Everywhere men lay dead or dying in both armies as Jackson rode westward for a late night conference with Lee and Longstreet at the former's headquarters on the Nine Mile Road.[43]

Lee was in the uncomfortable position of not knowing what McClellan would do: Would he bring up reinforcements and attempt to protect his supply bases on the Pamunkey; would he retreat down the Chickahominy toward his headquarters at Rooney's old home at White House; would he shift direction and move his army to the James and the protective cover of federal gunboats? As the generals pondered their options, Jackson was told to send Jeb Stuart and Ewell in the direction of Despatch Station on the Richmond and York River Railroad to intercept any movement north of the Chickahominy. At the same time, unbeknownst to Lee, McClellan solved his emergency. "On the evening of the 27th of June, I assembled the corps commanders at my headquarters, and informed them of the plan, its reasons, my choice of route and method of execution," Little Mac penned later: "The operations of this day proved the numerical superiority of the enemy, and made it evident that while he had a large army on the left bank of the Chickahominy, which had already turned our right, and was in position to intercept the communications at White House, he was also in large force between our army and Richmond. I there effected a junction of our forces." The instant McClellan decided to abandon the Pamunkey and combine his separated forces south of the Chickahominy, the campaign for Richmond took a new direction; for Lee it now became a running struggle to crush the federal army before it could reach the James.[44]

Saturday, June 28, was spent awaiting McClellan's next move; although Little Mac was urging his divisions southward through the expanses of White Oak Swamp, Lee did not know his whereabouts during much of the day, thus giving his adversary a twenty-four-hour head start. When Jackson awoke, following a fitful sleep on the ground near Jeb Stuart, he acted on Lee's instruction and ordered the cavalryman and Ewell on their mission down the Chickahominy. But Stuart went on another raiding expedition and failed to bring any reliable information about McClellan's whereabouts. Ewell, on the other hand, busied himself destroying depots of abandoned federal stores; "large quantities of supplies were captured, and for many days his troops dined in luxury on desiccated vegetables washed down by the coffee of Java."[45]

Tom Jackson, meanwhile, proceeded to rebuild the Grapevine Bridge at Lee's order; although it was located in front of his command, the the bridge was one of several—New, Duane's, Grapevine, Lower, Bottom's, Long—that spanned the sluggish Chickahominy between

Mechanicsville and Williamsburg. Uncharacteristically, Jackson, who was still suffering from fatigue after a week of constant warfare, did not drive his men to the task. "Jackson was long delayed repairing the Grapevine Bridge," says Longstreet: "He probably knew that the river was fordable at that position but preferred to pass his men over dry-shod." The bridge restored, Jackson and his staff crossed the Chickahominy as darkness approached to confer with Lee and Magruder, who held the Confederate left below the river. By this time, Lee had correctly surmised that McClellan was marching for the James, but the late hour prevented an attack.

As the three warriors sat astride their mounts, they were captivated along with everybody else in both armies by a spectacular train wreck. Without warning, the retreating federals loaded a train with unwanted ammunition at Savage Station and launched the unmanned engine down the Richmond and York Railroad at breakneck speed. When it reached the recently destroyed span over the Chickahominy, it "blew up with a roar which was heard for more than thirty miles—cars rolling, torn to pieces, into the river; the grimy engine hanging like some inanimate monster on the very brink of the trestle work, in the center of the stream, where by some strange chance it had not toppled over."[46]

"McClellan's only course seemed to me to make for the James river & thus open communications with his gun boats and fleet—though not yet certain of his route, the whole army had been put in motion upon this supposition," Lee informed Jefferson Davis on the morning of June 29 from his new headquarters along the Williamsburg Road. And the general commanding told Davis about his own plans: "Gen. Stuart is on the left bank [of the Chickahominy] watching his movements in that direction. General Jackson will cross to the right bank at Grapevine Bridge. Gen. Magruder pursuing down the Wms.Burg road. Gen. Huger on the Charles City, & Gen. Longstreet on the Darby Town." After Longstreet crossed by the New Bridge near Gaines Mill and Huger was withdrawn from the advance at Lee's command, Magruder suddenly held the Confederate front almost single-handedly; when Jackson did not march as anticipated, he not only held the front alone, but he also panicked at the prospect of facing McClellan without reinforcements.[47]

Joseph B. Kershaw's brigade of South Carolinians moved forward in "a spirited charge" about 4:30 P.M., although they had not previously been in battle; the brigade, which had been in Virginia before Manassas, had escaped actual combat under Joe Johnston, Longstreet, and now Magruder. Yet Kershaw, veteran of the Mexican War, legislator, and aristocratic lawyer, rammed the columns of Sumner, Franklin, and

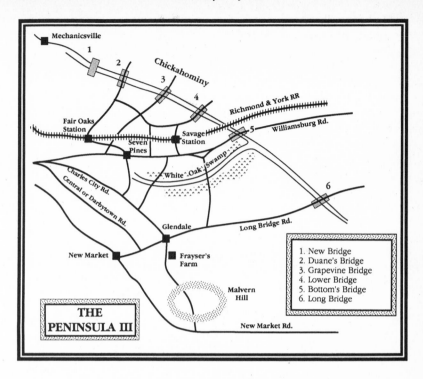

1. New Bridge
2. Duane's Bridge
3. Grapevine Bridge
4. Lower Bridge
5. Bottom's Bridge
6. Long Bridge

THE PENINSULA III

Heintzelman where the road from Grapevine Bridge crossed the railroad at Savage Station. The attack failed when Magruder did not send additional men as the South Carolinians were driven back. Magruder in fact was "a bundle of nerves" throughout the fight along the Williamsburg Road.

Prince John did not push the battle because of a mistaken belief that Jackson was unable to support his left flank by the Grapevine Bridge. Jackson, after all, had informed him that "other important duty" would detain his forces north of the Chickahominy, which heightened his anxiety. At the same time, Lee implored the hapless commander to attack the enemy's rear "rapidly and vigorously"; when Magruder again hesitated, Lee told him: "I learn from Major [Walter] Taylor that you are under the impression that General Jackson has not been ordered to support you. On the contrary, he has been ordered to do so; and to push the pursuit vigorously." Although Lee suffered 626 casualties at Savage Station to McClellan's 1,590, Jackson did not cross the Grapevine Bridge until the small hours of June 28.[48]

When Magruder protested his subsequent reprimand because of Savage Station and a further reluctance to attack at Malvern Hill a day or so later, he soon found himself far removed from the Virginia campaigns as commander of the District of Texas. But Jackson received no word of condemnation—at least not in public—for his renewed tardiness. "Jackson's unextenuated failure removed from the pursuit two thirds of the force planned by Lee and, after delaying and confusing Magruder's command for hours, exposed the attacking force to a severe repulse," observes a Lee biographer. "Magruder, though he floundered because of unfounded anxieties, as well as the uncertainties caused by Jackson and Huger, saved Lee's army from the effects of Jackson's torpor by not making a vigorous pursuit alone."[49]

When Jackson filed his own battle report some months later, he did not mention the affair, let alone admit that he had left Magruder to face the federals alone. Old Jack said only: "The 28th and 29th were occupied in disposing of the dead and wounded and repairing Grapevine Bridge, over the Chickahominy, which McClellan's forces had used in their retreat and destroyed in their rear. During the night of the 29th we commenced crossing the Chickahominy, and on the following morning arrived at Savage Station, . . . where a summer hospital, remarkable for the extent and convenience of its accommodations, fell into our possession." Although he reached the railroad one day late, Jackson found himself burdened with three thousand prisoners, of whom twenty-five hundred were sick and wounded. When Magruder was lambasted for his failure, Lee simply intoned that "Jackson's route led to the flank and rear of Savage Station, but he was delayed by the necessity of reconstructing Grapevine Bridge." Magruder's part in the June 29th fighting, Lee added, resulted in "a severe action [that] continued for about two hours when it was terminated by night."[50]

If Magruder was fearful lest Jackson would not support him at the critical hour, George Brinton McClellan was panic-stricken that Lee and Jackson would overwhelm his army; his telegraphic dispatches to Lincoln and the war office were laden with fears that Old Jack's command might tip the balance against him. McClellan was scared even though his army was far from beaten except in his own mind as July 30 dawned across the peninsula. Any other soldier worth his keep would have turned upon his undermanned pursuers with a vengeance. "Why! if I had twenty thousand more men, I would crush this rebellion," cried sixty-five-year-old General Edwin Sumner when ordered to evacuate his entrenchments around Savage Station. That old war-horse was not alone when he declared that he "would never leave a victorious field"; others including William B. Franklin and Samuel P. Heintzelman, also advised against further retreat. Although Sumner was threatened with arrest and other generals grumbled at abandoning the Chickahominy, McClellan, despite his apprehensions, did not appear throughout the day. While the Yankee commander went off to the James and conferred with his naval counterparts, other officers were left to handle Lee at a place known as Frayser's Farm.[51]

Throughout the night of June 29–30, McClellan had continued his headlong drive for the safety of the river flotilla. By noon, his "trains, reserve artillery, and rear guard" were beyond White Oak Swamp, a good five miles south of Savage Station. Here, the federal army drew itself into an inverted "L" formation, with W. F. Smith and Israel Richardson of Franklin's corps parallel to White Oak Creek and guarding the only bridge crossing; the remaining brigades extended three miles southward to a slight rise called Malvern Hill. Concentrated about a crossroads hamlet named Glendale, where the Charles City and Long Bridge Roads intersected, were the divisions of Slocum, Sedgwick, and McCall.

While McClellan ignored his generals, Lee, who made his camp with Longstreet's troopers, knew that he had to consolidate his seventy thousand effectives against the enemy's center. First, Theophilus Hunter Holmes, who had crossed the James during the Savage Station fighting, and strengthened by Henry A. Wise's brigade, was told to attack McClellan's wagons when they crossed the River Road at Malvern Hill. A command mix-up resulted when Magruder failed to reinforce him, and, caught in a tremendous cross fire from the river fleet, Holmes muffed an opportunity to destroy a large part of the federal army. Meanwhile, by Lee's own account:

> Longstreet and A. P. Hill, continuing their advance on the 30th soon came upon the enemy posted across the Long Bridge Road about one mile from its intersection with the Charles City Road. Huger's route led to his position, Jackson to the rear, and the arrival of their commands was waited to begin the attack. . . . Huger reported that his progress was obstructed, but about 4 P.M., firing was heard in the direction of the Charles City Road, which was supposed to indicate his approach. Longstreet immediately with one of his batteries gave notice of his presence. This brought on the engagement, but Huger not coming up and Jackson having been unable to force White Oak Swamp, Longstreet and Hill were without expected support.

Even so, when the battle ended around 9 P.M., Lee says: "Nearly the entire field remained in our possession, covered with the enemy's dead and wounded. Many prisoners, including a general of division [George A. McCall], were captured, and several batteries, with some thousands of small-arms taken." But he could not conceal his disappointment with Jackson and Huger: "Could the other commands [have] co-operated in the action the result would have proved most disastrous to the enemy." Their failure to reach the fighting at Frayser's Farm meant that Lee never got more than twenty thousand of his expected seventy thousand men into the fray; McClellan had escaped again![52]

While Lee watched the slaughter of thirty-six hundred Confederates in the company of President Davis, he must have felt let down and exasperated over Jackson's absence. Yet, when he opened his account of the battle, written some months after Jackson's triumphs at Cedar Mountain and Second Manassas, he was restrained as usual: "As Jackson advanced he captured such numbers of prisoners and collected so many arms that two regiments had to be detached for their security. His progress was arrested at White Oak Swamp. The enemy occupied the opposite side and obstinately resisted the reconstruction of the bridge." Throughout the campaign, Jackson had been posted on Lee's extreme left, which invariably placed him opposite the enemy's rear. It also meant that he constantly had to replace the spans destroyed by McClellan's retreating columns.[53]

Dr. McGuire again argues that Jackson was merely obeying orders at Frayser's Farm and had remained in place waiting further instruction from Lee: "The stream was impassable for infantry under fire, and impassable for artillery without a bridge. Jackson and his staff, with Colonel Munford's cavalry tested it, riding across through the quagmires that took us up to the girths of our horses; but with a fierce artillery attack he kept Franklin's and part of Sumner's corps from joining with McCall to resist the attack at Frayser's Farm. This attack General Jackson began with twenty-eight pieces of artillery at 12 o'clock that day." His guns opened hours before Longstreet and A. P. Hill commenced their advance on the enemy's center.

Edward Porter Alexander, who was also there and who visited the White Oak Swamp many times afterward, presents an entirely different view of Jackson's artillery duel with the enemy. Many contemporaries thought Jackson was purposely withholding his command from the bloodshed, and Alexander was clearly no exception. When Jackson contested the guns guarding the swamp bridge, he notes, "the Confederate batteries were ordered to open fire in their direction *guided by the sound*, for the forest in their front completely hid them from view. And, for the rest of the day, that absurd farce of war was played, our guns firing at the enemy's sound and their guns firing at ours. The enemy had the good luck to hit one of our cannoneers. Whether we hit any body or not I cannot find out. All four divisions of infantry laid there all day in the roads & slept there all night & never fired a musket." Longstreet, surprisingly, although normally critical, says only that "before noon of the 30th, Jackson encountered Franklin, defending the principal crossing of White Oak Swamp by the divisions of Richardson, W. F. Smith and Naglee's brigade." Later he suggests that Old Jack could have joined him and A. P. Hill long before the bridge had been restored.[54]

When Jackson did arrive, McClellan had long withdrawn toward the James. "About noon we reached White Oak Swamp and here the enemy made a determined effort and thereby to prevent an immediate junction between General Longstreet and myself," he wrote later. "A heavy cannonading in front announced the engagement of General Longstreet . . . and made me eager to press forward; but the marshy character of the soil, the destruction of the bridge over the marsh and the creek, and the strong position of the enemy defending the passage prevented my advancing until the following morning." But Jackson found time to forward a June 30 letter to Anna from his bivouac "Near White Oak Swamp." Following his customary endearments and a complaint about "a wet bed last night, as the rain fell in torrents," Jackson told his wife: "You must give fifty dollars for church purposes, and more should you be disposed." She was also admonished to keep a close watch over his church contributions. At a most critical time in the Seven Days campaign, Old Jack was concerned lest he not give the biblical "one tenth."[55]

Even as Jackson wrote to Anna and Lee pondered his next moves, McClellan cleverly drew the federal army into battle array along the crest of Malvern Hill, a process begun the previous day as the battle raged at Frayser's Farm. Situated roughly midway between White Oak Swamp and Harrison's Landing on the James, Malvern Hill is more like a gentle swell than anything resembling a hill. "It is an elevated platform rising to a height of 150 feet above the surrounding forests and embraced by two branches of Western Run, and possessing nearly every requirement for a strong defensive position." Then, continues a Virginia historian, "the open ground on top of the hill is about 1½ miles in length by half a mile in breath. Sloping gradually to the north, the northwest, and northeast, the hillsides were covered with wheat standing or in shock, to the edge of a wood some 800 yards from the crest." The left, or northeast part, of Malvern Hill provided an excellent place for artillery, and it could also be "flanked by fire from gunboats on the river."[56]

The hill was made into a veritable fortress by McClellan's chief of artillery, Colonel Henry J. Hunt, and Lee made a tactical blunder when he ordered a headlong assault. He had not seriously crippled the federal army by the start of July 1, and it was now or never; McClellan had to be crushed at Malvern Hill or it would be too late to prevent his reaching the James. The result was an operation with little or no coordination between Lee's subordinate commanders: "There was a strange lack of concert," writes George Cary Eggleston, a careful student of war. "One division after another attacked without support and was beaten back for want of it. At no time did the Confederates hurl their whole force upon the enemy. They fought gallantly, but in detail, and therefore without effect." Lee even complained to Colonel Jubal A. Early, who led Elzey's brigade at Malvern Hill, that "I cannot have my orders carried out," even as the battle raged.[57]

The Confederates faced enormous topographical and tactical odds from the beginning. W. L. Allen, a chaplain with D. H. Hill's command and a native of the area, sent a chilling word up the chain of command: "Malvern Hill's commanding height, the difficulties of approach, its amphitheatrical form, and ample area, would enable McClellan to arrange his 350 guns, tier above tier, and sweep the plain in every direction." After Lee conferred with D. H. Hill and also with Longstreet and Jackson during the morning hours of July 1, he brushed aside Hill's objections to an attack in favor of Longstreet's recommendation to move forward; Old Pete had reconnoitered the countryside earlier and now he told Lee that his own gun emplacements would produce a Confederate cross fire, enabling his infantry to carry the heights. When Jackson arrived from White Oak Swamp, he, too, took one look and advised against attack.

The day belonged to Longstreet, who already thought of himself as Lee's second in command. The general commanding got bad advice, and, says a modern scholar, he never asked for it again. Afterward at Gettysburg, according to General William Nelson Pendleton, Episcopal clergyman and commander of the reserve artillery at Malvern Hill, Lee said: "Longstreet is a very good fighter when he gets in position and gets everything ready, but he is so *slow*." On July 1, 1862, it is easy to speculate that because of the previous heavy fighting, Longstreet knew that he and A. P. Hill would be held in reserve. And, though he accepted Longstreet's advice, Lee watched the unfolding drama from Jackson's lines.[58]

Not surprisingly, the federal officers who had crisscrossed the area for days knew the terrain better than the Confederates. McClellan and Hunt used that knowledge to great advantage, aligning the Army of the Potomac "in the form of a huge semicircle, its wings resting on the river, with the right at Huxall, where it was protected by the fire from the gunboats." Besides the guns of Franklin, Heintzelman, and Porter, continues a battle historian, "The reserve artillery under General Hunt, was posted by that able officer on the height on the west of the plateau and in front of the brick house. Batteries of 20-and 32-pounders, with rifled Napoleon guns formed a terrible array; below them were the infantry awaiting with confidence. Sixty pieces had a converging fire from Porter's line, and along the crest of the hill. Whenever one was needed, a battery made its appearance at the instant."[59]

As Lee gathered his legions, enemy guns were already blasting huge gaps in his lines. Jackson with D. H. Hill formed the left; Whiting and Ewell fought with Old Jack, although the Stonewall Brigade and part of Ewell's force were held in reserve; Huger was in the center and Prince John Magruder, "with his own and one of Huger's brigades," held the Confederate right. Jackson's command, which had been late for several days running, was suddenly thrown into the van after Lee sounded the forward. When D. H. Hill, who generaled Jackson's right, advanced at six o'clock, July 1, a disastrous mix-up caused him to charge Hunt's belching cannon alone; "he took his men," observes Frank Vandiver, "into a slaughter pen which bathed the slopes of Malvern Hill in Southern blood." And Fitz-John Porter would write later: "With a determination to capture our army, or destroy it by driving us into the river, brigade after brigade rushed at our batteries, but the artillery of both Morell and Couch mowed them down with shrapnel, grape and canister, while our infantry, withholding their fire until the enemy were in short range, scattered the remnants of their columns, sometimes following them up and capturing prisoners and colors."[60]

When Hunt's fearsome cannonade opened, Sandie Pendleton, one of Jackson's aides, thought it "the most awful artillery fire I ever imagined." Our boys "suffered terribly, rather more than the enemy," he added in a letter to his mother. Pendleton's companions, one federal officer speculated, rushed the guns because their canteens were filled with an effective nineteenth-century palliative: whiskey and gunpowder. Tales of raw courage abound of the fighting and dying at Malvern Hill, although, comments artilleryman William Poague, "John Craig, a blustering bully on the streets of Lexington couldn't stand the racket and broke for the rear." Yet most Confederate soldiers did what was expected: Poague, who fought his battery in support of D. H. Hill until "the enemy ceased," looked up momentarily from the ghastly business to discover "Old D. H. sitting with a leg over the pommel chatting with Whiting and both smoking cigars."[61]

A shot nearly hit Jackson as he sat writing a dispatch from horseback during the early maneuvering; several were killed by the explosion, which threw splinters and dirt over his copy book. Later, as he watched with Lee and Dick Ewell, it became painfully clear that General William N. Pendleton, father of Jackson's aide, Sandie Pendleton, had not received word to deploy the reserve artillery during the prebattle conferences—a lapse that doomed Lee's chances of crushing McClellan's army. Jackson, nonetheless, at one point left Lee's side for the front when several of his guns came under fire. When he reached the flash point with Sandie Pendleton and Kyd Douglas, according to the latter: "A shell which struck in front of the General, and threw a shower of dirt over the whole party, while the General's horse squatted to the ground in fright. . . . He got little farther, for a staff officer came up like a charge of cavalry and with a salute said, 'General Lee presents his compliments and directs you to return at once.' " Jackson, who could never deny his chief, complied immediately. His near fanatical loyalty to Lee on the battlefield was not lost on the commanding general; Jackson, unlike Longstreet and others, was a hands-on subordinate, always ready for action, but action that was obedient to Lee's wishes.[62]

At the Malvern Hill slaughterhouse, when D. H. Hill heeded the wrong signal to advance and got himself caught in Hunt's withering cannon fire, Jackson himself wrote: "I ordered that portion of General Ewell's division held in reserve and Jackson's division to his relief; but from the darkness of night, and the obstruction caused by the swamp and undergrowth, through which they had to march, none reached him in time to afford him the desired support." Dabney says that Jackson sent the brigades of Trimble, Lawton, Winder, and Cunningham, but that they "could only hold their ground, and maintain an uncertain conflict." In his own battle report, D. H. Hill relates nothing about his brother-in-law's failure to send a relief column other than: "Brigadier-General Winder was sent up by Major-General Jackson, but he came too late. . . . Finally Major General Ewell came up but it was after dark and nothing could be accomplished." Before the battle terminated around ten o'clock, Hill continues: "My division fought an hour or more the whole Yankee force without the assistance from a single Confederate soldier. The front line of the Yankees was twice broken and in full retreat, when fresh troops came to its support. At such critical junctures the general advance of the divisions on my right and left must have been decisive."[63]

Jackson's inability to advance notwithstanding, he was among the first to sense that McClellan was done with the peninsula when darkness halted the fighting. "At one o'clock he was awakened by several brigade commanders" who wanted to renew the fight, as his wife tells the story. "Jackson listened indifferently, asking a few brief questions, and said if at ease in the matter, 'No, I think he will clear out in the morning.' " When he did "clear out," McClellan had lost about fifteen thousand dead, wounded, and missing since the clash at Oak Grove Church on June 25, although Lee's casualties were higher at 20,600—fifty-three hundred of his men had been squandered at Malvern Hill. Lee had taken the worst of it in body count, but he had achieved his great purpose with the help of Tom Jackson and the Valley Army; he had driven McClellan and the federal Goliath from the southern citadel at Richmond. Of greater importance, however, the Army of Potomac had not been destroyed in July 1862. Lee and Jackson would be obliged to fight it another day![64]

12

Manassas Again

After several days spent watching McClellan from his headquarters at Dr. Poindexter's house near the Malvern Hill battlefield, Robert E. Lee concluded that the Army of the Potomac no longer posed a threat. In spite of the great resources at his command, Little Mac showed no disposition to renew the contest, although he continued to bombard his Washington superiors with requests for additional troops. Before he returned to his old quarters in the Dabbs House nearer Richmond, Lee dispatched daily communiqués to President Davis describing the federal entrenchments. While his often-detailed reports barely mention Jackson, he agreed with Old Jack that a renewed assault on the peninsula was out of the question. "After a thorough reconnaissance of the enemy on James River, I found him strongly posted and effectively flanked by his Gunboats," he informed Davis. "In the present condition of our troops I did not think proper to risk an attack, on the results of which so much depended." Lee ordered a few rounds from his artillery, but the return fire forced him to retire. "One shot from a gunboat went through an oak 30 inches in diameter and took off the head of one of my men, John Brown, of our ambulance force, 400 yards in the rear of the battery," one of Jackson's men wrote afterward.[1]

Lee had no sooner arrived at his old headquarters on the Nine Mile Road than he told Davis that he was reorganizing "our forces for active operations." From the moment of Malvern Hill, he had been concerned about regimental reorganization because "we have lost many valuable officers whose places must be supplied, and our thinned ranks must be filled as rapidly as possible." Although he ridded himself of several officers of questionable ability—John Magruder, Theophilus Holmes, and Benjamin Huger—his new army structure was unquestionably linked to his plans for renewing the fight. "Having learned through the newspapers and other sources," writes General Long, "that there was a difference of opinion between General McClellan and Mr. Lincoln in regard to future operations, and knowing the Federal President's anxiety concerning the safety of his capital, Lee rightly concluded that any movement in that direction would cause McClellan's opinion to be overruled and the Army of the Potomac withdrawn from the James for the defense of Washington." To carry out these plans, Lee needed trusted subordinates who were fighting men as well as men who would faithfully execute his wishes.[2]

After Lee posted a skeletal force to watch the federal encampment, he issued orders on July 8 for the army to abandon its positions along the James. Importantly, Jackson was told to assume a new bivouac "on the Mechanicsville Pike, north of Richmond," while Longstreet, D. H. Hill, and others were kept south and east of the capital. If Lee resolved to march northward, he plainly wanted Old Jack to take the van. Under the completed reorganization, Jackson had his own division of four brigades as well as Ewell's division—eight brigades in all. Longstreet was given the bulk of the army—his own division plus those of A. P. Hill, D. R. Jones, D. H. Hill, Richard H. Anderson, and Lafayette McLaws, or a total twenty-nine brigades. The six brigades of D. H. Hill's division were led by Roswell S. Ripley, an Ohio native who took a near-fatal bullet at Antietam. D. H. Hill himself had a separate command of six brigades south of the James, where he used his artillery to harass McClellan. Lee assigned other units to Jeb Stuart's cavalry and Pendleton's artillery reserve.

On paper, Longstreet had the larger force but he was held close to headquarters and even as the army marched for the Rapidan, Lee was never far from his side; although Jackson had the smaller number of men, Lee obviously retained his faith in Old Jack's ability for isolated command. His desultory movements on the peninsula had been forgotten as Lee entrusted him with a sizable portion of the army beyond his immediate grasp.[3]

"My position is about three miles north of James River, and twenty-five miles below Richmond," Jackson told his wife on July 8. As he awaited Lee's marching orders, his old physical complaints reappeared. "During the past week I have not been well," he informed Anna. "I have suffered from fever and debility, but through the blessing of an ever-kind Providence I am much better." After all, if a man cannot complain and elicit sympathy from his own wife, to whom can he turn?

When Jackson arrived at his new station on the Mechanicsville Road, he slipped into Richmond on Sunday, July 13, to worship with the Presbyterian congregation of Dr. Moses Hoge; accompanied by Sandie Pendleton, Kyd Douglas, and Dr. McGuire, it was Old Jack's first appearance in the capital following his rise to recognition. "It was a great comfort to have the privilege of a quiet Sabbath within the walls of a house dedicated to the service of God," he wrote home the following day. But, notes young Pendleton's biographer, "Jackson's presence was discovered, and the congregation pressed around him, squeezing his protective staff into a corner. Finally, an elderly lady seized his arm and hurried him, uneasy and confused into the street. Captain Hugh White of the Stonewall Brigade, and a witness of this demonstration of affection, smiled, he wrote, 'to see the Old Hero conquered and made to run.' " While he was in the city, Jackson made a courtesy visit to a home that had lost a son in the recent campaign. But the following day, July 14, he told Anna: "Please direct your next letter to Gordonsville, and to continue to address me there until you hear otherwise. Everyone doesn't know the meaning and location of *Headquarters, Valley District.*"4

Although Lee certainly meant to worry Lincoln by marching northward, as General Long suggests, the decision to hurry Jackson forward was prompted by the president's own reorganization. McClellan's bellyaching and his defensive posture led Lincoln to appoint Major General John Pope as commander of a new federal army while the peninsula fighting was yet underway. A presidential order of June 26 told the story: "The forces under Major Generals Fremont, Banks, and McDowell, including the troops under Brigadier General [Samuel D.] Sturgis at Washington, shall be consolidated and form one army, to be called the Army of Virginia." At the same time, Lincoln telegraphed McClellan that his complaining "pains me very much," but added that new troops would join him when available. Still, Washington's focus had shifted from Little Mac's schemes several days before Lee forced his Army of the Potomac to seek sanctuary along the James: "The Army of Virginia shall operate in such manner as, while protecting western Virginia and the National Capital from danger or insult, it shall in the speediest manner attack and overcome the rebel forces under Jackson and Ewell, threaten the enemy in the direction of Charlottesville, and render the most effective aid to relieve General McClellan and capture Richmond." A big order that!5

The Kentucky-born Pope had graduated in the West Point class of 1842; a veteran of Mexico and the Indian wars, Lincoln called him to command after his success in directing the Army of Mississippi "in the capture of New Madrid, Island No. 10, and the advance upon and siege of Corinth." Although he did not take field command until July 29—two days after Jackson established himself at Gordonsville—Pope sought an immediate concentration of "his scattered army" of 38,500: Fremont, 12,000; Banks, 8,000; McDowell, 18,500; plus an additional 5,000 cavalry. "My first objective," he said later "was to bring the three corps of the army together, or near enough together to be within supporting distance of one another, and to put them in as efficient a condition for active service as was possible with the time and means at my disposal." Not content with a mere assembly of his troops, which now included Brigadier General Franz Sigel, who replaced onetime presidential candidate John C. Fremont, Pope, full of exuberance, issued his famous bombast to the Army of Virginia on July 14. After recounting that his command in the west had always faced its adversaries, he continued: "I presume that I have been called here to pursue the same policy and to lead you against the enemy. It is my purpose to do so, and that speedily. . . . Let us look before us and not behind. Success and glory are in the advance, disaster and shame lurk in the rear. Let us act on this understanding, and it is safe to predict that your banners shall be inscribed with a glorious deed and that your names will be dear to your countrymen forever."[6]

As Pope lingered in Washington, conferring with Lincoln and the war cabinet, he told reporters that his headquarters "would be in the saddle" and he also started to incur great hostility in both the Union and Confederate camps. McClellan was almost jubilant when Lee and Jackson crushed him at Second Manassas, and another Union general let it be known around Washington that he "did not care for Pope one pinch of owl dung." And his additional directives aroused a usually serene Lee. Pope intended to strip the Virginia countryside by issuing papers "payable at the conclusion of the war, upon sufficient testimony being furnished that such owners have been loyal citizens of the United States since the date of the vouchers." Other Virginians would presumably lose their property forever if seized by Yankee foragers. Not only would their property be confiscated but, according to Pope's Order No. 7, civilians were told to avoid the federal army:

> It is, therefore, ordered that whenever a railroad, wagon-road, or telegraph is injured by parties of Guerrillas, the citizens living within five miles of the spot shall be turned out in mass to repair the damage. . . . If a soldier, or a legitimate follower of the army be fired upon from any house, the house shall be razed to the ground, and the inhabitants sent prisoners to the headquarters of this army. If such an outrage occurs at any place

distant from settlements, the people within five miles around shall be held accountable and made to pay an indemnity sufficient for the case.

And, if that were not enough, Pope issued another dictate, which demanded the arrest of "disloyal male citizens" within his lines. An oath of allegiance would be demanded and if the arrested citizen refused: "He shall be conducted south, beyond the extreme pickets of this army, and be notified that if found again anywhere within our lines, or at a point in the rear, they will be considered as spies and subjected to the extreme rigor of military law."[7]

Pope's arrest orders incited a storm among the Confederate high command. After consultation with President Davis, Lee "informed the federal authorities that unless they were rescinded General Pope and his officers would not, if captured, be treated as prisoners of war." Jackson, with Ewell's division, was rushed toward the rail junction at Gordonsville, Lee wrote afterward, "to restrain, as far as possible, the atrocities which [Pope] threatened to perpetuate upon our defenseless citizens." Yet he never lost his sense of humor at the approaching contest: "When you write to Rob [his youngest son] again," he implored Mrs. Lee on July 28, "tell him to catch Pope for me, and also bring in his cousin, Louis Marshall. I could forgive the latter's fighting against us, but not his joining Pope."[8]

Rob, Jr., who joined Jackson's command at Gordonsville, indicates that he visited with his father while the army "lay inactive around Richmond." Although others draw upon this account to suggest that Lee called upon his wife and daughters in Richmond, the writings of Robert E. Lee, Jr., are not clear about dates other than to say: "He was the same loving father to us all, as kind and thoughtful to my mother, who was an invalid, and of us, his children, as if our comfort and happiness were all he had to care for." Lee was unquestionably near the city, but he was also an extremely busy man trying to anticipate the next moves of Pope and McClellan. A letter dated July 9—the very day Jackson marched into Gordonsville—says that he would "come in when I can but I have much to do & do not know when it will be." Lee wanted his wife to see after his laundry before his arrival and to look for "a pair of spectacles" and some "thinner clothes." And, in the same letter: "I have just returned to my old quarters dear Mary & am filled with gratitude to our Heavenly father for the mercies He has extended to us. Our success has not been as great or complete as I would have desired, but God knows what is best for us. Our enemy has met with a heavy loss from which he will take some time to recover & then recommence his operations." As he prepared to renew the fight, Lee's journeys into Richmond would have taken place between July 9 and August 16, when he accompanied Longstreet northward. However, his voluminous correspondence with Jefferson Davis and his field commanders suggest that he spent little time away from his Dabbs House headquarters.[9]

While Jackson bided his time at Gordonsville with fourteen thousand men and Pope gathered upward of fifty thousand north of the Rappanahannock, Lee was in near constant communication with the Valley Army. His General Orders 150, dated July 13, announced: "Major General Jackson, with his own and Ewell's division, will immediately proceed to Louisa Court-House, and if practicable to Gordonsville, there to oppose the reported advance of the enemy from the direction of Orange Court-House." One week later, Lee admonished Jackson "to get definite information of Pope, his numbers, etc. You must keep your troops well in hand and your cavalry well behind him, so that he cannot strike you an unexpected blow should you not be strong enough to strike at him." And he closed: "If Pope gets far enough, could you swoop down north of the Rappanhannock, suddenly uniting with Stuart, and clear the left bank opposite Fredericksburg?" On July 27, Lee fired off another message: "I want Pope suppressed," he said. "The course indicated in his orders, if the newspapers report them correctly, cannot be permitted and will lead to a retaliation on our part. You had better notify him at the first opportunity."

Jeb Stuart was sent to reckon Pope's line of march, which the cavalryman accomplished on August 5 in a series of running battles with the federal infantry; Stuart also informed Lee that besides the army under Pope, a sizable force had occupied Fredericksburg. While he remained near New Market checking an abortive movement by McClellan toward Malvern Hill, Jackson was instructed: "If you were strong enough to bear down all opposition in your front the force at Fredericksburg might be neglected, for it would be sure to fall back if that in your front was suppressed. . . . I ventured to suggest for your consideration not to attack the enemy's strong points. . . . I would rather you should have easy fighting and heavy victories." Finally, as Jackson prepared the attack at Cedar Mountain, Lee told him to strike Pope on the march and thus draw his army from its strong positions: "Relying upon your judgment, courage, and discretion, and trusting to the continued blessing of an ever-kind Providence, I hope for victory."[10]

Lee clearly perceived the greater danger to lie in northern Virginia, and, as he inundated Jackson with instructions, Pope confirmed his suspicions by ordering a march on Culpeper. While Lee and Jackson watched the northern approaches, Lincoln had been adjusting his own war machine by appointing Henry Wager Halleck to overall command of the federal armies. Although Halleck had graduated third in the West Point class of 1839, and was known as "Old Brains" throughout the army because of his writings—he had recently translated Antoine Jomini's writings on Napoleon into English—he was not regarded as either a fighting man or a strategist. But Lincoln valued his reputed administrative ability and entrusted him to bring order from the separated commands of Pope and McClellan. Halleck, described as "a man completely lacking in physical attractiveness or charm—pop-eyed, flabby, surly and crafty," set off instantly to confer with McClellan at Harrison's Landing.[11]

But, writes Halleck biographer, Stephen Ambrose, "he was not always a willing tool in Lincoln's hands." He listened to McClellan's renewed arguments that victory was possible on the peninsula with additional troops and Pope's contention that McClellan was needed in northern Virginia to help his own drive toward Richmond. In the end, Halleck summoned Ambrose Burnside to Fredericksburg from North Carolina, and also sent the famous telegram to McClellan: "It is determined to withdraw your army from the Peninsula to Aquia Creek." He acted, Ambrose continues, "on the doctrine of concentration on the vital point" advocated by his hero Jomini: "McClellan wanted to combine the principles of concentration, offensive movement and maneuver, by sending Pope's men to the army around Petersburg, but Halleck felt that when McClellan's army was annexed to Pope's Washington was secure from attack and the possibilities of a move on Richmond were improved." The same transports used to ferry Burnside from the Carolina coast were sent to gather the Army of the Potomac "huddled along the banks of the James." As McClellan told his wife that "the rascals" were out to get him, Pope still in Washington, was instructed "to prevent concentration of Lee's army upon our forces on the Peninsula, while in the confusion incident to the removal, and while the corps composing them are separated."[12]

Pope put Halleck's grand strategy into operation on the morning of August 8 by sending thirty thousand men roaring into Culpeper, twenty-six miles north of Jackson's force at Gordonsville. Jackson, however, did not wait for a concentration of the federal armies; nor did he concern himself about worrying Lincoln by menacing Washington. The moment word reached him that Pope was on the move, he sprang to action without awaiting specific instructions from the Dabbs House. Lee had stationed him at "the vital point," and he meant to stop the Yankee horde before it could unite.

Upon receiving word that Pope was keeping headquarters in the saddle, a yarn swept the Gordonsville encampment about a supposed message from Jackson to his adversary: "It is strange that a General would have his headquarters where his hindquarters ought to be." Their antics aside, Jackson's foot cavalry faced a hot, dry march with the thermometer above ninety degrees when it broke camp; notes John Casler of the 33rd Virginia, "several men dropped dead in the ranks from sunstroke" as the army advanced on the Rapidan. Casler and his comrades were on the move because Jackson did not realize that the entire Army of Virginia was gathering on his front. "Having received information that only part of General Pope's army was at Culpeper Court-House, and hoping through the blessing of Providence to be able to defeat it before re-enforcements should arrive there, Ewell's, Hill's, and Jackson's divisions were moved on the 7th in the direction of the enemy," Old Jack noted in his battle summary. After spending the morning of August 7th attending a court-martial in Ewell's camp at Liberty Mills, northeast of Gordonsville, Jackson did not commence the march until late afternoon. By nightfall, his army was bivouacked around Orange Court House—eighteen miles south of Culpeper.[13]

Jackson had known Ambrose Powell Hill since their cadet days at West Point, and he apparently harbored a long dislike for the man Lee mustered to reinforce the Valley Army; perhaps a prudish Jackson knew that Cadet Hill had been sent down from the academy seventeen years before with a venereal complaint. A strained relationship worsened on the night of August 7–8, when a tight-lipped Jackson, still unable to share confidences, unexplainedly changed his marching sequence for the following morning: "On that night orders were received by me from Major-General Jackson to move at dawn in the morning, and in the following order, viz: Ewell's, Hill's, and Jackson's divisions," Hill penned afterward. "At the appointed time I was ready, with the head of my leading brigade resting near the street down which I understood Ewell was to pass, and ready to take my appointed place in the column of march. A little after sunrise a division commenced passing, which I supposed to be Ewell's. One or two brigades having passed, I recognized it to be Jackson's and learned that Ewell had taken another route. . . . Of this no intimation had been given me." Because of "the misconception"—Dabney's phrase—Jackson was obliged to cancel his attack until August 9, after Hill covered but one mile from Orange, while Ewell and Jackson had marched nearly eight. "The element of surprise in which Jackson had based his entire offensive was gone; Winder was ill; Ewell was swearing in exasperation; Hill was angry, and Jackson was livid," observes Hill's biographer.[14]

In Jackson's own words: "On the 9th as we arrived in about 8 miles of Culpeper Court-House, we found the enemy in our front, near Cedar Run, and a short distance west and north of Slaughter Mountain." The enemy confronting him was Banks's division of Pope's army and the force would have been larger had Franz Sigel not lost his way to the front. At Slaughter Mountain, commonly called Cedar Mountain after nearby Cedar Run, Jackson placed Winder's division astride the main Orange-Culpeper thoroughfare with Ewell occupying the western slopes of the mountain itself in a concave line. Almost immediately, Charles S. Winder was killed while arranging his men: "Our first position was just on the right of the road, one gun being stationed on it." Then, says William Poague, "had we remained here we would have been captured. But fortunately the guns had been moved some 400 or 500 yards to the right to get a better chance at a Yankee battery which had been annoying us, one shot from which had killed our commander, General Winder, right beside my left gun." Jackson had an affinity for all of the men who commanded his old brigade, and the death of the Maryland-born Winder affected him deeply. Although William B. Taliaferro took charge, Old Jack told his wife on August 11 that Winder "was mortally wounded whilst ably discharging his duty at the head of his command, which was the advance of the left wing of the army." And in his official account Jackson called his comrade "richly endowed with those qualities of mind and person which fit an officer for command. . . . he was rapidly rising to the front rank of his profession." A magnanimous Jackson added that his death was "severely felt."[15]

Shortly after Taliaferro took command, the Confederate left and the Stonewall Brigade particularly "were badly mauled" by a frontal assault. The surprise thrust by Banks against first Ewell and then Jackson's division "caused the Confederate center and nearly the whole line to give away in confusion." It came while Jackson was awaiting the arrival of A. P. Hill's Light Division, which came on the field in rapid time following a forced march from Orange. Though Hill dispatched Edward Lloyd Thomas' brigade to reinforce Jubal A. Early, whose men were in the thick of it, Jackson's division not only became a "disorganized mob" it actually began to disintegrate. "At this moment of disaster," reads one account,

Jackson appeared, amid the clouds of smoke, and his voice was heard rising above the uproar and the thunder of guns. . . . Galloping to the front, amid the heavy fire directed upon his disordered lines, now rapidly giving way—with eyes flashing, his face flushed, his voice rising and ringing like a clarion on every ear, he rallied the confused troops and brought them into line. . . . The presence of Jackson, leading them on in person, seemed to produce an indescribable influence on the troops, and as he rode to and fro, they greeted him with resounding cheers. This was one of the few occasions when he is reported to have been mastered by excitement.[16]

In spite of Old Jack's heroics, A. P. Hill clearly gave him the fire-power to drive Banks from the field. Lawrence O'B. Branch, a onetime North Carolina congressman, and his Tarheels immediately attacked down the Orange-Culpeper road assisted by the brigades of Dorsey Pender and J. J. Archer. Hill's drive, Jackson himself noted, "met the Federal force, flushed with their temporary triumph, and drove them back with terrible slaughter through the wood." Ewell, meanwhile, still holding the Confederate right, was able to direct a murderous fire into the final rout. But the main action fell upon A. P. Hill, who rushed his Light Division onto the field, in Jackson's own words, "at the critical moment." As the fight unfolded, a brigade commander named Henry Prince was taken by some of Hill's men: "The Federal general was brought before Hill as minie balls whistled around. The suave Prince stood stiffly at attention and said to Hill, 'General, the fortunes of war have thrown me into your hands.' 'Damn the fortunes of war, General!' Hill shouted. 'Get to the rear! You are in danger here.' "[17]

Perhaps Hill performed too well—his recent biographer proclaims it "Hill's victory at Cedar Mountain"—because he soon incurred Jackson's displeasure on another field. Most of the Confederate high command thought the triumph belonged to Jackson, not Hill. When Pope's men arrived under a flag of truce after the contest to carry away their dead, relates Dabney: "The Federals with one consent, were loud in their praises of Jackson, and declared that if they had such Generals to lead them, they also could win victories and display prowess." Lee likewise considered it Jackson's honor, and says only in his battle summary: "By a general charge the enemy was driven back in confusion, leaving the ground covered with his dead and wounded," after Hill came up. Nor does he mention Hill in his customary letter to Jackson: "I congratulate you most heartily on the victory God has granted you at Cedar Run. . . ." Again, Jackson had accomplished what Lee envisioned—he hit the enemy head on with his separate army in a bloody clash. Although he suffered thirteen hundred dead and wounded, he effectively checked Pope for another two weeks, until Lee was able to advance toward the Rapidan with Longstreet and the main army. [18]

When he returned to the old camp at Gordonsville, Jackson dashed off a note to Lee at the Dabbs House: "God blessed our arms with another victory," he said, and he told Lee that "the enemy, according to prisoners, consisted of Banks' McDowell's and Sigel's commands." Lee also knew that McClellan's stirrings on the peninsula meant that sooner or later the armies of Pope and Little Mac would combine against him. An odd saga commenced to unfold in which Pope demanded McClellan's troops before Lee and Jackson could unite against him at the time Lee resolved to hit Pope before McClellan's arrival. Lee started Longstreet toward the Rapidan on the 13th, and other commands including Richard H. Anderson's were hurried toward the rendezvous. "Unless I hear from you to the contrary I shall leave for [Gordonsville] at 4 A.M., tomorrow," he wired Jefferson Davis on the 14th. "The troops are accumulating there & I must see that arrangements are made for the field. I received a letter today from General Longstreet requesting my presence. I will keep you informed of anything of importance that transpires."

The developing scenario called Lee northward before he could visit Mrs. Lee in Richmond. He had wanted to come, he told Custis in a note, also on the 14th, but "my after movements depend on circumstances that I cannot foresee." In a postscript, Lee was the personal man as well as warrior: "I send my straw hat which please give room to. Also a summer under-jacket which I find in my trunk. If you have the key put it in, or ask your mother to mend it & keep it for me." As he traveled to join Jackson, Lee must have been near his wife. "I passed by you Friday morning when you were asleep," a later note from Orange implied. "I looked very hard but could see no body. I should have liked so much to stop and to have waked you up. I was afraid at such an hour I should not have been welcome."[19]

Lee reached Gordonsville late on the 14th and immediately conferred with Jackson, although Old Jack, unlike Longstreet, would never ask for Lee's presence at a troublesome time. The next day, August 15, he traveled onward to Clark's Mountain, "a bold hill" a few miles beyond Orange, where the Rapidan bends around its northwestern reaches; from the crest, Lee gazed at Pope's army north of the river, with its outriders reaching from Raccoon Ford to the base of the Blue Ridge. Then and there, he decided to strike across the Rapidan; his first attempt, however, was unsuccessful when Jeb Stuart failed to get his cavalry beyond the river on the 18th and nearly got himself captured at Verdiersville; Stuart even lost his hat and plume during the famed episode in which enemy raiders overwhelmed his camp, but Lee had more to worry about than cries of "whar's your hat," which taunted the cavalryman upon his return. Jackson, too, had been forced back after an initial crossing of the Rapidan, which caused Lee to devise a new plan. The next day, August 19, he issued General Orders No. 185 for a renewed attack: Longstreet, with twenty-one infantry brigades and supporting artillery, would cross at Somerville Ford east of the railroad connecting Orange and Culpeper; Jackson and the left flank of the army would force the river at Raccoon Ford beyond the railroad.[20]

Several factors, including freshets feeding the Rapidan and Rappahannock, another failure by Stuart to disrupt federal supply lines, and continued problems of communication within the army, prevented Lee from crushing Pope between the two rivers. The Confederate thrust had frightened Halleck and Pope into withdrawing the Army of Virginia north of the Rappahannock until reinforcements could arrive from the peninsula. Although Lee advanced to the river on August 20–21, he was unable to engage Pope or to thwart the arrival of McClellan's old command. Heintzelman and Porter reached northern Virginia first, but poor docking facilities at Aquia Creek prompted Halleck to divert Franklin and Sumner to Alexandria; although Keyes stayed at Yorktown until September 3, the remainder of Little Mac's once-proud army was soon available for Pope's use. The federal army facing Lee's fifty-five thousand men across the Rappahannock numbered seventy-five thousand by August 26, with more troops on the way; Lee, however, had no prospect of additional reinforcements.

Lee informed President Davis on August 23 that high water and enemy spies had foiled the earlier attack. Two days later, he told his wife that he was "too busy for visiting," and confided that the struggle would soon reopen: "The rains have however ceased now and I trust the river will soon fall. I think we shall change the theater of war from James River to north of the Rappahannock. That is part of the advantage I contemplated. If it is affected for a season, it will be a great gain. . . ." And, Jackson, "now preparing himself to separate from the rest of the army, pass around Pope to the westward, and place his corps between him and Washington," at Jeffersonton near the Rappahannock, scribbled a "hurried note" to his own wife: "The enemy has taken a position, rather several positions, on the Fauquier side of the Rappahannock. I have only time to tell you how much I love my darling pet." Lee and Jackson

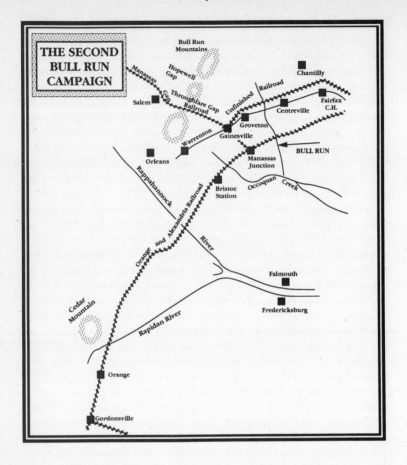

THE SECOND
BULL RUN
CAMPAIGN

Bull Run
Mountains

Hopewell
Gap

Manassas

Chantilly

Railroad

Salem

Throughfare Gap
Railroad

Unfinished

Fairfax
C.H.

Centreville

Groveton

Gainesville

Warrenton

BULL RUN

Orleans

Manassas
Junction

Rappahannock

Occoquan Creek

Bristoe
Station

Orange and Alexandria Railroad

River

Falmouth

Fredericksburg

Cedar
Mountain

Rapidan River

Orange

Gordonsville

remained in constant touch while preparing the new offensive, yet neither man, now or at other times, seems to have mentioned the other in their personal letters. Although Lee frequently discussed mutual acquaintances with his wife, Jackson was surprisingly silent about his meetings with Lee in his letters to Anna.[21]

Mary Anna Jackson is correct that her husband was getting ready to separate from Lee once more; because of Lee's new assault on John Pope, Jackson left the Rappahannock on August 25 with twenty-five thousand "foot cavalry," who had been ordered to cook three days' rations for a march upon the federal supply depot at Manassas Station. Eben Swift, a careful student of Lee's generalship, makes the powerful argument that he was driven by three considerations: "First, that McClellan's troops from the Peninsula were near at hand hurrying to join Pope; second, that Pope's morale had been shaken by his retreat from the Rapidan; third, that an attack on the weakest point of an enemy will cause him to abandon his own plans in order to meet that attack. . . . Altogether there seems to have been a big factor of safety which was accurately estimated by Lee in this move." Most significantly, when Lee decided to gamble in the face of conventional military wisdom—to split his own smaller force in front of Pope's larger one, he turned again to the one soldier he trusted to execute his wishes: Thomas J. Jackson.[22]

Although Lee followed with Longstreet's command within forty-eight hours, Jackson set out from his camp of thirty-six hours at Jeffersonton on the Warrenton Turnpike to accomplish Lee's plan. He also proved that he could be a stern taskmaster before he left—that he could and did enforce a hard discipline. Jackson ordered three men condemned for desertion taken to an open field and blindfolded. Records Edward Moore, who marched with the Rockbridge Artillery: "They were directed to kneel in front of their open graves, and a platoon of twelve or fifteen men, half of them with their muskets loaded with ball, and half with blank cartridges (so that no man would feel he fired the fatal shot), at the word 'Fire!' emptied their guns at close range. Then the whole division marched by within a few steps to view their lifeless bodies." Presumably, a grim-visaged Jackson witnessed the whole affair.[23]

"I do not believe there was a man in the corps who knew our destination," James M. Hendricks writes, as Jackson set his columns in motion. Besides being told to cook three days' rations, each man was issued sixty rounds of ammunition. Shrouded in secrecy as always, the force, composed of Jackson's own division, now commanded by Taliaferro, Ewell's division, and two brigades of cavalry, marched from Jeffersonton to Amissville and across the Rappahannock via the Hinson Mills Ford to

Orleans. The artillery was pulled "with difficulty up the narrow and rock-ribbed road beyond the river, and pushed forward with the utmost speed." Lee's aide, William Snow, termed it "a gigantic task." Jackson tented the first night at the small hamlet of Salem on the Manassas Gap Railroad in Fauquier County. Throughout that hot, August day Hendricks continues, "each felt that something extraordinary was contemplated and nerved himself for the expected task. We did not always follow roads, but went through cornfields and bypaths, waded streams, and occasionally we marched right through someone's yard." While his corps tramped through one well-manicured lawn, the lady of the place charged out to confront the foot cavalry. "At first she seemed dumbfounded, but she soon expressed her thoughts: 'get out of here. Who told you to come through here?'. . . . A lank old Reb in Company B directed her to Jackson, who just at the time was passing. 'That old fellow over there with the greasy cap riding the sorrel hoss is the cause of all this!' She bolted for him. I saw him smile. I do not know what she said; but she carried her point and we defiled."[24]

Jackson the disciplinarian could also cast a spell amounting to awe over his troops. In an oft-repeated tale by Dabney and John Esten Cooke, both writing within months of his death, Jackson placed himself upon a crag beside the roadway near Salem during the first day's march. A great cheering commenced when his men saw him, but word swept the ranks to pass in silence. "As they passed, they raised their caps, and waved them around their heads, and the enthusiastic love which beamed on every countenance, showed how hard it was to suppress the usual greeting. Those who saw General Jackson that evening as he sat on his horse, cap in hand, with the westering sun shining full on his firm face, could not say he was without *pride*. He was full of it!" reads one account. And Jackson could be appreciative as well as proud. Both chroniclers agree that he turned to subordinates and boasted: "Who could fail to win victories with those men!"[25]

Jackson passed through the lightly defended, but rocky, defiles of Thoroughfare Gap in the Bull Run Mountains; then it was down the Manassas Gap Railroad onto the Manassas Plain. Old Jack reached the Orange and Alexandria, a few miles south of Manassas Junction "after sunset" on August 26. Jeb Stuart and the cavalry had already rendezvoused with him at Gainesville, so that enemy horsemen guarding the way station at Bristoe were quickly subdued. "As we approached Bristoe Station the sound of cars coming from the direction of Warrenton Junction was heard, and General Ewell divided his force so as to take simultaneous possession of the two points of the railroad," Jackson himself wrote. "Colonel T. T. Munford, with the Second Virginia Cavalry, co-operated in this movement. Two trains of cars and some prisoners were captured, the largest portion of the small Federal force at that point making its escape." Although Jackson "fell on the place like a thunderbolt," Kyd Douglas leaves a more vivid account of the fight: "Instantly a train of cars, loaded with stores, came dashing past. The dismounted cavalry poured an ineffective volley into it, but it rushed on its way and bore the alarm to Manassas Junction." Munford's failure alerted Pope that Jackson was now between the Army of Virginia and Washington.[26]

"Notwithstanding the darkness of the night and the long and arduous march of the day," Lee writes, "General Jackson determined to lose no time in capturing the enemy depot at Manassas Junction, about 7 miles distant on the road to Alexandria." Old Isaac Trimble and Jeb Stuart sped through the night, and Jackson himself followed the next morning; he left Ewell's division and Colonel Thomas Rosser's Fifth Virginia Cavalry at Bristoe Station to watch Pope's rear on the Rappahannock. Aroused to action, the federal high command dispatched a force under General George Taylor to oppose Jackson's raid on the vital rail junction: "After a sharp encounter the enemy was routed and driven back, leaving his killed and wounded on the field, General Taylor himself being mortally wounded in the pursuit," Lee's battle account continues: "The troops remained at Manassas Junction during the rest of the day supplying themselves with everything they required from the captured stores."

They not only found a storehouse of supplies, but they also ransacked everything in sight. What took place after Taylor gave up the fight was told and retold until the last Confederate muster; it must have been a glorious time for Jackson's half-starved campaigners, who had tramped more than fifty miles in two days. While Hendricks says, "we never had rations issued so liberally," another trooper gathered up "a tooth-brush, a box of candles, a quantity of lobster salad, a barrel of coffee, and other things which I forgot." According to John Esten Cooke: "Eight pieces of artillery; seventy-two horses and equipments; three hundred prisoners; two hundred negroes [sic]; two hundred new tents; seventy-five additional horses, exclusive of artillery horses; ten locomotives; two railroad trains of enormous size, with many millions worth of stores; fifty thousand pounds of bacon; one thousand barrels of pork; several thousand pounds of flour, and a large quantity of forage fell into Jackson's hands." After each man took what he could carry, great plumes of smoke rolled over the Manassas countryside as the remainder was burned.[27]

Robert E. Lee, meanwhile, had marched with Longstreet's corps along the same path—across the Rappahannock at Hinson's Mill Ford to Salem and down the Manassas Gap Railroad toward Thoroughfare Gap. Jackson was exposed and alone beyond the Bull Run Mountains, and, writes General Long, "unless the mountains could speedily be passed by Longstreet's corps the force under Jackson might be assailed by the whole of Pope's army, and very severely dealt with." When Lee and Longstreet reached the gap "about noon of the 28th," they could hear a roaring cannonade in the distance, which signaled the renewed battle between Jackson and Pope; yet Lee retained the great serenity and firmness that characterized his generalship. "That he was lost in deep reflection as he surveyed the mountain pass in front was evident, yet neither in looks nor words did he show that he was not fully the master of himself and of the occasion," Long continues. When "a Mr. Robinson who lived near the gap" extended a dinner invitation to Lee and his staff, it was willingly accepted; "and this meal was partaken of with as good an appetite and with as much geniality of manner as if the occasion was an ordinary one, not a moment in which victory or ruin hung trembling in the balance."

Long also relates the amusing incident in which a lady of the neighborhood rode out to meet Lee "in the family carriage drawn by a pair of handsome and spirited horses." The party, which included her daughters, was intercepted by enemy horsemen, who appropriated her team for the federal cavalry. "When General Lee rode up to the spot he found the distressed party in a house by the wayside, in which they had taken refuge. With his usual gallantry and courtesy, he dismounted and strove to cheer up the unfortunate lady, expressing his deep sympathy with her mishap, and regretting his inability to relieve her from her difficulty by supplying her with another pair of horses." Lee's chivalry aside, he had to get more than half of his army onto the Manassas Plain to save Jackson from disaster. Unbeknownst to Pope—who would carp about it later— General Irvin McDowell, a man who knew something about Manassas, had detached James B. Ricketts with Buford's cavalry to guard Thoroughfare Gap. Although outnumbered, the small band of federals facing Longstreet's command was able to thwart the Confederate advance for several hours. The delaying action obliged Lee and Longstreet to use nearby Hopewell Gap, and it also prevented a linkup with Jackson until the following day.[28]

What Lee and his marching companions heard through Hopewell and Thoroughfare Gaps was the hotly disputed fight at Groveton, in which Stonewall Jackson upset the grand design of Major General John Pope.

Following the episodes at Bristoe and Manassas Junction, Jackson withdrew a mile or so toward the northwest to await Lee's arrival. In fact, he ordered a concentration of Ewell, Taliaferro, and A. P. Hill beyond the turnpike connecting Warrenton and Centreville. Although A. P. Hill did not reach the battlefield until after nightfall because of an abortive march across the Bull Run fords into Centreville, Old Jack positioned himself along Stony Ridge or Sudley Mountain. On the morning of August 28, he lay entrenched behind a partially constructed railroad grade across the Warrenton Turnpike from Henry House Hill in plain sight of the spot where the deceased Bernard Bee had dubbed him "Stonewall."[29]

The night before, Pope, who had convinced himself that Jackson was withdrawing toward the safety of Thoroughfare Gap, commenced a series of unbelievable blunders. At 9 A.M., August 27, he ordered his entire command to concentrate around Manassas Junction. "At daylight tomorrow morning," he summoned McDowell, "march rapidly on Manassas Junction. We had a severe fight with them to-day, driving them back several miles along the railroad. If you will march promptly and rapidly, at the earliest dawn of day . . . , we shall bag the whole crowd." When Pope, by his own account, reached the Junction around noon on the 28th and found the place abandoned, he issued new orders to head for Centreville on the pretext that A. P. Hill had been observed marching through the town. At the instant, Banks, Porter, Reno, Heintzelman, Sigel, Reynolds, and McDowell altered their lines of march to comply with the new directive. Although Pope, in his haste to crush Jackson, did not know it, his new order destroyed any advantage he might have enjoyed. In other words, except for James B. Ricketts and Buford's cavalry at Thoroughfare Gap as well as Rufus King's command, he had not a man between Jackson and Lee, who was closing with Longstreet's corps. And, as Jackson, with no thought of withdrawing westward, realized that King was marching across his front—along the Warrenton Turnpike to reach Centreville, he jumped at the opportunity to hit a part of Pope's separated army.[30]

The three-hour battle near Groveton on August 28 was a stubborn, brutal affair that ended in stalemate, although King, as Jackson puts it, "slowly fell back, yielding the field to our troops." Jackson knew from captured dispatches and Jeb Stuart's intelligence that an enemy force was closing on his position. It started around 6 P.M., when Old Jack "attacked with two divisions (the Stonewall Brigade, then under General Taliaferro, and Ewell's division), and the fight on the Union side was sustained by King's division alone." Jackson's corps suffered heavy command losses when both Taliaferro and Ewell, who lost a leg, were wounded. A. P. Hill, who spent much of the day countermarching from Centreville because of Jackson's persistent secrecy, though he went into line on Jackson's left flank, arrived too late for the battle.[31]

Unluckily, Jackson's adversary was Colonel John Gibbon and the renowned Black Hat Brigade—named for a distinctive headdress—over a one-mile battlefront. Gibbon, described as "steel-cold, the most American of Americans with his sharp nose and up-and-down manner of telling the truth, no matter whom it hurt," like Jackson, was not a man to run. His brigade of sturdy Wisconsin farmers—soon dubbed the Iron Brigade at Antietam—suffered 33 percent casualties at Groveton. Jackson himself wrote: "The conflict was fierce and sanguinary. Although largely re-enforced, the Federals did not attempt to advance, but maintained their ground with obstinate determination." Abner Doubleday sent two regiments to help the Iron Brigade, but, writes Gibbon in his battle report: "Of the conduct of my brigade it is only necessary for me to state that it nobly maintained its position against heavy odds. The fearful list of killed and wounded tells the rest. The troops fought most of the time not more than 75 yards apart. The total loss of the brigade was, killed, 133; wounded, 539; missing, 79. Total, 751, or considerably over one-third the command." Gibbon's four and Doubleday's two regiments, he added, "sustained for over an hour the fire of two of Ewell's brigades, commanded by Jackson in person."[32]

When Jackson learned that Rufus King and Gibbon were marching past the railroad cut, he quickly placed "the batteries of Woodring, Poague, and Carpenter in front of Starke's brigade and above the village of Groveton, and, firing over the heads of the skirmishers, they poured a heavy fire of shot and shell upon the enemy." A murderous return fire forced his artillery to take new positions, when a stand of trees rendered some of the guns ineffective. "Owing to the difficulty of getting artillery through the woods, I did not have as much of that arm as I desired at the opening of the engagement." Thereupon, Jackson continues, "this want was met by Major Pelham, with the Stuart Horse Artillery, who dashed forward on my right and opened upon the enemy at a moment when his services were much needed."

Twenty-four-year-old John Pelham, soon to die during the Chancellorsville campaign, was in charge of the cannon that always accompanied Stuart's cavalry. Born in Alabama, he had been a West Point undergraduate at the outbreak of war and soon gained a reputation for steadiness under fire as well as for numerous amours with Richmond belles. Blue eyed and fair haired, Pelham moved two Blakely guns against the Iron Brigade. "At one time the bluecoats advanced within fifty yards of

Pelham's fieldpieces, whereupon General Jackson sent word for him to pull his guns back. However, the pole on his right gun had been shattered by an enemy shell making the cannon difficult to move. Hence Pelham remained where he was and directed its fire while the other Blakely kept shifting position to avoid taking a direct hit."[33]

Around nine o'clock, both sides decided to halt the bloodshed. King and Gibbon, in spite of the Iron Brigade's heroic performance, fell back toward Centreville during the night; Ricketts, still guarding Thoroughfare Gap against Longstreet's advance, joined the retreat. With prophetic insight, Jackson added to his battle summary: "Although the enemy moved off under cover of night and left us in quiet possession of the field, he did not long permit us to remain inactive or in doubt as to his intention to renew the conflict." Losses were high on both sides as James Cooper Nisbet, who fought with his fellow Georgians, noted that "braver men never went into battle." And, as Jackson remained secure behind his Groveton fortifications and waited for Lee's help, Pope sat more confused than ever in his Centreville headquarters. "He now saw plainly that he had been outgeneraled, having misinterpreted Jackson's purposes," observes one of his officers, O. O. Howard. "In fact he helped Stonewall to concentrate his brigades where Longstreet might join him."[34]

Pope's new attack was unleashed at 7:00 A.M., August 29, when the batteries of Jesse Reno and John Reynolds opened against Jackson's extreme right. The federal general remained convinced that he was advancing upon a retreating Jackson, and that his troops would have an easy time with Old Jack while his own army concentrated to meet Lee and Longstreet. Although Pope's fury was directed at William Starke, who had replaced Taliaferro as commander of the Stonewall Brigade, it was soon shifted to A. P. Hill, who held Jackson's left flank. "Hill's position formed an obtuse angle which pointed toward the Federal lines," writes Hill's biographer.

Edward Thomas' Georgians fanned out for battle along the wooded tongue to Gregg's right. However, for some unexplained reason, Hill left a gap between the two brigades unattended. The opening was about 175 yards wide. Almost as bad, in front of it was a chasm six to ten feet deep, behind which advancing troops were not visible. Hill apparently never saw the gap and Jackson never checked the line. It was clearly Hill's failure at a critical moment and it nearly cost Jackson his entrenchments along the railroad; foreign-born Franz Sigel not only found the break but he lost no time in trying to smash through Hill's separated units under Maxey Gregg.[35]

With an eye on the dust kicked up by Longstreet's columns, Jackson ordered two of Ewell's regiments into the fray. Despite reinforcements, the federals lunged at the hiatus in six separate assaults and were beaten back each time; Ewell's men fired point-blank into the surging enemy; writes Dabney: "The struggle raged until the cartridges of the infantry were in many places exhausted. When Hill sent word to the gallant Gregg to ask if he could hold his own, he answered, 'tell him I have no ammunition, but I will hold my position with the bayonet.'" In one exchange of gunfire, Ewell himself went down, his right knee shattered beyond repair; Drs. McGuire and S. B. Morrison, Ewell's regimental surgeon, removed the leg at a field hospital, while some of Jackson's men farther down the line, threw rocks at the foe.[36]

The melee along Jackson's front peaked around 2 o'clock in the afternoon. And though Longstreet's lead columns swung into position astraddle the Warrenton Turnpike on the Confederate right by noon, Jackson fought alone throughout the 29th. Lee, who established his headquarters "on a tree stump about a mile from the front," repeatedly urged Longstreet to attack and therefore relieve the pressure on Jackson. Bullheaded and hesitant to commit his men without first surveying the field, Longstreet resisted Lee's "suggestion" that he advance until nearly dark; after hours of procrastination, he sent John Bell Hood and his Texans "to drive the enemy back (on Jackson's right) with great vigor capturing a number of prisoners, a cannon, and three colors," according to Dabney. "Darkness then closed the bloody day, and the Confederates on every side withdrew to lie upon their arms upon their selected lines of combat." Hood says the battle halted after he rode to the rear "to inform Generals Lee and Longstreet of the facts": The late-hour rush had caused "the Federals and Confederates to become so intermingled that commanders of both armies gave orders for alignment, in some instances, to the troops of their opponents."[37]

While Lee struggled to bring order out of confusion, Edward Moore, one of Jackson's cannoneers, surveyed the battlefield at nightfall and found more than dead bodies: "On the ground where some of the heaviest fighting took place there stood a neat log house, the home of a farmer's family. From it they had, of course, hurriedly fled, leaving their cow and a half-grown colt in the yard. Both of these were killed. I saw also, on the field, a dead rabbit and a dead fieldlark—innocent victims of man's brutality."[38]

As Longstreet quibbled with Lee over committing his troops, Jackson met Pope's onslaught without reinforcements. When federal raiders threatened his rear during Sigel's assault, Pelham and the Horse Artillery drove them off but not before "a few wounded men and their ambulances were captured." Otherwise, Old Jack stood alone! When darkness halted the slaughter, Jackson, like his troopers, dropped among the fallen for a few hours rest. "We were sitting by the fire drinking coffee out of our tin cups," records Dr. McGuire, who gave Jackson a report of the day's killed and wounded. "I said, 'we have won this battle by the hardest kind of fighting.' He answered me very gently and softly, 'No, no; we have won it by the blessing of Almighty God.' " Later, as the chaplains offered prayers of supplication and thanksgiving, Jackson's entire bivouac erupted into a giant camp meeting. Dabney says that "many were the brave men who joined in these strange and solemn meetings, whose next worship was offered in the upper sanctuary."[39]

Lee, who rode to the front with a navy Colt tucked in his saddle, was nearly captured when a troop of Buford's cavalry swooped down on Longstreet's lead column marching from Thoroughfare Gap; afterward, he traveled further back in the ranks for the remainder of the day. Throughout the march, cannon fire could be heard in the distance, which spread a feeling of urgency among officers and common soldiers alike. "The day was warm, the roads dusty, and the men suffered for lack of water," observes David Johnston, who tramped with the Seventh Virginia Infantry. "It was pathetic to see the boys with feet bare and bleeding endeavoring to keep pace with their comrades." In the face of such hardship and effort to reach the front, it is difficult to fathom Longstreet's reticence to relieve the pressure on Jackson.[40]

Although Lee repeatedly "suggested that he attack Pope's left once his troops were deployed," Old Pete merely undertook a reconnaissance to determine the lay of the land. Longstreet admits Lee "hesitated" when told that the lateness of the hour precluded an attack until the following morning; he also confirms that Jeb Stuart rode into Lee's headquarters with news of Pope's troop dispositions and seconded his argument to wait. Stuart even lay on the ground with his head perched on a rock for a short nap while Lee and Longstreet debated their next moves. "We remained, until late in the afternoon, spectators of the heavy engagement of Jackson's troops with the enemy," Hood writes. Lee finally *ordered* his reticent officer to send Hood forward with two brigades, although Longstreet's carps in his memoir that Jackson and A. P. Hill had "attacked too much in detail to hold even the ground gained." A touchy political balance that plagued the Confederate effort may have induced Lee to go easy with his direct commands to Longstreet, who had close ties to South Carolina and other Deep South politicians miffed at Virginia's domination of the army. More generous interpreters of Lee's motives ascribe a desire to let those doing the fighting make their own command decisions. It is interesting to note, however, that Jackson's battle report says only: "During the day the commanding general arrived and also General Longstreet with his command."[41]

John Pope also had difficulty with recalcitrant generals at the Second Manassas. His troubles commenced when Stuart met with Lee and Longstreet along the Gainesville roadway, and, using a map, pointed out the best means of "helping Jackson." Stuart also warned that a part of Fitz-John Porter's command was dangerously close to Longstreet's own flank; he ordered his cavalrymen to cut pine branches and drag them along the hot Virginia roads. The resulting dust clouds had the desired effect of persuading Porter and McDowell to withdraw in opposition to a directive from Pope to attack the Confederate right. Pope, who either did not know or did not appreciate that Lee and Longstreet were on the field, finally issued "a direct order" at 4:30 P.M. for Porter to advance. Although he made ready to comply and directed George W. Morell to prepare the assault, Porter decided to hold back because of approaching darkness, the same argument Longstreet used to evade Lee's instructions. Porter's failure to act, which resulted in his court-martial and dismissal from the army within the month, unquestionably contributed to Lee's great triumph the next day in spite of Longstreet's bungling. Through the years, Porter has enjoyed many defenders and President Grover Cleveland even restored his rank, but the fact remains that had he obeyed Pope's order Lee would have experienced difficulty in deploying across the Warrenton Turnpike during the afternoon and evening.[42]

"When the battle ceased on the 29th of August, we were in possession of the field on our right, and occupied on our left the position held early in the day, and had every right to acclaim a decided success," Pope himself argues. "What that success might have been, if a corps of twelve thousand men who had not been in battle that day had been thrown against Longstreet's right while engaged in the severe fight that afternoon I need not indicate." Had Porter attacked at the same time Hood's Texans were on the prowl, Pope reasoned, it would have upset Lee's strategy: "To say that General Porter's non-action during the whole day was unexpected and disappointing, and that it provoked the severest comment on all hands, is to state the facts mildly."[43]

When dawn broke on August 30, Lee, who made his headquarters close to Longstreet, had roughly fifty thousand troops "in a flattened crescent" beyond and south of the Warrenton Turnpike. Heavy casualties had reduced Jackson's effectives to seventeen thousand, while Longstreet with Richard H. Anderson's newly arrived division had about thirty thousand; Stuart's cavalry added another twenty-five hundred and Lee had twenty thousand men in reserve and marching toward northern Virginia—Lafayette McLaws and D. H. Hill with seven thousand each, James A. Walker's division of four thousand, Wade Hampton's cavalry of fifteen hundred, and William Nelson Pendleton's reserve artillery of one thousand. Jackson was still ensconced along the railroad, although part of his force had fallen back to a stand of trees to confuse the enemy; Longstreet's line ran off to the south at an obtuse angle to Jackson and in some respects their commands were actually separated.

"The far-seeing eyes of the great soldier who commanded the southern army had embraced at a glance the whole situation of things, and his plans were formed," observes John Esten Cooke. "The design was to envelop the enemy, as it were, and occupy a position from which he could be struck in front, flank, and rear at the same moment if he made a single error." But a previously obscure colonel of artillery, a member of Longstreet's command, named Stephen D. Lee, held the key to both wings of Lee's army. His eighteen guns had been placed "on a crest" between Longstreet and Jackson, where they would determine the entire battle. If ever a soldier was in the right place at the right time, it was S. D. Lee at the Second Manassas.[44]

The first day had been but a prelude to the bloodletting of August 30, although John Pope, ignorant as ever of Lee's intentions, had a formidable array to send against the Confederates. Except for Nathaniel P. Banks, Pope now had his entire army at hand, a total of sixty-five thousand men; he even summoned Fitz-John Porter from his isolated position on Longstreet's right flank. He also had Edwin Sumner and William B. Franklin as well as the divisions of Jacob Cox and Samuel Sturgis—forty-two thousand additional men—part of McClellan's Peninsula army, marching from Alexandria, a mere twenty-five miles away. Although he could count on 100,000 men to hurl against Lee and Jackson, he made a fatal error; Pope persisted in the belief that only Jackson remained in force and that he, Lee, and the rest of the Confederate force was retreating to the safety of Thoroughfare Gap. When the fight broke on August 30, no one but John Reynolds—soon to die at Gettysburg—and James B. Ricketts faced Longstreet's wing of Lee's combined army.[45]

Except for an occasional picket shot, both armies waited in deathly solitude for the opening round; "Saturday morning, the 30th was clear and warm. The stillness seemed unnatural—or was the calm repose of the thousands dead. The resigned silence of the thousands living," records Kyd Douglas. Jackson did not think Pope would fight for the third day running, yet he spent the morning riding to and fro, checking every military detail. Young Theodore Hartman, who fought with the Fourteenth Tennessee Infantry, reported that he heard a rider approach him along the railroad bed around 3 P.M. "Upon looking around I saw General Jackson on his old claybank, unattended by an aide or courier. As he neared me and was about to pass on I halted him, shouted, and said: 'General, this is our extreme left; the enemy is right out there.' " After Hartman pointed the way to safety, Jackson returned his salute and rode off in "the right direction." Earlier, he had ridden the half mile or so to army headquarters to discuss strategy with not only Lee but also Longstreet and Stuart; he found Lee convinced that Pope, braggart though he was, could not pass the opportunity to attack. Marse Robert cautioned his generals to be on guard, and while the anxiety of waiting pressed upon both armies, the opening shot rang out, although accounts differ on the exact time.[46]

Kyd Douglas, who remained near Jackson throughout the day, said that Old Jack was writing an afternoon dispatch to Lee when Pope's guns opened. " 'Notwithstanding the threatening movements of the enemy, I am still of the opinion expressed this morning that he does not intend to attack us. . . .' A single gun was fired and General Jackson got up hastily and handing me the unfinished note, said, 'That was the opening signal for a general attack.' " Pope's attack, wave after wave of bluecoated infantry, was aimed at Jackson's position along the railroad once Reynolds and other Union officers convinced him that Lee was not retreating. Longstreet and the Confederate right were all but forgotten when Pope "advanced his powerful infantry against Jackson, whose single line behind the friendly shelter of railroad cuts and embankments received this mighty array with tremendous volleys of musketry, hurling back line after line, only to be replaced by fresh assailants." During this part of the fight, General Long continues, "the roar of musketry gave place to the clash of bayonets, and at one point, after the Confederates had exhausted their ammunition, the assailants were repelled with stones which had been thrown up from a neighboring excavation."[47]

At a critical juncture, Jackson hurried a rider to Lee's headquarters with a plea for reinforcements. Longstreet was quickly told to send additional infantry to his beleaguered comrade; instead, he showed a long sought-after initiative by ordering "Bachman's and Reilley's batteries of Frobel's battalion," which had been dueling with the enemy at long range, to join the eighteen guns of S. D. Lee. With Fitz-John Porter's columns in his direct front, Old Pete decided against sending slow-moving infantry when massed artillery would be instantly effective. The two extra batteries, writes an expert on Confederate artillery,

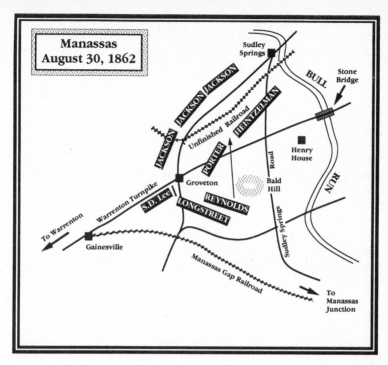

"added all that was needed to put an end to the attack. Before the second battery, Reilley's with its howitzer section gained its position, the enemy began to retire, and in 10 minutes after the effect of the guns began to be felt, Porter's troops gave up the contest and retired in confusion to the woods through which they advanced." John Esten Cooke cites "an eye-witness" who reported: "As shell after shell burst in the wavering ranks, and round shot ploughed broad gaps among them, you could distinctly see, through the rifts of smoke, the Federal soldiers falling and flying on every side." As Porter struggled to reverse the disaster, Lee had a signalman ask Jackson if he yet required reinforcements. "No!" came the reply in semaphore: "The enemy are giving away."[48]

The horrible carnage wreaked by Stephen Lee's artillery was evident to both armies as Lee ordered Longstreet forward, but Old Pete was on the move before the dispatch reached him. Pope had made the ensuing slaughter much easier by withdrawing Reynolds and Ricketts from Longstreet's front, thereby weakening his entire left. Lee personally joined the pursuit, accompanied by his aide, Walter Taylor, who wrote later: "Our attention was attracted by a Federal officer who lay upon the ground wounded. . . . Before I could speak to him he said: 'Is Frank Huger here?' I replied that Huger was just not here at that point. Then he said: 'Is Ramseur here?' Again I replied in the negative, and then I asked: 'Why do you ask for Huger and Ramseur?' 'Oh,' he replied, 'They are old friends of mine and fellow cadets at West Point.' " Lieutenant W. W. Chamberlain, an aide to General George Sykes, later died from his wounds.

Pope, who lost 1,747 killed, 8,452 wounded, and 4,263 missing, could not sustain the losses, and broke off the fight in the late afternoon, but Lee's army also suffered during Longstreet's counterattack. The First Virginia Infantry Brigade, for instance, had less than eighty men standing when the killing ended. Also among the dead at Second Manassas was Colonel Fletcher Webster, only son of Daniel Webster.[49]

Pope's blunders had enabled the Confederacy to win big, although Lee, always alert to every opening, had been quick to exploit his every weakness. Union positions at Bald Hill, Henry House Hill, and Young's Branch, all fell in sequence until one o'clock in the morning, when Colonel Thomas Kane's battalion of Pennsylvania Bucktails destroyed the Stone Bridge over Bull Run to cover the retreat into Centreville. "It was a severe defeat for General Pope; but it was nothing else," says one historian. "It was not a rout nor anything like a rout. The army retired under orders, and though, of course, there were many stragglers, it retreated in good order." Because the Army of the Potomac remained a potent force, Lee realized that pursuit was necessary to check Pope before he could reach the Washington entrenchments. And it was Jackson again, and not Longstreet, to whom he turned on the night of August 30; by daybreak, August 31, instead of preparing for the Sabbath, Stonewall Jackson, with orders from Lee to turn Centreville and stop the retreat, had his troops on the march.[50]

As Pope headed eastward on his path to Washington, Jackson marched north across Bull Run at Sudley Ford; followed by Longstreet, he struck the Little River Turnpike and sped eastward toward Germantown and Fairfax Court House. A mile or so west of Germantown—where the Little River and Warrenton Turnpike intersect before reaching Fairfax— Old Jack deployed his troops and waited. In front of Ox Hill, a gentle swell in the Manassas Plain near the village of Chantilly, he made ready to meet Pope with his force facing southwest—A. P. Hill near the Warrenton Pike, Ewell's division, commanded by Alexander Lawton, on the extreme right or Little River roadway, and William Starke, with Jackson's own division in the center. Jackson had again outmarched the slow-moving Longstreet and was forced to fight alone throughout September 1.

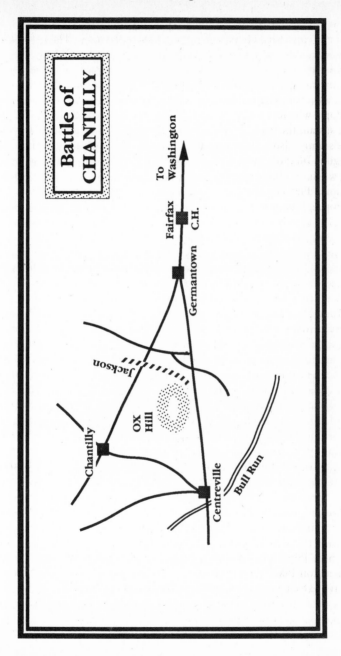

Battle of CHANTILLY

"A cold and drenching thunder-shower swept over the field, striking directly into the faces of our troops," Jackson writes. The brigades of Lawrence Branch and J. M. Brockenbrough charged the enemy, "but so severe was the fire in the front and flank of Branch's brigade as to produce in it some disorder and falling back. The brigades of Gregg, Thomas, and Pender were then thrown into the fight. Soon a portion of Ewell's division became engaged." And, Jackson continues: "The conflict now raged with great fury, the enemy obstinately and desperately contesting the ground until their generals (Kearny and Stevens) fell in front of Thomas' brigade, after which they retired from the field." Darkness broke off the engagement without decisive result, and, records Edward P. Alexander: "At Ox Hill on September 1 a part of Jackson's forces encountered a strong rear guard & received a temporary check, but Pope made no halt outside of the strong chain of fortifications guarding Washington on the south."[51]

Lee had set out to worry Abraham Lincoln and worry him he did, with Longstreet and Jackson within fifteen miles of the federal capital. Lincoln was clearly disturbed as he ordered government clerks to begin drilling along Washington streets, and sent the federal treasury to New York; a gunboat was anchored in the Potomac "to carry the President away if necessary." Although he was mightily upset with McClellan's boast "to let Pope get out of his scrape," Lincoln knew that a new federal commander was unavoidable following the fiasco at Manassas; as Mc-Clellan, who was the only ranking officer in the east, was having breakfast at his H Street home, the president and General Halleck "appeared at his front door unannounced." With considerable trepidation, they handed George Brinton McClellan the Army of the Potomac for the second time. The date was September 2, one day after Ox Hill, and within two weeks McClellan would again fight Lee and Jackson, not on the soil of Virginia but sixty miles to the northwest, in Maryland. As Pope's legions straggled into the city rehashing the earlier retreat from the same battlefield, McClellan rode out to meet them on the roadway from Centreville and Fairfax; hundreds of bluecoats cheered Little Mac's return until he could hardly proceed among the throngs who "hugged his horse's legs and caressed its head and mane."[52]

The troops under Jackson and Longstreet had an even greater cause to cheer in the battle's aftermath. "The great advantage of the advance of the army," Lee telegraphed President Davis on September 3, "is the withdrawal of the enemy from our territory and the hurling back upon their capital two great armies from the banks of the James and the Rappahannock." McClellan and Pope had not only been beaten, but Union losses outnumbered Lee's casualties by a significant margin: sixteen thousand to nine thousand. Following Ox Hill, Lee's combined force lay very close to the Potomac, which no doubt influenced the decision to launch his subsequent Maryland invasion. Although numerous factors played on Lee's mind, including a need to replenish the army's larder while Virginia farmers harvested their crops unmolested by marching armies, his military momentum and the forward position of the army became key factors. "The present seems to be the most propitious time since the commencement of the war for the Confederate army to enter Maryland," he told Davis. On the same evening, as the army dried out from the pelting rains of September 1, Lee rode into Jackson's camp at Pleasant Valley near Chantilly. The next morning, September 4, the bloodletting on Cedar Mountain, Manassas, and Ox Hill notwithstanding, it was Jackson who again led the way northward through Dranesville and Leesburg to the Potomac crossing at White's Ford.[53]

Since he was constantly on the move, Lee had no time for letters to his wife and daughters. After the battle of August 31, he did not recognize Rob, Jr., who had served a gun under S. D. Lee, when the two passed within fifteen feet of each other; Lee was "greatly amused" to encounter his youngest son with blackened hands and face from "powder-sweat and his clothing covered with the red soil of the region." And he must have opened the Maryland campaign in considerable discomfort. While he watched the Manassas fighting, his horse had bolted, pulling him to the ground; both his hands were broken in the mishap, which necessitated the use of an ambulance for several days. Perhaps Lee's inability to write and a reluctance to use clerks prevented personal letters to his family. Even Jackson was too preoccupied for letters to his beloved *esposa*; yet, two days before his conference with Lee at Pleasant Valley, he wrote a penitent note to Anna from Ox Hill: "The Lord has answered our prayers; He has again placed us across Bull Run; and I pray that He will make our arms entirely satisfactory. . . . God has blessed and preserved me through His great mercy. . . ."[54]

13

"Maryland, My Maryland"

When Lee hurried Jackson toward the Potomac ahead of the main army on September 4, 1862, he again demonstrated confidence in his capabilities of command; Old Jack was once more in the van as he spearheaded the Maryland invasion. Still uncomfortable from his injuries at Manassas, Lee established his headquarters "two miles from Fredericktown" on September 7, two days after Jackson's crossing at White's Ford; he informed Jefferson Davis that "all divisions have crossed the Potomac, unless it may be Genl. [John G.] Walker's from whom I have heard nothing." The Confederate high command was apprehensive about this grand intrusion into northern territory, which prompted Lee to dispatch daily—sometimes even more frequently—letters to the president in Richmond. These communiqués in the *Official Records* are concerned with not only military matters but also with diplomatic efforts to bring Maryland into the Confederate camp. Although Lee launched the campaign in high spirits, he was obliged to inform Davis: "Notwithstanding individual expressions of kindness that have been given, and the general sympathy in the success of the Confederate States, situated as Maryland is, I do not anticipate any general rising of the people in our behalf."[1]

If Marylanders did not flock to Lee's standard, there were still compelling reasons to commence the cross-Potomac incursion. He could not attack Washington, Fitzhugh Lee argues, "because his numbers were too few"; if he were to keep the Confederate momentum gained during the Seven Days and Second Manassas, Lee had no option but to move away from Virginia. He could hardly remain fixed on the Manassas plain with Lincoln and McClellan gathering an even larger force near the federal capital. A triumph on northern territory might bring diplomatic recognition of the Confederate nation from England and France, or it might cause Lincoln to ask for terms and let the South go in peace. By encouraging the Copperhead movement, Lee might yet induce the Old Line State to join the South, thereby surrounding the enemy capital with hostile territory. A decisive victory on northern soil could well dampen Unionist resolve to continue the war, and it would surely boost Confederate morale. Moreover, if Lee could not attack Washington, neither could McClellan move against Richmond while he remained north of the Potomac.[2]

As Jackson marched on White's Ford, a nasty incident took place between Old Jack and A. P. Hill, who still commanded the Light Division. On the night of September 3–4, Jackson had told his subordinate commanders to move out at 4:00 A.M. sharp, but when that time arrived Hill's men were not moving and Maxey Gregg's brigade was filling its canteens. Angered at the delay and already miffed at Hill, Jackson not only chastised his general for disobeying his orders but told Gregg to move. Hill objected to Old Jack's harsh treatment, and reportedly asked Jackson to take his sword; as all three officers—Jackson, Hill and Gregg—were getting steamed up, Old Jack ordered Hill to the rear, placed him under arrest, and entrusted the Light Division to Lawrence Branch. The matter created a wound that never healed, although Jackson rescinded his order long enough for Hill to lead his men at Antietam. Both Jackson and Hill were probably at fault, and because Lee was too preoccupied with strategy to intervene, the dispute continued to fester until Jackson's death.[3]

"The 10th Va. Regt. of infantry, preceded by a band and bearing a Virginia flag, was in the advance; as a band reached the Maryland shore it struck up the air, 'Maryland, My Maryland,' amid shouts of the soldiers," notes Jed Hotchkiss. "It was a noble spectacle, the broad river, fringed by the lofty trees in full foliage; the exuberant wealth of autumnal wild flowers down to the very margin of the stream and a bright green island stretched away to the right." Jackson was one of the first across, and he was immediately treated to a melon feast along with many of his men. "Our crossing was unexpected by the enemy and therefore unopposed," Hotchkiss continues. "General J. had a fine horse presented to him and we were cordially invited to many houses. The General ordered a field of corn to be purchased and the roasting ears given to the men and the husks and stalks to the horses. . . ." But the following day, September 6, Jackson was thrown from the animal that had been presented by well wishers in Frederick; he was shaken badly enough to turn over his command temporarily to D. H. Hill. James Dabney McCabe says,

"[T]his act of admiration, came very near proving fatal to him, for he had barely mounted the horse before the animal became frightened, threw him, and came near breaking his neck."[4]

Jackson, who established close contact with Lee during the Frederick bivouac, had recovered sufficiently to attend church services the next day, Sunday, September 7; according to Kyd Douglas, who went along, Old Jack had a special pass issued to leave camp: "Guard and Pickets— Pass Genl. T. J. Jackson and two staff officers and attendants to Frederick to church, and to return tonight." He apparently signed his own order to attend the German Reformed Congregation of the Reverend Dr. Zacharias because a Presbyterian service could not be located. Douglas describes Jackson sitting in the back of the church, where he had difficulty hearing and promptly went to sleep, dropping his hat to the floor. And, Douglas maintains, he even slept through the closing prayer: "The Doctor was afterwards credited with much loyalty and courage because he prayed for the President of the United States in the presence of Stonewall Jackson." When he wrote to Anna the next morning, Old Jack confessed to falling asleep but said nothing about the pro-Union supplications, which he probably did not hear. "The minister is a gifted one, and the building beautiful," he added.[5]

The brazenness of Zacharias reinforces John Esten Cooke's contention that the venture was "not encouraging from the inception." Months of constant warfare had reduced the Army of Northern Virginia to a bare-bones existence. When Lee crossed the Potomac, his was "a strange and motley army." Moreover, continues, Robert Selph Henry, "men were dressed in anything and everything. The fine militia uniforms of the year before had disappeared, and the regulation gray, which had a blue tinge, was disappearing. . . . After all, though, it was not rags and tatters that mattered so much at that season. It was the lack of shoes, a lack that the Confederate army was never able to supply." The "motley" invaders induced the state's governor to telegraph Lincoln: "Jackson's troops are represented to be in very bad condition, a large portion of them without shoes or hats, and with ragged clothing."[6]

Union-loving Maryland was openly hostile to Lee's ragtag army, which led the abolitionist poet John Greenleaf Whittier to pen his well-known "Barbara Friechie":

> Up rose old Barbara Friechie then,
> Bowed with her fourscore years and ten;
> Bravest of all in Frederick town,
> She took up the flag the men hauled down;

In her attic window the staff she set,
To show one heart was loyal yet.
Up the street came the rebel tread,
Stonewall Jackson riding ahead.
Under his slouched hat, left and right
He glanced; the old flag met his sight.
'Halt!'—the dust-brown ranks stood fast.
'Fire!'—out blazed the rifle blast;
It shivered the window, pane and sash;
It rent the banner with seam and gash.
Quick, as it fell from the broken staff,
Dame Barbara snatched the silken scarf;
She leaned far out on the window sill,
And shook it forth with a royal will.
'Shoot, if you must, this old gray head,
But spare your country's flag,' she said.
A shade of sadness, a blush of shame,
Over the face of the leader came;
The noble nature within him stirred
To life at the woman's deed and word:
'Who touches a hair of yon gray head
Dies like a dog! March on!' he said.

Honor to her! and let a tear
Fall, for her sake, on Stonewall's bier.

Whittier employed considerable poetic license to present his flawed account. He had gotten the tale from Mrs. E.D.E.N. Southworth, "a popular novelist he had met when he was corresponding editor of the *National Era.*" Mrs. Southworth had heard about Dame Friechie and the Union flag from a Friechie relative and relayed it to the poet. Whittier's poetry notwithstanding, Anna Jackson cites another relative, Valerius Ebert, who claimed that Jackson and his men trooped down another Frederick street three hundred yards from her residence and that Mrs. Friechie, then ninety-six years of age, was bedfast at the time. The aged lady no doubt shared the sentiments of those young girls who lined the streets waving the Stars and Stripes and shouting patriotic slogans. Whether she had waved her flag at a passing column of Union soldiers instead of Jackson's veterans, Whittier had put her into the American lexicon.[7]

Undeterred by Unionist outpourings, Lee, at the behest of Jefferson

Davis, issued a "Proclamation to the People of Maryland" on September 8, which had but one purpose—to lure the state into the Confederacy:

> Under the pretense of supporting the Constitution, but in violation of its most valuable provisions, your citizens have been arrested and imprisoned upon no charge and contrary to all forms of law. The faithful and manly protest against this outrage made by the venerable and illustrious Marylander, to whom in better days no citizen appealed for right in vain, was treated with scorn and contempt; the government of your chief city has been usurped by strangers; your legislature has been dissolved by unlawful arrest of its members; freedom of the press and of speech has been suppressed. . . .

Lee and the Confederates were now prepared to help a sister state throw off its "foreign yoke"; after saying that the Army of Northern Virginia would respect all shades of opinion and enforce the law equally, he announced: "While the Southern people will rejoice to welcome you to your natural position among them, they will only welcome you when you come of your own free will."

Davis and Lee were adamant that the army observe complete propriety while north of the Potomac; strict orders passed through the ranks to do nothing that might aggravate the local citizenry long before the official proclamation. "Never before had the world beheld the spectacle of a hostile army, in an enemy's territory, conducting itself with perfect regard for the rights of property and the feelings of the inhabitants." But, added John Esten Cooke, "the recruits did not appear."[8]

Lee was more concerned with a worsening military situation, as McClellan advanced on Frederick from the Washington defenses; he realized that federal garrisons of twenty-five hundred men at Martinsburg and nine thousand at Harpers Ferry, both commanded by General Dixon S. Miles, would jeopardize his lifeline with the Shenandoah Valley. He could not withdraw behind either the Catoctin Range or South Mountain—the northern extension of the Blue Ridge—while these forces remained in place; moreover, Harpers Ferry was a tempting prize to snatch from the enemy. When Lee decided to issue the famous General Order 191 on September 9, one day after his proclamation, the stage was set for battle. His scheme called for Jackson to again take the lead and to detach himself from the main army while he stayed close to Longstreet and the rest. As had been the case when he marched against Pope at Cedar Mountain on the eve of Second Manassas, Old Jack was the soldier tapped to capture Harpers Ferry.

"The army will resume its march to-morrow [September 10], taking the Hagerstown Road. General Jackson's command will form the advance, and, after passing Middletown, with such portion as he may select, take the route toward Sharpsburg, cross the Potomac at the most convenient point, and by Friday morning take possession of the Baltimore and Ohio Railroad, capture such of them as may be at Martinsburg, and intercept such as may attempt to escape from Harpers Ferry." Longstreet was directed to march through Turner's Gap in South Mountain to Boonsboro, while Lafayette McLaws with Richard H. Anderson proceeded through Middletown to Maryland Heights, overlooking Harpers Ferry from the north. John G. Walker was ordered to the Loudoun Heights on the south flank of Harpers Ferry to cooperate with Jackson and McLaws. The rear guard was entrusted to D. H. Hill, who followed the main force under Longstreet. Jeb Stuart with the cavalry was posted to screen the army against McClellan's oncoming hosts of more than eighty thousand.[9]

Although Jackson marched at dawn on September 10, a dramatic turn in the war occurred three days later, when McClellan came into possession of Lee's Order 191. Private B. W. Mitchell, Company F, Twenty-seventh Indiana Volunteers, stumbled across a copy wrapped around three cigars, intended for D. H. Hill at the latter's campsite near Frederick. According to F. W. Palfrey, the campaign's most careful student, "it appears at this time General D. H. Hill was in command of a division which had not been attached to or incorporated with either of the two wings of the army, and that one copy of Special Orders No. 191, was sent to him directly from headquarters, and that General Jackson also sent him a copy, as he regarded Hill in his command, and that the order sent from headquarters was carelessly left by some one in Hill's camp. While the other, which was in Jackson's own hand, was preserved by Hill." Civil War chroniclers from 1862 to the present have speculated about subsequent events once McClellan had the plan at his disposal. When D. H. Hill argued in a published article after the war that the "Lost Dispatch" actually helped the Confederate cause, Lee responded in a February 1868 letter to his onetime subordinate: "At the time the order fell into Genl. McClellan's hands, I considered it a great calamity & subsequent reflection has not caused me to change my opinion." Lee concluded with his only comment on the matter: "I do not know how the order was lost, nor until I saw Genl. McClellans [*sic*] published report after the termination of the war did I know certainly that it was the copy addressed to you. From what I have stated you will see that I do not concur with you in the opinion that its having fallen into Genl.

McClellan's hands was a 'benefit' but on the contrary, 'an injury of Confederate arms.' "[10]

When McClellan received Lee's order on September 13, he instantly realized (1) that the Army of Northern Virginia had been divided and (2) that Lee's intent was the capture of Harpers Ferry as well as the outpost of Martinsburg. And he immediately appraised Lincoln of the windfall: "I think Lee has made a great mistake, and that he will be severely punished for it. The army is in motion as rapidly as possible. I hope for a great success if the plans of the rebels remain unchanged. I have all the plans of the rebels, and will catch them in their own trap, if my men are equal to the emergency. . . ." Yet Little Mac, still obsessed with visions of superior Confederate numbers, knew that only fast marching would allow him to destroy part of Lee's army overlooking Harpers Ferry before the remainder could concentrate against him. On the night of September 13, only two of D. H. Hill's brigades held the South Mountain passes, and they were shortly detected by the federal cavalry under Alfred Pleasonton. At the very time he needed to move quickly, McClellan spent the 13th at his headquarters in Frederick drafting a plan to advance through Crampton, Turner's and Fox's Gaps to hit McLaws on the Maryland Heights. His main force under Burnside would attack through Turner's Gap on the road from Frederick through Boonsboro to Hagerstown, while William B. Franklin was ordered to seize Crampton's Gap, six miles to the south. "Having gained the pass, your duty will be first to cut off, destroy, or capture McLaws' command and relieve General Miles. . . ." That done, Franklin was told to march against D. H. Hill and Longstreet with help from Miles or to prevent Jackson from recrossing the Potomac. "My general idea is to cut the enemy in two and beat him in detail," McClellan declared. [11]

Franklin was instructed to march at daybreak on September 14, the same day McClellan informed his wife that he expected "a serious engagement today & perhaps a general battle—if we have one at all during the operation it ought to be today or tomorrow." McClellan's modern biographer observes: "Sunday, September 14, was the first of five consecutive days in which General McClellan was in close contact with all or some part of Lee's forces. Not once in that time would he discover, by observation or intuition or with the aid of the Lost Order, his opponent's critical situation or the true strength of his army." Lee, near Hagerstown with Longstreet, had divided his force (McClellan thought he had 120,000 men, about twice his actual numbers) precisely because he counted upon his adversary's "slows." Now that McClellan had Lee's order—a Confederate sympathizer who knew of the find had brought word to Lee—a new plan was needed to counter the federal threat to his rear. "It had not been the intention of Lee to oppose the passage of the enemy through South Mountain, as he desired to draw McClellan as far as possible from his base, but the delay in the fall of Harpers Ferry now made this necessary," observes John Esten Cooke. "It was essential to defend the mountain-defiles to insure the safety of the Confederate troops at Harpers Ferry." Lee could not allow Jackson's mission to be threatened, and when word of Franklin's advance reached him on the Boonsboro-Hagerstown pike, he turned with Longstreet to contest the passes. Shortly after Little Mac reached a base camp on the east side of South Mountain to watch the melee, Lee came up with Longstreet and personally took command. [12]

Battles at Turner's and Fox's Gaps, where General Sir Edward Braddock had crossed South Mountain during the French and Indian War, as well as Crampton's Gap, developed simultaneously. It was approaching noon before Ambrose Burnside opened the northernmost fight at Turner's Gap; although Hill had ordered up his remaining brigades and Lee hurried Longstreet's force toward the mountain, he fought alone for much of the day. Samuel Garland, one of Hill's brigade commanders, had already been killed before Longstreet's arrival; before the fighting ended, Union general Jesse Reno also fell mortally wounded, and a future president of the United States named Rutherford B. Hayes was hit so badly that he had to leave the field. D. H. Hill argues that Longstreet and Lee did not appear until 4 P.M., although both had reached the fighting much sooner following a thirteen-mile trek from Hagerstown. Although Hill remained critical, Lee noted in his battle summary that "Longstreet advanced rapidly to his support and immediately placed his troops in support. . . . Under General Longstreet's directions, our right was soon restored and firmly resisted the attacks of the enemy from the east." John B. Hood's Texans, who came up with Longstreet, managed to carry the crest for a moment following a bloody bayonet charge. [13]

Burnside's superior numbers soon caused Lee to call off the fight, Hood's momentary success notwithstanding. Despite Lee's good words, D. H. Hill wrote in his own report that Longstreet's men "took wrong positions, and, in their exhausted condition after a long march they were broken and scattered." Nor was the irascible Hill stinting in his own praise:

> Should the truth ever be known, the battle of South Mountain, as far as my division was concerned, will be regarded as one of the most remarkable of the war. The division had marched all the way from Richmond and the

straggling had been enormous in consequence of heavy marches, deficient commissariat, want of shoes, and inefficient officers. Owing to these combined causes, the division numbered less than 5,000 men on the morning of September 14. . . . This small force successfully resisted, for eight hours, the whole Yankee army, and, when its supports were beaten, still held the roads, so that our retreat was effected without the loss of a gun, a wagon, or an ambulance.

At Turner's and Fox's Gaps, approximately twenty-eight thousand federals—not quite the entire army—were thrown against seventeen thousand Confederates, counting Longstreet's command, before Lee called off the fight after the onset of darkness. Losses for Burnside—killed, wounded, and missing—reached 1,813, while Hill and Longstreet lost nearly 2,700 men.[14]

Meanwhile, the fight of Crampton's Gap nearer Harpers Ferry and the Potomac turned into a rout once the slow-moving Franklin reached the summit around noon. This passage at the rear of McLaws on the Maryland Heights remained completely unguarded through the night of September 13 and part of the 14th, when Jeb Stuart became concerned; and, taking a closer look himself, rode personally to the headquarters of McLaws overlooking Harpers Ferry. Howell Cobb and his Georgians were dispatched to the gap, which they held stubbornly for several hours. McLaws, who was directing a cannonade at the Harpers Ferry garrison, became alarmed when he heard the battle raging between Cobb and Franklin about five miles to the northeast; he was even heading for the fight himself when an approaching courier told him the news: "Franklin's superiority of force was such that he gained the crest after a spirited action of three hours," observes General Palfrey. "He lost five hundred and thirty men, and estimated the enemy's killed and wounded at about the same; but he took from him four hundred prisoners, a gun, and three colors." Had he moved a few hours sooner, Franklin could have taken Crampton's Gap for the asking. Although forced to withdraw from both passes, Lee had accomplished his hastily drawn mission for September 14; he had given Jackson time to concentrate on Harpers Ferry.[15]

Around 8:00 P.M., Lee sent a cryptic message to McLaws telling him to break off the fight. "The day has gone against us," he said from his headquarters at the Widow Herr's Tavern opposite Turner's Gap, as he informed McLaws that the army was preparing to withdraw toward Sharpsburg and the Potomac crossings. "I now consider it safe to say that General McClellan has gained a great victory over the rebel

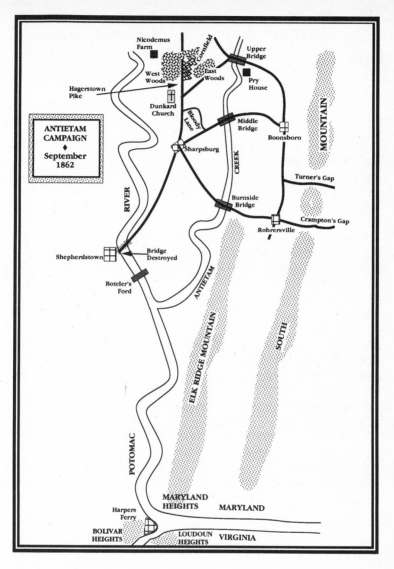

ANTIETAM
CAMPAIGN
♦
September
1862

Nicodemus
Farm

Upper
Bridge

Cornfield

West
Woods

East
Woods

Pry
House

MOUNTAIN

Hagerstown
Pike

Dunkard
Church

Bloody
Lane

Middle
Bridge

Boonsboro

Sharpsburg

CREEK

Turner's Gap

RIVER

Burnside
Bridge

Crampton's Gap

Rohrersville

Shepherdstown

Bridge
Destroyed

Boteler's
Ford

ANTIETAM

ELK RIDGE MOUNTAIN

SOUTH

POTOMAC

MARYLAND
HEIGHTS

MARYLAND

Harpers
Ferry

BOLIVAR
HEIGHTS

LOUDOUN
HEIGHTS

VIRGINIA

army in Maryland between Frederickstown and Hagerstown," a jubilant Abraham Lincoln telegraphed to Judge Jesse Kilgore DuBois, one of his political friends in Illinois. "He is now pursuing the flying foe." But Lee was not fleeing; instead of crossing the Potomac as intended, he took up a defensive position along a line of rolling hills overlooking nearby Antietam Creek. With nineteen thousand men and a summons for Jackson to join him at the double quick, Lee and the Army of Northern Virginia prepared to renew the fight.[16]

About the time D. H. Hill was looking out from Turner's Gap in utter dismay at Burnside's approaching columns, Jackson reached the federal positions on Bolivar Heights around eleven o'clock during the morning of September 13; he marched through Middletown, Boonsboro, and Williamsport, and "recrossed the Potomac into Virginia at White's Ford," to reach Martinsburg, twelve miles west of Harpers Ferry. William Poague, who traveled with him, records that Jackson was nearly captured on the way "by a reconnoitering detachment of Federal cavalry." A better reception awaited him in Virginia than in Maryland; he was nearly mobbed by grateful citizens who looked upon him as a savior. "He gave his autograph generously, cut a button from his coat for a little girl, and then submitted patiently to an attack by others, who soon stripped the coat of the remaining buttons." Old Jack spent one day, September 12, in Martinsburg before his advance through Halltown to Bolivar Heights; he no sooner arrived than couriers were dispatched to McLaws and Walker beyond the Potomac after a prearranged signal system failed to locate his compeers.[17]

McLaws and Walker were in position soon enough, and writes a local historian: "About two P.M. the Confederates began a furious artillery fire simultaneously from Maryland and Loudoun Heights and from Sandy Hook. The Federal artillery replied with much spirit and for a time silenced the Loudoun batteries. The enemy also opened with other guns from the Charlestown and Shepherdstown roads." Throughout September 14, Jackson prepared to capture the Harpers Ferry garrison, which had been augmented by Julius White's three thousand infantry from Martinsburg.

Confederate success was insured when Old Jack directed A. P. Hill "to move along the left bank of the Shenandoah and thus turn the enemy's flank and enter Harpers Ferry." Hill, whose guns joined in the cannonade on the 14th, found a flaw in the Union defenses as he neared the river; "to his amazement he discovered an elevation on the Federal left that was occupied by infantry but unsupported by artillery," writes his biographer. "Hill immediately sent the brigades of Pender, Archer, and Brockenbrough—with Thomas in reserve—to seize the eminence while Gregg and Branch proceeded along the riverbank and established a foothold on the Federal left and rear." Hill wrote in his official report that "the fate of Harpers Ferry was sealed" when the Light Division unlimbered its nine rifled guns, eight Napoleons, and thirteen short-range pieces within 1,000 yards of the Federal lines."

Always the wary warrior, Jackson made further preparation by ordering Stapleton Crutchfield, his artillery officer, to move ten guns across the Potomac under cover of darkness. These cannons, borrowed from Ewell's division, were positioned under Walker's guns atop Loudoun Heights to fire on Harpers Ferry in reverse. "This arrangement of the Confederate forces," comments Dabney, "is a no more beautiful instance in the whole history of the military art, of a grand combination absolutely complete and punctual, irrevocably deciding the struggle before it was begun. . . ." The early bombardment during September 14 was a mere rehearsal for things to come; when dawn broke on September 15, Jackson was able to open a blistering fire from seven different points.[18]

As both armies slept at their guns through the night of September 14–15, a troop of twenty-five hundred Union cavalry broke out of Jackson's noose. Although Jackson had warned his officers to watch for an escape attempt, Miles agreed to the scheme after Hasbrouck Davis, grandson of historian George Bancroft, convinced him that cavalry could no longer help his beleaguered command. Guided by an old settler named Noakes, Davis and his men moved northward "right under the guns of McLaws" and "but 178 of those who started were missing when the escapees reached Greencastle, Pennsylvania, at between eight and nine o'clock the next morning." Jackson, however, was seemingly unaware of the exploit when he sent an 8:15 P.M. message to Lee: "Through God's blessing, the advance, which commenced this evening, has been successful thus far. . . . The advance has been directed to resume at dawn to-morrow morning. . . . Your dispatch respecting the movements of the enemy and the importance of concentration has been received." He also hoped for divine sanction of a "complete success" on the 15th, and most scholars agree that Jackson's assurances persuaded Lee to halt his rush for the Potomac; he was now prepared to challenge the whole federal army solely on the conviction that Old Jack thought he could win at Harpers Ferry.[19]

When Jackson's guns opened on the 15th, the struggle had become anticlimactic; because each Confederate gunner had preset his sights, the federal batteries were silenced within an hour. When William Poague informed Colonel Andrew Grigsby, his brigade commander, that he had seen a white flag on Bolivar Heights, he was told to keep firing: "He either could not or would not see the flag, which now looked like a small tent fly, and ordered 'd-n their eyes, give it to them.' After this we fired very slowly. After a while here comes a courier from 'Old Jack' on the extreme right with orders to 'cease firing, enemy at Harpers Ferry has surrendered.' " Although Jackson had directed A. P. Hill to charge through the abatis, the federals had lost their momentum following the barrage. And, observes Jubal A. Early, when the surrender did come "very hearty cheers went up along the line, as we were thus saved from the necessity of an assault, which if stubbornly resisted would have resulted in the death of many of us."[20]

Sporadic firing after the surrender resulted in the unfortunate death of General Miles, so that Julius White, who afterward became ambassador to Argentina, handed the garrison over to Old Jack. He left the details of capitulation to A. P. Hill, and, by his own account, reached "the vicinity of Sharpsburg after a severe night's march." Besides the eleven thousand–man garrison, the Confederates captured "75 pieces of artillery, some 13,000 small arms, and other stores." But Jackson had only one goal after Harpers Ferry and that was to join Lee at the earliest possible moment; when he crossed the Potomac, a breathless messenger rode up to say "McClellan was within an hour's march with an enormous army." Then, avows John Esten Cooke, "Jackson turned around and said: 'Has he any cattle with him?' The reply was that he had thousands. 'Well,' said Jackson, with his dry smile, 'You can go. My men can whip any army that comes well provisioned.' " His jocularity aside, Jackson and his men waded the Potomac at Shepherdstown and reached Sharpsburg on the afternoon of the 16th; without a moment's rest since leaving Frederick on September 10, Old Jack now had his troopers ready to help Lee meet McClellan and the Army of the Potomac.[21]

After the surrender, Jackson dashed off two letters, which, not surprisingly, employed the same language. During the 16th, presumably after he had conferred with Lee and after he had established his headquarters "at the farm of Davis Smith near Sharpsburg," he wrote to Colonel R. H. Chilton, Lee's adjutant general. "Yesterday crowned our army with another brilliant success in the surrender at Harpers Ferry of Brigadier General White. . . . Our losses were small." And to Anna on September 15: "It is my grateful privilege to write that Our God has given us a brilliant victory. . . . The action commenced yesterday, and ended this morning in capitulation. Our Heavenly Father blesses us exceedingly." Jackson was not a man to understate his achievements.[22]

The great battle, "the bloodiest single day of the Civil War," which developed the morning after Jackson rejoined Lee, unfolded in three distinct phases; although Lee had chosen the field west of Antietam Creek, McClellan's erratic attacks determined the course of action. Phase one started at dawn on the Confederate left, and lasted until roughly 10 A.M., around the Miller cornfield and nearby Dunkard Church; Jackson played a prominent role in this contest. Phase two, from 9:30 through 1:30 P.M., involved the murderous confrontation along the Sunken Road opposite Lee's center; the concluding stage was fought between 1:00 and 5:30 P.M., astraddle the lower or Burnside Bridge, when A. P. Hill marched on the field from Harpers Ferry. Significant confusion exists about the number engaged in both armies: General Long puts the figures at McClellan, ninety thousand, and Lee, forty thousand; Livermore insists Lee had fifty-one thousand effectives throughout the seventeenth; and an official government publication says it was McClellan, seventy-five thousand, Lee, forty-five thousand. A handout given to Antietam Battle Park visitors lists 12,410 Union and 10,700 Confederate casualties.[23]

"My plan for the impending engagement," McClellan wrote after the war, "was to attack the enemy's left with the corps of Hooker and Mansfield, supported by Sumner's and if necessary Franklin's and as soon as matters looked favorably there to move the corps of Gen. Burnside against the enemy's extreme right, upon the ridges running to the south and rear of Sharpsburg, and having carried their positions to press along the crest toward our right; and whenever either of the flank movements should be successful to advance our centre with all their force then disposable." McClellan, however, did a poor job of communicating with his division commanders, so that no one fully understood his plan for "whipping Bobby Lee" when the fight started; furthermore, he made no serious attempt to locate Lee's exact position. As Jackson came up with the divisions of Lawton and J. R. Jones, Lee had already arrayed his men in a curving line from the Potomac near its juncture with Antietam Creek to a point on the Potomac north of Sharpsburg. His defenses paralleled the Sharpsburg-Hagerstown Pike about one-half mile west of the sluggish Antietam, which is a mill stream that originates near Greencastle, Pennsylvania, and strikes the Potomac between Shepherdstown and Harpers Ferry.[24]

In order to prepare for his "general engagement," McClellan directed Joe Hooker to cross the Antietam by the Upper Bridge around 2 P.M. on September 16. Anticipating the coming fury, Lee had pointedly asked

John Bell Hood and his Texans to bolster his left, although Jeb Stuart and the cavalry held the extreme flank. Then, in the midst of a day-long artillery duel, Hood's brigades absorbed the initial federal assault north of Sharpsburg. "With George Gordon Meade's Pennsylvania Reserves (Division) in the van, Hooker's Corps advanced cross-country during the late afternoon, struck the Hagerstown road, turned south and deployed for action against the Confederate left flank." And, continues a brigade historian, "the Texans succeeded in driving part of the First Pennsylvania Rifles (Bucktails) and the Third Regiment of the Pennsylvania Reserves upon Truman Seymour's brigade, which was in support of the Federal skirmish line. With the coming of darkness the firing gradually subsided, and both sides bivouacked for the night on the battlefield—close enough for Hood's men to hear the enemy reinforcing his position in their immediate front." In all of Lee's army, only Hood saw direct action during the 16th.[25]

Hooker's late-afternoon assault accomplished little, because approaching darkness precluded a follow-up attack. What it did do was alert Lee that McClellan's main thrust would be directed at his left on the next morning. Throughout the night of September 16–17, he worked furiously to strengthen his lines after Jackson as well as McLaws and Walker arrived from Harpers Ferry. Jackson's command was thrown along the left to replace Hood, who had been allowed to withdraw after his bout with Hooker. Hood himself had ridden to Lee's tent and asked that his men be given an opportunity to replenish themselves, but he was referred to Old Jack. Following another ride through the drizzly night, Hood found him " 'alone lying upon the ground, asleep by the root of a tree.' Upon hearing Hood's plea for the relief of his half-starved troops, Jackson immediately ordered Lawton's and W. H. Trimble's Brigades to replace his troops. Before ordering the movement, however, Jackson first exacted a promise from Hood that he would come to the assistance of Lawton and Trimble if he was called upon to do so."[26]

Jackson now had the Stonewall Brigade, temporarily headed by Andrew Grigsby, nearby with his other units, including Ewell's division (now commanded by Lawton), in the West Woods beyond the Hagerstown Pike and North of Dunkard Church. E. E. Stickley relates that sharpshooters in both armies kept up a steady fire through much of the night; when "some boys" grew anxious, Grigsby, who surely enjoyed Old Jack's confidence, took time to soothe their fears. Around 11 o'clock he told them: "Boys, no-fight to-night. You can lie down and get some sleep." If men on the line were bothered about the coming battle, Jackson went back to sleep with Lee's great appreciation. "Part of General Jackson's corps have reached us and the rest are approaching except General A. P. Hill's division, left at Harpers Ferry to guard the place and take care of public property," he wrote to President Davis on the 16th. "The enemy have made no attack up to this afternoon, but are in force in our front." Lee also added a telling postscript about the capture of Harpers Ferry: "The indomitable Jackson and his troops gives us renewed occasion for gratitude to Almighty God for his guidance and protection."[27]

"Your dispatch of to-day received. God bless you, and all with you," a jubilant Lincoln telegraphed to McClellan on the afternoon of September 15. "Destroy the rebel army if possible," the president added, and Little Mac, armed with that petition, unleashed his drive against Lee forty hours later at 3 o'clock A.M., according to Private Stickley. The storm fell on Jackson as Fighting Joe Hooker opened the assault with ten brigades under Abner Doubleday, James B. Ricketts, and Gordon Meade. McClellan had all but told Lee that his left would receive the first blow, and writes a poetic Yankee: "Before dawn there was an outburst of cannon thunder. The roosters at Miller's, Poffenberger's, Mumma's and other neighboring farm houses crowed lustily. As soon as it was light— so that objects could be seen at close range—the battle on the Federal right began. . . . We could see the flashes of fire from the muskets; here and there a battery hurried into position and opened fire—the rebels answering gun for gun and 'Hell had let loose.' "[28]

Jackson's line, including the commands of Lawton and J. R. Jones, did not have a man to spare when the battle started. During the night, Lawton had been posted in a cornfield east of the Hagerstown Pike and three hundred yards beyond the main positions. When the federals under Doubleday hit that patch of corn, a wholesale slaughter on both sides ensued. "In the time I am writing this," Joe Hooker put in his battle summary, "every stalk of corn in the northern and greater part of the field was cut as closely as could have been done with a knife, and the slain lay in rows precisely as they had stood in their ranks a few moments before. It has never been my fortune to witness a more bloody, dismal battlefield." That was after he had seen Confederate bayonets glistening in the morning sun and ordered his batteries to rake the field with canister and shell.[29]

Lawton was cut to pieces in the opening melee as were other outfits; the Louisiana Tigers, commanded by Henry T. Hays, went into the thirty-acre cornfield with 550 men and within thirty minutes "over 60 percent of the brigade had fallen, 45 dead, 248 wounded, and 2 missing." The Sixth Louisiana, which started with twelve officers, had five killed and seven wounded within a matter of minutes. Unit after unit lost so many men that Jackson had to withdraw in order to regroup. And Old Jack himself did not escape harm's way; as he rode before his position after daybreak, the "Yankees spied him," writes R. H. Daniels, who fought with Company K, Fourth Georgia Regiment. "The first shell passed over him, the second just to the rear and a little above him, and the third shell struck his horse just back of the saddle. As the horse went down Gen. Jackson jumped to the ground, and, one of his aides dismounting, he vaulted into the saddle, and immediately ordered us to 'attention' and to 'left wheel.'" Stonewall said nothing about the incident in his battle report.[30]

At 6:00 A.M., Hood reentered the fray when Jackson pulled parts of his command to the safety of the West Woods and Dunkard Church. "For two hours, from 7 to 9 A.M., the Texas Brigade, with the First Texas far in advance, held tenaciously to Miller's Cornfield and that section of the pike that ran along its west side," writes Hood's biographer. So many men fell that Hood was afraid his horse might trample the dying and wounded under his feet. Joined by a section of D. H. Hill's command, Hood's regiments pushed the enemy until he reached a line of six 12-pound Napoleon guns that sent them reeling back at point-blank range.[31]

Around 7:30 A.M., Hooker was reinforced by Joseph K. F. Mansfield, who had camped in his rear through the night. The resulting fight, says historian Burke Davis, "all but wrecked the Confederate army," as Lee, who had arrived on the field, pulled men from elsewhere to stem the incursion. Almost immediately, Mansfield, nephew of Lee's West Point instructor Jared Mansfield, fell mortally wounded. Joe Hooker, too, received a painful wound in the heel, while riding into the pasture south of the cornfield on his white charger to direct events personally. The ground around the Dunkard Church he had contended for since dawn was finally within his grasp when a rebel sharpshooter put a bullet through his foot. He tried to stay on the field but could not; "weak and faint from the loss of blood, he was taken to the rear." When he reached the Philip Pry house, where McClellan had his headquarters, ambulances were sent for his return to the battle, but he was through for the day. Years later when Fighting Joe revisited the battlefield, he was able to locate the spot of his wounding "where the big walnut trees stood about 75 yards from where the Smith house now stands (1906) along the Smoketown Road."[32]

Mansfield's charge was blunted when Jeb Stuart's horse artillery opened from the Nicodemus Hill near the Potomac. John Pelham had massed between fifteen and twenty guns, Blakleys and Napoleons, and when Stuart said "shoot" the resultant fire shattered the federal right. "As the Yankees pushed ahead over the dead and wounded in the cornfield, Pelham's five batteries showered them with a devastating fire of grape and canister that surprised them as they had not seen Pelham change position," notes his biographer. "One bluecoat who saw 4,000 of his comrades slaughtered during the assaults, described Pelham's devastating fire as 'artillery hell.' " During the fighting, Heros Von Borcke, the big Prussian who acted as Stuart's chief of staff, saw the horrors of war at close quarters: "At the moment of passing the 3rd Virginia Cavalry, as I was exchanging some friendly words with its gallant commander, Colonel Thornton, a piece of shell tore off his left arm very near the shoulder, from which wound he died in a great agony a few hours afterward." Nor was Jackson's inner circle immune from the bloodbath, as William E. Starke, commanding Jackson's division, was killed and had to be replaced by Andrew Grigsby as the Confederate lines sagged from the return fire.[33]

As Pelham fired from his position one-half mile to the west, the federal left under General George S. Green drove Hood unmercifully toward the Dunkard Church. Lee and Jackson summoned Jubal Early from the Nicodemus Hill, where he had been guarding Stuart's guns, after Hood signaled that all would be lost without reinforcements. Senior brigade commander Early was put in command of Ewell's division and rushed to Hood's relief following the wounding of McLaws. "Discovering that Green's bluecoats were moving to the rear of the Dunkard Church and threatening to take the whole Confederate line in reverse, Old Jube gave orders for an attack. With the 4th Virginia regiment leading the advance, the other troops joined in. The brigade attacked so vigorously that it drove the Unionists entirely out of the woods." And if Old Jube's biographer thinks highly of his man, Jackson was equally laudatory: "General Early attacked with great vigor and gallantry the columns on his right and front," reads his battle summary.[34]

While Early and Hood stabilized Jackson's front, another specter loomed when Edwin Vose Sumner charged out of the West Woods and made straight for the front. The scene of battle now shifted a few hundred yards north of Dunkard Church—destroyed in a 1921 storm but rebuilt for Antietam Battle Park visitors—to the East Woods, where Old Jack gathered additional reinforcements. Here behind trees and limestone outcroppings, Jackson waited for the renewed assault. "By this time the expected re-enforcements (consisting of Semmes's and Anderson's brigades and a part of Barksdale's, of McLaws's division) arrived, and the whole, including Grigsby's command, now united, charged upon the enemy, checking his advance, then driving him back with great slaughter and beyond the wood, and gaining possession of our original position," Jackson himself reflected. What he failed to say was that his ambush of the unsuspecting Major General John Sedgwick, whose statue today overlooks the Hudson at West Point, produced a virtual bloodletting. Within twenty minutes, twenty-two hundred officers and men, nearly half of his command, fell dead or wounded. Sedgwick himself was shot three times, although he lived to fight again before his death during the Wilderness campaign.[35]

The cost in lives had been enormous, although the Confederate left managed to hold. Yet Lee retained a calm dignity throughout the ordeal. "It was about noon of September 17, 1862, that I saw Gen. Robert E. Lee riding along the firing line," comments C. A. Richardson, Company B, 15th Virginia Infantry. "He was inquiring for General Jackson. I heard him make the inquiry of several officers, and was so impressed with his noble bearing, the stately appearance of the man, and his good substantial mount that I was induced to ask an officer near me if he was not some general officer. I received the prompt reply that it was Gen. Robert E. Lee." Richardson adds that he wore no sign of rank during the battle.

Noble though he was—what Thomas L. Connelly has termed the "Marble Man"—Lee could also be a stern disciplinarian when the occasion demanded. Although he might excuse A. P. Hill's refusal to march at Jackson's beckoning or send John Bell Hood back into the fray at Antietam—he had absconded with several captured ambulances at Harpers Ferry—he took a dim view of shirking in the midst of battle. As Lee sat astride his horse—which had to be held by an orderly because of his injured hands—he espied a man near the Dunkard Church coming toward him with a dead pig in tow. "With disaster so close, and straggling one of its chief causes, Lee momentarily lost control and ordered Jackson to shoot the man as an example. Instead, Jackson gave the culprit a musket and placed him where the action was hottest for the rest of the day. He came through unscathed and was afterward known as the man who had lost his pig but saved his bacon."[36]

After the deadly clash on the Confederate left ended around noon, Lee had plenty to occupy his attention as McClellan shifted "his piecemeal attacks" to other parts of the field. Jackson, however, was done with Antietam once the Sumner-Sedgwick assault terminated. "In the afternoon in obedience to instructions from the commanding general, I moved to the left with a view to turning the Federal right, but I found his numerous artillery so judicially established in their front and extending so near to the Potomac, which here makes a remarkable bend . . . as to render it inexpedient to hazard the attempt," Jackson comments. And when the day ended after the renewed killing around the Sunken Road and at the Burnside Bridge, Jackson still held the Confederate left. His tired veterans slept on the very field they had occupied at the break of dawn; if Old Jack had not gained territory, he had not given ground before McClellan's masses.[37]

Although McClellan's strategy called for an attack against Lee's left and then his right, the battle developed differently when William H. French strayed away from Hooker and stumbled into D. H. Hill's command at a place afterward enshrined in the national memory as the Sunken Road, or Bloody Lane. In the beginning, Lee did not have a center; he had concentrated his forces on the left around Dunkard Church, Cornfield, and West Woods, and on his right near the lower bridge, or, as it became known, Burnside Bridge. The center was a thin line of skirmishers connecting his two flanks. At the first sign of trouble, Lee rode to the crest overlooking the Sunken Road with Longstreet and D. H. Hill to observe the gathering reinforcements for French's advance. Then, as he ordered Richard H. Anderson, who had just arrived from Harpers Ferry, to march for the Confederate center, a Yankee battery sighted Hill, who had separated slightly from the other two. "While viewing the field a puff of white smoke was seen to burst from a cannon's mouth about a mile off," Longstreet observes. "I remarked, 'There is a shot for General Hill,' and, looking toward him, saw his horse drop on its knees. Both forelegs were cut off just below the knees." Although unhurt, Hill had two additional horses shot from under him during the day.[38]

Hill's two brigades spread between Lee's two flanks were driven before French's onslaught to a defensive position along the Sunken Road. "Worn down by farm use and the wash of heavy rains, this natural trench joins the Hagerstown Pike 500 yards south of the Dunkard Church. From this point the road runs about 1,000 yards, then turns south toward the Boonsboro Pike. That first 1,000 yards was soon known as the Bloody Lane." Although parts of Hill's command had fought with Jackson and Hood earlier in the morning, the two remaining units put up a spirited defense while waiting for Anderson. They were forced back from the Hagerstown Pike into the Sunken Road, in Hill's own words, "after Captain Thompson, Fifth North Carolina, cried out, 'They are flanking us!' This cry spread like an electric shock along the ranks, bringing up vivid recollections of the flank fire at South Mountain. In a moment they broke and fell to the rear."[39]

Anderson arrived around 11 o'clock with three thousand troops, which emboldened Hill to renew the fight with French, who had been reinforced by Israel B. Richardson. Known throughout the army as "Fighting Dick," Richardson and his men managed to bring up additional batteries to rake Hill's positions. "The Confederate battle line in the Sunken Road, the strongest defensive position on the battlefield, collapsed completely," says a recent chronicler. "Rebel soldiers by the hundreds were seen clambering out of the road and running for the rear. It was a mix-up in orders that caused the line to be abandoned, the only significant command failure in Lee's army that day." Like the panic that drove them into the roadbed, a new order shouted by Colonel J. N. Lightfoot of the Sixth Alabama prompted several regiments to join in a headlong flight for the Hagerstown Pike. When his line commenced to buckle, D. H. Hill had no choice but to leave the Sunken Road—now the Bloody Lane—for safer ground. But, notes Edward Porter Alexander, "some congenital defect made McClellan keep Fitz-John Porter's five large corps entirely out of action, although they stood there looking on about 20,000 strong within a mile of our centre." Instead of coming to the front himself to assess the immediate situation, Little Mac remained ensconced in his Pry House headquarters.[40]

Hill was able to avert a complete rout by rallying some of his spent troops; in his own words, he "found a battery concealed in a cornfield, and ordered it to be moved upon the Yankee columns. . . . It was moved out most gallantly, although exposed to a terrible direct reverse fire from the long-range Yankee artillery across the Antietam. . . . The battery unlimbered, and with grape and canister drove the Yankees back." Because McClellan chose not to attack in force—he was apparently afraid Lee would counterattack along the federal right—Hill was able to fix his lines west of the Hagerstown Pike and to the south of Jackson and Hood. The unquenchable Hill, author of mathematics texts in more peaceful times, gathered about two thousand of his veterans for another charge at the converging enemy, but his valor came to nothing. When Lee filed his account some weeks later, he said only that the "small force" rallied by D. H. Hill "and the well-directed fire of the artillery, under Captain Miller of the Washington Artillery, and Captain Boyce's South Carolina battery, checked the progress of the enemy, and in about an hour and a half he retired." What he did not say was that his army had nearly collapsed before the federal pounding; had Abraham Lincoln dispatched a more assertive warrior instead of the snaillike McClellan, the result could have been much different.[41]

The killing had been among the worst for the entire war as both sides grasped the importance of the Sunken Road fight. "The Confederates had great advantages of position, as the old road and the rails piled before it placed them, as it were, in a fort, and they got some guns into place from which they were partially able to enfilade the Federal line." But Hill's men also suffered. When a group of local farmers toured the field after the battle, a dead Confederate who had been shot seven times was discovered hanging across a rail fence. A single split-rail with seventeen bullet holes was found. Perhaps most remarkable of all was "the man with a two-horse spring wagon who came to the Roulette farm and drove to where the [observation] tower now stands and gave to a number of Union soldiers bread, ham, cakes, and pies that had been sent by some of the good ladies, but no one knows who he was or where he came from." Federal authorities after the war attempted unsuccessfully to locate the unidentified samaritan in order to recognize his bravery.[42]

The third phase started in earnest around noon or shortly after, when Ambrose Everett Burnside commenced a serious effort to force the lower bridge across the Antietam. Actually, three bridges of similiar masonry construction spanned the stream, but the lower one—forever known as the Burnside Bridge—was the scene of a bloody struggle extending over several hours; since early morning, McClellan had dispatched numerous couriers directing Burnside to cross the stream with the Ninth Corps when he realized that Lee's right had to be turned or the battle would be lost. And, importantly, if successful south of Sharpsburg proper, the federal army would block Lee's direct line of retreat down the Harpers Ferry Turnpike. With his back to the Potomac, Lee began to exercise great concern about this part of his defenses after the Sunken Road struggle. Although McClellan did not know it, the Confederate right, under D. R. Jones had been weakened by the transfer of men and cannon to help Jackson and D. H. Hill; nevertheless, two Georgia brigades under Robert A. Toombs stood between the Ninth Corps and destruction of Lee's southern flank when the guns opened.[43]

Lee had the continued good fortune of facing another Union officer without the will to fight; one McClellan biographer makes the flat statement that "exercising initiative was the furthest thing from General Burnside's mind." Burnside, born in an Indiana log cabin thirty-eight years before and a West Point graduate, was so dilatory in carrying the bridge that McClellan himself became disillusioned with his onetime friend. It took him from 8:00 A.M. until noon to cross, and then another two hours before he ordered his men to attack the crest overlooking the creek. "Burnside's tentatives were frivolous in their character; and hour after hour went by during which the need of his assistance became more and more imperative and McClellan's command more and more urgent," notes William Swinton. "Five hours, in fact passed, and the action on the right had been *concluded* . . . before the work on the left that should have been done in the morning was accomplished." Burnside's inaction had enabled Lee to save Jackson's flank by pulling troops from Jones and Toombs.[44]

Although Toombs, according to his own words, never had more than 403 infantrymen to hold the bridge, Burnside was confronted with some difficult terrain that turned the federal left into a killing field; although nearby fords permitted men to wade the Antietam, the bridge itself—twelve feet wide and 125 feet long—was approached from the east by an exposed road that was easily covered by Toombs's sharpshooters. McClellan himself had recognized the dilemma on the evening of September 16 and visited the bridge; he made troop dispositions to assist a crossing of the triple-arched span constructed in 1836. "The whole Ninth Corps, except Willcox's division, was moved forward and to the left to the rear slope of the ridges on the left bank of the Antietam, its centre being nearly opposite the stone bridge." Despite Burnside's formidable array, Toombs held the high ground; his position, he writes, "lay in the fact that, the nature of the ground on the other side, the enemy were compelled to approach mainly by the road which led up to the river for near 300 paces, parallel with my line of battle, and distant therefrom from 50 to 150 feet, thus exposing his flank to a destructive fire the most of that distance." Once across the stream, the road into Sharpsburg met a steep hill of one hundred or so feet before it reached the plain extending into the city. It was here, on the hillside above the Antietam, in still-discernible rifle pits, that Toombs's Georgia boys held the entire Ninth Corps in check. "At between 9 A.M. and 10 o'clock," Toombs continues, "the enemy made his first attempt to carry the bridge by a rapid assault, and was repulsed with great slaughter, and at irregular intervals, up to about 1 o'clock, made four other attempts of the same kind, all of which were gallantly met and successfully repulsed by the Twentieth and Second Georgia."[45]

The riflemen under Toombs, who told his wife that he intended to leave the army as soon as he had distinguished himself in a major battle, were forced to abandon their positions during the early afternoon; in his own words: "The enemy despairing of wresting the bridge from the grasp of its heroic defenders, and thus forcing his passage across the river at this point, turned his attention to the fords. . . . , and commenced moving fresh troops in that direction by the left flank." A sizable force under Isaac P. Rodman did cross by a ford below the bridge and attack

Toombs from his right; beyond that, his men had run out of ammunition as his lines began to retreat. Without adequate reserves the Georgians were forced back almost to the streets of Sharpsburg. The disintegrating southern lines had reached such a state that Lee arrived to direct several batteries into place to challenge Burnside's headlong rush toward Sharpsburg and the Harpers Ferry Pike. About this time, he also sent word for Jackson to start his abortive counterattack against the federal right to relieve the pressure.[46]

At the critical moment, when all seemed lost, General Ambrose Powell Hill arrived on the field and probably extended the Civil War for another thirty-one months. "When General Lee found that General Jackson had left six of his brigades under General A. P. Hill to receive property and the garrison surrendered at Harpers Ferry, he sent orders for them to join him, and by magic spell he arrived on the field to meet the final crisis," notes Longstreet who had nominal command of the Confederate right. The instant Hill got that message to come at the double-quick, he set the Light Division in motion for the front. It came from Lee and not the cantankerous Jackson, and he ignored Old Jack's dictate to rest marching troops ten minutes out of every hour. With cannon booming on the horizon Hill crossed the Potomac by the Boteler Ford and made straight for Lee, often whacking straggling troopers with his own sword. "Lee was anxiously looking southward at two-thirty, as seconds seemed to tick the death knell of his army." And, continues A. P. Hill's biographer, "suddenly over a rise appeared a group of officers on frothing horses. It was Hill. He had covered seventeen miles in seven hours." He reined his horse in front of Lee by the Harpers Ferry roadway, and without a moment's respite the Light Brigade was ordered to reinforce D. R. Jones and Toombs.[47]

Lee was so elated by Hills's arrival that observers say he embraced him—a rare thing for the aloof commander. After a brief exchange, Hill immediately sent two of his brigades southward as protection against federals who might cross by another span below the Burnside Bridge. The brigades of Branch, Gregg, and Archer were hurled against Burnside's center, while those of Toombs, Kemper, and Garnett opposed his right. D. H. Hill even sent some of his guns from the Sunken Road, and the Washington Artillery along with the batteries of S. D. Lee and B. W. Frobel were rushed into the fray. "The strong battle concentrating against General Burnside seemed to spring from the earth as his march bore him farther from the river," Longstreet continues. "Outflanked and staggered by the gallant attack of A. P. Hill's brigades, his advance was arrested." By 7 o'clock, Hill used the artillery amassed by Lee to force the Ninth Corps back to the very crest overlooking the stream. And when Stonewall Jackson, who surely remembered his tiff with Hill, filed his account of the day, he said only: "I refer you to the report of Maj. Gen. A. P. Hill for the operations of his command in the battle of Sharpsburg. Arriving upon the battlefield from Harpers Ferry at 2:30 o'clock of the 17th, he reported to the commanding general, and was directed by him to take position on the right." Old Jack's reticence aside, A. P. Hill had been in the right place at the right time to save Lee's army from almost certain annihilation.[48]

As the great battle wound down, Lee met with his generals at a makeshift headquarters "on the road near the village" and received their reports. Although the army was in no condition to renew the contest, he determined to hold his ground throughout the 18th; "a part of his line was withdrawn to the range of hills west of the town, which gave him a very strong and much better field than the previous day," writes General Long. When Lee learned that fifteen thousand fresh troops were marching to join McClellan, he had no choice but to order a general withdrawal south of the Potomac; Longstreet himself and all of his biographers comment on Lee's exclamation, "Ah! here is Longstreet; here is my warhorse," when he appeared at the late-evening conference. But when the army headed south, Old Jack was placed in charge of the rear guard. Not Longstreet but Stonewall Jackson was the man tapped to insure the army's safety.[49]

Jackson, too, had been at the roadside meeting and he understood the importance of an unhampered retreat. "Early on the morning of the 19th we recrossed the Potomac into Virginia near Shepherdstown," reads his battle report; and in a burst of familial pride, Anna adds: "General Jackson . . . sitting on his horse in the middle of the Potomac, for hours watched the passage of the troops across the stream. Not until he had seen the last man and the last gun safely upon the Virginia side did he cross over himself." But the crossing became a near disaster when William Nelson Pendleton, Lee's chief of artillery, failed to get his guns in place to ward off any pursuing federals. Jackson rushed back to the river from his Martinsburg camp to resist a two thousand-man force including the 118th Pennsylvania, which managed to get a toehold south of the river. A. P. Hill was again sent into the vortex as Lee and Jackson sat atop the bank watching hundreds of hapless federals cut down in midstream while they sloshed for safety. The action developed so quickly that Fitz-John Porter did not have time to send reinforcements, and by "midmorning" it had ended with an enormous loss of life.[50]

After the "Affair at Boteler's Ford," the army bivouacked along

Opequon Creek, then Martinsburg, and finally Bunker Hill in present Berkeley County, West Virginia. It was a time to rest and replenish the ranks; about the moment Abraham Lincoln arrived to walk over the Antietam battlefield and to reach his conclusion to replace McClellan with Burnside as commander of the Army of Potomac, Lee and Jackson found time to write their loved ones after weeks of constant combat. When Lee wrote home "not long after the battle," he told his wife that he "had not laid eyes on Rob" since the 17th. "My hands are improving slowly and with my left hand I am able to dress and undress myself, which is a great comfort. My right is becoming of some assistance, too, though it is still swollen, and sometimes painful. . . . I am now able to sign my name." Later, on October 26, Lee again wrote his wife, this time to lament the death of their daughter Annie Carter Lee: "When I reflect on how she will escape in life, brief and painful at best, and all we may hope she will enjoy with her sainted grandmother, I cannot wish her back. I know how much you will grieve, and how much she will be missed." The beloved daughter had passed away six days earlier at a North Carolina spa.[51]

While Jackson remained at Bunker Hill, relates his wife, an "old woman" stormed into his headquarters looking for her son, "John," saying only that the boy was a member of "Jackson's company." Her persistent inquiries irked some of his junior officers, who had more urgent duties at hand, "but when Jackson came in and heard her simple story, he listened with as much politeness as if she were a grand lady, and . . . he ordered that every company of his corps should be searched for 'John' who was at last found to the indescribable delight of his loving old mother." And, in a letter dated October 6 to his *esposa*, Jackson told Anna about "two nice sponge-cakes" from ladies of the neighborhood and also admonished her to send a contribution to the local Bible Society.[52]

As the Army of Northern Virginia awaited the next battle, it became clear that Lee's tactical advance into Union territory failed to achieve any real purpose; he had neither crushed McClellan nor gained a foothold north of the Potomac. Although Lee himself rarely sought excuses for his failures, he told Jefferson Davis on September 21 that "a great many men belonging to the army never entered Maryland" due to straggling and desertions; he may have temporarily checked McClellan, but he urged the president to seek special legislation to deal with the problem before his next move: "For it is still my desire to threaten a passage into Maryland, to occupy the enemy on this frontier, and if my purpose cannot be accomplished, to draw them into the Valley, where I can attack them to advantage." But Lee had to wait until the following summer before he could mount another northern offensive—an offensive that not only took place after Jackson's death but also ended in the disaster of Gettysburg. Thousands of words have been penned about the Antietam campaign, yet none describes its failure better than those of Lee's nephew, himself a participant in the brutal fighting: "He added but few recruits, lost ten thousand men, and fought a drawn battle, which for the invading army was not a success." Nor was the hoped-for diplomatic recognition of the Confederate nation by England and France forthcoming.[53]

14

Fredericksburg

In the weeks following Antietam, Lee and Jackson remained near each other at "the Rehabilitation Camp" along the Opequon until October 28, when Lee accompanied Longstreet's corps to Culpeper; Jackson was left to keep McClellan out of the Shenandoah Valley, as Lee again placed his confidence in Old Jack's ability to act alone. Concerned with harmony before the next battle, Lee sought to reconcile the festering dispute between Jackson and A. P. Hill at the former's headquarters while he remained near Martinsburg. Although Jackson preferred to forget past differences following Hill's brilliant performance during the Maryland campaign, Hill would not let the matter rest; he demanded a resolution of the charges against him. Lee's pleas for moderation could not persuade either man to budge. Sketchy accounts of the meeting indicate that Lee merely patched an uneasy truce between the two warriors. "The three generals were closeted in Jackson's tent for some time, after which Lee mounted Traveller and rode away," comments a Hill biographer. "Hill grimly spurred his horse in another direction and Jackson strode back to his quarters. No word of the proceedings was ever revealed by the participants, but whatever the nature of Lee's appeal, it failed to mend the rift." From that moment, Hill and Jackson maintained only formal communications; Lee abandoned the inquiry, but an icy civility permeated each man's relations with the other until Jackson's death.[1]

While encamped in northern Virginia, Lee received a visit from Colonel Garnet Wolseley, later Field Marshal Wolseley of the British Army. Wolseley had been posted in Canada with several contingents in the aftermath of the *Trent* Affair, in which two Confederate envoys had been forcibly removed from a British ship by the federal navy and which had momentarily threatened an outbreak of hostilities between England and the United States. Accompanied by two London correspondents, Wolseley made his way first to Lee's headquarters and then Jackson's. Published accounts of his meeting with "the Confederate generals" afford modern readers an insight into the life-style of both while in the field. In contrast to the pomp and show of European armies, Wolseley found Lee's camp free of outward display. "It consisted of about seven or eight pole tents, pitched, with their backs to a stake-fence, upon a piece of ground so rocky that it was unpleasant to ride over it, its only recommendation being a little stream of good water which flowed close to the general's tent." A number of slaves who acted as servants and several enlisted couriers, however, either slept in the wagons or under them in the brisk autumn weather. Lee still suffered from his earlier fall, although Wolseley found him "a strongly built man, about five feet eleven in height. . . . His hair and beard are nearly white; but his dark brown eyes still shine with all the brightness of youth, and beam with a most pleasing expression." He was proud of his victories in the fall of 1862 and "confident of ultimate success under the blessing of the Almighty, whom he glorified for past successes, and whose aid he invoked for all future operations."

At Jackson's headquarters, Wolseley was greeted by a general who wanted to expound on his own journey through the English countryside a decade earlier; Old Jack even launched into a discourse about the Durham Cathedral, which he had once visited. "With him we spent a most pleasant hour, and were agreeably surprised to find him very affable, having been led to expect that he was silent and almost morose. . . . He has a broad open forehead, from which the hair is well brushed back; a shapely nose, straight, and rather long; then colourless cheeks, with only a very small allowance of whisker; a clearly-shaped upper lip and chin. . . . and I have only to add, that a smile seems always lurking about the mouth when he speaks. . . ." Lee and Jackson, the Englishman found, were revered by their troopers; Lee was "regarded in the light of an infallible Jove"; Jackson was looked upon "as a Napoleon, who is idolised with that intense fervour which, consisting of mingled personal attachment and devoted loyalty, causes them to meet death for his sake, and bless him when dying."[2]

Not content to bask in past triumphs, Lee ordered Jeb Stuart on the 8th with eighteen hundred cavalry and four pieces of artillery to search out McClellan and the federal army. The mounted troop crossed the Potomac at McCoy's Ford the next morning, "moved north through Maryland and Pennsylvania, and camped at Chambersburg," a federal depot without a garrison. Then, continues a 1906 study, "he there took prisoners and paroled all the sick and wounded in the hospitals, seized 500 remounts, cut the telegraph wires, obstructed the railroad communication with Washington, destroyed all the arms, ammunition, and clothing stored in the town, and a train of loaded cars on the railroad." When Stuart reached Lee's camp on the 14th, he had covered 126 miles, and he had again ridden around McClellan. He had not only thrown Washington and the northern generals into an unbelievable panic, he had done it without losing a single man.[3]

While Stuart was rounding up several hundred Pennsylvania horses for the Army of Northern Virginia and pinpointing McClellan's whereabouts, word arrived from Richmond that Stonewall Jackson had been promoted lieutenant general. Six additional officers were raised to the same rank by an October 11 act of Congress—James Longstreet, Leonidas K. Polk, Theophilus H. Holmes, William J. Hardee, E. Kirby Smith, and John C. Pemberton. With the new appointments, Lee immediately reorganized his army into two corps—the First under Longstreet and the Second under Old Jack. Lee used the new scheme throughout the Fredericksburg campaign, with Longstreet's division commanders being major generals Lafayette McLaws, Richard H. Anderson, and John B. Hood, and Brigadier General Robert Ransom. Jackson's Second Corps included major generals D. H. Hill and A. P. Hill, and Brigadier General William B. Taliaferro, who commanded Jackson's own division. Only the Reserve Artillery under Pendleton remained beyond the control of Longstreet and Jackson; interestingly, despite their differences, A. P. Hill remained a part of Jackson's command.[4]

Before Lee again divided his army on October 28 and moved to Culpeper as a counter to McClellan's belated offensive, he found time to mingle with several local families. Although he steadfastly refused to bivouac in Virginia plantation houses, he was not adverse to an occasional visit. Nevertheless, he was sometimes obliged to take a backseat to the ever-popular Jackson as the army rested in the valley; "while dining at a hospitable house on the Opequon not far from Leetown" with Old Jack, Longstreet, and Stuart, "the lady of the mansion said that it was like the famous breakfast at the Castle of Tillietudlem, and that General Lee's chair should be marked and remembered." But, John Esten Cooke proceeds, "it was said that General Jackson was regaled with the choicest portions of the banquet, and that for him she arrayed herself in her best silk and assumed her most winning smiles." Lee's letter of October 26 to his wife—written two days before his departure from Jackson—indicates he was grieving mightily over the recent death of his daughter

Annie; Colonel Wolseley is quick to note that his hands had not mended after the fall at the Second Manassas.[5]

Jackson stayed in the valley first at Bunker Hill and then Winchester for another month before orders arrived from Lee to cross the Blue Ridge. His presence became a nagging thorn in McClellan's side because he was not only on his own but also because he was a constant threat to Washington itself. A letter from Bunker Hill on October 13 indicates he had attended church services conducted by Dr. Joseph C. Stiles; Jackson thought highly of the Richmond-based minister, who "labored in a work of grace" while the Second Corps awaited its next move. A wave of revivalistic fervor in fact swept through both of Lee's corps in the weeks following Antietam. But Jackson had the enemy on his mind as well as the salvation of his troops. Although disappointed when unable to accompany Stuart on the Chambersburg raid, Jackson soon wreaked his own destruction on the enemy. "Remaining with his command for some time in the neighborhood of the Potomac, he inflicted great damage upon the Baltimore and Ohio railroad, tearing up the track and burning bridges," writes an early biographer. "That portion of the road extending from Sir John's run in Morgan County to a point within a few miles of Harpers Ferry, a distance of forty miles was entirely destroyed." At Bunker Hill, Jackson, like Lee, lived in a tent, and told his wife that he suffered from "the cold, damp weather."[6]

By the 20th, a week or so before Lee and Longstreet left for Culpeper, Jackson's camp life improved. "Last night was very cold, but my good friend Dr. Hunter McGuire secured a camp-stove for me, and in consequence, to-day, I am comparatively quite comfortable," he informed his wife. "Don't send me any more socks, as the ladies have given me more than I could probably wear out in two years. God, through kind friends, is showering blessings upon me. . . . Let the soldiers have all of your blankets." Although Private John Casler says nothing of interest "transpired" while the Second Corps remained at Bunker Hill, other troopers under Old Jack suffered in the cold weather. The Louisiana Tigers—part of Ewell's Division—were so demoralized that "between September 1 and November 23, 1862, nine men deserted from Company H of the 15th Louisiana; and Colonel [Edmund] Pendleton claimed that nearly half of Francis T. Nicholls' brigade was absent without leave in Richmond that December." Yet, Jackson closed the letter of October 20: "I am in a Sibley tent, which is a beautiful shape, and I am sure you would enjoy being in it for a while."[7]

When Jackson penned a December 1862 note of appreciation to Major Robert L. Dabney, who had resigned as his chief of staff, he acknowledged that all was not well: "Many of our soldiers are barefoot. It is gratifying to see that many are enlisted in behalf of our suffering soldiers." And, he added, "it appears to me that if we go into winter quarters unusual efforts should be made for the spiritual improvement of the army." Besides his duties as aide-de-camp, Dabney, who officiated at the funerals of both Lee and Jackson, also endeared himself to Jackson by holding regular services for the troops. But the Presbyterian cleric was too old and ill equipped for the rigors of camp life; and though Jackson thought highly of his services, Dr. McGuire felt he had been out of place from the beginning: "The Doctor wore the black Prince Albert coat to which he had been accustomed, a beaver hat, and the usual dress of a Presbyterian clergyman, and he also carried an umbrella of a dull brown or bluish color." Dabney's peculiar dress—until fellow officers gave him an "ill-fitting" major's uniform—evoked loud guffaws when he first appeared at headquarters. Upon Dabney's resignation to resume teaching at the Union Theological Seminary in Richmond, Jackson named young Sandie Pendleton as his replacement.[8]

Jackson, anxious for good relations with the surrounding neighborhood, enforced strict rules to prevent the destruction and burning of rail fences by the army. The prohibition resulted in D. H. Hill sending an unredeemed "burner" to Jackson's tent after he found the man incorrigible. When asked why he persisted, as John Esten Cooke tells the story: " 'Well, general,' returned the reprobate, 'you see I've been enlisted eight months now in General Hill's division, and in all that time I never could get a good look at you, so I thought I would steal fence rails; I knew they would take me up and then send me to you, so I would see you.' " Jackson listened, and then ordered the man to sit all afternoon on the head of a barrel in front of his open command tent "so he can look at me as much as he likes."[9]

When Old Jack moved into more comfortable quarters at Winchester, where he remained until November 22, he called at the home of Dr. McGuire's father on several occasions. One visit in particular brought a demand that he sit for a local photographer. "But when the photograph was about to be taken, the photographer pointed out that one of Jackson's buttons was missing. Jackson produced the button from his pocket, asked for a needle and thread, and said that to save time he would sew it on himself. He did not do it very skillfully; and the button, the third from the top on his left breast was out of line." Yet the famous picture of the dignified warrior is probably his best likeness.

Although he remained only a short time in Winchester, Jackson told his wife: "Our headquarters are about one hundred yards from Mr.

Graham's, in a large white house back of his, and in full view of our last winter's, where my *esposa* used to come and talk to me. Wouldn't it be nice for you to be here again? But I don't know how long you could remain. . . ." Always at ease with Presbyterian ministers, Jackson apparently enjoyed the hospitality of the Reverend James Graham and his family amid the gathering battle; also adding to his lightness of spirit was the expectation that he would soon be a new father.[10]

The conviviality of Winchester was brushed aside when a November 20 dispatch from Lee ordered him out of the valley. Although he was on the march two days later, events in Washington and within the federal army had been underway for some time that demanded his presence elsewhere. McClellan, like Lee, was not anxious to renew the fight in the weeks following Antietam; when he did cross the Potomac at Berlin on October 26, he did so at the persistent prodding of Abraham Lincoln. McClellan was still McClellan! He took nine days to cross the river, and, writes his biographer: "He told Washington nothing of his plans, although it was quickly apparent that he was paying no heed to the president's injunction that he march swiftly along the chord of a circle to get between General Lee and his capital. Instead he advanced cautiously, taking eleven days to cover the first thirty-five miles."

As McClellan lay concentrated about Warrenton, Lee was already in position with Longstreet at Culpeper to block his further advances upon Richmond. Although McClellan reported 120,000 men upon reentering Virginia to Lee's 78,000, the fast-moving Confederate had outmarched him and had once again divided his army by leaving Jackson detached in the Shenandoah Valley. Lincoln, unable to abide McClellan's "slows," told Halleck, still his chief of staff, to replace him with Major General Ambrose Everett Burnside. After the transfer of command at Warrenton on November 7, McClellan bade his troops farewell and left the army for a political career that included the 1864 Democratic nomination to oppose Lincoln and later he was elected governor of New Jersey. "The adored commander," was missed by his men, writes Thomas F. Galwey of the Eighth Ohio Infantry. "A very mutinous feeling was apparent everywhere. . . . The soldiers who followed him for so long a time were at least as well qualified to criticize his movements as the pettifoggers who had control, in a large degree, of the legislature." For all his faults, McClellan was still the toast of the Yankee army; when Lee heard the news, he shared the opinions of Galwey and his fellow bluecoats. On more than one occasion, Lee spoke out in defense of his old opponent. When asked in later years which "was the ablest of the Union generals

. . . he answered bringing his hands down to the table with emphatic energy, 'McClellan, by all odds!' "[11]

By all accounts, Burnside was not anxious for the job thrust upon him; an arms manufacturer in Rhode Island before the war as well as governor and United States senator before his death in 1881, Burnside caused General Oliver O. Howard, who observed him closely during the Fredericksburg campaign, to note: "When he came to Warrenton to command the Army of the Potomac, then over 100,000 strong, his whole character appeared to undergo a change. A large, brave prepossessing man, popular with his associates, he was accustomed to defer greatly to the judgment of his chosen friends. . . . Indeed, he was urged to shoulder the burden, and at last did so." From the beginning, however, Burnside was under no misapprehension. Although he did not want the job, he would have to do what McClellan had not—act!

Burnside's first order of command was a complete restructuring of the army. The result was three grand divisions under his direct authority, each consisting of two army corps and a brigade of cavalry; Major General Edwin V. Sumner was given the Right Grand Division, composed of the Second and Ninth Army corps; the Center Grand Division went to Major General Joseph "Fighting Joe" Hooker, with the Third and Fifth corps; Major General William B. Franklin's Left Grand Division had the First and Sixth Army corps. The cavalry and artillery were parceled out among the Grand Divisions. Unlike Lee, Burnside found himself with an unworkable military organization when the time for battle arrived; "it proved unwieldy except when the army operated in columns along separate routes," observes one authority. "One more headquarters had been placed between the commanding general and the divisions which were his basic maneuver elements. The size of this new unit also proved too large to be used as a reserve force, and in the coming battle one of the grand divisions was, in effect, never used as a unit but was broken up to provide reinforcements for the other two grand divisions. . . ."[12]

Burnside also did what any new commander is supposed to do—he altered McClellan's plan of moving on Richmond via Culpeper, Gordonsville, and the Orange and Alexandria Railroad; instead, he proposed to send units toward the gaps in the Blue Ridge as feints, while his main army marched "straightaway to Falmouth, seized the heights beyond, and held them preparatory to future movements." The operation depended upon the infamous pontoon bridges to cross the river in front of Fredericksburg; here the scheme went sour from the beginning.

Burnside placed too much confidence in Henry W. Halleck to produce the pontoons and also to repair the railroad from Aquia Creek to supply his force. Halleck apparently left a strategy session believing that Burnside intended to cross above Fredericksburg where the river was fordable, while the general commanding meant to span the Rappahannock at Fredericksburg proper. Whatever the reason, Burnside's bridges were not on hand when the campaign started to unfold.[13]

The three grand divisions were set in motion for the Rappahannock on November 15, eight days after McClellan's disposal. Sumner and the Right Grand Division reached Falmouth two days later, and though the old warrior wanted to charge the river immediately, Burnside said, "No! Wait until I arrive." A Confederate artillery detachment blasted away at the first units, which forced them to fall back momentarily. "One of Sumner's officers saw a steer start from the south side and wade slowly to the north bank of the Rappahannock," writes O. O. Howard. "The commander of the leading brigade, whose attention was called to the fact, went to the animal and measured the height the water had reached on his side; it did not reach three feet." Although informed of developments, Burnside chose not to act, but slowly, inexorably, concentrated his army on the Stafford Heights overlooking Fredericksburg. Abraham Lincoln even journeyed by ship to Aquia Creek for "a long conference," yet Burnside remained fixed in his plan to reach Richmond by the Fredericksburg crossing. Four days after the meeting, Lincoln sent his annual message to Congress, which, surprisingly, said nothing about the developing campaign. But it did summarize what was on the president's mind as Burnside made ready to renew the fight: "One section of the country believes slavery is *right,* and ought to be extended, while the other believes it is *wrong,* and ought not to be extended. It is the only substantial dispute."[14]

At the very moment, Lincoln, Burnside, and the Army of the Potomac again pushed the abolitionist crusade into the southland, Robert E. Lee and Thomas Jonathan Jackson prepared to dispute the Union hordes poised at Richmond, although the initial diversionary thrusts toward his base at Culpeper momentarily confused Lee. "I am operating to baffle the advance of the enemy and retain him among the mountains until I can get him separated so that I can strike him. His force will thus be diminished and disheartened. His sick and stragglers must be going back. His advance cavalry is along the line of the Rappahannock River. . . ." But Burnside's real stratagem reached Culpeper soon enough, and by November 18–19 lead units of Longstreet's First Corps accompanied by Lee himself began marching into Fredericksburg from the west. The new federal commander had waited too long![15]

"Burnside is concentrating his whole army opposite Fredericksburg," Lee informed Jefferson Davis on the 20th; and it was soon obvious that he needed Jackson. No fewer than twenty communiqués passed between the two from November 18 through December 3, although the *Official Records* do not contain Jackson's messages to Lee, which were apparently lost. "It is certainly important to deceive the enemy as long as possible as to position and intentions, provided it is rendered that a junction can be made before a battle, and this latter point we must always keep in view, as necessary to enable us to resist the large force now on the Rappahannock," Lee informed Jackson on November 19. Four days later, as Burnside brought up additional men, he added: "I do not see at this distance, what military effect can be produced by the continuance of your corps in the valley."

Jackson already knew that a juncture was in the offing, and by November 25 he was heading down the Valley Pike toward Strasburg; that was hours after Lee had told the president he thought "from the tone of the Northern papers, it is intended that General Burnside shall advance from Fredericksburg to Richmond. . . ." Lee also told Davis: "I have waited to the last moment to draw Jackson's corps to me, as I have seen that his presence on their flank has embarrassed their plans and defeated their first purpose of advancing upon Gordonsville and Charlottesville." An additional message to Jackson implored him to hurry toward Fredericksburg by the best possible route.[16]

Mrs. Jackson says that Old Jack was eight days on the march to join Lee; although he wanted him to cross the Blue Ridge at Chester Gap and to approach Fredericksburg from the north, Jackson was already committed to a path that took him further south. He traveled down the Great Valley of Virginia for the last time to New Market, according to Kyd Douglas, "then turning to the east over the Massanutten and the Shenandoah Luray Valley, then into the Blue Ridge and over it at Fisher's Gap to a different county of Virginia—to Madison Court House and Orange Court House." As Jackson neared the tidewater, Lee thought it best he go into camp "on Massaponax Creek at a convenient distance from the railroad." Lee was uncertain, by his own admission, where Burnside might attempt to span the river and he wanted the Second Corps in position to march in any direction.[17]

Jackson did not reach his new bivouac at the plantation home of Thomas C. Chandler until December 1; he digressed slightly from his eastward march to confer with Lee at the latter's headquarters on the Mine Run Road not far from Fredericksburg. Then, as his divisions trudged through a snowstorm by several roads, Jackson scratched a December 4 letter to his wife: "At present I am fifty miles from Richmond, and one mile from Guiney's Station, on the railroad from Richmond to Fredericksburg. Should I remain here, I do hope you and baby can come to see me before spring, as you can come on the railroad." But Jackson only stayed at the Chandlers until December 12, when he took the Telegraph Road toward Lee at Fredericksburg.[18]

News that he had become the father of a baby daughter reached Jackson during his march out of the valley, and his letters to Mrs. Jackson over the next weeks are those of a contented family man. Julia Laura Jackson (1862–1889), who was born November 23, and named after Jackson's mother and sister, became the wife of William E. Christian in 1885; today she lies buried with her father, mother, and husband in the Jackson Cemetery at Lexington. Jackson was beside himself when a letter addressed to "My own dear Father" arrived at his Guiney Station encampment. Written by his sister-in-law, Mrs. Harriet Irwin, and signed, "Your dear little wee Daughter," it playfully described the child's arrival: ". . . I am a very tiny little thing. I weigh only eight and one half pounds, and aunt Harriet says I am the express image of my darling papa, and so does our dear friend, Mrs. Osborn, and thus my mother. My aunts both say that I am a little beauty. My hair is dark and long, my eyes are blue, my nose straight just like Papa's, and my complexion not all red like most young ladies of my age, but a beautiful blending of the lily and the rose." Following a quick note of gratitude to Mrs. Irwin, Jackson wrote a tender, reassuring letter to his wife lest she be disappointed the child had not been a boy: "Thank sister H——— very kindly, and give the baby daughter a shower of kisses from her father, and tell her that he loves her better than all the baby-boys in the world, and more than all the other babies in the world."[19]

Family matters also pressed upon Lee as tension mounted along the Rappahannock. One day after the birth of Jackson's child, Lee poured out his grief for his own daughter. "The death of my dear Annie was indeed to me a bitter pang," he wrote on November 24. "But the Lord gave and the Lord has taken away; blessed be the name of the Lord. In the hours of night, when there is nothing to lighten the full weight of my grief, I feel as if I should be overwhelmed. I had always thought, if God should spare me a few days of peace after this cruel war was ended, that I should have her with me. But year after year my hopes go out, and I must be resigned." Besides the welfare of his own family, Lee fretted about others caught up in the campaign. "People," he told his daughter Mary, "have been abandoning their homes day and night, during all of this inclement weather, cheerfully and uncomplainingly, with only such assistance as wagons and ambulances could afford—women, girls, and children, trudging through the mud and bivouacking in the open field. . . ."[20]

The forced evacuation, which had been ordered by Sumner, was only part of Burnside's plan. A December 6 dispatch to Jefferson Davis warned that his entire force was concentrated "between the Potomac and Rappahannock," but, Lee added, he "could discover no intentions of his advancing, or of transferring his troops to other positions. Scouts on both flanks north of the Rappahannock report no movements, nor have those stationed on the Potomac discovered the collection of transports or the passage of troops down that river." Two days later, Lee learned through another of his scouts that "reinforcements are still coming to General Burnside's army." And, he warned Davis, "two regiments left Alexandria while he was there, and four were waiting for transportation to Aquia Creek. Three regiments of cavalry were also marching by land and a large pontoon train was moving through Dumfries while he was in that vicinity." Thus, by December 9–10, Lee surely knew that Burnside would bridge the Rappahannock at some point; when he did so during the early hours of December 11, another message was hurried to General Pendleton: "Ascertain the best position for the two big guns and bring them to bear."[21]

Although Lee had placed Longstreet's corps along Marye's Heights and adjacent crests overlooking Fredericksburg and the river from the west, Jackson remained at Guiney Station when the battle opened. Throughout the preliminary buildup, Lee and Jackson, who were in constant touch, were uncertain where the federal pontoons would be used. For that reason, D. H. Hill was kept at Port Royal to the east and twenty miles below Fredericksburg. "Between him and Longstreet was the division of Early; and the remainder of Jackson's Corps was held in reserve about Guiney Station, ready to support either point," notes Dabney. "The cavalry division of Stuart guarded the course of the Rappahannock for many miles above and below. . . . The defensive force may be stated with substantial, although not with exact correctness, at sixty-five thousand men of all arms." Jackson, meanwhile, who commanded about fifteen thousand men, made his own preparations for battle by writing to his wife and sister-in-law in North Carolina and by trying out a new coat, a gift from Jeb Stuart and Major Von Borcke. Jed Hotchkiss, his topographer, also procured a replacement for "the famous old grey cap," which Jackson had worn since December 1861 "through all of the marches, battles, and camps of that eventful intervening period." Once outfitted for the coming campaign, Jackson gave the relic to Hotchkiss when the latter arrived at Guiney Station with the new cap.[22]

Unbeknownst to Lee, Burnside had difficulty getting his pontoons into position for the assault on Fredericksburg. A comedy of errors ensued when they were first sent to Harpers Ferry, then had to be rerouted to the Rappahannock, some overland, some by steamer. Heavy mud along the winter roads of northern Virginia turned the enterprise into a nightmare for Burnside's engineers and teamsters. Although "the bridging equipment" was in place by November 26, the federal commander waited another two weeks to cross the river because of supply problems. After General Hunt, his artillery chief, amassed nearly 150 pieces to sweep Fredericksburg and the plain behind it, orders to proceed were issued on December 10: "Two bridges to be thrown across at the upper end of Fredericksburg, one at the lower end, and two a mile below, making the distance between the extreme bridges nearly two miles. Each bridge to be covered by artillery and a regiment of infantry. Heads of bridge trains to arrive at bank of river at 3 A.M., material to be unloaded and boats in the water by daylight, and bridges to be finished in two or three hours if not interrupted by the enemy."[23]

General William Barksdale, who held the water's edge, reported through the night of December 10–11 that sounds from the other side indicated bridging operations were underway; Lafayette McLaws, who was Barksdale's superior officer, allowed the work to proceed uncontested because of heavy mists along the Rappahannock, later described by Edward P. Alexander: "This peculiar fog which limited vision to less than 100 yards, strongly resembled the haze of Indian summer, but was very dense, returned nightly during the struggle, and generally prevailed until nearly noon, and it was of material advantage to the Federals in veiling their movements and masses of troops from the Confederate artillery." The span in front of Fredericksburg was about thirty feet across before the vapors lifted enough to allow Barksdale's Mississippians to pour a killing fire into the "pontooniers." A signal from two Confederate pieces also aroused Lee's army to action, but, Alexander continues: "In no battle during the war was the Confederate artillery ammunition more defective than in that of Fredericksburg. There were three or four Whitworth Rifles which fired wonderfully far, and with great accuracy, but they were only supplied with solid shot, and but scantily with these. The two thirty-pound Parrotts did wonderful practice until they were burst one at the thirty-ninth round and the other at the fifty-fourth. . . ." Other guns were so unreliable that Lee would not permit them to be fired over the heads of infantry.

A combined fire from Barksdale's riflemen and Pendleton's artillery drove back Sumner's first attempt to bridge the river. Finally, in desperation, Burnside ordered Hunt's guns to sweep the city and particularly the buildings sheltering several hundred Confederate sharpshooters; "it is impossible to fitly describe the effects of this iron hail hurled against the small band of defenders and into the devoted city," observes McLaws. "The roar of the cannon, the bursting shells, the falling walls and chimneys, and the flying bricks, and other material dislodged from the houses by the iron balls and shells, added to the fire of the infantry from both sides and the smoke from the guns and from the burning houses, made a scene of indescribable confusion, enough to appall the stoutest hearts." Although repeated attempts were made to proceed with the pontoons, Barksdale's men drove them back in spite of the heavy shelling; at the suggestion of General Hunt, federal soldiers were loaded into individual pontoons, and using them as boats, paddled across as quickly as possible. Protected by the sharp riverbanks and Hunt's cannon, the Mississippians were soon driven from their pits and what was left of Fredericksburg.[24]

Meanwhile, downriver, where no brick buildings screened the marksmen, Franklin's Left Grand Division made a nearly unopposed crossing. They even came over with a band playing and flags unfurled before the lead regiments. Union reinforcements stormed across the bridges throughout December 12, as thousands of bluecoated soldiers took up positions beyond the reach of Longstreet's guns located on the high ground behind the city. By nightfall, Burnside had the bulk of his army beyond the Rappahannock. Sumner was on the right in Fredericksburg proper; Franklin who had held the Union left was clustered around Hamilton's Crossing and Deep Run with his back to the river, while Fighting Joe Hooker was poised to cross the upper bridges at the first ring of battle. When darkness settled over the valley of the Rappahannock on the twelfth, Lee sent an ominous message to Richmond: "The enemy passing over all of last night and to-day by the different bridges. They are massed under protection of their guns on the north bank of the river, beyond the reach of which they have not ventured. . . ."[25]

Stonewall Jackson heard the firing and knew from experience that Lee needed the Second Corps. Burnside's occupation of Fredericksburg mandated his quick march from Guiney Station by the Telegraph Road, and he dispatched orders for Jubal A. Early, who commanded Ewell's division, and D. H. Hill to close on Hamilton's Crossing from their encampments at Buckner's Neck and Port Royal. Following a 4 A.M. breakfast, Old Jack proceeded directly "to the brow of a hill towards Fredericksburg where our heavy guns were placed," but he departed shortly to oversee his own divisions. Throughout the twelfth, Jed Hotchkiss continues, "the day was spent getting the troops into position. . . . There was some skirmishing on our left. Gen. Jackson rode all along the lines, as did Gens. Lee and Stuart. Late in the afternoon the General rode down to the river, from Hamilton's Crossing, and examined the country to and near the river bank; we then rode back to our camp, the General whistling as we went along." Although D. H. Hill, who had an eighteen-mile trek, did not arrive until the next day, Jackson had his corps in line on Lee's right by nightfall on the twelfth. Beyond Hood's division, which formed Longstreet's extreme right, Jackson placed Taliaferro and Early on the crest above Hamilton's Crossing with A. P. Hill in their front along the Richmond, Fredericksburg, and Potomac Railroad. Jeb Stuart, with Pelham's horse artillery, formed the far right flank extending down to the Rappahannock.[26]

Part of Lee's preparation was the construction of a crude pathway known as the Military Road, to connect Prospect Hill occupied by Jackson with Longstreet's right; placed above the crest overlooking Hamilton's Crossing, it was designed to insure effective communication between both wings of the army. Once Burnside learned of its existence from "a Negro line-crosser whose home was in the vicinity," he devoted his immediate strategy of December 12–13 to its capture. "I wanted to obtain possession of that new road, and that was my reason for making an attack on the extreme left," he afterward told the Committee on the Conduct of the War. "I did not intend to make the attack on the right until the position had been taken; which I supposed would stagger the enemy, cutting their line in two; and then I proposed to make a direct attack on their front, and drive them out of their works." Burnside had been obsessed with attacking Lee before Jackson could join him from the Shenandoah Valley, and now he called on Franklin to attack the Confederate left on Prospect Hill, thereby seizing the Military Road and isolating Old Jack from the rest of the army. Sumner, reinforced by part of Hooker's Grand Division from across the Rappahannock, was instructed to pummel Marye's Heights once the road had been captured. Although he hoped that its possession would "force the Confederates out of their entrenchments" when they could be captured in flank, written instructions to his commanders were not issued until 7:30 A.M., December 13, just two and a half hours before the attack started.[27]

Lee had established his headquarters "on a small hill with a good plateau, from which he had a fair view of Sumner's attack on Longstreet, as well as Franklin's on Jackson." When Jackson rode up for an early morning conference, G. Moxley Sorrel, a member of Lee's staff, continues, "we broke into astonished smiles. He was in a spick and span new overcoat, new uniform with rank marks, fine black hat, and a handsome sword. We had never seen the like before, and gave him our congratulations on his really fine appearance. He said he 'believed it was some of his friend Stuart's doings.'" R. K. Charles, who was also present, says that Old Jack "seemed a little ashamed" of the getup and that following a brief word with Lee "he went off and leaned against a pine, looking at the ground."

Longstreet was also at hand, and as the generals conferred on their foggy precipice, Charles observes, "nothing could be seen and heard, except that indescribable buzz, that so plainly tells the trained soldier that an army is going into battle." Earlier, Old Pete and Lee had inspected the lines atop Marye's Heights to make certain all was ready; they took breakfast together at the "Randolph Mansion" located at the base of the hill below Longstreet's positions before Jackson's arrival. When the fog finally cleared, Lee, Longstreet, and Jackson, accompanied by Colonel Arthur Lyon Freemantle of the British army, gazed transfixed at the "magnificient" Union army, 120,000 strong and arrayed for battle. One observer said the shimmering flags and long blue lines resembled a giant parade ground; each man knew that hard fighting lay ahead, and, as they studied Franklin's masses on their right, a light-hearted Longstreet called out: "'Jackson, what are you going to do with all of those people over there?' 'Sir,' said Stonewall, with great fire and spirit, 'we will give them the bayonet.'" Sorrel's account is silent if Lee joined in the banter as Jackson galloped off to rejoin his command.[28]

As the mist lifted in front of Prospect Hill, one of the war's heroic feats began to unfold, as Gordon Meade advanced against Jackson's center with five thousand men. Young John Pelham immediately sensed a grand opportunity to hit the Union flank as it crossed the Richmond Pike. Without a moment's hesitation, he sped from Stuart's encampment east of Hamilton's Crossing with two guns—a Blakely rifle and a twelve-pound Napoleon. Then, with the entire army watching from the high ground, he opened fire "at 500 yards right up the road into the blue masses of the enemy." Burnside's timetables were thrown into turmoil when four or five Union batteries had to be diverted from Meade's assault to silence his guns. Although "the obstreperous Blakely," as Douglas Southall Freeman puts it, was knocked out of action, Pelham fired away with the remaining Napoleon.

The twenty-four-year-old artilleryman rode into the fray "with a red and blue striped necktie around his hat given to him to wear as a talisman by Captain Phillips, an English officer with the Grenadier Guards, who had obtained furlough from his regiment stationed in Canada." The Napoleon continued to do its work "for more than half an hour" as he served the gun himself at one point while constantly shifting his position to avoid the return fire. Lee watched the selfless display of Anglo-Saxon manhood with several staff officers, and notes Pelham's biographer, he cried out: " 'It is glorious to see such courage in one so young.' And in his official report of the battle General Lee added an immortal luster to the deed of valor he had witnessed by making reference to the part played by the 'gallant Pelham.' " Since Lee rarely mentioned lesser officers and enlisted men in his dispatches, his admiration is all the more remarkable. Jackson likewise singled him out in his own battle summary: ". . . Pelham, with part of Stuart's Horse Artillery, was soon engaged with the artillery of the enemy, and a brisk and animated contest was kept up for about an hour."[29]

Despite calls from Stuart to abandon his lonely platform, Pelham kept at it with a simple: "Tell the General, I can hold my ground." His ammunition exhausted, he at last withdrew to safer surroundings and was placed in charge of a battalion of artillery that included several pieces of the Rockbridge Artillery under William Poague. "He had delayed Meade's advance forty-five minutes," continues his biographer. "This in itself was of no particular value, but what grew out of it was; for Franklin was so afraid of an attack upon his left flank, that Doubleday's division of five thousand men, intended as a support for Meade, was diverted to the left as a precaution, and was not engaged the whole day. If it could have supported Meade and Gibbon in the grand assault at one o'clock, Jackson's lines might have been broken." In the later fighting, however, Pelham's guns were ineffective because of the terrain, but his escapade had not only slowed Franklin's momentum it had also captured the admiration of both armies.[30]

"The enemy next directed his artillery on the heights held by Lieutenant Colonel Walker, and upon the wood generally occupied by our troops evidently with a view of causing us to disclose whatever troops or artillery were there," Jackson writes about the battle following Pelham's withdrawal.

When he found no response he advanced about 11 o'clock by the flank parallel to the Port Royal Road nearly to the road from thence to Hamilton's Crossing, now unimpeded in his march. Facing to the front, he advanced in line of battle across the plain, straight upon the position occupied by Walker. His batteries reserved their fire until the enemy's lines came within 800 yards, when the fourteen guns opened, pouring such a storm of shot and shell into his ranks as to cause him first to halt, then to waver, and at last seek refuge by flight.

But Franklin directed a renewed cannonade preparatory to a third assault; this time, the Union artillery carried the moment with a thirty-minute barrage that led "the rebel gunners to call their position Dead Horse Hill."[31]

Franklin's main thrust around one o'clock was directed at the exposed brigade of James H. Lane of A. P. Hill's division; Jackson in fact had accurately predicted the storm might break here, although he apparently made no effort to strengthen the position. A. P. Hill had spread out along Prospect Hill from Hamilton's Crossing to a point near Hood's brigade of Longstreet's corps; from left to right, it was Pender, Thomas, Lane, Gregg, Archer, and Brockenbrough posted along Lee's Military Road. Jubal A. Early and Taliaferro were above the road, while D. H. Hill occupied the crest. But, writes Dabney, A. P. Hill's position "did not form a continuous line; for the brigade of Lane in the centre was advanced two hundred yards to the front, to occupy a tongue of woodland which here projected itself far into the plain. This patch of forest was low and marshy; and behind it the ridge sunk almost to the same level; so that no position for artillery could be obtained upon Jackson's centre. Behind the interval thus left between the brigades of Archer and Lane, was placed that of Gregg." That gap surrounding a rivulet flowing into the Rappahannock determined the course of battle along Jackson's front for the next two hours.[32]

"A splendid line of breastworks had been made around Marye's Hill and extended along the line of Generals Longstreet and D. H. Hill," writes J. H. Worsham, Twenty-first Virginia Infantry, which left A. P. Hill's command largely unprotected. His men had no choice but to stand and fight once Franklin charged into the gap, although Lane and Archer tried to stem the onslaught, which swept past them, smashing into the brigade of Maxey Gregg. The South Carolinian was totally surprised, notes Edward P. Alexander, "by this force advancing through the dense forest and General Gregg himself was killed while beating down his men's muskets to stop the firing upon what he mistook for a Confederate brigade." Gregg, who was struck in the spine, did not die until later in the evening as a gigantic outburst of the northern lights was dancing across the horizon. A lawyer who dabbled in astronomical observation,

Gregg had joined the Confederacy at the first outbreak of fighting; following action in the Peninsula campaign, he served under Jackson at Cedar Mountain, Second Manassas, and the Antietam, where he had a horse shot from under him. As Gregg lay dying, Jackson, who had fallen asleep at the close of battle, arrived at his tent to comfort his fallen comrade.[33]

But the question remains: Why had that dreadful gap been allowed to persist after Lee and Jackson both inspected the ground well before the opening gun? In his battle report, Jackson says merely: "The enemy continued to press forward, and before General A. P. Hill closed the interval which he had left between Archer and Lane it was penetrated, and the enemy, pressing forward in overwhelming numbers through that interval turned Lane's right and Archer's left." Lee does not mention a gap or interval in his summary of December 14 sent to the secretary of war, but his formal report filed in April 1863 says that "an interval" existed in Hill's line, but, unlike Jackson, he ascribes no blame for its existence. Hill "downgraded" the incident when he posted his own report, but his major biographer calls him "delinquent." In spite of his festering grudge against Jackson and the recent death of a beloved daughter, Hill's lapse cannot be excused. It nearly cost Lee a great victory.[34]

While Burnside remained at the Phillips House north of the Rappahannock and depended upon T.S.C. Lowe's balloons for information from the front, "Old Jube" Early crashed down the hill to save Hill's command. Lee's adjutant general, Walter H. Taylor, as well as Jackson himself in the *Official Records,* maintains that Early, reinforced by Taliaferro, was ordered into the fray once Old Jack recognized the danger. Ere Jackson's command, at least two officers, including Ham Chamberlayne, rode into Early's headquarters asking for help at "an awful gap" in Hill's lines. And when Early published his 1912 memoir, it was clear that he acted on his own initiative: "It was so serious an emergency that I determined to act upon it at once notwithstanding the previous directions from General Jackson to hold my division in readiness for another purpose and I accordingly ordered Atkinson to advance with his brigade." Followed by Taliaferro, Early "plugged the gap," and his troops counterattacked with such enthusiasm that Meade— reinforced by Gibbon—was driven back to the railroad embankment and across the Rappahannock River plain. Early's headlong rush carried his men to the point of being nearly overwhelmed before they were recalled to safety.[35]

Jackson pushed to the front ordering up additional artillery to support Early's assault. "Those who saw him at that hour, will never forget the expression of intense but suppressed excitement which his face displayed," observes John Esten Cooke. "The genius of battle seemed to have gained possession of the great leader, ordinarily so calm, and his countenance glowed as from the glare of a great conflagration." Logistical realities, however, forced him to abandon the enterprise, but not before he stopped Burnside's attack on Lee's right. With something under fifteen thousand men, Jackson had checked Franklin's fifty-five thousand, part of them from Hooker's Center Grand Division, with considerable slaughter to the enemy. Old Jack's maneuvering was so successful that Lee "regarded the affair as nothing more than a heavy demonstration to feel his position, not a definite trial of strength with the whole Confederate army." When Burnside sent an appeal to renew the fight to relieve the pressure on Sumner and Hooker, who were later cut to pieces at the famed Sunken Road, General William Buel Franklin conveniently chose to ignore the order; he had no inclination to tangle with Jackson a fourth time in a single day. "When night fell there were no longer forty thousand men in the Left Grand Division, and we had gained no important advance," acknowledges William F. Smith, who generaled the Sixth Army corps under Franklin.[36]

Although Burnside later complained to the Committee on the Conduct of the War that Franklin's failure to carry the Confederate right had cost the battle, the great encounter was won by Lee's superior defensive position and his strategy of "I am the spider; won't you come into my trap?" In fairness, Burnside argued also that the late arrival of his pontoons had given Lee time to concentrate his army. Nowhere was Lee's plan more apparent than his placement of men and artillery on the Confederate left, which stretched from Marye's Heights directly behind the city of Fredericksburg across the smaller Lee's Hill to connect with Jackson and the Military Road. In front of Marye's Hill, with the Marye family mansion at its crest, ran the famed Telegraph Road, or Sunken Road, which Longstreet called the "salient point." "A stone wall, partly enclosing a field fronting the mansion, ran along the side of the road," says C. C. Cummins, a participant in the battle. "In exacavating the road at the foot of the hill the dirt was thrown up over this wall and thus formed what goes down in history as the Sunken Road."

Longstreet's First Corps, which made up the left, was composed of Richard H. Anderson's division on the extreme left, Lafayette McLaws and Robert Ransom in front of the mansion, with John Bell Hood and George Pickett on the right. "The Eighteenth and Twenty-fourth Georgia Regiments, Cobb's Legion, and the Twenty-fourth North Carolina regiment were in the Sunken Road," reads Longstreet's own account.

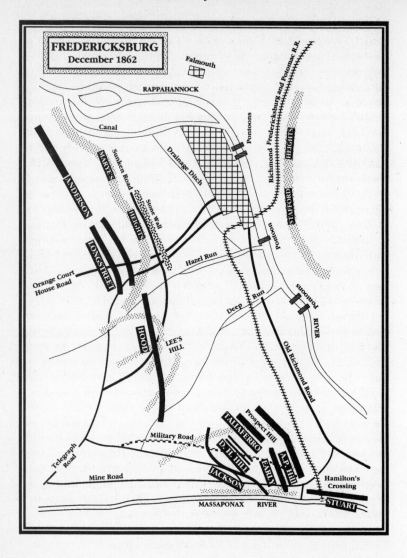

FREDERICKSBURG
December 1862

Falmouth

RAPPAHANNOCK

Canal

Richmond Fredericksburg and Potomac R.R.

Pontoons

Drainage Ditch

STAFFORD HEIGHTS

MARYE'S

Sunken Road

ANDERSON

Stone Wall

HEIGHTS

Pontoon

LONGSTREET

Orange Court
House Road

Hazel Run

Deep Run

Pontoons

RIVER

HOOD

LEE'S
HILL

Old Richmond Road

Prospect Hill

TALIAFERRO

Military Road

D. H. HILL

A.P. Hill

Telegraph
Road

JACKSON

EARLY

Hamilton's
Crossing

Mine Road

STUART

MASSAPONAX   RIVER

Other units were sent to reinforce those at the wall, while the Washington Artillery from New Orleans with more than fifteen guns on Lee's Hill was held in waiting to sweep the field. "Not a rabbit could cross that plain and live," snorted General—then Colonel—Edward P. Alexander, as Lee and Longstreet awaited Burnside's advance.[37]

Shortly before 11:00 A.M., when Sumner ordered French's division forward, Lee had taken the precaution of drawing Pickett's division and part of Hood's to Marye's Hill. When all was ready, no army of equivalent strength on earth could have carried Lee's left. Sumner sent other waves forward under Hancock, Howard, Couch, and Sturgis after French's initial blow. A drainage ditch sliced diagonally across the plain, which complicated the federal advance and made it easier for the infantrymen of Cobb, now reinforced by Kershaw's South Carolinians, to find their mark; the artillery atop Marye's Heights and Lee's Hill made the area between Fredericksburg and the Sunken Road into a slaughter pen. "The enemy riddled every moving thing in sight: horses tied to the wheels of a broken gun-carriage behind us; pigs that incautiously came grunting across the road; even chickens were brought down with an accuracy of aim that told of a fatally short range, and of a better practice than it would have been wise for our numbers to face," writes General John W. Ames, who fought under Sumner. "They applauded their own success with a hilarity we could hardly share in, as their chicken-shooting was across our backs, leaving us no extra room for turning." Ames adds that his "most distinct memory of the war" was lying flat on his "belly" and looking over the wall to see the unconcerned marksmen laughing and joking as they fired at point-blank range into his hapless comrades.[38]

Lee watched the afternoon butchery from the headquarters he shared with Longstreet, and at one point J. William Jones has him calling out: "It is well that this is so terrible, or else we might grow fond of it." Fitzhugh Lee notes that the "battle of Fredericksburg was a grand sight Lee witnessed from Lee's Hill in the center of his lines, and Burnside through his field glasses from a more secure position, two miles in the rear of the battlefield, with the river flowing between himself and his troops." Lee's formidable position, he continues, "made the whole affair into a farce." Nevertheless, it was no bed of roses for the Confederates that cold December day. General T. R. R. Cobb was shot dead while directing his troops behind the wall, and amid the killing, General John R. Cooke, a brother-in-law to Jeb Stuart and cousin to John Esten Cooke, was "struck a glancing blow on the forehead by a minie ball" that broke the skull. Cooke, however, was more fortunate than many of his compeers; he became a successful Richmond businessman for twenty-five years after the war.[39]

Lee stayed close to Longstreet throughout the fight, according to General Long, "so that he was able to keep his hand on the reign of his 'old war-horse' and to direct him where to apply his strength." A renewed assault commenced around 3:00 P.M., when Hooker and the Center Grand Division took over from the disheartened Sumner. Although he protested loudly about the needless destruction of his command, Fighting Joe had no choice but to obey Burnside's directive and advance toward Lee's waiting guns. About the time Jackson was securing his position along Franklin's front, Hooker directed a series of new attacks under Charles Griffin, Andrew A. Humphreys, Amiel W. Whipple, and George Getty, who went last and attempted to carry the wall from the flank. None of these attempts were any more successful than those under Sumner.

The slaughter did not end until nightfall, when a great sigh of relief swept the Union ranks that men could at last arise from their "bellies" under the shield of darkness. As dawn broke on Sunday, December 14, frost-encased bodies were found strewn throughout the plain in the eerie morning fog. Stories of piled corpses and still-dying federals have become a part of the national folklore. Lee sent a flag of truce to Burnside requesting that he bury his dead, in what must have been one of the war's largest funerals. "A remnant of what was left of the Irish brigade come over with their native farming implement, the spade," reports C. C. Cummins who became a Texas judge after the war. "They dug a large trench the length of a modern [1915] dreadnaught and the width of the height of a man and were as long a time in placing the bodies side by side as it took the gunners to lay them out there."

Cummins closes with a tale about a "New Foundland dog who kept a faithful vigil by the side of his dead master, an officer" for two days as the burying operations continued. "With mournful mien and downcast countenance he followed the corpse to the trench, and when he saw the hostile dirt cover his master in a hostile land, he exhibited a human sympathy in his mourning, more so than any there in human shape." The federal army had paid a terrible price at Fredericksburg, and when Lee filed his formal report four months later, he said Burnside made six distinct assaults on the wall, although others have set the figure higher. "Notwithstanding the havoc caused by our batteries, the enemy pressed on to within 100 yards of the foot of the hill, but here encountered the deadly fire of our infantry." Thousands of Burnside's troops had fled in confusion toward Fredericksburg and the pontoon bridges, Lee added.[40]

"I rode into Fredericksburg by the road that ran between Marye and the stone wall, and just at that fatal point I halted to look up on the left at Marye," writes R. K. Charles, who carried Lee's burial request to Burnside.

There was hardly a twig as big as the little finger that was not scratched by a missle; in one thin telegraph pole I counted thirteen Minie balls. And then I looked to the right over the wall. The Federal dead lay there as they had fallen. . . . I stood before that 'somber, fatal, terrible stone wall' utterly amazed at the extent of the slaughter. The line of dead began about fifty yards from the wall, piled upon each other, and thence extended back for acres, and the mutilation of the bodies was the most terrible description, showing the havoc of grape and canister.

Casualty figures also confirm the Confederate triumph: Burnside had lost ten thousand killed and wounded to Lee's forty-six hundred; losses to the Army of the Potomac exceeded ten percent of Burnside's effectives.[41]

The federal march on Richmond had been stopped for the time being, although Lee had gained little more than an enhanced military reputation. The northern Goliath remained on Virginia soil! But the victory, coupled with another at Chancellorsville a few months later, may have contributed to Lee's feelings of superiority over the generals sent against him that led to the disaster at Gettysburg in July 1863. When the Pennsylvania fight unfolded without Jackson's steadying influence, Lee repeated Burnside's mistake and charged a fortified position without hope of success other than a blind trust in the gods of war. In the winter of 1862, Lee and Jackson were triumphant, yet they made preparation to receive a renewed assault during December 14–15, although Burnside did not move as expected. The Yankee army by December 16, Lee informed the secretary of war, had "disappeared from our front." To the total dismay of Lincoln, who had just telegraphed that "we have every confidence in your judgment and ultimate success," Ambrose Burnside had abandoned the fight.[42]

Lee waited on the Rappahannock until late April, and though he dispatched Jeb Stuart upon a scouting-destroy mission in late December, Jefferson Davis records: "Excepting a cavalry engagement near Kelly's Ford on March 17th nothing of interest transpired during this period of inactivity." But the raid that cost the life of John Pelham lay in the future as Lee maintained his headquarters "at a point midway between Fredericksburg and Hamilton's Crossing, selected on account of its accessibility." General Long, who stayed with Lee through a difficult winter, continues: "It consisted of four or five wall tents and three or four common tents, situated at the edge of an old pine field, and not far from a fine grove of forest trees, from which was obtained an abundant supply of excellent wood, while the branches of the old field-pine served to fortify the tents against the cold of winter and to make shelter for the horses." While he waited, Lee spent considerable time writing daily letters to Secretary of War Seddon because President Davis was away from the capital on a tour of Tennessee and Alabama.

In addition to routine matters, Lee informed Richmond on January 10 of "the absolute necessity . . . to increase our armies, if we desire to oppose effectual resistance to the vast numbers that the enemy is precipitating upon us." Although Longstreet was in the south gathering additional troops, Lee set his strength on December 31 at 70,972 effectives: First Corps, 27,608; Second Corps, 30,060; Stuart's cavalry, 8,814; and the artillery under Pendleton, 4,490. "The great successes with which our efforts have been crowned, under the blessing of God, should not betray our people into the dangerous delusion that the armies now in the field are sufficient to bring this war to a successful and speedy termination."[43]

The heart/chest disorders that plagued Lee through much of the winter apparently did not commence until early 1863, as his letter writing continued from "Camp Fredericksburg." Lee sent messages of condolence on the 18th to South Carolina governor Francis W. Pickens, lamenting the death of Maxey Gregg, and to General Howell Cobb, a one-time Georgia governor, on the loss of his brother, T.R.R. Cobb, in the recent fighting. Lee was as attuned to his political position as ever, although a December 16 letter to his wife commented on things military: "Yesterday evening I had my suspicions they might return during the night, but . . . this morning they were all safe on the north side of the Rappahannock. They went as they came—in the night. They suffered terribly as far as the battle went, but it did not go far enough to satisfy me. . . . The contest will have now to be renewed, but on what field I can not say." Lee, who had the task of freeing the Arlington slaves in accordance with his father-in-law's will, told his wife that it was impossible for him to see after their needs, but that he wanted all "placed to the best advantage"; he even agreed that they could leave Virginia if they wished. Perhaps a lingering melancholia over Annie's death induced him to pen several December–January letters to sixteen-year-old Mildred and to Agnes, six years younger, in which he complained of weariness and a desire "to be reunited with my family once again."[44]

At the urging of Jeb Stuart, who recognized that Burnside was on the run, Jackson wanted to resume the battle, but Lee said, "No!" It was time to rest. Old Jack nonetheless asked Pelham to superintend his lines during the night, in case the Union commander had a change of heart. "When Jackson inspected, in the morning, the defenses which had thus risen like magic, he turned to Stuart who accompanied him: 'Have you another Pelham? If so, I wish you would give him to me,' " relates John Esten Cooke, who says that he remembered every word. "These works saved hundreds of lives during the cannonade that soon began," although Burnside did not follow with his infantry. Jackson kept his headquarters near the front until December 16, when complaining of an earache, he moved to Moss Neck or Corbin Hall, a few miles down the Rappahannock. "One of the handsomest residences in Virginia," it was the home of Richard Corbin, scion of an old plantation family, then serving as a private with the Ninth Virginia Infantry.[45]

"What excitement we had making the General comfortable for the night," notes a family member, when Jackson arrived at the household composed of women and children. "Next morning I had several long tables set, and, having killed our winter 'porkers' (in lieu of the fatted calf), we were able to serve a pretty fair wartime repast of sausage, pork steaks, waffles, muffins, etc., for our distinguished guests. After breakfast I asked General Jackson to take one of the wings of the house for his headquarters, but he replied that he would prefer to use the 'office' in the yard; that the house 'was too luxurious for a soldier, who should sleep in a tent.' These were his words." Although Jackson declined to stay in the mansion, he did accept accommodation in an outbuilding used to conduct plantation business in more peaceful times. Its well-stocked library and pleasant surroundings made the place into a favorite retreat for Jackson. Both Old Jack and his staff were warmly received by the Corbin clan, who kept them supplied with food and amusement. Janie Corbin, five-year-old daughter of the house, records Kyd Douglas, "with her wealth of light golden hair, her large trustful eyes, 'the sweetest eyes ever seen,' and her perfect unspoiled ways" became his daily companion. While he organized and awaited the next campaign, Jackson took a fancy to the child, who was allowed to visit "his office" every afternoon.[46]

Jackson's letters home say nothing about Lee, although he told Anna the enemy had been "repulsed at all points" when he wrote on the 16th. The new daughter had apparently been sick enough to require medical attention, and Jackson was ever the concerned father. "I was made very happy at hearing through my baby daughter's last letter that she had entirely recovered, and that she 'no longer saw the doctor's gray whiskers.' I was much gratified to learn that she was beginning to notice and smile when caressed. I tell you, I would love to caress her and see her smile. . . ." Two days later, he told Anna about Mrs. Corbin's great hospitality. Moss Neck, he said, "is one of the most beautiful buildings I have seen in this country," and he told her that he had much work to get done before the army marched.[47]

"To Generals Longstreet and Jackson great praise is due for the disposition and management of the respective corps," Lee comments in his official account of Fredericksburg. "Their quick perception enabled them to discover the projected assaults upon their positions, and their ready skill to devise the best means to resist them." Although he paid his two commanders an equal tribute, he decided to celebrate Christmas with Jackson at Moss Neck following Longstreet's departure for the south. Jackson had invited Lee, Stuart, Pendleton, and several others, including Kyd Douglas, to a gay event filled with good food and fellowship. "I had the good fortune to secure a fine turkey; a bucket of oysters came down the river; a box was received by the general from some Staunton ladies, containing a variety of good things; and our dinner was quite well set forth," says James P. Smith, a member of Old Jack's staff. Lee took one look at the menu and accused his hosts of "playing like soldiers," saying they were living the good life. The high point by all accounts was the shenanigans of Jeb Stuart: "On this occasion he made himself very merry at finding Jackson in the office of old Mr. Corbin, whose walls were decorated with pictures of race-horses, fine stock, gamestock, and a famous *rat-terrier*," Smith continues. "To the great amusement of Jackson and his guests, Stuart pretended to regard these as General Jackson's *own selections*, and as indications of his *private tastes—indicating a great decline in his moral character*, which would be a grief and disappointment to the pious ladies of the old south."[48]

Kyd Douglas and Mrs. Jackson state positively that the merriment took place on December 25, although Von Borcke hints it was really a Christmas Eve gathering, as Stuart left early the next morning for his raid northward. Lee opens a yule letter to Arlington by saying he would "commence this holy day by writing" but he says nothing about the fête with Jackson and the others. "But what a cruel thing is war, to separate and destroy families, and mar the purest joys and happiness God has granted us in this world; to fill our hearts with hatred for our neighbors, and to devastate the fair face of this beautiful world!" Jackson, too, found time for a Christmas letter to Anna, in which he also ignored the banquet and explained that he could not leave camp even to visit his new daughter; he had to set an example to the thousands of "absentees by remaining at the post of duty."[49]

The Christmas gala was an apt culmination for the Confederate successes of 1862, and President Davis is correct that nothing of importance occurred in Virginia until the incident at Kelly's Ford in March, although Braxton Bragg fought the Yankees to a standstill through the first days of January in the Stones River campaign around Murfreesboro, Tennessee. And Burnside attempted one last assault, the famed Mud March, which took place during January 20–23, when he fixed on the idea to attack Lee by marching up the Rappahannock and hitting his rear flank by the upper fords; it was essentially the plan reemployed by Joe Hooker during April–May 1863, but the January roads were nothing more than quagmires following heavy rains and snow. Although Burnside was obliged to abandon the enterprise after his troops became hopelessly bogged down, Lee knew about the venture from the onset; several countermeasures were implemented, including a movement of Edward P. Alexander's artillery, whose men stumbled across a cache of whiskey and had to be reprimanded. Lee's dispositions to guard against attack were also thwarted by the severe weather and the affair ended without bloodshed, as well as Burnside's dismissal from command. "The storm [that] has culminated here is a deep snow, which does not improve our comfort. It became particularly hard on some of our troops I was obliged to send eleven miles up the Rappahannock to meet a recent move by General Burnside," Lee told his wife on January 29. The Fredericksburg campaign was over when he added: "Burnside's schemes have apparently been frustrated."[50]

15

"I Have Lost My Right Arm"

Following Burnside's final assault on Marye's Heights and the ill-fated Mud March, the two armies lay astride the Rappahannock until spring. The Army of the Potomac numbered approximately 124,000 men with another twelve thousand organized into cavalry units; concentrated among the Stafford hills opposite Fredericksburg and to the west toward Falmouth, it occupied the river's north bank, within easy shooting distance of Lee's army. Some of the bluecoated units extended to the Potomac to guard the railroad from Aquia Creek to Falmouth. A steady flow of supplies reached the federal army by water and rail, a flow that Lee was powerless to check. [1]

Common soldiers and low-ranking officers billeted themselves in tents or makeshift lodgings, while the general officers sought accommodations in plantation homes around Fredericksburg and Falmouth. Like their southern antagonists, the Unionists suffered through a cold, damp winter. The harsh weather along with the disillusionment that permeated the recently beaten army led to soaring desertion rates among federal troops. Joe Hooker, who generaled the Center Grand Division at Fredericksburg, thought the morale problem stemmed from Burnside's policy on absences, which allowed wide discretion to individual commanders; five days after he assumed command, Hooker implemented a uniform plan for leaves. His General Order Number 3, among other things, required his personal approval for "commanders of corps, divisions, and cavalry brigades" to go home. Leaves for enlisted men were restricted to "two for every 100 on duty." More reorganization followed for troopers and officers alike, as a cold and shivering army awaited its marching orders. [2]

Across the river, Lee was safely ensconced behind his old ramparts from the Fredericksburg fighting. The Rappahannock itself added to his well-being, and he had taken the precaution of fortifying every ford and potential crossing for miles in either direction. Yet the overwhelming might of the North continued to raise an ominous threat. Official reports of both armies told the story: Lee had but sixty-two thousand men, three thousand of them mounted under Stuart, to face first Burnside's and then Hooker's 124,000. Professor Tom Jackson held the extreme right at Port Royal, where the width of the river reached one thousand feet. Extending west along the Rappahannock, Jackson's command spread to Hamilton's Crossing, a distance of ten miles. Longstreet was looking for supplies and recruits in North Carolina during most of the winter, although two of his divisions under Lafayette McLaws and Richard H. Anderson held the high ground beyond Hamilton's Crossing. The ever-faithful Jeb Stuart had his cavalry units on guard to the west of Falmouth towards the Rapidan. [3]

Although Lee's men were not as generously provisioned as their Union counterparts, most "made themselves very comfortable," notes John H. Worsham. "Huts were made of any material that could be gotten, and in any way the architect of the party thought best." Most habitations were made from timbers, because few men had tents unless they had been lucky enough to filch them from some Yankee quartermaster. The rebels became adept at building "shebangs," which could be constructed without difficulty. "All a man had to do was put up a couple of forked sticks, with a pole across the forks, and lean bushes against the side toward the wind." While the southerners sat out the winter in makeshift lodgings, a renewed religious upheaval swept the army. Led by William B. Owen, a chaplain with Barksdale's Mississippians, it became "one of the most powerful revivals witnessed during the war." J. C. Stiles, a Presbyterian divine who worked with Owen, said afterward that "a morning and afternoon prayer meeting and a preaching service at night" were held daily in a hastily built chapel. [4]

As the Confederates prayed and fought the cold, Burnside asked to be removed from command; after considerable soul-searching, a president desperate for victory handed the army to Joe Hooker on January 26. Even his letter of appointment reflected Lincoln's distress: ". . . I believe you to be a brave and skillful soldier, which of course, I like. . . . I have heard in such a way as to believe it, of you recently saying that both the Army and the Government needed a dictator. Of course, it is not for

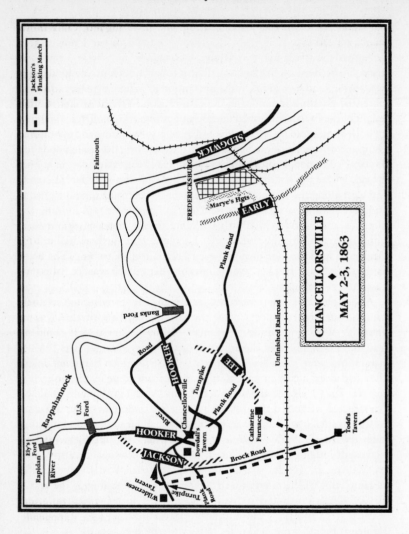

Jackson's Flanking March

Falmouth

SEDGWICK

FREDERICKSBURG

Marye's Hgts

EARLY

Plank Road

Banks Ford

Unfinished Railroad

CHANCELLORSVILLE
MAY 2-3, 1863

Road

HOOKER

Chancellorsville

Turnpike

LEE

Plank Road

Catharine Furnace

Rappahannock

U.S. Ford

River

HOOKER

Dowdall's Tavern

Brock Road

Todd's Tavern

Ely's Ford

Rapidan

River

JACKSON

Wilderness Tavern

Turnpike

Plank Road

this, but in spite of it, that I have given you the command. Only those generals who gain successes can set up dictators. What I now ask is military success and I will risk the dictatorship."

Once Hooker got his desertion problem under control, he moved quickly to reorganize the army and to bolster morale. The Grand Divisions of Burnside were replaced by army corps—several of them under new commanders: John Reynolds, Darius Couch, Daniel E. Sickles, George Gordon Meade, John Sedgwick, Oliver O. Howard, and Henry W. Slocum. By April 30, when the Chancellorsville campaign opened, Hooker had several infantry and a newly organized cavalry corps under George Stoneman to oppose Lee, Jackson, and Longstreet. He even designed a series of badges or insignia to help with command recognition under fire.[5]

The same Hooker who criticized Burnside at Fredericksburg and once called Lincoln "a played out imbecile" was now in command—the fourth general to face Robert E. Lee since the Seven Days. He was a West Point man, class of 1839, with Braxton Bragg, John Sedgwick, Jubal A. Early, and John Pemberton. And Hooker had personal difficulties that raised eyebrows inside the army and at Washington—even today some insist that the popular term for prostitutes derives from his name. In spite of his shortcomings, Hooker became a popular leader with the troops. Not since McClellan had Lincoln found an officer to equal Hooker's hold over the rank and file. After Halleck, still chief of staff in Washington, told him on March 27 that the time for action had arrived, he got busy with new preparations. Abraham Lincoln himself visited army headquarters to discuss strategy and to spur him forward. "On to Richmond" became the great cry for Hooker and his command—and the new chief of the Army of the Potomac set about drafting his final plans. If the Confederate capital could be captured, then all would be well—or so Fighting Joe Hooker thought.[6]

Whatever his plan to reach Richmond, two formidable obstacles lay in Hooker's path: Lee and Jackson still held the high ground opposite Fredericksburg, and the very terrain made any forcing of the Rappahannock a dangerous if not impossible enterprise. At Falmouth, two miles upstream from Fredericksburg, the Rappahannock changes from a tidal river to an upland stream; moreover, Banks Ford close to Fredericksburg and United States Ford further upstream were the only natural crossing points east of the Rapidan. Lee had fortified both against any intrusion, which prompted Hooker to seek another route. He therefore decided to attack the Confederate left and rear by hitting across the Rappahannock at Kelly's Ford and then over the Rapidan at Germanna and Ely's Fords;

once behind Lee, other Union forces could cross by the fords nearer Fredericksburg.

The plan, which called for a force under Sedgwick to make a feint in front of Fredericksburg, put Hooker and Lee on a collision course at a crossroads tavern called "Chancellorsville." The battlefield was not a town or even a village but a single building dating from 1816; erected by George Chancellor, a Spotsylvania County innkeeper, it was a large brick structure ten miles west of Fredericksburg and widely known for its genial hospitality. Meanwhile, a plank road "was completed to Orange Court House, forty miles west of Fredericksburg, in the 1850s. The surface consisted of planks, eight-feet long and three or four inches thick, laid on enormous stringers. This planking covered half the road-bed, the righthand side coming eastward, the side of the more heavily loaded wagons."

The Orange Plank Road, built parallel to an earlier turnpike, was part of the nineteenth-century phenomenon that swept the country to get travelers out of axle-deep mud which characterized the public roads. Built as toll roads by private entrepreneurs, the plank roads soon criss-crossed the country. And the Fredericksburg-Orange Court House road diverged frequently from the older turnpike to take advantage of favorable land contours. George Chancellor's inn—operated by others in 1863, and soon to become Hooker's headquarters—lay at a converging point of the two highways. A railroad had also started west from Fredericksburg in the late 1850s—the unfinished railroad of the Fredericksburg fighting—but it was not completed until 1878.[7]

Although Halleck offered advice, Hooker developed his own plans to attack—and in the utmost secrecy. The chief of staff wanted General John Dix, an aging veteran of the War of 1812, whom Hooker had dispatched to Fort Monroe, to attack from the south, but that scheme never developed. Amid boasts of "God help the rebels," Fighting Joe forged his strategy. Finally, in early April, he sent General Daniel Butterfield on a personal mission to the White House with completed plans. Lincoln gave his assent on April 12, and the following day Hooker issued his marching orders: Each man was issued "five days of hard bread, coffee, sugar, and salt . . . small arms to be carried will be 150 rounds—60 on the person—the full complement on the pack train and the balance to be in the train, ready to start first when the trains move. . . . Surplus clothing of the troops, beyond the extra shirt, pair of socks and drawers should be stored under the supervision of the quarter-master. . . ." Hooker was now ready to do what McClellan, Pope, and Burnside, could not—"whip Bobby Lee."[8]

Beyond the Rappahannock, Lee sifted through daily reports to pinpoint every federal move. With Longstreet, Hood, and Pickett south of Richmond, it was Marse Robert and Jackson who kept the vigil. "General Hooker is obliged to do something, I do not know what it will be," Lee wrote to his daughter Agnes on February 6: "He is playing a Chinese game trying what frightening will do. He runs out his guns, starts his wagons and troops up and down the river, and creates an excitement generally. Our men look on in wonder, give a cheer, and all subsides into *status quo ante bellum. . . .*"[9]

Lee told Agnes that men and animals were suffering from the cold, and that roads around the camp were "wretched, almost impassable." We also get a glimpse that he was not in the best of health: "I am so cross now that I am not worth seeing anywhere." General Long notes that Lee contracted a sore throat, which resulted in "a rheumatism of the heart-sac." In March, he was forced to take to his bed, although the fever was intermittent, with occasional discomfort in the upper chest. Lee almost certainly suffered from pericarditis, an inflammation of the heart often induced by pneumonia; Long suggests that his fatal heart collapse seven years later stemmed from his 1863 difficulties.[10]

All of Lee's Chancellorsville letters are headed "Camp Fredericksburg." Although Robert E. Lee, Jr., who stayed in camp through the winter, says his father never complained, there can be little doubt that winter life in makeshift quarters took their toll on the fifty-six-year-old general. He retained his earlier camp from the December fighting located between Hamilton's Crossing and Fredericksburg on the road to Bowling Green; wood for heat and cooking came from a handy stand of pine trees. "Notwithstanding there was near-by a good house vacant, he lived in his tents," his son continues: "His quarters were very unpretentious, consisting of three or four 'wall-tents' and several more common ones. . . . Though from the outside they were rather dismal, especially through the dreary winter time, within they were cheerful, and the surroundings as neat and comfortable as possible under the circumstances." Lee remained at Camp Fredericksburg because of its accessibility to the troops guarding the fords upstream and to Jackson at Port Royal a few miles to the east.[11]

"I owe Mr. F. J. Hooker no thanks for keeping me here. He ought to have made up his mind long ago what to do," Lee told his wife on February 23. And while the army wrestled with foot-deep snows, Lee carried on a lively correspondence with Richmond about the need for army reorganization. Since early January, he had pleaded with Secretary of War Seddon, a onetime Virginia congressman, for more men to bolster his defenses. Despite his illness, Lee traveled to Richmond during mid-March to confer with Jefferson Davis about the army; he told the president that his greatest difficulty was "causing his orders and regulations to be obeyed."

Lee also pointed out that several of his divisions were larger than Winfield Scott's army in Mexico; size alone had become an organizational headache, since nothing in the old army had prepared Lee for the sheer numbers of his command. And, while he did not name specific officers, Lee was obviously disturbed that his commands were not always carried out. "I think [it] important and indeed necessary to simplify the mechanism of our army as much as possible, yet still to give it sufficient power to move and regulate the whole body," was his recommendation.[12]

At this point, while he struggled with his health and read an Episcopalian journal called *The Churchman*, Lee made known his estimate of Jackson and Longstreet, who remained his top subordinates. In a March 27 letter to Mrs. Lee, he talked about Jackson's "fine candid and fresh expression, so charming to see and so attractive to the beholder." But it was different with Longstreet, who had become jealous of Jackson and also chafed under Lee's scrutiny; he wanted an independent command away from the main army. On March 21, the same day he told Davis that his orders were not always obeyed, Lee also wrote to Longstreet: ". . . I am confident that at all times and in all places you will do all that can be done for the defence [sic] of the country and advancement of the service, and are ready to cooperate or act singly as circumstances dictate. . . ."[13]

Now on station near Petersburg, where he guarded Lee's southern flank at Suffolk, Longstreet had been talking with Seddon in Richmond, a few miles away. Although Old Pete ignores Lee's letter in his *Memoirs*, he does say that he approached Seddon on his way north to join the army at Chancellorsville. But when Longstreet asked that he be sent with the divisions of Pickett and Hood to join Braxton Bragg in Tennessee, the war secretary said no. Longstreet reached Chancellorsville after the battle but before Jackson's death, where he found Lee in "sadness, notwithstanding his brilliant victory." Lee's contemplation of the subsequent Pennsylvania operation notwithstanding, Longstreet advised a defensive posture and again asked for a transfer to the west. "His plans or wishes announced, it became useless and improper to offer suggestions leading to a different course." Still, Longstreet had his own clout within government and army circles; after Jackson's death, when Lee did restructure his force into three corps, he was given command along with Jubal A. Early and A. P. Hill. Since Longstreet's recalcitrance to obey orders at Gettysburg six weeks later probably cost the battle, if not the entire Confederate cause, Lee would have been better served with his "Old War-Horse" elsewhere. His ill feelings aside, Longstreet was magnanimous toward his fallen comrade. The Confederacy in May 1863 "faced a future bereft of much of its hopefulness," he noted after Jackson's funeral. [14]

With Lee in camp near Hamilton's Crossing and Old Jack at Moss Neck, where he remained until mid-March, the two soldiers remained in close contact through the harsh season. John Esten Cooke records that Lee told others during January, "he wished he had a dozen Jacksons as his lieutenants." And if Longstreet was envious of the rapport between Jackson and Lee, Jeb Stuart surely was not; "General Stuart again repeats that 'Jackson is a man of *military genius*'—and I reply 'that it hits it exactly: he certainly has the knack of whipping Yankees,' " Cooke put in his diary for January 31. [15]

Throughout February and early March, Jackson, Lee, Old Jack's artillery chief Stapleton Crutchfield, and Jefferson Davis carried on a lengthy correspondence over reorganization of Jackson's artillery arm. Although Davis, who always kept a tight rein over the army, ultimately settled the issue, Jackson uncharacteristically told Lee: "I have had much trouble resulting from incompetent officers having been assigned to duty with me regardless of my wishes. Those who assigned them have never taken the responsibility of incurring the odium which results from such incompetency." Jackson and Lee had their camps in such close proximity that little need existed for formal communications, which made Old Jack's outburst all the more remarkable, and he had put it in writing. Yet Jackson had other upheavals to resolve at Moss Neck. When several men were caught stealing chickens, he had a death sentence carried out over the strong objection of General Elisha F. Paxton, a University of Virginia trained lawyer and commander of the Stonewall Brigade, who prepared an elaborate legal defense. Little wonder that Kyd Douglas was moved to comment: "In this case General Jackson was hard as nails; in the performance of duty he always was. I never knew him in such a case to temper justice with mercy; his very words were merciless." [16]

Another nasty incident occupied Jackson during his stay at Moss Neck when Isaac R. Trimble was promoted major general and put in charge of Jackson's old division, which had been officered by William B. Taliaferro for several months. Miffed at being passed over, Taliaferro threw his weight around before relinquishing command, which angered E. F. Paxton, who was one of his subordinates. Paxton said Taliaferro "abused his power as a superior officer" and preferred charges. Although Lee—with plenty on his mind—rejected Paxton's plea for court-martial proceedings, he sided with Taliaferro. Jackson, however, refused to second Taliaferro's elevation to higher rank, which paved the way for his exit to the Georgia coast. It became a nerve-racking business for all concerned; sadly, Paxton, who emerged with Jackson's blessing, was killed in the Chancellorsville fighting.[17]

While Lee watched Hooker's every move and Jackson reorganized his artillery branch, the opening move took place March 16–17 at Kelly's Ford on the Rappahannock. With Confederate pickets ranging twenty-five miles upriver, Fighting Joe became alarmed at constant cavalry thrusts by units under Fitz Lee and Jeb Stuart along his right flank. Something must be done, he reasoned, and he tapped General William W. Averell, a West Point man in the same class as Fitz Lee and veteran of the Indian wars, to attack his classmate's cavalry at Culpeper, where he held the extreme Confederate left. "We ought to be invincible," Hooker told Averell, "and by God, sir, we shall be. You have got to stop these disgraceful cavalry 'surprises.' I'll have no more of them. I give you full power over your officers, to arrest, cashier, shoot—whatever you will—only you must stop these surprises. And by God, sir, if you don't do it, I give you fair notice, I will relieve the whole of you and take command of the cavalry myself."[18]

With Hooker's ultimatum ringing in his ears, Averell moved toward his foe by way of Kelly's Ford with twenty-one hundred sabers on March 16; but Fitz Lee had his own spy system and, following a short delay to collect his force, he rode from Culpeper with eight hundred horsemen. The ensuing melee at the Rappahannock was "the best cavalry fight of the war," said Hooker's chief of staff Daniel Butterfield, the same man who argued Hooker's strategy with Abraham Lincoln. Averell, who became a millionaire with several electrical inventions after the war, claimed that he drove the enemy from the field and that only their hasty retreat behind infantry breastworks saved them from destruction.

"Had Fitz Lee been able to mount all the troopers on his rolls," says John W. Thomason, the biographer of Jeb Stuart, "and if his horses had not been, by reason of overwork, in such poor condition, not a man of Averell's would have been allowed to recross the Rappahannock." Importantly, it was completely a cavalry engagement; except for a handful of federal riflemen behind a stone wall, the entire action was fought on horseback. And it was a sharp little fight, with Averell sustaining 78 losses to 133 for the Confederates; historians to this day debate the winner. Kelly's Ford alerted Lee that he was now facing a rejuvenated federal cavalry; and he recalled the divisions of Pickett and Hood, over Longstreet's objection in the belief that Hooker had started his grand offensive.[19]

Tragically, the episode resulted in the death of John Pelham, the gallant Pelham of Stuart's horse artillery. Jeb Stuart was at Culpeper to attend a court-martial, and Pelham, who wanted to court a young lady there, had accompanied his chief. Heros Von Borcke, Stuart's aide-de-camp, tells what happened: "When one of our regiments advancing to charge was received with such a terrible fire as to cause it to waver, Pelham galloped to them shouting, 'Forward, boys! Forward to victory and glory!' and at the same moment a fragment of a shell, which exploded close over his head, penetrated the back part of the skull and stretched the young hero insensible on the ground." He was taken to a private residence in Culpeper, where he died the same evening.[20]

Pelham's death was felt deeply throughout the army. Stuart, who had seen the boy gunner through every major battle, was crushed. Jackson had expressed his admiration previously: "An army should have a Pelham on each flank," after watching him in action at Antietam. Lee, who had dubbed him the "gallant Pelham" at Fredericksburg, was equally gracious in his praise after the Kelly's Ford incident. Upon his recommendation to Jefferson Davis, the senate confirmed his posthumous promotion to lieutenant colonel.[21]

Meanwhile, Jackson moved his headquarters from Moss Neck to a tent at Hamilton's Crossing. Although he had insisted all along that Hooker would open his campaign on Lee's right flank below Fredericksburg, Kelly's Ford had aroused new fears. Marse Robert, prostrate with illness, intended to march quickly in whichever direction his foe decided to strike, and now he needed Old Jack to strengthen his left and center. Jackson's move, however, was marred by news that his little friend, five-year-old Janie Corbin, had died from some childhood fever.

As clearing weather made a clash with Hooker inevitable, Jackson grew anxious about his own wife and daughter, and incessant letters to Anna could not fill the void. On February 23, Old Jack lamented that he had not seen his esposa for nearly a year and that he had never seen his daughter. "But it is important that I and those at headquarters, should set an example by remaining at the post of duty," he added. Jackson's letters to his wife, always full of endearments, were different from Lee's missives to Mrs. Lee. Although Lee was ever solicitous of his wife's health and well-being, his matter-of-fact approach never equaled Jackson's intimacy. "I am beginning to look for my darling and my baby," Old Jack wrote home on April 18—and two days later, another letter said he had found accommodations for her and the child in the Yerby home, a plantation house near his new headquarters. Jackson personally traveled to Guiney Station to meet his family on April 20; Mrs. Jackson has left at least two accounts of the connubial visit that followed. Disaster and death might lie on the horizon, but Jackson was sublimely happy to have "his darlings" near. "The father entered the coach to receive us, his overcoat dripping with rain, but his face aglow with happiness. Baby could not be taken from him until we arrived at Mr. Yerby's and then I shall never forget the exquisite picture of love. During that short time he was rarely without the baby in his arms. Now he would go to the mirror and hold the chubby bundle up for inspection. 'Miss Jackson, look at yourself!' he would say. . . ."

Jackson arranged for the child's christening on April 23 by his friend and chaplain, the Reverend B. T. Lacy, who officiated before a gathering of staff officers and army friends. Lee was there and characteristically paid his respects to Anna and the child. "It was during this visit that General Jackson had his last picture taken. I arranged his hair myself, for it had grown in long ringlets, and he sat in the hall of the Yerby house, where the wind blew in his face and brought a slight frown to his countenance."

Anna had prepared herself to leave on instant notice, which came on April 29; "a hasty good-by and he was gone, and I heard nothing but the terrible rattle of musketry." His wife and daughter had been at Hamilton's Crossing for nine days when Hooker commenced his grand assault. [22]

Anna Jackson had indeed heard the opening sounds of Chancellorsville and, whether she sensed danger or not, she instinctively knew that her husband meant to fight. Jackson had laid it on the line two weeks earlier when marching orders had been cut for the Second Corps: ". . . each division will move precisely at the time indicated . . . the troops are to have a rest of ten minutes each hour. The rate of march is not to exceed 1 mile in twenty-five minutes. . . . Any one leaving his appropriate duty, under the pretext of taking care of the wounded will be promptly arrested. . . ." Though Lee and Old Jack had considered every tactical possibility, Hooker's fast march to the Rapidan caught them by surprise. Abner Doubleday, a participant in the battle, maintains that Lee was stunned by Hooker's audacity. [23]

With the divisions of Meade, Howard, and Slocum in the van, Hooker crossed the Rappahannock on the night of April 28–29, and made for the Rapidan at Germanna and Ely's Fords. William "Little Billy" Mahone, destined for greater renown when he "plugged" the Crater attack at Petersburg a year later, first encountered the advancing federals at the Rapidan crossings. Hooker had marched eastward to turn Lee's rear and left flank while he left a small force under John Sedgwick to threaten Fredericksburg. And Jubal Early, whom Lee put in command at Marye's Heights, when he divided his army on the 30th, soon faced a federal probe along his front at Deer Run. But the storm was behind Lee, where Mahone and Carnot Posey of Richard H. Anderson's command fell back from the Rapidan following a hurried conference at Chancellorsville. For the time being, Anderson decided to entrench around Tabernacle Church, about halfway between Hooker's front lines and Fredericksburg.[24]

Besides the crossings at Germanna and Ely's Fords, Hooker dispatched additional columns against Lee and Jackson in addition to Sedgwick's feint at Fredericksburg. First, his cavalry commander, Alfred Pleasonton, was put in motion one day earlier, with instructions to cut Lee's communications south of the Rappahannock. Hooker had convinced himself that once Lee lost direct contact with Richmond, he would begin a general withdrawal southward. Pleasonton's mounted units did succeed in temporarily disrupting traffic on the Richmond and Fredericksburg Railroad, which delayed Mrs. Jackson's arrival at her husband's sickbed following the tragedy of May 2, but Freeman labels Pleasonton's raid a grave error because it enabled Jackson to march unhindered around Hooker's right flank in the ensuing battle. As Jackson lay dying from his wounds, writes Freeman, he considered "this the prime defect in Hooker's plan of operations."[25]

Daniel Sickles, later commandant of the Carolinas during Radical Reconstruction, completed Hooker's attack when he crossed by the United States Ford; his force was reinforced by Couch's division, thereby bolstering the federal left and depriving Confederate access to the river crossings. Small wonder that Lee was momentarialy disorganized by the four-pronged thrust of Hooker's 130,000 men.[26]

Still, Lee and Jackson were astir at the first notice of trouble. When Old Jack left his wife in the care of Dr. Lacy on the morning of April 29, he rode immediately to Early's headquarters on the Old Stage Road, which led south to Richmond. Within minutes, Lee had arrived from Camp Fredericksburg and, following an intense consultation, the two warriors decided to wait before joining the march. Lee then spent the day poring over battle reports from his far-flung units; he was convinced the chief threat lay along his left, but Sedgwick's posturing—marching and countermarching opposite Fredericksburg—raised doubts in that otherwise clear mind. While he pondered, Lee communicated with his generals throughout the day and sent urgent telegrams to Richmond. In the first, he said the enemy had crossed the river, but "I could not learn their strength, but infantry is said to have crossed with cavalry. . . . Their intention I presume, is to turn our left, and probably get into our rear." Lee again asked for reinforcements; another wire to Jefferson Davis asked him to order up Longstreet's division still detached from the army.

Jackson, meanwhile, spent the 29th gathering and concentrating the second corps nearer Fredericksburg. Units downriver toward Port Royal were recalled as well as the divisions of Raleigh Colston, A. P. Hill, and Robert E. Rodes. Lee instructed Lafayette McLaws of Longstreet's corps to cooperate with Jackson; "leave your sharpshooters," he instructed the Georgian, West Pointer, and veteran of Mexico, "and take a position in the rifle-pits, so as to maintain the heights back of the town, as in December." Those sharpshooters and Barksdale's batteries would make it hot for Sedgwick when he did decide to force the Rappahannock. Old Jack remained in his camp at Hamilton's Crossing for the night in heavy meditation. When he left the next morning (April 30) to confer with Lee, according to Vandiver who summarizes Dabney, he returned to his tent for a moment of prayer. "Faithful Jim Lewis, holding Little Sorrel's reins, motioned to silence the staff workers. 'Hush,' he said, 'the general is praying. . . .' Fifteen minutes passed and then Old Jack came out, gave some final instructions, and rode off. That was the last time he used the tent."[27]

Rain fell throughout the 29th and when Jackson rode out the next morning to study Sedgwick's emplacements beyond the river, he encountered a fog-enshrouded Rappahannock. The sound of guns had aroused his fighting blood as he sat astride his mount gazing at Henry Hunt's artillery atop the Stafford Heights and awaiting Lee's arrival. Jackson wanted to charge straight across the river; but Marse Robert, always the vigilant captain said no. Couriers from Anderson had confirmed his suspicions that the bluecoats were coming from behind—on the roads that converged on Chancellorsville.

Hooker moved forward on the 30th; by nightfall, he had replaced Billy Mahone as guest in the Chancellorsville tavern. Although Hooker knew from captured dispatches that Lee was still at Fredericksburg, he committed the big blunder of the campaign when he hesitated at the first sound of Anderson's guns. Fighting Joe's indecision meant that Jackson could move the next morning to help Anderson's isolated command.

Anderson's refusal to budge before the entire weight of the federal army gave Lee enough time to focus his counterattack. When a staff officer asked Anderson about Lee's order to stand firm, that soldier did not equivocate: "And promptly," notes his biographer, "came the answer, clear and true. 'Fight, General Lee says so.' "[28]

Back on the Rappahannock, Lee and Jackson renewed their council of war. Old Jack asked for time to reconnoiter Sedgwick's emplacements before a decision was made to march down the Plank Road to meet Hooker. It did not take long for him to agree with Lee: This was no place for a Confederate counterattack. Lee had already decided to split the army once more. "Learning yesterday afternoon that the enemy's right wing had crossed the Rapidan," he telegraphed the war office, "and its head had reached the position on our extreme left. To arrest their progress I determined to hold our lines in the rear of Fredericksburg with part of the force and endeavor with the rest to drive the enemy back to Rapidan." The wire sent at twelve noon again asked for additional troops; Jubal Early would stay on the Rappahannock, while Jackson prepared to reinforce a beleaguered Anderson. Lee's Special Order No. 121, spelled it out: McLaws and Jackson would detach skeleton forces to help Early and with the remainder of their commands march "at daylight tomorrow morning (May 1) . . . and make arrangements to repulse the enemy."[29]

At 11 o'clock sharp, May 1, Hooker started his advance by driving four columns straight at Lee with every expectation of success: On the left, Meade's corps marched by the poorly defined River Road. Sykes took the center and proceeded down the Turnpike, while the right under Slocum and the doomed Howard followed the Plank Road. Part of Couch's division was ordered southward toward Todd's Tavern on the road to Orange Court House. In his eagerness, Hooker had apparently discounted serious opposition until he reached the old breastworks at Fredericksburg. But first McLaws, who arrived to confront Sykes, and then Jackson brought their reinforcements to Anderson. Professor Jackson was anxious for the fight, and from the moment of his arrival told Anderson to stop his defensive tactics and to prepare a forward march.

Hooker and Jackson slammed together about a mile and a half east of Chancellorsville in the tangled undergrowth known as the Wilderness, which hampered movement on both sides; decayed corpses were found in the same undergrowth a year later, when Lee and Ulysses S. Grant fought over the identical ground. Once contact had been made and the defensive lines established, Lee spent the rest of May 1 sending feints against Hooker's divisions trying to probe his positions. When he telegraphed a status report to Jefferson Davis later in the day, he again lamented the absence of Longstreet's divisions.

By nightfall, the Confederate works stretched from Mott's Run, across the Plank Road, to Catharine Furnace, a mile or so to the southeast. McLaws with Barksdale and Wilcox held the extreme right near the Rappahannock; Anderson was in the center astride the Plank Road opposite Slocum, while Stonewall Jackson with Colston, A. P. Hill, and Rodes was on the left along and south of the road. Jeb Stuart's cavalry units at the furnace held the extreme left. Throughout the day, Hooker's strategy had become obvious; he meant to stand on the defensive behind his abatis fortifications. Jackson, always impatient to get at the enemy, was nearly killed during the day while trying to probe the Union flank. He had joined Stuart and several aides along the Confederate left near Catharine Furnance and rode to a small knoll searching for suitable gun emplacements; two unseen batteries opened on the small party at close range. "Horses and men were knocked over, kicking, . . . and nobody understands how any person came from the place alive. As for Stuart and Stonewall, their work was not yet done," writes Stuart's biographer, John W. Thomason.[30]

Indeed, the federal army was in a strong defensive position at eventide. Yet Hooker had a problem that proved fatal on the morrow; his extreme right flank—the Eleventh Corps under Oliver O. Howard with its high concentration of German troops—according to military parlance, "was in the air." It rested on no natural barrier but merely ended in the dense growth of the wilderness. Hooker himself recognized the problem and dispatched a brigade from Sickles's corps to bolster the line; outraged that anyone would question his soldierly abilities or the bravery of his command, Howard said the help was unwanted and sent the reinforcements back to headquarters.[31]

Then, as nightfall fell over the Wilderness crossroads, the sound of axes could be heard in every direction as Johnny Reb and Billy Yank piled additional abatis along their fronts. Jackson again inspected Hooker's positions later in the evening with Captain Alexander C. Haskell and immediately rode to confer with Lee "under some pine trees on the left of the Plank Road, just where the Confederate line crossed it." Although Jackson thought Fighting Joe would leave during the night and reposition himself beyond the river, Lee said otherwise. "He hoped Jackson was right," Vandiver notes, "but he felt sure that Hooker had made his big push here and could hardly give it up without a serious contest. Admittedly, his plans were obscure, but that he would retreat after light contact appeared unlikely." Strong federal entrenchments near the Rappahannock, where Meade held the keep, demanded that Lee and Jackson find another way to get at Hooker's flank.

This conference and another that followed early on May 2 have spawned a debate among scholars that will not cease: Who first conceived the masterstroke that followed—Lee or Jackson? The widely held notion that Chancellorsville "was directed and executed by Jackson," according to Major T.M.R. Talcott, was first suggested in 1875 by Major John W. Daniel; Talcott, an aide to Lee throughout the campaign, thought Daniel made his suggestion before the Fifth Annual Reunion of the Army of Northern Virginia. Every writer from Dabney in 1866 has been forced to grapple with the dilemma. Douglas Southall Freeman says flat out: "Lee's was the responsibility, Lee's the decision." For Dabney, "General Lee had promptly concluded, that while, on the one hand, immediate attack was proper, some more favorable place for assault must be sought, by moving further toward Hooker's right." When Fitz Lee and Stuart confirmed Hooker's weakness, "General Jackson now proposed to throw his command entirely into Hooker's rear," Dabney continues, "availing himself of the absence of Federal cavalry, and the presence of the Confederate horse, and to assail him from the west in concert with McLaws and Anderson." General Long suggests the flanking movement was jointly conceived.[32]

In the intervening years, each man has found his champion. "The point is not material," notes John Esten Cooke, biographer of both Lee and Jackson, and a participant at Chancellorsville: "The plan was adopted, and Lee determined to detach a column of about twenty thousand men under Jackson to make the attack the next day." It came about, as Cooke points out, after Stuart joined the Lee-Jackson conference with news that the federal right was "in the air." In the discussions that followed, both men fixed upon Howard. After Lee departed for the night, Old Jack, acting upon a suggestion by the Reverend Lacy, sent Jed Hotchkiss to seek information from Colonel Charles Wellford, operator of a local smelting furnace. Awakened from his slumbers, Wellford told Hotchkiss what he wanted to hear. An uncharted lane, cut through the Wilderness by his own workers, indeed led to the Plank Road behind Hooker.[33]

A disturbing incident took place the next morning; as Jackson was preparing to eat breakfast in the chilly dawn, his sword suddenly crashed to the ground. "While we were still talking the general's sword, which was leaning against a tree, without apparent cause fell to the ground," relates General Long, who acted as Lee's staff officer: "I picked it up and handed it to him. He thanked me and buckled it on. It was now dawn, the troops were on the march, and the bivouac was all astir. After a few words with General Lee he mounted his horse and rode off. This was the last meeting between Lee and Jackson." Ill omen or not, the incident was not lost on the assembled staff officers. They had read their history at West Point and the University of Virginia, and they knew that Charles I had his standard blown over "on a hillock at Nottingham" at the start of the English Civil War two hundred years earlier. They also knew that Charles Stuart lost his head on the block at Whitehall after his cavaliers had gone down to defeat before the hosts of Oliver Cromwell. And when Jackson bade farewell to Lee at the start of his march to the Plank Road, at least one observer noted: "His face was flustered."[34]

In those early morning hours of May 2, Lee had made his way to Jackson's fire from his own tent. As they sat on cracker boxes—left by fleeing federals the day before—they were joined by Jed Hotchkiss, who spread a map before them; he had charted the path suggested by Wellford's son, who agreed to act as guide. "General Lee then said," the Hotchkiss account continues: " 'General Jackson, what do you propose to do?' He replied, 'Go around here,' moving his finger over the road I had located on the map. General Lee said, 'What do you propose to make the movement with?' 'With my whole corps,' was the answer. General Lee then asked, 'What will you leave me?' 'The divisions of Anderson and McLaws,' said Jackson. General Lee, after a moment's reflection, remarked, 'Well, go on. . . .' " After some last-minute conversation in which Lee ordered Stuart to move the cavalry with him, Jackson rose and with a salute, told Lee: "My troops will move at once, sir."[35]

And move they did that May dawn! Jackson had twenty-eight thousand men at his disposal when he struck for Hooker's rear with the commands of Rodes, Colston, and A. P. Hill; with the army now split, Lee had but fourteen thousand effectives to oppose the federals in front of Chancellorsville. It was a twelve-mile trek along the Brock Road to the Old Turnpike, and Jackson's medical chief, Dr. Hunter McGuire, later reminisced that he would never forget the intensity of Jackson's face. "Press forward, Press Forward" was his steady admonition. "Every man in the ranks knew that they were engaged in some great flank movement, and they eagerly responded and pressed on at a rapid gait," McGuire notes.

Federal pickets spotted Jackson's quick-marching columns when he emerged out of the underscrub into the clearing around Catharine Furnace. Men along Howard's right, among others, reported the news to headquarters, but neither Hooker nor Howard took notice. They remained strangely indifferent and said that Jackson was withdrawing southward toward Gordonsville to protect the railroad link to Richmond. "Why any one would suppose that Lee would part with half his army, and send it away to Gordonsville where there was no enemy and nothing to be done, is more than I can imagine," Abner Doubleday writes with consternation. Although Hooker was unmoved by Jackson's movements, several of his subordinates grew alarmed as the day wore on. General Carl Schurz, later U.S. senator from Missouri and Secretary of the Interior under Rutherford B. Hayes, even acted on his own to strengthen Howard's flank. But Schurz and the others had waited too long; Jackson, like a caged tiger, was ready to pounce.[36]

Old Jack called a temporary halt around 1 P.M., after a breathless Fitz Lee met him at the Brock Road-Plank Road intersection. Stuart's cavalrymen had seen Howard's flank and the sprawling federal army from a hillock vantage point, and he summoned Jackson to see for himself. Without demur, the general and a staff officer joined Stuart for a quick reconnaissance. Just beyond the Plank Road, the small group rode into the brush and up a small rise. Unbelievably, Jackson gazed upon the unsuspecting enemy—thousands of bluecoated federals cooking, mending clothes, smoking, even slaughtering beefs. He had intended to hit Hooker down the Plank Road, where Hooker's flank was exposed, but now a new opportunity beckoned; with scarcely a word to break his concentration, he returned to his waiting columns. "Onward," he bade his commanders, "to the Turnpike."[37]

When Jackson's force reached the road at 2 o'clock, it was roughly six miles from Lee and Anderson. At the turnpike, his lines were formed perpendicular to the road and extending a mile in either direction; Rodes took the lead, with A. P. Hill closing the rear, as the mighty force prepared to march. Brigades under McGowan and Lane were held in reserve at the Brock Road junction, while Fitz Lee and Paxton (who was killed in the attack) moved down the Plank Road. As Jackson gazed eastward past the clearings around Talley's Farm, the Wilderness Church, and Melzi Chancellor's tavern, he already knew his next move. He scrawled a hasty note to Lee by resting his order book against Little Sorrel's saddlehorn. "Near 3 P.M. General, the enemy has made a stand at Chancellors which is about 2 miles from Chancellorsville. I hope as soon as practicable to attack. I trust that an ever kind Providence will bless us with great success." And he added a postscript: "The lead division is up and the next two appear to be well closed." It was the last thing written by Stonewall Jackson, and it is entirely fitting that it should be to his commanding general and compatriot. At 5 P.M., Jackson turned to Rodes, who once applied for his old teaching slot at VMI, and asked, "Are you ready, sir?"[38]

It was a glorious day for southern arms when Rodes moved forward straight down the turnpike; Jackson's grey line advanced so quickly that scarcely a northern soldier was ready for the onslaught. Confusion and panic gripped the Union high command—one federal officer, Lieutenant Colonel Levi Smith of the 128th Pennsylvania, rode up to D. H. Hill and James H. Lane, another VMI man, "waving a white flag and inquired whether Lane's troops were Union or Confederate." Lane considered this an improper use of a flag of truce and ordered the man arrested. Hooker himself only became alarmed when droves of forest creatures—foxes, rabbits, deer—frightened by the oncoming rebels, darted through his camp. Jackson was constantly near the van as Rodes's troopers, animals, and Yankee pickets came crashing down the turnpike in one twisted mass.

Oliver O. Howard, whose Eleventh Corps lost upward of three thousand men and was nearly decimated in the attack, later wrote in his battle report: "At about 6 P.M. I was at my headquarters, at Dowdall's Tavern, when the attack commenced." Within three minutes, he was at the front, where he saw "that the enemy had enveloped my right, and that the First Division was giving way." Howard was not a man to discount the "masterstroke" perpetrated upon him by Lee and Jackson: "Though constantly threatened and apprised of the moving of the enemy, yet the woods was so dense that he was able to mass a large force, whose exact whereabouts neither patrols, reconnaissances, nor scouts ascertained. He succeeded in forming a column opposite to and outflanking my right." Jackson's movement around Hooker had done the job. "By panic produced by the enemy's reverse fire, regiments and artillery were suddenly thrown upon those in position," Howard concludes.[39]

But Confederate organization began to crumble with the onset of darkness. Some federal resistance, largely ineffective, developed along the center, although Jackson's major problem remained the dense underscrub. Many Confederate units became entangled and separated from their commands in spite of his call to "press forward." Finally, around 8 P.M., Rodes ordered a halt and asked that D. H. Hill's command rush forward to help stabilize the front. When the fight resumed Sunday morning, Lee telegraphed the triumph to Richmond: "Yesterday General Jackson, with three of his divisions, penetrated the rear of the enemy, and drove him from all his positions from the Wilderness to within 1 mile of Chancellorsville. . . . Many prisoners were taken, and the enemy's loss in killed and wounded large."[40]

Lee's wire also carried the worst possible news. "I regret to state that General Paxton was killed, General Jackson severely, and Generals Heth and A. P. Hill, slightly wounded." Stonewall wounded! Word of the catastrophe shot through the southern nation like a tocsin; it carried a foreboding that the invincible Lee-Jackson team was broken. "From the cities of the Atlantic coast to the far-off settlements of Texas the news that Stonewall had fallen came as a stunning blow," G.F.R. Henderson observes. Although Lee's initial wire did not express alarm, Jackson's worsening condition and death one week afterward devastated the country. Longstreet's appraisal of Jackson was universally shared by his southern compatriots. "His example, let us hope and believe, will survive him," editorialized the Richmond *Enquirer,* "and in the coming fight let Jackson's men show to the world that a dead Jackson shall win in the field."[41]

Northern papers, while happy to be done with a formidable adversary, were uniformly generous with praise for the fallen warrior! "It is agreed on all hands," said the New York *Herald*—the same paper he scanned for war news in Lexington—"that Jackson was the most brilliant General developed by the war. . . . he resembled Napoleon in his early career more than any other general of modern times." The Washington *Chronicle* called him a "noble Christian, a brave soldier, and a pure man." But its widely noted article by John Forney labeled him a religious zealot who perverted his great powers in the secessionist cause. "Mahomet, Cyril, Philip of Spain, Loyola, Xavier, Bloody Mary, several of the Popes of Rome, Robespierre, George III, and Joe Smith are familiar instances of enthusiasm, fanaticism, and obstinacy, combined with that curious obliquity of reasoning powers which is one of the most puzzling characteristics of the human mind. Jackson belonged to this class of men." Forney hoped the Almighty would balance his Christian virtues against his rebel sins. The writer sent a copy of his work to Abraham Lincoln, who responded that his was a "manly" appraisal of the dead hero.[42]

Jackson's death came eight days after three bullets struck him on the night of May 2; following his brilliant, but headlong, rush at Hooker's rear columns, he had ridden down the Plank Road—which converged with the turnpike—toward Chancellorsville to scout the land after Rodes halted to reorganize. Old Jack meant to block any federal retreat to safety across the United States Ford, while A. P. Hill moved to the front. Disaster came when his standing order that pickets were always to be positioned beyond the line at the end of a day's advance was disobeyed. In the exhilaration and disarray of the federal rout, advance sentries had not been posted, although Fitz Lee had rushed guns forward to pound the enemy at Chancellorsville. A return cannonade down the wilderness forced Jackson and his party to seek cover.

When he learned that the enemy was near—Dabney says Jackson was one hundred yards beyond the Confederate front—he turned back. Men were tired and excited after the day's march, and though a North Carolina brigade opened fire at the approaching horsemen, Old Jack escaped into the undergrowth. Back on the pike, tragedy soon struck. Dabney continues: "As the party approached within twenty paces of the Confederate troops, these, evidently mistaking them for cavalry, stopped and delivered a deadly fire. So sudden and stunning was this volley, and so near at hand, that every horse that was not shot down, recoiled from it in panic, and turned to rush back, bearing their riders toward the approaching enemy." Luckily, Jackson was able to check Little Sorrel after the horse darted into low-hanging branches, knocking his cap to the ground and lacerating his face.[43]

Jackson sustained three wounds in the blistering cross fire: one in the right hand while alerting his companions to danger, and two in the left arm, one of which apparently damaged the main artery. The major wound was three inches below the shoulder. Although others were shot—some of them killed—Old Jack's staff managed with difficulty to get him to a field hospital at Dowdall's Tavern. Before treating his own wounds, A. P. Hill, who had ridden to the same vantage point, removed Jackson's epaulets to conceal his identity. Enemy units remained dangerously near; Jackson, who wanted to avoid panic among the ranks, told his staff to say "a Confederate officer had been wounded" as he was carried from the field. William Dorsey Pender, who had taken command of Hill's division, recognized Jackson and asked what he should do with his disorganized troops. "Almost fainting with anguish and loss of blood, he still replied, in a voice feeble but full of its old determination and authority, 'General Pender, you must keep your men together, and hold your ground.' This was the last military order ever given by Jackson," Dabney records.[44]

John Esten Cooke says that Jackson was shot in front of the Van Wert residence about two miles west of Chancellorsville. Today a stone column stands over the "exact spot" near the battlefield visitors' center. A still-conscious Jackson knew that he had been wounded by his own men as Hunter McGuire and three other doctors probed his injuries. Dr. Richard R. Barr, a surgeon in one of Hill's brigades, who examined him on the field, had already determined that the arm was broken, a fact confirmed by Jackson himself. Although an earlier tourniquet had been applied, Barr did not prescribe another because the bleeding had ceased. Yet McGuire resolved to amputate the left arm about two inches below the shoulder after Jackson told him to do what he thought best. Following the operation, Jackson told bystanders that he had never favored the use of chloroform in cases where death might be imminent. "But it was," Jackson said, "the most delightful sensation I ever enjoyed. . . . I had enough consciousness to know what was doing; at one time I thought I heard the most delightful music that ever greeted my ears. But I should dislike above all things to enter eternity in such a condition."[45]

Although Lee, the epitome of Anglo-Saxon self-control, had a half-won battle to direct, he was obviously shaken by the tragedy. Jackson had been his companion in arms since the first days of Civil War, and now that ever-faithful lieutenant lay wounded. The void created by his subsequent death surely contributed to Lee's lackadaisical handling of the army at Gettysburg a month later, when he had to fight his first major battle without him. It is true that Lee had much on his mind after Chancellorsville, including the wounding and capture of Rooney at Brandy Station and the heavy decision to invade Pennsylvania. But his first letters to Jackson and others following the misfortune reflect his deep sense of loss.

When first told that Old Jack had been hurt, Lee sent an immediate note of good cheer: ". . . I cannot express my regret at the occurrence. Could I have directed events, I should have chosen for the good of the country to be disabled in your stead." The victory at Chancellorsville, Lee said, was "due to your skill and energy." Jeb Stuart took command of the Second Corps when Jackson was carried from the field, and in two dispatches during the early hours of May 3 Lee urged him to press the advantage. Lee wanted his army reunited at the expense of Hooker's right wing—to continue Jackson's attack. According to Mrs. Jackson, always anxious for her husband's place in history, Lee turned to several staff officers: " 'Ah, any victory is dearly bought which deprives us of the services of Jackson, even for a short while. He was then told that Jackson had said, 'the enemy should be pressed in the morning.' 'Those people shall be immediately pressed,' he replied.' " When the May 3 note was read to Jackson in the field hospital at Melzi Chancellor's, Old Jack, suffering mightily after the amputation, was equally appreciative of his commander. "Better that ten Jacksons should fall than one Lee."

Robert E. Lee, Jr., who remained near his father, has Jackson saying he would follow Lee "blindfolded" because he was so "cautious." That confidence was more than reciprocated in a follow-up note to Jackson: "You are better off than I am, for while you have only lost your left, I HAVE LOST MY RIGHT ARM." Eyewitness accounts of what transpired in McGuire's surgery and in Lee's command tent after the wounding abound. All agree that Lee was exceptionally generous toward his fallen friend and comrade. "I do not know how to replace him—God's will be done. I trust He will raise up someone in his place," he wrote to Mrs. Lee on May 11. But that warrior never emerged for Lee or the Confederacy.[46]

Fearful that Jackson might fall into the hands of enemy raiders, Lee directed his removal to Guiney Station. Jed Hotchkiss took "a company of pioneers" to smooth the road ahead of Jackson's ambulance for the twenty-five-mile trip via Spotsylvania Court House; though he objected to officers, including his aide Captain James P. Smith and McGuire, accompanying him because of his strictness about men leaving their post to attend the wounded, Lee overrode him and ordered the entourage to proceed. "The rough teamsters sometimes refused to move their loaded wagons out of the way for an ambulance, until told that it contained Jackson, and then, with all possible speed, they gave way, and stood with their hats off, and weeping, as he went by," records Anna Jackson. At Spotsylvania Court House, he was greeted by tearful townspeople, who "offered all the poor delicacies they had." He was conscious and hopeful upon reaching the home of Thomas C. Chandler at Guiney Station on the evening of May 4. During the previous winter, Jackson had visited in the house while the army was encamped nearby at Moss Neck; since the main house was filled with sick and wounded, he was placed in an outbuilding used by the family son, Dr. Joseph Chandler, as a physician's office. He stayed there under the constant attention of McGuire until his death six days later.[47]

Jackson appeared in command of his faculties following the bonejarring ride to Chandler's place; McGuire and his colleagues found no reason for immediate alarm. The wounded soldier asked an attendant if he knew where the Scriptures offered guidance to officers for writing their battle reports. When a bemused young captain said no, Jackson told him to look at Joshua's battle with the Amalekites: "It was clearness, brevity, fairness, modesty, and it traces the victory to the right source— the blessing of God." The Almighty and things religious in fact were never far from his mind throughout his suffering. Once he engaged Captain Smith in a discussion about the location "of the headquarters of Christianity after the crucifixion." Smith, a theological student before the war, suggested several likely spots—Antioch, Iconium, Rome, Alexandria. Uncomfortable though he was, Jackson implored his aide to find a map and "show me precisely where Iconium was."[48]

Meanwhile, Lee and Stuart—the latter's troops charged into battle with yells of "Remember Jackson"—renewed the fight with Hooker on May 3. But the Chancellorsville campaign became anticlimactic after Jackson had done his work in the Wilderness. Although Hooker became "hopelessly confused" during the last phases of the fight, he ordered Sedgwick to recross the Rappahannock on May 3, while he took a defensive position around Chancellorsville. Ever cautious, Sedgwick managed to dislodge Early's troops from Marye's Heights for a brief time. But the triumph was short-lived because Lee completed his "masterpiece" by leaving Stuart only twenty-five thousand men to confront Hooker and marching east along the Plank Road to relieve Early. In spite of a sharp little fight around Salem Church, the combined forces of Lee and Old Jube had driven the federals north of the Rappahannock by May 6.

After Jackson's flanking movement, "Hooker became very despondent," notes Darius N. Couch, commander of his Second Corps. "I think his being outgeneraled by Lee had a good deal to do with his depression." And Hooker's discomfort was compounded by a cannon shot that struck his headquarters in the Chancellor House; though stunned and knocked to the ground, he was able to mount his horse and ride to safety. By nightfall, Fighting Joe had withdrawn to a new position between Chancellorsville and the Rappahannock. Following a hurried conference with his commanders, he signaled a general retreat across the United States Ford to join Sedgwick, which ended the Battle of Chancellorsville. Masterpiece that it was for Confederate arms, and though Hooker had been trounced, the federals were still on the Rappahannock miles inside southern territory.[49]

About the time Hooker withdrew to his old campgrounds opposite Fredericksburg, Anna Jackson and her child reached Guiney Station on Thursday, May 7, after a torturous journey. What she encountered was heartrending; Jackson had contracted pneumonia—probably induced by an injury to his lung after his fall from a battlefield litter that greatly aggravated his already precarious condition. "When he left me on the morning of the 29th, going forth so cheerfully and bravely to the call of duty, he was in the full flesh of vigorous manhood, and during that last, blessed visit, I never saw him look so handsome, so happy, and so noble. *Now*, his fearful wounds, his mutilated arm, the scratches upon his face, and, above all, the desperate pneumonia, which was flushing his cheeks, oppressing his breathing, and benumbing his senses, wrung my soul with such grief and anguish as it had never before experienced." Anna Jackson did not leave his side until the end, except to nurse her infant.

Jackson was patently a sick man. Two physicians, Drs. David Tucker and S. B. Morrison, were brought from Richmond to consult with McGuire. Although "morphia," which had been administered to help him rest, caused lapses into semiconsciousness, Jackson recognized Morrison, a kinsman of his wife. "As Dr. Morrison was examining the patient, he looked up pleasantly at him and said, 'that's a familiar face.' " Anna read to him, sang hymns, and tried to comfort his last hours; as they talked, he expressed a desire to be buried in Lexington near the VMI campus. He told his wife that she was "much loved," and when Anna asked what she should do after his death, he told her to return to her father's North Carolina home.

Saturday afternoon, May 9, he asked to see the Reverend Lacy, and though his "respiration was now very difficult," he could not be dissuaded from the visit. Soldier and chaplain talked about the need for Sabbath observance among the troops. Lacy wanted to remain in the sickroom as the end approached, but Jackson declined his offer; the chaplain should proceed with his customary Sunday sermons. Again, according to Anna, "when Major (Sandie) Pendelton came to his bedside about noon he inquired of him, 'who is preaching at headquarters today?!' When told that Mr. Lacy was, and that the whole army was praying for him, he said, 'thank God; they are very kind.' " At headquarters that Sunday morning, Lee, of course, asked Lacy about Jackson. Lacy replied that death was imminent. "Surely General Jackson must recover. God will not take him from us, now that we need him so much. Surely he will be spared to us, in answer to the many prayers which are offered for him." Lee sent a special message of fidelity to Guiney Station, and though he did not visit his comrade, observers noted that Lee's "voice became choked with emotion, and that he turned away to hide his intense feeling."

The ravages of pneumonia caused the doctors to tell Jackson on Sunday morning that he would not recover—about the same time Lacy was delivering the sermon that Jackson would surely have attended under better circumstances. With Christian resolve, he told McGuire, "I will be the infinite gainer to be transplanted."* "He sank rapidly," Anna wrote in a September 1864 letter to Sister Laura at Beverly: "Just before 4 o'clock, his blessed spirit was with the Saviour he so loved while on

---

* Anna, in her 1864 letter says, "transplanted"; in her *Memoirs*, it's "translated."

earth. He looked so *noble* in death, so *natural*, so *beautiful*, I could have gazed on his face forever!" The distraught wife retrieved a lock of hair for Laura. Captain William Snow sets the time of death at 3:30, Sunday, May 10; though accounts differ on the exact moment, they agree on his last feverish words. "Very good! Very good! It is alright," he told Anna. Then, "Tell A. P. Hill to prepare for action." And the final, most famous, "Let us cross over the river and rest under the shade of the trees." Thomas Jonathan Jackson was dead at three months and nineteen days past his thirty-ninth birthday.[50]

"That evening the news went abroad," writes Kyd Douglas, "and a great sob swept over the Army of Northern Virginia; it was the heartbreak of the Confederacy." Lee, who did not visit the dying man nor did he attend his funeral, notified Secretary of War Seddon of the death on Sunday evening: It was his "melancholy duty," Lee said, and he asked that an "escort of honor" meet the body in Richmond. The following day, he issued General Orders No. 61, announcing Jackson's death to the army: "The daring, skill and energy of this great and good soldier, by decree of an all wise Providence, are now lost to us. . . . Let his name be a watchword to his corps, who have followed him to victory on so many fields. Let officers and soldiers emulate his invincible determination to do everything in the defense of our beloved country."[51]

Lee did not follow the Jackson cortege to Richmond because of a continued federal threat. All participants in the Chancellorsville campaign agree that the commanding general was both shaken and magnanimous toward the fallen hero. Colonel Charles Marshall, one of Lee's aides, said he could "never forget the pain and anguish that passed over his face" when told of the wounding. All the more so as Marshall looked on while Lee read Jackson's dispatch congratulating him on "the great victory" at Chancellorsville without mention of his own troubles. And Kyd Douglas says Jackson was dying from the first moment.

At the invitation of Governor Letcher, the body lay in state at the governor's mansion. On Tuesday, May 12, "an immense military and civic pageant," proceeded to the capitol building; the first men of the Confederacy were there to pay their respects to the popular Jackson, including Jefferson Davis and the entire cabinet. Old Jack's fellow officers—Generals Longstreet, Ewell, Elzey, Winder, Garnett, Kemper, and Corse, and Commodore French Forrest—acted as official pallbearers. The body was interred on May 15 at Lexington in the Valley of Virginia that Jackson loved so dearly. The military loss to Lee and the Confederacy almost defies analysis—the partnership born at Richmond in April 1861, when Jackson marched his VMI cadets into Camp Lee—

was now shattered. Lee would never find another lieutenant to carry Jackson's load. Jackson was popular in every part of the southern nation—his bold exploits, his fast marches with the foot cavalry, and his stout nickname gained on the field at Manassas had seized the public imagination. Jefferson Davis telegraphed that spirit to Lee on May 11 as Jackson's body made its way to Richmond: "A national calamity has befallen us," the president said.[52]

16

An Epilogue: Without
Jackson

Although Robert E. Lee could become teary eyed, and on occasion
maudlin, when discussing religious matters, he consistently kept an
outward calm during the war. Even the setbacks at Gettysburg and
Appomattox did not disrupt his soldierly demeanor; nevertheless, he
became visibly disturbed upon hearing of Jackson's death in May 1863
and that of his daughter Annie seven months earlier. That Lee's composure slipped over the loss of his trusted right arm was entirely understandable, because Jackson was not only his faithful lieutenant but also
his friend. Perhaps it was impossible for him to separate the two emo-
tions following his unflinching reliance upon Jackson's willingness to
undertake any assignment and to do so without questioning his motives.
"From the opportunities I had to form a conception of the character of
General Jackson I was convinced that he deserved all of the great confidence in which he was held by General Lee, and that was a high honor
for anyone," Lafayette McLaws penned after the war. "There was no
other such character in our army, for in addition to the qualities I have
stated, in which he stood eminent, he had a sublime faith in the justice of
our cause, and often acted as if he was, on special and desperate occasions, asking for God's aid for success." What more could Lee demand
from any man than a blind obedience to the Confederate nation. And
though he sought other men to replace the "indomitable Jackson," such
men were never found. [1]

Lee, who died in October 1870, lived another seven years after Jackson's death; when he passed away at age sixty-three, he had lived twenty-
four years longer than his valued helpmate. The elder general said little

about Jackson in his latter years, but when he did mention his contribution to the Confederacy, it was always with feeling. When a lady correspondent asked him for authentic information concerning Jackson's war record, he referred her to Dabney's great biography of 1866 as the best source. In an October 1867 letter to Dr. A. T. Bledsoe, editor of the *Southern Review* in Baltimore, Lee spoke out on Jackson the soldier after the journal published a delayed account of Chancellorsville. "I have learned from others that the various authors of the life of Jackson award to him the credit of the success gained by the Army of Northern Virginia when he was present, and describe the movement of his corps or command as independent of the general plan of operations and undertaken at his own suggestion and upon his own responsibility." Although Lee had not read the piece, he heaped praise upon his old comrade: "I have the greatest reluctance to do anything that might be considered detracting from his well-deserved fame, for I believe no one was more convinced of his worth or appreciated him more highly than myself; yet your knowledge of military affairs, if you have none of the events themselves, will teach you that this could not have been so. Every movement of an army must be well considered and properly ordered, and every one who knew General Jackson must know that he was too good a soldier to violate this fundamental principle." Complimentary though he was of Jackson's war record, Lee nonetheless made it clear that he had been in charge. [2]

Jackson's eagerness to undertake independent orders had insured Lee's great successes throughout the battles of 1862; at Chancellorsville, he had been the supreme isolated commander. "The most general instructions were all that he ever needed," Lee said afterward. Their communications were so clear that a spoken word was often unnecessary; each instinctively knew the other's thoughts. When an excited staff officer rushed into Lee's headquarters on the eve of Chancellorsville to say Hooker was crossing the Rappahannock in force, R. E. Lee, Jr., has his father replying playfully: "Well, I heard firing, and I was beginning to think it was time some of you lazy young fellows were coming in to tell me what it was about. Say to General Jackson that he knows just as well what to do with the enemy as I do." [3]

Throughout the valley campaign, the Seven Days, when he held the Confederate left north of the James, and at the Second Manassas, when he took the van northward to Cedar Mountain and crushed John Pope at Groveton, Jackson had been at his best while operating away from the main army; it was the same story in Maryland, when he separated himself to reduce Harpers Ferry and then rejoined Lee at Antietam; on the march southward, "Longstreet's Corps and Lee's Headquarters after recrossing the Potomac had encamped close to the Martinsburg road about six miles from Winchester. Jackson had isolated the 2nd Corps as usual, which rested at Bunker Hill, six miles further north." As Lee concentrated the army in front of Fredericksburg during the winter of 1862, he posted Jackson at Guiney Station so that he could rendezvous wherever the federal army decided to span the Rappahannock; when that fight unfolded, Old Jack reacted quickly to help repulse Burnside's Grand Divisions, and at Chancellorsville in May 1863 his independent march by the Catharine Furnace Road to attack Hooker's rear has become legendary.

Little wonder that young Ham Chamberlayne wrote to his mother from Camp Davidson near Chancellorsville: "Jackson's death was a blow to us but we can spare him better now than we could have done before the battle of Kernstown." And a "Federal Soldier," identified as M. Quad, summarizes Jackson's battles through the Maryland campaign: "Without him Longstreet and Hill would have been pressed back, routed, annihilated." But it was Jackson's British biographer, G.F.R. Henderson, who best recounts his great penchant for autonomous service. "Throughout the whole of his soldier's life he was never entrusted with any detached mission which he failed to execute with complete success," he wrote in Anna Jackson's 1895 *Memoir*.[4]

Lee was forced to begin an immediate search for someone to replace his fallen lieutenant. Jeb Stuart was placed in temporary command of the Second Corps on the field at Chancellorsville, but it was soon apparent that without Old Jack the Army of Northern Virginia required a complete reorganization. Jackson had endorsed Stuart from his deathbed, but the great cavalryman, while he knew about fighting on horseback, had little experience with Lee's grey lines. An infantryman was needed! In the reorganization of May–June 1863—before the army headed north without Jackson, Lee embraced Richard Stoddart Ewell, who had returned from his wounds at Groveton "with a peg leg and a pretty new wife."

Instead of the two corps under Longstreet and Jackson, Lee divided his seventy-three thousand–man force into three, generaled by Longstreet, A. P. Hill, and Ewell. Already disappointed at finding a fit substitute for Old Jack, he created a new Third Corps under Hill, "made up of parts of the First and Second." But the new scheme was in trouble from the beginning because the ever-quarrelsome Longstreet felt himself slighted. Old Pete thought that he was the man of the hour following Jackson's death, and he even conferred with Secretary of War Seddon on how best to proceed. "Too much Virginia," Longstreet wrote in his memoirs about the new army structure.[5]

"I grieve much over the death of General Jackson," Lee told John Bell Hood as he took the army into Pennsylvania a scant seven weeks after Old Jack's funeral; and, "I agree with you in believing that our army would be invincible if it could be properly organized and officered. There never were such men [as Jackson] in the army before." Lee's misgivings were soon put to the test when he was forced into combat at Gettysburg without Jackson's steadying influence. When the great battle opened on July 1, Ewell, at the head of Jackson's old command, initially drove Meade's army eastward to the famed Cemetery Ridge; but there he hesitated, although Lee had ordered him to attack "if possible." Ewell's defeatism at dusk on the first day at Gettysburg remains an imponderable of the entire war as he allowed the federals a respite to reinforce their already formidable positions. Lafayette McLaws, himself a participant in the fight, was convinced that had Jackson been beside Lee "when the enemy were in full retreat and in confusion upon the hill and ridge on which the battles of July 2 occurred, there would have been no delay in the onward march of his then victorious troops."[6]

Neither Longstreet nor Ewell had any stomach for charging the federal lines on Cemetery Ridge and the Round Tops when the battle reopened on July 3. Old Pete's recalcitrance at Gettysburg probably cost Lee a great victory, notwithstanding the awesome fighting at places immortalized in the American saga—Devil's Den, Peach Orchard, Wheat Field, Culp's Hill. "Jackson would not have hesitated," McLaws argues, "when he saw the chance of success offered by the evident confusion of the retreating foe, but would have gone forward, with his characteristic dash and daring, and these important positions would have doubtless been ours."

On that fateful third day—the high-water mark of the southern war effort—when George Pickett led the disastrous charge against Meade's entrenched federals atop Cemetery Hill, a bullheaded Longstreet did not move as ordered. Although Longstreet spent years trying to justify his behavior on July 3, 1863, William Nelson Pendleton, who later preached Lee's funeral, remains adamant that Old Pete had simply ignored his instructions throughout the Gettysburg fight! The tragedy of July 3 was complete when Pickett lost seventy-five hundred men in less than an hour and forced Lee to summon a general retreat into Virginia; stoical under every military circumstance, Lee kept his counsel about the failures of Longstreet and Ewell. "It was my fault," he said. But McLaws says flat-out that the events of July 3 "would never have occurred" had Jackson been there. "Jackson was needed," offers Douglas Southall Freeman, but Lee's anguish is best captured by J. William Jones, the

Baptist minister who knew him during the post-Appomattox years: "I had the privilege of hearing General Lee, in his office at Lexington, pronounce a glowing eulogy on Jackson, in which he said with far more than his accustomed warmth and feeling. 'He never failed me. Why, if I had had Stonewall Jackson at Gettysburg I should have won that battle, and if I had won a decided victory there we would have established the independence of the Confederacy.' " Lee clearly suggested that Old Jack would not have dissuaded the attack on Meade but would have carried the day by obeying his instructions.[7]

Lee was a beaten man after Gettysburg, yet he managed to fight on for another twenty-two months. "God's will be done," he wrote, as he faced an uncertain future without Jackson. In early August 1863, Lee, in a lengthy letter to Jefferson Davis, offered to resign because of the Pennsylvania defeat. Rumors and strong talk about the campaign raced through the army, and when several southern newspapers joined the clamor, he confessed that he did not know how far the discontent reached into the ranks. Lee had thought himself invincible with Jackson at his side, and now his army lay in shambles. "The general remedy for the want of success in a military commander is his removal," he informed the president: ". . . I, therefore, in all sincerity, request your Excellency to take measures to supply my place. I do this with the more earnestness, because no one is more aware than myself of my inability to discharge the duties of my position. I cannot even accomplish what I myself desire. How can I fulfill the expectations of others?"

Davis replied six days later, and, understandably, rejected his pleas about being unpopular in the army; he also lamented Lee's poor health and wished him a quick recovery from "the lingering effects of the illness you suffered last spring." The resignation letter had complained of an increasing physical discomfort, which suggests additional heart difficulties: "I sensibly feel the growing failure of my bodily strength. . . . I am becoming more and more incapable of exertion, and thus prevented from making the personal examination, and giving the personal supervision to the operations which I feel to be necessary." Lee also mentioned his failing eyesight and said he had to rely upon others to make battlefield decisions. Although he lived another seven years, there can be no doubt that the near-constant angina during his Lexington years originated from the attack suffered at Fredericksburg during the winter of 1862–1863.[8]

No significant operations developed until the following spring, although a nasty little fight took place in late November–early December 1863 at Mine Run, a tributary of the Rapidan, where Lee lay encamped with the Army of Northern Virginia. Gordon Meade was searching for a path around the Confederate entrenchments in the wilderness, a tangled mass of second growth south of the river, before he was hurled back by Lee's tattered and now-thinning force. Two years of constant warfare without any hope of resupply or reinforcement was already taking its toll upon southern fighting élan, but Abraham Lincoln's appointment of Ulysses S. Grant to command all Union forces in March 1864 presented Lee with a new sort of adversary for the remainder of the war. Always before, the Yankee generals had halted after a major fight, which afforded Lee time to regroup and replenish his veterans. But not so with this new general from the west—the victor of Forts Donelson and Henry, Shiloh, Vicksburg, and, most recently, Chattanooga. Grant pursued him over the next months with a bulldog determination that gave the Army of Northern Virginia no rest.

Grant rightly perceived that his main obstacle was Lee's army beyond the Rapidan-Rappahannock line, and it was here that he assumed personal charge. At the same time he undertook his campaign to capture Richmond, Benjamin F. Butler, a political general and sometime politician from Massachusetts, was ordered to march toward the prize from Fortress Monroe; German-born Franz Sigel was sent up the Shenandoah Valley and told to wreck Lee's breadbasket; and, "Little Phil" Sheridan was dispatched on a cavalry thrust at Richmond itself, which ended in the death of Jeb Stuart in the scrap at Yellow Tavern a few miles north of the Confederate capital. Not content with this multipronged attack, Grant summoned his compatriot William Tecumseh Sherman to march through Georgia, where he fought Joe Johnston and later John Bell Hood to a standstill. Sherman's capture of Atlanta, immortalized in Margaret Mitchell's *Gone With the Wind,* and his subsequent march to Savannah drove home the horrors of Civil War. As Lee faced his pursuers, writes Robert Selph Henry, "he knew what his soldiers did not— that Grant, determined and tenacious, had the whole immense resources of the United States and the entire confidence of that government at his command; and that this time there was to be no letting go, no giving up, no going back."9

Although Lee prepared to face the onslaught with every available resource, he has met considerable criticism over the years for concentrating on Virginia and neglecting other parts of the Confederacy. Whatever his thoughts about other theaters of war, Lee could do little to supply other southern armies prior to the spring of 1865, when he was made overall commander, and then it was too late to help even himself. "In truth, Lee seems to have been less than fully responsive to the problems of the west, partly out of Virginia parochialism—he always regarded his sword as first serving his state of Virginia—and partly in adherence to his military philosophy," notes a modern scholar. "The vast expanses of the Mississippi Valley did not afford opportunity for the limited manpower of the Confederate armies to mount an offensive which could hope for decisive effects." Beyond that, any disposition of troops in some grand strategy was essentially a political decision that President Davis was hesitant to relinquish. The main battlefield in the minds of Lee and Davis was Virginia, because each knew instinctively that Confederate fortunes hinged upon a successful defense of the Old Dominion. If Virginia fell, then the entire southern war effort fell with it.

Lee was probably correct that the west could not be defended with the resources at hand. When Grant plunged headlong through Tennessee and Mississippi during 1862–1863, he told the president that he had no spare units for strapped commanders in the west. Lee did send Longstreet into southwestern Virginia and other forces into North Carolina, but he did so to protect his railroad links between Richmond and the lower South. Although some of his maneuvers appeared offensive in nature, Lee was forced to concentrate first and last on Virginia. In short, he was too preoccupied with his own Army of Northern Virginia to worry about the west.[10]

Davis as political overseer certainly acquiesced in Lee's stubborn defense of Virginia, which led to some uneasy moments as Sherman drove his armies into the southern heartland during 1864. Georgia governor Joseph E. Brown resisted Confederate conscription laws because his men were needed at home and threatened to make a separate peace for his state when additional aid was not forthcoming to repel the invaders. Lee was far too busy on the battlefield to worry about a tiff between the president and a governor, although he remained adamant that the enemy lay in northern Virginia. But Brown's recalcitrance throughout 1863–1865 both weakened southern resolve to pursue the war and deprived the Army of Northern Virginia of men and supplies. The Georgian was a constitutional purist who thought Davis and his Richmond bureaucrats formed a conspiracy to deprive the people and the state of their rights. "Among the more prominent military commanders, he had praise for only Lee, Beauregard, and Johnston," says his biographer. Ironically, Brown thought Lee could have won had Davis not overruled his tactical decisions.[11]

Meanwhile, the one-sided fight to capture Richmond started May 4, 1864, when Grant urged his 102,000-man army across the Rapidan to confront Lee's sixty-four thousand, and while Lee and the South could expect no succor, the federal force was soon increased by another sixteen thousand. He was not only outnumbered two-to-one, but Lee was still a sick man. "I want all of the help I can get now," he wrote to Custis on April 9. "I feel a marked change in my strength since my attack last spring at Fredericksburg, and am less competent for my duty than ever before." For all of his difficulties, Lee was nothing short of brilliant in the campaign of attrition that followed. But the Wilderness fighting of May 5-6 over part of the old Chancellorsville battlefield took a heavy toll, as Longstreet fell wounded with a bullet through the throat and shoulder. Although he recovered, Old Pete, despite his faults, was lost to Lee for the remainder of 1864. First Jackson, now Longstreet, wounded, and Stuart killed at Yellow Tavern on May 11! When Richard H. Anderson was put in Longstreet's place, Lee found himself fighting with a new cadre of subordinate commanders.

In the brutal combat along the Rapidan, Lee himself was nearly captured on May 9 at the widow Tapp's farmhouse, while sitting under a tree with A. P. Hill and Jeb Stuart. Luckily, the bewildered federal officer in charge of a small troop did not recognize his quarry and withdrew quickly upon learning that he had blundered into the Confederate lines. And Lee, caught up in the excitement of battle, had to be sent to safety with the cry, "General Lee to the rear!" as he sought to lead John Gregg's command into the fray. The wilderness ended with tremendous losses on both sides, as men stumbled across unburied skeletons from the Chancellorsville fighting; the ghost of Jackson seemed near, as Lee's troopers lay on their arms unable to sleep because of smoldering underbrush set ablaze during the battle.[12]

Grant did not retreat but kept moving to Lee's right—"sidling" on the drive to Richmond. By May 8, his columns were clustered about the crossroads at Spotsylvania Court House, which forced Lee to move south in pursuit. The battle or siege at Spotsylvania, which lasted from May 7 through May 20, witnessed an evolution in trench warfare that prefigured World War I when Lee dug in to protect himself against Grant's superior numbers. Attack after attack upon a salient in the Confederate entrenchments known as the Mule Shoe or Bloody Angle failed to crush Lee's army in spite of Grant's famous telegram to Lincoln that he intended "to fight it out on this line if it takes all summer."

Both armies suffered unbelievably high losses at Spotsylvania. Besides the tremendous casualty rate, General John Sedgwick was shot dead by a Confederate sniper on May 7, and Lee himself was exposed to real danger for the first time in the war. Traveller reared after becoming frightened and pawed the air when a shot passed under his belly, almost hitting Lee's stirrup. After Grant's furious assault at the Bloody Angle, in which Winfield Scott Hancock took two thousand prisoners and twenty cannon, Lee and Ewell were able to hold their own, although the famed Stonewall Brigade was captured almost to the man. Once Grant found it impossible to go through his Confederate foe, he merely sidled again on the night of May 20 and continued the march on Richmond.[13]

When Grant reached the North Anna on the morning of May 23, in the words of Fitzhugh Lee, "he found Lee there too." But without Jackson, there was no lieutenant ready for a separate action against the federal flanks; Lee was forced to concentrate his force without Old Jack or Stuart to undertake a detached action. Although an attack was launched by the Union hordes, Grant called off the fight because he did not like the odds and continued his southward march. Lee had hoped to blunt his opponent's momentum but fell sick during the North Anna stalemate, perhaps even lapsing into a feverish delirium; Colonel Charles S. Venable, his aide-de-camp, has him repeating over and over: "We must strike them. We must not let them pass again!" While he kept a watchful eye on Grant at Hanover Junction (or North Anna), he had recovered sufficiently to dash off a letter to Mrs. Lee: "I begrudge every step he takes toward Richmond."[14]

But the Yankee Goliath again marched by the right to reach Cold Harbor on the old Seven Days battlefield by the morning of May 31. Not far from the place where Jackson had held Lee's northern flank at Gaines Mill two years earlier, the two armies clashed near a now-famous tavern that served no warm food. Again Lee was entrenched and ready for one of the bloodiest spectacles of the war; this time, the southern ranks had been swelled by several thousand reinforcements, including the command of John C. Breckinridge, which had recently defeated Sigel's army at New Market in the Shenandoah Valley. At Cold Harbor on the morning of June 3, writes Lee's nephew, "nearly all of the one hundred and thirteen thousand troops, in double lines of battle six miles long, sprang to arms at half-past four in the morning, and, in obedience to the customary order 'to attack along the whole line,' assailed the army of Lee and were terribly slaughtered at every point."

Grant's assault was finally canceled when thirteen thousand Union troopers lay dead or dying. Northern soldiers pinned names and addresses on their coats in anticipation of another charge, but Grant said no. The cost was too great. He even wrote in his postwar memoir that he regretted the huge loss of life. When the Cold Harbor affray died down, it was discovered that Grant had lost fifty thousand men and Lee thirty-two thousand in the month of constant maneuvering. That was 41 percent of the Army of the Potomac and 46 percent of all Confederate forces operating in Virginia; for Lee, these were men who could not be replaced by a manpower-starved South. "I have only one earthly want, that God in his infinite mercy will send our enemies back to their homes," he wrote to Custis a few weeks later. [15]

After Cold Harbor, Lee's military situation became desperate, if not sad; he was now threatened anew as Grant crossed the James to a position south of Richmond. Although Longstreet rejoined the army in October during the siege of Petersburg, Colonel Walter Taylor, Lee's aide-de-camp, thought the absence of Jackson had compounded Lee's troubles throughout the Wilderness campaign. "I only wish the general had good lieutenants," he writes. Both armies soon commenced to entrench south and east of Petersburg until parallel lines extended more than twenty-five miles around the city. Grant now intended to move on Richmond from the south, but his army which had been fighting by day and marching by night for a month was in need of rest.

As he worked to fortify his position opposite Lee's interior lines, Grant approved a questionable scheme to permit a group of Pennsylvania coal miners to dig a tunnel across no-man's-land to a point under the Confederate lines. Once packed with powder, the giant mine exploded in the early hours of July 30, hurling several Confederate companies into the air and leaving the renowned "Crater," which measured "one hundred and seventy feet long, sixty feet wide, and thirty feet deep" in the midst of Lee, entrenchments. As federal troops rushed into the "hole" before "Little Billy" Mahone drove them back, casualties reached thirty-eight hundred for Grant to Lee's twelve hundred. Grant labeled the incident "a stupendous failure," and after the excitement died down, the impasse became a series of thrusts and counterthrusts for the remainder of the year. In reality, observes historian Allan Nevins, it was "not a true siege for the town was never invested, but a beleaguerment, resembling that of Stalingrad in the Second World War." Lee fought his war of attrition until the spring of 1865, when Grant's greater numbers forced him to abandon Petersburg and thus Richmond itself. Throughout the last months of 1864, however, the incessant attention to military detail began to affect Lee. "But what care can a man give to himself in time of war," he asked Mrs. Lee on September 18: "It is from no desire of exposure or hazard that I live in a tent, but from necessity. I must be where I can speedily attend to the duties of my position, and be near or accessible to the officers with whom I have to act. I have been offered rooms in the houses of our citizens, but I could not turn the dwellings of my kind hosts into a barrack, where officers, couriers, distressed women, etc., would be entering day and night." [16]

The Congress made Lee commander in chief of all Confederate armies in January 1865, largely because of growing discontent with the president's war policies; when Davis urged him to undertake a last effort to break the siege, he directed General John B. Gordon to capture a fortified place in the federal lines called Fort Stedman, not far from the Appomattox River. Although Gordon carried Stedman and several smaller forts on March 25 with a loss of thirty-five hundred men including nineteen hundred captured, it proved a temporary gain in the great game of upsmanship with Grant. After his last battle at Five Forks with even heavier losses on April 1, Lee was forced to leave the trenches and start his march westward along the Appomattox, with the illusory hope of joining his old comrade Joe Johnston in North Carolina. As he prodded his hungry band from Petersburg, word arrived that A. P. Hill lay dead with a bullet through the heart—shot down by a band of Union stragglers. Those present said a tear welled in Lee's eyes when he heard the news: "He is at rest, and we who are left are the ones to suffer." One can only imagine what foreboding rushed over Lee when he received the news at the same time that the Army of Northern Virginia lay dying itself. As Jefferson Davis collected the Confederate archives and what remained of the treasury before leaving a burning Richmond for the safety of the Carolinas, Abraham Lincoln arrived to sit with Grant "on the Petersburg Court House steps." Lee's army, reduced to a mere thirty thousand from desertions and lack of food, put up what resistance it could to the constant sniping by Sheridan's cavalrymen. Finally, in response to earlier offers to end the one-sided struggle, he dispatched his own message to Grant's headquarters: "Received your note this morning with reference to the surrender of this army. I now request an interview in accordance with that purpose."[17]

With that communiqué, Lee ended the foremost military career in the American saga—a career that had been reinforced in large measure by the devoted generalship of Thomas Jonathan Jackson. Others had helped, including Longstreet, who stayed with Lee to the end, but it was the "indomitable Stonewall" who abetted the great victories of 1861–1862; after Chancellorsville, there had been no further triumphs, only destruction and a winding down of the Confederate military machine. The record is silent whether Lee thought of his fallen comrade while riding to the famed interlude with Ulysses S. Grant in Wilmer McLean's living room in Appomattox.

As he left on April 9, "wearing a new uniform with embroidered belt and new gauntlets, high boots with red silk stitchings at the top and gold spurs at the heels, a sash and a gilded presentation sword whose hilt was formed in the head of a lion," he uttered a few words to General Pendleton, his artilleryman; Lee was not certain what faced him—he even thought that he might become Grant's prisoner. Fortunately, it never came to that. After the preliminary greetings—they had not met since Mexico—Grant dictated his terms: "Officers and men of Lee's command were to be released on giving their paroles not to take up arms against the United States until exchanged; arms, artillery, and public property were to be turned over." The private horses and baggage of the officers were not included in the order, nor their side arms. All accounts say that Lee was visibly moved by Grant's leniency, especially when he allowed private soldiers to keep their horses and mules so they might "work their little farms." The administration was magnanimous in victory, and as a sign of healing, Lee neither offered his sword nor did Grant ask for it. Defeat for the Confederacy did not imply humiliation for its military chieftain.[18]

The work with Grant done, Lee received his veterans one last time, finished some details of the surrender, and mounted Traveller for the ride into Richmond to rejoin his wife and daughters. A black trooper had been posted at her front door to guard against intruders; whether his presence was intentional or not, it symbolized what the great struggle had been about. Lee, the man who had opposed slavery and a dissolution of the Union, and who "displayed every art by which genius and courage can make good the lack of numbers and resources" during four years of warfare, like his countrymen North and South, faced a changed world. The titanic effort to preserve the Old South, the South of magnolia-scented plantations and mint juleps, had ended in failure; different men from the North meant to create a social revolution that would raise former slaves to positions of responsible citizenship. But that social realignment lay with the era that followed Appomattox; in retrospect, Lincoln and the administration had to await the destruction of Robert E. Lee and the Army of Northern Virginia before proceeding with a new social agenda. Military matters had to be reconciled first.

Richmond was a city in shambles when Lee reached the Franklin Street house that had been loaned to his family by a wealthy Scottish philanthropist; Lee in fact was broke and without assets after confiscation of his Washington and Arlington properties because of unpaid taxes. Food and daily sustenance became a dilemma for the family in those first weeks after Appomattox. Yet Lee made several crucial decisions that influenced the remainder of his life; first, he resolved to stay in Virginia and to cast his fortunes with the state of his birth at the same time other Confederate leaders were seeking greener pastures in the West or abroad. He also sought a pardon for his wartime activities from the Lincoln administration, thereby setting a good example for other Confederates to peacefully accept the authority of a united country.

Unable to find respite from an avalanche of callers and well-wishers in Richmond, he wrote General Long during May 1865: "I am looking for some quiet little house in the woods where I can procure shelter and my daily bread if permitted by the victor. I wish to get Mrs. Lee out of the city as soon as possible." His hopes materialized when friends arranged the use of Derwent, a modest two-story house on the Cumberland County plantation of Mrs. Randolph Cocke, about thirty-five miles west of Richmond. Located near Cartersville on the Powhatan County line, the home had the advantage that Mrs. Lee, now invalided, could reach it by boat on the James River and Kanawha Canal. Here, in comparative quiet, Lee was able to rest, collect his thoughts, and sort through numerous offers of position until August 1865, when he accepted the presidency of Washington College.[19]

When the unsolicited invitation to Lexington was carried to Derwent by Judge John W. Brockenbrough, college rector, Lee's response indicated that his health remained a problem: "The proper education of youth requires not only great ability, but, I fear, more strength than I now possess, for I do not feel able to undergo the labor of conducting classes in the regular course of instruction. I could not therefore undertake more than a general administration and supervision of the institution," he told college officials. "Oh! what a change in his appearance," writes Channing Smith, one of Mosby's cavalrymen, who saw him briefly before he left Richmond. "The last time I saw him he was in the fullest glory of his splendid manhood, and now pale and wan with the sorrow of blighted hopes." Yet, Lord Wolseley, later commander in chief of the British army, found him the perfect gentleman during those trying days after Appomattox: "I was seated in his parlor on Franklin Street, Richmond, talking with his daughter when the general entered the room. Never can I forget his gentle manner as he extended his hand, and put me at my ease with a few cordial words of welcome. . . ."

School trustees quickly relieved him of any teaching or instructional obligations, so that he could assume the respected duties of a college president. When he reached Lexington on September 18, 1865, astride Traveller—they were still fast companions—Lee would live his remaining four and one-half years in the proximity of Stonewall Jackson's legacy. Although some have encouraged the notion that he was drawn to Lexington because of Jackson, his correspondence suggests that he came because he needed a job and that he rejected all offers of unearned emolument. Even so, the fact remains that Jackson not only taught at adjoining VMI, but he also lay buried near both campuses. An artist named A. J. Volck even produced a widely distributed lithograph, "Lee Kneeling at the Grave of Jackson," although right reason would indicate that Lee was far too concerned with college matters and daily living to brood over the glory days of 1861–1863 with Jackson at his side.[20]

Stonewall Jackson's home on Washington Street during his VMI days sat just around the corner from Lee's new college office. And Jackson undoubtedly walked through the Washington College campus on his daily trips to the lecture room. The Lee-Jackson relationship was cemented further when Lee brought his family to live in a home once occupied by Old Jack. "This was the 'Old President's House,' in which General Lee lived for several years before the present President's House was erected," writes Washington and Lee professor Franklin L. Riley. It was the same residence where Jackson had lived with his first wife, Elie Junkin, in the home of her father, Dr. George Junkin, president of the college and one of Lee's predecessors. "But whether in the old or new house, the home of General Lee was always open to the students; and whatever awe 'the President' may have inspired, Mrs. Lee and her accomplished daughters were able to make even the most diffident forget their embarrassment."[21]

Lee spent the Lexington years guarding his student charges and overseeing a significant growth of the college. "The faculty before Lee's accession to the presidency, had consisted of five men, the president, who taught moral philosophy, and four professors, teaching Latin, Greek, mathematics, and chemistry and natural philosophy," Riley records. "The number of students had been less than one hundred. During the five years of General Lee's presidency the number of professors was more than trebled; the number of students was quadrupled, and the endowment of the institution was increased many fold." According to John Esten Cooke, he only appeared in public "two or three times," including his testimony at hearings in Richmond concerning a possible treason trial for Jefferson Davis; he was also summoned before the notorious Congressional Committee on Reconstruction during March 1866 to share his views on a variety of issues facing the South. After being questioned at length about the loyalty of former secessionists in the event of a foreign war, he was asked about the welfare of southern blacks, whom he said were capable of being educated. Lee had expressed a somewhat different view when visiting his cousin, Thomas H. Carter, the previous year. "I have always observed that wherever you find the Negro, everything is going down around him, and wherever you find the white man you see things around him improving!" And when asked if he had ever taken an oath of fidelity to the Confederate government, like much of his congressional testimony, Lee gave a qualified and evasive answer. "I do not recollect having done so, but it is possible that when I was commissioned I did; I do not recollect whether it was required; if it was required, I took it, or if it had been required I would have taken it; but I do not recollect whether it was or not."[22]

His hesitancy to appear in public led him to reject the governorship in 1867 because "it would be injurious to Virginia." Lee also engaged in considerable letter writing to secure funds for the college; although he decided not to write his own account of the war, he never forgot his famous companion in arms. "It is pleasant as well as profitable to contemplate his character, to recall his patriotism, his piety, and his unselfish nature," he wrote an admirer in 1866 about Jackson. "The early instructions of his mother, who he seems never to have forgotten, may have had great influence in shaping his course through life." And, two years later, when a correspondent sent an overcoat belonging to Jackson, Lee dispatched it immediately to Mrs. Jackson, still living in North Carolina: "It has appeared to me most proper that this relic of your husband, though painfully recalling his death, should be possessed by you, and I take pleasure in transmitting it to you." Lee also conveyed his "warmest admiration and regard for her great and good husband."[23]

Occasional trips to the White Sulphur Springs in West Virginia and visits with numerous cousins around the state followed. In May 1869, Lee called at the White House at Grant's urging, but the famous encounter did not go well, with Lee appearing awkward and reticent to speak. When Grant had learned that his old adversary was in Baltimore to help a group of Shenandoah civic leaders bring a railroad through Lexington, the president extended a purely social invitation. "You and I, General, have more to do with destroying railroads than building them," Grant had gestured, but notes one biographer, "Lee was not amused." Increasingly poor health may have influenced the disappointing session, because Lee was now having extreme difficulty; "I perceive no change in the stricture in my chest. If I attempt to walk beyond a slow gait, the pain is always there," he wrote to Mrs. Lee in the spring of 1870, while on a tour of the south with his daughter that lasted from March until May, undertaken in the forlorn hope that it might restore his health; he called upon former Confederate associates, visited his father's grave in Georgia, and finally returned to Rooney's plantation at White House for a family reunion with his wife and grandchildren.[24]

Although the southern tour was a great triumph, Lee was wearied by the crowds of enthusiastic admirers who greeted his every turn. He was back in Lexington by May 28 and despite his efforts to maintain a brave front his basic problem had not improved. Acquaintances were saddened at his deteriorating appearance throughout the summer; finally, on Wednesday, September 28, after a full day at the college, he returned to the president's house at 3 P.M., and departed for a business session of his church vestry from 4 P.M., until later in the evening. "Lee did not return home until 7 o'clock, finding the family waiting tea for him. He started to ask a blessing, when he was smitten with the fatal disease from which he died soon after 9 o'clock on the morning of October 12."[25]

Doctors treated him for what was termed "venous congestion," according to General Long, with some initial success. "But on the afternoon of October 10 his pulse accelerated and his hurried breathing betokened a serious relapse. At midnight a chill of exhaustion supervened, and the intelligence of his critical condition was broken to the family. Through the next day he rapidly sank, and his dissolution was felt to be imminent at any hour." Lee died without struggle thirteen days after he was first stricken. In an ironic twist, he spoke of A. P. Hill during his last moments, as Jackson had done on his own deathbed seven years earlier; Lee's last words were also a throwback to former days: "Strike the tent," he called out as death approached. He was laid to rest on October 15 in a specially built vault in the Lee Chapel on the Washington College (now Washington and Lee University) campus. Today it is topped by a life-sized marble likeness by the sculptor Edward V. Valentine; less than a mile distant is the grave of Jackson, "Mighty Stonewall," under a monument bearing his erect statue by the same artist.

Lee's funeral service was conducted by Dr. William Nelson Pendleton, the artilleryist who lies buried at Lexington within a few paces of Jackson; Dr. W. S. White, pastor of the Lexington Presbyterian Church, 1848–1867, who conducted Jackson's own funeral, also spoke, as did the Reverend J. William Jones, Lee's biographer and onetime Confederate chaplain. Pendleton built his eulogy around Psalm 37, which he related to Lee's life and career:

> . . . Mark the perfect man, and behold the upright; for the end of that man is peace.
> . . . And the Lord shall help them, and deliver them; he shall deliver them from the wicked, and save them because they trust in him.[26]

Notes

CHAPTER 1

1. Clifford Dowdey, *Lee* (Boston: Little, Brown and Company, 1965), pp. 8–10; Edmund Jennings Lee, *Lee of Virginia, 1642–1892* (Philadelphia: Franklin Publishing Company, 1895), pp. 51–52.

2. Charles Royster, *Light-Horse Harry Lee and the Legacy of the American Revolution* (New York: Alfred A. Knopf, 1981), pp. 71–72; Elizabeth Cometti and Festus P. Summers, *The Thirty-Fifth State: A Documentary History of West Virginia* (Morgantown: West Virginia University Library, 1966), pp. 16–18; John W. Wayland, *Stonewall Jackson's Way: Route, Method, Achievement* (Staunton, VA: McClure Company, 1940), pp. 199–205.

3. Douglas Southall Freeman, *R. E. Lee: A Biography* (New York: Charles Scribner's Sons, 1934), I, p. 161; Henry Lee, *Memoirs of the War in the Southern Department of the United States; with a biography of the author by Robert E. Lee* (New York: University Publishing Company, 1869), pp. 15–16.

4. Robert Lewis Dabney, *Life and Campaigns of Lieut.-Gen. Thomas J. Jackson* (New York: Blelock and Company, 1866), pp. 1–8; Mary Anna Jackson, *Memoirs of Stonewall Jackson by His Widow* (Louisville, KY: Prentice Press, 1895), pp. 2–10; Frank E. Vandiver, *Mighty Stonewall* (New York: McGraw-Hill, 1957), pp. 1–14; G. F. R. Henderson, *Stonewall Jackson and the American Civil War* (London: Longmans, Green, and Company, 1906), I, pp. 4–6; Roy Bird Cook, *The Family and Early Life of Stonewall Jackson* (Charleston, WV: Educational Foundation, reprint, 1967), pp. 1–27. Other valuable Jackson ancestral material can be found in Thomas Jackson Arnold, *Early Life and Letters of General Jackson* (New York: Thomas H. Revell Company, 1916), pp. 1–49.

5. Walter P. Webb, ed., *The Handbook of Texas* (Austin: Texas State Historical Association, 1952), I, p. 452; Arnold, *Life and Letters of Jackson*, p. 24; Thomas Carey Johnson, *The Life and Letters of Robert Lewis Dabney* (Richmond: Presbyterian Committee on Publication, 1903), passim. The Jed Hotchkiss Papers in the

Library of Congress, Washington, D.C., abound with letters from Dabney describing the Virginia campaigns in great detail.

6. James G. Leyburn, *The Scotch-Irish: A Social History* (Chapel Hill: University of North Carolina Press, 1962), pp. 83–182; Charles R. Hanna, *The Scotch-Irish: Or the Scot in Britain, North Ireland, and North America* (New York: G. P. Putnam Sons, 1902), passim; Richard C. Davids, *The Man Who Loved a Mountain* (Philadelphia: Fortress Press, 1970), p. 2.

7. Anna Jackson, *Memoirs of Jackson*, pp. 2–4; Dabney, *Life and Campaigns of Jackson*, pp. 5–7.

8. Cook, *Early Life of Jackson*, pp. 11–12; Anna Jackson, *Memoirs of Jackson*, pp. 2–4.

9. Cook, *Early Life of Jackson*, pp. 13–15; Dabney, *Life and Campaigns of Jackson*, p. 8.

10. U.S. Congress, *Biographical Directory of the American Congress, 1774–1961* (Washington, DC: U.S. Government Printing Office, 1961), pp. 1110–11; Arnold, *Early Life and Letters of Jackson*, pp. 40–42.

11. Stephen W. Brown, *Voice of the New West: John G. Jackson, His Life and Times* (Macon, GA: Mercer University Press, 1985), passim; C. Peter Magrath, *Yazoo: Law and Politics in the New Republic* (New York: W. W. Norton and Company, 1966), pp. 44–45.

12. U.S. Congress, *Biographical Directory of the Congress 1774–1961*, pp. 1110–11; Noel B. Gerson, *Light-Horse Harry Lee: A Biography of Washington's Great Cavalryman* (Garden City, NY: Doubleday and Company, 1966), pp. 214–18.

13. Royster, *Light-Horse Harry Lee*, passim; Gerson, *Light-Horse Harry*, passim.

14. Freeman, *Lee*, I, pp. 14–15; Thomas E. Templin, "Henry 'Light-Horse Harry' Lee: Kentucky's Last Virginia Governor," in *Kentucky Profiles: Biographical Essays in Honor of Holman Hamilton* (Frankfort, KY: Kentucky Historical Society, 1982), pp. 47–49; David H. Fischer, *The Revolution of American Conservatism: The Federalist Party in the Era of Jeffersonian Democracy* (New York: Harper and Row, 1965), pp. 140–75.

15. Henry Lee, *Memoirs*, pp. 55–56; Burton J. Hendrick, *The Lees of Virginia: Biography of a Family* (Boston: Little, Brown and Company, 1935), 406–7.

16. Templin, "Light-Horse Harry Lee," pp. 49–50; Marshall Smelser, *The Democratic Republic, 1801–1815* (New York: Harper and Row, 1968), pp. 285–87.

17. E. J. Lee, *Lee of Virginia, 1642–1892*, p. 413.

18. Henry Lee, *Memoirs*, pp. 65–66.

19. J. William Jones, *Personal Reminiscences, Anecdotes, and Letters of General Robert E. Lee* (New York: D. Appleton and Company, 1874), p. 145.

20. A. L. Long, *Memoirs of Robert E. Lee: His Military and Personal History* (Secaucus, NJ: Blue and Gray Press, reprint, 1983), p. 30; Henry Kyd Douglas, *I Rode with Stonewall* (Chapel Hill: University of North Carolina Press, reprint, 1968), p. 234.

21. Henry Lee, *Memoirs*, p. 74.

22. Hendrick, *The Lees of Virginia*, p. 406.

23. Henry Lee, *Memoirs*, p. 56; Gerson, *Light-Horse Harry*, p. 318.

24. Arnold, *Early Life and Letters of Jackson*, pp. 205, 239, 242.

25. John G. Gittings, *Personal Recollections of Stonewall Jackson* (Cincinnati: Editor Publishing Company, 1899), pp. 3–4; Cook, *Early Life of Jackson*, p. 21.

26. Cook, *Early Life of Jackson*, p. 21; Cornelius J. Heatwole, *A History of Education in West Virginia* (New York: Macmillan, 1910), pp. 128–30; William Couper, *Claudius Crozet* (Charlottesville: University of Virginia Press, 1936), pp. 73–85; see also Bernard L. Allen, *Four Lectures on the Significance of the Neale and Jackson Families of Wood County West Virginia* (Parkersburg, WV: Data/Day, 1990), p. 6, for a different view of Jackson's birth.

27. Cook, *Early Life of Jackson*, pp. 19–21; Arnold, *Early Life and Letters of Jackson*, pp. 25–47.

28. Vandiver, *Mighty Stonewall*, pp. 2–4; Anna Jackson, *Memoirs of Jackson*, pp. 14–15; Cook, *Early Life of Jackson*, pp. 20–22.

29. Arnold, *Early Life and Letters of Jackson*, pp. 27–28.

30. Anna Jackson, *Memoirs of Jackson*, p. 16; Cook, *Early Life of Jackson*, pp. 20–22.

31. Cook, *Early Life of Jackson*, pp. 35–41; Arnold, *Early Life and Letters of Jackson*, pp. 32–33.

32. Festus P. Summers, *Johnson Newlon Camden: A Study in Individualism* (New York: G. P. Putnam's Sons, 1937), pp. 15–16, 33; John Alexander Williams, *West Virginia and the Captains of Industry* (Morgantown: West Virginia University Library, 1976), passim; Cook, *Early Life of Jackson*, pp. 49–56; Dabney, *Life and Campaigns of Jackson*, p. 13.

33. Arnold, *Early Life and Letters of Jackson*, p. 33; Stephen B. Oates, *With Malice Toward None: The Life of Abraham Lincoln* (New York: Harper and Row, 1977), pp. 15–16; Carl Sandburg, *Abraham Lincoln: The Prairie Years* (New York: Charles Scribner's Sons, 1947), I, pp. 84–85.

34. John Selby, *Stonewall Jackson as Military Commander* (London: B. T. Batsford, Ltd., 1968), p. 32; Vandiver, *Mighty Stonewall*, pp. 10–11; Anna Jackson, *Memoirs of Jackson*, pp. 27–28; Cook, *Early Life of Jackson*, pp. 54–56.

35. E. J. Lee, *Lee of Virginia 1642–1892*, p. 425; Dumas Malone, ed., *Dictionary of American Biography* (New York: Charles Scribner's Sons, 1933), 11, p. 108.

36. Dowdey, *Lee*, p. 39.

37. Thomas L. Connelly, *The Marble Man: Robert E. Lee and His Image in American Society* (New York: Alfred A. Knopf, 1977), pp. 4–12; Louis Pendleton, *Alexander H. Stephens* (Philadelphia: George W. Jacobs and Company, 1908), p. 280.

38. Freeman, *Lee*, I, pp. 30–31.

39. R. A. Brock, *Gen. Robert Edward Lee: Soldier, Citizen, Christian* (Richmond: B. F. Johnson Publishing Company, 1897), pp. 149–51.

40. Dowdey, *Lee*, p. 42; Brock, *Gen. Robert E. Lee*, p. 151; Benjamin Hallowell, *The Autobiography of Benjamin Hallowell* (Philadelphia: Friends Book Association, 1883), passim; Bruce Ray Smith, "Benjamin Hallowell of Alexandria: Scientist, Educator, Quaker Idealist," *Virginia Magazine of History and Biography* 85 (July 1977): 340–43.

CHAPTER 2

1. Fitzhugh Lee, *General Lee* (New York: D. Appleton and Company, 1894), p. 22; Marquis James, *Andrew Jackson: Portrait of a President* (New York; Gossett and Dunlap, reprint, n.d.), pp. 10–11; Douglas Southall Freeman, *R. E. Lee: A Biography* (New York: Charles Scribner's Sons, 1934), I, p. 43.

2. "Cadet Record Card: Robert E. Lee"; "Cadet Record Card: Thomas Jonathan Jackson," United States Military Academy, West Point, New York; Charles D. Rhodes, *Robert E. Lee: West Pointer* (Richmond, Garrett and Massie, 1932), p. 10–11. Frederick T. Hill, *On the Trail of Grant and Lee* (New York: D. Appleton and Company, 1911), p. 11.

3. J. William Jones, *Life and Letters of Robert Edward Lee: Soldier and Man* (New York: Neale Publishing Company, 1906), pp. 28–29; Thomas J. Fleming, *West Point: The Men and Times of the United States Military Academy* (New York: William Morrow and Company, 1969), pp. 45–47; Stephen E. Ambrose, *Duty, Honor, Country: A History of West Point* (Baltimore: John Hopkins University Press, 1966), pp. 69–74.

4. "Cadet Record Card: Robert E. Lee"; Rhodes, *Lee: West Pointer*, p. 17.

5. Mark M. Boatner, *The Civil War Dictionary* (New York: David McKay Company, 1959), passim; this source conveniently lists the year of graduation and class standing for all major officers during the Civil War era; Clement Eaton, *Jefferson Davis* (New York: Free Press, 1977), pp. 12–15; Julian Symons, The *Tell-Tale Heart: The Life and Works of Edgar Allan Poe* (New York: Harper and Row, 1978), pp. 39–41; Ambrose, *Duty, Honor, Country*, pp. 156–57.

6. Frederick Rudolph, *The American College and University: A History* (New York: Vantage Press, 1962), p. 119; Eben Swift, "The Military Education of Robert E. Lee," *Virginia Magazine of History and Biography* 35 (April 1927): 104–5; Ambrose, *Duty, Honor, Country*, p. 95.

7. Eben, "Military History of Lee," p. 105; James W. Pohl, "The Influence of Antoine de Jomini on Winfield Scott's Campaign in the Mexican War," *Southwestern Historical Quarterly* 77 (July 1973): pp. 86–88; see also, Grady McWhiney, "Who Whipped Whom: the Confederate Defeat Reexamined," *Civil War History* 11 (March 1965): 5–26.

8. Ambrose, *Duty, Honor, Country*, p. 187; Freeman, *Lee*, I, pp. 79–82; Rhodes, *Lee: West Pointer*, pp. 20–21.

9. Freeman, *Lee*, I, pp. 79–82; Henry Alexander White, *Robert E. Lee and the Southern Confederacy* (New York: G. P. Putnam's Sons, 1910), p. 26; Margaret Sanborn, *Robert E. Lee: The Complete Man* (Philadelphia: J. B. Lippincott Company, 1967), p. 363.

10. James T. Flexner, *George Washington: The Forge of Experience, 1732–1775* (Boston: Little, Brown and Company, 1965), pp. 357–58; Burton J. Hendrick, *The Lees of Virginia: Biography of a Family* (Boston: Little, Brown and Company, 1935), p. 406; Rhodes, *Lee: West Pointer*, p. 25; see also Benson J. Lossing, *Recollections and Private Memoirs of Washington* (New York: Derby and Jackson, 1860).

11. Edmund Jennings Lee, *Lee of Virginia, 1642–1892* (Philadelphia: Franklin Publishing Company, 1895), p. 414; Fitzhugh Lee, *General Lee*, 23; White, *Lee and the Southern Confederacy*, p. 26.

12. J. William Jones, *Personal Reminiscences, Anecodotes, and Letters of General Robert E. Lee* (New York: D. Appleton and Company, 1874), p. 363; Clifford Dowdey, *Lee* (Boston: Little, Brown and Company, 1965), pp. 53–55; Sanborn, *Lee: The Complete Man*, pp. 357–58.

13. John Richard Alden, *The South in the Revolution, 1763–1789* (Baton Rouge: Louisiana State University Press, 1957), p. 97; Betsy Fancher, *Savannah: A Renaissance of the Heart* (New York: Doubleday and Company, 1976), p. 59; Boatner, *Civil War Dictionary*, p. 508.

14. Matthew Paige Andrews, *Virginia: The Old Dominion* (Garden City, NY: Doubleday and Company, 1937), pp. 58–59; George G. Shackelford, "Lieutenant Lee Reports to Captain Talcott on Fort Calhoun's Construction on the Rip Raps," *Virginia Magazine of History and Biography* 60 (1952): 461–63.

15. *National Cyclopaedia of American Biography* (New York: James T. White and Company, 1906), 13, p. 405; Fitzhugh Lee, *General Lee*, p. 27; Virginius Dabney, *Virginia: The New Dominion* (Garden City, NY: Doubleday and Company, 1971), p. 297.

16. Long, *Memoirs of Lee*, p. 32; Rhodes, *Lee: West Pointer*, p. 25; Dowdey, *Lee*, p. 53.

17. Long, *Memoirs of Lee*, 33; Edward A. Pollard, *Lee and His Lieutenants* (New York: E. B. Treat and Company, 1867), p. 43; Norma B. Cuthbert, "To Molly: Five Early Letters from Robert E. Lee to His wife, 1832–1835," *Huntington Library Quarterly* 15 (May 1952): 265; Frederick Warren Alexander, *Stratford Hall and the Lees* (Oak Grove, VA: privately printed, 1912), p. 277.

18. Fitzhugh Lee, *General Lee*, pp. 27–28; John B. Duff and Peter M. Mitchell, eds., *The Nat Turner Rebellion: The Historical Event and the Modern Controversy* (New York: Harper and Row, 1971), p. 99; Herbert Aptheker, *Nat Turner's Slave Rebellion* (New York: Humanities Press, 1966), pp. 55, 152; Virginius Dabney, *Virginia: The New Dominion*, p. 226; see also, Stephen B. Oates, *The Fires of Jubilee: Nat Turner's Fierce Rebellion* (New York: Harper and Row, 1971).

19. White, *Lee and the Southern Confederacy*, p. 79; Cuthbert, "Lee's Letters to His Wife," p. 270; Shackelford, "Lee Reports to Captain Talcott," p. 469.

20. Long, *Memoirs of Lee*, pp. 36–37; Cuthbert, "Lee's Letters to His Wife," p. 271.

21. Fitzhugh Lee, *General Lee*, p. 28; W. Cleaver Bald, *Michigan in Four Centuries* (New York: Harper and Row, 1961), pp. 194–96.

22. John Esten Cooke, *A Life of Gen. Robert E. Lee* (New York: D. Appleton and Company, 1871), p. 19; Ambrose, *Duty, Honor, Country*, p. 95; Cuthbert, "Lee's Letters to His Wife," pp. 270–74.

23. E. J. Lee, *Lee of Virginia*, p. 496; William P. Snow, *Lee and His Generals* (New York: Fairfax Press, reprint, 1982), p. 23; U.S. Congress, *Biographical Directory of the Congress, 1774–1961* (Washington, DC: U.S. Government Printing Office, 1961), p. 1207.

24. John Esten Cooke, *Life of Lee*, p. 19; Long, *Memoirs of Lee*, pp. 42–43; Stella M. Drumm, "Robert E. Lee and the Improvement of the Mississippi River," *Missouri Historical Society Collections* 6 (February 1929): 157–62.

25. Jones, *Life and Letters of Lee*, pp. 32–34; Jones, *Reminiscences of Lee*, p. 368; interestingly, Lee's numerous letters reproduced in the volumes by Jones are statesmanlike and formal while those from sources other than the Lee family—such as the works by Cuthbert and Drumm cited above—have a much more earthy quality.

26. E. J. Lee, *Lee of Virginia*, p. 455; Alexander, *Stratford Hall and the Lees*, p. 277; Jones, *Reminiscences of Lee*, p. 369.

27. Long, *Memoirs of Lee*, p. 41; Jones, *Reminiscences of Lee*, p. 369; Roy Bird Cook, *The Family and Early Life of Stonewall Jackson* (Charleston, WV: Education Foundation, reprint, 1967), pp. 27, 47; J. Hop Woods, "Stonewall Jackson in West Virginia," *Confederate Veteran* 24 (1916): 493.

28. Hill, *On the Trail of Grant and Lee*, p. 14; Cuthbert, "Lee's Letters to his Wife," p. 170.

29. Long, *Memoirs of Lee*, p. 46; Freeman, *Lee*, I, p. 191; An Ex-Cadet (James Dabney McCabe), *The Life of Thomas J. Jackson* (Richmond: James E. Goode, 1864), p. 12.

30. Cook, *Family and Early Life of Jackson*, pp. 59ff.; Otis K. Rice, *West Virginia: A History* (Lexington: University Press of Kentucky, 1985), p. 78; Thomas C. Miller, *History of Education in West Virginia* (Charleston, WV: Tribune Printing Company, 1904), p. 269.

31. Mary Anna Jackson, *Memoirs of Stonewall Jackson by His Widow* (Louisville: Prentice Press, 1895), p. 31; Festus P. Summers, *Johnson Newlon Camden: A Study in Individualism* (New York: G. P. Putnam's Sons, 1937), p. 33.

32. Cook, *Early Life and Family of Jackson*, p. 85.

33. Ibid., p. 89–91; Anna Jackson, *Memoirs of Jackson*, p. 32; W. D. Barger, "Scenes of Jackson's Boyhood," *Confederate Veteran* 22 (July 1914): 323; Stephen W. Brown, *Voice of the West: John G. Jackson, His Life and Times* (Macon, GA: Mercer University Press, 1985), p. 2.

34. Anna Jackson, *Memoirs of Jackson*, p. 33; Cook, *Early Life and Family of Jackson*,

p. 93; "Academic Record of Thomas Jonathan Jackson," Typescript, U. S. Military Academy.

35. Ambrose, *Duty, Honor Country*, p. 103; Lloyd Lewis, *Captain Sam Grant* (Boston: Little, Brown and Company, 1950), pp. 88–89; Anna Jackson, *Memoirs of Jackson*, p. 576.

36. Robert L. Dabney, *Life and Campaigns of Lieut.-Gen. Thomas J. Jackson* (New York: Blelock and Company, 1866), pp. 33–34; Anna Jackson, *Memoirs of Jackson*, p. 38; John Esten Cooke, *Stonewall Jackson: A Military Biography* (New York: D. Appleton and Company, 1866), p. 13.

37. Dabney, *Life and Campaigns of Jackson*, p. 35; Cook, *Early Life and Family of Jackson*, p. 94; Thomas Jackson Arnold, *Early Life and Letters of General Thomas J. Jackson* (New York: Fleming Revel Company, 1916), p. 65.

38. "Academic Record of Jackson"; Arnold, *Life and Letters of Jackson*, p. 70.

39. "Academic Record of Jackson"; "Cadet Record Card: Robert E. Lee," pp. 2–5; James L. Morrison, Jr., *The Best School in the World": West Point, the Pre-Civil War Years, 1833–1866* (Kent: Kent State Unversity Press, 1986), pp. 108–9.

40. Pollard, *Lee and His Lieutenants*, p. 179; Arnold, *Life and Letters of Jackson*, pp. 70–71; Frank E. Vandiver, *Mighty Stonewall* (New York: McGraw-Hill, 1957), pp. 42–47.

41. Dowdey, *Lee*, p. 73; Fitzhugh Lee, *General Lee*, p. 30.

42. Bertram Wyatt-Brown, *Honor and Violence in the Old South* (New York: Oxford University Press, 1986), p. 56; E. J. Lee, *Lee of Virginia*, p. 455; Drumm, *"Lee and the Mississippi River,"* p. 169; Alexander, *Stratford Hall and the Lees*, p. 277.

43. Avery O. Craven, ed., *To Markie: The Letters of Robert E. Lee to Martha Custis Williams* (Cambridge: Harvard University Press, 1933), p. 9; Jones, *Life and Letters of Lee*, p. 76.

44. Jones, *Life and Letters of Lee*, p. 38; Dowdey, *Lee*, p. 76.

45. Freeman, *Lee, I*, pp. 187–91; White, *Lee and the Southern Confederacy*, p. 31.

46. Long, *Memoirs of Lee*, p. 67

CHAPTER 3

1. Thomas J. Arnold, *Early Life and Letters of General Thomas J. Jackson* (New York: Fleming Revell Company, 1916), p. 91.

2. Fitzhugh Lee, *General Lee* (New York: D. Appleton and Company, 1894), pp. 34–36, 42–44.

3. John Edward Weems, *To Conquer a Peace: The War Between the United States and Mexico* (Garden City, NY: Doubleday and Company, 1947), p. 9; Seymour V. Connor and Odie B. Faulk, *North America Divided: The Mexican War, 1846–1848* (New York: Oxford University Press, 1971), pp. 28–29.

4. Joseph Milton Nance, *After San Jacinto: The Texas-Mexican Frontier, 1836–1841* (Austin: University of Texas Press, 1963), pp. 227–30; Herbert Gambrell, *Anson Jones, Last President of Texas* (Garden City, NY: Doubleday and Company, 1948), p. 54; Alwyn Barr, *Texans in Revolt: The Battle for San Antonio, 1835* (Austin: University of Texas Press, 1990), pp. 1–4.

5. George Winston Smith and Charles Judah, *Chronciles of the Gringos: The U.S. Army in the Mexican War, 1846–1848* (Albuquerque: University of New Mexico Press, 1968), p. 1.

6. Otis A. Singletary, *The Mexican War* (Chicago: University of Chicago Press, 1960), pp. 25–27; Winfield Scott, *Memoirs: Written by Himself* (New York: Sheldon and Company, 1867), II, p. 450.

7. Edward A. Pollard, *Lee and His Lieutenants* (New York: E. B. Treat and Company, 1867), p. 45.

8. Roy Bird Cook, *The Family and Early Life of Stonewall Jackson* (Charleston, WV: Education Foundation, reprint, 1967), p. 102; Frank E. Vandiver, *Mighty Stonewall* (New York: McGraw-Hill, 1957), pp. 42–44.

9. Winfield Scott, *Memoirs*, II, p. 520–24.

10. Avery O. Craven, ed., *To Markie: The Letters of Robert E. Lee to Martha Custis Williams* (Cambridge: Harvard University Press, 1933), pp. 17–18; Cook, *Family and Early Life of Jackson*, p. 99.

11. Cadmus Wilcox, *History of the Mexican War* (Washington, DC: Church News Publishing Company, 1892), p. 5; Vandiver, *Mighty Stonewall*, p. 40; Arnold, *Life and Letters of Jackson*, p. 93; Jack Zinn, *R. E. Lee's Cheat Mountain Campaign* (Parsons, WV: McClain Publishing Company, 1974), pp. 112–13.

12. Cook, *Family and Early Life of Jackson*, p. 20.

13. Arnold, *Life and Letters of Jackson*, p. 78; Cook, *Early Life and Family of Jackson*, p. 112; Vandiver, *Mighty Stonewall*, p. 19.

14. Arnold, *Life and Letters of Jackson*, pp. 80–81.

15. Edmund Jennings Lee, *Lee of Virginia, 1642–1892* (Philadelphia: Franklin Publishing Company, 1895), p. 456; J. William Jones, *Life and Letters of Robert E. Lee: Soldier and Man* (New York: Neale Publishing Company, 1906), p. 40.

16. Douglas Southall Freeman, *R. E. Lee: A Biography* (New York: Charles Scribner's Sons, 1934), I, p. 203; Frederick Warren Alexander, *Stratford Hall and the Lees* (Oak Grove, VA: privately printed, 1912), p. 277; Clifford Dowdey, *Lee* (Boston: Little, Brown and Company, 1965), p. 722.

17. Walter P. Webb, ed., *The Handbook of Texas* (Austin: Texas State Historical Association, 1952), I, pp. 44, 395; Freeman, *Lee*, I, pp. 203–4.

18. Thomas Bangs Thorpe, *Our Army on the Rio Grande . . .* (Philadelphia: Cary and Hart, 1846), pp. 38–41; Oliver P. Chitwood, *John Tyler, Champion of the Old South* (New York: Russell and Russell, reprint, 1964), p. 351; James Longstreet,

From Manassas to Appomattox: Memoirs of the Civil War in America (Philadelphia: J. B. Lippincott and Company, 1903), pp. 18–19.

19. Connor and Faulk, *North America Divided*, pp. 40–41; Edward D. Mansfield, *The Mexican War: A History of Its Origin* (Cincinnati: H. W. Derby and Company, 1849), pp. 9–25.

20. Holman Hamilton, *Zachary Taylor: Soldier of the Republic* (Hamden, CT: Archon Books, reprint, 1966), pp. 176ff.

21. Connor and Faulk, *North America Divided*, pp. 30–33; Charles Sellers, *James K. Polk: Continentalist* (Princeton: Princeton University Press, 1966), II, pp. 406–9.

22. Hamilton, *Taylor: Soldier of the Republic*, p. 79.

23. Jack Bauer, *Zachary Taylor: Soldier, Planter, Statesman of the Old Southwest* (Baton Rouge: Louisiana State University Press, 1985), pp. 166–84; Charles A. McCoy, *Polk and the Presidency* (Austin: University of Texas Press, 1960), p. 94; Holman Hamilton, *The Three Kentucky Presidents: Lincoln, Taylor, Davis* (Lexington: University Press of Kentucky, 1978), pp. 24–25.

24. Dumas Malone, ed., *Dictionary of American Biography* (New York: Charles Scribner's Sons, 1936), 20, p. 513.

25. Robert S. Henry, *The Story of the Mexican War* (New York: Bobbs-Merrill Company, 1950), p. 181.

26. Fitzhugh Lee, *General Lee*, p. 34; Jones, *Life and Letters of Lee*, p. 50.

27. Frank G. Hanighen, *Santa Anna: Napoleon of the West* (New York: Coward-McCann, 1934), pp. 196–208; Wilfred H. Callcott, *Santa Anna: The Story of an Enigma Who Was Once Mexico* (Norman: University of Oklahoma Press, 1936), pp. 241–45; Hamilton, *Taylor: Soldier of the Republic*, p. 224.

28. Freeman, *Lee*, I, pp. 210–13; Henry, *Story of the Mexican War*, p. 182.

29. Arnold, *Life and Letters of Jackson*, p. 80; Lenoir Chambers, *Stonewall Jackson: The Legend and the Man to the Valley* (New York: William Morrow and Company, 1959), p. 82.

30. Arnold, *Life and Letters of Jackson*, p. 89.

31. G. F. R. Henderson, *Stonewall Jackson and the American Civil War* (London: Longmans, Green and Company, 1906), I, p. 27; Dabney H. Maury, *Recollections of a Virginian in the Mexican, Indian, and Civil Wars* (New York: Charles Scribner's Sons, 1894), p. 28; Vandiver, *Mighty Stonewall*, p. 21.

32. Cook, *Family and Early Life of Jackson*, pp. 99–100.

33. Fitzhugh Lee, *General Lee*, p. 8.

34. Jones, *Life and Letters of Lee*, pp. 42–45; J. William Jones, *Personal Reminiscences, Ancedotes, and Letters of General Robert E. Lee* (New York: D. Appleton and Company, 1874), pp. 288ff.; Freeman, *Lee*, I, pp. 214–16; Walter H. Taylor, *Four Years with General Lee* (New York: D. Appleton and Company, 1877), pp. 49ff.;

A. L. Long, *Memoirs of Robert E. Lee: His Military and Personal History* (Secaucus, NJ: Blue and Gray Press, reprint, 1983), pp. 49–51; Thomas L. Connelly, *The Marble Man: Robert E. Lee and His Image in American Society* (New York: Alfred A. Knopf, 1977), pp. 40–41 (both quotes).

35. Long, *Memoirs of Lee*, p. 51.

36. Robert W. Johannsen, *To the Halls of Montezumas: The Mexican War in the American Imagination* (New York: Oxford University Press, 1985), p. 91.

37. Chambers, *Stonewall Jackson*, I, p. 85.

38. Johannsen, *To the Hall of Montezumas*, p. 89.

39. James I. Robertson, *General A. P. Hill: The Story of a Confederate Warrior* (New York: Random House, 1987), p. 17; Conner and Faulk, *North America Divided*, p. 108; Arnold, *Life and Letters of Jackson*, p. 85.

40. General Daniel H. Hill, "The Real Stonewall Jackson," *Century Magazine* 25 (February 1894): 623–24.

41. Alfred Hoyt Bill, *Rehearsal for Conflict: The War with Mexico, 1846–1848* (New York: Alfred A. Knopf, 1947), pp. 204–7; Arnold, *Life and Letters of Jackson*, p. 85.

42. Bill, *Rehearsal for Conflict*, pp. 208–12.

43. Jones, *Life and Letters of Lee*, p. 42.

44. Long, *Memoirs of Lee*, p. 51; Fitzhugh Lee, *General Lee*, p. 35.

45. John H. Schroeder, *Mr. Polk's War: American Opportunism and Dissent, 1846–1848* (Madison: University of Wisconsin Press, 1973), p. 62; Henry, *Story of the Mexican War*, pp. 198–99.

46. Hamilton, *Taylor: Soldier of the Republic*, p. 229; William P. Snow, *Lee and His Generals* (New York: Fairfax Press, reprint, 1982), p. 23.

47. Jones, *Life and Letters of Lee*, pp. 40–42; Freeman, *Lee*, I, pp. 218–22; Wilcox, *Mexican War*, p. 237.

CHAPTER 4

1. Douglas Southall Freeman, *R. E. Lee: A Biography* (New York: Charles Scribner's Sons, 1934), I, p. 259; Robert L. Dabney, *Life and Campaigns of Lieut.-Gen. Thomas J. Jackson* (New York: Blelock and Company, 1866), p. 42; Alfred Hoyt Bill, *Rehearsal for Conflict: The War With Mexico: 1846–1848* (New York: Alfred A. Knopf, 1947), p. 213.

2. An Ex-Cadet (James Dabney McCabe), *The Life of Thomas J. Jackson* (Richmond: James E. Goode, 1864), p. 13; Mary Anna Jackson, *Memoirs of Stonewall Jackson by His Widow* (Louisville, KY: Prentice Press, 1895), p. 55.

3. Vincent J. Esposito, *The West Point Atlas of American Wars* (New York: Frederick A. Praeger, 1960), I, p. 15; Thomas Jackson Arnold, *Early Life and Letters of General Thomas J. Jackson* (New York: Fleming H. Revell Company, 1916), pp. 84–

85; Ellsworth Eliot, *West Point in the Confederacy* (New York: G. A. Baker and Company, 1941), pp. xxv–xxviii; Frank H. Smyrl, *Texas in Gray: The Civil War Years, 1861–1865* (Boston: American Press, 1983), pp. 11–15.

4. Bill, *Rehearsal for Conflict*, pp. 267–69; Robert S. Henry, *The Story of the Mexican War* (New York: Bobbs-Merrill Company, 1950), pp. 267–69.

5. Raphael Semmes, *Service Ashore and Afloat during the Mexican War* (Cincinnati: W. H. Moore and Company, 1851), passim; Edward Boykin, *Ghost Ship of the Confederacy: The Story of the Alabama and Her Captain Raphael Semmes* (New York: Funk and Wagnalls Company, 1957), pp. 32–33.

6. Bill, *Rehearsal for Conflict*, p. 217.

7. Fitzhugh Lee, *General Lee* (New York: D. Appleton and Company, 1894), p. 37.

8. Dabney H. Maury, *Recollections of a Virginian in the Mexican, Indian, and Civil Wars* (New York: Charles Scribner's Sons, 1894), p. 35.

9. Seymour V. Connor and Odie B. Faulk, *North America Divided: The Mexican War, 1846–1848* (New York: Oxford University Press, 1971), p. 111; Arnold, *Life and Letters of Jackson*, p. 84.

10. Henry, *Story of the Mexican War*, p. 285.

11. Bill, *Rehearsal for Conflict*, pp. 225–29; A. L. Long, *Memoirs of Robert E. Lee: His Military and Personal History* (Secaucus, NJ: Blue and Grey Press, reprint, 1983), p. 52.

12. Henry, *Story of the Mexican War*, p. 285; U.S. Grant, *Personal Memoirs* (New York: Charles L. Webster and Company, 1885), I, p. 133; Arthur D. H. Smith, *Old Fuss and Feathers: The Life and Exploits of Lt.-General Winfield Scott* (New York: Greystone Press, 1937), pp. 278–85; Horace Porter, "Lee . . . Facing Grant: The Surrender at Appomattox Court House," in Ned Bradford, ed., *Battles and Leaders of the Civil War* (New York: Appleton-Century Crofts, 1956), p. 609.

13. J. William Jones, *Life and Letters of Robert E. Lee: Soldier and Man* (New York: Neale Publishing Company, 1906), p. 51.

14. Long, *Memoirs of Lee*, p. 53.

15. Arnold, *Life and Letters of Jackson*, pp. 89–90; Dabney, *Life and Campaigns of Jackson*, pp. 42–43; Lenoir Chambers, *Stonewall Jackson: The Legend and the Man to the Valley* (New York: William Morrow and Company, 1959), I, p. 92.

16. John Esten Cooke, *Stonewall Jackson: A Military Biography* (New York: D. Appleton and Company, 1866), pp. 14–15; Roy F. Nichols, *Franklin Pierce: Young Hickory of the Granite Hills* (Philadelphia: University of Pennsylvania Press, 1931), p. 213.

17. Arnold, *Life and Letters of Jackson*, pp. 91–92.

18. Bill, *Rehearsal for Conflict*, p. 258; Arnold, *Life and Letters of Jackson*, pp. 129–30; Frank E. Vandiver, *Mighty Stonewall* (New York: McGraw-Hill, 1957), pp. 31–32.

19. Jones, *Life and Letters of Lee*, p. 52; John Edward Weems, *To Conquer a Peace: The War Between the United States and Mexico* (New York: Doubleday and Company, 1974), p. 370.

20. Roy Bird Cook, *The Family and Early Life of Stonewall Jackson* (Charleston, WV: Education Foundation, reprint, 1967), pp. 102–3; Markenfield Addey, *The Life and Military Career of Thomas Jonathan Jackson* (New York: Charles T. Evans, 1863), pp. 17–19. The Addey volume contains interesting anecdotes about Jackson and has some interest because it was published immediately after his death; however, it has factual errors and should be consulted with caution.

21. Dabney, *Life and Campaigns of Jackson*, p. 44.

22. Cook, *Early Life of Jackson*, p. 102; Arnold, *Life and Letters of Jackson*, p. 134.

23. W. A. Croffut, ed., *Fifty Years in Camp and Field: Diary of Major-General Ethan Allen Hitchcock, USA* (New York: G. P. Putnam's Sons, 1901), p. 259.

24. Grady McWhiney and Perry D Jamieson, *Attack and Die: Civil War Tactics and the Southern Heritage* (Tuscaloosa: University of Alabama Press, 1982), p. 38.

25. Robert W. Johannsen, *To the Halls of Montezuma: The Mexican War in the American Imagination* (New York: Oxford University Press, 1985), p. 132; McWhiney and Jamieson, *Attack and Die*, p. 154.

26. Cadmus Wilcox, *History of the Mexican War* (Washington, DC: Church News Publishing Company, 1892), pp. 349–53; Winfield Scott, *Memoirs: Written by Himself* (New York: Sheldon and Company, 1867), II, pp. 460–61.

27. Long, *Memoirs of Lee*, pp. 54–56; G. F. R. Henderson, *Stonewall Jackson and the American Civil War* (London: Longmans, Green and Company, 1906), I, p. 36; Mark M. Boatner, *The Civil War Dictionary* (New York: David McKay Company, 1959), p. 418; Douglas Southall Freeman, *Lee*, I, pp. 249–72, entitles his chapter on Lee at Contreras and Churubusco, "Laurels in a Lava Field."

28. Justin H. Smith, *The War with Mexico* (New York: Macmillan Company, 1919), I, pp. 103, 378; Henry, *Story of the Mexican War*, p. 330; Dabney, *Life and Campaigns of Jackson*, p. 46.

29. Eliot, *West Point in the Confederacy*, pp. xxv–xxviii; An Ex-Cadet (McCabe), *Life of Jackson*, pp. 16–17; Arnold, *Life and Letters of Jackson*, pp. 131–34.

30. Scott, *Memoirs*, II, pp. 469–75; Henry, *Story of the Mexican War*, pp. 334–35; Smith, *War with Mexico*, I, pp. 109ff.

31. Connor and Faulk, *North America Divided*, pp. 125–26; Smith, *War with Mexico*, I, p. 99.

32. Wilcox, *History of the Mexican War*, pp. 380–81.

33. Henry Alexander White, *Robert E. Lee and the Southern Confederacy* (New York: G. P. Putnam's Sons, 1910), p. 42; Freeman, *Lee*, I, p. 269, speculates that the letter was written to Mrs. Lee, which seems unlikely since it does not appear in Jones.

34. Esposito, *West Point Atlas*, I, p. 15; Connor and Faulk, *North America Divided*, pp. 126–27.

35. Eliot, *West Point in the Confederacy*, pp. xxv–xxvii; Vandiver, *Mighty Stonewall*, p. 36.

36. Henry, *Story of the Mexican War*, pp. 348–50; Johnston is quoted in Long, *Memoirs of Lee*, p. 71.

37. Anna Jackson, *Memoirs of Jackson*, p. 41; Vandiver, *Mighty Stonewall*, p. 36.

38. Weems, *To Conquer a Peace*, pp. 414–415; White, *Lee and the Southern Confederacy*, p. 43.

39. Smith, *War With Mexico*, I, p. 403; Vandiver, *Mighty Stonewall*, p. 36; Dabney, *Life and Campaigns of Jackson*, p. 46; Croffut, ed., *Fifty Years in Camp and Field*, p. 397.

40. White, *Lee and the Southern Confederacy*, p. 43; Edward D. Mansfield, *The Mexican War: A History of Its Origin* (New York: A. S. Barns and Company, 1849), p. 273. Other writers say the castle was two hundred feet above the surrounding plain. See George Winston Smith and Charles Judah, *Chronicles of the Gringos: The U.S. Army in the Mexican War, 1846–1848* (Albuquerque: University of New Mexico Press), p. 257; Vandiver, *Mighty Stonewall*, p. 38.

41. Bill, *Rehearsal for Conflict*, p. 292; Smith and Judah, *Chronicles of the Gringos*, p. 273.

42. Clifford Dowdey, *Lee* (Boston: Little, Brown and Company, 1965), pp. 93–94; Boatner, *Civil War Dictionary*, p. 416; Bill, *Rehearsal for Conflict*, p. 293.

43. Otis A. Singletary, *The Mexican War* (Chicago: University of Chicago Press, 1960), p. 96.

44. White, *Lee and the Southern Confederacy*, p. 45; Scott, *Memoirs*, II, pp. 520–21; Anna Jackson, *Memoirs of Jackson*, pp. 41–43.

45. Dabney, *Life and Campaigns of Jackson*, p. 48; Addey, *Life and Career of Jackson*, pp. 19–22; An Ex-Cadet (McCabe), *Life of Jackson*, pp. 15–18; Anna Jackson, *Memoirs of Jackson*, pp. 41ff.; Arnold, *Life and Letters of Jackson*, pp. 114–17; John Esten Cooke, *Stonewall Jackson*, pp. 16–18.

46. Arnold, *Life and Letters of Jackson*, p. 143; Long, *Memoirs of Lee*, p. 64; Sir Frederick Maurice, *Robert E. Lee: The Soldier* (Boston: Houghton Mifflin and Company, 1925), p. 36.

47. John H. Schroeder, *Mr. Polk's War: American Opposition and Dissent, 1846–1848* (Madison: University of Wisconsin Press, 1973), p. 156; Arnold, *Life and Letters of Jackson*, p. 137; Fitzhugh Lee, *General Lee*, pp. 43–45; Lee's letter to Mrs. Smith Lee, February 13, 1848, contains a detailed summary of his thoughts on the war and ensuing peace transactions. See also his letter to Smith Lee, March 4, 1848, in Jones, *Life and Letters of Lee*, pp. 56–57.

48. Jones, *Life and Letters of Lee*, p. 56; Arnold, *Life and Letters of Jackson*, p. 138; Dowdey, *Lee*, pp. 93–94.

49. Anna Jackson, *Memoirs of Jackson*, p. 48; Jones, *Life and Letters of Lee*, p. 55; Fitzhugh Lee, *General Lee*, p. 45.

50. Arnold, *Life and Letters of Jackson*, pp. 132, 136; Avery O. Craven, ed., *To Markie: The Letters of Robert E. Lee to Martha Custis Williams* (Cambridge: Harvard University Press, 1933), p. 21; Wilcox, *History of the Mexican War*, pp. 710–711.

CHAPTER 5

1. Frank E. Vandiver, *Mighty Stonewall* (New York: McGraw-Hill, 1957), p. 45; Robert L. Dabney, *Life and Campaigns of Lieut.-Gen. Thomas J. Jackson* (New York: Blelock and Company, 1866), p. 58; Thomas Jackson Arnold, *Early Life and Letters of General Thomas J. Jackson* (New York: Fleming H. Revell Company, 1916), p. 141.

2. Arnold, *Life and Letters of Jackson*, pp. 142, 157, 164–69; Duman Malone, ed., *The Dictionary of American Biography* (New York: Charles Scribner's Sons, 1933), 11, pp. 105–6.

3. Arnold, *Life and Letters of Jackson*, p. 147; Charles H. Ambler, *Waitman Thomas Willey: Orator, Churchman, Humanitarian* (Huntington, WV: Standard Printing and Publishing Company, 1954), pp. 42, 83; Richard O. Curry, *Radicalism, Racism, and Party Realignment: The Border States During Reconstruction* (Baltimore: Johns Hopkins University Press, 1969), p. 82; U.S. Congress, *Biographical Directory of the American Congress, 1774–1961* (Washington, DC: Government Printing Office, 1961), p. 662.

4. Arnold, *Life and Letters of Jackson*, pp. 147ff.; Dabney, *Life and Campaigns of Jackson*, p. 65; Erasmus D. Keyes, *Fifty Years Observation of Men and Events* (New York: Charles Scribner's Sons, 1884), p. 198.

5. Mary Anna Jackson, *Memoirs of Stonewall Jackson by His Widow* (Louisville, KY: Prentice Press, 1895), p. 49; D. H. Hill, "The Real Stonewall Jackson," *Century Magazine* 25 (February 1894): 623–24; Arnold, *Life and Letters of Jackson*, p. 149; Roy Bird Cook, *The Family and Early Life of Stonewall Jackson* (Charleston, WV: Education Foundation, reprint, 1965), p. 108.

6. W. H. Purcell, "The Brief Stay of Stonewall Jackson at Fort Meade" [Conclusion], *Polk County Historical Quarterly* 3 (March 1976): 2; Arnold, *Life and Letters of Jackson*, p. 169; Vandiver, *Mighty Stonewall*, pp. 56–70.

7. Virginia Bergman Peters, *The Florida Wars* (Hamden, CT: Archon Books, 1979), p. 267; Max Reif, "Early History of Fort Meade," *Polk County Historical Quarterly* 3 (June 1976): 2.

8. W. H. Purcell, "The Brief Stay of Stonewall Jackson at Fort Meade," *Polk County Historical Quarterly* 2 (December 1975): 2; Arnold, *Life and Letters of Jackson*, pp. 169–170; Vandiver, *Mighty Stonewall*, p. 59.

9. Hill, "The Real Stonewall," p. 625; Lenoir Chambers, *Stonewall Jackson: The Man and the Legend to the Valley* (New York: William Morrow and Company, 1959), pp. 167–69; see also National Archives Publication No. 617, *Returns from U.S.*

Military Posts, 1800–1916, one microfilm roll of which is devoted to Fort Meade, December 1848–August 1857.

10. Anna Jackson, *Memoirs of Jackson,* pp. 55–56; Arnold, *Life and Letters of Jackson,* pp. 172–73.

11. Charles H. Ambler and Festus P. Summers, *West Virginia: The Mountain State* (Englewood Cliffs, NJ: Prentice-Hall, 1957), p. 168; Virginius Dabney, *Virginia: The New Dominion* (New York: Doubleday and Company, 1971), pp. 222–23; Arnold, *Life and Letters of Jackson,* pp. 171–72.

12. Arnold, *Life and Letters of Jackson,* p. 174; Anna Jackson, *Memoirs of Jackson,* p. 58; Vandiver, *Mighty Stonewall,* p. 70; Cook, *Early Life of Jackson,* p. 116.

13. Dabney, *Life and Campaigns of Jackson,* p. 62; William Couper, *One Hundred Years at VMI* (Richmond: Garrett and Massie, 1939), I, p. 253; Francis B. Heitman, *Historical Register and Directory of the United States Army* (Washington, DC: U.S. Government Printing Office, 1903), p. 568.

14. Margaret Junkin Preston, "Personal Reminiscences of Stonewall Jackson," *Century Magazine* 32 (1886): 921; Couper, *One Hundred Years at VMI,* I, p. 263; Francis H. Smith, *The Virginia Military Institute: Its Building and Rebuilding* (Lynchburg, VA: T. P. Bell Company, 1912), p. 138; Dabney, *Life and Campaigns of Jackson,* p. 81.

15. Hill, "The Real Stonewall," p. 625; Dabney, *Life and Campaigns of Jackson,* pp. 71ff.

16. "The tombstone reads Elinor; the marriage license record reads Eleanor, but was crudely changed to read Elinor . . . ; her sister in her fascinating diaries used the spelling Eleanor, and Jackson's letters say 'Elie.' " See Couper, *One Hundred Years at VMI,* I, p. 291. Her photograph is reproduced on p. 205, Arnold, *Life and Letters of Jackson.* Jackson's nephew uses the spelling Eleanor.

17. Hill, "The Real Stonewall," p. 625; D. X. Junkin, *George Junkin, D.D., LLD.* (Philadelphia: J.P. Lippincott and Company, 1971) p. 553; Elizabeth Junkin Allan, *The Life and Letters of Margaret Junkin Preston* (Boston: Houghton Mifflin and Company, 1903), pp. 60–61; Vandiver, *Mighty Stonewall,* p. 119.

18. Jackson remained in the Junkin home until Elie's death in 1854; Lee later lived there until a new president's home was constructed on an adjacent lot on the Washington College campus. See Couper, *One Hundred Years at VMI,* I, pp. 291–92.

19. Hill, "The Real Stonewall," p. 625; Anna Jackson, *Memoirs of Jackson,* p. 57.

20. Arnold, *Life and Letters of Jackson,* p. 205; Allan, *Life and Letters of Margaret Junkin Preston,* p. 62.

21. Arnold, *Life and Letters of Jackson,* p. 204; Suzanne Christoff, Assistant Archivist, USMA, to P.D.C., June 23, 1988; Dabney, *Life and Campaigns of Jackson,* p. 69.

22. Robert E. Lee, Jr., *Recollections and Letters of General Robert E. Lee* (Garden City, NY: Garden City Publishing Company, 1904), p. 4; Burton J. Hendrick, *The Lees of Virginia: Biography of a Family* (Boston: Little, Brown and Company, 1935), p. 227.

23. Fitzhugh Lee, *General Lee* (New York: D. Appleton and Company, 1894), pp. 49–50; R. E. Lee, Jr., *Recollections and Letters of Lee*, p. 5; Frederick Warren Alexander, *Stratford Hall and the Lees* (Oak Grove, VA: Privately printed, 1912), p. 227; Douglas Southall Freeman, *R. E. Lee: A Biography* (New York: Charles Scribner's Sons, 1934), I, pp. 301–3.

24. Avery O. Craven, ed., *To Markie: The Letters of Robert E. Lee to Martha Custis Williams* (Cambridge: Harvard University Press, 1933), p. 28; R. E. Lee, Jr., *Recollections and Letters*, pp. 10–11.

25. W. P. Craighill, "Baltimore and Its Defenses," *Maryland Historical Magazine* I (1908): 28–40.

26. Holman Hamilton, *Zachary Taylor: Soldier in the White House* (Hamden, CT: Archon Books, reprint, 1966), p. 159; R. E. Lee, Jr., *Recollections and Letters*, p. 11.

27. A. L. Long, *Memoirs of Robert E. Lee: His Military and Personal History* (Secaucus, NJ: Blue and Grey Press, reprint, 1983), pp. 72–73; Clement Eaton, *Jefferson Davis* (New York: Free Press, 1977), p. 68; Holman Hamilton, *Taylor: Soldier in the White House*, p. 200.

28. Eaton, *Jefferson Davis*, pp. 85–86; Henry Alexander White, *Robert E. Lee and the Southern Confederacy* (New York: G. P. Putnam's Sons, 1910), p. 48.

29. James L. Morrison, *"The Best School in the World": West Point, the Pre-Civil War Years, 1833–1866* (Kent: Kent State University Press, 1985), pp. 90–94.

30. R. E. Lee, Jr., *Recollections and Letters of Lee*, p. 11; O. O. Howard, *Autobiography of Oliver Otis Howard* (New York: Baker and Taylor Company, 1907), II, p. 49; Burke Davis, *JEB Stuart: The Last Cavalier* (New York: Fairfax Press, reprint, 1988), p. 23.

31. Craven, ed., *To Markie*, p. 46.

32. R. E. Lee, *Recollections and Letters*, p. 13; J. William Jones, *Life and Letters of Robert E. Lee: Soldier and Man* (New York: Neale Publishing Company, 1906), p. 68.

33. Ellsworth Eliot, *West Point in the Confederacy* (New York: G. A. Baker and Company, 1941), pp. xxii—this source says thirteen entered the Confederate army; Freeman lists fourteen; R. L. Lee, Jr., *Recollections and Letters*, pp. 12–13; Douglas Southall Freeman, *R. E. Lee: A Biography* (New York: Charles Scribner's Sons, 1934), I, p. 346; Stanley Weintraub, *Whistler: A Biography* (New York: Waybright and Talley, 1974), pp. 14–25; Tom Prideaux, *The World of Whistler, 1834–1903* (New York: Time-Life Books, 1970), pp. 18–20.

34. Phillip A. Bruce, *History of the University of Virginia, 1819–1919* (New York: Macmillan Company, 1921), p. 78; Couper, *One Hundred Years at VMI*, I, p. 280; Rossiter Johnson, ed., *The Twentieth Century Biographical Directory of Notable Americans* (Detroit: Gale Research Company, reprint, 1968), II, unpaged.

35. Thomas J. Jackson to Judge J. J. Allen, December 28, 1853, the University of

Virginia Archives, Alderman Library, Charlottesville; Stephen W. Brown, *Voice of the New West: John G. Jackson, His Life and Times* (Macon, GA: Mercer University Press, 1985), p. 203; Jim Comstock, ed., *The West Virginia Heritage Encyclopaedia* (Richwood, WV: Jim Comstock, 1976), 21, p. 4670.

36. Thomas J. Jackson to Board of Vistors, University of Virginia, January 2, 1854, Virginia Historical Society Library, Richmond.

37. Robert E. Lee to Board of Vistors, University of Virginia, January 26, 1854, Virginia Historical Society Library, Richmond.

38. D. H. Hill to Board of Vistors, University of Virginia, January 2, 1854, the University of Virginia Archives, Alderman Library, Charlottesville; J. L. Campbell to Board of Vistors, Ibid., the Hill-Campbell letter is erroneously dated January 2, 1853; Esmarch S. Gilbreath and John H. Wise, "Chemical Education: The View from W & L," *The Alumni Magazine of Washington and Lee University* 51 (July 1976), p. 16.

39. Couper, *One Hundred Years at VMI*, p. 182.

40. Malone, ed., *Dictionary of American Biography*, II, pp. 364–65; Bruce, *History of the University of Virginia*, p. 78; Dabney, *Life and Campaigns of Jackson*, p. 70; Arnold, *Life and Letters of Jackson*, p. 206.

41. Eaton, *Jefferson Davis*, p. 86; Craven, ed., *To Markie*, p. 49.

42. Eben Swift, "The Military Education of Robert E. Lee," *The Virginia Magazine of Biography and History* 37 (April 1927): 107–8.

CHAPTER 6

1. Elizabeth Preston Allan, *The Life and Letters of Margaret Junkin Preston* (Boston: Houghton Mifflin and Company, 1903), p. 84; John Esten Cooke, *Stonewall Jackson: A Military Biography* (New York: D. Appleton and Company, 1866), pp. 24–25; Frank E. Vandiver, *Mighty Stonewall* (New York: McGraw-Hill, 1957), pp. 96–97.

2. Margaret Junkin Preston, "Personal Reminiscences of Stonewall Jackson," *Century Magazine* 16 (1886): 930; D. H. Hill, "The Real Stonewall Jackson," *Century Magazine* 25 (February 1894): 624; Warner J. Richards, *God Bless Our Arms: The Religious Life of Stonewall Jackson* (New York: Vantage Press, 1986), p. 35.

3. Thomas Jackson Arnold, *Early Life and Letters of General Thomas J. Jackson* (New York: Fleming H. Revell Company, 1916), pp. 209–10.

4. Ibid., pp. 219–20.

5. Mary Anna Jackson, *Memoirs of Stonewall Jackson by His Widow* (Louisville, KY: Prentice Press, 1895), p. 83; William Couper, *One Hundred Years at VMI* (Richmond: Garrett and Massie, 1939), I, p. 291; Hill, "The Real Stonewall Jackson," p. 626; Vandiver, *Mighty Stonewall*, p. 104

6. Arnold, *Life and Letters of Jackson*, p. 219.

7. Clifford Dowdey, *Lee* (Boston: Little, Brown and Company, 1965), p. 101; Douglas Southall Freeman, *R. E. Lee: A Biography* (New York: Charles Scribner's Sons, 1934), I, pp. 330–31.

8. Robert E. Lee, Jr., *Recollections and Letters of General Robert E. Lee* (Garden City, NY: Garden City Publishing Company, 1904), p. 12; J. William Jones, *Personal Reminiscences, Anecdotes, and Letters of General Robert E. Lee* (New York: D. Appleton and Company, 1875), pp. 416–17.

9. Richard M. McMurry, *John Bell Hood and the Southern Confederacy* (Lexington: University Press of Kentucky, 1982), p. 14; A. L. Long, *Memoirs of Robert E. Lee: His Military and Personal History* (Secaucus, NJ: Blue and Gray Press, reprint, 1983), pp. 74–76; Charles P. Roland, *Albert Sidney Johnston: Soldier of Three Republics* (Austin: University of Texas Press, 1964), pp. 170–171.

10. Charles P. Roland and Richard C. Robbins, eds., "The Second Cavalry Comes to Texas: The Diary of Eliza (Mrs. Albert Sidney) Johnston," *Southwestern Historical Quarterly* 60 (April 1957): 465–66.

11. J. William Jones, *Life and Letters of Robert Edward Lee: Soldier and Man* (New York: Neale Publishing Company, 1906), p. 79.

12. Long, *Memoirs of Lee*, p. 78; Freeman, *Lee*, I, pp. 363–78.

13. Clear Fork of the Brazos, where Camp Cooper was located.

14. Fitzhugh Lee, *General Lee* (New York: D. Appleton and Company, 1894), pp. 61–66; Dowdey, *Lee*, p. 107; Roland and Robbins, eds., "The Second Cavalry Comes to Texas," pp. 479, 494–95.

15. Carl Cone Rister, *Robert E. Lee in Texas* (Norman: University of Oklahoma Press, 1946), pp. 20, 27.

16. Ibid., p. 23.

17. Rister, *Lee in Texas*, pp. 23, 52; Fitzhugh Lee, *General Lee*, p. 59; Walter P. Webb, ed., *The Handbook of Texas* (Austin: Texas State Historical Association, 1954), II, p. 44.

18. Jones, *Life and Letters of Lee*, p. 80; Fitzhugh Lee, *General Lee*, p. 59.

19. Jones, *Life and Letters of Lee*, p. 80; John Bell Hood, *Advance and Retreat: Personal Experiences in the United States and Confederate Armies* (New Orleans: G.T. Beauregard, 1880), p. 8.

20. Jones, *Life and Letters of Lee*, p. 81; Webb, ed., *Handbook of Texas*, I, p. 631.

21. Jones, *Life and Letters of Lee*, pp. 82–83; Fitzhugh Lee, *General Lee*, pp. 62–63.

22. Arnold, *Life and Letters of Jackson*, p. 228; Roy Bird Cook, *The Family and Early Life of Stonewall Jackson* (Charleston, WV: Education Foundation, reprint, 1967), pp. 135–38.

23. Arnold, *Life and Letters of Jackson*, pp. 232–33.

24. Arnold, *Life and Letters of Jackson*, p. 231; Cook, *Family and Early Life of Jackson*,

p. 38; William P. Snow, *Lee and His Generals* (New York: Fairfax Press, reprint, 1982), p. 178.

25. Elizabeth Cometti and Festus P. Summers, eds., *The Thirty-Fifth State: A Documentary History of West Virginia* (Morgantown: West Virginia University Library, 1966), p. 191; Cook, *Early Life of Jackson*, p. 138.

26. Robert L. Dabney, *Life and Campaigns of Lieut.-Gen. Thomas J. Jackson* (New York: Blelock and Company, 1866), p. 93.

27. Dabney, *Life and Campaigns of Jackson*, p. 80; John Esten Cooke, *Stonewall Jackson*, p. 39; Preston, "Personal Reminiscences of Jackson," p. 934.

28. Dabney, *Life and Campaigns of Jackson*, p. 82; Stephen B. Oates, *To Purge This Land with Blood: A Biography of John Brown* (New York: Harper and Row, 1970), pp. 68–69.

29. Eugenia Morrison married Rufus Barringer in 1854; she died in 1858. A North Carolina lawyer and legislator, Barringer fought on the peninsula, and at Second Manassas, Antietam, Fredericksburg, Chancellorsville, and Brandy Station, before his capture in 1865. He made general rank in June 1864 and suffered three wounds during the war. See Dumas Malone, ed., *The Dictionary of American Biography* (New York: Charles Scribner's Sons, 1928), 1, p. 649.

30. Mary Anna Jackson, *The Memoirs of Stonewall Jackson by His Widow* (Louisville, KY: Prentice Press, 1895), pp. 99–103.

31. Ibid., p. 104; Vandiver, *Mighty Stonewall*, pp. 113–15; Arnold, *Life and Letters of Jackson*, pp. 255–56; An Ex-Cadet (James Dabney McCabe), *The Life of Thomas J. Jackson* (Richmond: James E. Goode, 1864), p. 24.

32. Charles P. Roland, *Albert Sidney Johnston: Soldier of Three Republics* (Austin: University of Texas Press, 1964), p. 184; Long, *Memoirs of Lee*, pp. 79–80.

33. Freeman, *Lee*, I, pp. 379ff.; Dowdey, *Lee*, p. 111; Robert E. Lee, Jr., *Recollections and Letters of General Robert E. Lee* (Garden City, NY: Garden City Publishing Company, 1904), p. 20.

34. Jones, *Life and Letters of Lee*, p. 87; Dowdey, *Lee*, p. 112; Robert E. Lee, *Recollections and Letters of Lee*, p. 20.

35. Avery O. Craven, ed., *To Markie: The Letters of Robert E. Lee to Martha Custis Williams* (Cambridge: Harvard University Press, 1933), pp. 54–56; Dowdey, *Lee*, p. 116.

36. Richard O. Boyer, *The Legend of John Brown: A Biography and a History* (New York: Alfred A. Knopf, 1973), pp. 525ff.; Oates, *To Purge This Land with Blood*, pp. 97–177; Paul D. Casdorph, "Brown Faces the Gallows," *West Virginia Hillbilly* 27 (November 1985): 19.

37. The Dred Scott decision of 1857.

38. Frederick Douglass, *The Life and Times of Frederick Douglass* (New York: Collier Books, reprint, 1962), pp. 318–24; William E. B. DuBois, *John Brown* (Millwood, NY: Kraus-Thompson, reprint, 1973), pp. 225–27; Jeffrey Rossbach, *John Brown*,

The Secret Six, and A Theory of Slave Violence (Philadelphia: University of Pennsylvania Press, 1982), pp. 313–16; Paul D. Casdorph, "John Brown's Letters," *West Virginia Hillbilly* 27 (October 1985): 27.

39. John W. Thomason, *JEB Stuart* (New York: Charles Scribner's Sons, reprint, 1958), p. 49; Oates, *To Purge This Land with Blood*, p. 298; Casdorph, "John Brown's Letters," p. 29.

40. Jones, *Life and Letters of Lee*, p. 106; Elijah Avey, *The Capture and Execution of John Brown* (Chicago: Afro-Am Press, reprint, 1969), pp. 83–85; Snow, *Lee and His Generals*, pp. 32–33: Casdorph, "John Brown's Letters," p. 27.

41. Robert E. Lee, Jr., *Recollections and Letters of Lee*, p. 22; Long, *Memoirs of Lee*, p. 86; Jones, *Life and Letters of Lee*, p. 106.

42. Cometti and Summers, eds., *The Thirty Fifth State*, p. 270; Casdorph, "John Brown's Letters," p. 19; Rossbach, *Brown and the Secret Six*, pp. 220, 229.

43. Fitzhugh Lee, *General Lee*, pp. 75–76; Burke Davis, *They Called Him Stonewall: A Life of Lt. General T. J. Jackson, C.S.A.* (New York: Fairfax Press, reprint, 1988), pp. 5–6.

44. Robert E. Lee, Jr., *Recollections and Letters*, p. 22; Fitzhugh Lee, *General Lee*, pp. 75–76; Burke Davis, *JEB Stuart: The Last Cavalier* (New York: Fairfax Press, reprint, 1988), p. 16; Jones, *Life and Letters of Lee*, pp. 105–6.

45. Anna Jackson, *Memoirs of Jackson*, pp. 130–31.

46. Dowdey, *Lee*, p. 120; Rister, *Lee in Texas*, p. 131.

47. Webb, ed., *Handbook of Texas*, I, p. 417; Stephen B. Oates, ed., *Rip Ford's Texas* (Austin: University of Texas Press, 1963), pp. 503–5.

48. Lyman L. Woodman, *Cortina: Rogue of the Rio Grande* (San Antonio: Naylor Company, 1950), pp. 53–61; Walter P. Webb, *The Texas Rangers: A Century of Frontier Defense* (Austin: University of Texas Press, reprint, 1965), pp. 173–93; Jones, *Reminiscences of Lee*, p. 380.

49. Jones, *Reminiscences of Lee*, pp. 381–83.

50. Jones, *Reminiscences of Lee*, p. 381; Freeman, *Lee*, II, p. 135; Robert E. Lee, Jr., *Recollections and Letters of Lee*, p. 24.

51. Webb, *Texas Rangers*, pp. 206–7; this source photographically reproduces the Lee-Lea Correspondence; Donald Braider, *Solitary Star: A Biography of Sam Houston* (New York: G. P. Putnam's Sons, 1974), p. 59.

52. Rister, *Lee in Texas*, pp. 133–37.

53. Fitzhugh Lee, *General Lee*, p. 77; Rupert N. Richardson, *Texas: The Lone Star State* (Englewood Cliffs, NJ: Prentice-Hall, 1961), pp. 150–53; Webb, ed., *Handbook of Texas*, I, p. 385.

54. Robert M. Hughes, *General Johnston* (New York: D. Appleton and Company, 1893), p. 33; Malone, ed., *Dictionary of American Biography*, 10, p. 63.

55. Hughes, *General Johnston*, p. 34.

56. Alfred Hoyt Bill, *Rehearsal for Conflict: The War with Mexico, 1846–1848* (New York: Alfred A. Knopf, 1947), p. 51; Roland, *Albert Sidney Johnston*, passim; James H. Wilson, *Under the Old Flag* (New York: D. Appleton and Company, 1912), pp. 321–24.

57. Hughes, *General Johnston*, p. 34.

58. Dowdey, *Lee*, p. 124.

CHAPTER 7

1. Mary Anna Jackson, *Memoirs of Stonewall Jackson by His Widow* (Louisville, KY: Prentice Press, 1895), p. 132; Frank E. Vandiver, *Mighty Stonewall* (New York: McGraw-Hill, 1957), p. 126.

2. Thomas J. Arnold, *Early Life and Letters of General Thomas J. Jackson* (New York: Fleming H. Revell Company, 1916), p. 278.

3. Ibid., pp. 305–7.

4. Jennings C. Wise, *The Military History of the Virginia Military Institute from 1839 to 1865* (Lynchburg, VA: J. P. Bell Company, 1915), pp. 121–22; Dumas Malone, ed., *The Dictionary of American Biography* (New York: Charles Scribner's Sons, 1935), 22, p. 264; *In Memoriam: Francis H. Smith, Father and Founder of the Virginia Military Institute* (New York: Knickerbocker Press, pamphlet, 1890), p. 18.

5. Wise, *Military History of VMI*, p. 121.

6. Malone, ed., *Dictionary of American Biography*, 14, p. 261.

7. Wise, *Military History of VMI*, p. 126; Anna Jackson, *Memoirs of Jackson*, p. 133.

8. Arnold, *Life and Letters of Jackson*, pp. 135, 385.

9. Eric Foner, *Free Soil, Free Labor, Free Men: The Ideology of the Republican Party before the Civil War* (New York: Oxford University Press, 1970), pp. 127–29; George H. Mayer, *The Republican Party, 1854–1964* (Oxford University Press, 1964), pp. 60–61, 66.

10. Stephen Vincent Benet, *John Brown's Body* (New York: Holt, Rinehart and Winston, reprint, 1960), pp. 40, 52, 54.

11. Dwight L. Dumond, *The Secession Movement, 1860–1861* (New York: Macmillan, 1931), p. 33; James M. McPherson, *Ordeal by Fire: The Civil War and Reconstruction* (New York: Alfred A. Knopf, 1982), p. 136; James G. Randall and David H. Donald, *The Civil War and Reconstruction* (Lexington, MA: D. C. Heath and Company, 1969), p. 127.

12. David M. Potter, *The Impending Crisis, 1848–1861* (New York: Harper and Row, 1976), pp. 401–28; Robert W. Johannsen, *Stephen A. Douglas* (New York: Oxford University Press, 1973), pp. 749–73.

13. Potter, *Impending Crisis*, pp. 428ff.; Malone, ed., *Dictionary of American Biography*, 6, p. 226; Henry H. Simms, *A Decade of Sectional Controversy, 1851–1861* (Chapel Hill: University of North Carolina Press, 1942), p. 202–03.

14. Wise, *Military History of VMI*, p. 26.

15. Ibid., p. 126; Anna Jackson, *Memoirs of Jackson*, p. 142.

16. Robert Franklin Maddox, "The Presidential Election of 1860 in Western Virginia," *West Virginia History* 25 (April 1963): 224; Elizabeth Cometti and Festus P. Summers, eds., *The Thirty-Fifth State: A Documentary History of West Virginia* (Morgantown: West Virginia University Library, 1966), p. 285.

17. Potter, *Impending Crisis*, pp. 485–513; E. Merton Coulter, *The Confederate States of America, 1861–1865* (Baton Rouge: Louisiana State University Press, 1950), pp. 1–32; Frank H. Smyrl, *The Twenty-Eighth Star: Texas during the Period of Early Statehood, 1846–1861* (Boston: American Press, 1983), pp. 38–43.

18. Douglas Southall Freeman, *R. E. Lee: A Biography* (New York: Charles Scribner's Sons, 1934), I, p. 413; Mark M. Boatner, *The Civil War Dictionary* (New York: David McKay Company, 1962), p. 87.

19. Carl Coke Rister, *Robert E. Lee in Texas* (Norman: University of Oklahoma Press, 1946), pp. 146–49; Walter P. Webb, ed., *The Handbook of Texas* (Austin: Texas State Historical Association, 1952), I, p. 64, II, p. 144.

20. Simms, *Decade of Sectional Controversy*, pp. 233–34; Charles H. Ambler and Festus P. Summers, *West Virginia: The Mountain State* (Englewood Cliffs, NJ: Prentice-Hall, 1958), pp. 187–94; Oliver P. Chitwood, *John Tyler: Champion of the Old South* (New York: Russell and Russell, reprint, 1964), pp. 436–48.

21. Ambler and Summers, *West Virginia: The Mountain State*, pp. 193–94; W. A. Swanberg, *First Blood: The Story of Fort Sumter* (New York: Charles Scribner's Sons, 1957), pp. 291–311.

22. Clifford Dowdey, *Lee* (Boston: Little, Brown and Company, 1965), p. 127; Webb, ed., *Handbook of Texas*, I, pp. 495, 847, II, p. 161; Philip Silver Klein, *James Buchanan: A Biography* (University Park: Pennsylvania State University Press, 1962), pp. 398–401.

23. Anna Jackson, *Memoirs of Jackson*, p. 139; Arnold, *Life and Letters of Jackson*, p. 318.

24. Anna Jackson, *Memoirs of Jackson*, p. 143.

25. Wise, *Military History of VMI*, p. 133.

26. Ibid., pp. 140–41.

27. Frank E. Vandiver, *Mighty Stonewall*, p. 133; Anna Jackson, *Memoirs of Jackson*, p. 148.

28. Anna Jackson, *Memoirs of Jackson*, p. 148; Wise, *Military History of VMI*, p. 136.

29. Dowdey, *Lee*, p. 128; J. William Jones, *Personal Reminiscences, Anecdotes, and*

Letters of General Robert E. Lee (New York: D. Appleton and Company, 1874), p. 136.

30. William E. Smith, *The Francis P. Blair Family in Politics* (New York: Macmillan Company, 1933), II, pp. 17–18; Jones, *Reminiscences of Lee*, p. 138.

31. Carl Sandburg, *Abraham Lincoln: The War Years* (New York: Harcourt, Brace and Company, 1939), I, p. 519; Rister, *Lee in Texas*, p. 165.

32. Robert E. Lee, Jr., *Recollections and Letters of General Robert E. Lee* (Garden City, NY: Garden City Publishing Company, 1904), pp. 26–28.

33. Ibid., 28; Ambler and Summers, *West Virginia: The Mountain State*, p. 190.

34. Dowdey, *Lee*, p. 172; Jones, *Reminiscences of Lee*, p. 140.

35. Anna Jackson, *Memoirs of Jackson*, p. 148.

CHAPTER 8

1. Mary Anna Jackson, *Memoirs of Stonewall Jackson by His Widow* (Louisville, KY: Prentice Press, 1895), p. 149.

2. James N. Bosang, *Memoirs of a Pulaski Veteran* (Pulaski, VA: Privately printed, 1912), p. 4.

3. Jennings C. Wise, *The Military History of the Virginia Military Institute from 1839 to 1865* (Lynchburg, VA: J. P. Bell Company, 1915), p. 146.

4. Lenoir Chambers, *Stonewall Jackson: The Legend and the Man to the Valley* (New York: William Morrow and Company, 1959), I, p. 280; Anna Jackson, *Memoirs of Jackson*, p. 149.

5. Anna Jackson, *Memoirs of Jackson*, p. 150; Secretary of War, *The War of the Rebellion: A Compilation of the Official Records of the Union and Confederate Armies* (Washington, DC: Government Printing Office, 1880ff.), Ser. 1, Vol. 2, p. 784, hereafter cited as *O.R.*

6. Anna Jackson, *Memoirs of Jackson*, p. 150; Wise, *Military History of VMI*, pp. 148–49.

7. Thomas Jackson Arnold, *Early Life and Letters of General Thomas J. Jackson* (New York: Fleming H. Revell Company, 1916), p. 331.

8. Frank E. Vandiver, *Mighty Stonewall* (New York: McGraw-Hill, 1957), p. 136; Douglas Southall Freeman, *Lee's Lieutenants: A Study in Command* (New York: Charles Scribner's Sons, 1942), I, pp. 720, 730.

9. Clifford Dowdey, *Lee* (Boston: Little, Brown and Company, 1965), p. 145; Mark M. Boatner, *The Civil War Dictionary* (New York: David McKay Company, 1959), p. 161.

10. Dowdey, *Lee*, p. 713; Dumas Malone, ed., *The Dictionary of American Biography* (New York: Charles Scribner's Sons, 1936), 18, p. 283.

11. Malone, ed., *Dictionary of American Biography*, 18, p. 281; George G. Shackelford, "Lieutenant Lee Reports to Captain Talcott on Fort Calhoun's Construction on the

Rip Raps," *Virginia Magazine of History and Biography* 60 (April 1952): 458–87; *O.R.*, Ser. 1, Vol. II, p. 876.

12. Anna Jackson, *Memoirs of Jackson*, p. 154; Vandiver, *Mighty Stonewall*, p. 136; William Couper, *One Hundred Years at VMI* (Richmond: Garrett and Massie, 1939), II, p. 112.

13. A. L. Long, *Memoirs of Robert E. Lee: His Military and Personal History* (Secaucus, NJ: Blue and Gray Press, reprint, 1983), p. 112.

14. Malone, ed., *Dictionary of American Biography*, 11, p. 374; Boatner, *Civil War Dictionary*, p. 489.

15. Burke Davis, *The Gray Fox: Robert E. Lee and the Civil War* (New York: Fairfax Press, reprint, 1981), pp. 30–31; Jefferson Davis, *The Rise and Fall of the Confederate Government* (New York: Thomas Yoseloff, reprint, 1958), I, p. 340; Long, *Memoirs of Lee*, pp. 112–13.

16. Long, *Memoirs of Lee*, p. 113; Frank E. Vandiver, *Plowshares into Swords: Josiah Gorgas and Confederate Ordnance* (Austin: University of Texas Press, 1952), passim; Malone, ed., *Dictionary of American Biography*, 7, pp. 428–30.

17. U.S. Congress, *Biographical Directory of the American Congress, 1774–1961* (Washington, DC: Government Printing Office, 1961), p. 1650; Vernon L. Parrington, *Main Currents in American Thought* (New York: Harcourt, Brace, and World, reprint, 1958), II, p. 82; Clement Eaton, *A History of the Southern Confederacy* (New York: Macmillan Company, 1958), p. 47; also, Alexander H. Stephens, *A Constitutional View of the Late War between the States* (Philadelphia: National Publishing Company, 1868–1870, 2 vols.).

18. Eaton, *Southern Confederacy*, pp. 47–48; Malone, ed., *Dictionary of American Biography*, 17, p. 573.

19. Robert E. Lee, Jr., *Recollections and Letters of General Robert E. Lee* (Garden City, NY: Garden City Publishing Company, 1904), p. 29.

20. Ibid., pp. 29–31; Malone, ed., *Dictionary of American Biography*, 12, pp. 475–76; Boatner, *Civil War Dictionary*, pp. 475–76.

21. Emory M. Thomas, *The Confederate Nation, 1861–1865* (New York: Harper and Row, 1979), pp. 99–101; Eaton, *Southern Confederacy*, p. 53.

22. Clement Eaton, *Jefferson Davis* (New York: Free Press, 1977), pp. 137–38; Jefferson Davis, *Rise and Fall of the Confederate Government*, I, p. 339.

23. Long, *Memoirs of Lee*, pp. 103–04; William P. Snow, *Lee and His Generals* (New York: Fairfax Press, reprint, 1982), p. 45.

24. Malone, ed., *Dictionary of American Biography*, 9, p. 134; *O.R.*, Ser. 1, Vol. 2, pp. 867ff.

25. Boatner, *Civil War Dictionary*, p. 63; Malone, ed., *Dictionary of American Biography*, 7, p. 205; Burke Davis, *Gray Fox*, p. 31.

26. Malone, ed., *Dictionary of American Biography*, 9, p. 126; Eaton, *Jefferson Davis*,

pp. 181–82; see also, J. H. Wheeler, *Reminiscences and Memoirs of North Carolinians* (Columbus, OH: Columbus Print Company, 1884).

27. Long, *Memoirs of Lee*, p. 104; T. Harry Williams, *P. G. T. Beauregard: Napoleon in Gray* (Baton Rouge: Louisiana State University Press, 1954), pp. 66–80; Boatner, *Civil War Dictionary*, p. 55.

28. Malone, ed., *Dictionary of American Biography*, 7, p. 159; Jack Zinn, *Lee's Cheat Mountain Campaign* (Parsons, WV: McClain Publishing Company, 1974), passim.

29. Gilbert E. Govan and James W. Livingood, *A Different Valor: The Story of General Joseph E. Johnston, C.S.A.* (Indianapolis: Bobbs-Merrill Company, 1956), p. 137; James I. Robertson, *The Stonewall Brigade* (Baton Rouge: Louisiana State University Press, 1963), pp. 7–10.

30. *O.R.*, Ser. 1, Vol. 2, pp. 807–08.

31. G. F. R. Henderson, *Stonewall Jackson and the American Civil War* (London: Longmans, Green and Company, 1906), I, pp. 114–16.

32. William W. Bennett, *A Narrative of the Great Revival Which Prevailed in the Southern Armies* (Philadelphia: Claton, Remsen, and Haffelfinger, 1877), p. 99; Robertson, *Stonewall Brigade*, pp. 26–27.

33. John N. Opie, *A Rebel Cavalryman under Lee, Stuart, and Jackson* (Chicago: W. B. Conkey Company, reprint, 1972), pp. 19–20.

34. *O.R.*, Ser. 1, Vol. 2, p. 809; Vandiver, *Mighty Stonewall*, pp. 140–42.

35. *O.R.*, Ser. 1, Vol. 2, pp. 824–25.

36. Ibid., pp. 832, 836.

37. Festus P. Summers, *The Baltimore and Ohio Railroad in the Civil War* (New York: G. P. Putnam's Sons, 1939), pp. 17, 65–69; Elizabeth Cometti and Festus P. Summers, *The Thirty-Fifth State: A Documentary History of West Virginia* (Morgantown: West Virginia University Library, 1966), pp. 217–222; Opie, *Rebel Cavalryman*, p. 20.

38. Summers, *Baltimore and Ohio Railroad in the Civil War*, p. 67.

39. Freeman, *Lee's Lieutenants*, 3, p. 167; Chambers, *Stonewall Jackson*, I, p. 320; Vandiver, *Mighty Stonewall*, pp. 142–43.

40. Anna Jackson, *Memoirs of Jackson*, pp. 151–53.

41. *O.R.*, Ser. 1, Vol. 2, pp. 849, 860; Sir Frederick Maurice, *An Aide-de-Camp of Lee* (Boston: Little, Brown and Company, 1927), pp. 8–10; J. G. Randall and David Donald, *The Civil War and Reconstruction* (Lexington, MA: D. C. Heath and Company, 1969), pp. 360–62.

42. *O.R.*, Ser. 1, Vol. 2, pp. 844–46; Anna Jackson, *Memoirs of Jackson*, p. 57.

43. *O.R.*, Ser. 1, Vol. 2, pp. 872–76; Robert M. Hughes, *General Johnston* (New York: D. Appleton and Company, 1893), p. 40.

44. Anna Jackson, *Memoirs of Jackson*, pp. 157–58.

45. Robert E. Lee, Jr., *Recollections and Letters of Lee*, pp. 30–31.

46. Ibid., pp. 31–32; *O.R.*, Ser. 1, Vol. 2, pp. 808–9, 863, 866–67.

47. Otis K. Rice, *West Virginia: A History* (Lexington: University Press of Kentucky, 1985), pp. 120–45; Charles H. Ambler and Festus P. Summers, *West Virginia: The Mountain State* (Englewood Cliffs, NJ: Prentice-Hall, 1958), pp. 195–228; *O.R.*, Ser. 1, Vol. 2, p. 810.

48. George B. McClellan, *Report of the Organization and Campaigns of the Army of the Potomac* (Freeport, NY: Books for Libraries, reprint, 1970), pp. 16–17.

49. Boyd B. Stutler, *West Virginia and the Civil War* (Charleston, WV: Education Foundation, 1963), p. 10; McClellan, *Report of the Army of the Potomac*, p. 16; *O.R.*, Ser. 1, Vol. 2, p. 833; Rice, *West Virginia: A History*, p. 125.

CHAPTER 9

1. Vincent J. Esposito, *The West Point Atlas of American Wars* (New York: Frederick A. Praeger Publishers, 1959), I, p. 20; Oliver O. Howard, *The Autobiography of Oliver Otis Howard* (New York: Baker and Taylor Company, 1907), p. 146; James B. Fry, *McDowell and Tyler in the Campaign of Bull Run* (New York: D. Van Nostrand, 1884), pp. 6–10; Mark M. Boatner, *The Civil War Dictionary* (New York: David McKay Company, 1959), p. 531; Kenneth P. Williams, *Lincoln Finds a General: A Military Study of the Civil War* (New York: Macmillan Company, 1964), I, pp. 66–68.

2. Williams, *Lincoln Finds a General*, I, p. 60; William C. Davis, *Battle at Bull Run: A History of the First Major Campaign of the Civil War* (Garden City, NY: Doubleday and Company, 1977), pp. 69–70.

3. Douglas Southall Freeman, *Robert E. Lee: A Biography* (New York: Charles Scribner's Sons, 1934), I, p. 512; Secretary of War, *The War of the Rebellion: A Compilation of the Official Records of the Union and Confederate Armies* (Washington, DC: Government Printing Office, 1880ff.), Ser. 1, Vol. 2, p. 849, hereafter cited as *O.R.*

4. *O.R.*, Ser. 1, Vol. 2, p. 847; A. L. Long, *The Memoirs of Robert E. Lee: His Military and Personal History* (Secaucus, NJ: Blue and Gray Press, reprint, 1983), p. 112; Burke Davis, *The Gray Fox: Robert E. Lee and the Civil War* (New York: Fairfax Press, reprint, 1981), pp. 30–32.

5. William Swinton, *Campaigns of the Army of the Potomac, 1861–1865* (New York: Charles Scribner's Sons, 1882), pp. 44–45; *O.R.*, Ser. 1, Vol. 2, p. 5; Davis, *Battle at Bull Run*, pp. 132ff.

6. Mary Anna Jackson, *Memoirs of Stonewall Jackson by His Widow* (Louisville, KY: Prentice Press, 1895), p. 159.

7. Ibid., p. 162; Thomas Jackson Arnold, *Early Life and Letters of General Thomas J. Jackson* (New York: Fleming H. Revell Company, 1916), p. 332.

8. Edward A. Pollard, *Lee and His Lieutenants* (New York: E. B. Treat and Company,

1867), p. 185; Joseph E. Johnston, *Narrative of Military Operations* (Bloomington: Indiana University Press, reprint, 1959), p. 17; William Thomas Poague, *Gunner with Stonewall* (Jackson, TN: McCowat-Mercer Press, reprint, 1957), pp. 6–7.

9. Johnston, *Narrative of Military Operations*, p. 27; John O. Casler, *Four Years in the Stonewall Brigade* (Girard, KS: Appeal Publishing Company, 1906), pp. 21–26; James I. Robertson, *The Stonewall Brigade* (Baton Rouge: Louisiana State University Press, 1963), pp. 10–11; Robert G. Tanner, *Stonewall in the Valley* (Garden City, NY: Doubleday and Company, 1976), pp. 33–34.

10. Johnston, *Narrative of Military Operations*, p. 30; *O.R.*, ser. 1, Vol. 2, pp. 184–85; Frank E. Vandiver, *Mighty Stonewall* (New York: McGraw-Hill, 1957), pp. 148–50.

11. *O.R.*, Ser. 1, Vol. 2, p. 185.

12. John Esten Cooke, *Stonewall Jackson: A Military Biography* (New York: D. Appleton and Company, 1866), p. 53; Poague, *Gunner with Stonewall*, pp. 52–53; Susan P. Lee, *Memoirs of William Nelson Pendleton* (Philadelphia: J. B. Lippincott Company, 1893), pp. 145–46.

13. John W. Thomason, *JEB Stuart* (New York: Charles Scribner's Sons, reprint, 1958), p. 97; Burke Davis, *JEB Stuart: The Last Cavalier* (New York: Fairfax Press, reprint, 1988), pp. 56–57; *O.R.*, Ser. 1, Vol. 2, p. 185; Johnston, *Narrative of Military Operations*, pp. 30–31.

14. Poague, *Gunner with Stonewall*, p. 7.

15. Anna Jackson, *Memoirs of Jackson*, pp. 166–67.

16. Ibid., pp. 167–68; An Ex-Cadet (James Dabney McCabe), *The Life of Thomas J. Jackson* (Richmond: James E. Goode, 1864), p. 33; Vandiver, *Mighty Stonewall*, pp. 146–47.

17. Johnston, *Narrative of Military Operations*, pp. 30–31; An Ex-Cadet (McCabe), *Life of Jackson*, p. 36.

18. Davis, *Battle at Bull Run*, pp. 79, 165; Robert Selph Henry, *The Story of the Confederacy* (New York: Bobbs-Merrill Company, 1936), pp. 52–54; Edwin S. Barrett, *What I Saw at Bull Run* (Boston: Beacon Press, 1886), pp. 11–13; Daniel Tyler, *Autobiography and War Record* (New Haven, CT: Privately printed, 1883), p. 48.

19. *O.R.*, Ser. 1, Vol. 2, p. 655; Fitzhugh Lee, *General Lee* (New York: D. Appleton and Company, 1894), p. 106.

20. Robert E. Lee, Jr., *Recollections and Letters of General Robert E. Lee* (Garden City, NY: Garden City Publishing Company, 1904), p. 36; *O.R.*, Ser. 1, Vol. 2, p. 507; C. Vann Woodward and Elisabeth Muhlenfeld, eds., *The Private Mary Chesnut: The Unpublished Civil War Diaries* (New York: Oxford University Press, 1984), p. 97.

21. Clifford Dowdey, *Lee* (Boston: Little, Brown and Company, 1965), p. 159; Clement Eaton, *Jefferson Davis* (New York: Free Press, 1977), pp. 137–38; Robert E. Lee, Jr., *Recollections and Letters of Lee*, p. 37.

22. Esposito, *West Point Atlas*, I, p. 20; Howard, *Autobiography*, pp. 146–47.

23. T. Harry Williams, *P. G. T. Beauregard: Napoleon in Gray* (Baton Rouge: Louisiana State University Press, 1954), pp. 77–79; Robert M. Johnston, *Bull Run: Its Strategy and Tactics* (Boston: Houghton Mifflin Company, 1913), pp. 84, 159–61.

24. Louis A. Sigaud, "Mrs. Greenhow and the Confederate Spy Ring," *Maryland Historical Magazine* 41 (September 1946): 173–75; *O.R.*, Ser. 1, Vol. 2, p. 504; Williams, *Lincoln Finds a General*, I, p. 86.

25. Johnston, *Bull Run*, p. 151; Anna Jackson, *Memoirs of Jackson*, p. 177; Johnston, *Narrative of Military Operations*, pp. 33–35.

26. James Franklin, "Incidents at the First Manassas Battle," *Confederate Veteran* 2 (October 1894): 292; Joseph M. Hanson, *Bull Run Remembers* (Manassas, VA: National Capital Publishers, 1961), p. 3; Tyler, *Autobiography*, pp. 53–54.

27. D. B. Conrad, "History of the First Battle of Manassas and the Organization of the Stonewall Brigade," *Southern Historical Society Papers* 20 (1892): pp. 83–85; Robertson, *Stonewall Brigade*, pp. 36–37.

28. Conrad, "History of Manassas," p. 83; John Esten Cooke, *Wearing of the Grey* (Bloomington: Indiana University Press, reprint, 1959), p. 35; D. H. Hill, "The Real Stonewall Jackson," *Century Magazine* 25 (February 1894): 625.

29. Williams, *Lincoln Finds a General*, I, p. 90; Tyler, *Autobiography*, p. 52; Douglas Southall Freeman, *Lee's Lieutenants: A Study in Command* (New York: Charles Scribner's Sons, 1942), I, p. 87; George Baylor, *Bull Run to Bull Run; or, Four Years in the Army of Northern Virginia* (Richmond: B. F. Johnson Publishing Company, 1900), pp. 19–22.

30. Swinton, *Campaigns of the Army of the Potomac*, p. 49; Davis, *Battle at Bull Run*, p. 66.

31. John Selby, *Stonewall Jackson as Military Commander* (London: B. T. Batsford, 1968), pp. 19–21; Vandiver, *Mighty Stonewall*, p. 161; *O.R.*, Ser. 1, Vol. 2, p. 461.

32. Jackson's letter to Bennett is reproduced in John Esten Cooke, *Stonewall Jackson*, appendix, unpaged; it contains much information found in his official battle report in the *O.R.*; see also Henry, *Story of the Confederacy*, p. 57.

33. Davis, *Battle at Bull Run*, p. 196; *O.R.*, Ser. 1, Vol. 2, p. 482.

34. Henry Kyd Douglas, *I Rode with Stonewall* (Chapel Hill: University of North Carolina Press, reprint, 1968), p. 10; *O.R.*, Ser. 1, Vol. 2, p. 482.

35. Johnston, *Bull Run*, p. 202; Charleston *Mercury*, July 25, 1861.

36. Robertson, *Stonewall Brigade*, p. 189; Douglas, *I Rode with Stonewall*, p. 227; Roy Bird Cook, *The Family and Early Life of Stonewall Jackson* (Charleston, WV: Education Foundation, reprint, 1967) pp. 169–70; Freeman, *Lee's Lieutenants*, I, p. 734; for a detailed analysis of the name "Stonewall" and its origins, see, Freeman, *Lee's Lieutenants*, I, pp. 733–34; J. M. Johnston, *Bull Run*, pp. 202–3; Selby, *Stonewall Jackson*, pp. 28–31.

37. J. M. Johnston, *Bull Run*, p. 303; John Esten Cooke, *Stonewall Jackson*, p. 466; Anna Jackson, *Memoirs of Jackson*, pp. 177–79.

38. Henry, *Story of the Confederacy*, pp. 59–60; Vandiver, *Mighty Stonewall*, pp. 162–64; John H. Worsham, *One of Jackson's Foot Cavalry* (Jackson, TN: McCowat-Mercer Press, reprint, 1964), pp. 12–13.

39. Bruce Catton, *Terrible Swift Sword* (Garden City, NY: Doubleday and Company, 1963), p. 1; Roy P. Basler, ed., *The Collected Works of Abraham Lincoln* (New Brunswick, NJ: Rutgers University Press, 1953), 4, pp. 457–58, 5, p. 98; Margaret Leech, *Reveille in Washington* (New York: Time Incorporated, reprint, 1962), pp. 128–31.

40. Winston Churchill, *A History of the English Speaking Peoples: The Great Democracies* (New York: Dodd, Meade and Company, 1958), p. 182; Fitzhugh Lee, *General Lee*, pp. 112ff.; Woodward and Muhlenfeld, eds., *The Private Mary Chesnut*, p. 106; Davis, *Gray Fox*, pp. 33–34.

41. George B. McClellan, *Report of the Organization and Campaigns of The Army of the Potomac* (Freeport, NY: Books for Libraries Press, reprint, 1970), p. 98; Boyd B. Stutler, *West Virginia and the Civil War* (Charleston, WV: Education Foundation, 1963), p. 74; Otis K. Rice, *West Virginia: A History* (Lexington: University Press of Kentucky, 1985), pp. 130–31.

42. Walter H. Taylor, *Four Years with General Lee* (New York: D. Appleton and Company, 1877), pp. 16–20; Jack Zinn, *Lee's Cheat Mountain Campaign* (Parsons, WV: McClain Printing Company, 1974), p. 67; William L. Wessels, *Born to Be a Soldier: The Military Career of William Wing Loring* (Fort Worth: Texas Christian University Press, 1971), pp. 57–58.

43. R. E. Lee, Jr., *Recollections and Letters of Lee*, pp. 38–39.

44. Ibid., p. 43; Long, *Memoirs of Lee*, p. 120; John Levering, "Lee's Advance and Retreat in the Cheat Mountain Campaign in 1861 Supplemented by the Tragic Death of Colonel John A. Washington of His Staff," *Military Essays and Recollections: Military Order of the Loyal Legion of the United States, Illinois Commandry* (Chicago: Cottens and Bealton Company, 1907), 4, pp. 29–32.

45. Stutler, *West Virginia and the Civil War*, pp. 95–96; Charles H. Ambler, "General R. E. Lee's Northwest Virginia Campaign," *West Virginia History* 5 (January 1944): 108; R. E. Lee, Jr., *Recollections and Letters of Lee*, p. 40.

46. Taylor, *Four Years with General Lee*, pp. 22–33; Long, *Memoirs of Lee*, p. 112; P. S. Hagy, "The Cheat Mountain Campaign," *Confederate Veteran* 23 (March 1915): 122–23.

47. Stutler, *West Virginia and the Civil War*, pp. 96–99; A. C. Jones, "The Mountain Campaign Failure," *Confederate Veteran* 22 (July 1914): 305; Zinn, *Lee's Cheat Mountain Campaign*, p. 112ff. Although I have relied heavily upon Stutler, D. S. Freeman, *Lee*, I, pp. 554ff., probably contains the best account of the Cheat Mountain fiasco.

48. Stutler, *West Virginia and the Civil War*, p. 97; R. E. Lee, Jr., *Recollections and Letters of Lee*, p. 45.

49. Clifford Dowdey, ed., *The Wartime Papers of R. E. Lee* (Boston: Little, Brown and Company, 1961), pp. 75–76; John Purifay, "Letters on the West Virginia Campaign," *Confederate Veteran* 34 (June 1926): 216–17; Fitzhugh Lee, *General Lee*, p. 127.

50. Long, *Memoirs of Lee*, pp. 127–28; William McComb, "Tennesseans in the Mountain Campaign," *Confederate Veteran* 22 (May 1914): 210.

51. Dumas Malone, ed., *The Dictionary of American Biography* (New York: Charles Scribner's Sons, 1931), 20, pp. 423–25; Stutler, *West Virginia and the Civil War*, pp. 69–73; Jacob D. Cox, *Military Reminiscences of the Civil War* (New York: Charles Scribner's Sons, 1900), I, pp. 68–79; see also Terry Lowry, *The Battle of Scary Cheek: Military Operations in the Kanawha Valley, April–July 1862* (Charleston, WV: Pictorial Histories Publishing Company, 1982).

52. *O.R.*, Ser. 1, Vol. 5, p. 805, and passim: Terry Lowry, *September Blood: The Battle of Carnifex Ferry* (Charleston, WV: Pictorial Histories Publishing Company, 1985), pp. 72–122; Stutler, *West Virginia and the Civil War*, p. 150.

53. Robert W. Barnwell, "The First West Virginia Campaign," *Confederate Veteran* 38 (April 1930): 150; Taylor, *Four Years with General Lee*, p. 33; Robert E. Lee, Jr., *Recollections and Letters of Lee*, p. 49; significant differences in transcription exist between Dowdey, ed., *Wartime Papers of Robert E. Lee*, and the collection of letters by Robert E. Lee, Jr. Compare Dowdey, p. 78, and Robert E. Lee, Jr., p. 49, and passim. To this author, Lee, Jr., appears the more plausible.

54. Thomas L. Broun, "General Robert E. Lee's War-Horses: Traveller and Lucy Long," *Southern Historical Society Papers* 18 (1890): 386–88; Long, *Memoirs of Lee*, p. 132; see also, Tim McKinney, *Robert E. Lee At Sewell Mountain* (Charleston, WV: Pictorial Histories Publishing Company, 1990).

55. A Member of the Family, "General Robert E. Lee's War-Horses," *Southern Historical Society Papers* 19 (1891): 334; Long, *Memoirs of Lee*, p. 133; "A Member of the Family" says Lee bought the horse in South Carolina.

56. Robert E. Lee, Jr., *Recollections and Letters of Lee*, p. 51.

CHAPTER 10

1. Clifford Dowdey, *The Seven Days: The Emergence of Lee* (Boston: Little, Brown and Company, 1964), p. 72; Randolph H. McKim, *The Soul of Lee* (New York: Longmans, Green and Company, 1918), pp. 41–44; Secretary of War, *The War of the Rebellion: A Compilation of the Official Records of the Union and Confederate Armies* (Washington, DC: Government Printing Office, 1880ff.), Ser. 1, Vol. 5, pp. 855–83, hereafter cited as *O.R.*

2. Stephen W. Sears, *George B. McClellan: The Young Napoleon* (New York: Ticknor and Fields, 1988), p. 164; David E. Johnson, *The Story of a Confederate Boy in the*

Civil War (Portland, OR: Glass and Prudhomme Company, 1914), p. 79; John O. Casler, *Four Years in the Stonewall Brigade* (Marietta, GA: Continental Book Company, reprint, 1951), p. 56.

3. Mary Anna Jackson, *Memoirs of Stonewall Jackson by His Widow* (Louisville, KY: Prentice Press, 1895), p. 195.

4. Ibid., pp. 189–91.

5. Joseph E. Johnston, *Narrative of Military Operations* (Bloomington: Indiana University Press, reprint, 1959), pp. 78–81.

6. Robert G. Tanner, *Stonewall in the Valley* (Garden City, NY: Doubleday and Company, 1976), pp. 42–43; John Esten Cooke, *Stonewall Jackson: A Military Biography* (New York: D. Appleton and Company, 1866), pp. 85–86; Casler, *Four Years in the Stonewall Brigade*, pp. 57–58.

7. *O.R.*, Ser. 1, Vol. 5, p. 965; Frank E. Vandiver, *Mighty Stonewall* (New York: McGraw-Hill, 1957), p. 186; James I. Robertson, *The Stonewall Brigade* (Baton Rouge: Louisiana State University Press, 1963), pp. 51–54.

8. *O.R.*, Ser. 1, Vol. 5, p. 965; William L. Wessels, *Born to Be a Soldier: The Military Career of William Wing Loring* (Fort Worth: Texas Christian University Press, 1971), p. 58; Robert L. Dabney, *Life and Campaigns of Lieut.-Gen. Thomas J. Jackson* (New York: Blelock and Company, 1866), p. 57.

9. Anna Jackson, *Memoirs of Jackson*, p. 209; G. F. R. Henderson, *Stonewall Jackson and the American Civil War* (London: Longmans, Green and Company, 1906), I, 182; Archie P. McDonald, ed., *Make Me a Map of the Valley: The Civil War Diary of Stonewall Jackson's Topographer* (Dallas: Southern Methodist University Press, 1973), pp. xvii–xxi.

10. Anna Jackson, *Memoirs of Jackson*, p. 216; Dabney, *Life and Campaigns of Jackson*, p. 261; W. W. Goldsborough, "How Ashley Was Killed," *Southern Historical Society Papers* 21 (1893): 224.

11. *O.R.*, Ser. 1, Vol. 5, p. 965.

12. Dabney, *Life and Campaigns of Jackson*, p. 261; Casler, *Four Years in the Stonewall Brigade*, p. 61; see *O.R.*, Ser. 1, Vol. 5, pp. 369ff., for dispatches from Nathaniel P. Banks about the episode.

13. Anna Jackson, *Memoirs of Jackson*, pp. 211, 216, 239.

14. Vandiver, *Mighty Stonewall*, p. 186; John H. Worsham, *One of Jackson's Foot Cavalry* (Jackson, TN: McCowat-Mercer Press, reprint, 1964), p. 26; Henry Kyd Douglas, *I Rode with Stonewall* (Chapel Hill: University of North Carolina Press, reprint, 1968), p. 20.

15. Boyd B. Stutler, *West Virginia and the Civil War* (Charleston, WV: Education Foundation, reprint, 1963), pp. 153–55; An Ex-Cadet (James Dabney McCabe), *The Life of Thomas J. Jackson* (Richmond: James E. Goode, 1864), pp. 49–52; *O.R.*, Ser. 1, Vol. 5, pp. 393–95.

16. *O.R.*, Ser. 1, Vol. 5, p. 1053; Wessels, *Born to Be a Soldier*, p. 60; Johnston,

Narrative of Military Operations, pp. 87–89; John Esten Cooke, *Stonewall Jackson*, p. 97.

17. Vandiver, *Mighty Stonewall*, p. 194; Douglas, *I Rode with Stonewall*, pp. 27–28.

18. Walter H. Taylor, *Four Years with General Lee* (New York: D. Appleton and Company, 1877), p. 37; Emory M. Thomas, *The Confederate Nation, 1861–1865* (New York: Harper and Row, 1979), p. 125; E. Merton Coulter, *The Confederate States of America, 1861–1865* (Baton Rouge: Louisiana State University Press, 1950), pp. 352–54.

19. Henry Alexander White, *Robert E. Lee and the Southern Confederacy* (New York: G. P. Putnam's Sons, 1910), pp. 126–27; *O.R.*, Ser. 1, Vol. 6, p. 328.

20. Robert E. Lee, Jr., *Recollections and Letters of General Robert E. Lee* (Garden City, NY: Garden City Publishing Company, 1904), p. 57; J. William Jones, *Personal Reminiscences, Anecdotes, and Letters of Robert E. Lee* (New York: D. Appleton and Company, 1874), p. 359; *O.R.*, Ser. 1, Vol. 6, p. 366; A. L. Long, *Memoirs of Robert E. Lee: His Military and Personal History* (Secaucus, NJ: Blue and Grey Press, reprint, 1983), p. 135.

21. *O.R.*, Ser. 1, Vol. 6, p. 327; Taylor, *Four Years with Lee*, pp. 36–37; John Esten Cooke, *A Life of General Robert E. Lee* (New York: D. Appleton and Company, 1871), p. 46; Long, *Memoirs of Lee*, p. 143.

22. Robert E. Lee, Jr., *Recollections and Letters of Lee*, pp. 59, 61; Fitzhugh Lee, *General Lee* (New York: D. Appleton and Company, 1894), p. 129.

23. Long, *Memoirs of Lee*, p. 143; James M. McPherson, *Battle Cry of Freedom: The Civil War Era* (New York: Ballantine Books, 1988), p. 373; White, *Lee and the Confederacy*, p. 131.

24. Kenneth P. Williams, *Lincoln Finds a General: A Military Study of the Civil War* (New York: Macmillan Company, 1964), I, p. 138; Sears, *McClellan*, p. 168; Joel Cook, *The Siege of Richmond: A Narrative of Military Operations of Major-General George B. McClellan, May and June 1862* (Philadelphia: George W. Childs, 1862), pp. 1–18.

25. White, *Lee and the Confederacy*, p. 131; Clifford Dowdey, *Lee* (Boston: Little, Brown and Company, 1965), pp. 192ff.; Robert S. Henry, *The Story of the Confederacy* (New York: Bobbs-Merrill Company, 1936), pp. 139–40; John Esten Cooke, *Life of Lee*, pp. 53–55.

26. Anna Jackson, *Memoirs of Jackson*, p. 239; Henderson, *Jackson and the Civil War*, I, pp. 330–35; Millard K. Bushong, "Jackson in the Shenandoah," *West Virginia History* 27 (January 1966): 90.

27. R. A. Brock, ed., "The Valley after Kernstown—The Jackson-Harman Letters," *Southern Historical Society Papers* 19 (1891): 318; Sears, *McClellan*, pp. 170ff.; George B. McClellan, *Report of the Organization and Campaigns of the Army of the Potomac* (Freeport, NY: Books for Libraries Press, reprint, 1970), p. 154.

28. Dowdey, *Lee*, p. 190; Johnston, *Narrative of Military Operations*, pp. 114–16; Clement Eaton, *Jefferson Davis* (New York: Free Press, 1977), p. 157.

29. T. T. Munford, "Reminiscences of Jackson's Valley Campaign," *Southern Historical Society Papers* 7 (1879): 523; William Thomas Poague, *Gunner with Stonewall* (Jackson, TN: McCowat-Mercer Press, reprint, 1957), pp. 248, 250.

30. Robertson, *Stonewall Brigade,* pp. 79–81; Douglas, *I Rode with Stonewall,* p. 36; Mark M. Boatner, *The Civil War Dictionary* (New York: David McKay Company, 1959), pp. 324–25.

31. Vandiver, *Mighty Stonewall,* pp. 210ff.; Tanner, *Stonewall in the Valley,* p. 139; Edward A. Moore, *The Story of a Cannoneer under Stonewall Jackson* (Lynchburg, VA: J. P. Bell Company, 1910), pp. 37–40.

32. Douglas, *I Rode with Stonewall,* pp. 42ff.; Percy Gatling Hamlin, *Old Bald Head: General R. S. Ewell, The Portrait of a Soldier* (Strasburg, VA: Shenandoah Publishing Company, 1940), pp. 80–83; Dabney, *Life and Campaigns of Jackson,* p. 337; John H. Worsham, "Jackson's Valley Campaign," *Southern Historical Society Papers* 38 (1910): 327.

33. *O.R.,* Ser. 1, Vol. 12, Pt. 2, pp. 868, 872, 878; Francis F. Wayland, ed., "Fremont's Pursuit of Jackson in the Shenandoah Valley: The Journal of Colonel Albert Tracy, March–July 1862," *Virginia Magazine of History and Biography* 70 (January 1962): 169–71; Hamlin, *Old Bald Head,* pp. 81–82.

34. John W. Fravel, "Jackson's Valley Campaign," *Confederate Veteran* 7 (1898): 418; Anna Jackson, *Memoirs of Jackson,* p. 255; Vincent J. Esposito, *The West Point Atlas of American Wars* (New York: Frederick A. Praeger Publisher, 1960), I, p. 50.

35. Fravel, "Jackson's Valley Campaign," p. 418; Bushong, "Jackson in the Shenandoah," p. 92; Dabney, *Life and Campaigns of Jackson,* p. 353.

36. Taylor, *Four Years with Lee,* p. 38; John Esten Cooke, *Life of Lee,* pp. 58–61; Burke Davis, *JEB Stuart: The Last Cavalier* (New York: Fairfax Press, reprint, 1988), pp. 139–41; Margaret Sanborn, *Robert E. Lee: The Complete Man* (Philadelphia: J. B. Lippincott Company, 1967), p. 62.

37. Dowdey, *Lee,* pp. 198–201; John Bell Hood, *Advance and Retreat: Personal Experiences in the United States and Confederate Armies* (New Orleans: G. T. Beauregard, 1880), pp. 21–23; *O.R.,* Ser. 1, Vol. 11, Pt. 2, pp. 275–76.

38. *O.R.,* Ser. 1, Vol. 12, Pt. 3, pp. 895–97; Hamlin, *Old Bald Head,* pp. 88–89.

39. *O.R.,* Ser. 1, Vol. 11, Pt. 1, pp. 701–9; Vol. 12, Pt. 3, p. 898; Anna Jackson, *Memoirs of Jackson,* p. 259; Dowdey, *Seven Days,* pp. 73–75; Johnston, *Narrative of Military Operations,* p. 129.

40. John M. Patton, "Reminiscences of Jackson's Infantry ('Foot Cavalry')," *Southern Historical Society Papers* 8 (1880): 141; John W. Wayland, *Stonewall Jackson's Way: Route, Method, Achievement* (Staunton, VA: McClure Company, 1940), pp. 202–5.

41. Kyd Douglas, *I Rode with Stonewall,* p. 52; Louis Sigaud, *Belle Boyd: Confederate Spy* (Richmond: Dietz Press, 1940), pp. 45–49; Bell I. Wiley, *Confederate Women* (Westport, CT: Greenwood Press, 1975), pp. 143–45.

42. Tanner, *Stonewall in the Valley,* pp. 221–23; Henry, *Story of the Confederacy,* p. 146; William Allan, *History of the Campaign of Gen. T. J. (Stonewall) Jackson in the*

Shenandoah Valley of Virginia (Dayton, Ohio: Morningside Book Shop, reprint, 1974), pp. 182ff.

43. Tanner, *Stonewall in the Valley*, pp. 226–28; Moore, *Cannoneer under Stonewall*, pp. 54–57; George Cary Eggleston, *The History of the Confederate War: Its Causes and Conduct* (New York: Sturgis and Walton Company, 1910), I, p. 384.

44. Allan, *Jackson in the Shenandoah*, pp. 115–17; Vandiver, *Mighty Stonewall*, pp. 259–61; Dabney, *Life and Campaigns of Jackson*, p. 384; Anna Jackson, *Memoirs of Jackson*, p. 265.

45. Roy P. Basler, ed., *The Collected Works of Abraham Lincoln* (New Brunswick, NJ: Rutgers University Press, 1953), 5, pp. 231–33; Henry, *Story of the Confederacy*, p. 146; Carl Sandburg, *Abraham Lincoln: The War Years* (New York: Harcourt, Brace, and Company, 1939), I, pp. 490–91.

46. *O.R.*, Ser. 1, Vol. 12, Pt. 1, pp. 707–8; Tanner, *Stonewall in the Valley*, pp. 239–40; William H. Condon, *Life of Major General James Shields* (Chicago: Blakey Printing Company, 1900), pp. 227–28.

47. Robertson, *Stonewall Brigade*, p. 103; *O.R.*, Ser. 1, Vol. 12, Pt. 3, pp. 907–8.

48. Clarence Thomas, *General Turner Ashby: The Centaur of the South* (Winchester, VA: Eddy Press, 1907), p. 155; James B. Avirett, *The Memoirs of General Turner Ashby and His Compeers* (Baltimore: Selby and Dulany, 1867), pp. 222–23; Dabney, *Life and Campaigns of Jackson*, p. 401.

49. Tanner, *Stonewall in the Valley*, pp. 286–89; Casler, *Four Years in the Stonewall Brigade*, p. 86; John Selby, *Stonewall Jackson: As Military Commander* (London: B. T. Batford, Ltd., 1968), pp. 86–87; Poague, *Gunner with Stonewall*, pp. 26–27.

50. Selby, *Stonewall Jackson*, pp. 87–88; Dabney, *Life and Campaigns of Jackson*, pp. 153–55; Allan Nevins, *Fremont: The West's Greatest Adventurer* (New York: Harper and Row, 1928), II, pp. 636–37.

51. Tanner, *Stonewall in the Valley*, pp. 290–92; Richard Taylor, *Destruction and Reconstruction* (New York: D. Appleton and Company, 1879), pp. 74–78; Allan, *Jackson in the Shenandoah*, pp. 204–8.

52. Anna Jackson, *Memoirs of Jackson*, p. 283; John Esten Cooke, *Stonewall Jackson*, p. 192; Hunter McGuire, "General T. J. ('Stonewall') Jackson, Confederate States Army," *Southern Historical Society Papers* 25 (1897): 105.

CHAPTER 11

1. Walter H. Taylor, *Four Years with General Lee* (New York: D. Appleton and Company, 1877), p. 40; James Longstreet, *Manassas to Appomattox: Memoirs of the Civil War in America* (Philadelphia: J. B. Lippincott Company, 1903), p. 113; Fitzhugh Lee, *General Lee* (New York: D. Appleton and Company, 1894), p. 144.

2. Longstreet, *Manassas to Appomattox*, p. 112; Burke Davis, *Gray Fox: Robert E. Lee and the Civil War* (New York: Fairfax Press, reprint, 1981), pp. 78–80.

3. Longstreet, *Manassas to Appomattox*, pp. 112–14; Jefferson Davis, *The Rise and Fall*

of the Confederate Government (New York: Thomas Yoseloff, reprint, 1958), I, p. 31; James I. Robertson, *A. P. Hill: The Story of a Confederate Warrior* (New York: Random House, 1987), pp. 78–80.

4. Fitzhugh Lee, *General Lee*, p. 152; Forrest Conner, ed., "The Letters of Lieutenant Robert H. Miller to His Family," *Virginia Magazine of History and Biography* 70 (January 1962): 83; Margaret Sanborn, *Robert E. Lee: The Complete Man, 1861–1870* (Philadelphia: J. B. Lippincott Company, 1967), p. 57.

5. Robert E. Lee, Jr., *Recollections and Letters of General Robert E. Lee* (Garden City, NY: Garden City Publishing Company, 1904), pp. 73–74.

6. John Esten Cooke, *A Life of General Robert E. Lee* (New York: D. Appleton and Company, 1871), pp. 61–62; Sanborn, *Robert E. Lee*, p. 58; Clifford Dowdey, ed., *The Wartime Papers of Robert E. Lee* (Boston: Little, Brown and Company, 1961), pp. 189–90.

7. Cooke, *Life of Lee*, p. 56; Gilbert E. Govan and James W. Livingood, *A Different Valor: The Story of General Joseph E. Johnston, C.S.A.* (Indianapolis: Bobbs-Merrill, 1956), p. 143; Robert M. Hughes, *General Johnston* (New York: D. Appleton and Company, 1893), pp. 136ff.

8. Vincent J. Esposito, *The West Point Atlas of American Wars* (New York: Frederick A. Praeger Publisher, 1959), I, p. 44; Govan and Livingood, *A Different Valor*, pp. 142–45; A. L. Long, *Memoirs of Robert E. Lee: His Personal and Military History* (Secaucus, NJ: Blue and Grey Press, reprint, 1983), p. 157.

9. Robert Selph Henry, *The Story of the Confederacy* (New York: Bobbs-Merrill, 1936), p. 148; Govan and Livingood, *A Different Valor*, p. 146; Robertson, *General A. P. Hill*, p. 63.

10. Joel Cook, *The Siege of Richmond: Military Operations of Major-General George B. McClellan* (Philadelphia: George W. Childs, 1862), pp. 188–90; Henry, *Story of the Confederacy*, p. 149; Stephen W. Sears, *George B. McClellan: The Young Napoleon* (New York: Ticknor and Fields, 1988), p. 195.

11. G. J. Fiebeger, *Campaigns of the American Civil War* (West Point: USMA Printing Office, 1914), p. 39; Thomas L. Livermore, *Numbers and Losses in the American Civil War 1861–1865* (Boston: Houghton Mifflin Company, 1900), p. 81; Gustavus W. Smith, *The Battle of Seven Pines* (New York: C. G. Crawford, Printer and Stationer, 1891), pp. 82, 142.

12. Long, *Memoirs of Lee*, p. 159; Joseph E. Johnston, *Narrative of Military Operations* (Bloomington: Indiana University Press, reprint, 1959), p. 185; Govan and Livingood, *A Different Valor*, p. 156.

13. Jefferson Davis, *The Rise and Fall of the Confederate Government* II, p. 129; George Cary Eggleston, *The History of the Confederate War: Its Causes and Conduct* (New York: Sturgis and Walton Company, 1910), I, p. 397; Dowdey, ed., *Wartime Papers of Lee*, p. 190.

14. Grady McWhiney and Perry D. Jamieson, *Attack and Die: Civil War Tactics and the Southern Heritage* (Tuscaloosa: University of Alabama Press, 1982), p. 164; Mary

Anna Jackson, *Memoirs of Stonewall Jackson by His Widow* (Louisville, KY: Prentice Press, 1895), p. 290; Robert L. Dabney, *The Life and Campaigns of Lieut.-Gen. Thomas J. Jackson* (New York: Blelock and Company, 1866), p. 431.

15. Sears, *McClellan*, p. 199.

16. Secretary of War, *The War of the Rebellion: A Compilation of the Official Records of the Union and Confederate Armies* (Washington, DC: Government Printing Office, 1880), Ser. 1, Vol. 11, Pt. 3, pp. 589–90, hereafter cited as *O.R.;* John Bell Hood, *Advance and Retreat: Personal Experiences in the Union and Confederate Armies* (New Orleans: G. T. Beauregard, 1880), pp. 24–25; Douglas Southall Freeman, *Lee's Lieutenants: A Study in Command* (New York: Charles Scribner's Sons, 1942), I, pp. 489ff.

17. *O.R.*, Ser. I, Vol. 11, Pt. 3, p. 590; Charles P. Snow *Lee and His Generals* (New York: Fairfax Press, reprint, 1982), pp. 380–82; John W. Thomason, *JEB Stuart* (New York: Charles Scribner's Sons, reprint, 1958), pp. 140ff.

18. Heros Von Borcke, *Memoirs of the Confederate War for Independence* (New York: Peter Smith, reprint, 1938), I, pp. 21–22; Thomason, *JEB Stuart*, p. 143; William W. Hassler, *Colonel John Pelham: Lee's Boy Artillerist* (Richmond: Garrett and Massie, 1960), p. 36.

19. Burke Davis, *JEB Stuart: The Last Cavalier* (New York: Fairfax Press, reprint, 1988), pp. 112–16; Thomason, *JEB Stuart*, p. 144.

20. Bruce Catton, *Terrible Swift Sword* (Garden City, New York, Doubleday and Company, 1963), p. 322; Thomason, *JEB Stuart*, pp. 151, 154–155; Sears, *McClellan*, p. 202.

21. Frank E. Vandiver, *Mighty Stonewall* (New York: McGraw-Hill, 1957), p. 286; Anna Jackson, *Memoirs of Jackson*, pp. 282–83; Roy Bird Cook, *The Family and Early Life of Stonewall Jackson* (Charleston, WV: Education Foundation, reprint, 1967), pp. 167–68.

22. Bell I. Wiley, *The Life of Johnny Reb: The Common Soldier of the Confederacy* (Indianapolis: Bobbs-Merrill Company, 1943), p. 54.

23. *O.R.*, Ser. 1, Vol. 11, Pt. 3, p. 602; Dabney, *Life and Campaigns of Jackson*, p. 434.

24. An Ex-Cadet (James Dabney McCabe), *The Life of Thomas J. Jackson* (Richmond: Thomas E. Goode, 1864), p. 109; Dabney, *Life and Campaigns of Jackson*, pp. 435–36; Vandiver, *Mighty Stonewall*, pp. 291–92; John Esten Cooke, *Stonewall Jackson: A Military Biography* (New York: D. Appleton and Company, 1866), p. 205.

25. John O. Casler, *Four Years in the Stonewall Brigade* (Marietta, GA: Continental Book Company, reprint, 1951), pp. 86–87; Dabney, *Life and Campaigns of Jackson*, p. 435.

26. *O.R.*, Ser. 1, Vol. 11, Pt., 3, p. 590; Henry Kyd Douglas, *I Rode with Stonewall* (Chapel Hill: University of North Carolina Press, reprint, 1968), pp. 98–99; Vandiver, *Mighty Stonewall*, p. 292.

27. Longstreet, *Manassas to Appomattox*, p. 120; Dabney, *Life and Campaigns of Jackson*, p. 438; *O.R.*, Ser. 1, Vol. 11, Pt. 2, pp. 498–99.

28. Vandiver, *Mighty Stonewall*, pp. 294ff.; Robertson, *General A. P. Hill*, p. 66; Longstreet, *Manassas to Appomattox*, pp. 120–22; Clifford Dowdey, *The Seven Days: The Emergence of Lee* (Boston: Little Brown and Company, 1964), p. 148; Kenneth P. Williams, *Lincoln Finds a General: A Military Study of the Civil War* (New York: Macmillan Company, 1964), 1, pp. 218–22.

29. Dabney, *Life and Campaigns of Jackson*, p. 436; Percy Gatling Hamlin, *"Old Bald Head": General R. S. Ewell* (Strasburg, VA: Shenandoah Publishing House, 1940), p. 108; James I. Robertson, *The Stonewall Brigade* (Baton Rouge: Louisiana State University Press, 1963), pp. 114–16.

30. Alexander S. Webb, *The Peninsula: McClellan's Campaign of 1862* (New York: Jack Brussel, Publisher, reprint, 1959), p. 120; *O.R.*, Ser. 2, Vol. 11, Pt. 2, pp. 804–7.

31. *O.R.*, Ser. 1, Vol. 22, Pt. 3, p. 620, Ser. 1, Vol. 22, Pt. 2, p. 553; William T. Poague, *Gunner with Stonewall* (Jackson, TN: McCowat-Mercer Press, reprint, 1957), p. 29.

32. Robertson, *General A. P. Hill*, pp. 74–75; George Cary Eggleston, *The History of the Confederate War* (New York: Sturgis and Walton Company, 1910), p. 400; William Swinton, *Campaigns of the Army of the Potomac* (New York: Charles Scribner's Sons, 1882), p. 151.

33. John Bowers, *Stonewall Jackson: Portrait of a Soldier* (New York: William Morrow and Company, 1989), p. 249; Long, *Memoirs of Lee*, p. 171; Douglas Southall Freeman and Grady McWhiney, eds., *Lee's Dispatches: Unpublished Letters of General Robert E. Lee to Jefferson Davis and the War Department of the Confederate States of America, 1861–1865* (New York: G. P. Putnam's Sons, 1957), p. 15; *O.R.*, Ser. 1, Vol. 11, Pt. 2, p. 491.

34. E. P. Alexander, *Military Memoirs of a Confederate* (New York: Charles Scribner's Sons, 1908), p. 122; Vandiver, *Mighty Stonewall*, 308–9; An English Combatant, *Battlefields of the South from Bull Run to Fredericksburgh* (New York: John Bradburn, 1864), pp. 333–41.

35. John Esten Cooke, *Life of Lee*, pp. 81–82.

36. Long, *Memoirs of Lee*, p. 172; Robertson, *General A. P. Hill*, p. 81.

37. Burke Davis, *They Called Him Stonewall: A Life of Lt. General T. J. Jackson, C.S.A.* (New York: Fairfax Press, reprint, 1988), pp. 222–23; see also Dabney, *Life and Campaigns of Jackson*, p. 443.

38. Dabney, *Life and Campaigns of Jackson*, p. 444; Snow, *Lee and His Generals*, p. 193; Vandiver, *Mighty Stonewall*, p. 305.

39. *O.R.*, Ser. 1, Vol. 11, Pt. 2, p. 837; Swinton, *Campaigns of the Army of the Potomac*, pp. 149–50; Long, *Memoirs of Lee*, p. 172.

40. John Esten Cooke, *Life of Lee*, p. 84; John Esten Cooke, *Stonewall Jackson*, p. 220; Douglas, *I Rode with Stonewall*, p. 103.

41. Hunter McGuire, "General T. J. (Stonewall) Jackson, Confederate States Army," *Southern Historical Society Papers* 27 (1897): 97–98.

42. *O.R.*, Ser. 1, Vol. 11, Pt. 2, pp. 555–56; John Selby, *Stonewall Jackson: As Military Commander* (London: B. T. Batsford, Ltd., 1968), pp. 111–13; John Esten Cooke, *Stonewall Jackson*, p. 224; Anna Jackson, *Memoirs of Jackson*, p. 293.

43. William F. Fox, *Regimental Losses in the American Civil War, 1861–1865* (Albany, NY: Albany Publishing Company, 1893), pp. 543, 550; Robertson, *Stonewall Brigade*, p. 119; Burke Davis, *They Called Him Stonewall*, p. 228.

44. Freeman, *Lee's Lieutenants*, I, pp. 542ff.; George B. McClellan, *Report on the Organization and Campaigns of the Army of the Potomac* (Freeport, NY: Books for Libraries Press, reprint, 1970), pp. 354–55; Clifford Dowdey, *Lee* (Boston: Little, Brown and Company, 1965), pp. 261–63.

45. Burke Davis, *They Called Him Stonewall*, pp. 138–39; Webb, *On the Peninsula*, p. 136; Hamlin, "*Old Bald Head*," pp. 111–13.

46. Longstreet, *Manassas to Appomattox*, p. 134; Hamlin, "*Old Bald Head*," p. 114; Dabney, *Life and Campaigns of Jackson*, pp. 459–60; John Esten Cooke, *Stonewall Jackson*, p. 232.

47. Freeman and McWhiney, *Lee's Dispatches to Jefferson Davis*, p. 21; Webb, *On the Peninsula*, pp. 123–25.

48. Dowdey, *Seven Days*, pp. 278–79; Taylor, *Four Years with Lee*, p. 49; Fox, *Regimental Losses*, pp. 543, 551; see also, Freeman, *Lee's Lieutenants*, I, pp. 552–56.

49. John W. Schildt, *Stonewall Jackson Day by Day* (Chewsville, MD: Antietam Publications, 1980), p. 64; Henry, *Story of the Confederacy*, pp. 160–61; Dowdey, *Seven Days*, p. 279.

50. *O.R.*, Ser. 1, Vol. 11, Pt. 2, pp. 494, 555.

51. Sears, *McClellan*, pp. 216–18; Swinton, *Campaigns of the Army of the Potomac*, pp. 154–55; Fitzhugh Lee, *General Lee*, pp. 154–56.

52. *O.R.*, Ser. 1, Vol. 11, Pt. 2, p. 495; David E. Johnston, "Charge of Kemper's Brigade at Frazier's Farm," *Southern Historical Society Papers*, 18 (1892): 391–93; Robertson, *General A. P. Hill*, pp. 87–93.

53. Fox, *Regimental Losses*, p. 551; *O.R.*, Ser. 1, Vol. 11, Pt. 2, p. 495.

54. Hunter McGuire, *The Confederate Cause and Conduct of the War between the States* (Richmond: L. H. Jenkins Publisher, 1907), p. 200; Gary W. Gallagher, ed., *Fighting for the Confederacy: The Personal Recollections of General Edward Porter Alexander* (Chapel Hill: University of North Carolina Press, 1989), p. 108; Longstreet, *Manassas to Appomattox*, pp. 133, 140.

55. *O.R.*, Ser. 1, Vol. 11, Pt. 2, p. 557; Anna Jackson, *Memoirs of Jackson*, p. 297.

56. Jennings C. Wise, *The Long Arm of Lee: The History of the Artillery of the Army of Northern Virginia* (Lynchburg, VA: J. P. Bell Company 1915), I, p. 506; Mark M.

Boatner, *The Civil War Dictionary* (New York: David McKay Company, 1959) p. 506; Henry, *Story of the Confederacy*, p. 162.

57. Eggleston, *Confederate War*, p. 412; Dowdey, *Seven Days*, p. 326; Millard K. Bushong, *Old Jube: A Biography of General Jubal A. Early* (Shippensburg, PA: White Mane Publishing Company, 1955), pp. 60–61.

58. Wise, *Long Arm of Lee*, p. 223; Dowdey, *Seven Days*, p. 329; Sarah P. Lee, *Memoirs of William Nelson Pendleton, D.D.* (Philadelphia: J. B. Lippincott Company, 1893), p. 288.

59. Webb, *On the Peninsula*, pp. 154–55.

60. *O.R.*, Ser. 1, Vol. 11, Pt. 2, p. 496; Vandiver, *Mighty Stonewall*, p. 320, Wise, *Long Arm of Lee*, p. 232; *Battles and Leaders of the Civil War* (New York: Century Company, 1884), 11, pp. 406–27.

61. Sarah P. Lee, *Memoirs of Pendleton*, p. 196; Reid Mitchell, *Civil War Soldiers* (New York: Viking Penguin, 1988), p. 30; Poague, *Gunner with Stonewall*, p. 29.

62. Wise, *Long Arm of Lee*, pp. 233–34; Kyd Douglas, *I Rode with Stonewall*, p. 109; William Garrett Piston, *Lee's Tarnished Lieutenant: James Longstreet and His Place in Southern History* (Athens: University of Georgia Press, 1987), pp. 20–23.

63. *O.R.*, Ser. 1, Vol. 11, Pt. 2, pp. 558, 629; Dabney, *Life and Campaigns of Jackson*, pp. 471–72.

64. Anna Jackson, *Memoirs of Jackson*, p. 299; Fox, *Regimental Losses in the Civil War*, pp. 543, 551; Livermore, *Numbers and Losses in the Civil War*, pp. 140–42.

CHAPTER 12

1. Douglas Southall Freeman and Grady McWhiney, eds., *Lee's Dispatches: Unpublished Letters of General Robert E. Lee, C.S.A. to Jefferson Davis and the War Department of the Confederate States of America, 1861–1865* (New York: G. P. Putnam's Sons, 1957), p. 28; Douglas Southall Freeman, *R. E. Lee: A Biography* (New York: Charles Scribner's Sons, 1934), II, pp. 251–53; Fitzhugh Lee, *General Lee* (New York: D. Appleton and Company, 1894), pp. 164–66; William T. Poague, *Gunner with Stonewall* (Jackson, TN: McCowat-Mercer Press, reprint, 1957), p. 30.

2. Freeman and McWhiney, eds., *Lee-Davis Dispatches*, p. 32; A. L. Long, *Memoirs of Robert E. Lee: His Military and Personal History* (Secaucus, NJ: Blue and Gray Press, reprint, 1983), p. 183.

3. Secretary of War, *The War of the Rebellion: A Compilation of the Official Records of the Union and Confederate Armies* (Washington, DC: Government Printing Office, 1880ff.), Ser. 1, Vol. 11, Pt. 3, pp. 636–37, hereafter cited as *O.R.*; John Esten Cooke, *A Life of General Robert E. Lee* (New York: D. Appleton and Company, 1871), pp. 103–9; James Longstreet, *Manassas to Appomattox: Memoirs of the Civil War in America* (Philadelphia: J. B. Lippincott Company, 1903), pp. 153–55.

4. Mary Anna Jackson, *Memoirs of Stonewall Jackson by His Widow* (Louisville, KY:

Prentice Hall, 1895), pp. 302–3; W. G. Bean, *Stonewall's Man: Sandie Pendleton* (Chapel Hill: University of North Carolina Press, 1959), p. 70; Henry Kyd Douglas, *I Rode with Stonewall* (Chapel Hill: University of North Carolina Press, reprint, 1968), p. 119.

5. Roy P. Basler, ed., *The Collected Works of Abraham Lincoln* (New Brunswick, NJ: Rutgers University Press, 1953), 5, pp. 286–87; John Codman Ropes, *The Army under Pope* (New York: Charles Scribner's Sons, 1881), p. 209; Kenneth P. Williams, *Lincoln Finds a General: A Military Study of the Civil War* (New York: Macmillan, 1964), I, pp. 242ff.

6. Mark M. Boatner, *The Civil War Dictionary* (New York: David McKay Company, 1959), pp. 658–59; John Pope, "To Gain Time . . ." in Ned Bradford, ed., *Battles and Leaders of the Civil War* (New York: Appleton-Century-Crofts, 1956), p. 209; Ropes, *The Army under Pope*, pp. 173–74, this source includes a full text of Pope's several orders to the army.

7. Ropes, *The Army under Pope*, pp. 175–77.

8. J. William Jones, *Life and Letters of Robert Edward Lee: Soldier and Man* (New York: Neale Publishing Company, 1906), p. 188; *O.R.*, Ser. 1, Vol. 12, Pt. 2, p. 179; Robert L. Dabney, *The Life and Campaigns of Lieut.-Gen. Thomas J. Jackson* (New York: Blelock and Company, 1866), pp. 489–91; Robert E. Lee, Jr., *Recollections and Letters of General Robert E. Lee* (Garden City, NY: Garden City Publishing Company, 1904), p. 77.

9. R. E. Lee, Jr., *Recollections and Letters of Lee*, p. 75; Jones, *Life and Letters of Lee*, p. 185; Freeman, *Lee*, I, p. 254; Longstreet, *Manassas to Appomattox*, p. 159.

10. Robert Selph Henry, *The Story of the Confederacy* (New York: Bobbs-Merrill Company, 1936), p. 172; John W. Thomason, *JEB Stuart* (New York: Charles Scribner's Sons, reprint, 1958), pp. 212–16; *O.R.*, Ser. 1, Vol. 12, Pt. 3, pp. 915–916. Robert K. Krick, *Stonewall Jackson at Cedar Mountain* (Chapel Hill: University of North Carolina Press, 1990), p. 259.

11. Boatner, *Civil War Dictionary*, p. 367; Oliver Otis Howard, *Autobiography* (New York: Baker and Taylor Company, 1907), p. 259.

12. Stephen E. Ambrose, *Halleck: Lincoln's Chief of Staff* (Baton Rouge: Louisiana State University Press, 1962), pp. 66–69; Ropes, *The Army under Pope*, pp. 16–17; Stephen W. Sears, *George B. McClellan: The Young Napoleon* (New York: Ticknor and Fields, 1988), pp. 239–42.

13. John O. Casler, *Four Years in the Stonewall Brigade* (Marietta, GA: Continental Book Company, reprint, 1951), p. 103; *O.R.*, Ser. 1, Vol. 12, Pt. 2, p. 182; Frank E. Vandiver, *Mighty Stonewall* (New York: McGraw-Hill, 1957), p. 336; John Selby, *Stonewall Jackson as Military Commander* (London: B. T. Batsford, Ltd., 1968), p. 126.

14. *O.R.*, Ser. 1, Vol. 12, Pt. 2, pp. 214–15; Dabney, *Life and Campaigns of Jackson*, p. 493; James I. Robertson, *General A. P. Hill: The Story of a Confederate Warrior* (New York: Random House, 1987), pp. 12, 102.

15. Edward A. Moore, *The Story of a Cannoneer under Stonewall Jackson* (Lynchburg, VA: J. P. Bell Company, 1910), pp. 97–98—this source contains a detailed account of Winder's death; Poague, *Gunner with Stonewall*, p. 173; Anna Jackson, *Memoirs of Jackson*, p. 313; O.R., Ser. 1, Vol. 11, Pt. 2, pp. 182–83.

16. William Swinton, *Campaigns of the Army of the Potomac* (New York: Charles Scribner's Sons, 1882), p. 173; Millard K. Bushong, *Old Jube: A Biography of Jubal A. Early* (Shippensburg, PA: White Mane Publishing Company, 1955), pp. 74–75; John Estern Cooke, *Stonewall Jackson: A Military Biography* (New York: D. Appleton and Company, 1866), p. 260.

17. O.R., Ser. 1, Vol. 12, Pt. 2, p. 183; Percy Gatling Hamlin, *"Old Bald Head": General R. S. Ewell* (Strasburg, VA: Shenandoah Publishing House, 1940), pp. 118–22—Hamlin includes a lengthy letter from Ewell to his wife describing his part in the Cedar Mountain affray; Robertson, *General A. P. Hill*, pp. 104–7.

18. Robertson, *General A. P. Hill*, pp. 99ff.; Dabney, *Life and Campaigns of Jackson*, pp. 504, 508; O.R., Ser. 1, Vol. 12, Pt. 2, pp. 178, 185; Thomas L. Livermore, *Numbers and Losses in the Civil War in America* (Boston: Houghton Mifflin Company, 1900), p. 88.

19. Anna Jackson, *Memoirs of Jackson*, p. 313; C. Irvin Walker, *The Life of Lieutenant General Richard Heron Walker of the Confederate Army* (Charleston, SC: Art Publishing Company, 1917), pp. 99–100; Clifford Dowdey, ed., *The Wartime Papers of R. E. Lee* (Boston: Little, Brown and Company, 1961), pp. 254–57.

20. John W. Schildt, *Stonewall Jackson Day by Day* (Chewsville, MD: Antietam Publications, 1980), p. 70; Henry, *Story of the Confederacy*, p. 172; Burke Davis, *JEB Stuart: The Last Cavalier* (New York: Fairfax Press, reprint, 1988), pp. 161–65; Ropes, *The Army Under Pope*, p. 33.

21. G. J. Fiebeger, *Campaigns of the American Civil War* (West Point: USMA Printing Office, 1914), pp. 56–57; Dowdey, ed., *Wartime Papers of Lee*, p. 264; Anna Jackson, *Memoirs of Jackson*, p. 317.

22. Eben Swift, "The Military Education of Robert E. Lee," *Virginia Magazine of History and Biography* 35 (April 1927): 113; Burke Davis, *The Gray Fox: Robert E. Lee and the Civil War* (New York: Fairfax Press, reprint, 1981), p. 109; John Esten Cooke, *Life of Lee*, p. 115, Cooke calls Lee's plan "reckless."

23. Moore, *Cannoneer with Jackson*, p. 103.

24. James M. Hendricks, "Jackson's March to the Rear of Pope's Army," *Confederate Veteran* 17 (1909): 549; James I. Robertson, *The Stonewall Brigade* (Baton Rouge: Louisiana State University Press, 1963), pp. 142–43; William P. Snow, *Lee and His Generals* (New York: Fairfax Press, reprint, 1982), p. 197.

25. An Ex-Cadet (James Dabney McCabe), *The Life of Thomas J. Jackson* (Richmond: James E. Goode, 1864), pp. 134–35; Dabney, *Life and Campaigns of Jackson*, p. 517; John Esten Cooke, *Stonewall Jackson*, p. 275.

26. John H. Worsham, *One of Jackson's Foot Cavalry* (Jackson, TN: McCowat-Mercer Press, reprint, 1964), pp. 121–23; O.R., Ser. 1, Vol. 12, Pt. 2, p. 643; George Cary

Eggleston, *The History of the Confederate War: Its Causes and Conduct* (New York: Sturgis and Walton Company, 1910), pp. 420–21; Kyd Douglas, *I Rode with Stonewall*, p. 135.

27. *O.R.*, Ser. 1, Vol. 12, Pt. 2, pp. 559, 554; Hendricks, "Jackson's March to the Rear of Pope's Army," p. 281; Gary W. Gallagher, ed., *Fighting for the Confederacy: The Personal Recollections of General Edward Porter Alexander* (Chapel Hill: University of North Carolina Press, 1989), pp. 130–31; John Esten Cooke, *Stonewall Jackson*, p. 280.

28. Long, *Memoirs of Lee*, pp. 193–95; Longstreet, *Manassas to Appomattox*, pp. 175–79; Francis F. Wilshin, *Manassas (Bull Run)* (Washington, DC: National Park Service, 1953), pp. 26–27.

29. Williams, *Lincoln Finds a General*, I, pp. 318–21; Vincent J. Esposito, *West Point Atlas of American Wars* (New York: Frederick A. Praeger Publisher, 1959), I, p. 60; Vandiver, *Mighty Stonewall*, pp. 361–62.

30. Ropes, *The Army under Pope*, p. 61; Clifford Dowdey, *Lee* (Boston: Little, Brown and Company, 1965), pp. 289–91; *O.R.*, Ser. 1, Vol. 12, Pt. 2, p. 37; James Cooper Nisbet, *Four Years on the Firing Line* (Jackson, TN: McCowat-Mercer Press, reprint, 1963), p. 92.

31. *O.R.*, Ser. 1, Vol. 12, Pt. 2, p. 645; Swinton, *Campaigns of the Army of the Potomac*, p. 182; G. Moxley Sorrel, *Recollections of a Confederate Staff Officer* (New York: Neale Publishing Company, 1905), pp. 96–97.

32. Boatner, *Civil War Dictionary*, p. 341; *O.R.*, Ser. 1, Vol. 12, Pt. 2, pp. 398, 645; Percy Gatling Hamlin, *The Making of a Soldier: Letters of General R. S. Ewell* (Richmond: Whittet and Shepperson, 1935), p. 118; see also, Alan T. Nolan, *The Iron Brigade* (New York: Macmillan, 1961).

33. *O.R.*, Ser. 1, Vol. 12, Pt. 2, p. 645; Poague, *Gunner with Stonewall*, p. 37; William Woods Hassler, *Colonel John Pelham: Lee's Boy Artillerist* (Richmond: Garrett and Massie, 1960), p. 62.

34. *O.R.*, Ser. 1, Vol. 12, Pt. 2, p. 645; Nisbet, *Four Years on the Firing Line*, p. 92; W. G. Bean, *The Liberty Hall Volunteers: Stonewall's College Boys* (Charlottesville: University Press of Virginia, 1965), pp. 129–31; Oliver Otis Howard, *Autobiography*, I, p. 264.

35. Walter H. Taylor, *General Lee: His Campaigns in Virginia, 1861–1865* (Norfolk, VA: Nusbaum Book and News Company, 1906), p. 105; Selby, *Stonewall Jackson*, p. 140; Robertson, *General A. P. Hill*, pp. 119ff.

36. Dabney, *Life and Campaigns of Jackson*, pp. 127–30; Wilshin, *Manassas*, p. 31; Hamlin, *"Old Bald Head,"* pp. 127–30.

37. Fitzhugh Lee, *General Lee*, p. 191; William Garrett Piston, *Lee's Tarnished Lieutenant: James Longstreet and His Place in Southern History* (Athens: University of Georgia Press, 1987), pp. 23–24; John Bell Hood, *Advance and Retreat: Personal Experiences in the Union and Confederate Armies* (New Orleans: G. T. Beauregard, 1880), p. 35; Dabney, *Life and Campaigns of Jackson*, p. 530.

38. Moore, *Cannoneer Under Jackson*, p. 115.

39. Heros Von Borcke, *Memoirs of the Confederate War for Independence* (New York: Peter Smith, reprint, 1938), II, pp. 146–50; Hunter McGuire, *The Confederate Cause and Conduct of the War between the States* (Richmond: L. H. Jenkins, Publisher, 1907), p. 210; Dabney, *Life and Campaigns of Jackson*, p. 531.

40. Dowdey, *Lee*, p. 288; David E. Johnston, *The Story of a Confederate Boy in the Civil War* (Portland, OR: Glass and Prudhomme, 1914), p. 127.

41. Longstreet, *Manassas to Appomattox*, pp. 182–84; Emory M. Thomas, *Bold Dragon: The Life of J. E. B. Stuart* (New York: Harper and Row, 1986), p. 156; Dowdey, *Lee*, pp. 288–89; O.R., Ser. 1, VOl. 12, Pt. 2, p. 646.

42. Ropes, *The Army under Pope*, pp. 117–20; Thomas, *Bold Dragon*, pp. 155–56; T. Harry Williams, *Lincoln and His Generals* (New York: Alfred A. Knopf, 1952), pp. 162–63; Grady McWhiney and Perry D. Jamieson, *Attack and Die: Civil War Military Tactics and the Southern Heritage* (Tuscaloosa: University of Alabama Press, 1982), p. 134.

43. Wilshin, *Manassas*, pp. 31–32; Williams, *Lincoln Finds a General*, I, pp. 328–30; Pope, in Bradford, ed., "To Gain Time," p. 226.

44. E. P. Alexander, *Military Memoirs of a Confederate* (New York: Charles Scribner's Sons, 1908), pp. 211–13; Esposito, *West Point Atlas of American Wars*, I, p. 63; John Esten Cooke, *Stonewall Jackson*, p. 290.

45. Alexander, *Military Memoirs*, p. 211; Walter H. Taylor, *Four Years With General Lee* (New York: D. Appleton and Company, 1877), pp. 63–64; Swinton, *Campaigns of the Army of the Potomac*, pp. 188–90.

46. Kyd Douglas, *I Rode with Stonewall*, p. 139; Theodore Hartman, "With Jackson at Second Manassas," *Confederate Veteran* 24 (1916): 557; John Esten Cooke, *Life of Lee*, pp. 122–23.

47. Kyd Douglas, *I Rode with Stonewall*, p. 139; William P. Snow, *Lee and His Generals* (New York: Fairfax Press, reprint, 1982), pp. 68–70; Long, *Memoirs of Lee*, p. 198.

48. Jennings C. Wise, *The Long Arm of Lee: The History of the Artillery of the Army of Northern Virginia* (New York: Oxford University Press, reprint, 1959), p. 272; Herman Hattaway, *General Stephen D. Lee* (Oxford: University Press of Mississippi, 1976), pp. 49–51; John Esten Cooke, *Stonewall Jackson*, p. 297; Dowdey, *Lee*, p. 293; see also, L. Van Loan Naisawald, *Grape and Cannister: The Story of the Field Artillery in the Army of the Potomac, 1861–1865* (New York: Oxford University Press, 1960).

49. Taylor, *General Lee: His Campaigns*, pp. 114–17; Johnson, *Confederate Boy*, pp. 126–28; Charles T. Loehr, *War History of the Old First Infantry Regiment, Army of Northern Virginia* (Richmond: William Ellis Jones, Book and Job Printer, 1884), pp. 28–29.

50. O.R., Ser. 1, Vol. 12, Pt. 2, pp. 551ff.; Ropes, *The Army under Pope*, p. 111, John Esten Cooke, *Stonewall Jackson*, p. 303.

51. Ropes, *The Army under Pope*, pp. 148–49; *O.R.*, Ser. 1, Vol. 12, Pt. 2, p. 647; Gallagher, ed., *Fighting for the Confederacy*, p. 134.

52. Carl Sandburg, *Abraham Lincoln: The War Years* (New York: Harcourt, Brace and Company, 1939), I, p. 533; Sears, *McClellan*, pp. 259–60; J. G. Randall and David H. Donald, *The Civil War and Reconstruction* (Lexington, MA: D. C. Heath Company, 1969), p. 220.

53. Freeman and McWhiney, eds., *Lee-Davis Dispatches*, p. 62; William F. Fox, *Regimental Losses in the American Civil War* (Albany, NY: Albany Publishing Company), pp. 544, 550; Dowdey, ed., *Lee's Wartime Papers*, p. 292; Archie P. McDonald, ed., *Make Me a Map of the Valley: The Civil War Journal of Stonewall Jackson's Topographer* (Dallas: Southern Methodist University Press, 1973), pp. 76–78.

54. R. E. Lee, Jr., *Recollections and Letters of Lee*, pp. 76–77; Taylor, *General Lee: His Campaigns*, p. 115; Anna Jackson, *Memoirs of Jackson*, p. 327.

CHAPTER 13

1. John W. Schildt, *Stonewall Jackson Day by Day* (Chewsville, MD: Antietam Publications, 1980), p. 75; Secretary of War, *The War of the Rebellion: A Compilation of the Official Records of the Union and Confederate Armies* (Washington, DC: Government Printing Office, 1880ff.), Ser. 1, Vol. 19, Pt. 2, p. 298, hereafter cited as *O.R.;* Clifford Dowdey, ed., *The Wartime Papers of R. E. Lee* (Boston: Little, Brown and Company, 1961), p. 298.

2. John W. Schildt, *September Echoes: The Maryland Campaign of 1862* (Shippensburg, PA: Beidel Printing House, 1980), pp. 3–4; Fitzhugh Lee, *General Lee* (New York: D. Appleton and Company, 1894), p. 200; Robert S. Henry, *The Story of the Confederacy* (New York: Bobbs-Merrill Company, 1936), p. 181; Stephen W. Sears, *Landscape Turned Red: The Battle of Antietam* (New York: Ticknor and Fields, 1983), pp. 64–68.

3. James I. Robertson, *General A. P. Hill: The Story of a Confederate Warrior* (New York: Random House, 1987), pp. 130–33; Henry Kyd Douglas, *I Rode with Stonewall* (Chapel Hill: University of North Carolina Press, reprint, 1968), p. 147; John Bowers, *Stonewall Jackson: Portrait of a Soldier* (New York: William Morrow and Company, 1989), p. 292.

4. Archie P. McDonald, ed., *Make Me a Map of the Valley: The Civil War Journal of Stonewall Jackson's Topographer* (Dallas: Southern Methodist University Press, 1973), pp. 78–79; William A. Frassanito, *Antietam: The Photographic Legacy of America's Bloodiest Day* (New York: Charles Scribner's Sons, 1978), p. 37; An Ex-Cadet (James Dabney McCabe), *The Life of Thomas J. Jackson* (Richmond: James E. Goode, 1864), p. 150.

5. Frank E. Vandiver, *Mighty Stonewall* (New York: McGraw-Hill, 1957), p. 378; Kyd Douglas, *I Rode with Stonewall*, p. 150; Mary Anna Jackson, *Memoirs of Stonewall Jackson by His Widow* (Louisville, KY: Prentice Press, 1895), p. 332.

6. John Esten Cook, *Stonewall Jackson: A Military Biography* (New York: D. Ap-

pleton and Company, 1866), p. 309; Henry, *Story of the Confederacy*, p. 181; Kenneth P. Williams, *Lincoln Finds a General: A Military Study of the Civil War* (New York: Macmillan Company, 1964), I, p. 366.

7. W. J. Linton, *Life of John Greenleaf Whittier* (London: Walter Scott, Ltd., 1893), p. 136; Elizabeth Gray Vining, *Mr. Whittier* (New York: Viking Press, 1974), pp. 123–24; Anna Jackson, *Memoirs of Jackson*, pp. 333–34.

8. *O.R.*, Ser. 1, Vol. 19, Pt. 2, pp. 601–2; An English Combatant, *Battlefields of the South: Bull Run to Fredericksburgh* (New York: John Bradburn, 1864), pp. 467–69. John Esten Cooke, *Stonewall Jackson*, p. 312.

9. *O.R.*, Ser. 1, Vol. 19, Pt. 1, pp. 603–4; John Esten Cooke, *A Life of Gen. Robert E. Lee* (New York: D. Appleton and Company, 1871), pp. 133–34; George Cary Eggleston, *The History of the Confederate War: Its Causes and Its Conduct* (New York: Sturgis and Walton Company, 1910), pp. 427–8.

10. Francis Winthrop Palfrey, *The Antietam and Fredericksburgh* (New York: Charles Scribner's Sons, 1882), pp. 21–22; Hal Bridges, "A Lee Letter on the 'Lost Dispatch' and the Maryland Campaign of 1862," *Virginia Magazine of History and Biography* 66 (1958): 164–66; Schildt, *September Echoes*, pp. 19–20; see also Douglas Southall Freeman, *Lee's Lieutenants: A Study in Command* (New York: Charles Scribner's Sons, 1943), II, pp. 715–23.

11. Palfrey, *Antietam and Fredericksburgh*, pp. 22, 29; Walter H. Taylor, *General Lee: His Campaigns in Virginia, 1861–1865* (Norfolk, VA: Nusbaum Book and News Company, 1906), p. 126; *O.R.*, Ser. 1, Vol. 19, Pt. 1, pp. 45–46.

12. Stephen W. Sears, *George B. McClellan: The Young Napoleon* (New York: Ticknor and Fields, 1988), pp. 286–87; John Esten Cooke, *Life of Lee*, p. 135; *O.R.*, Ser. 1, Vol. 19, Pt. 1, p. 140; James Longstreet, *From Manassas to Appomattox: Memoirs of the Civil War in America* (Philadelphia: J. B. Lippincott, 1903), p. 224.

13. *O.R.*, Ser. 1, Vol. 19, Pt. 1, p. 140, 1021; Schildt, *September Echoes*, pp. 31ff.; Garry W. Gallagher, ed., *Fighting for the Confederacy: The Personal Recollections of General Edward Porter Alexander* (Chapel Hill: University of North Carolina Press, 1989), pp. 142–43; Harold B. Simpson, *Gaines Mill to Appomattox: Waco and McLennan County in Hood's Texas Brigade* (Waco, TX: Texian Press, 1963), pp. 102–3.

14. *O.R.*, Ser. 1, Vol. 19, Pt. 1, pp. 1020–21; G. Moxley Sorrel, *Recollections of a Confederate Staff Officer* (New York: Neale Publishing Company, 1905), p. 106; Thomas L. Livermore, *Numbers and Losses in the Civil War in America, 1861–1865* (Boston: Houghton Mifflin Company, 1905), pp. 144–45.

15. Kenneth P. Williams, *Lincoln Finds a General*, I, p. 381; John W. Thomason, *JEB Stuart* (New York: Charles Scribner's Sons, reprint, 1958), p. 276; Palfrey, *Antietam and Fredericksburgh*, p. 32.

16. *O.R.*, Ser. 1, Vol. 19, Pt. 2, p. 295; Schildt, *September Echoes*, p. 49; Carl Sandburg, *Abraham Lincoln: The War Years* (New York: Harcourt, Brace & Company, 1936), I, p. 35; Henry, *Story of the Confederacy*, p. 187.

17. *O.R.*, Ser. 1, Vol. 19, Pt. 1, p. 953; William T. Poague, *Gunner with Stonewall* (Jackson, TN: McCowat-Mercer Press, reprint, 1957), p. 43; John M. Shelby, *Stonewall Jackson As Military Commander* (London: B. T. Batsford, Ltd., 1968), p. 153; Vandiver, *Mighty Stonewall*, pp. 383–84.

18. Robertson, *General A. P. Hill*, p. 136; New York: Miles Clayton Huyette, *The Maryland Campaign and the Battle of Antietam* (Buffalo, New York: Privately printed, 1915), p. 20; Robert L. Dabney, *Life and Campaigns of Lieut.-Gen. Thomas J. Jackson* (New York: Blelock and Company, 1866), p. 554; J. Thomas Scharf, *History of Western Maryland* (Philadelphia: Louis H. Evarts, 1882), I, p. 238—this source contains a surprisingly detailed account of the entire Maryland campaign.

19. Stephen Z. Starr, *The Union Cavalry in the Civil War* (Baton Rouge: Louisiana State University Press, 1979), I, pp. 306–7; *O.R.*, Ser. 1, Vol. 19, Pt. 1, p. 951; Schildt, *September Echoes*, p. 51.

20. Dabney, *Life and Campaigns of Jackson*, p. 555; Poague, *Gunner with Stonewall*, p. 44; Jubal A. Early, *Lieutenant General Jubal Anderson Early: Autobiographical Sketch and Narrative of the War between the States* (Philadelphia: J. B. Lippincott, 1912), p. 137.

21. *O.R.*, Ser. 1, Vol. 19, Pt. 1, p. 955; John Esten Cooke, *Wearing of the Gray* (Bloomington: Indiana University Press, reprint, 1959), p. 39; E. E. Stickley, "Battle of Sharpsburg," *Confederate Veteran* 22 (1914): 66.

22. Schildt, *Jackson Day by Day*, p. 77; *O.R.*, Ser. 1, Vol. 19, Pt. 1, p. 951: Anna Jackson, *Memoirs of Jackson*, p. 338.

23. A. L. Long, *Memoirs of Robert E. Lee: His Military and Personal History* (Secaucus, NJ: Blue and Gray Press, reprint, 1983), p. 219; Livermore, *Numbers and Losses*, pp. 92–93; John Esten Cooke, *Life of Lee*, p. 141; Frederick Tilberg, *Antietam: National Battlefield Site—Maryland* (Washington, DC: Government Printing Office, reprint, 1961), pp. 15–17; "Antietam," National Park Service Imprint; see Palfrey, *Antietam and Fredericksburgh*, for even greater discrepancies in numbers.

24. George B. McClellan, *Report on the Organization and Campaigns of the Army of the Potomac* (Freeport, NY: Books for Libraries Press, reprint, 1970), p. 376; Vincent J. Esposito, *West Point Atlas of American Wars* (New York: Frederick A. Praeger Publishers, 1960), I, pp. 55–56.

25. Richard M. McMurry, *John Bell Hood and the War for Southern Independence* (Lexington: University Press of Kentucky, 1982), pp. 57–58; Harold B. Simpson, *Hood's Texas Brigade: Lee's Grenadier Guard* (Waco, TX: Texian Press, 1970), pp. 169–70; John Bell Hood, *Advance and Retreat: Personal Experiences in the United States and Confederate Armies* (New Orleans: G. T. Beauregard, 1880), pp. 41–42.

26. William Swinton, *Campaigns of the Army of the Potomac* (New York: Charles Scribner's Sons, 1882), p. 210; Fitzhugh Lee, *General Lee*, p. 213; Simpson, *Hood's Texas Brigade*, p. 170.

27. James I. Robertson, *The Stonewall Brigade* (Baton Rouge: Louisiana State University Press, 1963), p. 155; Stickley, "Battle of Sharpsburg," p. 66; *O.R.*, Ser. 1, Vol. 19, Pt. 1, p. 191.

28. McClellan, *Army of the Potomac*, p. 373; Palfrey, *Antietam and Fredericksburgh*, pp. 79–80; Huyette, *The Maryland Campaign*, p. 29.

29. Walter H. Taylor, *Four Years with General Lee* (New York: D. Appleton and Company, 1877), p. 69; Tilberg, *Antietam*, p. 22; James V. Murfin, *The Gleam of Bayonets: The Battle of Antietam and the Maryland Campaign of 1862* (New York: Thomas Yoseloff, 1965), pp. 220–21.

30. Swinton, *Campaigns of the Army of the Potomac*, pp. 211–13; Terry L. Jones, *Lee's Tigers: The Louisiana Infantry in the Army of Northern Virginia* (Baton Rouge: Louisiana State University Press, 1987), p. 130; R. H. Daniels, "The Battle of Sharpsburg," *Confederate Veteran* 9 (1901): 217.

31. Palfrey, *Antietam and Fredericksburgh*, p. 83; Simpson, *Hood's Texas Brigade*, p. 174; Selby, *Jackson as Military Commander*, p. 161.

32. Burke Davis, *They Called Him Stonewall: A Life of Lt. General Thomas J. Jackson, C.S.A.* (New York: Fairfax Press, reprint, 1988), pp. 330–33; Sears, *Landscape Turned Red*, p. 215; O. T. Reilly, *The Battlefield of Antietam* (Sharpsburg, MD: Privately printed, 1906), unpaged.

33. William W. Hassler, *Colonel John Pelham: Lee's Boy Artillerist* (Richmond: Garrett and Massie, 1960), p. 92; Philip Mercer, *The Life of the Gallant Pelham* (Kennesaw, GA: Continental Book Company, reprint, 1958), pp. 90–91; Heros Von Borcke, *Memoirs of the Confederate War for Independence* (New York: Peter Smith, reprint, 1938), I, p. 232; Robertson, *Stonewall Brigade*, p. 158.

34. John H. Worsham, *One of Jackson's Foot Cavalry* (Jackson, TN: McCowat-Mercer Press, reprint, 1964), pp. 88–89; Millard K. Bushong, *Old Jube: A Life of General Jubal A. Early* (Shippensburg, PA: White Mane Publishing Company, 1955), p. 99; *O.R.*, Ser. 1, Vol. 19, pt. 1, p. 956.

35. Sears, *Landscape Turned Red*, pp. 216ff.; Tilberg, *Antietam*, p. 30; *O.R.*, Ser. 1, Vol. 19, Pt. 1, p. 956.

36. C. A. Richardson, "General Lee at Antietam," *Confederate Veteran* 15 (1907): 411; Tilberg, *Antietam*, p. 25; Reilly, *Battlefield at Antietam*, unpaged.

37. *O.R.*, Ser. 1, Vol. 19, Pt. 1, pp. 956–57; Selby, *Jackson as Military Commander*, pp. 165–66.

38. G. J. Fiebeger, *Campaigns of the American Civil War* (West Point, NY: USMA Printing Office, 1914), p. 72; Fitzhugh Lee, *General Lee*, p. 212; Longstreet, *Manassas to Appomattox*, p. 254.

39. Tilberg, *Antietam*, p. 35; Swinton, *Campaigns of the Army of the Potomac*, p. 216; Palfrey, *Antietam and Fredericksburgh*, p. 93.

40. C. Irvine Walker, *The Life of Lieutenant General Richard Heron Anderson of the Confederate States Army* (Charleston, SC: Art Publishing Company, 1914), p. 109: Sears, *McClellan*, p. 312; Schildt, *September Echoes*, p. 83; *O.R.*, Ser. 1, Vol. 19, Pt. 1, pp. 1036–37; Gallagher, ed., *Fighting for the Confederacy*, p. 151.

41. Schildt, *September Echoes*, pp. 84–85; Taylor, *Lee: His Campaigns*, pp. 132–33; *O.R.*, Ser. 1, Vol. 19, Pt. 1, pp. 150, 1024.

42. Palfrey, *Antietam and Fredericksburgh*, p. 95; Reilly, *Battlefield of Antietam*, unpaged.

43. William P. Snow, *Lee and His Generals* (New York: Fairfax Press, reprint, 1982), pp. 76–77; Freeman, *Lee's Lieutenants*, II, p. 221–23; Frank E. Vandiver, *Their Tattered Flags* (New York: Harpers Magazine Press, 1970), pp. 154–55.

44. Clarence E. Macartney, *Lincoln and His Generals* (Freeport, NY: Books for Libraries Press, reprint, 1970), p. 117; Sears, *Landscape Turned Red*, p. 259; Swinton, *Campaigns of the Army of the Potomac*, p. 220.

45. Swinton, *Campaigns of the Army of the Potomac*, p. 220; Palfrey, *Antietam and Fredericksburgh*, p. 109; *O.R.*, Ser. 1, Vol. 19, Pt. 1, p. 890.

46. Freeman, *Lee's Lieutenants*, II, p. 221; Charles T. Loehr, *War History of the Old First Virginia Infantry Regiment, Army of Northern Virginia* (Richmond: William Ellis Jones, 1884), pp. 30–31; *O.R.*, Ser. 1, Vol. 19, Pt. 1, p. 890.

47. Longstreet, *Manassas to Appomattox*, p. 261; John Esten Cooke, *Life of Lee*, p. 147; Robertson, *A. P. Hill*, p. 143.

48. William W. Hassler, *A. P. Hill: Lee's Forgotten General* (Richmond: Garrett and Massie, 1957), pp. 104–6; Longstreet, *Manassas to Appomattox*, p. 261; Edward P. Alexander, *Military Memoirs of a Confederate* (New York: Charles Scribner's Sons, 1908), pp. 267–269; *O.R.*, Ser. 1, Vol. 19, Pt. 1, p. 957.

49. Alexander, *Memoirs of a Confederate*, p. 269; Long, *Memoirs of Lee*, p. 219; Longstreet, *Manassas to Appomattox*, p. 269; William Garrett Piston, *Lee's Tarnished Lieutenant: James Longstreet and His Place in Southern History* (Athens: University of Georgia Press, 1987), 26; Anna Jackson, *Memoirs of Jackson*, p. 344.

50. Reilly, *Battlefield of Antietam*, unpaged; C. A. Richardson, "Account of the Battle of Sharpsburg," *Confederate Veteran* 16 (1908): 21; Anna Jackson, *Memoirs of Jackson*, p. 344; Robertson, *General A. P. Hill*, pp. 149–50.

51. Fitzhugh Lee, *General Lee*, p. 216; J. William Jones, *Life and Letters of Robert Edward Lee: Soldier and Man* (New York: Neale Publishing Company, 1906), p. 199.

52. Kyd Douglas, *I Rode with Stonewall*, p. 190; Anna Jackson, *Memoirs of Jackson*, p. 346.

53. *O.R.*, Ser. 1, Vol. 19, Pt. 1, p. 143; Grady McWhiney and Perry D. Jamieson, *Attack and Die: Civil War Tactics and the Southern Heritage* (Tuscaloosa: University of Alabama Press, 1982), pp. 70–71; Fitzhugh Lee, *General Lee*, p. 215.

CHAPTER 14

1. Clifford Dowdey, ed., *The Wartime Papers of R. E. Lee* (Boston: Little, Brown and Company, 1961), pp. 325–26; William W. Hassler, *A. P. Hill: Lee's Forgotten*

General (Richmond: Garrett and Massie, 1957), p. 114; James I. Robertson, *General A. P. Hill: The Story of a Confederate Warrior* (New York: Random House, 1987), p. 154.

2. J. William Jones, *Life and Letters of Robert Edward Lee: Soldier and Man* (New York: Neale Publishing Company, 1906), p. 203; Frank E. Vandiver, *Mighty Stonewall* (New York: McGraw-Hill, 1957), pp. 423–24; An English Officer, "A Month's Visit to the Confederate Headquarters," *Blackwood's Magazine* 93 (January 1863): 18–21.

3. G. W. Redway, *Fredericksburg: A Study in War* (London: Allen and Unwin, Ltd., 1906), p. 18; Fitzhugh Lee, *General Lee* (New York: D. Appleton and Company, 1894), p. 219; John W. Thomason, *JEB Stuart* (New York: Charles Scribner's Sons, reprint, 1958), pp. 297–319.

4. James Longstreet, *From Manassas to Appomattox: Memoirs of the Civil War in America* (Philadelphia: J. B. Lippincott Company, 1903), pp. 290, 317–20; Burke Davis, *They Called Him Stonewall: The Life of Lt. General T. J. Jackson* (New York: Fairfax Press, reprint, 1988), p. 344; Robertson, *General A. P. Hill*, p. 154.

5. John Esten Cooke, *Stonewall Jackson: A Military Biography* (New York: D. Appleton and Company, 1866), p. 355; An English Officer, "Visit to Confederate Headquarters," p. 17.

6. Mary Anna Jackson, *Memoirs of Stonewall Jackson by His Widow* (Louisville, KY: Prentice Press, 1895), p. 348; James I. Robertson, *The Stonewall Brigade* (Baton Rouge: Louisiana State University Press, 1963), p. 171; An Ex-Cadet (James Dabney McCabe), *The Life of Thomas J. Jackson* (Richmond: James E. Goode, 1864), p. 167.

7. Anna Jackson, *Memoirs of Jackson*, pp. 349–51; John O. Casler, *Four Years in the Stonewall Brigade* (Marietta, GA: Continental Book Company, reprint, 1951), p. 118; Terry L. Jones, *Lee's Tigers: The Louisiana Infantry in the Army of Northern Virginia* (Baton Rouge: Louisiana State University Press, 1987), p. 142.

8. Thomas Cary Johnson, *The Life and Letters of Robert Lewis Dabney* (Richmond: Presbyterian Committee on Publication, 1903), p. 270; Henry Kyd Douglas, *I Rode with Stonewall* (Chapel Hill: University of North Carolina Press, reprint, 1968), p. 118; W. G. Bean, *Stonewall's Man: Sandie Pendleton* (Chapel Hill: University of North Carolina Press, 1954), p. 142.

9. Thompson, *Life and Letters of Dabney*, p. 275; John Esten Cooke, *Stonewall Jackson*, pp. 353–54.

10. Anna Jackson, *Memoirs of Jackson*, p. 352; John Selby, *Stonewall Jackson as Military Commander* (London: B. T. Batsford, Ltd., 1968), p. 169; Vandiver, *Mighty Stonewall*, pp. 415–16.

11. John Esten Cooke, *Stonewall Jackson*, pp. 362ff.; Stephen W. Sears, *George B. McClellan: The Young Napoleon* (New York: Ticknor and Fields, 1988), pp. 336–38; Thomas Francis Galwey, *The Valiant Hours* (Harrisburg, PA: Stackpole Company, 1961), p. 53; Jones, *Life and Letters of Lee*, p. 207.

12. Oliver Otis Howard, *Autobiography* (New York: Baker and Taylor Company,

1907), I, 314; William Swinton, *Campaigns of the Army of the Potomac* (New York: Charles Scribner's Sons, 1882), pp. 231–34; Vorin E. Whan, *Fiasco at Fredericksburg* (University Park: Pennsylvania State University Press, 1961), p. 1–3.

13. Whan, *Fiasco at Fredericksburg*, pp. 19–20; An English Combatant, *Battle-Fields of the South: From Bull Run to Fredericksburgh* (New York: John Bradburn, 1864), pp. 500–501.

14. Howard, *Autobiography*, I, p. 317; Roy P. Basler, ed., *The Collected Works of Abraham Lincoln* (New Brunswick, NJ: Rutgers University Press, 1953), 5, pp. 518ff.

15. Jones, *Life and Letters of Lee*, p. 199; Dowdey, ed., *Wartime Papers of Lee*, p. 326.

16. Douglas Southall Freeman and Grady McWhiney, eds., *Lee's Dispatches: Unpublished Letters of General Robert E. Lee, C.S.A. to Jefferson Davis and the War Department of the Confederate States of America, 1861–1865* (New York: G. P. Putnam's Sons, 1957), p. 66; Secretary of War, *The War of the Rebellion: A Compilation of the Official Records of the Union and Confederate Armies* (Washington, DC: Government Printing Office, 1880ff.), Ser. 1, Vol. 21, pp. 1021–29, hereafter cited as *O.R.*

17. Anna Jackson, *Memoirs of Jackson*, p. 346; *O.R.*, Ser. 1, Vol. 21, pp. 1033–37; Kyd Douglas, *I Rode with Stonewall*, p. 203.

18. Archie P. McDonald, *Make Me a Map of the Valley: The Civil War Journal of Stonewall Jackson's Topographer* (Dallas: Southern Methodist University Press, 1973), p. 96. John W. Schildt, *Stonewall Jackson Day by Day* (Chewsville, MD: Antietam Publications, 1980), pp. 84–85; Anna Jackson, *Memoirs of Jackson*, p. 362.

19. Roy Bird Cook, *The Family and Early Life of Stonewall Jackson* (Charleston, WV: Education Foundation, reprint, 1967), pp. 22–23; Anna Jackson, *Memoirs of Jackson*, pp. 359–63; Vandiver, *Mighty Stonewall*, pp. 418–19; Kyd Douglas, *I Rode with Stonewall*, p. 203; Cook, pp. 22–25, contains a first-rate account of Jackson's descendants.

20. Jones, *Life and Letters of Lee*, p. 200.

21. *O.R.*, Ser. 1, Vol. 21, pp. 1049, 1053, 1058; Swinton, *Campaigns of the Army of the Potomac*, pp. 239–41.

22. William T. Poague, *Gunner with Stonewall* (Jackson, TN: McCowat-Mercer Press, reprint, 1957), p. 52; Robert L. Dabney, *Life and Campaigns of Lieut.-Gen. Thomas J. Jackson* (New York: Blelock and Company, 1866), p. 598; McDonald, ed., *Make Me a Map of the Valley*, p. 98.

23. Redway, *Fredericksburg*, pp. 40–41, 94–96; Robert Selph Henry, *The Story of the Confederacy* (New York: Bobbs-Merrill Company, 1936), p. 209; Francis W. Palfrey, *The Antietam and Fredericksburgh* (New York: Charles Scribner's Sons, 1882), pp. 144–46.

24. Lafayette McLaws, "The Confederate Left at Fredericksburg," in *Retreat from Fredericksburg: Battles and Leaders of the Civil War* (New York: Thomas Joseloff,

reprint, 1956), p. 87; Edward P. Alexander, "The Battle of Fredericksburg," *Southern Historical Society Papers* 10 (1882): 387–88; Walter H. Taylor, *General Lee: His Campaigns in Virginia, 1861–1865* (Norfolk, VA: Nusbaum Book and News Company, 1906), pp. 143–44.

25. Alexander, "The Battle of Fredericksburg," p. 87; Vincent J. Esposito, *The West Point Atlas of American Wars* (New York: Frederick A. Praeger Publisher, 1959), I, p. 72; *O.R.*, Ser. 1, Vol. 21, p. 545.

26. *O.R.*, Ser. 1, Vol. 21, p. 1060; McDonald, ed., *Make Me a Map of the Valley*, p. 99; Burke Davis, *JEB Stuart: The Last Cavalier* (New York: Fairfax Press, reprint, 1988), pp. 352–53.

27. Whan, *Fiasco at Fredericksburg*, pp. 54–55; Redway, *Fredericksburg*, pp. 144–45; Esposito, *West Point Atlas of American Wars*, I, p. 72.

28. G. Moxley Sorrel, *Recollections of a Confederate Staff Officer* (New York: Neale Publishing Company, 1905), pp. 140–41; R. K. Charles, "Events in the Battle of Fredericksburg," *Confederate Veteran* 14 (1906): 66–67; Schildt, Jackson *Day by Day*, p. 89.

29. Douglas Southall Freeman, *Lee's Lieutenants: A Study in Command* (New York: Charles Scribner's Sons, 1943), II, p. 350; William W. Hassler, *Colonel John Pelham: Lee's Boy Artillerist* (Richmond: Garrett and Massie, 1960), pp. 144–49; Philip Mercer, *The Life of the Gallant Pelham* (Kennesaw, GA: Continental Book Company, reprint, 1958), pp. 134–37; *O.R.*, Ser. 1, Vol. 21, p. 631.

30. Edward P. Alexander, "The Battle of Fredericksburg—Paper No. 2," *Southern Historical Society Papers* 10 (1882): 446; Mercer, *The Gallant Pelham*, pp. 137–38; Poague, *Gunner with Stonewall*, p. 55.

31. *O.R.*, Ser. 1, Vol. 21, p. 631; John Esten Cooke, *Stonewall Jackson*, p. 372; Whan, *Fiasco at Fredericksburg*, p. 66.

32. Whan, *Fiasco at Fredricksburg*, pp. 59–61; Dabney, *Life and Campaigns of Jackson*, pp. 609–10; Palfrey, *Antietam and Fredericksburgh*, pp. 148–49.

33. John H. Worsham, *One of Jackson's Foot Cavalry* (Jackson, TN: McCowat-Mercer Press, reprint, 1964), p. 94; Alexander, "The Battle of Fredericksburg—Paper No. 2," p. 454; Mark M. Boatner, *The Civil War Dictionary* (New York: David McKay Company, 1959), p. 358; Kyd Douglas, *I Rode with Stonewall*, p. 206.

34. John Esten Cooke, *Stonewall Jackson*, p. 373; *O.R.*, Ser. 1, Vol. 21, pp. 547, 553, 632; Robertson, *General A. P. Hill*, pp. 160, 167–68.

35. Whan, *Fiasco at Fredericksburg*, p. 57; Taylor, *Lee: His Campaigns in Virginia*, p. 147; Millard K. Bushong, *Old Jube: A Biography of General Jubal A. Early* (Shippensburg, PA: White Mane Publishing Company, 1955), p. 111; Jubal A. Early, *Autobiographical Sketch and Narrative of the War between the States* (Philadelphia: J. B. Lippincott Company, 1912), p. 172.

36. John Esten Cooke, *Stonewall Jackson*, pp. 373–76; Selby, *Stonewall Jackson*, p. 117;

William F. Smith, "Franklin's 'Left Grand Division,' " *Battles and Leaders of the Civil War* (New York: Thomas Yoseloff, reprint, 1956), III, pp. 128–30.

37. C. C. Cummins, "The Sunken Road—The Slaughter Pen," *Confederate Veteran* 23 (1915): 358; Richard M. McMurry, *John Bell Hood and the War for Southern Independence* (Lexington: University Press of Kentucky, 1982), pp. 64–65; Esposito, *West Point Atlas of American Wars*, I, p. 72; Longstreet, *Manassas to Appomattox*, pp. 509–10.

38. Redway, *Fredericksburg*, pp. 208ff.; Esposito, *West Point Atlas of American Wars*, I, p. 72; James M. McPherson, *Battle Cry of Freedom: The Civil War Era* (New York: Ballantine Books, 1988), p. 572; John W. Ames, "In Front of the Stone Wall at Fredericksburg," *Battles and Leaders of the Civil War* (New York: Thomas Joseloff, reprint, 1956), III, p. 123.

39. A. L. Long, *Memoirs of Robert E. Lee: His Military and Personal History* (Secaucus, NJ: Blue and Gray Press, reprint, 1983), p. 239; Jones, *Life and Letters of Lee*, p. 208; Fitzhugh Lee, *General Lee*, pp. 230–31; H. A. Butler, "Fredericksburg— Personal Reminiscences," *Confederate Veteran* 14 (1906): 181.

40. Long, *Memoirs of Lee*, p. 240; Cummins, "The Sunken Road—The Slaughter Pen," p. 358; *O.R.*, Ser. 1, Vol. 21, p. 555.

41. Charles, "Events in the Battle of Fredericksburg," p. 68; Thomas L. Livermore, *Numbers and Losses in the Civil War in America, 1861–1865* (Boston: Houghton Mifflin Company, 1900), p. 96; Grady McWhiney and Perry D. Jamieson, *Attack and Die: Civil War Tactics and the Southern Heritage* (Tuscaloosa: University of Alabama Press, 1982), p. 8.

42. Eben Swift, "The Military Education of Robert E. Lee," *Virginia Magazine of History and Biography* 35 (April 1927): 119; *O.R.*, Ser. 1, Vol. 21, p. 1064; Redway, *Fredericksburg*, p. 231.

43. Jefferson Davis, *The Rise and Fall of the Confederate Government* (New York: Thomas Yoseloff, reprint, 1958), II, p. 350; Burke Davis, *JEB Stuart*, pp. 261–63; Long, *Memoirs of Lee*, p. 240; *O.R.*, Ser. 1, Vol. 21, pp. 1075, 1082, 1085.

44. *O.R.*, Ser. 1, Vol. 21, pp. 1067–68; Fitzhugh Lee, *General Lee*, p. 235; Jones, *Life and Letters of Lee*, pp. 211–12.

45. John Esten Cooke, *Surry of Eagle's Nest: Or Memoirs of a Staff Officer* (New York: G. W. Dillingham Company, 1866), p. 373; Mercer, *The Gallant Pelham*, p. 147; Kyd Douglas, *I Rode with Stonewall*, p. 207.

46. Roberta Cary Corbin Kinsolving, "Stonewall Jackson in Winter Quarters" *Confederate Veteran* 20 (1912): 25; Kyd Douglas, *I Rode with Stonewall*, pp. 210, 214; John W. Wayland, *Stonewall Jackson's Way: Route, Method, Achievement* (Staunton, VA: McClure Company, 1940), pp. 209–12.

47. Anna Jackson, *Memoirs of Jackson*, pp. 372–73.

48. *O.R.*, Ser. 1, Vol. 21, p. 556; Anna Jackson, *Memoirs of Jackson*, p. 373; Kyd Douglas, *I Rode with Stonewall*, p. 209.

49. Heros Von Borcke, *Memoirs of the Southern War for Independence* (New York: Peter Smith, reprint, 1938), II, p. 158; Jones, *Life and Letters of Lee*, p. 213; Douglas Southall Freeman, *R. E. Lee: A Biography* (New York: Charles Scribner's Sons, 1935), II, p. 479; Anna Jackson, *Memoirs of Jackson*, pp. 373–74.

50. Redway, *Fredericksburg*, pp. 250ff.; Gary W. Gallagher, ed., *Fighting for the Confederacy: Personal Reflections of General Edward Porter Alexander* (Chapel Hill: University of North Carolina Press, 1989), p. 189; Fitzhugh Lee, *General Lee*, p. 237.

CHAPTER 15

1. Abner Doubleday, *Chancellorsville and Gettysburg* (New York: Charles Scribner's Sons, 1908), pp. 1–2.

2. Secretary of War, *The War of the Rebellion: A Compiliation of the Official Records of the Union and Confederate Armies* (Washington, DC: Government Printing Office, 1880ff.), Ser. 1, Vol. 25, Pt. 2, pp. 10–11, hereafter cited as *O.R.*

3. C. Irvin Walker, *The Life of Lieutenant General Richard Heron Walker* (Charleston, SC: Art Publishing Company, 1917), pp. 131–32; Doubleday, *Chancellorsville and Gettysburg*, p. 2.

4. John H. Worsham, *One of Jackson's Foot Cavalry* (Jackson, TN: McCowat-Mercer Press, reprint, 1964), pp. 94–95; Robert Selph Henry, *The Story of the Confederacy* (New York: Bobbs-Merrill Company, 1936), p. 124; William W. Bennett, *A Narrative of the Great Revival Which Prevailed in the Southern Armies* (Philadelphia: Claxton, Remsen, and Haffelfinger, 1877), p. 251.

5. *O.R.*, Ser. 1, Vol. 25, Pt. 2, pp. 2–4, 111, 151; Doubleday, *Chancellorsville and Gettysburg*, pp. 2–3; Vincent J. Esposito, *West Point Atlas of American Wars* (New York: Frederick A. Praeger, 1960), I, pp. 83–84.

6. Walter H. Herbert, *Fighting Joe Hooker* (Indianapolis: Bobbs-Merrill Company, 1944), passim; Stephen B. Oates, *With Malice Toward None: The Life of Abraham Lincoln* (New York: Harper and Row, 1977), pp. 338, 345–47; Charles E. Macartney, *Lincoln and His Generals* (Philadelphia: Dorrance and Company, 1925), pp. 135–37; Dumas Malone, ed., *The Dictionary of American Biography* (New York: Charles Scribner's Sons, 1932), 9, pp. 196–98.

7. Ralph Happel, "The Chancellors of Chancellorsville," *Virginia Magazine of History and Biography* 71 (July 1963): 259–61.

8. John Bigelow, *The Campaign of Chancellorsville: A Strategic and Tactical Study* (New Haven, CT: Yale University Press, 1910), pp. 119–21; Stephen E. Ambrose, *Halleck: Lincoln's Chief of Staff* (Baton Rouge: Louisiana State University Press, 1962), pp. 132–33; *O.R.*, Ser. 1, Vol. 25, Pt. 2, pp. 203–4.

9. Robert E. Lee, Jr., *Recollections and Letters of General Robert E. Lee* (Garden City, NY: Garden City Publishing Company, 1903), p. 92.

10. A. L. Long, *Memoirs of Robert E. Lee: His Military and Personal History* (Secaucus,

NJ: Blue and Grey Press, reprint, 1983), p. 471; Clifford Dowdey, ed., *The Wartime Papers of R. E. Lee* (Boston: Little, Brown and Company, 1961), p. 421.

11. Long, *Memoirs of Lee*, pp. 228, 240; Robert E. Lee, Jr., *Recollections and Letters of Lee*, p. 85.

12. Robert E. Lee, Jr., *Recollections and Letters of Lee*, p. 93; Douglas Southall Freeman and Grady McWhiney, eds., *Lee's Dispatches: Unpublished Letters of General Robert E. Lee, C.S.A. to Jefferson Davis and the War Department of the Confederate States of America, 1861–1865* (New York: G. P. Putnam's Sons, 1957), p. 81; Dowdey, ed., *Wartime Papers of Lee*, p. 413.

13. Dowdey, ed., *Wartime Papers of Lee*, p. 416.

14. James Longstreet, *From Manassas to Appomattox: Memoirs of the Civil War in America* (Philadelphia: J. B. Lippincott Company, 1903), pp. 324–33; Malone, ed., *Dictionary of American Biography*, 16, p. 546; Paul D. Casdorph, "Future Bishop Gives Account of the Civil War," *West Virginia Hillbilly* 27 (October 1985): 10.

15. Jay B. Hubbell, "The War Diary of John Esten Cooke," *Journal of Southern History* 7 (November 1941): 537.

16. Freeman and McWhiney, eds., *Lee's Dispatches*, pp. 72–75; *O.R.*, Ser. 1, Vol. 25, Pt. 2, p. 633: Douglas, *I Rode with Stonewall*, p. 214.

17. Frank E. Vandiver, *Mighty Stonewall* (New York: McGraw-Hill, 1957), pp. 443–44; Douglas, *I Rode with Stonewall*, p. 213; Marcus J. Wright, *General Officers of the Confederate Army* (New York: Neale Publishing Company, 1911), pp. 72, 96.

18. Herbert, *Fighting Joe Hooker*, pp. 180–88; Stephen Z. Starr, *The Union Cavalry in the Civil War* (Baton Rouge: Louisiana State University Press, 1979), I, pp. 345–46; Fitzhugh Lee, *General Lee* (New York: D. Appleton and Company, 1894), p. 240.

19. Starr, *Union Cavalry in the Civil War*, I, p. 348; John W. Thomason, *JEB Stuart* (New York: Charles Scribner's Sons, reprint, 1958), p. 359.

20. Heros Von Borcke, *Memoirs of the Confederate War for Independence* (New York: Peter Smith, reprint, 1938), II, pp. 187–88.

21. Ibid.; William W. Hassler, *Colonel John Pelham: Lee's Boy Artillerist* (Richmond: Garrett and Massie, 1960), pp. 164–67; Thomason, *JEB Stuart*, pp. 350–63; *O.R.*, Ser. 1, Vol. 25, Pt. 2, pp. 640, 651, 658, 675.

22. Mary Anna Jackson, *Memoirs of Stonewall Jackson by His Widow* (Louisville, KY: Prentice Press, 1895), pp. 401–10; Mary Anna Jackson, "With 'Stonewall' Jackson in Camp: More Confederate Memories," *Hearst Magazine* 34 (1913): 392–94; Robert E. Lee, Jr., *Recollections and Letters of Lee*, pp. 90–95.

23. Doubleday, *Chancellorsville and Gettysburg*, pp. 3–4; *O.R.*, Ser. 1, Vol. 25, Pt. 2, p. 719; John Esten Cooke, *A Life of Gen. Robert E. Lee* (New York: D. Appleton and Company, 1871), pp. 228–29.

24. Ralph Happel, "Chancellors of Chancellorsville," p. 269; Jubal A. Early, *Auto-*

biographical Sketch and Narrative of the War between the States (Philadelphia: J. B. Lippincott Company, 1912), pp. 196–97.

25. Doubleday, *Chancellorsville and Gettysburg*, p. 4; Douglas Southall Freeman, *Lee's Lieutenants: A Study in Command* (New York: Charles Scribner's Sons, 1943), II, p. 646; *O.R.*, Ser. 1, Vol. 25, Pt. 2, p. 1065.

26. Early, *Autobiographical Sketch*, pp. 194–95; Freeman, *Lee's Lieutenants*, II, pp. 528–29; James M. McPherson, *Ordeal by Fire: The Civil War and Reconstruction* (New York: Alfred A. Knopf, 1982), p. 529.

27. Dowdey, ed., *Wartime Papers of R. E. Lee*, pp. 441–45; *O.R.*, Ser. 1, Vol. 25, Pt. 2, pp. 756–62; Vandiver, *Mighty Stonewall*, pp. 456–57.

28. Doubleday, *Chancellorsville and Gettysburg*, pp. 5–7; Walker, *Life of R. H. Walker*, p. 133; *O.R.*, Ser. 1, Vol. 25, Pt. 2, p. 756.

29. Freeman and McWhiney, eds., *Lee-Davis Dispatches*, p. 86; Vandiver, *Mighty Stonewall*, pp. 458–59; Joseph T. Derry, *Georgia*, in *Confederate Military History* 6 (Atlanta: Confederate Publishing Company, 1899), pp. 213–15.

30. Thomason, *JEB Stuart*, p. 376; Burke Davis, *They Called Him Stonewall: A Life of Lt. General T. J. Jackson, C.S.A.* (New York: Fairfax Press, reprint, 1988), p. 405; Doubleday, *Chancellorsville and Gettysburg*, p. 18.

31. G. F. R. *Henderson, Stonewall Jackson and the American Civil War* (New York: Fawcett Publications, reprint, 1962), II, p. 512; Doubleday, *Chancellorsville and Gettysburg*, p. 16.

32. T. M. R. Talcott, "General Lee's Strategy at the Battle of Chancellorsville," *Southern Historical Society Papers* 34 (1906): pp. 1–2; Freeman, *Lee's Lieutenants*, II, p. 541; Robert L. Dabney, *Life and Campaigns of Lieut.-General Thomas J. Jackson* (New York: Blelock and Company, 1866), p. 673; Long, *Memoirs of Lee*, pp. 254–55.

33. John Esten Cooke, *Life of Lee*, pp. 228–29; Davis, *They Called Him Stonewall*, pp. 408–9; Jed Hotchkiss and William Allan, "The Battlefields of Virginia: Chancellorsville," *Southern Historical Society Papers* 34 (1909): 3–9.

34. Vandiver, *Mighty Stonewall*, pp. 466–67; Long, *Memoirs of Lee*, p. 258; Alfred Burne and Peter Young, *The Great Civil War* (London: Eyre and Spottswood, 1959), p. 4; C. V. Wedgewood, *The King's War* (London: Collins, 1958), 118.

35. Hotchkiss and Allan, "The Battlefields of Virginia: Chancellorsville," p. 5.

36. William W. Hassler, *A. P. Hill: Lee's Forgotten General* (Richmond: Garrett and Massie, 1957), pp. 134–35; Bigelow, *Chancellorsville*, p. 275; Doubleday, *Chancellorsville and Gettysburg*, p. 26.

37. Bigelow, *Chancellorsville*, p. 282; Thomason, *JEB Stuart*, p. 378; Freeman, *Lee's Lieutenants*, II, pp. 552–53.

38. Anna Jackson, "With 'Stonewall' Jackson in Camp," p. 393, this source contains a facsimile of Jackson's note; Hassler, *A. P. Hill*, p. 135.

39. Hassler, *A. P. Hill*, p. 137; *O.R.*, Ser. 1, Vol. 25, Pt. 2, pp. 916, 630.

40. *O.R.*, Ser. 1, Vol. 25, Pt. 2, p. 768.

41. Ibid.; Henderson, *Jackson and the American Civil War*, II, p. 547; Charles P. Cullop, "English Reaction to Stonewall Jackson's Death," *West Virginia History* 29 (October 1967): 5.

42. New York *Herald*, May 14, 1863; Richmond *Enquirer*, May 19, 1863; Washington *Daily Chronicle*, May 13, 1863; Roy P. Basler, ed., *The Collected Works of Abraham Lincoln* (New Brunswick, NJ: Rutgers University Press, 1953), 6, p. 214.

43. Dabney, *Life and Campaigns of Jackson*, pp. 684–86; Bigelow, *Chancellorsville*, pp. 318–19.

44. Dabney, *Life and Campaigns of Jackson*, p. 690; Douglas, *I Rode with Stonewall*, p. 233.

45. C. B. Camerer, "The Last Days of 'Stonewall' Jackson," *Military Surgeon* 78 (1936): 136–37; John Esten Cooke, *Stonewall Jackson: A Military Biography* (New York: D. Appleton and Company, 1866), p. 427; Dabney, *Life and Campaigns of Jackson*, p. 696.

46. Robert E. Lee, Jr., *Recollections and Letters of Lee*, pp. 93–94; Anna Jackson, *Memoirs of Jackson*, p. 443; *O.R.*, Ser. 1, Vol. 25, Pt. 2, p. 769.

47. Dabney, *Life and Campaigns of Jackson*, p. 707; Anna Jackson, *Memoirs of Jackson*, p. 439; Wayland, *Stonewall Jackson's Way*, p. 210.

48. James Power Smith, " 'No, no, let us pass over the river, and rest under the shade of the trees,' " in Ned Bradford, ed., *Battles and Leaders of the Civil War*, p. 342; Anna Jackson, *Memoirs of Jackson*, pp. 445–46.

49. Darius N. Couch, "Outgeneraled by Lee," in Ned Bradford, *Battles and Leaders of the Civil War*, p. 330; Bigelow, *Chancellorsville*, p. 473; Thomason, *JEB Stuart*, pp. 388–94; Freeman, *Lee's Lieutenants*, II, pp. 644ff.

50. William P. Snow, *Lee and His Generals* (New York: Fairfax Press, reprint, 1982), p. 208; Roy Bird Cook, *The Family and Early Life of Stonewall Jackson* (Charleston, WV: Education Foundation, reprint, 1967), p. 147; Anna Jackson, *Memoirs of Jackson*, pp. 449–57.

51. Douglas, *I Rode with Stonewall*, p. 228; *O.R.*, Ser. 1, Vol. 25, Pt. 2, p. 793.

52. Douglas, *I Rode with Stonewall*, p. 229; Long, *Memoirs of Lee*, p. 260; *O.R.*, Ser. 1, Vol. 25, Pt. 2, p. 791.

CHAPTER 16

1. Marshall W. Fishwick, *Lee After the War* (New York: Dodd, Meade and Company, 1963), p. 93; Margaret Sanborn, *Robert E. Lee: The Complete Man* (Philadelphia: J. B. Lippincott Company, 1967), p. 386; Mary Anna Jackson, *The Memoirs of Stonewall Jackson by His Widow* (Louisville, KY: Prentice Press, 1895), p. 574.

2. Clifford Dowdey, *Lee* (Boston: Little, Brown and Company, 1965), pp. 732–34; A. L. Long, *Memoirs of Robert E Lee: His Military and Personal History* (Secaucus,

NJ: Blue and Grey Press, reprint, 1983), p. 235; Douglas Southall Freeman, *R. E. Lee: A Biography* (New York: Charles Scribner's Sons, 1935), Vol. 4, which contains an excellent account of Lee after the war, has repeated instances of his devotion to Jackson the soldier and man.

3. Robert E. Lee, Jr., *Recollections and Letters of General Robert E. Lee* (Garden City, NY: Garden City Publishing Company, 1903), pp. 94–95; Charles Bracelen Flood, *Lee: The Last Years* (Boston: Houghton Mifflin Company, 1981), p. 92.

4. G. W. Redway, *Fredericksburg: A Study in War* (London: Allen and Unwin, Ltd., 1906), p. 14; C. G. Chamberlayne, *Ham Chamberlayne—Virginian* (Richmond: Dietz Printing Company, 1932), p. 181; "A Federal Soldier's Opinion of Stonewall Jackson," *Southern Historical Society Papers* 10 (1878): 334; Anna Jackson, *Memoirs of Jackson*, p. 600.

5. Robert Selph Henry, *The Story of the Confederacy* (New York: Bobbs-Merrill Company, 1936), p. 270; John W. Thomason, *JEB Stuart* (New York: Charles Scribner's Sons, reprint, 1958), p. 390ff.; James Longstreet, *From Manassas to Appomattox: Memoirs of the Civil War in America* (Philadelphia: J. B. Lippincott Company, 1903), p. 332.

6. J. William Jones, *The Life and Letters of Robert Edward Lee: Soldier and Man* (New York: Neale Publishing Company, 1906), p. 247; William P. Snow, *Lee and His Generals* (New York: Fairfax Press, reprint, 1982), p. 370; Anna Jackson, *Memoirs of Jackson*, p. 570.

7. Anna Jackson, *Memoirs of Jackson*, p. 570; Susan P. Lee, *Memoirs of William Nelson Pendleton* (Philadelphia: J. B. Lippincott Company, 1893), p. 292; James W. McPherson, *Battlecry of Freedom: The Civil War Era* (New York: Ballantine Books, 1988), pp. 661–62; Jones, *Life and Letters of Lee*, p. 237.

8. Fishwick, *Lee After the War*, p. 209; Jones, *Life and Letters of Lee*, pp. 280–81; Dowdey, *Lee*, pp. 727–28.

9. J. G. Randall and David Donald, *Civil War and Reconstruction* (Lexington, MA: D. C. Heath and Company, 1969), p. 419; J. C. F. Fuller, *Grant and Lee: A Study in Personality and Generalship* (Bloomington: Indiana University Press, reprint, 1957), pp. 206–10; Henry, *Story of the Confederacy*, p. 355.

10. Russell F. Weigley, *The American Way of War: A History of United States Military Strategy and Policy* (New York: Macmillan, 1973), pp. 114–15; Herman Hattaway and Archer Allen, *How the North Won: A Military History of the Civil War* (Urbana: University of Illinois Press, 1983), p. 698.

11. T. Harry Williams, *The History of American Wars from 1745 to 1918* (New York: Alfred A. Knopf, 1981), p. 238; Joseph H. Parks, *Joseph E. Brown of Georgia* (Baton Rouge: Louisiana State University Press, 1977), p. 322.

12. Burke Davis, *Gray Fox: Robert E. Lee and the Civil War* (New York: Fairfax Press, reprint, 1981), p. 282; Clifford Dowdey, *Lee's Last Campaign: The Story of Lee and His Men against Grant—1864* (Boston: Little, Brown and Company, 1960), pp.

116–17; Edward Steere, *The Wilderness Campaign* (Harrisburg, PA: Stackpole Company, 1960), p. 405; Jones, *Life and Letters of Lee*, p. 304.

13. Nancy Scott Anderson and Dwight Anderson, *The Generals: Ulysses S. Grant and Robert E. Lee* (New York: Alfred A. Knopf, 1988), pp. 379ff.; Dowdey, *Lee's Last Campaign*, p. 210; Gene Smith, *Lee and Grant: A Dual Biography* (New York: McGraw-Hill, 1984), pp. 206–10.

14. Fitzhugh Lee, *General Lee* (New York: D. Appleton and Company, 1894), p. 338; Henry, *Story of the Confederacy*, p. 361.

15. Fitzhugh Lee, *General Lee*, pp. 341–42; Noah Andre Trudeau, *Bloody Roads South: The Wilderness to Cold Harbor* (Boston: Little, Brown and Company, 1989), pp. 298–99; Mark M. Boatner, *The Civil War Dictionary* (New York: Davis McKay Company, 1959), p. 165; Jones *Life and Letters of Lee*, p. 306.

16. Henry, *Story of the Confederacy*, p. 396; Allan Nevins, *The War for the Union: The Organized War to Victory, 1864–1865* (New York: Charles Scribner's Sons, 1971), 4, pp. 50–52; Fitzhugh Lee, *General Lee*, p. 344.

17. James I. Robertson, *General A. P. Hill: The Story of a Confederate Warrior* (New York: Random House, 1987), pp. 317–18; Freeman, *Lee*, 4, pp. 14–15; Smith, *Lee and Grant*, p. 266.

18. Anderson and Anderson, *The Generals*, pp. 453–55; Smith, *Lee and Grant*, p. 267; Randall and Donald, *Civil War and Reconstruction*, p. 526.

19. Freeman, *Lee*, 4, pp. 188ff.; Long, *Memoirs of Lee*, p. 539; Anderson and Anderson, *The Generals*, pp. 465–69.

20. Freeman, *Lee*, 4, p. 191; Lord Wolseley, "Glowing Tribute to General R. E. Lee," *Southern Historical Society Papers* 28 (1900): 111; Fishwick, *Lee After the War*, p. 181.

21. Franklin L. Riley, *General Robert E. Lee after Appomattox* (New York: Macmillan Company, 1922), pp. 22–24; Flood, *The Last Years*, p. 115.

22. Riley, *Lee After Appomattox*, p. 23; Robert E. Lee, Jr., *Recollections and Letters of Lee*, pp. 168–69; John Esten Cooke, *A Life of General Robert E. Lee* (New York: D. Appleton and Company, 1871), p. 477.

23. D. S. G. Cabell, "Lee as an Educator," *Southern Historical Society Papers* 17 (1889): 361; J. William Jones, *Personal Reminiscences, Anecdotes, and Letters of General Robert E. Lee* (New York: D. Appleton and Company, 1874), pp. 156–58.

24. Riley, *Lee After Appomattox*, p. 207; Anderson and Anderson, *The Generals*, p. 470; Dowdey, *Lee*, pp. 722–27.

25. Riley, *Lee After Appomattox*, p. 224.

26. Long, *Memoirs of Lee*, pp. 473–77; Anna Jackson, *Memoirs of Jackson*, p. 464; Henry Kyd Douglas, *I Rode with Stonewall* (Chapel Hill: University of North Carolina Press, reprint, 1968), p. 367.

Bibliography

BOOKS AND MONOGRAPHS

Addey, Markenfield. *The Life and Military Career of Thomas Jonathan Jackson.* New York: Charles T. Evans, 1863.

Alden, John Richard. *The South in the Revolution, 1763–1789.* Baton Rouge: Louisiana State University Press, 1957.

Alexander, Edward Porter. *Military Memoirs of a Confederate.* New York: Charles Scribner's Sons, 1908.

Alexander, Frederick Warren. *Stratford Hall and the Lees.* Oak Grove, VA: Privately printed, 1912.

Allan, Elizabeth Junkin. *The Life and Letters of Margaret Junkin Preston.* Boston: Houghton Mifflin Company, 1903.

Allan, William. *History of the Campaign of Gen. T. J. (Stonewall) Jackson in the Shenandoah Valley of Virginia.* Dayton, OH: Morningside Book Shop, reprint, 1974.

Allen, Bernard L. *Four Lectures on the Significance of the Neale and Jackson Families of Wood County, West Virginia.* Parkersburg, WV: Data/Day, 1990.

Ambler, Charles H. *Waitman T. Wiley: Orator, Churchman, Humanitarian.* Huntington, WV: Standard Printing and Publishing Company, 1954.

Ambler, Charles H., and Festus P. Summers. *West Virginia: The Mountain State.* Englewood Cliffs, NJ: Prentice-Hall, 1957.

Ambrose, Stephen E. *Duty, Honor, Country: A History of West Point.* Baltimore: Johns Hopkins University Press, 1966.

Ambrose, Stephen E. *Halleck: Lincoln's Chief of Staff.* Baton Rouge: Louisiana State University Press, 1962.

Anderson, Nancy Scott, and Dwight Anderson. *The Generals: Ulysses S. Grant and Robert E. Lee.* New York: Alfred A. Knopf, 1988.

Andrews, Matthew P. *Virginia: The Old Dominion.* Garden City, NY: Doubleday and Company, 1937.

An English Combatant. *Battle-Fields of the South: From Bull Run to Fredericksburg.* New York: John Bradburn, 1864.

An Ex-Cadet (James Dabney McCabe). *The Life of Thomas J. Jackson.* Richmond: James E. Goode, 1864.

Aptheker, Herbert. *Nat Turner's Slave Rebellion.* New York: Humanities Press, 1966.

Arnold, Thomas Jackson. *Early Life and Letters of General Jackson.* New York: Fleming H. Revell Company, 1916.

Avey, Elijah. *The Capture and Execution of John Brown.* Chicago: Afro-Am Press, reprint, 1969.

Avirett, James B. *The Memoirs of General Turner Ashby and His Compeers.* Baltimore: Selby and Dulany, 1867.

Bald, W. Clever. *Michigan in Four Centuries.* New York: Harper and Row, 1961.

Barr, Alwyn. *Texans in Revolt: The Battle of San Antonio, 1835.* Austin: The University of Texas Press, 1990.

Barrett, Edwin S. *What I Saw at Bull Run.* Boston: Beacon Press, 1886.

Basler, Roy P., ed. *The Collected Works of Abraham Lincoln.* New Brunswick, NJ: Rutgers University Press, 1953.

Bauer, Jack. *Zachary Taylor: Soldier, Planter, Statesman of the Old Southwest.* Baton Rouge: Louisiana State University Press, 1985.

Baylor, George. *Bull Run to Bull Run: Or Four Years in the Army of Northern Virginia.* Richmond: B. F. Johnson Publishing Company, 1900.

Bean, W. G. *The Liberty Hall Volunteers: Stonewall's Boys.* Charlottesville: University of Virginia Press, 1965.

Bean, W. G. *Stonewall's Man: Sandie Pendleton.* Chapel Hill: University of North Carolina Press, reprint, 1959.

Benet, Stephen V. *John Brown's Body.* New York: Holt, Rinehart and Winston, reprint, 1960.

Bennett, William W. *A Narrative of the Great Revival Which Prevailed in the Southern Armies.* Philadelphia: Claton, Remsen, and Haffelfinger, 1877.

Bigelow, John. *The Campaign of Chancellorsville: A Strategic and Tactical Study.* New Haven, CT: Yale University Press, 1910.

Bill, Alfred Hoyt. *Rehearsal for Conflict: The War With Mexico, 1846–1848.* New York: Alfred A. Knopf, 1947.

Boatner, Mark M. *The Civil War Dictionary.* New York: David M. McKay Company, 1959.

Bosang, James N. *Memoirs of a Pulaski County Veteran.* Pulaski, VA: Privately printed, 1912.

Bowers, John. *Stonewall Jackson: Portrait of a Soldier.* New York: William Morrow and Company, 1989.

Boyer, Richard O. *The Legend of John Brown: A Biography and a History.* New York: Alfred A. Knopf, 1973.

Boykin, Edward. *Ghost Ship of the Confederacy: The Story of the* Alabama *and Her Captain Raphael Semmes.* New York: Funk and Wagnalls Company, 1957.

Braider, Donald. *Solitary Star: A Biography of Sam Houston.* New York: G. P. Putnam's Sons, 1974.

Brock, R. A., ed. *Gen. Robert Edward Lee: Soldier, Citizen, Christian.* Richmond: B. F. Johnson Publishing Company, 1897.

Brown, Stephen W. *Voice of the West: John G. Jackson, His Life and Times.* Macon, GA: Mercer University Press, 1985.

Burne, Alfred, and Peter Young. *The Great Civil War.* London: Eyre and Spottswood, 1959.

Bushong, Millard K. *Old Jube: A Biography of Jubal A. Early.* Shippensburg, PA: White Mane Publishing Company, 1955.

Callcott, Wilfred H. *Santa Anna: The Story of an Enigma That Was Mexico.* Norman: University of Oklahoma Press, 1936.

Casler, John O. *Four Years in the Stonewall Brigade.* Marietta, GA: Continental Book Company, reprint, 1951.

Catton, Bruce. *Terrible Swift Sword.* Garden City, NY: Doubleday and Company, 1963.

Chamberlayne, C. G. *Ham Chamberlayne—Virginian.* Richmond: Press of the Dietz Printing Company, 1932.

Chambers, Lenoir. *Stonewall Jackson: The Legend and the Man to the Valley.* New York: William Morrow and Company, 1959.

Chitwood, Oliver P. *John Tyler: Champion of the Old South.* New York: Russell and Russell, reprint, 1964.

Churchill, Winston S. *A History of the English Speaking Peoples: The Great Democracies.* New York: Dodd, Mead and Company, 1958.

Cometti, Elizabeth, and Festus P. Summers. *The Thirty-Fifth State: A Documentary History of West Virginia.* Morgantown: West Virginia University Library, 1966.

Comstock, Jim, ed. *The West Virginia Heritage Encyclopaedia.* Richwood, WV: Jim Comstock, 1963.

Condon, William H. *Life of Major General James Shields.* Chicago: Blakely Printing Company, 1900.

Connelly, Thomas L. *The Marble Man: Robert E. Lee and His Image in American Society.* New York: Alfred A. Knopf, 1977.

Connor, Seymour V., and Odie B. Faulk. *North America Divided: The Mexican War, 1846–1848.* New York: Oxford University Press, 1971.

Cook, Joel. *The Siege of Richmond: Military Operations of Major-General George B. McClellan.* Philadelphia: George W. Childs, 1862.

Cook, Roy Bird. *The Family and Early Life of Stonewall Jackson.* Charleston, WV: Education Foundation, reprint, 1967.

Cooke, John Esten. *A Life of General Robert E. Lee.* New York: D. Appleton and Company, 1871.

Cooke, John Esten. *Stonewall Jackson: A Military Biography.* New York: D. Appleton and Company, 1866.

Cooke, John Esten. *Surry of Eagle's Nest: Or Memoirs of a Staff Officer.* New York: G. W. Dillingham Company, 1866.

Cooke, John Esten. *Wearing of the Grey.* Bloomington: Indiana University Press, reprint, 1959.

Coulter, E. Merton. *The Confederate States of America, 1861–1865.* Baton Rouge: Louisiana State University Press, 1950.

Couper, William. *Claudius Crozet.* Charlottesville: University of Virginia Press, 1936.

Couper, William. *One Hundred Years at VMI.* Richmond: Garrett and Massie, 1939.

Cox, Jacob D. *Military Reminiscences of the Civil War.* New York: Charles Scribner's Sons, 1900.

Craven, Avery O., ed. *To Markie: The Letters of Robert E. Lee to Martha Custis Williams.* Cambridge: Harvard University Press, 1933.

Croffut, W. A., ed. *Fifty Years in Camp and Field: Diary of Major-General Ethan Allen Hitchcock, USA.* New York: G. P. Putnam's Sons, 1901.

Curry, Richard O. *Radicalism, Racism, and Party Realignment: The Border States During Reconstruction.* Baltimore: Johns Hopkins University Press, 1969.

Dabney, Robert Lewis. *Life and Campaigns of Lieut.-Gen. Thomas J. Jackson.* New York: Blelock and Company, 1866.

Dabney, Virginius. *The New Dominion.* Garden City, NY: Doubleday and Company, 1971.

Davids, Richard C. *The Man Who Loved A Mountain.* Philadelphia: Fortress Press, 1970.

Davis, Burke. *JEB Stuart: The Last Cavalier.* New York: Fairfax Press, reprint, 1988.

Davis, Burke. *The Gray Fox: Robert E. Lee and the Civil War.* New York: Fairfax Press, reprint, 1981.

Davis, Burke. *They Called Him Stonewall: The Life of Lt. General T. J. Jackson, C.S.A.* New York: Fairfax Press, reprint, 1988.

Davis, Jefferson. *The Rise and Fall of the Confederate Government.* New York: Thomas Yoseloff, reprint, 1958.

Davis, William C. *Battle at Bull Run: A History of the First Major Battle of the Civil War.* Garden City, NY: Doubleday and Company, 1977.

Derry, Joseph T. *Georgia—Confederate Military History.* Atlanta: Confederate Publishing Company, 1899.

Doubleday, Abner. *Cancellorsville and Gettysburg.* New York: Charles Scribner's Sons, 1908.

Douglas, Henry Kyd. *I Rode With Stonewall.* Chapel Hill: University of North Carolina Press, reprint, 1984.

Douglass, Frederick. *The Life and Times of Frederick Douglass.* New York: Collier Books, reprint, 1962.

Dowdey, Clifford. *Lee.* Boston: Little, Brown and Company, 1965.

Dowdey, Clifford. *Lee's Last Campaign: The Story of Lee and His Men against Grant, 1864.* Boston: Little, Brown and Company, 1960.

Dowdey, Clifford. *The Seven Days: The Emergence of Lee.* Boston: Little, Brown and Company, 1964.

DuBois, William E. B. *John Brown.* Millwood, NJ: Kraus-Thomson, reprint, 1973.

Bibliography

Duff, John B., and Peter M. Mitchell, eds. *The Nat Turner Rebellion: The Historical Event and the Modern Controversy*. New York: Harper and Row, 1971.

Dumond, Dwight L. *The Secession Movement, 1860–1861*. New York: Macmillan, 1931.

Early, Jubal A. *Lieutenant General Jubal Anderson Early: Autobiographical Sketch and Narrative of the War between the States*. Philadelphia: J. B. Lippincott, 1912.

Eaton, Clement. *A History of the Southern Confederacy*. New York: Macmillan, 1958.

Eaton, Clement. *Jefferson Davis*. New York: Free Press, 1977.

Eggleston, George Cary. *The History of the Confederate War: Its Causes and Conduct*. New York: Sturgis and Walton Company, 1910.

Eliot, Ellsworth, Jr. *West Point and the Confederacy*. New York: G. A. Baker and Company, 1916.

Esposito, Vincent J. *West Point Atlas of American Wars, 1689–1900*. New York: Frederick A. Praeger, 1960.

Fancher, Betsy. *Savannah: Renaissance of the Heart*. New York: Doubleday and Company, 1976.

Fiebeger, G. J. *Campaigns of the American Civil War*. West Point, NY: USMA Printing Office, 1914.

Fischer, David H. *The Revolution of American Conservatism: The Federalist Party in the Era of Jeffersonian Democracy*. New York: Harper and Row, 1965.

Fishwick, Marshall W. *Lee after the War*. New York: Dodd, Meade and Company, 1963.

Fleming, Thomas J. *West Point: The Men and Times of the United States Military Academy*. New York: William Morrow and Company, 1969.

Flexner, James T. *George Washington: The Forge of Experience*. Boston: Little, Brown and Company, 1965.

Flood, Charles Bracelen. *Lee: The Last Years*. Boston: Houghton Mifflin Company, 1981.

Foner, Eric. *Free Soil, Free Labor, Free Men: The Ideology of the Republican Party before the Civil War*. New York: Oxford University Press, 1970.

Fox, William F. *Regimental Losses in the American Civil War*. Albany, NY: Albany Publishing Company, 1893.

Frassanito, William A. *Antietam: The Photographic Legacy of America's Bloodiest Day*. New York: Charles Scribner's Sons, 1978.

Freeman, Douglas Southall. *R. E. Lee: A Biography*. New York: Charles Scribner's Sons, 1934.

Freeman, Douglas Southall. *Lee's Lieutenants: A Study in Command*. New York: Charles Scribner's Sons, 1942.

Freeman, Douglas Southall, and Grady McWhiney, eds. *Lee's Dispatches: Letters of General Robert E. Lee, C.S.A. to Jefferson Davis and the War Department of the Confederate States of America, 1861–1865*. New York: G. P. Putnam's Sons, 1957.

Fry, James B. *McDowell and Tyler in the Campaign of Bull Run*. New York: D. Van Nostrand, 1884.

Fuller, J. C. F. *Grant and Lee: A Study in Personality and Generalship*. Bloomington: Indiana University Press, reprint, 1957.

Gallagher, Gary W., ed. *Fighting for the Confederacy: The Personal Recollections of General Edward Porter Alexander*. Chapel Hill: University of North Carolina Press, 1989.

Galwey, Thomas F. *The Valiant Hours*. Harrisburg, PA: Stackpole Company, 1961.

Gambrell, Herbert. *Anson Jones: The Last President of Texas*. Garden City, NY: Doubleday and Company, 1948.

Gerson, Noel B. *Light-Horse Harry Lee: A Biography of Washington's Great Cavalryman*. Garden City, NY: Doubleday and Company, 1966.

Gittings, John G. *Personal Recollections of Stonewall Jackson*. Cincinnati: Editor Publishing Company, 1899.

Govan, Gilbert E., and James W. Livingood. *A Different Valor: The Story of Joseph E. Johnston, C.S.A.* Indianapolis: Bobbs-Merrill Company, 1956.

Grant, Ulysses S. *Personal Memoirs*. New York: Charles L. Webster and Company, 1885.

Hallowell, Benjamin. *The Autobiography of Benjamin Hallowell*. Philadelphia: Friends Publishing Association, 1883.

Hamilton, Holman. *Zachary Taylor: Soldier of the Republic*. Hamden, CT: Archon Books, reprint, 1966.

Hamilton, Holman. *Zachary Taylor: Soldier in the White House*. Hamden, CT: Archon Books, reprint, 1966.

Hamilton, Holman. *The Three Kentucky Presidents: Lincoln, Taylor, Davis*. Lexington: University Press of Kentucky, 1978.

Hamlin, Percy Gatling. *"Old Bald Head": General R. S. Ewell*. Strasburg, VA: Shenandoah Publishing House, 1940.

Hamlin, Percy Gatling. *The Making of a Soldier: Letters of General R. S. Ewell*. Richmond: Whittet and Shepperson, 1935.

Hanighen, Frank G. *Santa Anna: Napoleon of the West*. New York: Coward and McCann, 1934.

Hanna, Charles R. *The Scotch-Irish: Or the Scot in Britain, North Ireland, and the United States*. New York: G. P. Putnam's Sons, 1902.

Hanson, Joseph M. *Bull Run Remembers*. Manassas, VA: National Capitol Publishers, 1961.

Hassler, William W. *A. P. Hill: Lee's Forgotten General*. Richmond: Garrett and Massie, 1957.

Hassler, William W. *Colonel John Pelham: Lee's Boy Artillerist*. Richmond: Garrett and Massie, 1960.

Hattaway, Herman. *General Stephen D. Lee*. Oxford: University Press of Mississippi, 1976.

Hattaway, Herman, and Archer Jones. *How the North Won: A Military History of the Civil War*. Urbana: University of Illinois Press, 1983.

Heatwole, Cornelius J. *A History of Education in West Virginia*. New York: Macmillan, 1910.

Heitman, Francis B. *Historical Register and Directory of the United States Army*. Washington, DC: Government Printing Office, 1903.

Henderson, G. F. R. *Stonewall Jackson and the American Civil War*. London: Longmans, Green and Company, 1906.

Hendrick, Burton K. *The Lees of Virginia: Biography of a Family*. Boston: Little, Brown and Company, 1935.

Henry, Robert S. *The Story of the Confederacy*. New York: Bobbs-Merrill, 1936.

Henry, Robert S. *The Story of the Mexican War*. New York: Bobbs-Merrill, 1950.

Herbert, Walter H. *Fighting Joe Hooker*. New York: Bobbs-Merrill, 1944.

Hill, Frederick T. *On the Trail of Grant and Lee*. New York: D. Appleton and Company, 1911.

Hood, John B. *Advance and Retreat: Personal Experiences in the United States and Confederate Armies*. New Orleans: G. T. Beauregard, 1880.

Howard, Oliver Otis. *Autobiography*. New York: Baker and Taylor, 1907.

Hughes, Robert M. *General Johnston*. New York: D. Appleton and Company, 1893.

Huyette, Miles Clayton. *The Maryland Campaign and Battlefield of Antietam*. Buffalo, NY: Privately printed, 1915.

In Memoriam. *Francis H. Smith, the Father and Founder of the Virginia Military Institute*. New York: Knickerbocker Press, 1890.

Jackson, Mary Anna. *Memoirs of Stonewall Jackson by His Widow*. Louisville, KY: Prentice Press, 1895.

James, Marquis. *Andrew Jackson: Portrait of a President*. New York: Gossett and Dulany, reprint, n.d.

Johannsen, Robert W. *Stephen A. Douglas*. New York: Oxford University Press, 1973.

Johannsen, Robert W. *To the Halls of Montezuma: The Mexican War in the American Imagination*. New York: Oxford University Press, 1985.

Johnson, Rossiter, ed. *The Twentieth Century Biographical Directory of Notable Americans*. Detroit: Gale Research Company, 1968.

Johnson, Thomas Cary. *The Life and Letters of Robert Lewis Dabney*. Richmond: Presbyterian Committee on Publications, 1903.

Johnston, David E. *The Story of a Confederate Boy in the Civil War*. Portland, OR: Glass and Prudhomme, 1914.

Johnston, Joseph E. *Narrative of Military Operations*. Bloomington: Indiana University Press, reprint, 1959.

Johnston, Robert M. *Bull Run: Its Strategy and Tactics*. Boston: Houghton Mifflin Company, 1903.

Jones, J. William. *Life and Letters of Robert Edward Lee: Soldier and Man*. New York: Neale Publishing Company, 1906.

Jones, J. William. *Personal Reminiscences, Anecdotes, and Letters of General Robert E. Lee*. New York: D. Appleton and Company, 1874.

Jones, Terry L. *Lee's Tigers: The Louisiana Infantry in the Army of Northern Virginia*. Baton Rouge: Louisiana State University Press, 1987.

Junkin, D. X. *George Junkin, D.D., LL.D.* Philadelphia: J. B. Lippincott and Company, 1871.

Keyes, Erasmus. *Fifty Years Observation of Men and Events.* New York: Charles Scribner's Sons, 1884.

Klein, Philip S. *James Buchanan: A Biography.* University Park: Pennsylvania State University Press, 1962.

Krick, Robert K. *Stonewall Jackson at Cedar Mountain.* Chapel Hill: University of North Carolina Press, 1990.

Lee, Edmund Jennings. *Lee of Virginia, 1642–1892.* Philadelphia: Franklin Publishing Company, 1895.

Lee, Fitzhugh. *General Lee.* New York: D. Appleton and Company, 1894.

Lee, Henry. *Memoirs of the War in the Southern Department of the States, with a Biography of the Author by Robert E. Lee.* New York: University Publishing Company, 1869.

Lee, Robert E., Jr. *Recollections and Letters of General Robert E. Lee.* Garden City, NY: Garden City Publishing Company, 1903.

Lee, Sarah P. *Memoirs of William Nelson Pendleton, D.D.* Philadelphia: J. B. Lippincott, 1893.

Leech, Margaret. *Reveille in Washington.* New York: Time Incorporated, reprint, 1962.

Lewis, Lloyd. *Captain Sam Grant.* Boston: Little, Brown and Company, 1950.

Leyburn, James G. *The Scotch-Irish: A Social History.* Chapel Hill: University of North Carolina Press, 1962.

Linton, W. J. *Life of John Greenleaf Whittier.* London: Walter Scott, Ldt., 1893.

Livermore, Thomas L. *Numbers and Losses in the American Civil War, 1861–1865.* Boston: Houghton Mifflin Company, 1900.

Loehr, Charles T. *War History of the Old First Infantry Regiment, Army of Northern Virginia.* Richmond: William Ellis Jones, Book and Job Printer, 1884.

Long, A. L. *The Memoirs of Robert E. Lee: His Military and Personal History.* Secaucus, NJ: Blue and Grey Press, reprint, 1983.

Longstreet, James. *From Manassas to Appomattox: Memoirs of the Civil War in America.* Philadelphia: J. B. Lippincott, 1903.

Lossing, Benson J. *Recollections and Memoirs of Washington.* New York: Derby and Jackson, 1860.

Lowry, Terry. *The Battle of Scary Creek.* Charleston, WV: Pictorial Histories Publishing Company, 1982.

Lowry, Terry. *September Blood: The Battle of Carnifex Ferry.* Charleston, WV: Pictorial Histories Publishing Company, 1985.

Macartney, Charles E. *Lincoln and His Generals.* Philadelphia: Dorrance and Company, 1925.

McClellan, George B. *Report of the Organization and Campaigns of the Army of the Potomac.* Freeport, NY: Books for Libraries Press, reprint, 1970.

McCoy, Charles A. *Polk and the Presidency.* Austin: University of Texas Press, 1960.

McDonald, Archie P., ed. *Make Me a Map of the Valley: The Civil War Journal of Stonewall Jackson's Topographer.* Dallas: Southern Methodist University Press, 1973.

McGuire, Hunter. *The Confederate Cause and Conduct of the War between the States.* Richmond: L. H. Jenkins, 1907.

McKim, Rudolph H. *The Soul of Lee.* New York: Longmans, Green and Company, 1918.

McKinney, Tim. *Robert E. Lee at Sewell Mountain.* Charleston, WV: Pictorial Histories Publishing Company, 1990.

McMurry, Richard M. *John Bell Hood and the War for Southern Independence.* Lexington: University Press of Kentucky, 1982.

McPherson, James M. *Battle Cry of Freedom: The Civil War Era.* New York: Ballantine Books, 1988.

McPherson, James M. *Ordeal by Fire: The Civil War and Reconstruction.* New York: Alfred A. Knopf, 1982.

McWhiney, Grady, and Perry D. Jamieson. *Attack and Die: Civil War Military Tactics and the Southern Heritage.* Tuscaloosa: University of Alabama Press, 1982.

Magrath, C. Peter. *Yazoo: Law and Politics in the New Republic.* New York: W. W. Norton and Company, 1966.

Malone, Dumas, ed. *The Dictionary of American Biography.* New York: Charles Scribner's Sons, 1928ff.

Mansfield, Edward D. *The Mexican War: A History of Its Origin.* New York: A. S. Barnes and Company, 1849.

Maurice, Sir Frederick. *An Aide de Camp of Lee.* Boston: Little, Brown and Company, 1927.

Maurice, Sir Frederick. *Robert E. Lee: The Soldier.* Boston: Houghton Mifflin Company, 1925.

Maury, Dabney H. *Recollections of a Virginian in the Mexican, Indian, and Civil Wars.* New York: Charles Scribner's Sons, 1894.

Mayer, George H. *The Republican Party, 1854–1964.* New York: Oxford University Press, 1964.

Mercer, Philip. *The Life of the Gallant Pelham.* Kennesaw, GA: Continental Book Company, reprint, 1958.

Miller, Thomas C. *History of Education in West Virginia.* Charleston, WV: Tribune Publishing Company, 1904.

Mitchell, Reid. *Civil War Soldiers.* New York: Viking Penguin, 1988.

Moore, Edward A. *The Story of a Cannoneer under Stonewall Jackson.* Lynchburg, VA: J. P. Bell Company, 1910.

Morrison, James L., Jr. *"The Best School in the World": West Point, The Pre–Civil War Years, 1833–1866.* Kent: Kent State University Press, 1986.

Murfin, James V. *The Gleam of Bayonets: The Battle of Antietam and the Maryland Campaign.* New York: Thomas Yoseloff, 1965.

Naiswald, L. VanLoan. *Grape and Canister: The Story of the Field Artillery in the Army of the Potomac, 1861–1865.* New York: Oxford University Press, 1960.

Nance, John Milton. *After San Jacinto: The Texas-Mexican Frontier, 1836–1841.* Austin: University of Texas Press, 1963.

National Cyclopaedia of American Biography. New York: James T. White Company, 1892ff.

Nevins, Allan. *Fremont: The West's Greatest Adventurer.* New York: Harper and Row, 1928.

Nevins, Allan. *The War for the Union: The Organized War to Victory.* New York: Charles Scribner's Sons, 1971.

Nichols, Roy F. *Franklin Pierce: Young Hickory of the Granite Hills.* Philadelphia: University of Pennsylvania Press, 1931.

Nisbet, James Cooper. *Four Years on the Firing Line.* Jackson, TN: McCowat-Mercer Press, reprint, 1963.

Oates, Stephen B. *The Fiery Jubilee: Nat Turner's Fierce Rebellion.* New York: Harper and Row, 1971.

Oates, Stephen B., ed. *Rip Ford's Texas.* Austin: University of Texas Press, 1963.

Oates, Stephen B. *To Purge This Land with Blood: A Biography of John Brown.* New York: Harper and Row, 1970.

Oates, Stephen B. *With Malice toward None: The Life of Abraham Lincoln.* New York: Harper and Row, 1977.

Opie, John N. *A Rebel Cavalryman with Lee, Stuart, and Jackson.* Chicago: W. B. Conkey Company, 1899.

Palfrey, James Winthrop. *The Antietam and Fredericksburgh.* New York: Charles Scribner's Sons, 1882.

Parks, Joseph H. *Joseph E. Brown of Georgia.* Baton Rouge: Louisiana State University Press, 1977.

Parrington, Vernon L. *Main Currents in American Thought.* New York: Harcourt, Brace and Company, reprint, 1958.

Pendleton, Louis. *Alexander H. Stephens.* Philadelphia: George W. Jacobs, 1908.

Peters, Virginia Bergman. *The Florida Wars.* Hamden, CT: Archon Books, reprint, 1979.

Piston, William Garrett. *Lee's Tarnished Lieutenant: James Longstreet and His Place in Southern History.* Athens: University of Georgia Press, 1987.

Poague, William T. *Gunner with Stonewall.* Jackson, TN: McCowat-Mercer Press, reprint, 1957.

Pollard, Edward A. *Lee and His Lieutenants.* New York: E. B. Treat and Company, 1867.

Potter, David M. *The Impending Crisis, 1848–1861.* New York: Harper and Row, 1976.

Prideaux, Tom. *The World of Whistler, 1834–1903.* New York: Time-Life Books, 1970.

Randall, James G., and David H. Donald. *The Civil War and Reconstruction.* Lexington, MA: D. C. Heath and Company, 1969.

Redway, G. W. *Fredericksburg: A Study in War.* London: Allen and Unwin, 1906.

Reilly, Oliver T. *The Battlefield of Antietam.* Sharpsburg, MD: Privately printed, 1906.

Rhodes, Charles D. *Robert E. Lee: West Pointer.* Richmond: Garrett and Massie, 1932.

Rice, Otis K. *West Virginia: A History.* Lexington: University Press of Kentucky, 1985.

Richards, Warner J. *God Bless Our Arms: The Religious Life of Stonewall Jackson.* New York: Vantage Press, 1982.

Richardson, Rupert N. *Texas: The Lone Star State.* Englewood Cliffs, NJ: Prentice-Hall, 1961.

Riley, Franklin L. *General Robert E. Lee After Appomattox.* New York: Macmillan Company, 1922.

Rister, Carl Coke. *Robert E. Lee in Texas.* Norman: University of Oklahoma Press, 1946.

Robertson, James I. *General A. P. Hill: The Story of a Confederate Warrior.* New York: Random House, 1987.

Robertson, James I. *The Stonewall Brigade.* Baton Rouge: Louisiana State University Press, 1963.

Roland, Charles P. *Albert Sidney Johnston: Soldier of Three Republics.* Austin: University of Texas Press, 1964.

Ropes, John Codman. *The Army under Pope.* New York: Charles Scribner's Sons, 1881.

Rossbach, Jeffery. *John Brown, the Secret Six, and a Theory of Slave Violence.* Philadelphia: University of Pennsylvania Press, 1982.

Royster, Charles. *Light-Horse Harry Lee and the Legacy of the American Revolution.* New York: Alfred A. Knopf, 1981.

Rudolph, Frederick. *The American College and University: A History.* New York: Vantage Press, 1962.

Sanborn, Margaret. *Robert E. Lee: The Complete Man.* Philadelphia: J. B. Lippincott Company, 1967.

Sandburg, Carl. *Abraham Lincoln: The Prairie Years.* New York: Charles Scribner's Sons, 1947.

Sandburg, Carl. *Abraham Lincoln: The War Years.* New York: Harcourt, Brace and Company, 1939.

Scharf, J. Thomas. *History of Western Maryland.* Philadelphia: Louis H. Everts, 1882.

Schildt, John W. *September Echoes: The Maryland Campaign of 1862.* Shippensburg, PA: Beidel Publishing House, 1980.

Schildt, John W. *Stonewall Jackson Day By Day.* Chewsville, MD: Antietam Publications, 1980.

Schroeder, John H. *Mr. Polk's War: American Opportunism and Dissent, 1846–1848.* Madison: University of Wisconsin Press, 1973.

Scott, Winfield. *Memoirs: Written by Himself.* New York: Sheldon and Company, 1867.

Sears, Stephen W. *George B. McClellan: The Young Napoleon.* New York: Ticknor and Fields, 1988.

Sears, Stephen W. *Landscape Turned Red: The Battle of Antietam.* New York: Ticknor and Fields, 1983.

Secretary of War. *The War of the Rebellion: A Compilation of the Official Records of the Union and Confederate Armies.* Washington, DC: Government Printing Office, 1880ff.

Selby, John. *Stonewall Jackson as Military Commander.* London: B. T. Batsford, Ldt., 1968.

Sellers, Charles. *James K. Polk: Continentalist*. Princeton: Princeton University Press, 1966.

Semmes, Raphael. *Service Ashore and Afloat during the Mexican War*. Cincinnati: W. H. Moore and Company, 1851.

Sigaud, Louis. *Belle Boyd: Confederate Spy*. Richmond: Dietz Press, 1940.

Simms, Henry H. *A Decade of Sectional Controversy, 1851–1861*. Chapel Hill: University of North Carolina Press, 1942.

Simpson, Harold B. *Gaines Mill to Appomattox: Waco and McLennan County in Hood's Texas Brigade*. Waco, TX: Texian Press, 1963.

Simpson, Harold B. *Hood's Texas Brigade: Lee's Grenadier Guard*. Waco, TX: Texian Press, 1970.

Singletary, Otis A. *The Mexican War*. Chicago: University of Chicago Press, 1960.

Smelser, Marshall. *The Democratic Republic, 1801–1815*. New York: Harper and Row, 1960.

Smith, Arthur D. H. *Old Fuss and Feathers: The Life and Exploits of Lt. General Winfield Scott*. New York: Grey stone Press, 1937.

Smith, Francis H. *The Virginia Military Institute: Its Building and Rebuilding*. Lynchburg, VA: J. P. Bell Company, 1912.

Smith, Gene. *Lee and Grant: A Dual Biography*. New York: McGraw-Hill Company, 1984.

Smith, George Winston, and Charles Judah. *Chronicles of the Gringoes: The U.S. Army in Mexico, 1846–1848*. Albuquerque: University of New Mexico Press, 1968.

Smith, Gustavus W. *The Battle of Seven Pines*. New York: C. G. Crawford, Printer and Stationer, 1891.

Smith, Justin H. *The War with Mexico*. New York: Macmillan Company, 1919.

Smith, William E. *The Francis P. Blair Family in Politics*. New York: Macmillan Company, 1933.

Smyrl, Frank H. *Texas in Gray: The Civil War Years, 1861–1865*. Boston: American Press, 1983.

Smyrl, Frank H. *The Twenty-Eighth Star: Texas during the Period of Early Statehood, 1846–1861*. Boston: American Press, 1983.

Snow, William P., *Lee and His Generals*. New York: Fairfax Press, reprint, 1982.

Sorrel, G. Moxley. *Recollections of a Confederate Staff Officer*. New York and Washington, DC: Neale Publishing Company, 1905.

Starr, Stephen Z. *The Union Cavalry in the Civil War*. Baton Rouge: Louisiana State University Press, 1979.

Stephens, Alexander H. *A Constitutional View of the Late War between the States*. Philadelphia: National Publishing Company, 1868–1870.

Stere, Edward. *The Wilderness Campaign*. Harrisburg, PA: Stackpole Company, 1960.

Stutler, Boyd B. *West Virginia and the Civil War*. Charleston, WV: Education Foundation, 1963.

Summers, Festus P. *The Baltimore and Ohio in the Civil War*. New York: G. P. Putnam's Sons, 1939.

Summers, Festus P. *John Newlon Camden: A Study in Individualism.* New York: G. P. Putnam's Sons, 1937.

Swanberg, W. A. *First Blood: The Story of Fort Sumter.* New York: Charles Scribner's Sons, 1957.

Swinton, William. *Campaigns of the Army of the Potomac.* New York: Charles Scribner's Sons, 1882.

Symons, Julian. *The Tell-Tale Heart: The Life and Work of Edgar Allan Poe.* New York: Harper and Row, 1978.

Tanner, Robert G. *Stonewall in the Valley: Thomas J. Jackson's Shenandoah Valley Campaign, Spring, 1862.* Garden City, NY: 1974.

Taylor, Walter H. *Four Years with General Lee.* New York: D. Appleton and Company, 1877.

Taylor, Walter H. *General Lee: His Campaigns in Virginia, 1861–1865.* Norfolk, VA: Nusbaum Book and News Company, 1906.

Thomas, Clarence. *General Turner Ashby: The Centaur of the South.* Winchester, VA: Eddy Press Corporation, 1907.

Thomas, Emory M. *Bold Dragon: The Life of J. E. B. Stuart.* New York: Harper and Row, 1986.

Thomas, Emory M. *The Confederate Nation, 1861–1865.* New York: Harper and Row, 1979.

Thomason, John W. *JEB Stuart.* New York: Charles Scribner's Sons, reprint, 1958.

Thorpe, Thomas Bangs. *Our Army on the Rio Grande.* Philadelphia: Cary and Hart, 1848.

Tilberg, Frederick. *Antietam: National Battlefield Site.* Washington, DC: Government Printing Office, 1961.

Trudeau, Noah Andre. *Bloody Roads South: The Wilderness to Cold Harbor.* Boston: Little, Brown and Company, 1989.

Tyler, Daniel. *Autobiography and War Record.* New Haven, CT: Privately printed, 1883.

U.S. Congress. *Biographical Directory of the American Congress, 1774–1961.* Washington, DC: Government Printing Office, 1961.

Vandiver, Frank E. *Mighty Stonewall.* New York: McGraw-Hill Company, 1957.

Vandiver, Frank E. *Plowshares into Swords: Josiah Gorgas and Confederate Ordnance.* Austin: University of Texas Press, 1952.

Vandiver, Frank E. *Their Tattered Flags.* New York: Harper's Magazine Press, 1970.

Vining, Elizabeth Gray. *Mr. Whittier.* New York: Viking Press, 1974.

Von Borcke, Heros. *Memoirs of the Confederate War for Independence.* New York: Peter Smith, reprint, 1938.

Walker, C. Irvin. *The Life of Lieutenant General Richard Heron Anderson.* Charleston, SC: Art Publishing Company, 1917.

Wayland, John W. *Stonewall Jackson's Way: Route, Method, Achievement.* Staunton, VA: McClure Company, 1940.

Webb, Alexander, S. *The Peninsula: McClellan's Campaign of 1862.* New York: Jack Brussell, Publisher, reprint, 1959.

Webb, Walter P. ed. *The Handbook of Texas.* Austin: Texas State Historical Association, 1952.

Webb, Walter P. *The Texas Rangers: A Century of Frontier Defense.* Austin: University of Texas Press, reprint, 1965.

Wedgewood, C. V. *The King's War, 1641–1647.* London: Collins, 1958.

Weems, John Edward. *To Conquer a Peace: The War between the United States and Mexico.* Garden City, NY: Doubleday and Company, 1947.

Weigley, Russel F. *The American Way of War: A History of United States Military Strategy and Policy.* New York: Macmillan Company, 1973.

Weintraub, Stanley. *Whistler: A Biography.* New York: Weybright and Talley, 1974.

Wessels, William L. *Born to Be a Soldier: The Military Career of William Wing Loring.* Fort Worth: Texas Christian University Press, 1971.

Whan, Vorin E. *Fiasco at Fredericksburg.* University Park: Pennsylvania State University Press, 1961.

Wheeler, J. H. *Reminiscences and Memoirs of North Carolina.* Columbus, OH: Columbus Print Company, 1884.

White, Henry Alexander. *Robert E. Lee and the Southern Confederacy.* New York: G. P. Putnam's Sons, 1910.

Wilcox, Cadmus. *History of the Mexican War.* Washington, DC: Church News Publishing Company, 1892.

Wiley, Bell I. *Confederate Women.* Westport, CT: Greenwood Press, 1975.

Wiley, Bell I. *The Life of Johnny Reb: The Common Soldier of the Civil War.* Indianapolis: Bobbs-Merrill Company, 1943.

Williams, John Alexander. *West Virginia and the Captains of Industry.* Morgantown: West Virginia University Library, 1976.

Williams, Kenneth P. *Lincoln Finds a General: A Military Study of the Civil War.* Macmillan Company, 1964.

Williams, T. Harry. *P. G. T. Beauregard: Napoleon in Grey.* Baton Rouge: Louisiana State University Press, 1954.

Williams, T. Harry. *The History of American Wars from 1745 to 1918.* New York: Alfred A. Knopf, 1981.

Wilshin, Francis F. *Manassas (Bull Run).* Washington, DC: National Park Service, 1953.

Wilson, James H. *Under the Old Flag.* New York: D. Appleton and Company, 1912.

Wise, Jennings C. *The Long Arm of Lee: The History of the Artillery of the Army of Northern Virginia.* New York: Oxford University Press, reprint, 1959.

Wise, Jennings C. *The Military History of the Virginia Military Institute, 1839 to 1865.* Lynchburg, VA: J. P. Bell Company, 1915.

Woodman, Lyman L. *Cortina: Rogue of the Rio Grande.* San Antonio, TX: Naylor Company, 1950.

Woodward, C. Vann, and Elisabeth Muhlenfeld, eds. *The Private Mary Chesnut: The Unpublished Civil War Diaries.* New York: Oxford University Press, 1984.

Worsham, John H. *One of Jackson's Foot Cavalry.* Jackson, TN: McCowat-Mercer Press, reprint, 1964.

Wright, Marcus J. *General Officers of the Confederate Army.* New York: Neale Publishing Company, 1911.

Wyatt-Brown, Bertram. *Honor and Violence in the Old South.* New York: Oxford University Press, 1986.

Zinn, Jack. *Lee's Cheat Mountain Campaign.* Parsons, WV: McClain Publishing Company, 1974.

ARTICLES

Alexander, Edward Porter. "The Battle of Fredericksburg." *Southern Historical Society Papers* 10 (1882).

Alexander, Edward Porter. "The Battle of Fredericksburg—Part 2." *Southern Historical Society Papers* 11 (1883).

Ambler, Charles H. "General R.E. Lee's Northwest Virginia Campaign." *West Virginia History* 5 (January 1944).

A Member of the Family. "General Robert E. Lee's War Horses." *Southern Historical Society Papers* 19 (1891).

Ames, John W. "In Front of the Stone Wall at Fredericksburg." In *Battles and Leaders of the Civil War,* New York: Thomas Yoseloff, reprint, 1956.

An English Officer. "A Month's Visit to Confederate Headquarters." *Blackwood's Edinburgh Magazine* 93 (January 1863).

Barger, W. D. "Scenes of Jackson's Boyhood." *Confederate Veteran* 22 (July 1914).

Barnwell, Robert W. "The First West Virginia Campaign." *Confederate Veteran* 38 (April 1930).

Bridges, Hal. "A Lee Letter on the 'Lost Dispatch' and the Maryland Campaign of 1862." *Virginia Magazine of History and Biography* 66 (1958).

Brock, R. A. "A Federal Soldier's Opinion of Stonewall Jackson." *Southern Historical Society Papers* 10 (1878).

Brock, R. A., ed. "The Valley after Kernstown: The Jackson-Harman Letters." *Southern Historical Society Papers* 19 (1891).

Broun, Thomas L. "General Robert E. Lee's War-Horses: Traveller and Lucy Long." *Southern Historical Society Papers* 18 (1890).

Bushong, Millard K. "Jackson in the Shenandoah." *West Virginia History* 27 (January 1966).

Butler, H. A. "Fredericksburg—Personal Reminiscences." *Confederate Veteran* 14 (1906).

Cabell, D. S. G. "Lee as an Educator." *Southern Historical Society Papers* 17 (1889).

Camerer, C. B. "The Last Days of 'Stonewall Jackson.' " *Military Surgeon* 78 (1936).

Casdorph, Paul D. "Brown Faces the Gallows." *West Virginia Hillbilly* 27 (November 1985).

Casdorph, Paul D. "Future Bishop Gives Account of the Civil War." *West Virginia Hillbilly* 27 (October 1985).

Casdorph, Paul D. "John Brown's Letters." *West Virginia Hillbilly* 27 (October 1985).

Charles R. K. "Events in the Battle of Fredericksburg." *Confederate Veteran* 14 (1906).

Conner, Forrest, ed. "Letters of Lieutenant Robert H. Miller to His Family." *Virginia Magazine of History and Biography* 70 (January 1962).

Conrad, D. B. "History of the First Battle at Manassas and the Organization of the Stonewall Brigade." *Southern Historical Society Papers* 20 (1892).

Couch, Darius N. "Outgeneraled by Lee." In Ned Bradford, ed., *Battles and Leaders of the Civil War*. New York: Appleton-Century-Crofts, 1956.

Craighill, W. P. "Baltimore and Its Defenses." *Maryland Historical Magazine* 1 (1908).

Cullop, Thomas L. "English Reaction to Stonewall Jackson's Death." *West Virginia History* 29 (October, 1967).

Cummins, C. C. "The Sunken Road—The Slaughter Pen." *Confederate Veteran* 23 (1915).

Cuthbert, Norma B. "To Molly: Five Early Letters from Robert E. Lee to His Wife, 1832–1835." *Huntington Library Quarterly* 15 (May 1952).

Daniels, R. H. "The Battle of Sharpsburg or Antietam." *Confederate Veteran* 9 (1901).

Drumm, Stella M. "Robert E. Lee and the Improvement of the Mississippi River." *Missouri Historical Society Collections* 6 (February 1929).

Franklin, James. "Incidents at the First Manassas Battle." *Confederate Veteran* 2 (1894).

Fravel, John W. "Jackson's Valley Campaign." *Confederate Veteran* 7 (1898).

Gilbreath, Esmarch, and John H. Wise. "Chemical Education: Two Views from W&L." *Alumni Magazine of Washington and Lee* 51 (July 1976).

Goldsborough, W. W. "How Ashley Was Killed." *Southern Historical Society Papers* 21 (1893).

Hagy, P.S. "The Cheat Mountain Campaign." *Confederate Veteran* 23 (1915).

Happel, Ralph. "The Chancellors of Chancellorsville." *Virginia Magazine of History and Biography* 71 (July 1963).

Hartman, Theodore. "With Jackson at Second Manassas." *Confederate Veteran* 24 (1916).

Hendricks, James M. "Jackson's March to the Rear of Pope's Army." *Confederate Veteran* 17 (1909).

Hill, D. H. "The Real Stonewall Jackson." *Century Magazine* 25 (February 1894).

Hotchkiss, Jed, and William Allan. "The Battlefields of Virginia: Chancellorsville." *Southern Historical Society Papers* 34 (1906).

Hubbell, Jay B. "The Civil War Diary of John Esten Cooke." *Journal of Southern History* 7 (November 1941).

Jackson, Mary Anna. "With 'Stonewall Jackson' in Camp: More Confederate Memories." *Hearst Magazine* 34 (1913).

Johnston, David E. "The Charge of Kemper's Brigade at Frazier's Farm." *Southern Historical Society Papers* 18 (1892).

Jones, A.C. "The Mountain Failure." *Confederate Veteran* 22 (1914).

Kingsolving, Roberta C. Corbin. "Stonewall Jackson in Winter Quarters." *Confederate Veteran* 20 (1912).

Levering, Jonn. "Lee's advance and retreat in the Cheat Mountain Campaign in 1861 supplemented by the tragic death of Colonel John A. Washington of his staff." In *Military Essays and Recollections, Military Order of the Loyal Legion of the United States, Illinois Commandry* Chicago: Cottens and Bealton Company, 1907.

McComb, William. "Tennesseans in the Mountain Campaign." *Confederate Veteran* 22 (1914).

McGuire, Hunter. "General T. J. (Stonewall) Jackson, Confederate States Army." *Southern Historical Society Papers* 27 (1897).

McLaws, Lafayette. "The Confederate Left at Fredericksburg." In *Battles and Leaders of the Civil War.* New York: Thomas Yoseloff, reprint, 1956.

McWhiney, Grady. "Who Whipped Whom: Confederate Defeat Reexamined." *Civil War History* 11 (March 1965).

Maddox, Robert F. "The Presidential Election of 1860 in Western Virginia." *West Virginia History* 25 (1963).

Munford, T. T. "Reminiscences of Jackson's Valley Campaign." *Southern Historical Society Papers* 7 (1878).

Patton, John M. "Reminiscences of Jackson's Infantry ('Foot Cavalry')." *Southern Historical Society Papers* 8 (1880).

Pohl, James W. "The Influence of Henri de Jomini on Winfield Scott's Campaign in the Mexican War." *Southwestern Historical Quarterly* 77 (July 1973).

Pope, John. "To Gain Time . . ." In Ned Bradford, ed., *Battles and Leaders of the Civil War.* New York: Appleton-Century-Crofts, 1956.

Porter, Horace. "Lee . . . Facing Grant: The Surrender at Appomattox Court House." In Ned Bradford, ed., *Battles and Leaders of the Civil War.* New York: Appleton-Century-Crofts, 1956.

Preston, Margaret Junkin. "Personal Reminiscences of Stonewall Jackson." *Century Magazine* 17 (1886).

Purcell, W. H. "The Brief Stay of Stonewall Jackson at Fort Meade." *Polk County Historical Quarterly* 2 (March 1976).

Purifay, John. "Letters on the West Virginia Campaign." *Confederate Veteran* 34 (1926).

Reif, Max. "Early History of Fort Meade." *Polk County Historical Quarterly* 3 (June 1976).

Richardson, C. A. "Account of the Battle of Antietam." *Confederate Veteran* 16 (1908).

Richardson, C. A. "General Lee at Antietam." *Confederate Veteran* 15 (1907).

Roland, Charles P., and Richard C. Robbins, eds. "The Second Cavalry Comes to

Texas: The Diary of Eliza (Mrs. Albert Sidney) Johnston." *Southwestern Historical Quarterly* 60 (April 1957).

Shackelford, George G. "Lieutenant Lee Reports to Captain Talcott on Fort Calhoun's Construction on the Rip Raps." *Virginia Magazine of History and Biography* 60 (1952).

Sigaud, Louis A. "Mrs. Greenhow and the Confederate Spy Ring." *Maryland Historical Magazine* 41 (September 1946).

Smith, Bruce R. "Benjamin Hallowell of Alexandria: Scientist, Educator, Quaker Idealist." *Virginia Magazine of History and Biography* 85 (July 1977).

Smith, James P. " 'No, no, let us pass over the river, and rest under the shade of the trees.' " In Ned Bradford, ed., *Battles and Leaders of the Civil War*. New York: Appleton-Century-Crofts, 1956.

Smith, William F. "Franklin's 'Left Grand Division.' " In *Battles and Leaders of the Civil War*. New York: Thomas Yoseloff, reprint 1956.

Stickley, E. E. "Battle of Sharpsburg." *Confederate Veteran* 22 (1914).

Swift, Eben. "The Military Education of Robert E. Lee." *Virginia Magazine of History and Biography* 35 (April 1927).

Talcott, T. M. R. "Lee's Strategy at the Battle of Chancellorsville." *Southern Historical Society Papers* 34 (1906).

Templin, Thomas E. "Henry 'Light-Horse Harry' Lee: Kentucky's Last Virginia Governor." In James C. Klotter and Peter J. Sehlinger, eds., *Kentucky Profiles: Essays in Honor of Holman Hamilton*. Frankfort: Kentucky Historical Society, 1982.

Wayland, Francis F. "Fremont's Pursuit of Jackson in the Shenandoah Valley: The Journal of Colonel Albert Tracy, March–July 1862." *Virginia Magazine of History and Biography* 70 (January 1962).

Wolseley, Lord Garnet. "Glowing Tribute to General Robert E. Lee." *Southern Historical Society Papers* 28 (1900).

Woods, J. Hop. "Stonewall Jackson in West Virginia." *Confederate Veteran* 24 (1916).

Worsham, John H. "Jackson's Valley Campaign." *Southern Historical Society Papers* 38 (1910).

MISCELLANEOUS SOURCES

"Academic Record Card of Thomas Jonathan Jackson." Typescript, United States Military Academy, West Point, New York.

"Antietam." Imprint, National Park Service, Antietam National Battlefield Park.

"Cadet Record Card of Robert E. Lee." Typescript, United States Military Academy, West Point, New York.

"Cadet Record Card of Thomas Jonathan Jackson." Typescript, United States Military Academy, West Point, New York.

Charleston *Mercury*, 1861.

Jed Hotchkiss Papers. Microfilm, Library of Congress, Washington, D.C.

New York *Herald*, 1863.

Bibliography

"Returns from U. S. Military Posts, 1800–1916." Microfilm, Publication Number 617, National Archives, Washington, D.C.

Richmond *Enquirer,* 1863.

T. J. Jackson Papers, Alderman Library, University of Virginia Archives, Charlottesville, Virginia.

T. J. Jackson Papers. Virginia Historical Society Library, Richmond, Virginia.

Index